Richard Elphick is professor of history at Wesleyan University. He is the author of *Kraal and Castle: Khoikhoi and the Founding of White South Africa* and editor (with Jeffrey Butler and David Welsh) of *Democratic Liberalism in South Africa: Its History and Prospect* (Wesleyan 1987). Hermann Giliomee is professor of political studies at the University of Cape Town. He is the author of *Die Kaap tydens die Eerste Britse Bewind* and co-author (with André du Toit) of *Afrikaner Political Thought: Analysis and Documents, 1780–1850*.

The other authors are James C. Armstrong, field director of the Library of Congress, Nairobi; William M. Freund, University of Natal, Durban; Leonard Guelke, University of Waterloo, Ontario; Martin Legassick, author and journalist, formerly of the University of Warwick; V. C. Malherbe, co-author of *The Khoikhoi Rebellion in the Eastern Cape (1799–1803)*; J. B. Peires, Rhodes University, Grahamstown; Robert Ross, University of Leiden; Gerrit Schutte, Free University, Amsterdam; Robert Shell, Princeton University; and Nigel A. Worden, University of Cape Town.

The Shaping of South African
Society, 1652–1840

The Shaping of South African Society, 1652–1840

EDITED BY
Richard Elphick and Hermann Giliomee

CONTRIBUTORS
James C. Armstrong
Richard Elphick
William M. Freund
Hermann Giliomee
Leonard Guelke
Martin Legassick
V. C. Malherbe
J. B. Peires
Robert Ross
Gerrit Schutte
Robert Shell
Nigel A. Worden

Wesleyan University Press
Middletown, Connecticut

This book is a revised edition of *The Shaping of South African Society,
1652–1820*. It is published simultaneously by Wesleyan University
Press in the United States and by Maskew Miller Longman Ltd. in
South Africa.

All inquiries and permissions requests should be addressed to
the Publisher, Wesleyan University Press, 110 Mt. Vernon Street,
Middletown, Connecticut 06457.

Library of Congress Cataloging-in-Publication Data

The Shaping of South African society, 1652–1840 / edited by Rich-
ard Elphick and Hermann Giliomee.—2nd ed., 1st Wesleyan ed.
    p.   cm.
  "A substantial revision and extension of The Shaping of South
African society, 1652–1820, published in 1979"—Pref.
  Bibliography: p.
  Includes index.
  ISBN 0-8195-5209-7—ISBN 0-8195-6211-4 (pbk.)
  1. South Africa—Social life and customs.   2. South Africa—
Ethnic relations.   3. South Africa—Race relations.   4. South
Africa —Social conditions.   5. South Africa—History—To 1836.
I. Elphick, Richard.   II. Giliomee, Hermann Buhr, 1938–   .
III. Shaping of South African society, 1652–1820.
DT761.s5   1989
968.03—dc19   88-36267
                                                                      CIP

Manufactured in the United States of America

First Wesleyan Edition, 1989

Wesleyan Paperback, 1989

EDITORS' DEDICATION
To Francine, Omay, Adrienne and Nenita

Contents

Figures

Tables

Contributors

James C. Armstrong has done extensive research on Cape slavery and the slave trade in the VOC period. He is Field Director of the Library of Congress in Nairobi, Kenya.

Richard Elphick is Professor of History at Wesleyan University, Middletown, Connecticut, U.S.A. He is the author of *Kraal and Castle: Khoikhoi and the Founding of White South Africa* (New Haven and London, 1977) and co-editor of *Democratic Liberalism in South Africa: Its History and Prospect* (Middletown, Ct. and Cape Town, 1987).

William M. Freund is Professor of Economic History at the University of Natal, Durban. He is the author of *Capital and Labour in the Nigerian Tin Mines* (Atlantic Highlands, N.J., 1981) and *The Making of Contemporary Africa: The Development of African Society since 1800* (Bloomington, 1984).

Hermann Giliomee, Professor of Political Studies at the University of Cape Town, has written *Die Kaap tydens die Eerste Britse Bewind* (Cape Town, 1975) and co-authored *Afrikaner Political Thought, 1780–1850* (Berkeley, 1981).

Leonard Guelke is the author of *Historical Understanding in Geography: An Idealist Approach* (Cambridge and New York, 1982) and numerous articles and papers on early South African historical geography. He is Professor of Geography at the University of Waterloo, Ontario, Canada.

Martin Legassick is an author and journalist who formerly taught at the University of Warwick and has written widely on South African history and politics. His Ph.D thesis (U.C.L.A., 1969) was entitled 'The Griqua, the Sotho-Tswana, and the missionaries, 1780–1840: the politics of a frontier zone'.

V.C. Malherbe co-authored *The Khoikhoi Rebellion in the Eastern Cape (1799–1803)* (Cape Town, 1984) and has published extensively on the history of the Khoisan.

J.B. Peires is Professor of History at the University of Transkei. He is the author of *The House of Phalo: A History of the Xhosa People in the Days of their Independence* (Johannesburg, 1981) and many articles on the history of the eastern Cape.

Robert Ross teaches at the University of Leiden in the Netherlands and is the author of *Adam Kok's Griquas: A Study in the Development of Stratification in South Africa* (Cambridge and New York, 1976) and *Cape of Torments: Slavery and Resistance in South Africa* (London, 1983).

Gerrit Schutte is Professor of the History of Netherlands Protestantism at the Free University in Amsterdam. He has written *De Nederlandse Patriotten en de Koloniën: Een onderzoek naar hun denkbeelden en optreden, 1770–1800* (Groningen, 1974) and has edited *Briefwisseling van Hendrik Swellengrebel Jr. oor Kaapse Sake, 1778–1792* (Cape Town, 1982).

Robert Shell's Ph.D thesis (Yale 1986) was entitled 'Slavery at the Cape of Good Hope, 1680-1731'. He has written articles on Cape slavery and Cape Islam and is now Assistant Professor of History at Princeton University.

Nigel A. Worden, Lecturer in History at the University of Cape Town, is the author of *Slavery in Dutch South Africa* (Cambridge, 1985) and articles on Cape slavery.

Abbreviations

Archives
Unless otherwise indicated, all documentary series are in the Cape Town depot of the South African State Archives. KA denotes the Koloniaal Archief, and KZ the Kamer Zeeland, series in the Algemeen Rijksarchief, The Hague. The KA series has recently been renumbered and given the designation VOC. Some chapters use the KA designation, some the VOC. Other series in the Algemeen Rijksarchief are prefaced by AR.

BPP	British Parliamentary Papers
DO	Deeds Office, Cape Town
LM	Leibbrandt's manuscripts
LMS	Archives of the London Missionary Society, School of Oriental and African Studies, London
MMS	Archives of the Methodist Missionary Society, London
PEMS	Archives of the Paris Evangelical Missionary Society, Paris
PRO	Public Record Office, London
Staf	Staffordshire County Record Office, Stafford, England

Other abbreviations

AYB	*Archives Yearbook for South African History*
DR	*Dagregister*
JAH	*Journal of African History*
KP	*Kaapse Plakkaatboek*, ed. M.K. Jeffreys *et al.*
RCC	*Records of the Cape Colony*, ed. G.M. Theal
Res	*Resolusies van die Politieke Raad* (Suid-Afrikaanse Argiefstukke)
Res	Resolution
RZA	*Reizen in Zuid-Afrika in de Hollandse Tijd*, ed. E.C. Godée Molsbergen
VOC	Dutch East India Company
VRJ	*Journal of Jan van Riebeeck*, ed. H.B. Thom
VRS	Van Riebeeck Society
XVII	Heren XVII

Conventions, terminology and units of currency

Glossary

Foreign words are italicised when they first appear. Unless defined in the text or self-explanatory, these words are briefly explained in the glossary at the end of the book.

Terminology

In this work the terms 'white' and 'European' are used interchangeably. The editors use the term 'European' in their own chapters for reasons explained in fn. †, p. 523. Those peoples whom modern scholars usually call 'San' are denoted in this book as '(Khoisan) hunter-gatherers' or 'Bushmen'; see fn. ‡, p. 4.

Units of currency

Almost all prices in this book are cited in guilders (florins), or rixdollars (in Dutch *rijksdaalders*). The guilder, which was used only in the Dutch period, was not a coin but purely a money of account. By VOC practice the guilder was deemed to be worth 20 stuivers in the Netherlands and 16 stuivers in the Netherlands Indies, including the Cape. Since the rixdollar was valued at 48 stuivers, it was worth 2.4 guilders in the Netherlands and 3 guilders in the Indies, a variance which allowed persons transferring money from the Indies to the Netherlands to make a gain on the exchange rate.

Under British rule, the pound sterling (consisting of 20 shillings) co-existed at the Cape with the rixdollar. Originally the rixdollar was worth four British shillings but its value declined steadily until it ceased to be legal tender in 1841 (See ch. 5, pp. 259–61).

Preface

This volume is a substantial revision and extension of *The Shaping of South African Society 1652–1820*, published in 1979. In 1982 the original edition also appeared in Afrikaans translation as *'n Samelewing in Wording: Suid-Afrika 1652–1820*.

Two chapters in this edition are completely new: chapter 5 on the Cape economy and chapter 10 on the Cape under the British, 1814–1834. Chapter 1 on the Khoisan and chapter 3 on the slaves have been extensively revised and extended to cover the period up to the 1830s, both with the help of new co-authors. Chapter 8 on the Northern Frontier has also been extended to the 1830s, while chapter 2 on the white settlers in the Company period has been substantially revised in the light of recent research. Chapter 9 on the Eastern Frontier is virtually unaltered but incorporates additional material appearing in the first edition as a separate chapter entitled 'The burgher rebellions on the Eastern Frontier, 1795–1815'. The editors' overview (chapter 11) has also been reworked in light of new contributions to this volume and other recent scholarship. The remaining three chapters (4, 6 and 7) have been altered only slightly from the original edition.

The editors are grateful to Mike Peacock, Managing Director of Maskew Miller Longman, for his support in bringing out this and the previous edition; to Colin Bower for his cheerful and professional supervision at all stages of publication; and to Karen Kowalski, Donna Scott and Frances Warren for expert typing. The University of Cape Town granted Hermann Giliomee research leave and financial support, while the Truman Institute of the Hebrew University of Jerusalem kindly provided him with a fellowship, and the editors with facilities to do final revisions.

RICHARD ELPHICK
HERMANN GILIOMEE
JERUSALEM, JUNE 1987

Introduction

Three hundred years ago the Cape Colony was a poor, underpopulated territory of interest to no one but its rulers, its inhabitants, its neighbours and a few inquisitive travellers. Yet in this colony there developed a complex society which in part prefigured that of modern South Africa. And South Africa is much that the early Cape Colony was not – rich, populous and of intense interest to the whole world.

This book is about the Cape in its formative years – 1652 to c. 1840. During this period two processes began which have since been the main themes of South African history: the integration of southern Africa into a world economy and the dominance of Europeans over blacks. Of course, not every feature of modern South Africa can be traced to this era. The conquest of most Bantu-speaking chiefdoms, the mineral revolution, urbanisation, the rise of Afrikaner nationalism – all followed this era and all were important. But each intensified, modified or extended patterns of social and economic organisation established in the early Cape Colony. This book attempts to analyse the development of these early patterns.

The book gives attention to all the peoples and classes who inhabited the Cape Colony: not only the European settlers who ruled it, but also the slaves, Khoikhoi, 'Bushmen', Bantu-speakers, free blacks and people of mixed descent. However, its focus is on the Cape Colony, not southern Africa as a whole. Thus contributors deal with groups who lived in colonial society or, like the Griqua, emanated from it. Communities indigenous to southern Africa – the Khoikhoi, hunter-gatherers and Bantu-speakers – are studied only in so far as they interacted with the colony.

The editors sought contributions from scholars who had done prolonged research in archives in South Africa, the Netherlands, or Great Britain. They did not wish to impose a uniform tone or conceptual scheme on these authors. Thus there are some overlaps between chapters and occasional differences of opinion, for example, on the relative importance assigned to race and class in social stratification.

Until fairly recently historians tended to treat the early Cape in isolation from the rest of the world. However, since the 1960s the developing field of African history has helped historians to see the Cape as part of the African continent, a viewpoint reflected in several chapters of this book. Moreover, there are other contexts in which the colony can be placed. It was, for example, a slave society; it bears comparison with many New World colonies and can be better understood through insights emerging from the historiography of comparative slavery. It was also a frontier society, and questions raised by the study of frontiers in America and elsewhere can appropriately be asked about the Cape. And, of course, the Cape Colony was by definition a colonial society, part of the vast empires of the Dutch East India Company (VOC) and, latterly, of the British and Batavian governments – a relationship which has been curiously under-researched in Cape historiography. The contributors to this book are aware of these perspectives and have read extensively in the comparative literature appropriate to their chapters. This reading is reflected in the questions they ask and the insights they offer: they have not tried to write systematic comparative history.

The book ends around 1840. It thus covers not only the establishment of a white-dominated social order in the VOC period but also the first serious challenges posed to that order in the early nineteenth century. By 1840 two vast and complex regions on the colony's borders – the northern areas heretofore dominated by the Griqua and the regions between the Fish and Kei occupied by the Xhosa – had become inextricably linked to the colony through trade, political influence, and missionary penetration. By 1840, too, colonial administration had been drastically modernised. Moreover, the colony's traditional labour systems had been profoundly shaken, though not overturned, by the extension of civil liberties to the Khoisan in 1828 and by the abolition of slavery, completed in 1838. Most of these events were intricately related to the origins of the Great Trek, the migration into the interior of many Afrikaner colonists in the 1830s. The Great Trek may be viewed as an attempt by Europeans to maintain and extend to new regions the social order whose development is traced in this book.

The volume consists of four parts. Part one deals with the major groups in the colony: chapter one with the Khoisan indigenes, chapter two with the free European agriculturalists (freeburghers), and chapter three with the Asian and African slaves. The final chapter of part one describes several processes of interaction among these three groups and introduces a fourth group, the free blacks.

Part two, consisting of a single chapter, offers a survey of the economic history of the Cape Colony, 1652–1835, and its links with the world economy.

Part three comprises five chapters linking governmental institutions and policies with socioeconomic developments at the Cape. Two chapters offer a synthetic and structural analysis of long periods normally fragmented by historians: the era of the Dutch East India Company rule (1652–1795) in chapter six, and that of the transitional British and Batavian regimes (1795–1820) in chapter seven. These chapters are followed by analyses of the most important Cape frontiers – the Northern Frontier to 1840 (chapter eight) and the Eastern Frontier to 1812 (chapter nine). The story of the Eastern Frontier after 1812 is continued in chapter ten as part of a broader analysis of the Cape under the Second British Occupation prior to the Great Trek.

In part four the editors review the development and maintenance of European domination throughout the entire period 1652–1840. This review is based not only on their own research but also on the preceding chapters of the book.

These eleven chapters do not deal with all the questions that can be asked about the early Cape. For example they offer relatively little on religious history, legal history, or the history of ideas or of the family. But in their strengths and weaknesses they are fairly reflective of the present state of documentation and research. We hope that this volume will stimulate further enquiry into the complex processes which first shaped South African society.

PART I

The Cape population

The Khoisan to 1828[*]

Richard Elphick and V.C. Malherbe

Jan van Riebeeck did not found the Cape Colony in an empty land. In 1652, when he set foot on the shores of Table Bay, the territories to the north and east had been occupied for centuries by the Khoikhoi ('Hottentots') and for millenia by hunter-gatherers ('Bushmen'). For the next 150 years the colony's expansion would be both hindered and assisted by these peoples. Yet until recently many writers on Cape history have dismissed them with a paragraph or even a sentence.[1] C.W. de Kiewiet's summary of Khoisan decline is typical:

> The Hottentots broke down undramatically and simply. Their end had little of the tragedy which lies in the last struggles of a dying race.[2]

The collapse of Khoisan in the face of colonial expansion was indeed 'undramatic' in that there were few decisive wars and few heroic personalities in the story. But it was scarcely 'simple'. It consisted of a complex web of social and economic processes which is difficult to reconstruct given the scantiness of our data.

At first the colony's contacts were mainly with Khoikhoi in the southwestern Cape. The pastoral society and economy of the Khoikhoi disintegrated rapidly, and most Khoikhoi were incorporated fairly easily into colonial society as a subordinate labouring class. By contrast the hunter-gatherers, the so-called Bushmen, seem to have put up more ferocious and protracted resistance, particularly in the late eighteenth century. How is this difference to be explained?

It is often assumed that the failure of the Khoikhoi was due to their small numbers[3] – perhaps about 50,000 in the whole of the southwestern Cape.[†] However, the population of the colony itself was

[*] We are grateful to Hermann Giliomee and Jeffrey Butler for critical comments on early drafts. We are also indebted to Nigel Penn who has generously shared with us his unrivalled knowledge of the Khoisan in the eighteenth century.
[†] The term 'southwestern Cape' is used in this chapter and in chapters 4 and 11 to denote lands south and west of a line running from the Oliphants River mouth to modern Tulbagh, and thence to the mouth of the Breede River.

also very small (only 394 Europeans and slaves in 1662, and 3,878 in 1714).[4] Population figures, though not irrelevant, do not tell the whole story. Neither does the catastrophic smallpox epidemic of 1713, which is often used to explain Khoikhoi decline. True, this disaster apparently swept away the majority of Khoikhoi in the southwestern Cape, but it merely consummated a long process of breakdown among Khoikhoi which was already far advanced by 1713. The first part of this chapter will be devoted to a description and explanation of that breakdown.

The Khoisan: Khoikhoi and 'Bushmen'

The term 'Khoisan' is a compound word devised by scholars and derived from names for the two groups into which Khoisan are conventionally divided: The Khoikhoi ('Hottentots'), who kept cattle and sheep, and the San ('Bushmen'), hunter-gatherers, who did not.[‡] The Khoisan were distantly related to the inhabitants of most of sub-equatorial Africa but over time their physical appearance had deviated markedly from that of most Africans. Their languages were characterised by the use of implosive consonants ('clicks') and belonged to a totally different language family from the Bantu languages.

The two groups are harder to distinguish than historians have usually assumed, and the relationships between them are complex. The hunter-gatherers were scattered throughout much of sub-equatorial Africa long before pastoralism or agriculture appeared in the region. Their economies varied with the terrain in which they lived, though they always consisted of some combination of hunting, fishing or gathering. These economies forced them into constant movement, but within very circumscribed areas. Over the many centuries that they occupied southern Africa, the languages of hunter-gatherers and some aspects of their material and

---

‡ No terminology can adequately describe the complex interactions between pastoralists and hunter-gatherers in this region. We use the term 'Khoikhoi' to refer to the Khoikhoi-speaking pastoralists and avoid 'Hottentot', a derogatory term. We prefer to call the hunter-gatherers 'Bushmen' rather than 'San', which was originally a pejorative word used by Khoikhoi. Our term 'Bushmen' covers *both* hunter-gathering communities whose ancestors had lived in the region before the Khoikhoi arrived *and* former Khoikhoi who later became hunter-gatherers. In writing about the southwestern Cape in the seventeenth century we refer mostly to Khoikhoi, because 'Bushmen' were largely peripheral to the colonial history of this area. By contrast, in writing of frontier regions to the north and east in later periods we often have recourse to 'Khoisan', a portmanteau word coined by scholars to refer both to Khoikhoi and 'Bushmen'. In these regions many of the people whom whites called 'Hottentots' were in fact of 'Bushman' origin.

intellectual culture diversified enormously. Because of this diversity, and because of the smallness and isolation of many of their communities, the 'Bushmen' had no overarching sense of group identity. Their heterogeneity was intensified by the fact that some of them were former Khoikhoi who had lost their livestock and reverted to a hunting-gathering economy.

In contrast the Khoikhoi were remarkably homogeneous. Though scattered over much of southern Africa, they all spoke closely related dialects of the same language and practised roughly the same culture. Unlike the 'Bushmen', they were aware of their cultural and historic bonds with others of the same community, often hundreds of miles away. Apparently all called themselves 'Khoikhoi' (or a dialectical variant thereof);[5] this term means 'men of men', and they used it to distinguish themselves both from Bantu-speaking cultivators and from 'Bushmen'.

The Khoikhoi orginated not (as has long been supposed) in northern or eastern Africa, but in or near northern Botswana, where one still finds 'Bushmen' hunters whose language and kinship structure closely approximate those of Khoikhoi. They were originally a hunter-gatherer community who stole or otherwise acquired livestock from early agricultural migrants into the region, probably speakers of Bantu or Central Sudanic languages.[6] The date of this 'pastoral revolution' cannot yet be established, though it was probably in the first millenium B.C. The pastoral revolution forced the Khoikhoi to move into new pastures to support their growing herds and flocks. The needs of their new economy, aided by a social structure which permitted easy fission of clans and chiefdoms, was the mainspring of their extraordinary expansion over southern Africa.[7]

The main directions of this expansion can only be speculatively reconstructed. Most likely the Khoikhoi first moved into the grasslands of Western Zimbabwe and the Transvaal (where they came into contact with Bantu-speaking cultivators) and hence to the tributaries of the Orange River. Here a split occurred: one group (consisting of the ancestors of the Cape Khoikhoi) passed down to the southern coast and then westward along the coastal plains to the Cape of Good Hope; the other group (ancestors of the Nama) pushed westward along the Orange until they neared the Atlantic coast, and then split into two groups, one moving north into Namibia, the other south towards the Cape. The Cape Khoikhoi and the southern wing of the Nama met again in the region 100 to 200 km north of the future Cape Town.[8] Those Khoikhoi who finally reached the southwestern Cape were pastoralists and planted no crops except *dagga*. This was so even though their ancestors had been in close contact with Bantu-speaking cultivators at different stages of their expansion.

The pastoralism of these Khoikhoi influenced their social and political structure in several ways. Since Khoikhoi herders had to move constantly and disperse widely in search of fresh pasture, their society was not based on the possession of land, but on small kin groups whose members were related to each other through the male line. Several of these patrilineal clans were often loosely organised together in a chiefdom§, whose chief could overrule the clan heads only if he was extraordinarily wealthy or talented. Political power at both chiefdom and clan level was weak and a function more of individual merit than of the legitimacy of the office or the command of force. Only rarely did a strong chief pass his rule on to an equally strong successor. Frequently one clan under a resourceful or resentful leader hived off into new pastures and soon ceased to pay any but ritual allegiance to its former chief. This tradition of fission favoured the rapid expansion of Khoikhoi, but also hindered their consolidation into large and stable political units.

The pastoralism of the Khoikhoi gave rise, not only to fragile social and political structures, but to an unstable economy as well. Domestic animals are extremely vulnerable as a form of individual or collective wealth. Khoikhoi pastoralists could quickly become impoverished through theft, disease, or drought. Since livestock was owned by families and individuals rather than by clans and chiefdoms, resources were not easily pooled in rebuilding herds after a disaster. An obvious strategy for the newly poor was to capture livestock from their neighbours, and thus to perpetuate the endemic (though not very bloody) warfare characteristic of the Khoikhoi. Thus the economic position of the wealthy was perpetually insecure, as was the political authority of rulers to the degree that such authority was tied to wealth.

Individuals and groups who had suddenly lost their livestock had two options other than 'going to war'. They could hire themselves out as herders for wealthy Khoikhoi, who would pay them in animals suitable for rebuilding their herds. Undoubtedly this was their preferred response.[9] Or, if the disaster had affected their neighbours as well, they could fall back on hunting and gathering. Even in times of prosperity the Khoikhoi continued to hunt and gather, and in times of distress they could rely on these as their sole means of subsistence.

§ Since we lack information on the lineage structure of most Khoikhoi communities, it is impossible to give a structural definition of the term 'chiefdom'. By this term we simply mean a group larger than a clan which regularly called itself, or was called by others, by a specific name.

Such former pastoralists (who in the Dutch period were called 'Bushmen' along with people who had never practised pastoralism) might also try to recover their stock by robbery and, if successful, return to their preferred economy of herding. In many areas of Khoikhoi habitation there thus recurred an 'ecological cycle' from pastoralism to hunting and back to pastoralism. The downward phase of the cycle was marked by a decline in the number of Khoikhoi engaged in pastoralism and by an increase of hunter-robbers; the upward phase was the exact reverse. This cycle was both a cause and an effect of the economic instability of Khoikhoi polities.[10]

Though all experienced intermittent poverty, some Khoikhoi lived in a most favoured region of Africa, namely the southwestern Cape. Here the heavy rainfall and excellent pastures supported a population which was rather high by Khoikhoi standards. All the chiefdoms of this area spoke approximately the same dialect and practised the same culture. Their chiefly lineages were related to each other and to other chiefs further east.[11] We call this cluster of chiefdoms the Western Cape Khoikhoi. The main groups of the cluster were the 'Peninsular'¶ clans and chiefdoms near Table Bay, the Cochoqua just to the north of the bay, the Guriqua to the north of the Cochoqua, and the Chainouqua and Hessequa, whose pastures stretched from Hottentots-Holland to near modern Swellendam (see Fig. 1.1, p. 9).

The lands of the Western Cape Khoikhoi were suitable for cultivation as well as for pastoralism, but before 1652 these Khoikhoi, unlike most pastoralists throughout the world, did not have to compete with cultivators for its use. Whenever they attained a measure of political and economic stability, their luxuriant pastures could support immense herds and flocks. These pastures, and the animals on them, were to make the Khoikhoi objects of envy when a new force arrived in the southwestern Cape, not from the interior of Africa, but from over the sea.

Frontiers of trade and agrarian settlement, c. 1590–1672

The European thrust into the lands of the Khoikhoi consisted of three distinct, though overlapping, phases. Each phase is identified by the European agents who were most prominent in relations with Khoikhoi

¶ A term which we have coined to refer to the Goringhaiqua, Gorachouqua, Goringhaicona and other scattered groups, all of which acknowledged the authority of a single overlord.

– the traders, the cultivators and the pastoral farmers (or *trekboers*). Each group of Europeans had a different impact on Khoikhoi and elicited from them a different response.

The first phase was a frontier** of trade and the political initiatives associated with trade. The European agents were 'servants' (employees) of trading companies of various European nations. From 1652, when Dutch traders founded a permanent colony, until about 1700, this frontier expanded from Table Bay throughout the southwestern Cape and bore initial responsibility for the decline of Khoikhoi in that region; in the eighteenth century it penetrated further into the interior. The agrarian frontier began in 1657, when the first free farmers were settled behind Table Mountain, and expanded outward well behind the first frontier, very rarely being the cutting edge of European advance. The third frontier, that of the European pastoralists, did not greatly affect the southwestern Cape; it originated on the fringes of the colony in the 1690s and moved inland into the drier regions to the north and east, gradually superseding the Company's frontier of trade as the chief threat to Khoikhoi in these regions.

The trading frontier was founded in the 1590s, when Dutch and English ships began to put in regularly at Table Bay en route between Europe and the Indies. The land near Table Bay was an ideal stop-over for the tired and sick crews of these ships, for it offered a benign climate and a regular supply of fresh water. Moreover, local Khoikhoi were willing to supply large quantities of beef and mutton, a boon to sailors who had been eating salty or rancid pork for months.

In the pre-colonial period, Khoikhoi were willing to barter sheep and cattle in large numbers, despite the high position these animals occupied in their economic and aesthetic value systems. This was because the Europeans from the ships offered Khoikhoi three products – tobacco, copper and iron – which satisfied a demand for narcotics and metals previously only incompletely met by trade with interior peoples. Thus Khoikhoi took to smoking tobacco as a substitute for the mild form of dagga which they used as a narcotic. They also bought copper beads and flat copper discs from the Europeans, using the metal for fashioning jewellery, just as they had done when it had reached them from distant peoples in modern Namibia and Botswana. There was a continuous market for copper among Khoikhoi both before and after 1652, and

** By a 'frontier' we mean a region where regular contact takes place between two or more culturally distinct communities, and where at least one of the communities is attempting to control the others but has not yet completely succeeded in doing so. This definition is substantially based on those of Martin Legassick and Hermann Giliomee.

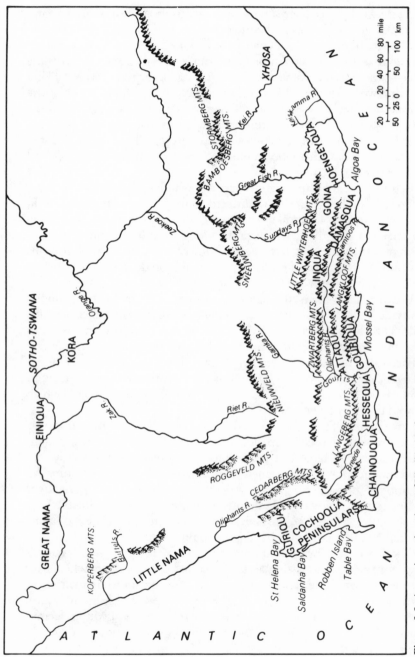

Figure 1.1 Approximate locations of Khoikhoi before contact with Europeans

Source: Richard Elphick, *Kraal and Castle: Khoikhoi and the Founding of White South Africa* (New Haven & London, 1977).
Reproduced by kind permission of Yale University Press.

trade networks in copper sprang up between those near Table Bay and other Khoikhoi peoples in the interior.[12]

The Khoikhoi used iron chiefly for making spear- and arrow-points. The market for iron was enormous from the early 1590s to 1610, by which time the chiefdoms near Table Bay had a surplus of it. No inland trade network developed for iron as it had for copper, perhaps because Khoikhoi at Table Bay were unwilling to pass it on to potential enemies. From 1610 the demand for iron became spasmodic, and after 1652 the Dutch government of the colony, realising the folly of improving the weapons of Khoikhoi who might become their enemies, embargoed further trade in the metal.[13]

Before 1652 the European traders were sailors from sundry nations, often sick and hungry, and uninhibited by long-range considerations in their treatment of Khoikhoi. In consequence the trade frequently degenerated into theft, which in turn led to reprisals from Khoikhoi. Moreover, because they lacked continuity of leadership, the Europeans were unable to impose a uniform price policy on the Khoikhoi: during the early seventeenth century the price for livestock rose steadily.

When in 1652 the Netherlands East India Company (VOC) founded a post at Table Bay, its goals were simply to regularise the benefits which sailors had long derived from the Cape stopover. Trade with Khoikhoi was thus a major concern of the early Dutch commanders. Copper and tobacco continued to be traded against sheep and cattle, but under different circumstances. The new Cape authorities were able largely to eliminate the violence of the early years and to impose controls which slowed the rise of prices.

The volume of the livestock trade grew slowly but steadily in response to a growing Dutch demand. Now that there was a permanent establishment at Table Bay, more ships called there than formerly, and their numbers continued to increase during the seventeenth century. An additional market for meat was created among the permanent population of soldiers and administrators; moreover, the hospital for ailing sailors needed a constant supply of mutton, and the Company wanted Khoikhoi oxen for hauling building materials.

The Khoikhoi always sold fewer livestock than the Dutch required, since for their precious animals they received only products which they deemed less valuable. They were particularly reluctant to part with beef cattle and tried to promote trade in sheep instead. To assure the future growth of their beef herds, they generally refused to sell young, fecund cows and urged the Dutch to accept sickly cows or oxen. Consequently the supply of beef cattle in Cape Town was inadequate. The Company was constantly forced to seek new trading partners, and the Dutch commanders had to lure traders from distant chiefdoms to the fort for barter.[14]

Dependent on the Khoikhoi for the colony's supplies and anxious to avoid costly wars at the Cape, the directors of the Company (the *Heren* XVII) made it a cardinal policy that the Khoikhoi were a free people; thus they were to be neither conquered nor enslaved, but were to be treated with respect and consideration. The first commander, Jan van Riebeeck (1652–62), was anxious to please the Heren XVII and to repair his career in the Company, which had been damaged by earlier indiscretions. Thus he conscientiously pursued the Company's mild policy (with which he himself did not always concur). He regularly entertained Khoikhoi delegates at the fort, controlled his subordinates who wished to plunder or punish the Khoikhoi, and offered gifts and services to Khoikhoi camped nearby.[15]

Nonetheless, several problems tried Van Riebeeck's forbearance. Chief among these were petty thefts by Khoikhoi, mainly of metal items, but also sometimes of the Company's livestock; the unwillingness of the Peninsulars (the chiefdoms and clans closest to the fort) to part with enough stock to feed the ships; and the belief, perhaps ill-founded, that Khoikhoi gave sanctuary to slaves fleeing the colony. All this was aggravated by the complex manoeuvres of the Khoikhoi interpreter, Harry, who used his knowledge of Dutch and his friendship with Van Riebeeck to enrich himself and gain political influence with the Peninsulars. Van Riebeeck repeatedly appealed to the directors to let him enslave the Peninsulars and confiscate their cattle. The directors never consented to such a drastic step, and toward the middle of his term at the Cape Van Riebeeck was reduced to seizing individual Khoikhoi chiefs as hostages until he gained satisfaction for his grievances. This tactic was generally successful in Van Riebeeck's time, but it naturally undermined much of the goodwill which the commander had so diligently nurtured by his other policies.[16]

Good relations were further strained when Khoikhoi discovered that the frontier was changing and that they were facing not only a trading post but also a growing agricultural community. The second frontier between Khoikhoi and Europeans, the frontier of agrarian settlement, was established in 1657 when the Company released some of its employees from their contracts and set them up as independent farmers (see ch. 2, p. 69ff). These *freeburghers* were to sell grain and meat to the Company at fixed prices, thus easing the colony's dependence on East Indian imports and on trade with Khoikhoi.

As soon as the freeburghers first put their land to the plough the Peninsular Khoikhoi realised that the European presence at the Cape would be permanent and most probably expansive. Khoikhoi resented not only the loss of exceptional pastures near Table Mountain, but also the way the new farms blocked their access to watering areas on the Cape Peninsula.[17] However, Gogosoa, the nominal head of all the Peninsulars, was too cautious and the other chiefs too divided to transform this widespread resentment into active resistance. This task was left to Doman, a man of common origin but uncommon skill, who had been an interpreter for the Company and had visited the Dutch holdings in Java. In May 1659 the Khoikhoi, under Doman's leadership, attacked suddenly and in force. They concentrated on the Europeans' food supply and in time destroyed most of the colonists' farms and stole the bulk of their cattle and sheep.

The Khoikhoi, however, were unwilling or unable to storm the well-gunned stockade to which the freeburghers had retired with their remaining livestock. The Dutch on their side lacked the information and mobility to locate the fast-moving Peninsulars and force them into battle. During this period of inaction Doman's coalition of Peninsulars began to disintegrate, especially after Doman himself was seriously injured in a skirmish on 19 July 1659. In April and May of 1660 the two leading Peninsular groups, the Goringhaiqua and Gorachouqua, made peace with the Company. The terms of the treaties reflected the ambiguous outcome of the war. The Khoikhoi kept the livestock they had seized and paid no reparations for the damage they had inflicted; but they recognised the sovereignty of the Company over the land where freeburghers had settled – a concession with ominous implications for their future.[18]

Frontiers of trade and agrarian settlement, 1672–1701

In the decades after the First Khoikhoi-Dutch War the Company's frontier of trade expanded much more rapidly than agrarian settlement, which remained very much under the supervision of the colonial government. Thus in 1679 and 1687, when Europeans under Company direction settled in Stellenbosch and Drakenstein, they came into contact with Khoikhoi who had long participated in the Company's trade and had long felt its political influence.

The Company's impact on Khoikhoi was gradual and cumulative rather than cataclysmic. Nonetheless, there was a decisive turning point in the mid-1670s when its commitment to Khoikhoi independence waned and when it began to impinge on Khoikhoi sovereignty in many ways – military, diplomatic, economic and judicial. In Van Riebeeck's day the Khoikhoi had been perceived as a threat to the colony's existence; but by the early 1670s the increasing number of Europeans and a series of defensive measures (watchhouses, mounted patrols and the famous almond hedge) had given the colony a new sense of security.

In part because of this new security, the directors of the East India Company were losing interest in the Khoikhoi. The Cape government no longer fed them long reports on the colony's relations with the Khoikhoi, and the Heren XVII were rarely moved to comment on, much less overrule, the actions of Cape officials. Consequently the Cape government became progressively bolder in dealing with Khoikhoi, a tendency which was to be greatly strengthened by the arrival in 1679 of the ambitious and forceful commander, Simon van der Stel.

Of the various prongs of the Company's assault on Khoikhoi independence the most dramatic was the military. Whereas the First Khoikhoi-Dutch War had led only to the discomfiture, not the total defeat, of the comparatively poor Peninsulars, the Second Khoikhoi-Dutch War (1673–77) affected most Khoikhoi of the southwestern Cape. The immediate cause was not the agricultural expansion of the colony but the alleged misdeeds of Gonnema, the influential chief of a sub-group of the Cochoqua to the north. Gonnema had visited the colony very early in its history[19] but had apparently seen little advantage in further contacts; thus unlike his fellow Cochoqua chief, Oedosoa, he avoided Europeans as much as possible.

In the early 1670s the colonial government became convinced that Gonnema was instigating a series of attacks on Europeans. In some of these incidents his people (or people in clans subject to him) assaulted farmers, and in others 'Bushmen' hunters, supposedly under his protection, ambushed and killed European hunters penetrating their territories. Only in one case did the Company's evidence clearly prove Gonnema's personal involvement; in most cases the government obtained its information from accusations made by Gonnema's Khoikhoi enemies, and it assumed that he had greater control over his subordinates than was probably the case.[20]

The war consisted chiefly of four punitive expeditions which the Company sent out against Gonnema: one in 1673, one in 1674 and two in 1676. In the first of these the Dutch gained an effortless and spectacular victory. This encouraged most chiefdoms and clans of the southwestern Cape to ally with the Company in the expectation of booty. Surrounded by covetous enemies, Gonnema adopted a defensive strategy – he apparently attacked the Company only once – and ordered his people to disperse their livestock and melt into the bush when a European expedition approached. After initial heavy losses the Cochoqua so perfected this technique that the frustrated expedition leaders took to attacking other Khoikhoi who had only tenuous connections with Gonnema's alleged crimes, thus spreading the destructive impact of the war even further. By 1677 it was clear that the war would yield little further booty to the Europeans and their allies. Accordingly, the colonial government (now under Joan Bax, a governor more sympathetic than his predecessors to Khoikhoi), concluded peace with Gonnema, who had long sought relief from the unequal conflict.[21]

In the peace treaty Gonnema promised to bring an annual 'tribute' of thirty cattle to the colony. Though the Company did not always insist on his strict compliance, Gonnema was sufficiently cooperative for the rest of his life (he died in 1685 or 1686) for both Europeans and Khoikhoi to realise that the strongest and most anti-Dutch of the Khoikhoi chiefs had been humiliated. The war accomplished more for the Dutch than merely the defeat of the Cochoqua. It also accelerated the Company's control over its Khoikhoi allies. During the conflict the government had forced various chiefdoms to stop communicating and trading with Gonnema. After the war it tightened control over them by insisting on regular payments from the cattle booty it had given them from Gonnema's captured herds. Most importantly, however, in 1676 and 1677 the Company had first asserted its right to adjudicate disputes among Khoikhoi clans or chiefdoms and to impose its decision by force.[22] On the arrival of Simon van der Stel in 1679 these interventions became more frequent and more blunt. The pretence that chiefs were respected allies was gradually dropped. Van der Stel also developed the practice of approving the installation of each new Khoikhoi chief: he ceremonially presented the new ruler with a cane of office with an engraved copper handle and bestowed on him a classical name like Hercules or Hannibal. These canes gave the chiefs a certain prestige as clients of the Company, but also made manifest their loss of independence and perhaps compromised them in the eyes of their followers.[23]

During the 1670s trading relations between the colony and the Khoikhoi also changed. The main participants in the older barter had been the Peninsulars, whose economy continued to decline after the First Khoikhoi-Dutch War until they were quite unable to satisfy the growing livestock demands of the colony. The government thus relied more and more on sending bartering expeditions to more distant peoples. This change was important to the Khoikhoi not only because the trading expeditions brought all of the Western Cape Khoikhoi into contact with the Company's trading network, but also because the repeated visits of armed soldiers strengthened the Company's capacity to interfere in Khoikhoi affairs.

Some of this long-distance trade was conducted by European officers, but not all: since the 1650s several enterprising Khoikhoi had enriched themselves by acting as middlemen in the trade between the colony and inland chiefdoms. At times these traders even blocked or disrupted trade into the colony in order to make their services indispensable.[24] Company officials almost always opposed them because they drove prices higher and, contrary to Company policy, traded with freeburghers. However, in the mid-1670s the government relaxed its hostility in one particular case and arranged for the most vigorous of the Khoikhoi entrepreneurs to be its agent.

Dorha (or Klaas as the Dutch called him) was a captain of one of the westernmost Chainouqua clans. He first gained prominence in the Second Khoikhoi-Dutch War and became the most eager and useful of the Company's Khoikhoi allies. Even before the war he had conceived the idea of bartering on behalf of the Dutch. By repeatedly proving his loyalty to the Company he induced the government to entrust him with increasing quantities of trade goods, which he exchanged inland for livestock, keeping a percentage of the acquired cattle for himself.

Klaas used his position to become a wealthy and influential chief, attracting many followers and concluding prestigious alliances with chiefs greater than he. The Company was delighted by this system which brought in livestock much more cheaply than the barter expeditions; and it also valued Klaas's endless supply of information and advice on Khoikhoi affairs.[25] It appeared that one Khoikhoi at least had learned to use the Dutch to enrich himself and his followers and to reverse the disintegration of traditional society which the colony's presence had encouraged.

Nevertheless this promising experiment failed. In 1693 Governor van der Stel, possibly anxious to seize Klaas's herds, suddenly abandoned the twenty-year alliance and ordered his soldiers, in company with Klaas's enemy Koopman, to attack Klaas's kraal. The latter was arrested and imprisoned on Robben Island; though Van der Stel later released him, he recovered only part of his former wealth and influence and was murdered in 1701 by Koopman. Van der Stel claimed that he had attacked Klaas to punish him for disloyalty to the Company. He provided only the slightest evidence to substantiate his charges and failed to convince either the Heren XVII or a number of observers at the Cape.[26] Nevertheless the damage had been done. All responses to the Dutch had failed: the open resistance of Doman, the cautious withdrawal of Gonnema, the eager co-operation of Klaas.

The fall of Klaas forced the Company to rely exclusively on its own trading expeditions. Most Khoikhoi were now so alarmed by the decline of their herds and flocks (a process described on pp. 18–21) that they did all they could to avoid the European traders; they tried to camouflage their true wealth and, failing all else, parted with only their sickliest animals. The Dutch officers now spent long hours convincing Khoikhoi chiefs to trade, first with arguments, then with threats. Prices were not allowed to rise; they were in fact lower after 1700 (when Khoikhoi sold under some duress) than in the 1660s (when they had sold willingly though cautiously). The trade was now enmeshed with the progressive subordination of Khoikhoi chiefs. In effect the government was inducing chiefs to sell part of their herds to avoid retaliation from the Company: trade had degenerated into the collection of tribute. More positively from the Khoikhoi point of view, the Company also offered to compliant Khoikhoi protection from their enemies, particularly 'Bushmen'.[27]

The decline of Khoikhoi chiefs and the increasingly coercive nature of the trade occurred concurrently with another major development – the intensification of labour relations between Khoikhoi and the colony. Ever since Van Riebeeck's time some Khoikhoi had worked in the colony as cook's aids, domestics, building labourers and dispatch runners. Because they feared thefts of livestock, Europeans did not hire Khoikhoi as herders or shepherds before the 1670s. However, the rapid expansion of the colony into Stellenbosch (1679) and Drakenstein (1687) greatly intensified the need for Khoikhoi labour.

Most farmers in these new settlements had fewer slaves than the farmers who remained in the older Cape district. According to the census of 1690 there was one slave in the Cape district for every nine cattle tended and for every *muid* of seed sown; in Drakenstein there was one slave for every sixty-three cattle and twenty muiden of seed.[28] Naturally, then, the new settlers turned to Khoikhoi to complement their slave force. The Khoikhoi, who were experiencing a rapid decline in their wealth and security, responded in large numbers. Most came to work on the farms. A few also made a meagre living in Cape Town, acting as porters for sailors and as errand boys for innkeepers and restaurateurs.[29]

Little is known about the conditions of employment on the farms in this early period. It seems that at first the Khoikhoi took employment for a season and left their families at home. By the mid-1690s some Khoikhoi were in permanent employment and lived with their families and livestock on the farmers' land, but in their own huts. In the early eighteenth century, if not before, servants were given space in one of the masters' main buildings. At first they served mainly as herders and shepherds, but by the turn of the eighteenth century they had learned how to cultivate, harvest, prune vines and drive wagons: in short, they did almost anything a slave could do. In 1695 Johannes Willem de Grevenbroek enthusiastically described the skills of Khoikhoi:

> They are apt in applying their hands to unfamiliar tasks. Thus they readily acquire the veterinary skill to cure scab in sheep, and they make faithful and efficient herds. They train oxen for use in ploughing . . . and are found exceedingly quick at inspanning or outspanning or guiding a team. Some of them are very accomplished riders, and have learned to break horses and master them . . . They make trusty bearers, porters, carriers, postboys and couriers. They chop wood, mind the fire, work in the kitchen, prune vines, gather grapes, or work in the wine press industriously . . . Without relaxation they plough, sow and harrow.[30]

The wages of these Khoikhoi were neither uniform nor regulated by government. The main attraction of life on a farm was a regular supply of tobacco, alcohol, bread, milk and vegetables, as well as increased security from the ravages of drought, wild animals and war. In addition some Khoikhoi were paid with a small number of calves or lambs.

As more and more Khoikhoi participated in the colonial economy the government deemed it necessary to assimilate them into the colony's legal system. The most decisive steps in this process were taken in 1671– 72. Before that time virtually all Khoikhoi had been regarded as members of independent clans or chiefdoms, and if the Dutch interfered in their affairs (as they rarely did) they did so as an act of 'foreign policy', without appeal to the laws of the Cape settlement. But in 1672 the Council of Justice passed judgement in two cases involving Khoikhoi, thus establishing their jurisdiction (1) over Khoikhoi who by culture, domicile and associations could be regarded as subjects of the colony rather than of a chief, and (2) over independent Khoikhoi involved in disputes with a European or slave.[31]

In general the Khoikhoi were given a fair hearing by the courts in cases where the Company itself was not a subject in the dispute. They were allowed to initiate proceedings and to testify against Europeans, and the judges sometimes decided in their favour. However, in one respect they did experience blatant discrimination: Europeans who had murdered Khoikhoi typically suffered confiscation of their goods and a period of banishment, whereas Khoikhoi who had murdered Europeans were routinely executed. It must, however, be remembered that only a minority of disputes between Khoikhoi and Europeans actually reached the courts. Most were settled informally by Company officials: in such cases the documentary evidence is inadequate for us to assess the quality of justice.[32]

The breakdown of the Western Cape Khoikhoi before 1720

By 1700 many (but not all) Western Cape Khoikhoi had become partially or totally dependent on the colony for their livelihood and security. The Company, not the settlers, had triggered the processes leading to this new dependence. It was the Company which consumed large numbers of Khoikhoi cattle, subordinated and humiliated the Khoikhoi chiefs, assimilated Khoikhoi into its legal systems, and instigated the expansion of the colony into Khoikhoi pastures. Only at the last stage did the freeburghers' role become decisive – in providing employment for impoverished Khoikhoi.

To say that the Company's operations were chiefly responsible for Khoikhoi collapse is not to imply that they were always intentionally so. It is true that from time to time the Company acted aggressively (e.g., against Gonnema and Klaas) but such acts were intermittent and only partially explain Khoikhoi decline. The Company did not have to be consistently aggressive; to some degree at least, Khoikhoi society fell apart as its age-old weaknesses were exacerbated by interaction with a more cohesive and powerful alien society. This proposition can be illustrated by posing and answering a difficult question. Why did Khoikhoi enter the colonial economy?

Two facets of the Khoikhoi economy – land and cattle – must be considered here: for pastoralists one without the other was useless. In later eras of South African history Europeans and Africans would clash mainly over land but, in this early period, the squeeze on land was the lesser threat to the Khoikhoi. This was because they, as transhumant pastoralists, were not ruined by the advent of European settlers in their midst as long as some good land between the farms remained unsown and accessible.

The loss of cattle and sheep was more ominous. From the mid-1660s Khoikhoi herds and flocks began a steady decline, first among the

Peninsulars, later among the more wealthy chiefdoms inland. Obviously the Company's trade contributed substantially to this loss. Between 1652 and 1699 its official papers record the purchase of 15,999 cattle and 36,636 sheep from Khoikhoi, and the actual figures were somewhat higher.[33] However, the original herds and flocks of the Western Cape Khoikhoi must have numbered well into the hundreds of thousands, and the Company's purchases were spread more or less evenly over half a century. Furthermore, as we noted, Khoikhoi were shrewd traders, reluctant to sell the healthy cows and ewes on which further growth of their livestock holdings depended. Thus the Company's trade accounts for only part of the decline.

It has sometimes been suggested that the freeburghers greatly contributed to Khoikhoi losses, both through robbery and illegal trade. However, the Company, in order to protect its monopoly, conducted a zealous campaign to protect the Khoikhoi from these dangers, and until about 1690 its control over the farmers was sufficiently tight that only minuscule numbers of livestock were traded or stolen.[34] We must note that the Company itself seized livestock in war, directing well-placed blows at the very wealthy Gonnema and at the rising entrepreneurs, Harry (in the 1650s) and Klaas (in the 1690s). But even when livestock thus obtained are added to the rest, the phenomenal decline of Khoikhoi herds and flocks is only partly explained.

We must remember that violent fluctuations between wealth and poverty had always been common among Khoikhoi. This resulted from their penchant for prolonged vendettas and stop-start wars, from their fluid political structure, and from the menace of drought, disease, and theft by 'Bushmen' hunter-robbers. The depredations by 'Bushmen' increased as Khoikhoi chiefdoms disintegrated, thus intensifying each downward phase of the 'ecological cycle'. It is not known to what degree the long decline after the 1650s was a normal phase in this recurring cycle of Khoikhoi history, and to what degree a product of European presence. But it is certain that the decline was prolonged and intensified by all the European demands on Khoikhoi livestock which we have enumerated. This was the case particularly after 1690, when the demands of both Company and freeburghers became increasingly peremptory.

Moreover, the colony's presence frustrated the normal mechanism whereby Khoikhoi society recovered from economic decline, namely the emergence of a military leader who captured sufficient livestock and recruited sufficient followers to create a growing economy and a secure society. The colony's demand for Khoikhoi labour deprived potential leaders of the impoverished individuals who would have been their most natural recruits. The periodic visitations of disease, almost certainly of European origin, also cut into the Khoikhoi population. But even more fundamentally, the colony made it impossible for Khoikhoi to recover through military aggrandisement; it did so by suppressing wars in its hinterland and by quashing leaders like Klaas and Harry who had made a successful start at accumulating herds and flocks. Faced with reduced security and a disintegrating economy, Khoikhoi naturally gravitated to the colonists' farms. This response was not alien to their traditions: it had long been customary for Khoikhoi who had lost stock to herd for wealthy kinsmen or neighbours and thus re-start their herds. But there was an important difference between the two cases. Khoikhoi who entered the colonial economy were disappointed in their expectation of livestock as their reward, the normal wages being food, lodging, and luxuries like tobacco. Those unable to rebuild their herds remained in the service of colonists and were thus permanently lost to independent Khoikhoi society. Numbers were also depleted when some Khoikhoi chose to trek inland from the southwestern Cape and thus delay for at least a century their showdown with the growing European power in southern Africa.

In the face of all these adverse developments the chiefs – who were weak at the best of times – failed to rally their followers to effective resistance or response. Indeed, by the turn of the eighteenth century the still independent Khoikhoi near the colony – the Peninsulars, Chariguriqua, Cochoqua and Chainouqua – had no visible leadership above the clan level. All groups were much less numerous than formerly (the overwhelming majority of some clans being on European farms) and owned small flocks and even smaller herds. In the southwestern Cape the demographic and economic base of Khoikhoi society was so small, and the political superstructure so feeble, that by the first decade of the eighteenth century the traditional order had disintegrated beyond recall.[35]

The Western Cape Khoikhoi received three further blows from the colony in the early eighteenth century. First came the rapid northward expansion of settlement into the Land of Waveren (Tulbagh basin) in 1700. Shortly thereafter, from 1701–03, farmers along the whole northern edge of the colony suffered from massive attacks on their livestock. Historians have usually called the attackers 'Bushmen', but many of them were in fact Khoikhoi who had lost livestock in the general decline and had seen in the colonial herds, particularly those in newly occupied Waveren, an opportunity to regain their wealth.[36] The Company and its Khoikhoi allies eventually learned how to contain these attacks, and in 1703 they fizzled out. But during the course of these hostilities the Khoikhoi allies of the Dutch, who had been safeguarding their dwindling livestock under Company protection, suffered severe losses.

The second blow to the Khoikhoi was the relaxation of the Company's control over freeburghers. The colony was now too big for officials to monitor its borders readily, and the Heren XVII made matters worse by vastly increasing the rights of freeburghers. From February 1700 to October 1702, and again after July 1704, the freeburghers were permitted to go inland and barter with Khoikhoi – a freedom that easily led to abuse. During the decade many cases of plunder came to light, the most notorious being an expedition in 1702 which ranged as far as the Xhosa and stole almost 2,000 cattle and 2,500 sheep from the Inqua (the largest Khoikhoi chiefdom between the Hessequa and the Xhosa).[37] In 1705 Landdrost Johannes Starrenburgh grimly described the plight of Khoikhoi north of Cape Town:

> . . . those who used to live contentedly under chiefs, peacefully supporting themselves by breeding cattle, have mostly all become Bushmen, hunters and robbers, and are scattered everywhere among the mountains.[38]

In these years the livestock holdings of the colonists jumped dramatically, in part at least because of trade and theft. During the eight years before the opening of the trade in 1700 their (probably under-reported) herds had grown by 3,712, their flocks by 5,449; in the first eight years of free trade the corresponding figures for growth were 8,871 and 35,562.[39]

However, the third and final blow made the others insignificant by comparison. In February 1713 a visiting fleet sent its linen ashore to be washed by the Company slaves in Cape Town. The laundry bore a smallpox virus which was to rage throughout the year, killing hundreds of Europeans and slaves. Its impact was even more severe on the Khoikhoi, who apparently had almost no immunity to it. Beginning with the Khoikhoi in Cape Town, it spread relentlessly to those on the farms and thence outward to the independent chiefdoms, who vainly tried to protect themselves by shooting down infected Khoikhoi that approached their settlements.[40]

We have only one contemporary estimate of the extent of Khoikhoi fatalities – namely that scarcely one in ten in the southwestern Cape survived. Since Khoikhoi virtually disappeared from the records of subsequent years, this assessment is probably not greatly overdrawn.[41] A society which had been in a protracted phase of economic and social decline was now almost annihilated.

The Khoisan and the trekboer frontier, 1720–1800

Just as these disasters were overtaking Khoikhoi in the southwestern Cape, the frontier of European pastoralism expanded in regions further to the north and east. The Land of Waveren was the first area of European settlement where climate, terrain and distance from markets favoured a predominantly pastoral rather than a mixed agricultural economy. Thereafter the challenge to Khoikhoi altered. Initiative passed from the Company to the European migrant farmers (trekboers), who were abandoning cultivation for ranching.

Smallpox continued its destructive course after 1713. From the southwestern Cape it spread north to the Tswana and then back to the Little Nama (around 1722–24), among whom it caused great disruption of social and economic life. In 1755 another smallpox epidemic broke out at the Cape and eventually spread at least to the Great Nama far to the north and to the Xhosa far in the east. Khoikhoi probably suffered further in even later outbreaks: in the 1780s, the traveller François le Vaillant learned that more than half of the Gona (by then the largest independent polity besides the Nama) had been killed in a single epidemic.[42]

Nor was smallpox the only catastrophe to overtake the inland Khoikhoi. After 1714, scab and other stock diseases swept through flocks and herds (see ch. 2, p. 80), endangering the colony's meat supply. The Company and freeburghers stepped up their demand for Khoikhoi animals, which were already depleted by these diseases and by 'Bushmen' raids. Both parties cajoled Khoikhoi into overselling and plundered them if they refused. The Khoikhoi responded with grim defiance, slaughtering their cattle rather than paying what they regarded as tribute. In 1727, when the Europeans' herds were recovering, the Company again banned bartering by freeburghers but continued to send its own expeditions, mainly to the Nama, for pack oxen and goats.[43]

Diseases, forced barter with the colony, and the rigours of a harsh environment appear to have triggered a severe economic downswing among the Khoikhoi living north and east of the colony. All eighteenth century descriptions show these people in a lamentable condition: poor, disunited, and in fear of 'Bushmen' robbers. Many poor Khoikhoi were forced to become hunters and robbers themselves. In 1752 one Dutch observer noted a group of Khoikhoi near the Gona, in the east:

> All these Hottentots, who formerly were rich in cattle, are now, through the thefts of the Bushmen, entirely destitute of them. Some have been killed and

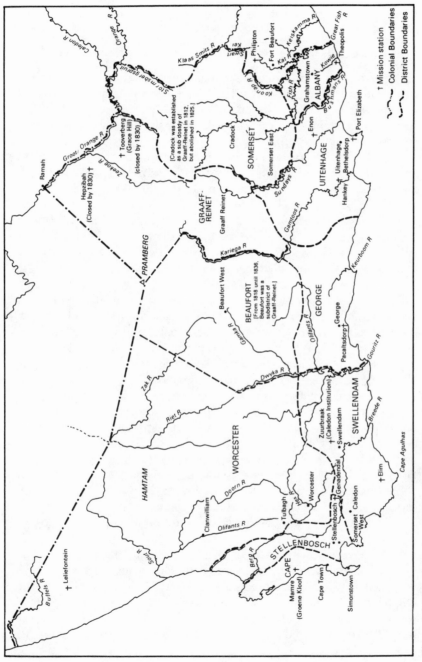

Figure 1.2 The colony about 1800 with district boundaries

some are scattered through wars with each other and with the Caffers. Those who are still found here and there consist of various groups which have united together. *They live like Bushmen* from stealing, hunting and eating anything eatable which they find in the field or along the shore . . . [Italics ours][44]

To Khoikhoi who still struggled to maintain some sheep and cattle, the trekboers may have appeared at first less as rivals than as champions of their pastoral way of life. In the 1730s O.F. Mentzel observed how the trekboers frequently settled at Khoikhoi kraals, thereby gaining access not only to the best supplies of water and pasture but also of labour. Some Khoikhoi acquiesced in their presence: the trekboers paid them and protected them from robbery while letting them retain their herds and flocks. Such Khoikhoi proved sturdy allies to the Europeans, protecting their livestock and their families as well as retrieving lost or stolen animals, even at great personal risk. On expeditions commanded by Europeans, they seized livestock, killed other Khoisan and took prisoners-of-war (mainly children), who became servants to the trekboers. Some even called themselves 'Boors' in referring to this close relationship with the colonists.[45]

The eastward expansion of the trekboers parallel to the south coast encountered little resistance from the Hessequa, Gouriqua and Attaqua, or even from the Inqua, who had been battered by the freeburgher expedition of 1702. Some Khoikhoi in this region were refugees from the colony: on the Zwartkops River Anders Sparrman found a group of 'Gunjemans Hottentots' who had migrated from the southwestern Cape. Most Khoikhoi who withdrew in this way were eventually overtaken by the colonists again. Sparrman also met Khoikhoi who protested the loss of pastures after a generation or so of trekboer occupation. A disgruntled captain near Mossel Bay informed him that whites forced their Khoikhoi neighbours to move almost daily. Formerly, he said, the Europeans had allowed chiefs, but not commoners, to stay on their land; but now, as the European population expanded, chiefs were also being removed. Attempts to displace Khoikhoi often led to brawls, retaliatory robberies and even to loss of life.[46]

Simultaneously with their eastward expansion, the trekboers also moved northward, close to the west coast. This prong of expansion was deflected eastward toward the Roggeveld by the lack of water beyond the Oliphants River mouth. It encountered relatively few Khoikhoi: rainfall was much less plentiful here than in the southwestern Cape, and the Khoikhoi thus pastured over greater distances and formed less populous and cohesive units.

Nevertheless, the northern prong of trekboers did meet periodic resistance beginning with the spate of attacks on the farmers of Waveren from 1701 to 1703 (see p. 20). The Dutch and their Khoikhoi allies referred to these resisters as 'Hottentots', more often as 'Bushmen', and sometimes as 'Bushmen-Hottentots'. Confusion in terminology reflected confusion in reality. In some cases the 'Bushmen' were aborigines, i.e., speakers of non-Khoikhoi languages and descendants of hunters who had inhabited the area before Khoikhoi herders had first arrived. In others they were actually Khoikhoi without cattle. In yet other cases 'Bushmen' raiding parties consisted of persons of both categories.[47] Thus as the eighteenth century progressed the distinctions between 'Bushmen' and Khoikhoi became more blurred. As a result the historian must increasingly resort to the portmanteau word 'Khoisan' (p. 4, fn ÷).

Even before the trekboers' arrival the 'Bushmen' had gained considerable experience of pastoralism from interaction with Khoikhoi. Either through theft or through working for Khoikhoi they had gained familiarity with sheep and cattle.[48] Though they apparently did not breed domestic animals themselves, they knew how to drive, corral and feed them. With the arrival of European pastoralists they sold stolen animals (particularly cows, whose reproductive capacity they did not value) in return for tobacco, dagga and other goods. They also understood much of the technology and economic mores of their European enemies. Increasingly, they used not only poisoned arrows and assegais but also stolen or bartered guns: commandos often found large caches of gunpowder and lead in their encampments. When attacking European farms the 'Bushmen' did more than steal livestock: they kidnapped the farmers' slaves, burned standing crops, and scattered harvested grains. Sometimes they even hauled away the grain in wagons or on pack oxen.[49]

Initially, in 1701, the Company garrisoned the threatened regions. At times, too, it tried to make peace with the Khoisan attackers. This mild policy occasionally succeeded, but officials and settlers more typically demanded retaliation. Thus the Company created the commando, an institution which would later become a symbol of the trekboer's considerable self-sufficiency. The earliest punitive expeditions consisted mainly of Company employees with only a smattering of freeburgher militia. In 1715 the first purely civilian commando was formed under freeburgher officers, but it and its successors continued to be subject to the Company's regulation and dependent on it for ammunition.[50]

Trekboer expansion aroused serious resistance in the Sandveld and

Bokkeveld, north of Piketberg. In 1738 some Khoisan servants accompanied a party of colonists on an illegal bartering and raiding expedition to the Great and Little Nama. Cheated of their promised share of the spoils, the Khoisan attacked their former employers. Other Khoisan soon entered the war, not only to capture livestock but also to regain their former lands. Khoisan raiders seized livestock, powder and lead, and burnt farms. The Company, aware that the trekboers had provoked these disturbances, tried to conciliate the Khoisan. However, a burgher revolt, led by Estienne Barbier, occurred in the northwest at this time (see ch. 6, pp. 308–09). Faced with the need to subdue both trekboers and Khoisan, the Company chose to defuse the burgher crisis by granting a reprieve to rebels who would join a commando against the Khoisan.[51]

The 'Bushman War' of 1739 was a turning point in the evolution of the commando. Freeburghers in threatened areas were for the first time made subject to compulsory commando service, though they were free to bring their Khoisan dependents along.[52] The commandos of 1739 were almost certainly more violent than their predecessors. They attacked all the Khoisan communities that they could find, sequestering livestock and weapons and killing or wounding their members. In one case a commander, while parleying with thirty or forty Khoisan, calmly ordered his followers to massacre them; he did so, he later explained, because he thought they would attack him later on.[53] During the year-long war it became apparent that the Company was less able, and less willing than formerly, to protect its Khoisan subjects and allies. At least a hundred Khoisan were killed and others lost livestock, pastures and watering places. Surviving captains accepted staffs of office from the Company and many Khoisan took service on the farms.[54]

The 1739 war not only secured the trekboers' hold on the best land south of Namaqualand and west of the Doorn River, but encouraged easterly expansion into the Hantam and Roggeveld (see fig. 2.1, p. 68). Independent Khoisan communities lived in the Roggeveld – some, perhaps, refugees from the southwestern Cape. As elsewhere, loss of livestock and land drove them to retaliatory thefts and arson. Commandos crushed this resistance during 1754–55 and several Khoisan leaders in the Roggeveld declared their submission to the Company. Fresh outbreaks of smallpox and cattle disease in 1755 further weakened such independent Khoisan as remained, and trekboer dominance was seldom challenged during the next fifteen years.[55]

In many respects the events of 1739 and 1754–55 presaged the much bigger 'Bushman wars' which began in 1770. By then trekboers had occupied the Sneeuwberg and the Camdebo. Impelled by the increase in their numbers and by the overgrazing of their pastures, the trekboers on the northern frontier demanded seasonal access to grazing north of the Roggeveld, Nieuweveld and Sneeuwberg.[56] However, the route to this good sheep country was blocked by determined Khoisan. An early sign that a century of European expansion was to be checked came in 1771 when Adriaan van Jaarsveld of the Sneeuwberg complained that 'Hottentots' were attacking the homesteads of the colonists. From what we know of the cultural identity of the Sneeuwberg Khoisan, they were probably longtime hunter-gatherers, but in some regions their numbers were swelled by former Khoikhoi pastoralists. Khoisan resistance was so fierce and so wide-ranging that fears were sometimes raised about the safety even of the long-settled Breede River Valley and the Land of Waveren. In 1790 two Khoisan bands said to be a thousand strong were active in the Koup.[57]

To combat this concerted resistance the government reconstituted the commando system: in 1774 it appointed a 'veldcommandant' to lead the first 'General Commando', a body of 250 men of whom Bastaards (see ch. 4, p. 201) and Khoisan formed more than half. The General Commando was empowered not simply to recover livestock and punish identifiable offenders but, where required, to wage war against all of the region's Khoisan. The slaughter was immense: 503 were killed by the commandos in 1774 and 2,480 between 1786 and 1795, according to records which are almost certainly incomplete.[58] Though the Khoisan took many thousand head of livestock and, time after time, drove colonists from their farms, the burghers with their guns and horses finally gained the upper hand.

These events were crucial not only to the allocation of resources on the northeastern frontier but to the shaping of labour relations within the colony itself. After many setbacks the General Commando cleared the way for an extension of the colonial boundary in 1798. The new line linked Plettenberg's Beacon in the east with the Riet River and the Buffalo River, which empties into the Atlantic north of the Kamiesberg. The 'good and faithful' Khoisan who participated in the campaign as partners with Europeans now faced harsh new realities. By implication the government had given the trekboers a free hand to exclude the Khoisan from any land which they coveted. More significantly, they had been allowed to capture and add to their labour force those Khoisan resisters whom they did not kill – women and children in almost every case. At the same time the colonial government introduced measures which coerced the Khoisan to meet manpower needs for agricultural production and for defence. They were forced to render military service without the prospect of either sharing in the spoils as in the past, or of earning burgher rights in the colony.[59]

By 1800 the domination of trekboers over Khoisan, in regions coveted for pastoralism, was almost complete. Starting in the late 1760s, the trekboers had also laid claim to the rich pasturelands east of the Gamtoos River, as far as the Great Fish. In 1786 the government recognised their de facto occupation of a vast region beyond the colonial frontier by establishing the district of Graaff-Reinet. The transformation of this regions's Khoisan into a labour force had followed a familiar course. Many became servants after a period of clientage; perhaps two thousand were captured in war; still others were indentured on the farms where they were born.[60] In 1797 John Barrow noted that there were no independent 'kraals' in Graaff-Reinet, nor even 'a score of individuals who are not actually in the service of the Dutch'.[61]

The Khoisan workforce on European farms, 1720–1803

Throughout the eighteenth century European farmers in the Cape Colony experienced severe labour shortages. Farms were large, white workers were few, and many farmers, particularly pastoralists, could not afford sufficient slaves. Khoikhoi were desirable farm labourers because of their long experience with the domestication of animals. Though they had not traditionally yoked their oxen, they had used them both as pack and riding animals. Their expertise in the training and handling of draught animals prepared them for ploughing and driving wagons on arable farms, while their skill in the management of flocks and herds ensured their importance to European graziers. The fact that Khoikhoi provided the colonists both with livestock and the labour to manage it was, as S.D. Neumark noted, a combination 'for which there is hardly any parallel in colonial history'.[62]

Both Khoikhoi men and women milked the farmers' cows, there being no taboo in Khoikhoi culture against female contact with cattle. In addition, they knew how to slaughter; to treat skins and hides; to render animal fat; and to manufacture skin bags, *veldschoenen*, whips and thongs. These skills enabled their employers to capitalise on the by-products, not only of pastoralism, but also of the hunt. With little additional training the Khoikhoi could make butter and soap, both important sources of revenue for the trekboers. The Khoikhoi women also worked as cooks,

domestics and nannies – especially on the frontier where there were
fewer slaves than in the southwestern Cape. Women made the reed mats
which trekboers used in fashioning Khoikhoi-style homes and in
covering their wagons.[63]

As for the 'Bushmen', many were at first less adept at pastoral tasks
than the Khoikhoi though apparently they picked up these skills quickly.
Like the Khoikhoi, 'Bushmen' were employed to hunt wild animals,
from which the master claimed meat for home consumption and
valuable skins, horns and tusks. Thunberg found farmers who made
their Khoisan servants hunt their own food: the farmers supplied the
ammunition and received the animal skins in return. As hunters and
armed herdsmen, many Khoisan became expert handlers of firearms.
This skill made them more valuable allies, or more dangerous enemies,
depending on the circumstances.[64]

As guides and interpreters, as well as drivers and leaders of oxen, the
Khoisan played a major part in the colonists' trade with the Xhosa and
other peoples. Butchers also hired Khoisan to drive livestock from the
frontier: on one drive from Sneeuwberg, John Barrow saw some 500
cattle and 5000 sheep. It was difficult and dangerous work to find
grazing and to protect the drive from thieves who lurked near the most-
travelled routes.[65] Similarly Khoisan wagoners carried the products of
farm and hunt to Cape Town, which for 150 years remained the sole
entrepôt in the colony. When farmers made these trips themselves, they
sometimes left Khoisan men and women in control of entire farms and
their enormous herds and flocks.

Travellers in the Cape Colony were sharply divided on how well the
farmers treated their servants. Some described colonists who were brutal
and serenely indifferent to suffering and death among their Khoisan
employees. Such observations are buttressed by the court records which
portray a high level of violence in master-servant relations. But we also
have vignettes in the travel literature of happy farms where Khoisan
received considerate treatment and looked to their employers with
evident affection.[66] By their very nature, isolated farms do not lend
themselves to generalisation.

The court records give the impression that Khoisan had access to the
courts when they needed protection against both whites and slaves. This
impression may, however, be misleading.[67] In one notable case in 1774,
where a string of violent disputes led to the death of a Khoisan youth, it
seems that the matter reached the court only because neighbours had
reasons of their own to intervene. As late as 1795, Landdrost H.C.D.
Maynier of Graaff-Reinet found it necessary to proclaim to burghers in

his district: 'I will and shall open my court to the heathen'.[68]

Though wages were invariably described as 'low', concrete details are scarce: the earnings of Khoisan farm labourers were seldom recorded before November 1799, when a register of labour contracts was introduced in the district of Graaff-Reinet. As a consequence it is very difficult to determine trends over time. One thing, however, is clear: rations almost always formed a major part of the wage. Mentzel said that 'every Cape farmer' needed 50 to 100 pounds of tobacco annually for his Khoisan and slaves. At the end of an extensive tour of the colony in 1797, Barrow observed that the farmer's work was done for him by Khoisan who 'cost him nothing but meat, tobacco and skins'.[69] Shortly after the end of the nineteenth century Hinrich Lichtenstein visited a farmer in Bruintjes Hoogte who slaughtered 600 sheep a year to feed his large household; by contrast, Lady Anne Barnard, in roughly the same period, believed that bread and melons were the normal fare of the Khoisan nearest to Cape Town.[70]

Besides tobacco and food, payments in kind included beads, flints and tinder boxes, knives, clothing (generally second-hand) and, perhaps, an ox or a small number of breeding animals. In the 1770s farmers on the Rivier Zondereind, near Tijgerhoek, paid their Khoisan rations of food and tobacco as well as an annual wage of one or two sheep and their lambs, or one cow and calf, or their value in cash. A heifer per annum seems to have been the standard wage in the north and northeast around 1775, but by 1793 the farmers preferred to pay workers in cash or in manufactured goods.[71]

Elsewhere cash wages were rare. In 1799 in the eastern district of Graaff-Reinet the landdrost was the only important employer paying an annual wage in cash. Cash may have been paid to casual workers more often than to full-time servants. Janze Spielman, a Khoikhoi of Bethelsdorp, stated that day labourers in Uitenhage had earned two skillings a day, or four skillings if they were sawyers or artisans. It was not necessarily advantageous to wage-earners to be paid in cash rather than in kind; on the contrary, in a time of rising prices, the conversion of rations to a cash wage might leave workers worse off than before.[72] The wages cited so far were paid to able-bodied Khoisan men; in 1809 Colonel Richard Collins observed that 'a female obtains much less' and that children were required to work from an early age in return for their rations. For a year's work many women were given only food and a suit of clothes.[73]

As in the previous period, Khoisan in the eighteenth century often kept their own stock on the farms, using cows' and ewes' milk to supplement their rations. In 1798 the only known census of Khoisan livestock holdings was carried out in Graaff-Reinet district: around 1,350 Khoisan on European-owned farms declared an average of five cattle and twenty-three sheep each.[74] By allowing this custom, farmers could secure the labour they required without resorting to force. The farmers' dependence on Khoisan labour in areas with a harsh environment and sparse population produced a short-lived paternalism. For example, in the Roggeveld between 1750 and 1770 not only were some Khoisan given grazing for their stock, but the trekboers also protected them from VOC agents who forced them to barter against their wish. However, at about the same time in a more heavily populated area near the Gamtoos in the east, an independent Khoisan was ordered to 'decamp' because 'he had too many cattle, and thus injured the pasture of' the European settlers. As the best land passed into European hands, the independence which Khoisan had derived from possessing stock diminished. They remained largely dependent on the farmers for grazing rights, even if they built up their herds and flocks to the point where they could aspire to an independent life. As pressures on the environment increased, so too did Khoisan complaints that farmers were seizing their animals. For example, in 1796 two contract workers in Graaff-Reinet charged that their employers were keeping them in service by holding sixteen of their cows and twenty-two of their sheep.[75]

Partly because of the low wages paid to Khoisan labourers, the farmers seem to have experienced great difficulty in finding and retaining adequate labour. Another reason for this labour shortage was the unwillingness of many Khoikhoi pastoralists to sign on for long periods. Thus throughout the century 'Bushmen' were assiduously 'tamed' to swell the labour force. Khoikhoi servants sometimes assisted in this by kidnapping 'Bushmen' and farmers came to rely upon distributions of child prisoners-of-war.[76]

Since labour contracts between Europeans and Khoisan were not written before 1799, they were easily broken by either party. Khoisan frequently alleged that their employers would not pay them the agreed wage, or that they were withholding part of their wage to recover debts or the cost of lost livestock. The burghers' common complaint was that Khoisan deserted before completing their contracts. At first the farmers relied on their own methods to control their labour force, which included (besides seizing workers' livestock) thrashing their labourers severely, chasing runaways and holding children hostage to force their parents' return.[77] It is clear that in the eighteenth century the government neither countenanced these customs nor took active measures to suppress them – unless a Khoisan had been murdered in the process. As its controls over the trekboers weakened, so did its capacity, and perhaps its will, to check the inevitable abuses of a labour system in which employees were impoverished, unorganised, and largely ignorant of the laws of the society in which they lived.

Farmers, however, asked more of government than non-intervention in labour relations. In 1721 a group of farmers objected to feeding the children born from unions between Khoisan women and slave men; these children were technically free and could not be forced to work when they reached maturity. Thus the farmers petitioned the Council of Policy to declare that such children could be apprenticed for a fixed number of years. The Council did not act on the request. It was not until 1775 that the governor approved a regulation in Stellenbosch which allowed a 'Bastaard Hottentot' child (i.e. one of Khoisan-slave ancestry) to be apprenticed to age twenty-five. Though subject to provisions designed to protect the child (see ch. 9, p. 449), this '*inboek*' system was a key step legislating the subservience of the labour force – especially since it was afterwards construed by the farmers to apply to all Khoisan children, not those with slave fathers alone.[78] The request passed over in 1721 may have received favourable attention in 1775 because, in addition to the ever-present labour shortage, there was now a military crisis as well. The last three decades of the eighteenth century were to see restrictive regulations which served not only to tie labour down but to identify new categories of men who could be made to serve in the commandos. Every year the local officials compiled lists of Khoisan and Bastaard-Hottentots residing in their districts; though designed to prevent runaway slaves from passing as free persons, these lists could also be used to pin-point men eligible for military service. In 1781 the first Khoisan and Bastaards were called up into a unit of their own, as we shall see. These decades represent, therefore, a crucial stage during which the rights and duties of the 'free' Khoisan were redefined.[79]

Limitations on freedom of movement also date from this period. In 1780 Stellenbosch officials asked that 'free Bastaard-Hottentots' be required to carry passes, like slaves. The Council of Policy withheld permission on this request. However, in 1787, the free movement of Khoisan, Bastaards and Bastaard-Hottentots around Cape Town was curtailed: a lapsed proclamation of 1755, which had required Bastaard-Hottentot women in Cape Town to be domiciled with burghers, was resuscitated and extended to include men as well. Pass systems were later introduced for Khoisan in Swellendam (1797) and Graaff-Reinet (1798). The pass system was designed not only to prevent servants from deserting but to stop burghers from poaching their neighbours' servants. It was thus a fierce competition for labour which gave birth to the pass system in South Africa.[80]

The Company added to the farmers' discontent by also competing for the services of Khoisan. In 1793 the farmers of Stellenbosch and Drakenstein complained that the Company's demand for Khoisan on commandos and in public works interfered with their labour supply. The Company and (after 1795) the British government also employed small numbers as messengers, interpreters and spies, and as intermediaries in their dealings with the Xhosa.[81] Progressively the surviving leaders of the Khoisan became dependents of the Company. Whereas before they had been wooed with gifts to secure peaceful co-existence and friendly trade, they now earned meagre rewards for the services which government exacted of them. In serving both the government and the colonists these Khoisan abetted the expansion of the colony.

The main way to resist servitude was to desert. As hiding-places grew scarcer within the colony, deserters lurked near farms, stealing to feed themselves, or cast their lot with communities beyond the moving frontier. Both as bandits inside the colony and as allies of 'Bushmen' and Xhosa beyond the frontier, deserters had an unsettling effect on farm servants, whose grievances were seldom heeded or redressed. Their example was not lost on Khoisan servants, who still vividly recalled a time before their land and livestock had been lost. The possibility that Khoisan servants might unite in revolt had first been realized in 1739, but the most important uprising occurred at the end of the century on the Eastern Frontier. Beginning in March 1799 hundreds of servants left farms in the region and waged a four-year war not so much to improve working conditions as to reclaim the 'country of which our fathers have been despoiled'.[82] This war of independence (1799–1803) was linked with a conflict between Xhosa and colonists (the Third Frontier War) in which Khoisan and Xhosa were allies (see ch. 9, p. 440).

The Khoisan rebels formed themselves into bands led by captains. Their command structure appears to have been an adaptation of the old system of social organisation based on clans. Maynier used the word 'confederacy' to describe these bands in combination. Among the captains whom the records name – the Stuurman brothers, Boezak, Bovenlander, Wildeman, Jan Kaffer, Hans Trompetter, Ourson, to mention a few – Klaas Stuurman appears as the most important spokesman but his primacy was often repudiated by other captains. In April 1799, Stuurman implored a British military contingent near Algoa Bay to rescue his people from the oppressive 'yoke of the Boers'. Before long, however, he and some followers found cause to doubt British intentions towards themselves and fled to the Zuurveld Xhosa, who already harboured many Khoisan refugees.[83]

In June 1799 a party of some 150 Xhosa and Khoisan defeated a strong burgher commando which the British had authorised to expel the Xhosa across the Fish River and to compel the Khoisan to return to the farms. The following month the Khoisan mustered 300 armed and mounted men for a raid down the Long Kloof in the district of Swellendam.[84] They seized livestock and wagons, ammunition and firearms, and forced most of the eastern colonists to abandon their farms. Acting Governor Francis Dundas went to the frontier, taking Maynier, on whom he relied to end the war. Maynier's strategy was to deal separately with the Khoisan and their Gqunukhwebe or Xhosa allies. Persistently, the lines of cleavage in frontier society were exploited by both sides: by the Khoisan who perceived the tensions between the Dutch colonists and the British government, especially where the fractious burghers of the eastern districts were concerned; and by the government which, in its negotiations, always strove to separate the Khoisan from the Xhosa.[85] Maynier's intervention resulted in some eighteen months of relative calm, but the fragile peace was disturbed by two burgher assaults on the Graaff-Reinet drostdy in mid-1801; then, in November, war broke out again.

Initially the central government's attitude to the war was fairly even-handed. As late as December 1801 an important official condemned the frontier farmers who, 'by their excessive and general cruelty have at length provoked these humble pacific people to acts of revenge'.[86] But soon after the fighting was renewed, the tide of official opinion turned. The killing of a field cornet in his home and the fresh wave of attacks on farms enraged colonists and government alike. By this time the economic consequences of a renewed war had also come into focus: meat production by frontier graziers and livestock trade with the Xhosa had both seriously declined. In Cape Town, as a result, 'butcher's meat [had] become very dear'.[87] The British, whose first occupation of the Cape was nearly at an end, were obliged to rely on burgher commandos once again to quell the raiders, who were striking deep into the colony throughout 1802. After months of inconclusive warfare and the loss of important leaders on both sides, the fighting died down. It fell to the new Batavian regime (see ch. 8, p. 441) to arrange a peace settlement in May, 1803.

The uprising failed in part because of divisions among Khoisan, and between Khoisan and their Xhosa comrades-in-arms. Some Khoisan resisted recruitment to the rebel cause. To such hesitant Khoisan, rebel recruiters would reply: 'Go but your way, we will murder all the Christians, and all of you'.[88] There were also divisions over tactics: Stuurman was prepared to negotiate a peace in return for some land in the eastern districts; other captains wanted to pursue a struggle for complete independence to the bitter end.

The rising of servants against masters in 1799–1803 had resulted in bitterness equalling that between trekboer and independent Khoisan on earlier frontiers.[89] Its most significant outcome was that government had been forced to intervene decisively, not only to police the frontier but to restore the dominance of white masters over their Khoisan servants.

Khoisan subservience mitigated and confirmed, c. 1790 to 1819

In the 1790s two new developments counteracted, in small degree, the decades-long transformation of the independent Khoisan into a class of wage labourers who were only partially free. One was the creation of a Corps (later Regiment) of Bastaards and Khoisan in 1793 (see ch. 7, p. 337).[90] The other was the arrival of European missionaries (see ch. 7, pp. 339–43). The options presented to Khoisan by the Cape Regiment and the missions became apparent in the terms offered to the rebels in 1802–03: those who agreed to lay down arms could enlist or enter a mission station rather than serving on a European farm.

From the 1670s the VOC had enjoyed the support of Khoisan allies in its wars with other Khoisan and in its preparations against external attack. It regarded colonial Khoisan and 'Bastaard Hottentots' as subjects whom it protected and who should hence contribute to their own defence.[91] In 1759, in response to the threat posed to Dutch colonies by the Seven Years War in Europe, the Company called on Khoisan who could handle guns to join the burghers, their slaves and *knechts*, to make ready to defend the Cape. In the event, no invasion occurred. In 1781 Khoisan and Bastaards were first formed into a separate unit when Governor Joachim van Plettenberg received news of the outbreak of the Fourth Anglo-Dutch War. Within a month, four hundred recruits were formed into a light infantry regiment; but in 1782, when mercenaries from Europe strengthened the garrison, the unit was disbanded. Once again, in 1793, when it appeared that French revolutionary forces would overrun Holland, the VOC ordered the burghers to send to the capital 'all Bastaards and other Hottentots' who could handle firearms, and the so-called 'Corps Pandoeren' was formed.[92]

The government of the first British occupation (1795 to 1803) decided to maintain the Corps of 'Hottentots' as a frank exercise in 'ethnic management'. The acting governor, General Sir James Craig, doubted if he could control a fractious white citizenry which had only been weakly governed in the past. Thus he admitted that, in retaining the Corps, he was 'actuated more by political than military views'. Barrow agreed that 'from their rooted antipathy to the boors' Khoisan in an armed unit could be relied on to 'quell any disturbances' and would become attached to the new regime.[93] Additional advantages of such a unit were the low cost of 'native' troops compared to imported garrisons and the benefits to those troops (and by extension, to society as a whole) of the presumed 'civilising' function of their training. A final argument, and a compelling one, extolled the unique skills of the Khoisan as trackers and guides.

During the Van Jaarsveld Rebellion in 1799 (see ch. 9, p. 440), a detachment of Khoisan was marched with other British units to the eastern Cape. This was the first occasion on which these Khoisan soldiers were employed to settle internal disputes among whites. Despite vehement burgher opposition, they remained on active service throughout the Third Frontier War (1799–1803). In 1801 the Corps was renamed the Cape Regiment. After retaking the Cape in 1806 the British called for the Khoisan unit to be established on the same footing as the Crown's other troops of infantry. Though a line regiment, it was 'colonial' in the sense that it was available only for service at the Cape.[94]

After several inactive years, detachments were sent to the frontier in 1810 and 1811 when fears of a Xhosa incursion were on the increase. The Regiment performed well in the Fourth Frontier War (1811–12), convincing Governor Cradock that it should be stationed permanently in the eastern Cape. In 1812 its headquarters was moved from Cape Town to a spot which took its name, Grahamstown, from Lieutenant-Colonel John Graham who commanded the Regiment from 1806.

Some Khoisan on farms volunteered for the Regiment: a VOC officer claimed that when they were brought to Cape Town they sometimes took the chance to desert their employers and enlist.[95] But generally the government conscripted Khoisan by ballot or district quotas in order to overcome the shortage of volunteers. The colonists, who saw the unit as a threat to their labour supply as well as a potential instrument against themselves, often contributed to the poor response of the Khoisan: some drove the recruiters from their farms, or spread false rumours about conditions in the service. Even without these disincentives many Khoisan were loath to enlist. In 1811 William Burchell reported a Khoisan soldier's view that most resented the 'exact and regular' routines of military life.[96]

Khoisan in missions and in semi-independent groups also resisted recruitment to the Regiment. The missions were under constant pressure to furnish soldiers, pressure which was hard to resist given their dependence on government patronage. In 1796, the military persuaded reluctant Khoisan at the Genadendal mission that they stood to forfeit the protection and support of government if they did not enlist.[97] The Stuurman community near the Gamtoos quarrelled with a recruiting officer in 1808; its leader, David Stuurman (a brother of Klaas), declined the staff of office which signified his duty to assist recruitment. The Bethelsdorp missionaries (under whose pastoral wing the community fell) were caught in the middle of this dispute: constantly prodded by government to supply recruits, they were accused by members of Stuurman's group of seeking 'merely to tame the Hottentots for military service'.[98] The subtlety which recruiting officers needed to fill quotas was well expressed in 1813 by W.S. van Andringa, landdrost of Stellenbosch. He explained that it was fatal to admit to Khoisan that they were free to choose whether to sign on or not.[99]

Though Khoisan soldiers widely resisted their initial recruitment, some were attracted to re-enlist after their first seven-year term of service; this was especially true after 1813 when a pension plan was introduced. Eventually a nucleus of career soldiers emerged. Soldiers became eligible for pensions after twenty-one years of service, or when they were discharged on account of injury or chronic ill health. Pensions were fixed at half-pay, on a sliding scale determined by rank: a discharged private received a skilling (6 pence) per day.[100]

Although the burghers had continually complained that the Regiment drained off labour, and the missionaries that it hindered Christian work, the officials by and large praised it unstintingly. However, service in the Regiment opened few doors for the Khoisan. No Khoisan attained a higher rank than sergeant, while Europeans filled all commissioned, and some non-commissioned ranks. As a visitor to the Cape was later to observe, 'absurdly settled usages' prevented the preferment of worthy men if they were 'Hottentots'.[101] On discharge, ex-soldiers had no option but to work for the burghers – unless they gained access to a mission or an independent kraal, and such access was not always easy. A discharged soldier could even be a focus of alarm. In 1810, when the frontier situation appeared threatening, the landdrost of

Uitenhage implored that none of the men serving there or in Graaff-Reinet should be discharged in those districts lest they 'commit acts of outrage' and entice the Xhosa to 'involve the country in a war'. Dr. John Philip of the London Missionary Society (LMS) later reported that a European officer who esteemed Khoisan in uniform could see no contradiction in despising the people as a whole: 'To the Hottentot soldier he would attach the ideas associated with British valour – with the Hottentot bondman he would associate feelings of contempt'.[102]

The impact of the Regiment on Khoisan and Bastaards must have been considerable: the LMS missionary, A.A. van der Lingen, who served as regimental chaplain, estimated that between 1806 and 1817 he had ministered to some 1,100 men, and also 400 women and numerous children who lived in the barracks with the men. Yet the Regiment's influence for good or ill is almost impossible to quantify. Collins was convinced that the Khoisan soldier's pay was good compared with that of a farm labourer but Major G. Tylden, a historian of the Regiment, states that 'the pay was small and deductions heavy and not always equitable'. The pension plan supported ex-soldiers and reduced the burden on missions and independent Khoisan groups responsible for invalids and 'worn out' men; yet in the 1840s the wife of a British officer would claim that the smallness of the pension and the difficulty of collecting payments deterred potential recruits.[103]

In 1814 a regimental school was founded at Grahamstown on the Lancastrian plan, whereby older pupils taught younger ones under supervision. Cradock wrote with pride of this 'extensive School' which promised to provide 'teachers . . . to all of the Hottentot nation who shall stand in need of instruction'; Lord Charles Somerset hailed it too, as one of the 'advantages . . . from forming [the 'Hottentot Community'] into a Military Corps'. Though the regimental school probably did not realise Cradock's ambitious claims for it, it was nonetheless the only source of formal education for Khoisan besides mission schools.[104]

Even more than the Regiment, Christian missions gave rise to the hope that Khoisan could be 'civilised' (i.e., acculturated) and their status in Cape society improved. In 1793 three Moravians returned to Baviaanskloof (later Genadendal) where their intrepid forerunner, Georg Schmidt, had worked from 1737 to 1744. Khoisan travelled great distances and defied hostile colonists in order to join the missionaries. They also manifested zeal for the Christian gospel and for the routines of mission life. All this was contrary to Schmidt's earlier experience, when the Hessequa among whom he worked were still relatively free and proved, with a few significant exceptions, indifferent to his teaching.[105] Bethelsdorp, the LMS station near Algoa Bay, was opened in 1803 among Khoisan who were only superficially more independent of the colonists than those in the vicinity of Baviaanskloof.[106] Though some frontier Khoisan hoped to join the Xhosa in a war against the colony like that of 1799–1803, the day-to-day reality of life for eastern Khoisan differed little from that of their fellows in the longer-settled west. In 1809 a census of Bethelsdorp residents revealed that almost a thousand individuals had been admitted – some 'from the woods', from 'Hans Trompetter's gang' or from 'Kaffer country' but more from the farms where the process of subordinating Khoisan was almost complete.[107]

In joining the missionaries, Khoisan also committed themselves to radical culture change. In theory, at least, they replaced their own cosmology with a Christian one; their traditional pastoralism with cultivation and trades; and their social system with broader loyalties to the church which transcended lineage and ethnic boundaries.[108] In 1804 Brother Boesak, a Bethelsdorp convert, described the struggle which conversion had caused between his two warring hearts: 'The one heart . . . will do nothing but sing all kinds of Hottentots and Boscheman's songs and all that is bad and the other heart strives to sing the praises of Christ'.[109] The great gift which Boesak and other converts received in return for surrendering their old beliefs was the experience of salvation through divine grace. Mission residents also received some protection from the hardships outside the station, and schooling and training in such skills as the missionaries happened to possess. They were also prodded to adopt 'square houses' and those consumer goods which were the emblems of a 'civilised' life.

At Bethelsdorp hunters, sawyers and timber merchants, transport riders, salt collectors and stocking knitters could make a fair living. Also, the services of certain skilled residents at Genadendal (a cartwright, a blacksmith, a cooper, a miller, several masons and midwives) were in demand by farmers in the neighbourhood, and some became 'quite well-to-do' as a result. Cutlers trained by the missionary Christian Kühnel, who had learned the craft at Herrnhut in Saxony, produced knives of the highest quality, which the colonists called 'herneuters'. Mission life gave a few Khoisan a measure of financial independence, but the shortage of suitable land on the overcrowded stations meant that most remained poor with no option but to hire themselves periodically to the farmers, or to enlist in the Regiment.[110]

Beginning in 1808, a number of new stations were founded for Khoisan which also admitted some Bastaards and freed slaves:

Groenekloof (Mamre) and Witterivier (Enon) by the Moravians; Theopolis, Hooge Kraal (Pacaltsdorp) and the 'Bushman' stations, Tooverberg (Grace Hill) and Hephzibah by the LMS; and Leliefontein in the Kamiesberg by the Wesleyans (see fig. 1.2, p.23). Opportunities opened up for zealous converts to become 'chapel servants' and overseers in the Moravian communities or deacons, elders and teachers in those of the LMS. In 1814 LMS representatives held an important conference at Graaff-Reinet to discuss calling 'missionaries . . . from among the Heathen'. Six men – four Griqua and two Khoisan – were raised to the rank of assistant missionary, without, apparently, being ordained.[111]

Cupido Kakkerlak, who was one of the six, had been among the earliest Khoisan baptised by Dr. J.T. van der Kemp, the first of the LMS missionaries. At Bethelsdorp Cupido had become moderately prosperous and figured prominently in the mission's life. His story provides a striking example of the hopes of Christian Khoisan and missionaries that a Khoisan middle-class would emerge and gain acceptance in colonial society. James Read was jubilant in 1814 when 'our Brother Cupido was taken for the first time to dine at the table of an African [i.e. Afrikaner] farmer'.[112] The successes which Cupido achieved – as sawyer, deacon, elder and assistant missionary – as well as the failure of his lonely mission to the wandering Kora east of Kuruman between 1817 and 1823, occurred mainly within the little world created by the mission society. However, missionaries and their sympathisers still hoped to assist ambitious Khoisan to enter colonial society on equal terms with other free inhabitants.

The advent of missionaries also meant that the grievances of the Khoisan were articulated more effectively than before. Van der Kemp and Read had vocally denounced the cruelties and injustices suffered by the Khoisan and had demanded the restoration of their status as free people. With missionary help, Khoisan were more inclined to seek reparation for injustice through the courts, particularly after 1811 when a circuit court was introduced. But by 1819, when their most ardent champion, Dr. John Philip of the LMS, arrived at the Cape, the subservience of most Khoisan had been entrenched. A series of colony-wide proclamations had enshrined restrictive practices previously upheld by custom or by local statute.

Lord Caledon's proclamation of 1 November 1809 was the first of these. It required that labour contracts be drawn up in triplicate so that master, servant and the authorities each possessed a record of the terms. It also laid down that all 'Hottentots' must have a 'fixed place of abode' registered with the *fiscal* or the *landdrost*. They must then apply to one of these officials for a 'certificate' (that is, a pass) before moving out of the district. However, servants also required passes stating that they had 'duly served out' their time before they could change jobs; they could be challenged by 'every one' to show the pass if they set foot beyond the place of their employment and, failing to do so, they could be delivered to the field cornet. Hence it was at the levels of the individual farm and the field cornet's ward (that is, a subdivision of the district) that Khoikhoi freedom of movement was in practice controlled. These requirements placed the Khoikhoi (they applied only to 'Hottentots') at the mercy of those most interested in tying them down.[113]

The proclamation of 1809 had no provision for the apprenticeship of young Khoikhoi. However, early in 1810 the Colonial Secretary advised J.G. Cuyler, the landdrost of Uitenhage, that 'where it is proposed to teach a Hottentot a trade or in case of great youth where early services scarcely compensate for their food and clothes', the Khoikhoi might 'bind themselves for a term of seven years'. At almost the same time the landdrost of Stellenbosch urgently enjoined the fiscal to permit the apprenticeship of Khoikhoi children (not just those with a slave father) 'until their twenty-fifth year'. In April 1812 Governor Cradock legislated a ten-year period of apprenticeship, from ages eight to eighteen, if the colonist had maintained a child in its first eight years. Child apprenticeship had the effect of immobilising parents who wished to preserve their family unit. In 1819 a further proclamation empowered the fiscal or landdrost to apprentice to a farmer orphans and other Khoikhoi children not in their parents' care to the age of eighteen. Its provisions were easily abused when officials imposed them on children who required no protection.[114] These laws referred only to 'Hottentots'; in 1817 a proclamation extended apprenticeship to certain categories of 'Bosjesman' children.[115] Designed ostensibly to protect the Khoisan, the main goal of all these laws was to secure for the burghers a stable labour force. They decreased mobility and probably depressed wages, though this is difficult to gauge.[116]

The web binding Khoisan in servitude was, however, more complex than this sequence of proclamations suggests. They were also excluded from land ownership – an exclusion which, if not explicit in law, was clear enough in fact to be addressed by the framers of Ordinance 50 of 1828, who emphasised that Khoisan had 'competency . . . to purchase or possess Land'.[117] Before 1828 there were only a handful of Khoisan or Bastaards who possessed land grants in the colony. The most notable example was Klaas Stuurman who, in the rebellion of 1799–1803, had claimed the region east of the Zwartkops River as 'my country'. After the rebellion collapsed, Stuurman was apparently the only rebel leader to receive a piece of land from the government. This grant, near the Gamtoos, was no larger than an ordinary farm. Five years later, after his death, the government expelled Stuurman's brother, David, along with some forty men, women and children who had moved onto the grant. The expulsion was prompted in large part by David Stuurman's willingness to give refuge to 'many Hottentots with whom he had no relationship' and by his failure to turn over to the government Khoisan accused of breaking labour contracts. Here, perhaps, is the key to the government's reluctance to give land to Khoisan: the fear that such land, like the missions, would offer Khoisan an escape from labour on farms.[118]

As free Khoisan were gradually reduced to conditions approaching serfdom, their leadership was also transformed. Long after most had been absorbed on European farms, their clan-based organization could quickly be revived, as in the servants' revolt of 1799–1803. The rebel Khoisan who remained east of the Sundays River for the better part of the war were organized under numerous captains; so were the more than 800 Khoisan who sought refuge in the village of Graaff-Reinet in 1801–02 (see ch. 9, p. 441). However, some of these latter captains had been appointed by Resident Commissioner Maynier. Increasingly, captaincies fell into the gift, not of the clan, but of whites. Indeed, Philip was to claim that by 1795 even local colonists might propose candidates for captain, although the final right of appointment belonged to the commander-in-chief. This fact underlines the white officials' preoccupation with the military function of captains, who above all were called upon to recruit Khoisan for the Regiment.[119] The government granted staffs of office to a number of captains between 1806 and 1809 in a drive to formalise the link between the Regiment and surviving semi-independent groups, not only of Khoikhoi pastoralists but also of 'Bushmen' hunters and Bastaards. The importance of Khoikhoi captains as recruiters is underscored by entries in the colony's accounts, viz.: 'Pay of Hottentot Captains for the purpose of encouraging them to promote the enlistment of recruits from their respective Kraals'.[120]

By 1819 the Khoisan in the colony were firmly in the grip of a system of labour repression based not only on labour legislation itself but on the absence of landholding and on the co-optation of their leadership. Against this massive system the material benefits provided by the missions and the Regiment must be seen more as palliatives than as genuine alternatives. However, the hope of a successful rebellion was not dead. An unknown number of Khoisan lived beyond the frontier, fuelling colonists' fears of a revived Khoisan-Xhosa alliance. In 1818 some Khoisan and the Xhosa chief Galata conspired to kill the landdrost of Uitenhage and drive out the white inhabitants. This plot, though it failed utterly, signified the enduring Khoisan claim to land and freedom.[121]

An attempt at emancipation, c. 1820–28

The 1820 census of the Cape Colony showed 26,975 Khoisan and Bastaards (see ch. 4, p. 202), who together formed 45 per cent of the labour force that was not European. The balance consisted of 1,932 free blacks and 31,779 slaves ('prize Negroes', that is, Africans freed by the Royal Navy from slaving vessels, were not enumerated).[122] 'Bushmen' were still being drawn into the labour force and subsumed under the category 'Hottentot': in 1807 the landdrost of Graaff-Reinet had pointed out that most of the 'Hottentots' in his district were 'generated from the Bosjesmen', a process which was still in evidence. From around 1823 there was also an influx of southern Tswana and other refugees from the Difaqane, called 'Mantatees' by the colonists. The employment of Xhosa by eastern frontier farmers had been forbidden in 1797 and remained illegal until the passage of Ordinance 49 in 1828. Slaves chiefly, but also prize Negroes and free blacks, comprised the work force in Cape Town and the arable southwest, although Khoikhoi were in demand for certain tasks, especially herding and wagondriving. In the eastern Cape, on the other hand, farmers looked to neighbouring Xhosa (despite the ban), chance arrivals from across the Orange and, above all, the Khoisan to fill their labour needs. By the 1820s slaves were also arriving in increasing numbers in the eastern Cape.[123]

With the incorporation of the Cape Colony into the dynamic trading system of the British Empire, conditions in the trekboer regions became increasingly diverse. In the Camdebo, the village of Graaff-Reinet and areas adjacent to Algoa Bay, both the economy and the population expanded more rapidly than elsewhere (see ch. 0, pp. 000–00, 000). This trend was intensified in 1820 when four to five thousand British settlers were placed in the Zuurveld, west of the Fish River, from where they soon fanned out, founding towns and promoting trade and agriculture (see ch. 10, pp. 472–75).[124] The resulting infusion of cash and the growth of consumer demand were felt at once by the established population. The British settlers, who were forbidden to have slaves, sought Khoisan workers at the Theopolis and Bethelsdorp missions. They hired as transport riders mission Khoisan who had invested in wagons and oxen. There was also employment for all sorts of construction workers – masons, thatchers and carpenters – and for wheelwrights and wagonmakers.[125] In these as in other respects, the British settlers set in train processes which soon distinguished the east from other parts of the colony.

Despite these developments, practices from earlier periods persisted into the 1820s. Commandos against 'Bushmen' continued to provide colonists with labour. Though the proclamation of August 1817 had forbidden 'manstealing', children who survived attacks on their communities could be assigned to farmers, first to be 'maintained' and then 'apprenticed' for a period of years. In wars of extermination against hunters the sparing of some, even for forced labour, struck contemporaries as 'humane'. In 1824 George Thompson found many such children in service to the farmers of the Onder Bokkeveld. Further east the landdrost of Cradock explained that '405 Bushmen above, and 437 under the age of 16' resided with farmers to whom they would be apprenticed when they had 'been severally maintained . . . for the periods required'.[126] Commandos also continued as instruments in the rivalry for booty and power on the open frontier, a fact understood by all the parties concerned. One Kora in the Winterveld even equated commandos with 'Bushmen' raiders, as 'people who come to murder and plunder'.[127]

Khoisan continued to be requisitioned for ill-paid public works in this period. Tasks such as building roads, preparing watercourses, driving wagons and delivering the post fell ever more upon the residents of mission stations. The Commissioners of Inquiry, sent in 1823 by the British government to investigate the condition of aborigines and slaves (see ch. 10, pp. 488–97), opposed the 'forced appropriation of the labour of Hottentots to public works and expeditions in which they had no interest'.[128] Officers of the Cape Regiment also scoured the missions for recruits. Most Khoisan remained reluctant to enlist, Landdrost van der Riet of George asserting that 'nothing but compulsion will induce the Hottentots to enter the Service'. By this stage some of the Khoisan captains had a keener sense of the extent to which recruiting officers depended on their aid: in 1823 'twelve fine lads' were selected by a Captain Aitchison, at Genadendal, after they had been 'paraded for my inspection by the Hottentot Captains (whose good offices I purchased by a small bribe)'.[129] Even in uniform, assemblies of Khoisan were perceived as convenient labour pools. In 1821 it became necessary for senior officers to rule that Khoikhoi soldiers should only be employed 'in regular routine of duty' and not, as before, detached as postmen, surveyers' assistants, ox-drivers for other regiments, or guards for the settlers' homes.[130]

Whereas in the past wages paid to the Khoisan were uniformly low, by the mid-1820s a wider range of salaries had developed. Cash wages were more common than formerly, but in many areas payments in kind (e.g. livestock and grain) remained the norm. Wages also showed more marked regional differences than before. In Clanwilliam where the farmers were said to be 'little better off than the Hottentots', farm workers were paid 2 to 3 rixdollars per month. In Uitenhage the rate varied from 5 to 12 rixdollars per month, and in Stellenbosch some Khoisan received up to 15 rixdollars. These rates refer to full-time workers under contract; during ploughing and harvesting the daily rates were 'much more'. They also refer to men in the prime of life: 'Bushmen' herders, female domestics, youths and apprentices worked merely for blankets, food and clothes.[131]

Janze Spielman, a Khoisan of Uitenhage where wages appear to have been relatively high, explained that the missionaries had informed the Khoisan 'of the value that they should put upon their labour . . .'[132] It is unlikely, however, that wages rose because of the missionaries' good advice alone. Enterprise had been stimulated by the opening of Algoa Bay to shipping and by the establishment of troops on the Eastern Frontier even before the 1820 settlers sparked an economic surge. By contrast, in the district of Clanwilliam north of Cape Town where, by the mid-1820s, the influence of missionaries and of the new commercial spirit was scarcely felt, 'the Hottentots very generally complained of the inadequate terms on which they were obliged to serve'. In Graaff-Reinet the ease with which 'Bushmen' servants were acquired was believed to keep wages particularly low.[133]

By the 1820s the thrust of the established missions to 'Hottentots' had changed. As one mission teacher explained, 'the Gospel is not now a novelty' and Khoisan 'normally profess Christianity': the excitement of conversion was therefore largely at an end. Philip aimed at an economic revitalisation of the LMS stations, whose depressed appearance played into the hands of the missionaries' critics. The injection of cash on the Eastern Frontier increased the buying power of some Khoisan and, at least for a time, abetted Philip's plans. Cape Town merchants opened shops at Bethelsdorp and Theopolis and experienced prompt rewards: in 1822 Ebenezer Kemp's store at Bethelsdorp sold goods valued at 20,000 rixdollars. The secretary to the landdrost of Uitenhage affirmed that Khoisan had come to value personal property and added: 'They are even inclined to luxuries, such as good clothes, and wearing shoes'.[134]

The encouragement of 'artificial wants', by which the missionaries hoped to inculcate the ethic of steady and gain-oriented work, exacerbated the problem of debt which had long bedevilled labour relations at the Cape. Detention of workers to repay debts incurred for medicines and other small items had been regulated by the labour law of 1809, but the provisions of this law were widely ignored. George Thompson was told in 1824 that farmers in the northwest ran their Khoisan servants into debt, 'a man having sometimes to serve two years to redeem the price of a suit of clothes worth 14 or 15 rixdollars'.[135]

In the 1820s, most of the old grievances of the Khoisan were still alive. They complained of being detained on the farms: when they wished to leave, their livestock was sometimes withheld or they were threatened with punishment by the field cornet. Moreover, servants were still tied down through the apprenticing of their children, which the proclamation of 1812 had allowed. Of all the regulations which inhibited the freedom of Khoisan, this last was deemed by the missionaries and their friends to be the most unfair. As Stockenstrom observed, this way of compensating employers for the maintenance of workers' dependents could not be justified: 'it is clear that the trifling quantity of food their children may require . . . was always taken into calculation in fixing those wages' which the parents were paid.[136]

Closely related to labour repression was the issue of land. The Commissioners of Inquiry found that, without legal justification, 'the Hottentots have been considered as being incapacitated by law from holding lands; and that, with a very few and late exceptions, they have never held any'.[137] Colonial Khoisan who possessed livestock were dependent upon farmers for their upkeep; there was seldom sufficient water or pasture in the wasteland between the farms. In 1829 the Khoisan Cobus Fortuin, who had twelve cows and sixty sheep, testified that he could not obtain wages because the right to graze his stock was 'considered sufficient payment for his labour'.[138] Philip was determined that the right of Khoisan to own land be clarified, though he foresaw that:

> . . . under the most favourable circumstances the great body of the Hottentots cannot be in any other condition than that of labourers for centuries to come. Individuals among the Hottentots . . . may, in thirty or forty years, rise to possess little farms.[139]

In 1824 George Thompson suggested that land should be purchased 'for industrious Hottentots all over the colony', who could then provide food and lodging to overcome the 'great evil the Hottentots and Bastaards endure on travelling through the colony'. As things stood they had no alternative when nightfall came but to creep into the servants' quarters on farms, thus inconveniencing the farmers.[140] However, no significant action was taken until 1829 when a settlement scheme was implemented at the Kat River for 'Hottentots of good character, or possessing property'. This project (which had some of the features of a military colony) evoked mixed reactions from the Europeans. Some believed that the Khoisan would prove to be as susceptible as others to 'the general effect which property produces', improving themselves once in possession of land. Others were alarmed, fearing a renewed Khoisan alliance with the Xhosa.[141]

The great increase of colonists after 1820 (see ch. 10, p. 472) ensured that the 'deficiency of labourers' – always an issue – was more keenly felt. In 1827 Lord Bathurst (Secretary of State for War and the Colonies) commissioned the Cape authorities to find out how the colonists of the frontier districts would react to the idea of indenturing other Bantu-speakers on the same terms as the 'Mantatees'. In Uitenhage a meeting of 'respectable inhabitants' agreed that labourers, especially herdsmen, were 'much wanted' and should be indentured for five to seven years.[142] Landdrost Stockenstrom of Graaff-Reinet argued, however, that apprenticeship had been counterproductive when applied to the Khoisan and would work no better if it were resorted to again. He advocated for Bantu-speakers what he had long advocated for the Khoisan, that they should be 'left to dispose of their labour as dear as they can, and to whom they please, [and] they should be allowed to lay out the fruits of their industry in whatever legal manner they think most of their advantage'. This view prevailed: the Council of Advice (which had superseded the Council of Policy in 1825) was persuaded to abandon the idea of apprenticeship and to adopt instead a system of passes and short-term labour contracts. The new law was issued on 14 July 1828 as Ordinance 49.[143]

Numerous individuals and interest groups – as well as the victims themselves – had lobbied tirelessly for the repeal of the proclamations which circumscribed the freedom and the fundamental rights of the Khoisan. Their efforts bore fruit on 17 July 1828 when Ordinance 50 became law. Passes (which had just been prescribed for immigrants from across the frontier by Ordinance 49) were abolished for the Khoisan, their right to land ownership was at last made clear, and they were no longer to be 'subject to any compulsory service to which other of His

Majesty's Subjects . . . are not liable'. Furthermore, their children could not be apprenticed without parental consent. Contracts of hire for periods of longer than a month had to be in writing and in no case should exceed a year. Ordinance 50 applied only to 'Hottentots and other free Persons of colour', excluding both whites and immigrants from beyond the colonial frontier. Philip would have preferred a colour-blind legal code. But, since the ordinance was a fait accompli, his next concern was to rule out future interference with these hard-won gains. Through his insistence, a clause was added to prevent its repeal or amendment without the prior approval of the Crown.[144]

Khoisan reaction to the ordinance was muted at first. According to James Read (then at Bethelsdorp): 'The Hottentots of this place have not been much elated by hearing of the liberty; in fact, it will not so much affect them, except in the pass system, which is now done with'. Soon afterwards he wrote that 'something more on the side of government was needed, that was to give land to the Hottentots'.[145] As we have seen, this came to pass, though on an inadequate scale, at the Kat River in 1829. A mere 2,114 Khoisan and Bastaards had moved there by 1833. Gratitude for Ordinance 50 was to run high among the recipients of land. As Andries Stoffels of the Kat River Settlement said: 'The 50 Ordinance came out, then did we first taste freedom . . . that other men eat so sweet . . . and now that it is mingled with Water & Ground it is 20 times sweeter than forced labour'.[146] When colonists complained that 'irregularities' arose from the new freedom of Khoisan, the Kat River residents had an unambiguous reply: 'Give us more land'.

Missionaries in general praised Ordinance 50. However, some (e.g. Read) perceived that legislation alone could not 'uplift' those who had been so long oppressed. They were aware that the Cape's history of slave-owning had moulded white attitudes and the racial order, to the detriment of 'free Persons of colour' as well as slaves. They added their voices to those of the Khoisan in asking for more land.[147] The settlers, by contrast, resented the loosening of longstanding labour controls. They channelled their resentment into demands for an act outlawing vagrancy – wandering, without a fixed habitation or apparent means of support – and for a restoration of powers taken away from local officers by Ordinance 50. The anti-vagrancy agitation grew in urgency early in the 1830s when the planned emancipation of the slaves became known.[148]

This agitation resulted in the draft vagrancy ordinance of 1834 which made vagrancy punishable, whether a crime was committed or not, and restored powers to field cornets which Ordinance 50 had abolished. The draft ordinance was eloquently condemned at mass meetings of

Khoisan. Kat River residents recalled their plight before Ordinance 50 had become law. Khoisan argued that if they were found on the road wearing clothes such as vagrants were thought to wear, they would be subject to the ills of the old system once again. Repeatedly they charged that their recent gains would be lost:

> What do the people want of us? . . . What have the Hottentots done? One ordinance comes in their favour to raise them, another soon comes to degrade them . . . they want to do away with the 50th ordinance which enables you to . . . [plant] barley and oats, and to make contracts for supplying the troops.[149]

If the fortunate few at the Kat River were alarmed, Khoisan in the colony at large had even more to fear. Though the draft ordinance claimed 'to include all persons', the impression remained that it was a 'law for slaves and Hottentots'. The Council passed the ordinance, but the Governor had come to doubt its efficacy and the Secretary of State for the Colonies rejected it in 1835.[150]

Ordinance 50 remained in force, and undiluted, until 1841. It helped a few Khoisan at the Kat River and elsewhere. Philip believed that the farmers were less willing to allow those with livestock to pasture their cattle near the farms than they had been when they could apprentice children as a matter of course. As for the mass of Khoisan, the liberty to seek work as they chose resulted in higher wages in some cases, though the level was in general still low. Leslie Duly concluded that Khoisan farmworkers experienced little positive change in their working conditions. Administrative difficulties with the new system of written contracts resulted in the circumvention of the Ordinance to the extent that one-month oral contracts, which were not subject to its provisions, were preferred. Thus breaches of contract seldom reached the courts. There is also little evidence of important benefits to those Khoisan who migrated to the towns. The failure of Ordinance 50 to achieve a real improvement in the status of most Khoisan was apparently due to the failure of government to implement the ordinance with this end in view.[151]

In 1834 attention was diverted from the Khoisan by the freeing of the slaves. Lord Glenelg, who was closely identified with the 'philanthropist' advocates of greater justice for colonised people and slaves, became Secretary of State for War and the Colonies in 1835. He seems to have believed that what was needed to do justice to the free people of colour at the Cape had already been done. In particular he opposed further land grants to them. Soon after taking office, Glenelg advised that 'settling Hottentots on lands of their own' would merely 'perpetuate their poverty and their depression in the social state'; to induce them 'to work for wages as labourers' was in the 'interests of all classes' at the Cape.[152] Glenelg well expressed the limits to 'Hottentot' emancipation as conceived by liberals in the governing classes. Their goal was to suppress legal discrimination and to reaffirm the rule of law. Never did they contemplate overturning a labour system which was the product of 180 years of Cape history – a system in which brown-skinned workers laboured cheaply and diligently for white-skinned farmers and entrepreneurs.

Conclusion

The Khoisan were the first indigenes of South Africa to be conquered by white settlers and also the first to be reduced to a form of forced labour akin to serfdom. Their history set precedents for the histories of numerous Bantu-speaking peoples, though it differed from theirs in three important respects: the role of the colonial government, the structure of the indigenous culture and economy, and the ideological climate in which the struggle was waged.

The Khoisan of the southwestern Cape were subordinated in the seventeenth century by the VOC, a commercial company interested chiefly in defending its settlement from attack and in obtaining livestock to feed its ships. At first it had relatively little interest in the Khoisan as labourers, relying instead on imported slaves. However, when white freeburghers began farming on an extensive scale the demand for labour increased. Trekboer pastoralists, who were less able than crop farmers to afford slaves, demanded from Khoikhoi not only land and livestock but also the labour to put both to productive use. Slowly the need to attract, and if necessary coerce, labour became a leading theme in settler-Khoisan relations. In this process the VOC was essentially passive. In the eighteenth century it turned over much of the jurisdiction of interior districts to the white farmers; thus for most of our period crucial patterns of labour relations were forged beyond the knowledge and control of the state.

It was the British government which, after 1795, first intervened decisively to codify and enforce the labour system established largely by the colonists themselves. This new governmental activism – which would thereafter be common in South African labour relations – was prompted both by a labour crisis and by severe strife with the Xhosa beyond the colony's eastern boundary. But it was also a sign of the British government's desire to obtain some legitimacy in the eyes of its (white) subjects and to establish a firm policy in areas where the VOC had been vague or silent.

Another distinguishing feature of the Khoisan story was the nature of indigenous society. Unlike Bantu-speaking peoples of the region, Khoisan did not cultivate the soil. Khoikhoi pastoralism and 'Bushman' hunting-gathering could not support nearly as many people as cultivation, and thus the Khoisan population was comparatively sparse. Moreover, the prestige of Khoikhoi chiefs was closely tied to the possession of livestock, a highly vulnerable form of wealth. After losing livestock to Dutch expeditions, most Khoikhoi leaders, unlike many Bantu-speaking monarchs of the nineteenth century, lost the authority to rally their followers to effective resistance. On the other hand, those who kept their livestock were open to attack in ways that the hunters were not. Throughout the eighteenth century so-called 'Bushmen' inflicted serious damage on frontier colonists and at times halted their advance. But in fact many of these 'Bushmen' were Khoikhoi who had lost their cattle; the comparative effectiveness of 'Bushman' strategies underscores the peculiar difficulties which Khoikhoi pastoralists faced when Europeans challenged their position at the Cape. The pastoralists' weaknesses profoundly shaped South African history by enabling a tiny population of European immigrants to gain a secure beachhead for further expansion into Africa.

The decline of the Khoikhoi was not merely a question of conquest. Perhaps more important was the close compatibility between colonial and Khoikhoi economies. The Khoikhoi had numerous skills which the farmers needed to conduct their ranching operations at the Cape; and Khoikhoi, faced with a loss of land and in many regions threatened by 'Bushmen', found that farms offered a refuge where they could maintain at least small numbers of livestock as well as their family life. The initial stages of working for whites seem to have harmonised with their traditional patterns of clientship. In fact, in many regions 'conquest' and 'incorporation' were aspects of the same process.

As chiefly power declined and the incorporation of Khoikhoi and of some 'Bushmen' increased, the period of primary resistance passed. As early as 1739 the VOC faced a rebellion in the north led in part by Khoisan who had laboured for white farmers. However, the most dramatic Khoisan rebellion was on the eastern frontier in 1799–1803, and here again the rebels were former farm workers. This was the last time when Khoisan rebelled under traditional leadership and the last time that they fought to regain their independence and the land they had lost. After their military defeat, Khoisan workers resisted their subordination through acts of defiance on the farms – slacking, arson, petty thefts – and banditry.

By this point the pastoral and hunting origins of the Khoisan no longer mattered much. In many ways their social position resembled that of the imported slaves, apart from the fact that they, unlike the slaves, could not be bought and sold. They were landless, largely immobile, and dependent on the settlers for the necessities of life. By the 1820s, however, a new generation of Khoisan had emerged, many of them mission-trained, who articulated demands for free labour conditions and access to land on the same basis as other free subjects of the Crown.

The story of the Khoisan frontier differs in a third way from that of subsequent South African frontiers. Throughout much of South African history white dominance of other groups has been fitfully challenged by ideological currents emanating from the centres of western civilisation. In the case of the Khoisan this was not true until the end of our period. Just as there was nothing markedly anomalous about the slave system at the Cape, so too the system of labour bondage imposed upon the Khoisan did not offend contemporary Western values. Though voices were occasionally raised against the brutality of white employers, no one before the turn of the nineteenth century considered it the duty of government to guarantee the right of indigenous people to own land, to sell their labour freely, or to move about without hindrance.

Early in the nineteenth century such demands were in fact raised among some missionaries and some liberals in sectors of British public life. In Ordinance 50 of 1828 (and subsequently in the abolition of slavery) the new liberal currents disturbed South African society. Nonetheless, as we have seen, the long-term effect seems to have been slight. For the first time, but not for the last, the white dominated social structure showed its capacity to endure change and outlast hostile impulses. The root of the liberals' failure was in part economic, in part political. By now whites had long been used to extensive farming with low capitalisation; the influx of new settlers after 1820 brought new attitudes, some capital, and an increased white population, but was not able to budge the essential nature of the Cape economy, namely, its heavy reliance on cheap, immobile labour. As for the Cape Regiment and the mission stations, they offered a haven, often only temporary, to a few Khoisan; the others had to labour on the farms.

The nature of political authority contributed greatly to this outcome. Though the British government of the period was not constitutionally bound by the will of the white colonists, it soon learned that it could not govern the Cape without either expending vast sums (which it was unwilling to do over long periods) or relying on the good will of the white inhabitants. Thus it found itself intervening, sometimes reluctantly, on behalf of the settlers and their labour system. Even at the point where it was most willing to defy settler opinion – in the late 1820s and early 1830s – it was not prepared to undertake a reshaping of the society, above all in land ownership, a prerequisite to realising its ostensible goals expressed in Ordinance 50 of 1828. Noting the plight of the Cape's working force, the British government put faith in the liberating capacity of free labour markets; observing that Khoisan were largely excluded from white society, it advocated assimilation through education and Christianisation. In the end neither markets nor missions accomplished the restructuring which only government could bring about. Thus most Khoisan remained alongside the newly freed slaves at the bottom of a society dominated by whites. A racial order had been created which, having survived both internal resistance and external displeasure, became a model, fixed in the minds of whites, which they carried with them to new regions and sought to inflict on new peoples.

Chapter One   Notes

1. Important exceptions are: Shula Marks, 'Khoisan Resistance to the Dutch in the Seventeenth and Eighteenth Centuries', *JAH*, XIII (1972), pp. 55–80; H.J. le Roux, 'Die Toestand, Verspreiding en Verbrokkeling van die Hottentotstamme in Suid-Afrika 1653–1713' (M.A. thesis, University of Stellenbosch, 1945). More recently H.C. Bredekamp has done a meticulous study of Khoikhoi-European relations in the period 1662–1679: *Van Veeverskaffers tot Veewagters: 'n Historiese ondersoek na betrekkinge tussen die Khoikhoi en Europeërs aan die Kaap, 1662–1679* (Bellville, 1982).
2. C.W. de Kiewiet, *A History of South Africa, Social and Economic* (Oxford, 1957), p. 20.
3. For a discussion of Khoikhoi population see Richard Elphick, *Kraal and Castle: Khoikhoi and the Founding of White South Africa* (New Haven and London, 1977), p. 23, n. 1.
4. KA 3974, 1 April 1662, n.p.; KA 4051, Opgaaf, 15 April 1714, p. 509. The former figure includes the garrison, the latter does not.
5. This assertion has been challenged by A.J. Böeseken. See her 'The meaning, origin, and use of the terms Khoikhoi, San and Khoisan', *Cabo*, I (1972), pp. 5–10; *Cabo*, II (1974), pp. 8–10; *Cabo*, II (1975), pp. 16–18; and Elphick's replies to her under the same title in *Cabo*, II (1974), pp. 3–7; *Cabo*, II (1975), pp. 12–15.
6. On the latter suggestion see Christopher Ehret, 'Patterns of Bantu and Central Sudanic Settlement in Central and Southern Africa', *Transafrican Journal of History*, III (1973), pp. 13, 64.
7. P.T. Robertshaw, 'The Origin of Pastoralism in the Cape', *South African Historical Journal*, X (1978), p. 131; Christopher Ehret, 'The First Spread

of Food Production to Southern Africa', *The Archaeological and Linguistic Reconstruction of African History*, ed. Christopher Ehret and Merrick Posnansky (Berkeley, Los Angeles and London, 1982), p. 162.

8. The arguments behind this reconstruction are found in Elphick, *Kraal and Castle*, pp. 14–21. Other views have been propounded more recently by archaeologists, in particular P.T. Robertshaw ('The Origin of Pastoralism'). For a brief introduction to the current debate and a restatement of Elphick's position see ch. 1 of the 1985 revision of *Kraal and Castle*: Richard Elphick, *Khoikhoi and the Founding of White South Africa* (Johannesburg, 1985).

9. Parkington argues that impoverished Khoikhoi did not naturally resort to a hunting-and-gathering lifestyle before the Dutch presence altered conditions in the southwestern Cape, but sought out still-wealthy pastoralists with whom they formed client relationships: John E. Parkington, 'Soaqua and Bushmen: Hunters and Robbers', *Past and Present in Hunter-Gatherer Studies*, ed. Carmel Schrire (Orlando, 1984), pp. 160–61.

10. The model of the 'ecological cycle' is defended in Elphick, *Kraal and Castle*, pp. 30–42. For evidence of Khoikhoi communities becoming totally reliant on hunting, gathering and robbery, see KA 4031, Dag Verhaal . . . Starrenburgh, 26 Oct. and 4 Nov. 1705, pp. 743v–44; *RZA*, III, 280; *The Journal of Hendrik Jacob Wikar (1779) and the Journals of Jacobus Coetsé Jansz (1760) and Willem van Reenen (1791)*, ed. E.E. Mossop and A.W. van der Horst (Cape Town, 1935), p. 315; George W. Stow, *The Native Races of South Africa* (London, 1905), pp. 276, 336.

11. Elphick, *Kraal and Castle*, pp. 49–53.

12. On pre-colonial Khoikhoi trade see Richard Hall Elphick, 'The Cape Khoi and the First Phase of South African Race Relations' (Ph.D. dissertation, Yale University, 1972), pp. 115–19. On trade networks from Table Bay see *VRJ*, I, 128 (14 Jan. 1653).

13. R. Raven-Hart, *Before Van Riebeeck: Callers at South Africa from 1488 to 1652* (Cape Town, 1967), pp. 15, 19, 20, 47, 48; Elphick, *Kraal and Castle*, p. 165, n. 33. The Company occasionally gave small amounts of iron as gifts to chiefs.

14. E.g., for the time of Van Riebeeck, *VRJ*, II, 370 (7 Nov. 1658); 378 (16 Nov. 1658); III, 5 (20 Jan. 1659); KA 3972, Van Riebeeck – XVII, 19 March 1660, p. 15.

15. *VRJ*, I, xxiv; 39 (11 May 1652); 270 (3 Nov. 1654).

16. KA 3967, Van Riebeeck – XVII, 22 April 1654, pp. 13–14; *VRJ*, II, 288–342 (22 June–21 Sept. 1658).

17. *Ibid.*, III, 176 (18 Jan. 1660); KA 3972, Van Riebeeck – Batavia, 29 July 1659, pp. 46–46v.

18. On the war see *VRJ*, III, 45–205 (19 May 1659 to 27 April 1660); Elphick, *Kraal and Castle*, pp. 110–15.

19. E.g., *VRJ*, I, 371 (27 Nov. 1655).

20. Gonnema's responsibility is assessed in Elphick, *Kraal and Castle*, pp. 127–30.

21. The main sources on the war are KA 3987, Dagelyckse aantekening . . . , 12–25 July, 1673, pp. 213–16v; KA 3988, DR, 24 March and 7–15 April

1674, pp. 103v–10; KA 3989, Dagelyckse aanteyckening . . . , 27 March – 17 April 1676, pp. 217v–24; KA 3989, DR, 1–19 Nov. 1676, pp. 334–39v.

22. KA 3989, DR, 23 and 25 Dec. 1676, pp. 367, 370v; KA 3990, DR, 17 and 19 Jan. 1677, pp. 245, 251v–52.

23. For examples of difficulties caused by the possession of the Company's canes, see KZ 3193, Dag Verhaal . . . Slotsbo, 18 and 24 Oct. 1712, n.p. Some Small Nama chiefs were apparently attacked because of their possession of the canes; others who had canes burned them as a sign of their unwillingness to trade further with the Dutch. These acts of defiance, it should be emphasised, took place at the fringes of the Company's sphere of influence, and were not duplicated among the Western Cape Khoikhoi.

24. For examples of informal blockades see *VRJ*, I, 273 (23 Nov. 1654); II, 36 (22 May 1656).

25. For the life of Klaas see Elphick, *Kraal and Castle*, pp. 141–48. A good survey of the advantages of Klaas's barter to the Company is found in KA 3977, S. van der Stel – XVII, 30 April 1684, pp. 416v–17v.

26. Van der Stel made his case in KA 4011, S. van der Stel – XVII, 9 May 1695, pp. 11–13. The Heren XVII rebuked him for his action and ordered Klaas released. This order reached the Cape after Van der Stel had already freed Klaas on his own initiative. The real reasons behind Van der Stel's actions have not been authoritatively determined, but for speculation on this subject see Elphick, *Kraal and Castle*, p. 146.

27. KA 4017, Declaration of Ambrosius Zassé and Jacob Leven, 23 Jan. 1699, pp. 350–55v; KA 4031, Dag Verhaal . . . Starrenburgh, 16 Oct. – 8 Dec. 1705, pp. 740–55; KZ 3193, Dag Verhaal . . . Slotsbo, 13 Oct. – 22 Nov. 1712, n.p.

28. KA 4005, Opgaaf of 1690, p. 82.

29. Charles Lockyer, *An Account of the Trade in India* (London, 1711), p. 298; *Collectanea* (Cape Town, 1924), pp. 114–17, 126.

30. *The Early Cape Hottentots*, ed. I. Schapera (Cape Town, 1933), pp. 271–73. We are grateful to Leonard Guelke for this reference.

31. KA 3984, Prosecution of Sara, 18 Dec. 1671, pp. 222v–24; Prosecution of Five Hottentots, n.d. [1672], pp. 382–87v.

32. For an extended discussion of Khoikhoi under Dutch justice see Elphick, *Kraal and Castle*, pp. 181–88.

33. We compiled sales figures from the dagregisters of the period, and tested them against the more reliable data in the Company's ledgers when such ledgers are available (1652–53; 1655–63; 1665–67).

34. Before 1690 all the illegal traders apprehended by the Company were convicted of trading fewer than ten animals, many of them only one or two.

35. For overviews of the state of Western Cape Khoikhoi in the early eighteenth century see KA 4031, Dag Verhaal . . . Starrenburgh, (1705), *passim*; KZ 3193, Dagh Verhaal . . . Slotsbo, (1712), *passim*; KA 4037, Dagverhaal . . . Hartogh, (1707), *passim*.

36. KA 4024, DR, 13 March 1701, p. 125; DR, 16 June 1701, p. 145.

37. KA 4027, Interrogations of Willem van Sijburg, Lambert Symonsz, Jacob Holland, David Pannesmit, and the Khoikhoi Soetekoek *et al.*, Oct. and Nov. 1702, pp. 442–56, 469–71.

38. KA 4031, Dag Verhaal . . . Starrenburgh, 4 Nov. 1705, p. 749v.
39. A.J.H. van der Walt, *Die Ausdehnung der Kolonie am Kap der Guten Hoffnung (1700–1779)* (Berlin, 1928), p. 15.
40. KA 4048, DR, 1713, *passim*.
41. KA 4050, DR, 13 Feb. 1714, p. 274v. For a review of the records after 1713 see Elphick, *Kraal and Castle*, p. 234.
42. *The Journals of Brink and Rhenius*, ed. E.E. Mossop (Cape Town, 1947), 'Dagh Register . . . Rhenius', 9, 14, 20 Oct. 1724, pp. 134, 140, 142; *ibid.*, 'Dag Register . . . Hop' (Brink), 6 Dec. 1761, p. 56; *Journal of Wikar*, 'Report to his Excellency Joachim van Plettenbergh' (by Wikar), 4 Sept. 1779, p.25; Staf D 593 /U/4/1/3, Journal van de vierde reyse van Captein R.J. Gordon, 26 July 1779, n.p.; François le Vaillant, *Voyage de Monsieur le Vaillant dans l'intérieur de l'Afrique* (Paris, 1790), II, 95; *RZA*, IV 'Journaal en verbaal eener landreyse . . . Janssens', 4 June 1803, p. 157; Henry Lichtenstein, *Travels in Southern Africa in the Years 1803, 1804, 1805, and 1806* (Cape Town, 1928, 1930), I, 110, 310–11; II, 311–12.
43. Rhenius, pp. xii–xiii and *passim*; H.B. Thom, *Die Geskiedenis van die Skaapboerdery in Suid-Afrika* (Amsterdam, 1936), pp. 47–48; *Res*, V, 329 (31 Jan. 1719); VI, 288 (9 March 1723); *KP*, II, 129–30, 167–69 (4/9 April 1727 and 8 Dec. 1739); O.F. Mentzel, *A Complete and Authentic . . . Description of the . . . Cape of Good Hope* (Cape Town, 1921, 1925, 1944), III, 123; KA 4093, Interrogation of Dragonder, 5 July 1729, p. 625v.
44. *RZA*, III, 'Joernaal . . . Beutler', 5 June 1752, p. 292. See also KA 4031, Dag verhaal . . . Starrenburgh, 4 Nov. 1705, p. 749v; and Rhenius, *passim*.
45. Mentzel, *Description*, I, 36, 83–84; III, 111; Donald Moodie, Afschriften [Cape Town Depot of the South African State Archives], XI, Evidence of Platje Swartland, 30 Dec. 1836.
46. Anders Sparrman, *A Voyage to the Cape of Good Hope . . . and to the Country of the Hottentots and the Caffres from the Year 1772–1776* (Cape Town, 1975, 1977), I, 230; II, 233 (the 'Gunjemans Hottentots' were presumably descendants of Gonnema's Cochoqua); KA 4116, Prosecution of Harmen Cloppenburg, 2 Jan. 1738, pp. 862v–68v.
47. This is seen clearly in connection with the 1739 disturbances; the insurgent leaders were brought to the Cape for interrogation and called themselves variously 'Nama' (i.e. Khoikhoi) and 'Bushmen'. See KA 4119, Res 13 March 1739, p. 240v.
48. Parkington, 'Soaqua and Bushmen', pp. 157–65.
49. KA 4093, Declaration of the Hottentot Schagger Jantje, 8 March 1729, p. 630; KA 4119, Report of Johannes Cruywagen, pp. 281v–82, 293; KA 4119, Aangenoomene Togt of Dagregister . . . Theunis Botha, pp. 357, 360–65, and *passim*.
50. On the evolution of the commando, see Petrus Johannes van der Merwe, *Die Noordwaarste Beweging van die Boere voor die Groot Trek (1770–1842)* (The Hague, n.d.), pp. 25–27 and ch. 8, pp. 361–63 in this volume.
51. N.G. Penn, 'The Frontier in the Western Cape, 1700–1740', *Papers in the Prehistory of the Western Cape, South Africa*, ed. John Parkington and Martin Hall (British Archaeological Reports Series 332, 1987), II, *passim*; S. Newton-King, 'Khoisan Resistance to Colonial Expansion, 1700–1828', *An Illustrated History of South Africa*, ed. T. Cameron and S.B. Spies

(Johannesburg, 1986), pp. 107–08.

52. LM 49, 'Bushmen depredations', pp. 54–63, 63–64, Res 2 and 25 June 1739; P.E. le Roux, *Die Verdedigingstelsel aan die Kaap onder die Hollands-Oosindiese Kompanje (1652–1795)*, (n.p., 1925), pp. 150–51.

53. LM 49, 'Namaquas', pp. 263–66; Report, J.P. Giebeler, 28 Nov. 1739; KA 4119, Res 8 Dec. 1739, pp. 395v–96.

54. Penn, 'The Frontier in the Western Cape', pp. 492–93.

55. Marks, 'Khoisan resistance', pp. 72–73; le Roux, *Verdedigingstelsel*, p. 152.

56. Penn has identified five resource areas, the retention of which was vital to the continued independence of the Khoisan, and where particularly fierce warfare between the Khoisan and the colonists was waged, i.e., the southwestern Cape, the west coast and Bokkeveld, the escarpment of the inland plateau formed by the Hantam, Roggeveld and Nieuweveld Mountains, Namaqualand, and the vicinity of the Orange River: see N.G. Penn, 'Pastoralists and Pastoralism in the Northern Cape Frontier Zone during the Eighteenth Century', *Prehistoric Pastoralism in Southern Africa*, ed. Martin Hall and Andrew B. Smith (Goodwin Series 5, S.A. Archaeological Society, June 1986), p. 64.

57. Donald Moodie, *The Record* (Cape Town, 1960), V, 34; Van der Merwe, *Noordwaartse Beweging*, pp. 10, 15, 19–20. Eighteenth-century travellers emphasised that the Sneeuwberg hunters spoke a language not mutually intelligible with Khoikhoi: this language is probably a member of Dorothea Bleek's 'Southern Bush' family. They were also the only hunter group among whom eighteenth-century observers found rock paintings. These facts together indicate that theirs was an aboriginal rather than a Khoikhoi culture. The main references on these people are cited in Elphick, *Kraal and Castle*, p. 28, n. 19 and p. 30, ns. 25, 26.

58. Le Roux, *Verdedigingstelsel*, pp. 156–70; Moodie, *The Record*, III, 28–30; Van der Merwe, *Noordwaartse Beweging*, pp. 28, 30, 53. See CO 4823, Barnard – Van de Graaff, 8 Aug. 1807, pp. 334–36 for British efforts to eradicate the attitudes which such eighteenth-century measures had encouraged, and to inculcate their own views regarding defence.

59. N. Penn, 'Labour, Land and Livestock in the Western Cape During the Eighteenth Century: The Khoisan and the Colonists', unpubl. paper, Western Cape Roots and Realities Workshop (Centre for African Studies, University of Cape Town, 1986), pp. 21–31.

60. Newton-King, 'Khoisan Resistance', pp. 109–11. Van der Merwe calculated that about one-quarter as many Khoisan were captured by the commandos as were killed: *Noordwaartse Beweging*, p. 53.

61. John Barrow, *Travels into the Interior of Southern Africa* (London, 1806), I, 93.

62. S. Daniel Neumark, *Economic Influences on the South African Frontier, 1652–1836* (Stanford, 1957) pp. 175–76: he refers to 'the native races' in this regard, possibly including Bantu-speakers as well as Khoikhoi; V.C. Malherbe, 'Diversification and Mobility of Khoikhoi Labour in the Eastern Districts of the Cape Colony Prior to the Labour Law of 1 November 1809' (M.A. Dissertation, University of Cape Town, 1978), pp. 32–33.

63. Women traditionally made mats: see I. Schapera, *The Khoisan Peoples of South Africa* (London, 1965), p. 316.

64. Charles Peter Thunberg, *Travels in Europe, Africa, and Asia, Made Between the Years 1770 and 1779* (London, 1795), I, 195. With the British occupation one finds references to Khoikhoi hired in the capacity of 'Gamekeeper', *RCC*, X, 138.

65. Barrow, *Travels*, I, 39. See *BPP*, 1835, XXXIX (50), p. 21: a commando was sent out 'on account of 11,000 sheep having been stolen from the butchers', 12 Feb. 1793.

66. Lichtenstein, *Travels*, I, 272; *RZA*, IV, Journaal . . . Janssens, 13 and 19 April 1803, pp. 110, 115; KA 4146, Prosecution of Hendrick Tessenaar and Anthony Minie, 3 Nov. 1746, pp. 1233v–36.

67. 'Early in the eighteenth century there were already a few cases of Khoikhoi bringing charges against burghers before colonial courts': *Afrikaner Political Thought, Analysis and Documents, I: 1780-1850*, ed. André du Toit and Hermann Giliomee (Cape Town, 1983), p. 9. In 1748 Commissioner Nolthenius supported the principle that Khoisan workers must be paid and, should the employer fail, his servants had the right to complain: see Anna J. Böeseken, 'Die Nederlandse Kommissarisse en die 18de Eeuse Samelewing aan die Kaap', *AYB* (1944), p. 77.

68. N.G. Penn, 'Anarchy and authority in the Koue Bokkeveld, 1739–1779: the banishing of Carel Buijtendag', *Kleio*, XVII (1985), pp. 35–37; J.S. Marais, *Maynier and the First Boer Republic* (Cape Town, 1962), p. 71; VC 68, no. 2, p. 70.

69. Mentzel, *Description*, I, 84; Barrow, *Travels*, II, 123; Moodie, *The Record*, V, 22. The register of labour contracts introduced by Maynier in Graaff-Reinet District in November 1799 is found in GR 15/43.

70. Lichtenstein, *Travels*, I, 446; Lady Anne Barnard, *South Africa a Century Ago (1797–1801)*, ed. H.J. Anderson (Cape Town, n.d.), p. 206.

71. Sparrman, *Voyage*, I, 181; Penn, 'Buijtendag', pp. 29–30 and n. 25; 1/STB 3/11, Depositions of Kiewit and Booy, 23 June 1775; Penn, 'Labour, Land and Livestock' pp. 29–30.

72. GR 15/43, Register of Labour Contracts, Nov. 1799 – Jan. 1801; BPP, 1835, XXXIX (50), p. 161; E.J. Hobsbawm and George Rudé, *Captain Swing* (1985), pp. 24–25.
Payment of casuals in kind, e.g. in grain, still frequently occurred; see Nigel Worden, *Slavery in Dutch South Africa* (Cambridge, 1985), p. 25.

73. *RCC*, VII, 111.

74. J 116, Graaff-Reinet Opgaaf, 1798. There were 8,947 Khoikhoi in the Graaff-Reinet District at this time according to Barrow: *Travels*, II, 83.

75. Penn, 'Labour, Land and Livestock', pp. 15–16, 18, 22, 29–30; Moodie, *The Record*, III, 3; BO 147, Ross-Bresler, 26 March 1796, pp. 76–77.

76. Sparrman, *Voyage*, II, 34. For a discussion of low wages in a situation of labour shortage see: H.A. Reyburn, 'Studies in Cape Frontier History. I. Labour, Land and Law', *The Critic*, III, 1 (Oct. 1934), pp. 46–47. J.S. Marais, *The Cape Coloured People, 1652–1937* (Johannesburg, 1968), pp. 129–31.

77. For a discussion of the nature of the master-servant relationship at this time see Newton-King, 'Khoisan Resistance', pp. 109–11. 'There is no law for

Hottentots', a knegt said in 1727 when explaining to a slave that he was less likely to be killed as this would involve his master in financial loss; Robert Ross, *Cape of Torments: Slavery and resistance in South Africa* (London, 1983), p. 43.

78. *Res*, VI, 128 (2 Sept. 1721); P.J. Venter, 'Die Inboek-stelsel, 'n Uitvloeisel van Slaverny in die Ou Dae', *Die Huisgenoot*, XVIII (1 June 1934), pp. 25, 59, 61; Barnard, *South Africa*, p. 203.

79. For links between new regulations affecting colonial Khoikhoi and the crisis on the northeastern frontier in the last three decades of the 18th century see Penn, 'Labour, Land and Livestock', pp. 25–27.

80. *Afrikaner Political Thought*, ed. du Toit and Giliomee, pp. 45-46; C 159, 13 March 1781, pp. 164–66; *KP*, III, n.d., pp. 15–16; *ibid.*, IV, 29 June 1787, pp. 8–11; 1/SWM 1/3, 4 Dec. 1797, pp. 330–32; GR 1/2, 2 July 1798, p. 174. For the opinion of the Commissioners of Inquiry as to the effect of the pass system on the Khoisan, see *RCC*, XXXV, Report . . . upon the Police, 10 May 1828, p. 147; *ibid.*, Report, p. 308.

81. 1/STB 10/6, Memorial to Commissioner-General of the Indies, May 1793; M. Whiting Spilhaus, *South Africa in the Making, 1652–1806* (Cape Town, 1966), p. 151.

82. Barrow, *Travels*, I, 403; GR 12/1A, C.J. Van Rooye[n] – Bresler, 6 April 1799.

83. BO 68, Barrow – F. Dundas, 15 April 1799, pp. 183–84; Barrow, *Travels*, I, 394–95. Susan Newton-King and V.C. Malherbe, *The Khoikhoi Rebellion in the Eastern Cape (1799–1803)* (Cape Town, 1984), *passim*.

84. *RCC*, II, Barnard – H. Dundas, 13 Sept. 1799, p. 481; *Transactions of the [London] Missionary Society* (London, 1804), I, 27 June 1799, p. 378; BO 227, P.H. van Rooyen – Field Cornets, 31 July 1799, p. 57.

85. See also, V.C. Malherbe, 'The Khoi Captains and the Third Frontier War', in Newton-King and Malherbe, *The Khoikhoi Rebellion*, pp. 82–84, 99, 117–19.

86. BO 157, Ross – Bresler, 21 Dec. 1801, p. 120.

87. Malherbe, 'The Khoi Captains', pp. 82, 120; BO 69, Bresler – F. Dundas, 10 Dec. 1801, p. 640; A 1415(74), Pt. B. Barnard – Macartney, 20 April 1802, p. 145.

88. BO 69, Nine Camdeboo Boers – F. Dundas, 21 Nov. 1801, p. 614.

89. At least thirty of the charges of cruelty to Khoikhoi presented by Van der Kemp and Read in 1811 apparently occurred during the war: Malherbe, 'The Khoi Captains', p. 106.

90. When Khoikhoi and Bastaards were first enrolled as a Corps in 1781–82, the unit was called the Corps Bastaard Hottentotten (400 men). After they were reassembled in 1793, the unit was called: the Corps Pandoeren, 1793–95 (135–210 men); the Hottentot Corps, 1796–1801 (about 300 men); Cape Regiment, 1801–03 (about 300 men); Oude Corps Hottentotten, 1803 (300 men); Corps Vrije Hottentotten, 1803–04 (300–400 men); Battaillon Hottentotsche Ligte Infanterie, 1804–06 (400–448 men); Cape Regiment, 1806–17 (500–800 men); Cape Corps of Infantry and Cavalry, 1817–27 (200–510 men); Corps of Cape Mounted Riflemen, 1827–70 (250–960 men). See Johannes de Villiers, 'Hottentot-Regimente aan die Kaap, 1781–1806', *AYB* (1970), II, 119;

G. Tylden, 'The Cape Coloured Regular Regiments, 1793 to 1870', *Africana Notes and News*, VII, 2 (March 1950), *passim*; Lennon William Swart, 'Some Aspects of the History of the Cape Regiment, 1806–1817' (B.A. Hons., University of Cape Town, Sept. 1978), *passim*.

91. Le Roux, *Verdedigingstelsel*, pp. 135–36; H.C.V. Leibbrandt, *Precis of the Archives of the Cape of Good Hope, Journal, 1662–1670*, 28 Aug. 1670, p. 324; *Early Cape Hottentots* ed. Schapera, p. 111.

92. *KP*, III, 14 Aug. 1759, p. 26; 2 April 1781, p. 116; IV, 30 April 1793, p. 198. In 1741 a similar call had gone out but no reference was made then to the Khoikhoi, although burghers had been required to offer their knegts and slaves, *ibid.*, II, 21 March 1741, pp. 198–200.

93. *RCC*, I, Craig – H. Dundas, 12, 14 April 1796, pp. 354, 359; Barrow, *Travels*, I, 402. For Craig's distrust of the Dutch burghers see *RCC*, I, Craig – H. Dundas. 27 Dec. 1795, pp. 269–70. In general it can be said that the composition of a nation's military depends less on a group's willingness to serve than on its perceived eligibility for military service – on grounds of loyalty above all else: Cynthia H. Enloe, *Police, Military and Ethnicity, Foundations of State Power* (New Brunswick, 1980), pp. 1–2; Ann Gregory and DeWitt C. Ellinwood, 'Ethnic Management and Military Recruitment in South and Southeast Asia', *Civil-Military Relations, Regional Perspectives*, ed. Morris Janowitz (London, 1981), pp. 95–96. The Khoikhoi were the 'only regular soldiers recruited in the country by . . . Dutch or British', as Reyburn pointed out, 'Cape Frontier History', p. 45.

94. *RCC*, IV, Proclamation, 19 April 1802, pp. 280–81. On 25 June 1801 the Cape Corps had been constituted as a full and equal British imperial regiment, a status which the unit regained in 1806: see de Villiers, 'Hottentot-Regimente', pp. 163–65; *RCC*, VI, Windham – Grey, 10 Nov. 1806, pp. 53–54.

95. VC 76, H.D. Campagne, p. 173.

96. Moodie, *The Record*, V, 22; CO 15, De Busche – ?, 7 July 1809, No. 59; *RCC*, I, Craig – H. Dundas, 12 April 1796, p. 354; 1/UIT 10/1, Circular, 18 April 1806; 1/UIT 15/1, Circular, 2 May 1806; William J. Burchell, *Travels in the Interior of Southern Africa* (London, 1953), I, 50.

97. Bernhard Krüger, *The Pear Tree Blossoms* (Genadendal, 1966), p. 78. In 1808 Collins found that the population of Genadendal was much reduced because almost 100 men, 'most of whom had families', were in the Regiment: *RCC*, VI, 348. At more or less the same time, some 50 men from Bethelsdorp were believed to be in the Corps, CO 2561, Van der Kemp – Col. Sec., 30 April 1807, No. 1.

98. 1/UIT 15/1, Cuyler – Col. Sec., 12 Jan. 1808; ZL 1/3/3, Box 3, Folder 5A, Read – ?, 30 Jan. 1808.

99. CO 2584, Van Andringa – Alexander, 2 March 1813. Thomas Baines related how, in 1848, some Khoikhoi in his party teased some Xhosa whom they met on the road from Shiloh to Burgersdorp: 'Pretending that they had authority to impress men for military service, our Hottentots now laid hold of one' whom they tied to a wagon. His friends were not amused and rescued him: Thomas Baines, *Journal of Residence in Africa, I, 1842–1853*, ed. R.F. Kennedy (Cape Town, 1961), p. 80.

100. The term of service seems to have ranged from one year to 'indefinite'

before 1814 when the first reference to a 7-year term (which had been standard in the British army since 1806) has been found: Krüger, *Pear Tree*, p. 78; CO 6167, Reynell – Anderson, 3 Jan. 1814; CO 2592, Fraser – Alexander, 28 Feb. 1814, No. 27; 1/UIT 10/3, Bird – Fraser, 25 June 1814, in No. 96; Edward M. Spiers, *The Army and Society, 1815–1914* (London, 1980), p. 52.

101. J.J. Freeman, *A Tour in South Africa* (London, 1851), p. 134. For praise of the Regiment see, e.g., *The Manuscripts of Robert Graham, Esq., of Fintry*, ed. C.T. Atkinson, (London, 1942), J. Graham–R. Graham, 14 Feb. 1812, pp. 106–07; 1/UIT 15/2, Cuyler – Alexander, 7 July 1814, No. 177; Barrow, *Travels*, I, 374–75; A. van Pallandt, *General Remarks on the Cape of Good Hope* (Cape Town, 1917), pp. 22–3, 28.

102. 1/UIT 15/1, Cuyler – Col. Sec., 10 June 1810, No. 27; John Philip, *Researches in South Africa* (New York, 1969), II, p. 314 n.*. In 1816 when 300 men were discharged from the regiment, even former mission residents were forbidden to go to the mission stations but had to seek work with the farmers, Jane Sales, *Mission Stations and the Coloured Communities of the Eastern Cape, 1800–1852* (Cape Town, 1975), p. 56.

103. J. de Villiers, 'Die Kaapse Regiment, 1806–1817', *South African Historical Journal*, VII (Nov. 1975), p. 17; Harriet Ward, *Five Years in Kaffirland, with Sketches of the Late War . . .* (London, 1848), II, 109–10; *RCC*, VII, Collins – Caledon, 6 Aug. 1809, pp. 111–12; Tylden, 'Cape Coloured Regular Regiments', p. 45.

104. *RCC*, IX, Cradock – Campbell, 10 Feb. 1814, p. 351; *ibid.*, XXVII, Somerset – Hay, 7 July 1826, and encl., pp. 42–43.

105. Kruger, *Pear Tree*, pp. 55–7; Richard Elphick, 'Africans and the Christian Campaign in Southern Africa', *The Frontier in History, North America and Southern Africa Compared* ed. Howard Lamar and Leonard Thompson (New Haven and London, 1981), p. 306.

106. It started with almost 300 men, women and children: see BR 293, Naamlyst, 1 Oct. 1803, pp. 127–29.

107. For names of the 629 then present at Bethelsdorp, see J 395; for names of 340 once resident, but absent for a year or more at the time of the census, see CO 6136. (Elsewhere, Van der Kemp claimed that 1,267 Khoikhoi had been admitted to Bethelsdorp by 1807: see CO 2561, Van der Kemp – Col. Sec., 30 April 1807, No. 1.) Where the column headed 'From what Place' is filled in, the names of farmers outnumber all other designations combined.

108. Elphick, 'Africans and the Christian Campaign', p. 282. For a discussion of cultural adaptation at the Cape in the 17th and the 18th centuries, see ch. 4, esp. pp. 225–30 in this volume.

109. ZL 1/3/2, Box 2, Folder 4E, Annual Report, 1804, Bethelsdorp.

110. John Campbell, *Travels in South Africa* (Cape Town, 1974), pp. 88–91; Krüger, *Pear Tree*, pp. 77, 112; P.J. van der Merwe, *Die Trekboer in die Geskiedenis van die Kaapkolonie (1657–1842)*, (Cape Town, 1938), p. 225.

111. ZL 1/3/5, Box 5, Folder 2F, Minutes, Graaff-Reinet Conference, Aug. 1814.

112. ZL 1/3/5, Box 5, Folder 3C, Read – LMS Directors, 2 May 1814; V.C.

Malherbe, 'The Life and Times of Cupido Kakkerlak', *JAH*, XX, 3 (1979), pp. 365–78.

113. Marais, *Cape Coloured People*, p. 116 and n. 3; *RCC*, VII, Proclamation, 1 Nov. 1809, pp. 211–16. In the opinion of the Commissioners of Inquiry, the application of the 1809 proclamation was far more restrictive than its clauses implied, *RCC*, XXXV, Report ... Hottentot and Bushman Population . . ., 28 Jan. 1830, pp. 316–17. See also, *ibid.*, Report . . . upon the Police . . ., 10 May 1828, pp. 149–50.

114. 1/UIT 10/1, Alexander – Cuyler, 22 March 1810, encl. in No. 55; 1/STB 1/29, Van der Riet – Truter, 1 April 1810, pp. 221–24. Cradock's proclamation followed a recommendation by the Commission of Circuit, 28 Feb. 1812, *RCC*, VIII, 302–03; *ibid.*, Proclamation, 23 April 1812, pp. 385–87; *ibid.*, XII, Proclamation, 9 July 1819, pp. 249–50; *ibid.*, XXXV, Report, pp. 320–25. Marais points out that the 1819 proclamation, 'or something like it', was preserved in later master-servant legislation: *Cape Coloured People*, p. 119, n. 2.

115. *RCC*, XI, Stockenstrom – Col. Sec., 5 May 1817, p. 327; *ibid.*, Proclamation, 8 Aug. 1817, pp. 365–67; *ibid.*, XIV, Stockenstrom, – Col. Sec., 5 June 1822, pp. 384–86; *ibid.*, Col. Sec. – Stockenstrom, 21 June 1822, pp. 409–10; *ibid.*, XXXV, Report, pp. 325–27.

116. W.M. Macmillan, *The Cape Colour Question, a Historical Survey* (Cape Town, 1968), pp. 157–70; Reyburn, 'Cape Frontier History', pp. 50–52; Marais, *Cape Coloured People*, pp. 121–31. For a discussion of how governments act to meet the labour needs of those on whom they rely to provide essential services, see Evsey D. Domar, 'The Causes of Slavery or Serfdom: a Hypothesis', *The Journal of Economic History*, XXX (March 1970), pp. 18–32.

117. Regarding the land issue, see: Philip, *Researches*, I, 277–78; Macmillan, *Cape Colour Question*, pp. 146–48; *Cape of Good Hope Ordinances, 1828*, Art. 3, Ordinance 50.

118. *BPP*, 1835, XXXIX (50), F. Dundas – Maynier, 29 Jan. 1800, p. 31; *RCC*, III, F. Dundas – Yonge, 20 Feb. 1800, pp. 53–54; S. Bannister, *Humane Policy; or Justice to the Aborigines of New Settlements* (London, 1968), Van der Kemp – Ross, 10 May 1802, pp. cxlvi–cxlviii; BR 301, Alberti – Janssens, 19 Dec. 1803, p. 62; GR 11/29, Cuyler – Stockenstrom, 23 May 1809, No. 526; *RCC*, VII, Journal . . . Collins, 1809, p. 56.

119. Philip, *Researches*, I, 55–56; Malherbe, 'The Khoi Captains', pp. 68, 90–91; BO 64, Faure – F. Dundas, 3 June 1799, pp. 14–15; CO 2582, Graham – Bird, 1 Sept. 1812, No. 24. At Griquatown, in 1813, captains were assigned military duties while civil affairs were placed in the hands of magistrates.

120. *RCC*, VI, Report . . . Collions, 30 May 1808, pp. 349–50; *ibid.*, XXXV, Expenditure of the Year 1827, p. 20.

121. V.C. Malherbe, 'David Stuurman: "Last Chief of the Hottentots"', *African Studies*, XXXIX (1980), esp. pp. 55–59; V.C. Malherbe, 'Hermanus and his Sons: Khoi Bandits and Conspirators in the Post-rebellion Period (1803–1818)', *African Studies*, XLI (1982), *passim*.

122. Some frontier Khoikhoi certainly eluded the census takers. Regarding the Kat River Settlement in 1829 Stockenstrom reported: 'I decoyed them

from those retreats where many of them were certainly not very comfortable, but where they were, at least, safe, and legally their own masters': *The Autobiography of the Late Sir Andries Stockenstrom, Bart.*, ed. C.W. Hutton (Cape Town, 1964), II, 358. A mere 362 'Hottentots' were counted in Cape Town in 1821: [W. Wilberforce Bird], *State of the Cape of Good Hope in 1822* (London, 1823), p. 338.

123. *RCC*, VI, Stockenstrom – Caledon, 17 July 1807, p. 183; *ibid.*, XXIX, Evidence of P.L. Cloete, 5 Dec. 1826, p. 442. 'Mantatee' derived from the widow of a Tlokwa leader, Mmanthatisi. For a discussion of schemes to alleviate the labour shortage by means of white indentured labourers, see Susan Newton-King, 'The labour market of the Cape Colony, 1807–28', *Economy and society in pre-industrial South Africa*, ed. Shula Marks and Anthony Atmore (London, 1980), pp. 182–92.

124. Basil A. le Cordeur, *The Politics of Eastern Cape Separatism, 1820–1854* (Cape Town, 1981), pp. 37–40.

125. Sales, *Mission Stations*, pp. 82, 84. It was claimed that some 40 Khoikhoi wagoners at Bethelsdorp earned Rds. 30–35 per week and some in other occupations earned Rds. 30–40 per week: *RCC*, XVI, Memorial of the LMS, 27 Aug. 1823, p. 217.

126. *RCC*, XI, Proclamation, 8 Aug. 1817, pp. 365–67; BPP, 1835, XXXIX (50), 56–110, 137, 143–44, 145; *ibid.*, Proclamation, 30 May 1827, p. 148; Marais, *Cape Coloured People*, pp. 19–25.

127. CO 439, Evidence of Ruiter, p. 606, No. 106. See also the deposition of Captain Uithaalder, Philip, *Researches*, II, 50–54. For a discussion of the role of commandos in a nomadic pastoralist society see Penn, 'Pastoralists and Pastoralism', p.66.

128. *RCC*, XVI, Memorial of the LMS, 27 Aug. 1823, pp. 215–23; *ibid.*, XXX, Philip – Directors of the LMS, Nov. 1826, in Hankey – Bathurst, 22 Jan. 1827, p. 156; *ibid.*, XXXV, Report . . . 28 Jan. 1830, pp. 340, 342–44.

129. CO 186, Aitchison – Bird, 12 March and 23 May 1823, pp. 149 and 243, Nos. 40 and 70.

130. *RCC*, XIV, Rogers – Jones, 28 Dec. 1821, pp. 220–21.

131. *RCC*, XXIX, Evidence before the Council of Policy, Dec. 1826, pp. 436–92; *ibid.*, XXXV, Report . . . 28 Jan. 1830, pp. 315, 318–20, 343.

132. *BPP*, 1835, XXXIX (50), 162. The Commissioners found some 6,000 Khoikhoi living on mission stations: *RCC*, XXXV, Report . . . upon the Police . . ., 10 May 1828, p. 147.

133. BPP, 1835, XXXIX (50), 136; *RCC*, XXXV, Report . . . 28 Jan. 1830, p. 315. Most servants in Clanwilliam District were 'Hottentots': CO 449, Wylde – D'Urban, 30 Jan. 1836, No. 11.

134. Macmillan, *Cape Colour Question*, p. 154, n. 1; Sales, *Mission Stations*, pp. 79–100; Philip, *Researches*, I, 204–06, 216–17; BPP, 1835, XXXIX (50), p. 147.

135. See e.g. James Read Jun. – Philip, 16 Nov. 1835, *The Kitchingman Papers*, ed. Basil le Cordeur and Christopher Saunders (Johannesburg, 1976), pp. 156–57; Philip, *Researches*, I, 365–66; CO 186, Armstrong – Bird, 4 April 1823, pp. 189–90, No. 54; BPP, 1835, XXXIX (50), 136. The missionaries sometimes took the line that if Khoikhoi were thought of as consumers, this would have advantages both for them and for the colony: *RCC*, XXX,

Philip – Directors of the LMS, Nov. 1826, in Hankey – Bathurst, 22 Jan. 1827, p. 162.
136. BPP, 1835, XXXIX (50), Stockenstrom – Bigge, 20 April 1824, p. 140; *ibid.*, Janze Spielman, p. 162. Somerset felt constrained to extend to 'Hottentots and prize negroes' the 'same considerate advantages' just conferred by his 'Magna Charta' upon the slaves: *RCC*, XVI, Proclamation, 1 Aug. 1823, pp. 174–75.
137. *RCC*, XXXV, Report . . . 28 Jan. 1830, p. 313. The 'few . . . exceptions' which the Commissioners mentioned probably referred to the isolated instances of Khoikhoi who occupied small farms and who, since the British takeover in 1814, appear to have held title to their land, see BPP, 1835, XXXIX (50), 135, 138, 139; *RCC*, XXIX, 467. For a discussion of the legal aspects see Leslie Clement Duly, *British Land Policy at the Cape, 1795–1844* (Durham, 1968), pp. 46–47, 61, 80 and n. 41.
138. Moodie, Afschriften, X, Deposition of Cobus Fortuin, July 1829.
139. Philip, *Researches*, I, 379. Philip likened the Khoikhoi to the British working class in an attempt to reassure the public at large that the extension of land ownership to 'Hottentots' would not lead to a drastic alteration of the social order.
140. BPP, 1835, XXXIX (50), 139.
141. BPP, 1835, XXXIX (50), 148; CO 2736, Van Ryneveld – Chief Sec., 5 Jan. 1832, and encls., No. 1; BPP, 1836, VII (538), 153–54. Each party settled at the Kat River was supposed to have 'not less than ten male adults capable of bearing arms': Marais, *Cape Coloured People*, p. 219.
142. AC 1, 29 Dec. 1826, pp. 487–88; *ibid.*, 6 March 1827, pp. 558–59. There had been a clamour from the British settlers for privileged access to free labour since they were denied slaves: e.g., *RCC*, XVI, Pigot – Wilmot, 20 June 1823, pp. 74–75.
143. *RCC*, XXXIV, Stockenstrom – Plasket, 20 Feb. 1827, pp. 378–81; AC 1, 21 April 1827, pp. 586–97; CCP 6/5/2, I, Ord. 49 of 1828, pp. 455–62. The proclamations of 1797, 1812 (in part) and 1820 prohibiting contact with 'tribes beyond the borders of the settlement', as well as the proclamation of 8 Aug. 1817, were repealed by Ordinance 49. The ordinance provided for 'the admission into the Colony of any Caffres, Gonaquas, Tambookies, Griquas, Bosjesmen, Bechuanas, Mantatees, Namaquas or other Natives of the Interior of Africa'.
144. Ordinance 50, *Cape of Good Hope Ordinances, 1828*; Macmillan, *Cape Colour Question*, pp. 213–19.
145. *Kitchingman Papers*, ed. le Cordeur and Saunders, Read Sen. – Kitchingman, 26 Aug. 1828, p. 98; ZL 1/3/9, Box 11, Folder 3D, Read – Orme, 30 July 1829.
146. A 50(4), Report of a Meeting held at Philipton, 5 Aug. 1834, p. 2.
147. E.g., W.B. Boyce, *Notes on South African Affairs* (Cape Town, 1971), pp. 126–32.
148. At the very moment when Ordinance 50 was passed, the governor informed the Advisory Council that a vagrant act had become 'more than ever necessary': AC 2, 17 July 1828, pp. 479–80.
149. Statement by Maurs Pretorius, 12 Aug. 1834, Philipton, in *South African Commercial Advertiser*, 6 Sept. 1834; Marais, *Cape Coloured People*, pp. 182–

83; Krüger, *Pear Tree*, pp. 189–90; Anderson – Kitchingman, 23 May 1834 and Read Sen. – Ellis, 3 July 1834, *Kitchingman Papers*, ed. le Cordeur and Saunders, pp. 121–22, 145.

150. 'A Hottentot', *South African Commercial Advertiser*, 25 June 1834; Edna Bradlow, 'The Khoi and the Proposed Vagrancy Legislation of 1834', *Quarterly Bulletin of the South African Library*, XXXIX, 3 (March 1985), pp. 99–105.

151. Marais, *Cape Coloured People*, pp. 184–86; LCA 6, Item 19, Memorial of John Philip, 29 May 1834; Leslie Clement Duly, 'A Revisit with the Cape's Hottentot Ordinance of 1828', *Studies in Economics and Economic History*, ed. M. Kooy (London, 1972), pp. 34–46. Galbraith believed that although the British government abolished slavery, the Khoikhoi's 'legal subservience' and the commando system, it did not 'impose an alternative system of order in accordance with humanitarian principles': John S. Galbraith, *Reluctant Empire* (Berkeley, 1963), p. 5. In some areas, wages fell because of the increase in the labour supply following Ordinance 49: Newton-King, 'The Labour Market', p. 207, n. 129.

152. GH 1/117, Glenelg – Napier, 9 Nov. 1837, pp. 134–35, No. 1783.

CHAPTER TWO

Freehold farmers and frontier settlers, 1657–1780*

Leonard Guelke

In 1652 the Dutch East India Company founded a refreshment station on the shores of Table Bay for the scurvy-ridden crews of its fleets plying between Europe and Asia. A few years later, in 1657, the Company gave out land at Rondebosch to former employees and encouraged them to settle. These settlers formed the nucleus of a permanent white population which grew slowly during the next two decades. In 1679 there were only 259 free people, of whom 55 were women and 117 were children,[1] and permanent settlement remained confined to the Cape Peninsula. From 1679 to 1717 the VOC attempted to stimulate agricultural production by granting land to settlers in fertile areas beyond the Cape Flats. When in 1717 this land granting policy was terminated, the free population numbered just about 2,000, including about 350 women.[2] This population was largely engaged in cultivation of wheat and grapes and in the raising of sheep and cattle.

After 1717 a growing number of settlers moved inland to join the few freeburghers who, since 1703, had established themselves as pastoralists or trekboers on land leased from the Company. From 1703 to 1780 the trekboers increased the area of white occupation almost tenfold as the Cape Colony grew from a compact settlement in the southwestern Cape to a vast, ill-defined area stretching almost to the Orange River in the north and to the Great Fish River in the east (Fig. 2.1, p. 68). During the same period there was a steady increase in the free population, which numbered 5,000 in 1751 and 10,500 in 1780.[3] In this population men consistently outnumbered women in a ratio of about 3:2 and children composed just over half the total. Most settlers lived on the land, and by 1780 a large majority of them were pastoralists. Cape Town was the only

* This chapter includes material from the author's 'Frontier Settlement in Early Dutch South Africa', reproduced with permission from the *Annals of the Association of American Geographers* LXVI (1976), and 'The Making of Two Frontier Communities' reproduced with permission of *Historical Reflections/Réflexions Historiques*, XII (1985).

town of significance and accounted for about one fifth of the free population, which included a number of free blacks.

This chapter deals with a period when settler expansion into the interior was largely unimpeded. Grazing land was generally available for those settlers who had the resources and desire for it with little opposition from the original inhabitants. This situation of an 'open' frontier was beginning to break down by 1780. In the north and northeast 'Bushman' hostility and arid conditions combined to check the settlers' expansion. In the east the numerous and well-organised Xhosa people proved a formidable barrier to further white expansion in that direction.

The Cape settlers were drawn from many sources. In the early years most of them were former VOC employees of Dutch or German origin. In the 1680s the original settlers were joined by more Company employees, including a number on their way home after working in the East.[4] Also among the settlers of this time were a number of former African and Asian slaves, some of whom became landholders. A few white colonists married former slave women, and their children were assimilated into the otherwise white community (see ch. 4, pp. 197-99). In 1685 the VOC offered free passages to immigrants from Europe, but few availed themselves of the offer.[5] The Company did, however, send a handful of women from Dutch orphanages as wives for established bachelor settlers.[6] It also arranged for 156 Huguenot refugees to be settled in South Africa, most of whom arrived in 1688.[7] A few immigrants intending to become freeburghers continued to arrive directly from Europe until 1707, when the scheme of free passages was terminated. Thereafter the growth in the free population was largely due to natural increase; but many Company employees, often after working for freeburghers, continued to take their discharges at the Cape and reinforced the rapidly growing white population.[8] The settler population was largely of Dutch, German and, to a lesser degree, French extraction.[9]

The Cape settlers came from widely different social and economic backgrounds. Most of them came as individuals or in families, not in groups. Among each of the major national groups (Dutch, German and French) were farmers, skilled artisans and labourers. Some were reasonably affluent, but many more were poverty-stricken immigrants from the lower rungs of European society. The VOC – with its low pay and high death rate – employed many down-at-heel adventurers, some of whom eventually became freeburghers.[10] There were also some well-educated and many talented individuals, especially among the

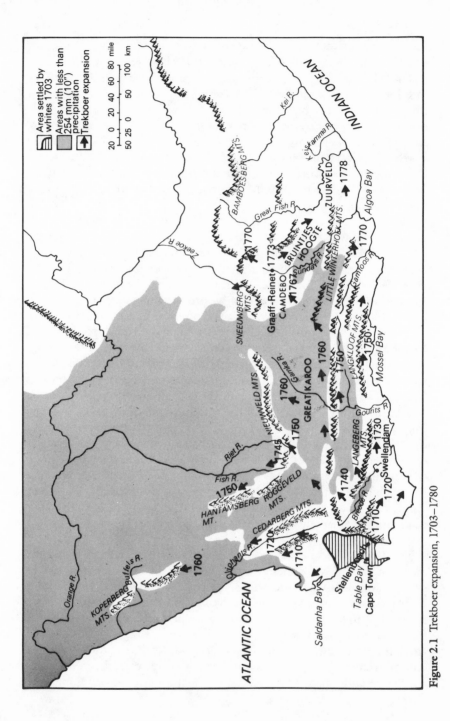

Figure 2.1 Trekboer expansion, 1703–1780

Huguenots and the German-speakers. Many of the latter had been unable to get ahead in the rigidly stratified and economically depressed societies of Central Europe recovering from the devastation of the Thirty Years War.[11] Almost all of them had been exposed to the individualistic and commercial values that were gradually spreading through Europe with the decline of feudalism, and could understand such values and survive in the colonial society at the Cape.

The failure of intensive agriculture, 1652–1679

The directors of the VOC were unprepared for the many difficulties encountered by the first Cape commander, Jan van Riebeeck, in establishing agriculture at the Cape. The memorandum of Janssen and Proot, which had prompted the VOC to establish a settlement on the African mainland, maintained that the agricultural potential of the Cape, with its fresh water, fertile soil and temperature climate, was outstanding.[12] Van Riebeeck, who had spent a few weeks at the Cape in 1648, concurred with this appraisal and suggested that there was nothing to prevent the Cape from rivalling Japan and northern China in the variety and abundance of its produce.[13] This view was reinforced when, shortly after his arrival at the Cape, Van Riebeeck inspected the land on the eastern side of Table Mountain. This land, he wrote, was so extensive that

> it would take a whole day to cover it by foot. According to our estimate it is a good 10 miles wide, traversed by the loveliest fresh rivers one could desire; even if there were thousands of Chinese or other tillers they could not take up or cultivate a tenth part of this land. It is moreover so fertile and rich that neither Formosa, which I have seen, nor New Netherlands, which I have heard of, can be compared with it.[14]

These appraisals of the resources of the Cape clearly assumed that intensive forms of agriculture would be adopted.

The first attempts to cultivate the Cape soil fell short of expectations. Unacclimatised wheat seed, poor tools, a shortage of draft animals, severe south-east winds and unenthusiastic labour were all problems in the early years.[15] Some of these difficulties were due to bad luck, others to lack of foresight and a lack of awareness that a considerable investment of capital and labour was needed to develop profitable agriculture on new land. As a result of this initial failure, Van Riebeeck suggested to the Heren XVII that they place agricultural operations in the hands of freemen or freeburghers who would, he felt, work harder on their own than they had as Company employees.

Van Riebeeck received prompt authorisation from the Heren XVII to settle freeburghers, but he considered it advisable in the light of previous experience to make some preliminary trials on the land designated for their use east of Table Mountain (Fig. 2.2, p. 72).[16] Early in May 1656 Van Riebeeck had five fields prepared at Rondebosch on which rice, oats, tobacco, beans and clover were sown.[17] All these crops, with the exception of rice, did well. Van Riebeeck was well satisfied when he visited Rondebosch in October:

> The haymakers . . . had gathered a large quantity of hay into heaps and were still busy mowing. The clover was especially fine, being knee high and standing very thick. It will be very useful for the horses during the dry season when there is hardly any grazing for them. As in the fatherland, hay will be collected annually for that purpose.[18]

The importance Van Riebeeck attached to clover is noteworthy. Clover was a key crop in Dutch rotation systems because it restored worked-out land and provided feed for additional livestock. The extra manure obtained from the livestock in turn permitted the intensive cultivation of land and high crop yields.

In February 1657 Van Riebeeck allocated land near the trial fields to the first freeburghers,[19] who remained subjects, though not employees, of the VOC; they acquired certain economic freedoms, most importantly the right to own land.[20] Obviously expecting them to employ intensive Dutch agricultural methods, Van Riebeeck granted the early freeburghers only 11.3 ha (28 acres) each. He recognised that freeburghers would need financial assistance, but did not succeed in convincing the Heren XVII, who placed tight restrictions on the credit that could be extended to them. Moreover, the Heren XVII set prices at which the Company would purchase the freeburghers' wheat, and these were low, because they were based on the prices in Europe.[21] Van Riebeeck sought to alleviate the labour shortage by importing slaves, who were made available to the freeburghers on credit. The early slaves were not efficient workers; many deserted while others were so intractable that their owners returned them to the Company.

Economic conditions at the Cape were not conducive to the system of intensive mixed farming on which Van Riebeeck had based his plans. Both the capital and labour for such a system were lacking and so the freeburghers concentrated on reducing their investment in both to a minimum. As a result they did not cultivate clover or other fodder crops, and instead pastured their livestock on the veld near their freehold land.

The purebred Dutch sheep, which did not do well on the natural pasture, were allowed to mingle with stock obtained from the Khoikhoi, and consequently disappeared as a distinctive breed.[22] Oxen, which could find their own food, replaced more efficient horses as plough animals, although most farmers retained a few horses for riding.

The freeburghers – even when dispensing with such labour-intensive practices as crop rotation, fallows, careful weeding and manuring – found the cultivation of wheat barely profitable, and turned elsewhere to make a living. The raising of livestock, which were purchased from the VOC and bartered or robbed from the Khoikhoi, became a mainstay of most farms. The freeburghers' reliance on pasturing their animals in the open veld weakened the link commonly found in Europe between cultivation and livestock farming. Although sheep and cattle were able to survive in the open throughout the year, they needed large areas of land, especially in the dry summer months. The dispersal of livestock made the collection of manure impractical, and longer fallow periods were required for the rejuvenation of soils. Freeburghers also took every opportunity to obtain extra income from non-farming activities. In 1660 a *plakkaat* prohibited freeburghers from collecting wood for foreign ships instead of using their oxen to plough fields.[23]

When Van Riebeeck left the Cape in 1662 he clearly recognised the extent to which his plans for the settlement had failed. In a memorandum to his successor he maintained that no more land for cultivation could be provided west of the Liesbeek River without reducing the already inadequate amounts of pasture available for livestock.[24] A large portion of an area which Van Riebeeck had expected to support thousands of families was now considered to be fully occupied with only about fifteen operating farms. This re-evaluation of the Cape's resources clearly stemmed from Van Riebeeck's recognition that intensive mixed farming had failed and that future development would have to be based on extensive methods.

For many years after Van Riebeeck's departure little was done to reinvigorate Cape agriculture, and the settlement remained dependent on imported rice to meet its cereal needs. The adoption of extensive methods of wheat farming on small farms made it imperative that the area under cultivation be expanded if the colony was ever to become self-sufficient in grain. Those freeburghers who survived on the land (and many did not) did so on the basis of extensive livestock farming and by taking advantage of non-farming opportunities such as wood hauling, hunting and fishing.[25] The Heren XVII, however, were loath to expend additional funds on the Cape, which had already proved to be something of a financial burden.

Figure 2.2 The southwestern Cape, c.1710

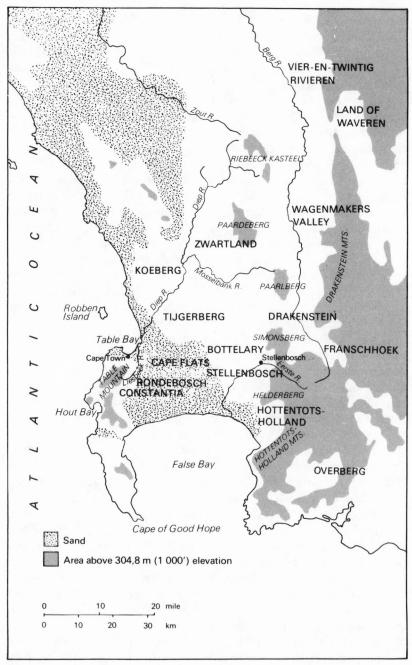

The occupation of Hottentots-Holland by Company soldiers in 1672 would probably have been followed by the permanent settlement of freeburghers beyond the Cape Flats had not the Second Khoikhoi-Dutch war (1673–77) postponed ideas of expansion; the settlement remained confined to the Cape Peninsula for another seven years. When in 1679 the VOC finally adopted a policy of expansion, fewer than half the 142 adult freeburghers had a stake in farming; the rest made a living as artisans and traders near the small village growing up on the shores of Table Bay.[26]

The adoption of extensive agriculture was a reversal of the agricultural intensification process of Western Europe and hence a development of major significance. It took place before the freeburghers had cultivated enough land either to keep themselves or to meet the cereal requirements of the VOC. Had the Heren XVII invested the capital needed to establish intensive agriculture firmly, or had they set wheat prices high enough to encourage the freeburghers themselves to make these investments, expansion beyond the Cape Peninsula would have been unnecessary, and a settlement such as the Heren XVII originally envisaged, confined to a defensible portion of the Cape Peninsula, might have emerged.

The southwestern Cape, 1679–1780

In 1679 Simon van der Stel arrived at the Cape with orders from the Heren XVII to begin new expansion. Under his policy, land in the new settlement of Stellenbosch was made available on a first come, first served basis.[27] No legal limits were placed on the size of an individual's claim, but it all had to be cultivated within three years or be forfeited. The freehold land grants which were finally authorised at Stellenbosch were usually smaller than initial claims, but they were three to six times larger than those of earlier times, ranging in size from 32 to 64 ha (80 to 160 acres).[28] Only between a fifth and a tenth of the land suitable for cultivation had been given out by 1687 when Simon van der Stel closed the Stellenbosch area to further settlement, although a few individual grants were made thereafter. The decision to limit the growth of settlement at Stellenbosch was probably taken on the urging of established farmers, who needed large areas of unallocated land as rough grazing for their livestock.[29]

In allowing settlers to claim their own land, Van der Stel avoided the mistake of imposing an unsuitable framework of landholding in advance of settlement. However, for Commissioner Hendrik Adriaan van Reede, who visited Stellenbosch in 1685, the disadvantages of Van der Stel's policy were more apparent than the advantages. Van Reede complained that all the good arable land next to rivers and streams had been given out (Fig. 2.3, p. 76), a situation which he predicted would give rise to many 'disputes, quarrels and unpleasantness', because future settlers would find themselves cut off from water.[30] In Van Reede's eyes the problem could have been avoided had land grants been rectangular and aligned at right angles to the streams. The disputes anticipated by Van Reede did not arise, however, because the land beyond the rivers was not allocated to settlers and remained in VOC hands. It would not have occurred to Van Reede, who assessed the situation in European terms, that Stellenbosch was close to being considered fully settled with about sixty land grants that comprised only about 5 per cent of the total area, including mountainous areas unsuitable for cultivation.[31]

As new lands were given out in Drakenstein, Paarl, Franschhoek, Tijgerberg, Wagenmakers Valley, the Land of Waveren and the Paardeberg, the general land policy adopted in Stellenbosch remained in force. Large areas of potentially cultivable land were not allocated and became available to freeburghers as rough grazing for their livestock. In the upper Berg River Valley, however, the policy of allowing freeburghers to stake out the boundaries of their own farms was replaced by one in which authorities allocated standard rectangular grants of 50.5 ha (125 acres),[32] a policy modification almost certainly stemming from Van Reede's criticism of Stellenbosch landholding (Fig. 2.3). In 1717, when the granting of new land ceased, there were about 400 freehold farms in the colony, covering in all 194 km² (75 square miles) (Table 2.1, p. 77).[33] This figure was remarkably low – even when one takes account of the vast areas unsuitable for cultivation – and represented only a small fraction of the area actually exploited by the colonists.

The land policy of Simon van der Stel helped early settlers to establish viable farms without much capital. Land, a factor in abundant supply, was substituted for scarce capital and labour. Yet, low as capital requirements were, most colonists could not meet them. Van der Stel described the measures he adopted to encourage agriculture:

> The poor and needy farmers who are in distressing circumstances were provided with enough land, animals and wheat seed to be repaid to the Company after the harvest; as without this measure the projected goal [of colonial self-sufficiency] could never have been reached; . . . it would be an absolutely impossible thing for a poor destitute people to have accomplished anything with empty hands, except with our encouragement.[34]

These measures would not have succeeded if settlers had not been able to use extensive methods of agriculture, giving a quick return on small amounts of invested capital.

The extensive methods of farming, under which each settler received a *de facto* land allocation equivalent to about 8 km^2 (3 square miles) including both an individual's freehold land and his or her 'share' of VOC pasture land, and the nature of the country with its large areas of mountains and sand flats, combined to scatter the population over a considerable area (Fig. 2.2, p. 72 and Table 2.1, p. 77). In the more closely settled areas of Stellenbosch and Drakenstein there were about two free people per 2.6 km^2 (1 square mile), and in Tijgerberg and Zwartland even lower densities. Sparse settlement meant that relatively few people could share the costs of providing transportation, which in the absence of navigable rivers had to be over land. Roads were supposed to be provided by local authorities (landdrost and heemraden) and supported by taxes and labour provided by settlers.[35] But the freeburghers evaded local taxes and delegated old slaves to do their corvée. In consequence Cape farmers were obliged to put up with rough tracks instead of roads, and the oxwagon became the most popular vehicle for transporting farm produce and supplies. Although oxen are slow-moving and cumbersome animals, they were well suited to haul heavy wagons over the Cape's sandy tracks and were able to thrive on rough forage along the route.

The poor transportation system worked against the exchange of goods and services between farm and village. In the vast area beyond the Cape Flats there was only one village, Stellenbosch, although a few artisans were scattered throughout the countryside (see ch. 6, p. 300). The lack of service centres meant that most Cape farmers had to be much more self-reliant than their European counterparts, and lost some of the advantages associated with specialisation and the division of labour. Yet, in spite of its drawbacks, dispersed settlement had obvious short-term economic advantages for settlers without capital. These advantages were most attractive in the early days of settlement. The first freeburghers benefitted from game and timber on or near their farms, and from nearby Khoikhoi labour. But as the game was destroyed and the timber used up, the disadvantages of dispersed settlement became more severe. However, an extensive agricultural system is not easily given up, once adopted. The problem is that the substantial benefits of close settlement are realised only gradually. Its disadvantages, however, appear immediately in the form of the longer and harder working hours necessary to maintain or increase the productivity of a fixed quantity of land.[36]

Figure 2.3 Patterns of landholdings in Stellenbosch and Drakenstein, 1680–1700

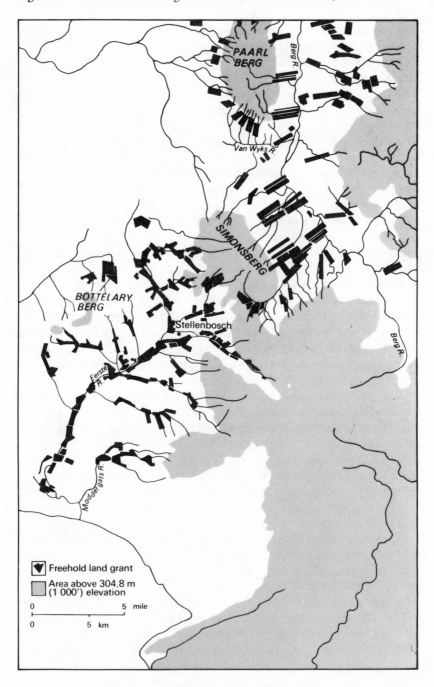

Freehold land grant

Area above 304,8 m (1 000') elevation

0	5 mile
0	5 km

Table 2.1   Freehold land grants, 1657–1717

District	Number of grants	Area of grants km² (square miles)	Total area settled† km² (square miles)
Cape	107	45.6 (17.6)	1,300 (500)
Stellenbosch	108	53.3 (20.6)	1,300 (500)
Drakenstein	189	94.0 (36.3)	3,900 (1,500)
Total	404	192.9 (74.5)	6,500 (2,500)

Source: DO, Old Cape Freeholds Vols. 1 and 2; Old Stellenbosch Freeholds Vols. 1 and 2.

† Approximate total of areas of more or less continuous settlement.

The expansion of the settlement created a demand for more labourers, largely met by importing African and Asian slaves sold to settlers on credit by the Company. More affluent settlers employed white servants in supervisory positions. Poorer settlers could not afford slaves and generally worked their own land, employing extra workers when needed.[37] The Khoikhoi, their traditional communities slowly disintegrating under the impact of European settlement, were particularly useful as casual labourers for settlers without slaves. But they also worked on large estates, especially at harvest time (see ch. 1, p. 17). In 1713 the Khoikhoi near the Cape were decimated by a smallpox epidemic, and their importance as labour declined sharply in the arable areas.

The Cape administration found it increasingly difficult to control the freeburghers seeking opportunities on the expanding frontiers of the settlement. In the 1690s a group of frontier traders was caught illicitly trading cattle between the Khoikhoi of the interior and the farmers of Stellenbosch and Drakenstein.[38] Although freeburghers were occasionally apprehended in illicit trading, the frontier was now too vast and the number of Company officials too few to stop it. The decrees or plakkaten issued and reissued against trade with the Khoikhoi bear testimony to the inability of the Company to control frontier activity.[39] The situation demanded more effective policing of the frontier rather than the promulgation of plakkaten with heavy penalties every trader was confident he could avoid.

As their flocks and herds increased, the freeburghers did not hesitate to use the pasture lands beyond the settled areas. In the dry summer months they commonly sent their livestock inland under the care of a son, trusted slave, or Khoikhoi. This incipient system of transhumance received a setback in 1692 when Simon van der Stel, anxious to reassert

Company control on the frontier, ordered freeburghers to keep their livestock within a day's journey of their freehold properties.[40] This measure appears to have been reasonably effective, perhaps because freeburghers were unwilling to risk heavy sentences merely for seeking good pasture for their stock.

In 1703, however, the administration of Willem Adriaan van der Stel reversed this policy and began issuing free grazing permits to all applicants, granting the exclusive use of a designated area for three to four months. The standard period of a grant was soon extended to six months, and rules were established to define its geographical limits. No grazing permit would be issued to a new applicant if his or her pasture would be within an hour's walk from the centre of an existing one. In practice this meant that each permit holder had exclusive control of a mimimum of 2,420 ha (6,000 acres). Theoretically these holdings were circular, though this meant little to the trekboers. As long as they did not infringe on their neighbours they had *de facto* control of all the land they could use, often twice or four times the theoretical minimum. After 1713 a small fee was charged for a grazing permit or permit for a loan farm (*leningplaats*) as these entities came to be known.[41] In the same year, permission to cultivate wheat on loan farms, heretofore granted only on an individual basis, was made a standard concession.[42]

In addition to trade and pasture, the remote regions of the colony offered incomparable hunting opportunities of which freeburghers had availed themselves from the earliest times. Small hunting parties were constantly setting out for a week or two in search of game, particularly hippopotamus and eland. A few freeburghers became professional elephant hunters and penetrated deep into the country.[43] Hunting expeditions provided colonists with cheap meat for themselves and their slaves, and more important, with knowledge of the resources of the interior. As agricultural opportunities in the settled areas declined, this knowledge was to be of value to many colonists who began to set themselves up as stock farmers.

In 1717 the Heren XVII decided not to encourage further European migration to the Cape but rather to continue reliance on slave labour for the development of the colony. Consequently they ordered the local authorities not to give out any more land in freehold,[44] though land was still available on loan as in earlier times. Many cultivators had commenced farming on a loan farm, a portion of which was later converted into a freehold farm. The latter possibility was now closed, but was reintroduced in 1743, when the holder of a loan farm was given the option of converting a portion of it (50.6 ha or 125 acres) into freehold

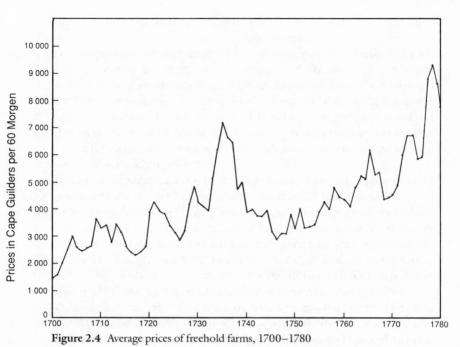

Figure 2.4 Average prices of freehold farms, 1700–1780

tenure on payment of a lump sum based on the value of the property. The occupant of such a property still had to pay the annual rent he or she had formerly paid on the loan farm. Only a handful of cultivators took advantage of this option. After 1717 an individual could acquire land for his own use through inheritance, by purchase, or by leasing a loan farm. In practice there was little distinction between freehold land and loan farms, whose leases became so secure that the fixed improvements (which could be sold) came to include the value of the land on which they stood.[45]

The VOC no longer desired a growing population of cultivators largely because it was experiencing difficulty in marketing Cape produce. In the absence of a large home population, Cape farmers were heavily dependent on passing ships for a market. The business generated by ships calling at Table Bay included sales to free-spending crews on shore leave and delivery of supplies directly to the ships. In times of war in Europe or Asia, troops were frequently stationed at the Cape and provided an additional market for Cape produce. From 1717 to 1780, except in the final decade, the number of ships calling at the Cape did not increase. The stagnation of this vitally important market had a detrimental effect on demand for arable produce, and freeburghers generally had to be content with selling to the VOC at low official prices. The VOC found a market for some of the surplus wheat by exporting about 5,000 muiden (15,500 bushels) annually to the East.[46] Wine farmers had more difficulty developing an export market, because Cape wine travelled badly and acquired a poor reputation abroad. Nonetheless, after 1743 some wine was exported annually to Batavia.[47]

The markets for meat and other pastoral products were also largely tied to the volume of shipping in Table Bay. The Company did not control the market for livestock as tightly as it controlled that for wheat and wine, and the price of meat and live animals tended to reflect supply and demand. Demand for livestock was reasonably stable, but drought and diseases occasionally reduced the supply and forced prices up. A particularly serious rash of diseases decimated Cape flocks and herds in the period 1714 to 1718.[48] Meat prices were high for a few years thereafter, but began a steady decline in the mid-1720s as the supply of animals increased. Live sheep, which fetched over 7 guilders in the early 1720s, usually sold for from 2 to 3 guilders after 1730.[49]

The effects of low prices for wheat and wine were not felt evenly by all cultivators, but varied according to the size of their operations. In general, large estates were more efficient than small ones, whose production costs tended to increase with time. The lack of a group of reliable and inexpensive artisans was one barrier to efficient production that was keenly felt by small and medium producers. Baron van Imhoff, who inspected the Cape in 1743, remarked:

> It seems incredible that a mason and a carpenter each earns from eight to nine schellingen [twenty schellingen equalled one guilder] a day and in addition receives food and drink and withal does not do as much as a half trained artisan in Europe. It is a burden this colony cannot bear and it certainly has a prejudicial effect on agriculture.[50]

The larger producers avoided the cost of hiring independent artisans by establishing their own specialised estate workshops which were staffed by skilled slaves.[51]

Small cultivators were also hard hit by the catastrophic decline in the number of Khoikhoi workers (see ch. 1, pp. 22–23). Unable to afford more than a few costly slaves of their own, they had to hire slaves from other freeburghers at busy times in the agricultural year.[52] More affluent farmers were also increasingly dependent on slave labour (Table 2.2, p. 82), but were able to achieve some economies by dividing farm tasks among a dozen or so slaves, each of whom might have a special skill.

In addition to gaining economic advantages from the size of their operations, wealthy farmers were often able to procure monopoly leases from the VOC. The holders of such leases, which were regularly auctioned by the Company, obtained the sole right of supplying the VOC or Cape public with a specific commodity such as meat, wine or beer. A monopoly lease provided an attractive investment opportunity for well-established freeburghers, and assured them a market for their own produce covered by the lease.

During the period 1720 to 1780 large fluctuations in land prices reflected the changing demand for agricultural products.[53] Although a sustained trend in land prices developed about 1755 and strengthened in the 1770s, an average farm of 60 morgen which sold for 4,200 guilders in 1721, would have fetched only *f*200 more in 1768 (Fig. 2.4, p. 79). The generally low land prices, however, did not make things much easier for a newcomer to get started in arable farming. In the seventeenth and early eighteenth centuries a new settler was able to commence farming on unimproved land which was obtained for nothing from the VOC. After 1717 a new cultivator was obliged to purchase a farm with its fixed improvements, which added little to the productive potential of the land. Indeed, there is considerable evidence to suggest that the productivity of cultivated land generally declined with use.[54] In addition to having to purchase land, which in spite of the trends referred to above still demanded a substantial capital outlay, a new arable farmer had also to acquire slaves, stock and equipment. The average cost of a working farm before 1770 was about 15,000 guilders, comprising 6,000 guilders for land, 2,000 guilders for slaves, and the rest for stock and equipment.[55] A new cultivator would have needed at least 5,000 to 10,000 guilders as a down payment for the purchase of such a working farm, depending on how much additional capital was available on loan.

The ability of a young person to take up arable farming was largely determined by the amount of capital able to be commanded. A number of sources of capital, both public and private, were available to freeburghers in the eighteenth century, but the most important was inheritance. Under the Cape system of partible inheritance the estate of a freeburger was normally divided equally between the surviving spouse and the children.[56] Each child, regardless of sex, was entitled to an equal portion of the children's half of the estate. These inheritance portions could be altered in a will, but no spouse or child could be disinherited of more than half of his or her standard portion. The standard inheritance portions, however, were seldom much altered even when a will was prepared.

The young adult children of the established freeburghers were in a good position to establish careers for themselves, but many young people were destined to inherit virtually nothing and consequently had limited access to loans. The German immigrant Mentzel noted that the difficulty of obtaining a loan was a major grievance of colonists.[57] The amount of capital an individual might assemble could also be affected by marriage, by the extent of the financial support of parents before their deaths, by the number of brothers and sisters with whom an inheritance had to be shared, and by many other factors. Poor but enterprising colonists were able to acquire capital through their own efforts. Elephant hunting, for example, offered good returns for a small investment. Nevertheless, only the children of the more affluent families were generally in a position to assemble the considerable amount of capital needed to become successful cultivators.

The size and gross value of working arable farms tended to increase from 1715 to 1780 while the inequalities among farmers also increased. This tendency was clearly revealed in the increasing number and the changing distribution of slaves employed by arable farmers (Table 2.2, p. 82). The number of male slaves in arable farming increased from 1,500 in 1716 to 2,800 in 1770; the number of cultivators who owned one or two slaves declined, but an increasing number of farmers owned ten or more.[58] Estate records reveal that many small farmers were deeply in debt and left no assets at all.[59] In the period 1731 to 1742 the average debt of estates with a gross value of less than 10,000 guilders was 4,170 guilders, which comprised fully 78.6 per cent of the average gross assets of these estates (Table 2.3, p. 82). While small cultivators found it increasingly difficult to secure a reasonable return on their invested capital, many large producers became exceptionally wealthy. In the period 1771–80 several colonists left estates with a net value of over 30,000 guilders; the largest, that of Martin Melck in 1776, was valued at 225,000 guilders.[60]

The white population was mainly native born by 1731 and exhibited great stability.[61] The majority of landowning whites had been born, lived and died in the same region. The white population was also highly stratified. Mentzel identified three classes of rural cultivator: the very wealthy plantation owner, the well-off gentry, and the hard-working 'yoeman' farmer.[62] In addition to this group of landed free people were a large number of landless white colonists, who made a living working for others, usually in supervisory roles. The white society, although it was divided on the basis of wealth, was a close-knit community. The wealthy and poor participated together in community activities. The small farmers were also often tied to the wealthier ones by debts.

Table 2.2 Distribution of slaves among cultivators‡

Source: KA 4053, 4144 and 4240 (Opgaaf Rolls).

| | Number of slaves held (adult males) | | | | | | | | |
| | 0 | | 1–5 | | 6–10 | | Over 10 | | |
Year	No. of cultivators	% of all cultivators	No. of cultivators	% of all cultivators	No. of cultivators	% of all cultivators	No. of cultivators	% of all cultivators	Total No. of cultivators
1716	40	17.7	90	39.8	53	23.5	43	19.0	226
1746	19	6.6	108	37.8	85	29.7	74	25.9	286
1770	11	3.6	108	35.1	98	31.8	91	29.5	308

‡ This table is concerned with adult slaves held by cultivators. Table 3.7 in the next chapter includes all slaves – men, women and children – and is not restricted to slave holders involved in arable farming.

Table 2.3 Estates of cultivators: Debts as a proportion of all assets, 1731–1780

| | Average gross value of estate (Cape guilders) | | | | | | | | |
| | Under 10,000 | | | 10,000 to 20,000 | | | Over 20,000 | | |
Period	No. of estates	Avg. debt	Avg. debt as a per cent of avg. assets	No. of estates	Avg. debt	Avg. debt as a per cent of avg. assets	No. of estates	Avg. debt	Avg. debt as a per cent of avg. assets
1731–1742	14	4,170	78.6	12	7,620	53.2	7	11,000	26.7
1751–1762	8	3,120	52.8	6	3,530	21.3	4	10,450	38.2
1770–1780	5	3,850	64.1	6	7,680	54.4	9	27,450	36.2

Source: Inventarissen, MOOC (Weeskamer), vols. 8/5 – 8/17 and Stel., 18/30 – 18/34.

The average hard-working farmers eked out an independent living for themselves, squeezed from above by large well-capitalized planters and spurred from the bottom by the examples of widespread poverty among landless whites who had difficulty finding reasonably well-paid employment in a slave society. The position of these small farmers was made even more uncomfortable by the presence of an administration that ruled in the interests of the wealthy burghers.[63] No matter how hard the small farmers tried they could not compete with the planters, and yet they needed to work reasonably hard simply to maintain their position as respectable farmers. Their weak economic position provided them with few opportunities of evading the VOC's marketing laws, which must have seemed especially oppressive to them as they struggled to survive as independent landholders.

At the pinnacle of white society was a small landed gentry, who lived well off large farms or plantations worked by scores of slaves.[64] There was some mobility in the social system, but only a few small farmers succeeded in becoming members of the landed gentry, usually by marriage. The rest of the white farmers by dint of steady hard work and with the help of slave and family labour kept themselves in the middle of free settler society at the Cape. Their values of hard work, order, discipline, and religious orthodoxy would have been inculcated in their children, who would have expected little help in their efforts to make a living for themselves. This group provided the majority of frontier family settlers, who began to move over the mountains in the early eighteenth century.

Frontier settlement, 1703–1780

From the earliest days of Dutch settlement at the Cape, Europeans had found attractive opportunities in the frontier regions.[65] There was good hunting, trade and prospects of pasture in abundance. A variety of inhabitants had availed themselves of these opportunities alone and in groups for shorter and longer periods.[66] In the eighteenth century, as the white population increased, so did the number of people active on the frontier. More and more loan farms were taken out at ever-increasing distances from Cape Town. The number of independent stockholders §

§ I define an independent stockholder as someone who is not engaged in commercial arable farming and who owns at least fifty sheep and twenty cattle. Almost all cultivators also possessed stock. Some of these took out loan farms on which their animals could graze during the dry summer months, but usually they pastured their sheep and cattle on the open veld near their cultivated lands.

numbered about 25 (one tenth of the 260 agricultural producers) in 1716, 225 in 1746 and 600 in 1770.[67] In 1770 they represented two thirds of all independent farmers. In other words, a rapid increase in the number of pastoralists took place while the number of arable farmers grew very slowly.

The rate and direction of settler expansion were largely a function of the nature of the terrain, the availability of permanent surface water, and the quality of pasture. The main areas settled before 1720 included the country to the north of the Berg River (Piketberg) and to the east of the Hottentots-Holland Mountains. In the 1720s the trekboers settled the Oliphants River Valley, the upper Breede River Valley and adjacent valleys and basins, and pushed eastwards in the coastal area to the area south of the Langeberg Mountains. The 1730s saw them entering the Little Karoo which, with the expanding area of settlement south of the Langeberg Mountains, became the district of Swellendam in 1745. In the north a group of trekboers crossed the arid plain between the Cape mountains and the Roggeveld escarpment in 1745 and occupied the most accessible portions of the interior plateau. The initial settlement expanded northwards and eastwards; the Hantam was occupied in the 1750s and the Nieuwveld in the 1760s. Settlement spread into the summer rainfall area in the late 1760s, and into the Camdebo (Graaff-Reinet area) and the Sneeuwberg Mountains. In the 1770s trekboers occupied the areas to the north and east of the Sneeuwberg Mountains, and to the southeast the country behind Bruintjes Hoogte. Meanwhile, in the south, Swellendam colonists pushed eastwards in the Little Karoo and the Langkloof. When, in 1770, the government made an abortive attempt to check further expansion at the Gamtoos River, a number of trekboers had already taken out loan farms beyond it. The eastward expansion continued, and by the late 1770s settlers had occupied the Zuurveld (see Fig. 2.1, p. 68).

Population densities were extraordinarily low everywhere in stock farming areas. The extremely dispersed settlement pattern was fostered in part by the arid and mountainous nature of much of the country, but more importantly by the system of land granting, which entitled each landholder to at least 2,420 ha (6,000 acres). Even the more fertile and better watered areas were sparsely inhabited. The country had almost certainly supported more nomadic Khoikhoi per square kilometer in the seventeenth century than it did trekboers, retainers and remnant Khoikhoi in the eighteenth. A well-endowed portion of the south coast, for instance, had 142 loan farms in an area of about 11,500 km² (4,450 square miles) (Fig. 2.5). Assuming that the average number of free persons in a household was seven and doubling this figure to include slaves and remnant Khoikhoi, the mean population density of the region would have been approximately one person per 5 km² (two square miles). In the arid regions the population density figures would have been lower; perhaps one person per 15 km² (six square miles).

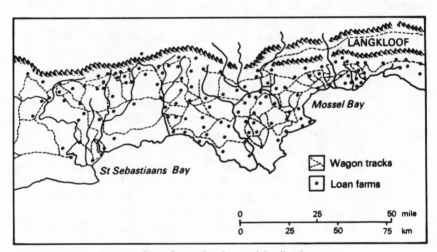

Figure 2.5 Distribution of loan farms: Southcentral Swellendam
After map A231, Van de Graaff collection

A major factor promoting the expansion of white settlement of the interior was the availability of land and the low capital requirement of stock farming. Land was available on the edge of the areas settled by whites for a small annual rent, and elsewhere in the older regions of white settlement by purchase of the *opstal* (as the house or other fixed improvements on a loan farm were designated) at a cost usually considerably lower than the cost of an arable freehold farm in the southwestern Cape. The average value of an opstal in stock farming areas ranged from 300 to 500 guilders compared with 6,000 to 10,000 guilders for an arable freehold farm.[68] In fact, in some areas an opstal could be purchased for as little as 100 guilders while a good arable farm could cost as much as 20,000 guilders. Moreover, the stock farmers did not have to purchase many slaves or expensive equipment. Their heaviest investment was for livestock. Assuming they could start with one horse, twenty cattle, fifty sheep, a wagon and a little equipment, their capital needs would amount to about 1,000 guilders.¶ Those lacking any capital resources whatsoever could become *bijwoners* (tenant farmers) on the properties of established settlers, looking after their patrons' stock on a system of shares. Many young men began their farming careers this way, and some ended them without ever achieving financial independence.

On the farms and cattle posts of the interior, colonists born in Africa and also a few European immigrants, learned to know and love the African veld. They became inured to the hardships of an isolated but independent way of life and mastered the skills and techniques necessary to survive in it. In the process sons lost the skills of their fathers, many of whom had been skilled artisans. The farming backgrounds of most colonists made them ill prepared for other kinds of work, but, more important, there was little non-farming employment in the arable farming areas and virtually none in the stock farming areas. There were a few opportunities for artisans near Cape Town, but they were not sufficiently attractive to encourage young colonists to become apprenticed in blacksmithing, carpentry or some other trade. The low level of business activity and the prospects of competition from slaves were the two main obstacles. When a need arose for more artisans, the positions were filled by slaves or ex-VOC employees born in Europe.

The gradual disintegration of the Khoikhoi communities in the interior provided trekboers with cheap labour. The Khoikhoi were excellent stockmen who were intimately acquainted with the local grazing and water resources. Moreover, they were particularly valuable to trekboers, often hard pressed for cash, as they were paid in kind – usually their keep and sometimes a small proportion of the increase of the stock they tended (see ch. 1, p. 30). The availability of Khoikhoi made it unnecessary for a trekboer to invest much capital in slaves. Occasionally Khoikhoi who were still adherents of surviving Khoikhoi communities would work for a trekboer for a year or two before returning to their people.[69] In the 1760s and 1770s the Khoikhoi workers were joined by captured 'Bushmen' women and children (see ch. 1, pp. 26-28).

Trekboers were not subsistence farmers, as has sometimes been argued. Throughout the years of colonial expansion they maintained

---

¶ It would have been broken down as follows: horse, 50; cattle, 150; sheep, 350; wagon, 300; rent on loan farm, 72; other equipment, 78. All figures are in Cape guilders.

economic links with the Cape, where there was a reasonably good demand for inland produce. Their expansion could not have taken place without guns, gunpowder, wagons and other manufactured items, obtainable only in exchange for the produce of the interior. Apart from essential goods and commodities, trekboers also needed some cash to pay district taxes and rents on their loan farms, although these could also be paid in kind. Though not subsistence farmers, neither were the trekboers profit-seekers who settled the frontier for commerical gain. Their movement was not sensitive to marketing opportunities for frontier produce. The marked increase in the number of loan farms in the early 1760s, for example, preceded, by a decade, the rapid build-up in the number of foreign ships calling at the Cape (Fig. 2.6, p. 88). One cannot argue that the trekboers moved inland in anticipation of the improved market of the 1770s, because this development was the result of complex international events beyond their competence to forecast. The picture is the same when settlement expansion is compared with meat prices. In the early 1740s applications for loan farms continued to be received by the Cape authorities when the meat market was flooded and prices were

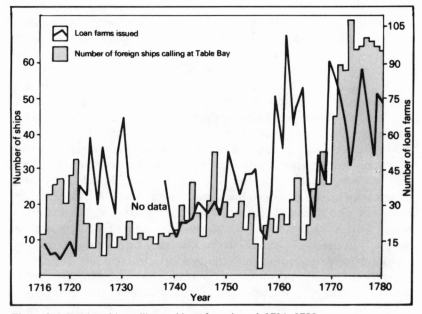

Figure 2.6 Foreign ships calling and loan farms issued, 1716–1780
Source: Coenraad Beyers, *Die Kaapse Patriotte*, 2nd ed. (Pretoria, 1967), pp. 333–35, and
Oude Wildschutteboeken, R.L.R., vols 3–26

exceptionally low. Had commericial considerations been foremost in the trekboer's mind, a marked decline in the number of new loan farms issued would have been expected.[70]

The trekboers were apparently moved by prospects other than those of commercial gain in settling the interior. The alternatives open to trekboers were few and unappealing. As we have seen, the high cost of an arable farm effectively excluded a large number of moderately well-off to poor persons from becoming cultivators. When such persons (worth, perhaps, 1,000 guilders) decided to put their capital into stock farms, they were taking the only action that offered them a reasonable chance of earning a living while preserving their independence. The applications for loan farms continued at all times, partly because there were no viable alternatives. Well-established cultivators did not sell their freehold farms to take up stock farming in the interior.[71]

The impressive estates of some of the cultivators confirm that arable farming could be profitable. The wealthier colonists of the Cape, who had a clear choice of where to invest their money, showed little interest in investing in the interior. The rich arable farmers often held loan farms for their stock, but these were not major assets. Rather than looking to the north or east for investment opportunities, the rich freeburghers looked west to Cape Town, where they competed with each other and with townsmen for the monopoly leases that were annually auctioned by the VOC.

The inland movement of trekboers, if not geared to market conditions, was economic in the sense that abundant land and resources provided the wherewithal for poorer white settlers to live in rough comfort despite their isolation. The general rule that a subsistence economy is undesirable because it inhibits effective deployment of human resources or regional specialisation broke down under the special conditions of Cape frontier settlement. Here a few settlers amidst abundant resources managed to achieve a modest standard of living with little participation in the exchange economy.

Access to the exchange economy was inhibited, particularly in the more remote sections of the colony, by excessively high transportation costs. True, slaughter stock could walk to market, but driving them hundreds of kilometres added considerably to their cost. The trekboers themselves did not normally accompany their animals to market, but turned them over to the employees of the meat contractors, who travelled the country districts buying up stock. Many inland farmers also produced butter, tallow, gum aloe and other produce on which heavy transportation costs could not be avoided. The difficulties of transport are clearly described in the following account of Anders Sparrman, a Swedish scientist who visited the Cape in the 1770s:

> Every peasant for such a journey as this [from just east of Mossel Bay to Cape Town] has two or three Hottentots, one to lead the oxen, and either one or two to drive the spare team; besides which his wife often goes with him, either for the purpose of having her children baptized at the Cape, or else for fear of being attacked by the Hottentots in her husband's absence. Thus, taking it at the lowest, and reckoning only three persons and twenty oxen for thirty days, it stands a great many farmers in ninety days of work of themselves and men, and six hundred of their cattle, in order to make one turn with their butter to the market, and so in proportion for such as are less distant. Hence it is evident, that many thousand days work are unnecessarily lost and thrown away every year.[72]

Sparrman was of the opinion that the days 'unnecessarily lost and thrown away' in transporting goods could be overcome if ships called at Mossel Bay or elsewhere along the eastern coast. The VOC, however, did not consider that the volume of trade merited the construction of the harbour and storage facilities, and the trekboers remained dependent on overland routes to Cape Town.

For the remoter inhabitants of the colony, such as those in the Sneeuwberg Mountains, Agter Bruintjes Hoogte or the Zuurveld, the journey to Cape Town and back might take three months or more. Travel was always demanding and often dangerous. The Scottish plant collector, Francis Masson, described the descent from the Roggeveld:

> We were furnished with fresh oxen, and several Hottentots, who, with long thongs of leather fixed to the upper part of our wagons, kept them from overturning, while we were obliged to make both the hind wheels fast with an iron chain to retard their motion. After two hours and a half employed in hard labour, sometimes pulling on one side, sometimes on the other, and sometimes all obliged to hang on with our whole strength behind the wagon, to keep it from running over the oxen, we arrived at the foot of the mountain, where we found the heat more troublesome than the cold had been at the top.[73]

The improvements made to a few of the passes closest to Cape Town barely shortened the enormous time many trekboers were obliged to spend on the road.

The high cost of transportation was also reflected in the prices of all items imported to the interior. The trekboers were under enormous economic pressure to reduce such items to a bare minimum. Imported items generally considered essential were guns, gunpowder, coffee, tea, tobacco, sugar, and (in the early days) soap. Guns and gunpowder were absolutely indispensable, but the teeming herds of game provided the trekboers with raw materials to make local substitutes for a number of manufactured items. For instance, the Swedish botanist, Carl Peter Thunberg, who visited the frontier in the 1770s, noted that 'thongs made of the hides of animals were everywhere used by the farmers instead of cords and ropes, both for the tackling of wagons and other purposes.'[74] Skins were also used for making saddle blankets, sacks, and even, among the poorest, for clothes.[75] Trekboers in remote areas appeared poverty-stricken to Europeans. Hendrick Swellengrebel Jr., a VOC official who made an inspection of the stock farming areas in 1776, attributed the appalling conditions in the Camdebo to the distance separating that region from Cape Town.[76] Thunberg observed that 'the farmers who live up-country, have generally the misfortune to be poorer, and to be subjected to greater expenses than others'.[77]

The poorly developed transportation system and low population densities also combined to prevent any significant labour specialisation. This situation was reflected in the complete absence of urban development. The administrative centre of Swellendam illustrates the point nicely. In 1745 a *drostdy* was established for the new district of Swellendam on the site of the present village of that name.[78] In 1750 the landdrost and heemraden of the new district discussed plans for controlling the growth of the village as artisans and others set up businesses to serve the farmers of the area.[79] The expected development never occurred. In 1774 no artisans were available to repair official buildings.[80] In 1777, over thirty years after the founding of the drostdy, Swellendam comprised but four houses, one of them used by the landdrost.[81]

In the absence of artisans and other specialists, the inhabitants of the frontier forfeited many of the economic advantages and social amenities derived from the division of labour. For the most part they did without physicians, blacksmiths, carpenters, wagonmakers, masons, teachers and the like. The early trekboers and their descendants had to be far more self-reliant than had hitherto been necessary for anyone at the Cape. In fact, the trekboers had no choice but to become jacks-of-all-trades, and probably masters of none. Trekboers would make use of artisans if business took them to Cape Town, but for everyday construction and maintenance work they were entirely dependent on their own resources. In the absence of frontier churches, religious services were often conducted on the loan farm by the trekboer, occasionally by a visiting preacher. Wealthier trekboers hired ill-qualified itinerant teachers, usually ex-Company servants, to instruct their children. Children of poorer people grew up without formal education.[82]

Although a pastoralist could get started with little capital, further investment brought limited returns. Unimproved pasture was the basic resource of the frontier regions, and the expansion of stock farming involved enlarging the area of activity rather than using the area already occupied more intensively. Such expansion was not conducive to dynamic regional development.

In fact the trekboers, far from improving their resource base, generally over-used it. There are numerous references to declining resources from the second half of the eighteenth century. In a petition to the Cape authorities in 1758, Swellendam officials partly blamed the deterioration of the veld for the poverty-stricken condition of the inhabitants of their district, and asked that rents on loan farms be lowered.[83] Similar complaints were made in later decades by district officials in Swellendam and Stellenbosch.[84] These officials, who were themselves frontier farmers, no doubt exaggerated the extent of resource deterioration to bolster claims for low rents or more land, but the truth of their contentions was confirmed by independent observers. In 1776 Hendrick Swellengrebel Jr. was appalled at the extent to which the pasture of the newly settled Camdebo had been destroyed, and anticipated that the region would have to be abandoned in a few years.[85] In the same year Robert Gordon reported that areas of Swellendam, which had once been rich in grasses, were covered with bushes which cattle refused to eat.[86] In the Bokkeveld he noted the spread of the unpalatable *renosterbos*.[87]

Unlike their arable counterparts, the stock farms, including the opstal, slaves, stock and equipment, tended to decline in value with time. In the period 1731–42 the average value of estates left by trekboers was 3,760 guilders; this figure had declined to 2,850 guilders by the period 1770–80.[88] The position of stock farming relative to arable farming was much less favourable toward the end of the period than it had been at the beginning (Table 2.4, p. 94). Wealth was fairly evenly distributed among stock farmers and tended to become even more so. Few stock farmers were wealthy. In the final period (1771–80) over two thirds of them left estates worth less than 2,500 guilders.

These figures suggest that the conditions which had allowed a small number of trekboers to obtain a modest livelihood as near-subsistence pastoralists were already beginning to break down before 1780. The advantages of a near-subsistence economy based upon extensive exploitation of resources had begun to disappear. The decline in the average value of trekboer estates from 1731 to 1780 suggests that the number of people that could comfortably be supported on a near-subsistence basis had been exceeded. The general economic rule that exchange economies are more efficient than subsistence ones was beginning to catch up with the trekboers as their population grew, as the resource value of the land declined, and as the average distance separating them from essential supplies and services increased. Stock farming had brought good returns on the investment of small amounts of capital, but further investments produced rapidly diminishing returns. Unlike the arable areas, where wealth became even more unevenly distributed and a small class of very rich farmers emerged, in the stock farming regions of the open frontier most people were rather poor, although they lived in rough comfort and were free of large debts.[89]

Frontiers of exclusion and inclusion

The frontier offered opportunities for a variety of people in different situations and with different objectives. Single men were able to use the frontier for hunting, trading and tending livestock for others, but these activities did not constitute settlement. Settlement occurred when whites occupied the frontier permanently, and this almost always involved family units. White men usually found wives from among the white inhabitants, but a few *eenlopendes* (single men) took Khoikhoi wives. Two distinct frontier communities emerged: one, which I will call the 'orthodox' or trekboer community, dedicated to the maintenance of an exclusivist 'European' way of life; the other or 'pluralist' community involved the blending of cultures and peoples within an informal social framework.

Although white women at the Cape were expected to marry (marriage was the only career for women), they or their fathers would have demanded some means of support from a prospective husband. This demand would have ruled out many adult males, who were barely able to support themselves, let alone wives and families. The frontier settlers who did acquire white wives were largely drawn from among the more sober and steady colonists, [90] many of whom had demonstrated their reliability by years of regular service for others on frontier loan farms.[91] In such service prospective settlers could acquaint themselves with frontier regions and assemble the capital they would need to set themselves up as independent graziers.

Most settlers of the frontier comprised remarkably stable communities, notwithstanding their isolated existence. The frontier couple, having settled on a suitable loan farm, typically occupied it for

Table 2.4   Cultivators and pastoralists: Net value of estates** (Cape guilders), 1731–1780

Period		1731–1742	1751–1762	1771–1780
	No.	33	18	20
Estates of	Total value	307,650	187,700	486,640
cultivators	Average value	9,300	10,430	24,330
	No.	24	36	27
Estates of	Total value	90,220	126,230	77,000
pastoralists	Average value	3,760	3,500	2,850
Average value of a pastoral estate as a per cent of an arable estate		40.4	33.6	11.7

Source: Inventarissen, MOOC (Weeskamer), vols. 8/5–8/17 and Stel., vols. 18/30–18/34.
** An estate inventory included stock, slaves, land, equipment, and all monetary assets and liabilities.

the rest of their lives. The evidence on which some historians, including P.J. van der Merwe, have concluded that most trekboers were nomads constantly on the move in search of game and pasture needs to be reassessed.[92] In analysing loan farm records, historians must distinguish between permanently occupied principal loan farms and temporarily occupied or unoccupied loan farms used to supplement the principal farms. For example, in 1731 principal loan farms had been occupied on average for twenty years by the same families.[93]

In addition to certain economic hardships, the frontier trekboers had to put up with severe social isolation. The day-to-day life on a loan farm was often monotonous, and was probably harder on women than on men. Men spent much time in the saddle supervising their workers or hunting with their sons. The sporting life, however, was not a substitute for a fuller social life, and isolation from the outside world tended to blunt the trekboers' intellectual development. The wives of the trekboers were responsible for running the home and rearing their numerous children. Much of the actual work about the house was done by Khoikhoi servants and slaves, and frontier women found themselves with time on their hands. But although frontier life was generally rather dull, there were times of excitement and even danger as violent clashes arose with the 'Bushmen', displaced from their hunting grounds by the trekboers.

European visitors were impressed by the egalitarianism and independent spirit of the trekboers. These characteristics were largely related to their economic circumstances. On their isolated farms, trekboers produced almost everything they needed and acquired other items directly from Cape Town. Trekboers were, therefore, largely independent of their neighbours for their economic well-being. If neighbouring trekboers quarrelled – and in an unsurveyed land there was much to quarrel about – there was little economic incentive for them to patch things up, neither side being likely to need the other's co-operation to maintain its economic position. Extreme individualism was further fostered by the absence of a non-farm rural population dependent on the farming community. Because artisans, retailers and innkeepers in rural areas are dependent on the goodwill of the entire farming community, people in such occupations typically manifest tolerance and flexibility, and actively promote these values within the whole society. Trekboer society lacked the cement that a community-minded, non-farm rural population could have provided and became, in consequence, even more atomised.[94]

The trekboers did, however, set some limits to their independent behaviour. They were noted for their hospitality to travellers. In a country without any stores, inns or guest houses, all travellers were dependent on farmers living along the road for refreshments and supplies. As all inland farmers were obliged to make occasional journeys to the Cape, everyone stood to benefit from an informal system of reciprocal help to travellers.[95] Another area in which inland inhabitants co-operated with each other was in the defence of their property against the 'Bushmen', whose attacks threatened the very existence of the settler community.

In their isolation the frontier settlers assumed many of the responsibilities of government. Though the VOC did not formally delegate any of its authority to the inhabitants, it failed to provide the personnel to administer the frontier, whose sparse numbers did not justify the expense needed to maintain Company authority. Not surprisingly, many frontier inhabitants came to regard the VOC as irrelevant to their survival. A resident of Swellendam probably spoke for the majority of frontier whites when he exclaimed that the entire Cape government was not worth a 'pipeful of tobacco'.[96] The frontiersmen were in many respects *the* government, and they used what power they had to protect their interests as they saw them.

Though the VOC was generally absent from the frontier, the orthodox inhabitants were unable to escape its influence. In assuming the government of their isolated estates with their mixed population of whites, slaves, Khokhoi and 'Bushmen', the family settlers based their actions on previous experience of VOC rule, from which they acquired their concepts of order and control. Although it was not possible to replicate the life of the southwestern Cape, the frontierspeople could adapt basic VOC concepts to the circumstances of their own lives. They accepted the notion that power was its own justification and that their subjects had to be awed and terrified into submission. In frontier conditions they could not awe the Khoikhoi and slaves with fanfare and fine dress, but they could emphasise their superiority as white Christians and insist on being addressed as 'baas' or 'master'. Khoikhoi and slave dependents were constantly reminded that they were inferior 'heathens' who had no rights other than those granted to them by their employers and overlords.

The orthodox frontier settlers also bolstered their authority by fear. Although lacking the sophisticated apparatus of torture available to the VOC, many would inflict severe physical punishment on those who dared to challenge their authority.[97] Severe whippings were routine and occasionally resulted in death.[98] Some farmers shot offending Khoikhoi in the legs, and occasionally resorted to outright executions. Although the VOC remained technically in control of frontier regions, *de facto* power was in the hands of individual white farmers, who had life-and-death power over their Khoikhoi and slave dependents.[99]

The whites feared they could be overwhelmed if they did not uphold authority constantly and with savage ferocity. Though this fear was not invented on the frontier, it acquired new life there and took on an intensified racial aspect, because the orthodox frontierspeople were dealing with people who were physically distinguishable from themselves. Although the VOC was not free of racism in its own policies, it rarely distinguished as sharply between whites and dependents who were not white as did settlers on the frontier.

In spite of the isolated settlement pattern which precluded regular church attendance, orthodox settlers made a deliberate effort to maintain and foster their religious heritage.[100] Regular devotional services, involving Bible reading and psalm singing, were a feature of orthodox frontier life.[101] These services were usually conducted by the farmer himself in the presence of his family and Khoikhoi and slave dependents.[102] The importance of religion in the daily lives of the majority of settlers is evident from the fact that whites often referred to themselves as 'Christians' and used this word to differentiate themselves from the slaves and the 'heathen' inhabitants of the country.[103] The significance of religion to the group solidarity of the orthodox settlers was well described by I.D. MacCrone:

For the frontier farmer, then, his religion was, first and foremost, a social fact and a jealously guarded group-privilege. By virtue of his religion, he justified his right to dominate the heathen by whom he was surrounded. They fell outside the pale, and their claims, therefore, could never compete on equal terms with those of the Christian group. The idea that Christians and non-Christians were, in any sense, equal, even before the law, or that an offence by a Christian against the person or property of a non-Christian, could be taken seriously or be dealt with as vigorously as a similar offence by a non-Christian, was entirely foreign to frontier mentality.[104]

Religion not only marked the boundaries of the white group but affirmed its superiority over the indigenous peoples.[105] It is not clear how far notions of identity and superiority derived from specifically Calvinist doctrines. However, the lack of missionary zeal in Cape Calvinism meant that scarcely any attempt was made by the VOC or anyone else to convert the Khokhoi to Christianity in contrast to the efforts of the Roman Catholic church in French Canada, Asia and Latin America. On the South African frontier the particularly exclusivist character of the Calvinism brought by the farmers from the southwestern Cape reinforced the idea that whites had a permanent monopoly on the Christian religion. Under this view, there was virtually no possibility of legitimate marital unions between black and white, and race relations were consequently given a sharper edge.

André du Toit has convincingly argued that the idea of a chosen people was not part of the eighteenth-century Afrikaner consciousness, as it later was in the twentieth century.[106] However, if the frontier people of the eighteenth century were not *a* chosen people, they were *chosen people* in the sense that they considered themslves as individuals and as families to have a special relationship with God that was denied to the 'heathens' among whom they lived. This sense of superiority had yet to be translated into a consciousness in which God was seen as favouring white settlers as a group, and giving them a historical destiny in Africa.

Although religion, as we have seen, tended to be the basis on which the orthodox frontier community differentiated itself from the Khoisan and slaves, there is evidence that race was as, if not more, important in defining the way the community conceived of its membership. The mixed-race offspring of white men and Khoikhoi women, notwithstanding their close cultural ties, were rarely incorporated into the orthodox white community. Such differentiation might have been justified on religious grounds, but there are also examples of outright racial discrimination. In 1780, the burghers Willem Plooy and Fredrick

Zeelen refused to let their sons do commando service on the grounds 'that they were regarded as bastards and consequently, were not judged good enough to participate in this burgher duty.'[107] This was so despite the fact that their parents were married and that they themselves had been baptised.[108] Their mothers, however, were non-European women, probably themselves of mixed racial ancestry.[109] When Sparrman observed the endogamy of white trekboers he used racial, not religious, categories. He wrote: ' . . . a great many of the whites have so much pride, as to hinder, as far as lies in their power, the blacks or their offspring from mixing with their blood . . .'[110]

This sense of racial identity was seen as a matter of community survival by orthodox settlers. On the frontier white men outnumbered white women about two to one for much of the eighteenth century. Settler women were regarded primarily as childbearers, and their worth on the frontier was tied to their scarcity. They had a vested interest in opposing any kind of race mixing, because if Khoikhoi women could be allowed to substitute for them, what little power they did have would have shrunk in a male-dominated social order. The orthodox settlers had, therefore, to insist on their racial 'purity' as a means of maintaining the social distinctions between whites and Khoikhoi, which were seen to be essential not only for frontier social order but also for survival of the white group. In 1758, a group of frontier residents submitted a request for a teacher to be sent out to them and in support of it made the point that the large number of 'barbarian and heathen people' threatened to overwhelm European society.[111] This sentiment was reiterated in a memorial of 1778, in which the inhabitants of the Camdebo region petitioned for a teacher and minister.[112] Although they could have exaggerated their fears to make their point, their memorial is nevertheless invaluable evidence on how frontier people saw themselves. Race mingling could only have posed a threat to a society dedicated to the maintenance of racial dominance and cultural survival.

There were other indications that the orthodox settler community had developed quite rigid views on the place of Khoikhoi and 'Bushmen' in the frontier scheme of things. The brief support given to the revolt of Estienne Barbier by established settlers of the northwest Cape was due to Barbier's espousal of a vigorous anti-Khoisan policy (see ch. 1, p. 26 and ch. 6, pp. 308–09). The sentiments were also found in other regions. A Swellendam burgher, one M. Botha, described landdrost Horak, who had sought to ensure some degree of equitable treatment of the Khoikhoi in his region, as a 'Hottentots' landdrost.[113] Such epithets were to have a long history in South Africa.

However, not all whites on the frontier conformed to the exclusivist pattern. Throughout the eighteenth century there were opportunities for eenlopende men in hunting, trading and herding. Such men were mainly temporary occupants of the frontier and would not have exerted much influence on the permanent settlers. Other single white men, however, adapted themselves to frontier life and learned to live with the Khoikhoi.[114] These men frequently took Khoikhoi as wives, but they maintained their European language and much of their culture. Although few in number, such examples provided a constant reminder that the indigenous people of the frontier had the potential of absorbing white settlers. They must have heightened the fears of the exclusivist white settlers and strengthened their resolve to maintain their own racial, religious and cultural identity.[115] The fact that the Dutch-speaking off-spring of white-Khoikhoi liaisons were not absorbed by the white population is evidence of a well-developed race prejudice among the orthodox frontier inhabitants rather than evidence of general racial tolerance on the frontier. Whites who lived with Khoikhoi women were cut off from the rest of the white community.

Little is yet known about the origins of those men who lived with Khoikhoi women and created pluralist frontier communities. Most were probably poor and would have had some difficulty finding white wives, but there were many poor white men who never married, yet remained within the orthodox community and accepted its values. The nonconformists were clearly intent on casting off some of the values of the VOC dominated society; the frontier allowed them not to perpetuate a way of life but to escape a social order which offered them little. In thus rejecting established values, they, unlike the orthodox settlers with their clearly defined social and religious objectives, apparently did not articulate an alternative ideology. The pluralist community of nonconformists evolved in a somewhat *ad hoc* manner and defined itself more in terms of what it rejected than of what it affirmed.

The appearance of a community of mixed white-Khoikhoi people on the eighteenth-century frontier is proof enough that a mingling of the races occurred.[116] The nature of the social and physical interaction between whites and Khoikhoi, however, is not easily reconstructed because of a paucity of evidence.[117] The frontier exposed people to the possibility of a variety of social-sexual relations. Hunters, traders and stockmen would have been able to indulge in illicit sexual activity with Khoikhoi women without incurring the social disapprobation of their community, provided they were sufficiently discreet. This kind of activity could also have taken place on the frontier farms of orthodox settlers. It seems likely that most offspring of such casual sexual encounters would have been assimilated within the culture of their Khoikhoi mothers. However, the fact that many of the offspring of white-Khoikhoi unions spoke Dutch and adopted new ways of living suggests that there were also reasonably stable male-dominated common law marriages between white men and Khoikhoi women.

The evidence for such stable unions is comparatively indirect because they existed on the fringes of the colony, unobserved by most travellers and unrecognized by officials and bureaucrats. There are, however, scattered references to white-Khoikhoi unions. For example, in 1768 *Secunde* (Deputy-Governor) J.W. Cloppenburg learned that the colonists Jan Ehrenkroon, Fredrick Zeelen and Hans Dietlof in Houteniqualand, who made a living as wood cutters, were living with 'Bastaard' and Khoikhoi women.[118] Ehrenkroon, recorded with a 'Bastaard' wife and children in the 1770 official census or *opgaaf*, is not among the old Cape families included in de Villiers-Pama's genealogy.[119] Frederick Zeelen married the mixed-blood mother of his children shortly after Cloppenburg's visit, and they were both baptised about the same time.[120] Hans Dietlof was the only one of this group who was living with a full-blooded Khoikhoi woman. There is no mention of Dietlof in the de Villiers-Pama genealogy, but he is listed in the 1770 opgaaf, as a single man.[121] It seems that from an official point of view Dietlof's Khoikhoi partner, and any children they might have had, did not exist. (For further evidence of white-Khoikhoi mixing see ch. 4 pp. 200-02).

It is impossible to say how many other men of European descent lived with Khoikhoi women, because many Khoikhoi wives and mixed children would not have been included in the opgaaf.[122] Nevertheless, there is no doubt that the number of people of mixed European-Khoikhoi descent increased steadily throughout the eighteenth century. The children of white-Khoikhoi informal marriages came to occupy an intermediate position between the orthodox settler community and the Khoikhoi people in the frontier social order. Orthodox settlers valued mixed-race people as reliable and trustworthy servants, but never accepted them as potential full members of the orthodox community. Indeed, the fact that the orthodox settlers were not prepared to accept the offspring of white-Khoikhoi unions is evidence enough of their consciousness as a distinct group identified both by race and religion.

Conclusion

The initial plan of the VOC to create a small, easily defensible settlement at the Cape was based on unrealistic assumptions about the ease with which agriculture could be established there and about the prospects of obtaining a regular supply of livestock from the Khoikhoi. The early freeburghers lacked the capital and labour to develop their lands along the intensive lines envisaged by Van Riebeeck, and many of them abandoned agriculture or left the colony. The freeburghers who persevered in agriculture devised their own ways of making a living, by putting more emphasis on trading and raising livestock and less on cultivation of wheat. In 1679, the VOC allocated new lands to settlers beyond the Cape Flats with a view to stimulating agricultural production. The land grants were now much larger, and it was assumed that much grazing land would be needed by settlers for their livestock. By 1700 Cape farmers raised ever increasing amounts of wheat, wine and livestock and re-invested most of their profits in slaves and land.

Wealth was unevenly distributed among the colonists of the southwestern Cape. There were wealthy planters with several farms, hard-working cultivators burdened by debt and many poor landless single men. As good arable land near the Cape became scarce and as the costs of arable farming increased, more and more settlers looked to the frontier.

The opportunities on the frontier were many, and colonists took advantage of them with different objectives and in different ways. Wealthier colonists made temporary use of inland pasture to supplement the pasture near their farms. Very poor, unattached single men went to the frontier to trade, rob, hunt and herd in the employ of others or on their own account. But it was the growing number of family settlers with a little capital, who sought to make a living as independent stock farmers on loan farms rented from the VOC, that provided the main basis of a new frontier economy and society.

Although the frontier was an attractive opportunity for a growing number of moderately-poor colonists who could not afford land in the southwestern Cape, it offered poor prospects for sustained growth. Its economy was primitive, and a large portion of its goods and services were produced and consumed at the same point. The frontier settler was largely dependent on the natural environment with, perhaps, a little home processing. Economic isolation made for a very marked degree of self-sufficiency on all frontier farms. Farm improvements waited on better transportation; improvements in transportation waited on an increase in population density; an increase in population density waited on farm improvements. As land was abundant on the open frontier, here was a vicious circle from which there was no escape. Lacking the basic requirements for sustained economic growth, the Cape interior remained economically stagnant for the greater part of the eighteenth century.

Notwithstanding the isolation and rough living associated with a near subsistence economy, most frontier family settlers were concerned to preserve their orthodox Christian way of life with its laws and social norms, above all the nuclear family. They defined themselves as a distinct community on the basis of their culture, religion and race and were at pains to preserve this lifestyle. There was, however, a minority of single men who settled the frontier permanently without finding white wives. These men created for themselves a new way of life in which the customs of Europe and the southwestern Cape were blended with those of the Khoikhoi among whom many of them lived and found sexual partners.

Although the nonconforming white frontiersmen were a significant frontier phenomenon and created a pluralist community of their own, such people had little standing with the orthodox white settlers and their effect on white South African values and social structures was slight. The orthodox settlers dominated the political, social and economic affairs of the frontier and imposed their values on all its people. In adapting firmly-held beliefs to frontier conditions, the orthodox settlers created a new community. This community was tough, individualistic and Christian white supremacist. It owed its ideology to the autocratic VOC-ruled slave society of the southwestern Cape, where European social values had already been substantially modified. Though none of these characteristics were new to the frontier, they were established there with particular determination. It was from the frontier regions that they were later taken further inland by the Voortrekkers, with major implications for all the peoples of southern Africa.

Chapter Two   Notes

1. C 499, Uitgaande Brieven, H. Crudop – XVII, 18 April 1679, p. 119.
2. KA 4053, Opgaaf Roll (1716); C. Beyers, *Die Kaapse Patriotte gedurende die Laaste Kwart van die Agtiende Eeu en die Voortlewing van hul Denkbeelde*, 2nd ed. (Pretoria, 1967), p. 341. The figure includes free blacks.
3. KA 4161, Opgaaf Roll (1751); *Kaapse Archiefstukken 1778–1783*, ed. K.M. Jeffreys (Cape Town, 1926–38), IV, 1 May 1780, pp. 355–57.
4. G.M. Theal, *History of South Africa before 1795* (London, 1927), II, 325.
5. C 416, Inkomende Brieven, XVII – Simon van der Stel, 8 Oct. 1685, p. 213.
6. Theal, *History of South Africa*, II, 316.
7. C.G. Botha, *The French Refugees at the Cape*, 3rd edn (Cape Town, 1970), p. 213.

8. L. Guelke, 'The Anatomy of a Colonial Settler Population: Cape Colony 1657–1750'. (forthcoming)
9. According to the research of J.A. Heese, the Afrikaner people (of 1807) were derived from the following ethnic groups: Dutch, 36.8 per cent; German, 35.0 per cent; French, 14.6 per cent; 'non-white', 7.2 per cent; other and indeterminable, 6.4 per cent: J.A. Heese, *Die Herkoms van die Afrikaner* (Cape Town, 1971), p. 21.
10. O.F. Mentzel, *A Geographical-Topographical Description of the Cape of Good Hope* (Cape Town, 1924), II, 21.
11. G. Barraclough, *The Origins of Modern Germany*, 2nd edn (Oxford, 1947), pp. 391–96.
12. H.C.V. Leibbrandt, *Précis of the Archives of the Cape of Good Hope: Letters and Documents Received, 1649–1662* (Cape Town, 1896–99), I, 26 July 1649, p. 12.
13. *Ibid.*, I, June 1651, pp. 18–29.
14. *Journal of Jan van Riebeeck, 1651–1662*, ed. H.B. Thom (Cape Town, 1954), 28 April 1652, pp. 35–36. This is hereafter cited as *VRJ*.
15. A.J. du Plessis, 'Die Geskiedenis van die Graankultuur in Suid-Afrika, 1652–1752', *Annals of the University of Stellenbosch*, Series B1, II, (1933) pp. 2–5 and 113.
16. H.M. Robertson, 'The Economic Development of the Cape under Jan van Riebeeck', *South African Journal of Economics*, XIII (1945), p. 77.
17. *VRJ*, II, 6 May 1656, pp. 32–33.
18. *Ibid.*, 24 Oct. 1656, p. 69.
19. *Suid-Afrikaanse Argiefstukke; Kaap: Resolusies van die Politieke Raad*, ed. A.J. Böeseken (Cape Town, 1957–62), I, 21 Feb. 1657, pp. 90–93.
20. *Ibid.*
21. C 409, Inkomende Brieven, XVII-Council of Policy, 16 April 1658, p. 1036.
22. H.B. Thom, *Die Geskiedenis van die Skaapboerdery in Suid-Afrika* (Amsterdam, 1936), p. 246.
23. *Kaapse Argiefstukke: Kaapse Plakkaatboek, 1652–1795*, ed. K.M. Jeffreys and S.D. Naudé (Cape Town, 1944–49), I, 26 Sept. 1660, p. 61.
24. *Belangrike Kaapse Dokumente: Memoriën en Instructiën 1657–1699*, ed. A.J. Böeseken (Cape Town, 1966), p. 39.
25. C 499, Uitgaande Brieven, H. Crudop-XVII, 18 April 1679, p. 119.
26. C 499, Uitgaande Brieven, Simon van der Stel-XVII, 27 March 1680, p. 477.
27. *Ibid.*, p. 514.
28. DO, Old Stellenbosch Freeholds, I.
29. L.T. Guelke, 'The Early European Settlement of South Africa' (Ph.D. diss., University of Toronto, 1974), p. 123.
30. H.A. van Reede, 'Joernaal van zijn Verblijf aan de Kaap', *Bijdragen en Mededelingen van het Historisch Genootschap*, LXII, 20 May 1685, pp. 122–23.
31. Guelke, 'European Settlement', pp. 119–23.
32. DO, Old Stellenbosch Freeholds, I and II.
33. Guelke, 'European Settlement', p. 179.
34. C 500, Uitgaande Brieven, Simon van der Stel-XVII, 23 April 1682, p. 39.
35. *Memoriën en Instructiën*, 16 July 1685, pp. 223–26; *Res*, III, 5 Aug. 1686,

pp. 140–42.
36. E. Boserup, *The Conditions of Agricultural Growth* (Chicago, 1965), p. 73.
37. Guelke, 'European Settlement', p. 160.
38. *KP*, I, 22 Jan. 1692, p. 282.
39. *Ibid.*, I, 8 Sept. 1693, p. 263.
40. *Ibid.*, 22 Jan. 1692, p. 263.
41. *Res*, IV, 3 July 1714, p. 412.
42. See P.J. van der Merwe, *Die Trekboer in die Geskiedenis van die Kaapkolonie (1657–1842)*, (Cape Town, 1938), pp. 63–132 for a detailed analysis of the origins and administration of the loan farm system.
43. The best account of hunting expeditions at the Cape is Mentzel, *Description of the Cape*, III, 125–26. Mentzel lived at the Cape in the early part of the eighteenth century.
44. C 436, Inkomende Brieven, 15 July 1717, p. 604. The views of the members of the Cape Council of Policy, whose advice was sought before the Heren XVII's decision on slavery was announced, are in *Reports of De Chavonnes and his Council and of Van Imhoff, on the Cape* (Cape Town, 1918). All but one councillor argued in favour of the retention of slavery.
45. This statement is based on an examination of the prices paid at public auctions for the fixed improvements or *opstal* of loan farms. MOOC series 10, Vendu Rollen, Vols. 6–14.
46. Du Plessis, 'Geskiedenis van die Graankultuur', p. 67.
47. J.I.J. van Rensburg, 'Die Geskiedenis van die Wingerdkultuur in Suid-Afrika tydens die Eerste Eeu, 1652–1752', *Archives Yearbook of South African History*, II (1954), pp. 1–96.
48. Thom, *Skaapboerdery*, pp. 47–48.
49. *Ibid.*, p. 50.
50. *Reports of de Chavonnes et al*, p. 137.
51. Items of equipment are listed under workshop headings in inventories of the larger estates; MOOC series 8, Inventarissen, Vols. 1–17.
52. A.J.H. van der Walt, *Die Ausdehnung der Kolonie am Kap der Guten Hoffnung (1700–1779)*, (Berlin, 1928), p. 40.
53. Data on land prices are in DO, *Transporten en Schepenenkennis* volumes, which are complete except for one year for the eighteenth century.
54. A. Sparrman, *A Voyage to the Cape of Good Hope, 1772–1776*, 2nd edn (London, 1786), I, 250–52.
55. Guelke, 'European Settlement', p. 277.
56. Theal, *History of South Africa*, III, 360.
57. Mentzel, *Description of the Cape*, II, 148–49.
58. Guelke, 'European Settlement', pp. 293–97.
59. Data from MOOC series 8, Inventarissen, Vols. 5–8.
60. St 18/31, Inventarissen, 24–26 June 1776, no. 17.
61. Guelke, 'A Computer Approach to Mapping the *Opgaaf*: The population of the Cape in 1731', *South African Journal of Photogrammetry, Remote Sensing and Cartography*, XIII (1983), p. 231.
62. Mentzel, *Description of the Cape*, III, 98–121.
63. L. Guelke and R. Shell, 'An Early Colonial Landed Gentry: Land and Wealth in the Cape Colony 1682–1731', *Journal of Historical Geography*, IX (1983), pp. 265–86.

64. *Ibid.*, p. 279. The gentry comprised about 10 percent of the census households.
65. The important studies of frontier expansion in eighteenth-century South Africa are: Van der Walt, *Die Ausdehnung*; Van der Merwe, *Die Trekboer*; P.J. van der Merwe, *Trek: Studies oor die Mobiliteit van die Pioniersbevolking aan die Kaap* (Cape Town, 1945); S.D. Neumark, *Economic Influences on the South African Frontier: 1652–1836* (Stanford, 1957). See also H. Giliomee, 'Processes in Development of the Southern African Frontier' and R. Ross, 'Capitalism, Expansion, and Incorporation on the Southern African Frontier', *The Frontier in History: North America and Southern Africa Compared*, ed. H. Lamar and L. Thompson (New Haven and London: 1981) pp. 76–119 and pp. 209–33.
66. Frontier activities can be traced in such primary sources as *Receiver of Land Revenue*, Vols. 1–32 and Stellenbosch 13/31 *Alphabeth van d'Eenlopende Personen*.
67. KA 4053, 4144, and 4240, Brieven en Papieren van de Caab Overgekomen, Opgaaf Rolls (1716, 1746, and 1770).
68. These data were obtained from estate inventories covering the period 1731–80: MOOC series 8, vols. 5–17 and Stel. series 18, vols. 30–34.
69. Jacob Koch of the Langekloof, an exceptional case, was reported to have employed as many as 100 Khoikhoi. See F. Masson 'An account of three journeys from Cape Town into the southern parts of Africa', *Philosophical Transactions of the Royal Society*, LXVII (1776), p. 29.
70. Neumark, *Economic Influences*, pp. 5, 17, 79.
71. *Ibid.*, p. 38.
72. Sparrman, *Voyage to the Cape*, I, 264.
73. Masson, 'Southern Parts of Africa', p. 315.
74. C.P. Thunberg, *Travels in Europe, Africa and Asia made between the Years 1770 and 1779*, 3rd edn (London, 1795), II, 52.
75. VC 595, Gordon Journals, p. 47; J. Barrow, *An account of Travels into the Interior of Southern Africa in the Years 1797 and 1798* (London, 1801), I, 105.
76. ACC 477, Swellengrebel Papers, p. 22.
77. Thunberg, *Travels*, II, 173.
78. Theal, *History of South Africa*, III, 71.
79. C 653, DR (Stellenbosch, Drakenstein en Swellendam), 18 March 1750, p. 815.
80. C 665, DR (Stellenbosch, Drakenstein en Swellendam), 11 Jan. 1774, pp. 344–45.
81. VC 592, Gordon Journals, p. 32.
82. C 311, Memoriën en Rapporten, 24 March 1778, p. 429.
83. SWM 1/1, Notulen van Landdrost en Heemraden, 24 Jan. 1758, pp. 424–47.
84. C 655, DR (Stellenbosch, Drakenstein en Swellendam), 15 June 1771, p. 65; C 310, Memoriën en Rapporten, 7 May 1776, p. 78.
85. ACC 447, Swellengrebel Papers, 31 Oct. 1776, p. 24.
86. VC 592, Gordon Journals, Oct. 1771, p. 34.
87. VC 593, Gordon Journals, 4 Dec. 1778, p. 163.

88. These data were obtained from estate inventories covering the period 1731–80: MOOC series 8, Inventarissen, Vols. 5–17 and Stel. series 18, Vols. 30–34. Estate inventories included the value of a deceased person's stockholdings.

89. Guelke, 'European Settlement', p. 327.

90. The conservative historian G.M. Theal was not entirely off base when he wrote that only the steadier elements in the population made a success of their careers. Theal, *History of South Africa*, III, 504.

91. The origins of settlers were traced using the eenlopende lists, which provided data on the employers of single freeburghers. Stellenbosch 13/31, Alphabeth van d'Eenlopende Personen.

92. See Van der Merwe, *Trek*, pp. 17–20 and pp. 61–120. Van der Merwe's image of people constantly on the move does, however, apply to many young single men and landless couples. People who had not yet found suitable affordable land were prepared to move in search of it.

93. South African Archives, RLR, Oude Wildschutteboeken, I–III.

94. Guelke, 'European Settlement', pp. 255–56.

95. Mentzel, *Description of the Cape*, III, 119.

96. Swellendam 3/12, *Verklarings in Kriminele Sake*, p. 40.

97. Barrow, *Travels into the Interior*, I, 145–46.

98. Swellendam 3/10, *Verklarings in Kriminele Sake*, p. 80.

99. When in 1787 a Khoikhoi named Daniel Dikkop, who had been accused of murdering a slave, was asked whether he knew that the penalty for murder was death, he replied that he did not and added, 'this sort of murder remains unpunished, and Europeans shoot Hottentots dead without anything being done about it'. Quoted by R. Ross, 'Oppression, Sexuality and Slavery at the Cape of Good Hope,' *Historical Reflections/ Réflexions Historiques*, VI (1979), pp. 421–33.

100. Van der Merwe, *Trekboer*, pp. 247–49.

101. *Ibid.*, pp. 249–54.

102. Heinrich Lichtenstein, *Reisen in südlichen Africa in den Jahren 1803, 1804, 1805, und 1806* (Berlin edition, 1911; reprint, Stuttgart: 1967), I, 268. The orthodox trekboers in conducting religious services in the presence of Khoikhoi underlined their 'outsider' status, rather than providing them with an opportunity to embrace Christianity.

103. The word 'Christian' was routinely used in official correspondence in referring to the white inhabitants of the Cape. It was also employed by visitors such as Sparrman who wrote about the Cape. The extent to which the idea of being Christian was an integral part of the frontier inhabitants' self-image comes out clearly in an incident related by Barrow, in which a colonist was flogged and put in irons by the British military authorities for ill-treating a non-Christian inhabitant of Graaff-Reinet. This colonist was indignant about his punishment and spent his first night in jail repeating the words 'My God! is dat een maniere om Christian mensch te handelen' (My God! is that a way to treat a Christian). Barrow, *Travels into the Interior*, I, 398.

104. MacCrone, *Race Attitudes*, p. 256.

105. Van der Merwe, *Trekboer*, p. 256–57 provides a summary of contemporary

evidence on this point.

106. Du Toit, 'No Chosen People,' p. 925.
107. SW 10/2: DR, n.p. (16 June 1780).
108. C.C. de Villiers and C. Pama, *Genealogies of Old South African Families* (Cape Town and Amsterdam, 1966), pp. 711, 1159.
109. *Ibid.*
110. Significantly, this observation on race prejudice was made by Sparrman, in the Houteniquas. *Voyage to the Cape*, I, 264.
111. C301, Memoriën en Instructiën, p. 20 (9 Jan. 1758).
112. C311, Memoriën en Requesten: Versoekskrif uit Camdebo, 24 March 1778, p. 429.
113. South African Archives, SW 3/12, Verklarings in Kriminele Sake, 16 Dec. 1767, p. 40.
114. MacCrone, *Race Attitudes*, p. 115.
115. *Ibid.*, pp. 125–36.
116. See E. Fischer, *Die Rehobother Bastards und das Bastardierungsproblem beim Menschen* (Graz, 1913) for an account of the origins of a mixed white-Khoikhoi community.
117. The Dutch kept no detailed records on the Khoikhoi and what information on them is available comes largely from criminal records and travellers' accounts of the interior.
118. The evidence of many visitors and officials needs careful interpretation. The remarks of J.W. Cloppenburg, for example, have to be analysed in their context. In these remarks, Cloppenburg made it clear that he was opposed to the kind of individual settlement occurring on the frontier. He thought that poorer settlers should work for wealthier ones rather than establish their own farms. This perspective coloured his remarks on the frontier inhabitants and their 'deterioration' and 'estrangement from religion'.

    The twelve adult males he encountered in Swellendam might not have been church members – the nearest church was at Tulbagh over 120 kilometres away – but one cannot conclude that they had 'given up' on religion. The evidence of other travellers and officials is that religion was maintained by the settlers themselves on their own farms. Cloppenburg, however, clearly encountered some individuals who had adapted their lives to the frontier situation and rejected the orthodox values of their community.
119. The wife of Jan Anton van Ehrenkroon is recorded in the 1770 census and an inventory of his estate was made in the usual way. See MOOC 8/50, 85.5.
120. Johan Fredrick Zeelen married Maria Stolts in 1769. His children were baptised one month after their marriage. De Villiers-Pama, *Genealogy*, p. 1159.
121. KA 4240, Opgaaf, 1770.
122. Although the number of white people who mingled with the Khoikhoi is impossible to estimate with any precision, it is known that the phenomenon was sufficiently widespread to have created real concern among orthodox settlers and some officials and to have resulted in the emergence of small mixed European-Khoikhoi communities. On the basis

of opgaaf, reports and travel accounts, it seems likely that the nonconforming frontiersmen would never have comprised more than 10 per cent of the white frontier population and probably substantially less than this figure.

The slaves, 1652–1834

James C. Armstrong and Nigel A. Worden

Long neglected, the history of the growth of a slave society at the Cape from the seventeenth to the early nineteenth centuries is a significant chapter in South African history and in the comparative history of slavery. Starting from zero in 1652, the Cape slave population rose to 36,169 in 1834, when the institution was abolished at the Cape, as in other British colonies. It has long been appreciated that the presence of slaves in such numbers, first under Dutch administration and then under British, must have had profound effects on the Cape Colony's social and economic development, but until recently it has received little detailed study.[1]

By the end of the sixteenth century, when the Dutch began to challenge Portugal's control of the Indies trade, domestic slavery had long disappeared from the Netherlands. However, in the following decades, the Dutch gained experience of slavery as their commerce expanded into the West and East Indies.[2] From the 1620s onwards the Dutch became involved in the slave trade from West Africa to the Americas, and their participation grew rapidly after they conquered northeastern Brazil in 1634–38.[3] In their Asian commerce, slaves were a significant, but never predominant factor, and the degree of Dutch involvement in the slave trade there never matched that in West Africa. However, in Asia slavery flourished in varying degrees in all the Dutch settlements, and slave trading figured in their activities throughout the seventeenth and eighteenth centuries, until it was finally abolished in 1855.[4]

The Netherlands came into contact with indigenous Asian slave-owning societies in the East Indies, India and Ceylon. There the institution of slavery had been long established even before the arrival of the Portuguese in the early sixteenth century. Forms of slavery throughout this vast region varied greatly, though in many cases slavery was based upon debt-bondage or upon capture of prisoners of war.[5]

However, the Portuguese had introduced to their Asian possessions concepts of servitude ultimately derived from the Roman law of slavery. The Dutch, when they established themselves in the Indies, did the same.

Thus from the beginning of the Dutch East India Company's activities in the Indies, slavery played an accepted and important part.[6] Under the governor-generalship of Laurens Real (1615–19) it became the basis for nutmeg cultivation on Amboina. Real's capable and ruthless successor, Jan Pieterzoon Coen (1619–23; 1627–29), encouraged its spread throughout the Company's territories. In time, large scale Company enterprises such as gold-mining at Salida on Sumatra (1670s–1739) and the construction of forts, as at the Cape (1665–79) and Ceylon (in the 1690s), relied heavily on slave labour.[7] Slave imports into Batavia alone reached about 1,000 per year in the seventeenth century and rose to about 3,000 annually in the 1770s.[8] While an adequate history of slavery during the Dutch administration of Batavia and other Asian possessions has yet to appear, it is clear that Cape slavery derived much of its form from this model, as well as many of its slaves from this region.

The slave trade and the origins of the Cape slaves

It is clear from the above, therefore, that the Dutch were well acquainted with slavery by 1652, when Jan van Riebeeck established the Company's refreshment station at the Cape. The introduction of slavery to the new colony came as a virtually fore-ordained, although incidental, consequence of its settlement. For the Company, a commercial enterprise whose resources were much over-extended even in its periods of prosperity, and which was always short of manpower, slavery solved otherwise intractable problems of labour supply.[9]

The East Indian experience of the Dutch meant that slavery came to the Cape fully developed, governed by laws already in force (the Statutes of India, 1642, and their amendments), and overseen by Company officials with experience of the institution in the East Indies. The forms which slavery assumed at the Cape were not influenced by pre-existent forms of bondage there, for there were none.

However, after the initial settlement of the Cape, it took some months for the extent of its labour needs to become apparent, and even longer before an initial supply of slaves was forthcoming.[10] Labour was needed for the cutting and hauling of timber and firewood; for the construction of the first mud Fort de Goede Hoop as well as storerooms, dwellings, a barn, a hospital; for fishing, sealing and whaling; for saltworks, brickmaking, cultivation, livestock-herding and exploration; and for the primary task of the refreshment post: the servicing of the transient VOC vessels and their scurvy-ridden crews. For these tasks the garrison, which numbered only about 100 to 200 in the first decade, was wholly insufficient. The other immediate source of labour was the visiting personnel of the Company's fleets. Available only intermittently, these crewmen were often too few and too sickly for the tasks at hand, and they sometimes lacked the necessary skills. Alternative sources of labour – convicts and the indigenous Khoikhoi population – were also unsuitable for the immediate needs of the Company's settlement; there were not enough convicts, and the Khoikhoi proved unwilling.

Van Riebeeck very soon concluded that slaves were essential. In May 1652, not two months after the establishment of the Dutch post at the Cape, he wrote to Batavia that slaves would be useful for the dirtiest and heaviest work.[11] Thereafter he frequently pleaded for slaves as well as for free Chinese and Mardijkers, emphasising the savings that their introduction might effect. The Council of India at Batavia, to which the Cape commander addressed these requests, was not able to send slaves, Chinese or Mardijkers to the Cape, however, and Van Riebeeck sought other means of supplying his settlement's needs. He hoped to supply both Batavia and the Cape with slaves from Antongil Bay in Madagascar, where the Dutch, from their initial settlement at Mauritius, had obtained slaves – a total of about 500 – between 1641 and 1647.[12] To these proposals he added that of supplying Mauritius with slave-grown provisions from the Cape, thereby saving Batavia the trouble. The first slaving voyage was attempted in 1654 by the *Roode Vos*, which was to proceed to Mauritius and thence to Antongil Bay, where it was ordered to buy thirty or forty slaves, including ten girls twelve to fifteen years of age.[13] This effort failed. The *Tulp* was despatched in the same year from the Cape to Antongil, but obtained only two slaves.[14] Antongil Bay at this period had ceased to be an effective slave outlet.

Prior to 1658 there was only a handful of personal slaves at the Cape, including a few in Van Riebeeck's household.[15] The first significant numbers were imported that year in two shiploads.[16] One, consisting of 228 slaves, was the result of a VOC expedition sent (with secret instructions from the *Heren XVII*) to Dahomey, which lay within the official monopoly area of the Dutch West India Company. Another shipload of 174 slaves, chiefly children, was the result of a chance capture by the Dutch of a Portuguese slaver bound to Brazil with Angolan slaves.[17] Of these initial slaves, some were sent on to Batavia, some retained by the Company and some assigned to the first freeburghers. These two shiploads of Angolan and Dahomean slaves were, excepting a few individuals, the only West African slaves brought to the Cape in the Company period.

Slaves were thereafter brought to the Cape mainly in three ways. Firstly, Company-sponsored voyages from the Cape visited slave outlets in Madagascar and, later on, in Mozambique and on the East African coast. Secondly, the Company's return fleets sailing each year from Batavia, and from Gale in Ceylon to the Netherlands, usually brought a few slaves to the Cape, occasionally for the Company's own use, but more often to be sold to individual burghers. Thirdly, foreign ships, including foreign slavers en route to the Americas from Madagascar, Mozambique and East Africa, sometimes sold slaves in Cape Town. It will be useful to examine each of these categories in turn.

Table 3.1   Company-sponsored slave voyages, 1652–1795[18]
(Number of slaves delivered to Cape in italics)

Region	1652–99	1700–49	1750–95	Totals
Madagascar	12*(1,069)*	9*(779)*	12*(977)*	33*(2,820)*
Mozambique, East African coast, and Zanzibar	–	–	5*(974)*	5*(974)*
Delagoa Bay	–	several *(c. 280)*	–	several *(c. 280)*
Dahomey	1*(226)*	–	–	1*(226)*
Totals	13*(1,290)*	9[+]*(c. 1,059)*	17*(1,951)*	39[+]*(c. 4,300)*

Company-sponsored slaving voyages, which are well documented, are summarised in Table 3.1. The predominance of Malagasy slaves, 65 per cent of the total, is apparent. Madagascar was a logical source of slaves for the Cape. It was relatively close, the navigational problems in reaching it were not great, and the Dutch had had some prior experience with slave trading there. However, their experience was limited to Antongil Bay (1641–47) and subsequently, in the 1660s, to St. Augustine's Bay.[19] Neither was a major slave port (see Fig. 3.1, p. 113).

Madagascar was a significant reservoir for the slave trade, however, particularly that conducted by 'Arab', i.e. Islamic, slave traders from East Africa, Oman and Surat, as well as by Portuguese slavers from Mozambique.[20] The reasons for Madagascar's long participation in the export trade in slaves are to be found in the fragmentation of political power there, which led to frequent warfare, and in the eventual rise of

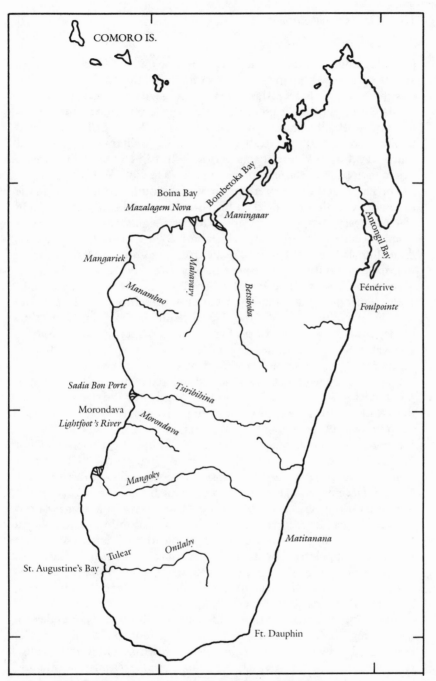

Figure 3.1 Madagascar and the Dutch Slave Trade, c. 1640–1786
Obsolete place-names are in italics

powerful kingdoms (Sakalava, Merina) whose military successes led to a stream of captive humanity. The main focus for this trade (until 1686) was the town of (Nova) Mazalagem, or Massailly, on a small island in Boina Bay on the northwest coast.[21] Mazalagem was then a considerable town of 6,000 inhabitants (far larger than Cape Town) and it conducted a sizeable volume of slave traffic, chiefly with 'Arab' traders, that was as much as 3,000 per year at this period.[22] In the 1660s English slavers began to appear at Mazalagem seeking slaves for the West Indies.

The Dutch at the Cape were ignorant of this outlet until 1672.[23] In the following year they captured an English vessel and brought its cargo of 184 Malagasy slaves to the Cape. The first significant Cape trade at Boina occurred in 1676 (the *Voorhout*: 279 slaves). For a century thereafter slaving voyages were made from the Cape to Madagascar, to Mazalagem and the nearby bay of Bombetoka (known to the Dutch as Maningaar) as well as to other Madagascar ports as changing patterns of trade demanded: St. Augustine's Bay, Tulear, Morondava, Foulpointe and Ft. Dauphin. In all, the VOC made 33 slaving voyages to Madagascar, 1654–1786, for the benefit of the Cape, plus a few more for slaves at its Salida gold mines. But the total number of slaves (2,820) thus exported to the Cape in this period was small in comparison to the overall scale of the Madagascar trade conducted by the 'Arabs' or that of the French, who after 1720 supplied Mauritius and Réunion with thousands of slaves for their sugar plantations there.[24]

Successful voyages usually originated at the Cape in May, taking about a month to reach Madagascar where, if competing traders had not depleted the stocks, trading for slaves might occupy three or four months. The return voyage might take five or six weeks with arrival at the Cape in December or January.[25] Voyages which varied from this pattern were usually not very successful, as they would arrive at Madagascar too early or too late for effective trading, and waste months in assembling a cargo. Slave raiding, i.e. the capture of people for their enslavement, was in general not practised by the Dutch, who were traders not raiders.

On arrival at a slaving port, the Company's *commies* or trade commissioner began negotiations with the local ruler or his emissaries. Typically these palavers were well-lubricated with alcohol. A small contingent of Company men would be left on shore to conduct day-to-day trading. Slaves, once acquired, would be sent to the ship for safe-keeping. Slaves were traded primarily for firearms, brandy and Spanish reals of eight, a medium of exchange widely used in Asian trade. Trading conditions varied greatly, depending on local circumstances and the presence or absence of competing slave traders. Prices also varied but averaged under 20 rixdollars per slave in the seventeenth century, and in the eighteenth century ranged from 20 to 30 rixdollars; higher prices were exceptional.[26]

Malagasy slaves of the Company were taken on these voyages as interpreters and were essential to the successful outcome of a trading venture. They are mentioned by name in the instructions given to the slaving captains on their departure from the Cape, together with the admonition that they be 'rather gently handled', thereby to ensure their co-operation. On virtually every voyage recorded, they did as was required of them.[27]

There was a long hiatus in the Company's trade with Madagasacar between 1715 and 1740, during which period the Company maintained its outpost at Delagoa Bay, the site of the future Maputo, between 1724 and 1732. However, Delagoa Bay produced few slaves, while causing much sickness among Company employees, and the post was abandoned.[28] Voyages to Madagascar resumed in 1740. No Dutch fort or 'factory' was ever established on Madagascar except for two men who were left at Antongil in 1641.[29]

The Company's attempts to obtain slaves from the East African coast north of Delagoa Bay were limited to the decade 1776–86 and were successful, although attended by heavy slave mortality. Five voyages obtained 1,387 slaves including some from Madagascar, although only 990 were landed at the Cape, a mortality rate of 28.6 percent. Slaves were bought at Zanzibar, the offshore island Oibo (Ibo) and Mozambique. The Company organised no slaving voyages at all after 1786.[30]

Virtually all the slaves obtained on these Company-sponsored voyages were destined for use by the Company at the Cape. In addition to those traded on Company account, however, some slaves were also obtained on these voyages by Company personnel in private trading. From incomplete records of slave sales *transporten* at the Cape, it seems likely that roughly 10 per cent should be added to the official figures to include slaves obtained in this manner. This private trade was conducted without the knowledge or approval of the Heren XVII or the Council of India. It was not mentioned in official correspondence, nor were the number of slaves privately acquired included in the official reports of these voyages. Indeed it was only after the Company ceased making slaving voyages, near the end of its administration, that the Heren XVII took any official cognizance of this individual trading by its Cape officials. It was then defended as a customary usage, without any specific known authorisation, which compensated the ships' officers and supercargoes for the dangers and discomforts they underwent in the trade, and as an encouragement for them to go on future voyages.[31]

The conduct of the Cape-based slave trade was affected by many factors, only one of which was the immediate labour needs of the Company at the Cape. The outbreak or anticipated outbreak of European wars, the wishes of the Heren XVII and the Batavian authorities, the lack of ships and specie, the activity of pirates and reports of poor trading conditions at the slaving ports, could all thwart a projected voyage.

The second major source of Cape slaves was Company shipping bound for Europe from the East Indies. Sporadically, and usually following wars or famines, the Batavian or Colombo authorities dispatched on the return fleets considerable numbers of slaves for the Company's use at the Cape. Thus in 1677, 93 'Tutucorin' slaves were sent from southern India; in 1712, 36 slaves arrived from Jaffnapatnam on Ceylon; in 1719 another 80 arrived from Jaffnapatnam, and there was a further shipment in 1754.[32] The overall contribution of these Company shipments to the Cape's slave population was small.

On the return fleets there was also a steady private trade in slaves from India and the East Indies conducted by Company officials for their own profit. Usually these officials were returning home themselves, but sometimes they remained in the Indies and entrusted their slaves to others for sale at the Cape. In conducting this trade the officials were taking advantage of (and stretching) a Company rule which allowed them to be accompanied by personal slaves as far as the Cape. There was no similar encouragement to bring slaves to the Netherlands where indeed they were legally free on arrival.[33]

The practice of bringing East Indian and Indian slaves on the homeward bound fleets was sporadic at first but became more frequent in the 1680s. The Council at Batavia attempted to regulate the passage of slaves to the Cape by requiring each slaveowner to obtain its permission for each slave sent. Members of the Council themselves often engaged in this trade. By 1713 the Heren XVII had become so concerned by the growth in this traffic, and by the smaller flow of slaves accompanying their masters to the Netherlands, that it required return passages for all slaves exported from the Indies to be paid in advance.[34] This requirement was plainly intended as a disincentive to the trade, to which the Company objected not on humanitarian grounds, but because it represented an unwelcome utilisation for private profit of the carrying capacity of the Company's ships. In 1716 Batavia issued a plakkaat against the clandestine transport of slaves, on pain of confiscation.[35]

Nevertheless the traffic, both open and covert continued, although on a smaller scale. C.P. Thunberg, writing in 1772, observed: 'The Company brings the greatest part of its slaves from Madagascar, whereas private persons buy their's [sic] of the officers belonging to the ships, as well Dutch as French, that are on their return home from the East Indies, seldom of the English and never of the Swedish'.[36]

The numbers involved in this traffic were never large, as space on the return fleets was usually at a premium.[37] The documentable numbers on Company vessels appear to have been about twenty to thirty a year, with the average being about twenty, exclusive of any clandestine trade.[38] However, the importance of these slaves in the Cape slave community was out of proportion to their numbers. They were in many instances skilled domestics or artisans of high value to their owners. Hence their chances of mild treatment and of longevity were probably better than those of most unskilled slaves.

In early 1767 the Council of Policy, reacting to a series of violent crimes by Indonesian slaves, resolved to ask Batavia to forbid the export of Buginese and other Eastern slaves to the Cape.[39] Batavia promptly complied and the export to the Cape of oriental slave men was prohibited, such slaves to be confiscated if found.[40] The trade in women slaves was not affected, nor was the practice, which continued till the end of the Company period, of permitting slaves to accompany their masters to the Netherlands. It is even doubtful that the export of slave men ceased, but it is difficult to document until the 1780s. In 1784 the earlier prohibition was repeated and a penalty of 300 rixdollars was added to that of confiscation.[41] However, the confiscation of slaves occurred very rarely, suggesting that the practice of sending male slaves to the Cape was winked at by officials both at Batavia and at the Cape.[42] In 1787 the prohibition was again promulgated and the following year the Heren XVII urged that the Cape authorities keep each newly arrived ship under the closest scrutiny the better to enforce the ban.[43]

Foreign ships were a third source of slaves for the Cape Colony. From 1664 to the 1720s these were chiefly British slavers taking slaves from Madagascar to Barbados and later to Virginia and Buenos Aires.[44] Initially they were interlopers seeking to avoid the Royal African Company's monopoly of the English West Africa slave trade. In Madagascar they traded at Mazalagem and at Morondava, known to them as 'Lightfoot's River' (Lahefoutsy's River).[45]

En route to the New World foreign slavers frequently stopped for refreshment at the Cape. Their willingness to sell slaves there depended on several factors. They had to balance the advantage of immediate sale at the Cape against an anticipated higher price in the New World, should their cargoes survive the risky middle passage across the Atlantic. If their slave cargoes were in ill health, or if prices were thought to be relatively low in the Americas (e.g. because of a depression in the plantation economy or because competitors were likely to beat them to their favoured ports), slaves might then be traded at the Cape. In practice these foreign slavers frequently sold only part of their cargo as a hedge against losses in transit and unpredictable market conditions in the Americas.

The Company rarely purchased slaves from transient slavers for its own use; hence most of these sales were to burghers or to Company officials. The Company's permission was required for such sales. Even where it was granted, records were not always kept.[46] Where it was not granted, the possibility of illicit trade arose. Partly for these reasons it is difficult to determine the total number of slaves imported to the Cape by foreign slavers (see p. 119).[47]

Nevertheless it is clear that for much of the period prior to the 1780s the number of slaves purchased annually was small relative both to the Cape slave population and to the numbers carried to the Americas past the Cape. In the 1780s, however, boom conditions at the Cape made it a profitable market for the slavers, who at this time were mostly French and Portuguese, and a few large shiploads were sold. For example in 1782 *L'Union* sold 279 slaves; in 1785 *L'Estrelle d'Afrique* sold 194 and *Le Télémacque* 75 slaves.[48] These three shiploads were purchased by the Company for resale to the burghers, the last two at the initiative of the Governor van de Graaff.[49] In 1786 Van de Graaff and his Council estimated the burghers' annual import needs at 200 to 300.[50] This was a level which foreign slavers were plainly able to supply. In addition to the sales from foreign slavers, there were also occasional sales of individual slaves from returning English and French East Indiamen, analagous to those made by the VOC return fleets.

From time to time Cape residents sought the Company's permission to engage in private trade, which would include slaving at Madagascar and along the East African coast. Such a request was made in 1687 following English reports that cheap slaves were obtainable at 'Lightfoot's River'. Governor Simon van der Stel forwarded the request to the Heren XVII, noting that free traders might prosecute the trade more zealously, but nothing came of this request.[51] In 1719 there were some persons residing in the colony with experience in trade and piracy at Madagascar, and they persuaded the Council of Policy to forward to the Heren XVII their request for a vessel to trade there.[52] There was no positive response, the Company being jealous of its trading monopoly.

Some years later, in 1731, the Heren XVII, perhaps prompted by the failure of the Delagoa Bay outpost, disinterred this request and indeed sought to encourage a free trading venture from the Cape to Madagascar; but by this time the earlier enthusiasm for such voyages had died at the Cape.[53] Free trade was again sought in 1745–46, in 1779 (in the petition of the burgher 'Patriots') and in 1784; it was finally permitted in 1791, too late to have any impact on the slave population of the Cape during the VOC's administration.[54]

These requests were fuelled by the apparent profitability of trading in slaves. Adult slaves were generally obtainable at Madagascar for prices ranging from 20 to 30 rixdollars and were saleable at the Cape for three to four times these figures. But the overheads were large and the risks considerable, as the Company's experience showed. The Company's own bookkeeping practices tended to conceal the true costs of its expeditions however. Vessel and crew overheads were not taken into account in calculating the real costs of these voyages; they were absorbed in the general expenses of the Company while only the purchase price and rations of the slaves were reckoned. The risks were also real, chiefly loss of slaves and seamen through illness and death, or escape. Shipboard slave revolts, although rare (e.g. *De Brak*, 1741; *Meermin*, 1776; *Zon*, 1775) were also a threat. Shipwreck was always a possibility, as was at times attack by pirates or rival traders. The VOC's *Westerwijk* was lost to pirates at Mazalagem in 1686.[55]

A cardinal question for the history of Cape slavery is of course how many slaves were imported into the Cape. Except for the Company slaves, which are well-documented (see p. 123) this is not a simple problem, as comprehensive VOC records, as communicated to the Heren XVII, are reticent on the dimensions of this import trade to burghers and officials.

Painstaking recent analyses of the transporten, notarial slave sale records, have produced a detailed picture of these sales for the period up to 1731, including much data about sellers, buyers, prices and geographical origins of slaves.[56] It seems probable that for the earlier part of this period the transporten are reasonably complete, and that conclusions based on them are firm. From 1717 onwards however, surviving transporten are fewer, and almost certainly are not an adequate reflection of all slave transactions. For the twelve years 1695–1707, for example, 1,194 slaves were imported into the Cape, an average of about 100 per year, plus another 650 or so on Company account.[57] However, for the twelve years 1717–29, a period of rapid slave population growth, the surviving transporten account for only 163 burgher slaves, plus another 103 purchased by Company officials for a total of 266.[58] Yet the opgaaf return (see p. 248) for 1718–29 shows a net increase of 1,472 burgher slaves, little of which can be attributed to natural increase.[59] It seems that the documentary record of transporten is very incomplete after 1717.

For most of the eighteenth century except for the 1740s, annual slave imports to the burghers and officials (excluding those imported by the Company for its own use) probably averaged c. 100–200. The 1740s were a time of higher slave mortality and insufficient imports, and the overall slave population fell in these years.[60] Future critical analyses of the opgaaf returns will doubtless refine this estimate somewhat.

From 1793–95 no slaves were imported. Under the First British Occupation (1795–1803) imports resumed, with the encouragement of the Burgher Senate.[61] In the first thirty-three months some 605 slaves were imported followed by an additional 400 in March 1799.[62] Permits for even larger numbers were granted by the Burgher Senate.[63] Altogether about 2,000 slaves were imported between 1795–1803, an average of about 250 per year.[64]

Under the Batavian Republic (1803–6), although its representatives at the Cape had reservations about the trade, the importation of slaves under licence was continued. Over 1,095 slaves, chiefly from Mozambique, were introduced.[65]

The Second British Occuption (1806) was soon followed by the passage of The Abolition of the Slave Trade Act (47 George III, Session I, c. 36) on 25 March 1807. By the terms of this act slaves could not be legally imported after 1 March 1808. However some 500 slaves were imported in 1806–8 before this terminal date.[66] There was also some illicit trading even after this embargo, but stiffer British penalties soon discouraged this trade. Moreover, a major source of labour for the Cape was created by the very fact of the British abolition of the trade. From 1808 slaves aboard slave ships were eligible for capture and 'liberation' by the British navy. These 'Prize Negroes' were released at Freetown, Sierra Leone and also at the Cape. No fewer than 2,100 slaves, almost all from Madagascar or Mozambique, were released at the Cape from December 1808 to December 1816.[67] 'Apprenticed' for fourteen years, they formed a major increment to the unfree labour of the Cape.

Because of the deficiencies in the archival record, the data are not sufficiently complete or sufficiently comparable to permit an analysis of the origins of the Cape slaves analogous to that of Heese on the freeburghers.[68] However it is plain that the major single regional source for Cape slaves during the Company period was Madagascar. A recent analysis of 3,283 slave imports 1680–1731 reveals that 1,595 or 48.5 per cent were of Malagasy origin, with India and Indonesia each contributing 15.8 per cent, and 19.8 per cent being of other or unidentified origins.[69] No fewer than 66 percent of the Company's direct imports came from Madagascar and officials and burghers also acquired many Malagasy slaves from transient merchants (Table 3.1, p. 112).

During the Company's administration, slaves from continental Africa were relatively few. They were imported only at the very beginning from West Africa and Angola, with a few score from Delagoa Bay during the Company's brief tenure (1724–32) there. After 1776 significant numbers, however, came from Mozambique and East Africa.

Asian slaves were drawn chiefly from Bengal, Malabar and Cormandel in India, from Ceylon and from Batavia and many of the outer islands of Indonesia, but especially from Macassar. These slaves formed a very heterogenous group, in which no single place of origin predominated.

The ethnic diversity of the Cape slaves meant linguistic diversity as well. Slaves from Angola, Dahomey, Madagascar, various Indonesian islands, India and the East African coast and its hinterland, brought their own languages with them, and consequently had difficulty in communicating among themselves and with their masters. Not surprisingly a lingua franca emerged; in fact there were two. Some slaves used a form of creolised Portuguese, which persisted throughout the Company period; its prevalence has long been a matter of scholarly contention.[70] But it is clear that most masters and slaves conversed in an evolving form of Dutch which developed into Afrikaans. Again, the extent of the slave contribution to this development has been hotly contested by Afrikaans linguists.[71] The details of this controversy need not detain us here. What is significant from the standpoint of the imported slaves is that their native languages were of only limited utility and survival value to them in their new home. A communal identity based on their traditional languages and cultures was rapidly eroded, even in the case of the relatively numerous Malagasy. Like the slaves who went to the American South, the slaves at the Cape appear to have quickly learned the language of their masters.[72]

As in other slave societies, the names given to slaves were often those assigned by their masters, and the original names of the imported slaves have usually been lost. The names were frequently identical to those used by Europeans: Andries, Anna, Catharina, David, etc. Others were distinctively slavish, and are rarely found among whites: Augustyn,

Fortuyn, Coridon, Cupido, Job, Scipio, Titus, Octavia, etc. Such names were used repeatedly, a practice which vexes the researcher attempting to identify individual slaves.

An exception to the pattern of renaming of slaves is found with the Company's slaves. The Company tended to preserve the original names of its slaves, especially when they were acquired from Madagascar. Hence lists of Company slaves abound with such Malagasy 'names' as Leidzare, Lambo, Ratzi, Calle, Mironde, Ingore, etc. Many of these appear to be descriptive terms applied at the time the slaves were acquired by the Dutch; e.g. Leidzare is *Lehilay Tsara*, which means 'good man'.[73] This practice was doubtless not due to any preference for the original names as such. But as the Company recorded the purchase of traded slaves under their original names, any change in those names might have suggested to the minds of visiting commissioners or other Company officials the substitution of slaves as well as names.

It is noteworthy that the Cape, unlike Latin America, did not adopt or evolve a complicated system of socio-racial terminology to distinguish between persons of various racial backgrounds. Slaves at the Cape, as in Indonesia, were *slaven* (singular *slaaf*) or *lijfeigenen*. These words were used interchangeably without distinctive connotations. Persons, whether slave or free, of African, Malagasy, Indian or Indonesian origin were all *zwarten* (blacks). The terms *heelslag* (full-breed) and *halfslag* (half-breed) were but rarely used. Even rarer was *mesties* (half-breed), a word of Portuguese usage. A person of colour who had been free in Indonesia was known there, and at the Cape, as a Mardijker. Slaves freed at the Cape became *vrijzwarten* (free-blacks). Further definition in racial terms was not needed. The term *kleurling* (coloured) did not emerge until the nineteenth century. It is possible that this lack of elaboration stems from the Dutch custom of referring to individuals by their place of origin (e.g. Jan van Ceylon), which may have made an additional scheme of racial classification redundant.

The Company slaves

The Company's labour force consisted primarily of slaves, but it also included Asian and Indonesian convicts (*bandieten*) sent by the Batavian and Ceylon authorities to serve out their sentences at the Cape. This latter group was distinct from that of the much smaller number of political exiles. The convicts lived in the slave lodge and at the outposts, and were generally treated like slaves. The more dangerous were kept in chains, as were unruly slaves. In theory convicts were free after completing their sentences, but they usually did not live to enjoy their freedom; in addition, the records of their cases were sometimes lost and they remained in captivity. The number of convicts fluctuated, but during much of the eighteenth century they were a significant part of the Company's adult labour force.

The Company's slaves are far better documented than the numerically more important slaves of the burghers. Relatively good information is available on their origins, living conditions, genealogies, deaths and manumissions. Population statistics are also fairly good, because the VOC as a business enterprise had both the motive and the means to keep an accurate check on its labour force. Very detailed figures are found in the *negotie-boeken* (trade ledgers) which, however, are not available for much of the eighteenth century, and in other Company documents. The size of the Company's slave force can be seen in Table 3.2 (p. 124) compiled from scattered but usually trustworthy sources.*

Moderate fluctuations in the Company's slave population took place from year to year. However, no dramatic growth is discernible in the totals which, having passed 300 in the late 1670s, rose only slowly into the eighteenth century and remained well below 1,000 during the whole of the VOC period. The very circumscribed nature of the Company's slave population was due to the Company's realistic calculation of its labour needs. Moreover, its economic needs were fairly constant, being linked mainly to activity in the port (which expanded only slowly) and to occasional construction projects in Cape Town. The Company played only the slightest role in enterprises in the interior. It did not participate as a producer in the expanding agricultural sector of the economy, which had a growing need of slaves, since it had handed over to the burghers most of its arable farming in 1657 and its pastoral activities in the 1690s. Before the settlement of Stellenbosch in 1679 the Company's slave force exceeded that of the burghers; in that year the Company had 310 slaves, the burghers 191. But thereafter the burghers' totals rose rapidly, surpassing those of the Company in 1692. In 1750 burgher slaves

* The Company sometimes reckoned its convicts as slaves, and in sources which give a single figure for slaves it is not always clear whether bandieten are included. Where possible a distinction has been made between the two in the table.

The figures also include slaves who had escaped and not been recovered, for no regular bookkeeping procedures existed for writing off successful escapes. For example, in 1753 there were no fewer than fifty such escaped slaves among the roughly six hundred slaves the Company then 'held'. (VOC 4191, Res 24 July 1753, pp. 470–72.)

Bookkeeping inconsistencies explain some of the seemingly rapid fluctuations of less than a hundred in totals from year to year, though a good part of the fluctuation is doubtless due to the arrival of new cargoes and to mortality from epidemics.

Table 3.2　Company slaves and convicts (*bandieten*), 1661–1793[74]

	Men	Women	Children	Total slaves	Convicts	Total forced labour
1661	22	34	11	67	–	–
1669	23	32	46	101	–	–
1679	67	121	122	310	–	–
1685	53	194	90	337	51	388
1693	152	170	†	322	49	371
1714	224	129	92	445	22	467
1727	266	228	103	597	104	701
1742	–	–	–	605	–	–
1752	253	179	74	506	138	644
1764	198	159	77	434	–	–
1777	281	166	112	559	122	681
1784	360	176	89	625	112	737
1789	–	–	–	–	–	946
1793	325	123	61	509	73	582

† Children included with adults

exceeded Company slaves by more than ten to one; in 1793 by almost thirty to one.

The very limited expansion of the Company slave population through most of the eighteenth century, despite continued infusions from outside, clearly suggests that mortality rates must have surpassed fertility rates among Company slaves. Low fertility cannot be attributed simply to a low ratio of women to men. In fact, as Table 3.2 indicates, the Company's slave women actually outnumbered the men in the seventeenth century. In the eighteenth century, however, Company slave men outnumbered the women, but never at ratios as disproportionate as among burgher slaves. The relatively balanced sex ratios among Company slaves may be due more to the working of various chance factors than to Company policy. Indeed, the Company consistently instructed its slavers to obtain male slaves whenever possible.

Moreover, the impact of sexual imbalance on fertility was offset by the frequent contacts which female Company slaves had with other slaves as well as with Europeans. In 1665 cash payment was given to slave women for bearing children, but this was soon dispensed with as unnecessary.[75] Many travellers observed that the Company's slave lodge served as a house of prostitution for visiting sailors and residents, and there is ample evidence that the children of Company slave women frequently had white fathers (ch. 4, p. 195).[76] Evidence regarding the attitude of the women to sexual exploitation is fragmentary and contradictory. On the one hand there are scattered references throughout the period to abortions and (rarely) to infanticides.[77] On the other hand there is the evidence of Peter Kolbe and others, who noted that Company slave women welcomed pregnancies, which freed them from work for six weeks before and after delivery.[78]

Some stable unions were formed between slaves in the lodge. Lasting attachments also occurred between European men and Company slave women. In a few cases the man purchased the freedom of his partner and subsequently married her.[79] More frequent, however, was the manumission of Company slave children by European men resident at the Cape, with the clear implication that the child's benefactor was his or her father.[80] However, the rate of both types of manumission was lower at the Cape than in many slave societies (ch. 4, pp. 204–14). Company slave manumission in the period 1715–92 totalled only 86, an average of about one slave per year. Thus the average manumission rate for Company slaves was about 0.17 per cent.

A crude measure of the fertility of Company slave women can be derived from the Company's ledgers, where annual totals of births are available for some years. It can be seen from Table 3.3 that roughly one in ten of the Company's woman slaves gave birth annually. When we recall that some of them were old it is clear that this fertility rate was very high. We do not know how many women were of childbearing age; probably a high percentage were so, in part because of the short life span of slaves and in part because of the Company's occasional manumission of its older slaves.

Table 3.3   Annual incidence of births among Company slave women[81]

	Number of Company slave women	Number of births	Ratio of women to births
1665	c. 30	9	3.3 : 1
1690	c. 120	13(+?)	9.2 : 1
1691	c. 120	12(+?)	10.0 : 1
1692	122	10	12.2 : 1
1769–70	c. 120	10	12.0 : 1
1777–78	166	17	9.8 : 1
1778–79	212	20	10.6 : 1

The number of Company slave children per slave woman varied from 0.4 to 1.4, the average being 0.64 (Fig. 3.2, p. 124). This ratio was comparable to but somewhat lower than that for burgher slaves, and much lower than the equivalent ratio among white freeburghers. (See Figures 3.4 and 3.5, page 131). For both Company and burgher slaves the ratio was affected by many factors other than birth and death rates, e.g. new imports of either women or children, escapes and manumissions.

Mortality rates among Company slaves were high, as can be seen from Table 3.4 below. The concentration of Company slaves in the lodge made them particularly liable to contagious diseases. Smallpox epidemics killed many: in 1713 about 200; in 1753 and 1754 about 300; in 1767, 67. Dysentery, measles and unnamed infectious diseases killed many more. The figures also include accidental deaths, suicides, murders and executions. However, the greatest threat was disease.

Table 3.4 Deaths among Company slaves[82]
(Mortality rates in parentheses)

1661	11 (16%)	1753/54	146 (25%)
1667/78	125 (39%)	1754/55	176 (40%)
1687	many	1755/56	58
1700/01	220 in six months	1756/57	21
1713	200 in six months	1767	67 (12%)
1715/16	56	1771	99
1716/17	15?	1774/75	98
1717/18	19	1777/78	154 (18%)
1718/19	122	1778/79	32
1719/20	96	1779/80	152
1731	55	1780/81	143
1741/42	48[+]	1781/82	60
1742/43	53	1782/83	46

New arrivals were particularly susceptible to mortal illnesses, although their deaths are often concealed in the overall mortality figures for a given year. For example, of the 221 Malagasy slaves of the *Joanna Catherina*, 129 died within fourteen months of their arrival in 1673. Of the *Voorhout's* 257 slaves (mostly children) landed in 1676, 92 were dead in three and a half months. Of the *Soldaat's* 119 slaves, the largest part were dead within a year of their arrival in 1697.[83]

A comparison of the birth and death statistics shows that deaths far exceeded births, and confirms the observation made above that the Company's slave force was not self-reproducing, but relied for its survival on replenishments from imports. In this respect it was similar not only to slave populations in the British West Indies and South America, but also to the burghers' slave force at the Cape (see p. 133). The slaves, excepting those who worked on outposts or for Company officials, were

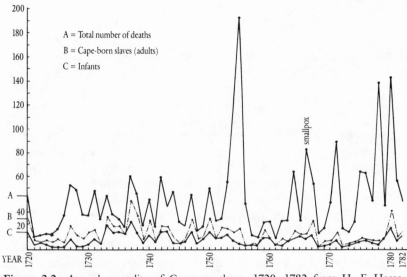

Figure 3.2   Annual mortality of Company slaves, 1720–1782 from H. F. Heese, 'Mortaliteit onder V.O.C. slawe, 1720–1782', *Kronos* II (1986, p. 13)

housed in the Company's slave lodge, a brick structure built in 1679.[84] This large building measured 86 by 42 metres; it had a central court where roll-call was taken and food prepared.[85] Men, women and children, as well as convicts, were kept in the lodge. On occasion, when the hospital was full, the lodge was also used to house the sick from the VOC fleets.[86] In Kolbe's time, pigs were kept in the courtyard.[87] Within the lodge there was no privacy, although in 1685 Van Reede ruled that men be separated from women and children from adults. However, this regulation was ignored.[88]

Daily control over the work of Company slaves was exercised by overseers (*mandoors*) who were slaves themselves. There were also paid overseers, either Europeans or free blacks. Responsibility for the slaves in the lodge was that of the European *opziender* (also called *oppermandoor, oppermeester*, or *opzichter*) who dwelt in a separate building adjoining the lodge. His duties included counting the slaves each day and locking them up at night. This was probably a brutalising job and it conferred only low status. The salary was initially meagre but it rose to 30 Cape guilders (10 rixdollars) a month, plus rations, by the end of the VOC period.[89]

A large number of the Company slaves were general labourers, available for a variety of tasks as needed. Others were stevedores, gardeners, domestics, masons, carpenters, coopers, smiths, nurses, herdsmen, chalk burners and so on. As noted above, some served as overseers of their fellow slaves. Some favoured slaves worked as domestics for the governor and other high officials, including the Dutch Reformed ministers (*predikanten*). A few were assigned to each of the outposts of the Company; for example, in 1793 slaves were located at Riet Valley, the River Zondereind, Klapmuts, Mossel Bay and False Bay.[90]

One special group were the so-called *Kaffirs*, eastern slaves or convicts who functioned as auxiliary police to apprehend escaped slaves and to act as disciplinarians. Punishments, whether judicial or not, were usually administered to slaves and sometimes to Europeans by these 'servants of justice.' On this account the Kaffirs were hated and feared by the slaves, and indeed by some whites. It is noteworthy that at the Cape this function was performed by Asians; at Batavia the Kaffirs were African slaves.[91]

The Company occasionally granted its slaves small rewards in return for meritorious work. For example, in the seventeenth century extra tobacco was passed out at the New Year, skilful brick-makers were given small cash payments, and slave children in school were eligible for prizes.[92] Malagasy slaves who served as interpreters on slave voyages were treated with special caution, and given special rewards, because of their critical role in the trade.[93]

The Company's outlay for its slaves' food and clothing naturally varied with the size of its slave force. The average cost of feeding and clothing a Company slave per year was in the eighteenth century only about 45 to 48 Cape guilders (15 to 16 rixdollars), a very low figure.[94] During the eighteenth century the Company's total expenditure for slave maintenance ranged from 20,000 to 30,000 Cape guilders (6,666 to 10,000 rixdollars) per annum until the 1780s, when it rose rapidly to a high of 63,365 guilders (21,122 rixdollars) in 1786–87.[95] These figures represented only about 4 to 7 per cent of the cost of administering the Cape. Although the actual amounts spent on the slaves increased, they formed a diminishing percentage of the Company's overall expenses at the Cape. The Company clearly paid very little for the indispensable labour which its slaves performed.

From the first British Occupation of the Cape in 1795, the Company, now called government, slaves, played an ever-diminishing role. From 534 slaves in 1795, their numbers gradually decreased under successive British, Batavian and British administrations.[96] In 1803, according to the long-serving overseer of the lodge, C.G. Höhne, there were 365 slaves in the lodge, 21 in Klapmuts, plus a few convicts.[97] By 1807, there were only 283, still housed in the lodge; schooling was now provided for the children.[98] Earl Caledon, the Governor, then felt that these slaves were no longer an asset to Government, and some were sold to 'respectable people' at £30 each.[99] Those remaining were, in March 1811, removed from the lodge, and settled in other rented premises.[100] In 1820 they were transferred to a new lodge in the Cape Town garden. Two years later, they numbered 'about 200 of various ages'.[101] By 1826 their numbers had fallen to 171, and their emancipation came in 1827, several years before that of the colonists' slaves.[102]

The colonists' slaves

After 1692, the number of slaves owned by colonists exceeded those of the Company and throughout the remainder of the VOC period the large majority of slaves at the Cape were privately-owned and were used as domestic servants or farm labourers. By 1795 the Cape's reported slave population of 16,839 consisted almost entirely of private slaves, the Company possessing only about 3 per cent of this figure.

The number of slaves at the Cape was systematically recorded in the VOC and early British period in the opgaaf rolls – tallies of the colonists

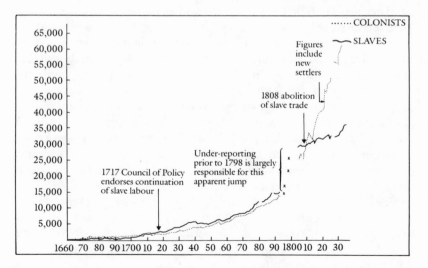

Figure 3.3   Colonists and colonists' slaves in the Cape Colony, 1660–1834
(Sources: Opgaaf rolls; C 06135, Statements of the Population and Quantity Lands at the Cape of Good Hope, 1806–1825 and Cape Blue Books).

and their property made by the authorities for taxation purposes – which were drawn up annually until 1825. Although there was some under-reporting, particularly in the remoter pastoral districts and possibly also in Cape Town, and evident inaccuracies by the 1780s, these census records do indicate the broad trends in slave numbers and regional distribution.[103]

Figure 3.3 shows the total number of slaves recorded. After a slow growth of numbers during the seventeenth century, the curve increases steadily during the Company period, and rises markedly between the late 1790s and the 1800s before levelling out during the nineteenth century. This pattern may be linked to three phases in the development of Cape slave society. In the first period (to c. 1717) slave numbers were small – there were only 350 privately-owned slaves in 1690 – and increased slowly. This was the period of slow initial development of the settlement's arable economy, when the demand for slave labour was relatively restricted. The drop from 2,012 slaves in 1712 to 1,788 in 1713 was caused by a smallpox epidemic which hit the Cape Town slaves especially badly, but it had little impact in the rural districts and imports rapidly offset the losses.[104]

In 1717, the Council of Policy gave its firm support for the continuation of slavery as the main source of labour, and this gave impetus to the second phase of development (c. 1717–1808) when the rapid expansion of the Cape economy and its farming population led to a marked increase in slave numbers. There were some fluctuations in this period of general increase. Growth was especially rapid between 1713 and 1738, a period of favourable economic expansion when the number of ships calling at the Cape reached heights not to be repeated until the 1770s (Fig. 2.6, p. 88). In the 1740s there was a short-term drop, partly caused by a decrease of imports, but also by an unusually high number of deaths among rural slaves, possibly the result of a measles epidemic. A decree of 1747 declared a day of prayer to atone for the sins of the inhabitants which had led 'Almighty God . . . to visit upon us for some period of time the heavy burden of a great number of deaths among our slaves.'[105] The second smallpox epidemic of 1755 is reflected in declining numbers of slaves, the more minor one of 1767 less so. Major imports in 1772–73 may have been responsible for the increase in that year, and the steep rise of the 1780s reflects a short-lived era of prosperity. This was brought to a halt in the 1790s by the outbreak of war in Europe and a subsequent economic slump.

There was a dramatic leap in the reported slave population from the last return under VOC rule (1795) of 16,839 slaves to 1798 when

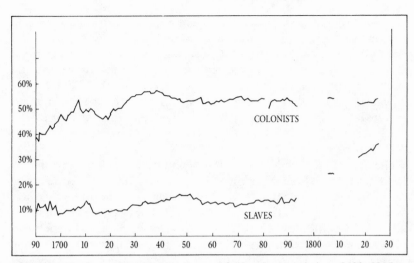

Figure 3.4 Percentage of children in slave and freeburgher populations, 1690–1825
(Sources: as for Figure 3.3)

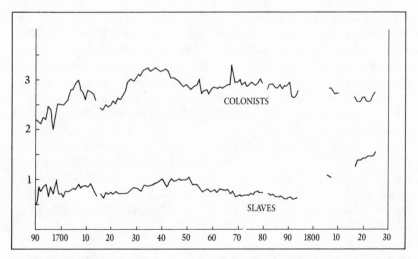

Figure 3.5 Number of children per adult female in slave and freeburgher populations,
1695–1825
(Sources: as for Figure 3.3)

25,754 were recorded. Some slaves were imported during this period, but the increase was primarily due to more effective administration of returns under British rule. In 1800, a proclamation stated that the opgaaf be administered under oath and with tough penalties for evasion and false returns.[106] Thus, the substantial increase in the 1798 figures indicates that the slave population was significantly larger in the last decades of Company rule than reported. Imports during the First British Occupation and the Batavian period continued to increase the totals to 29,861 in 1806.

The dependence of the Cape on slave imports was clearly revealed by the effects of the abolition of the slave trade after 1808 (p. 120). During this third and final phase, despite some allegations of smuggling, few slaves could have been landed in Cape Town and taken into the interior out of sight of the authorities.[107] Instead, slave-owners were dependent on demographic growth within the colony. Increasingly, rural slaves were Cape-born. By 1833, 20,409 of the total 38,343 slaves, or 53.2 per cent were less than twenty-five years old and so had been born in the colony after the ending of the slave trade.[108] Yet the level of natural reproduction was only sufficient to produce a small increase in the total population from 29,861 in 1806 to 36,274 at the time of emancipation in 1834.

These three phases, broadly corresponding to the three centuries, were also distinguished by different ratios between slaves and freemen, as Fig. 3.3 (p. 129) shows. Until about 1710, burghers outnumbered slaves, but for most of the eighteenth century slaves were slightly ahead. Nonetheless, the growth of the two groups was closely parallel, except during the prosperous 1720s and 1730s when the number of slaves surged briefly. After the ending of the slave trade, however, the settler population began to exceed that of the slaves. By the 1820s the increase in the number of colonists, boosted by settler immigration as well as natural reproduction, led to a substantial disparity between free and slave numbers.

Despite some similarity in their overall numbers, the slave and free populations differed markedly. During the VOC period, the male adult component of the burgher population was very much smaller than that of the slaves. As a result, adult slave men outnumbered adult burgher men by four to one in 1738 and almost three to one in 1768. These striking ratios may partly account for the burghers' fear of the slave population, a fear which may have been less had the two male populations been more equal in size. On the other hand, the number of adult female slaves was almost the same as the number of adult female burghers from 1710 to 1770. Yet the percentage of children in the burgher population was considerably higher than that amongst the slaves (Fig. 3.4). Moreover the average number of children per female slave was consistently lower than that amongst the colonists (Fig. 3.5).

These differences reflect the fact that during the VOC period the gowth of the slave population depended more on imports than on internal reproduction. More slave men than women were imported to serve the labour demands of the colony. Moreover, natural reproduction levels were insufficient to produce a normal sexual balance of the kind found amongst the burgher population. This position changed after the ending of the slave trade in 1808. Increase was now entirely dependent on natural reproduction. By the time slavery came to an end, the gap between the numbers of slaves of each sex had narrowed considerably (Table 3.5).

Table 3.5 Number of males and females in slave population[109]

	Males	Females	Number of males per female
1738	4,602	1,155	3.98
1768	6,243	2,464	2.53
1806	19,346	10,515	1.84
1825	19,063	13,767	1.38
1834	19,580	16,589	1.18

During the nineteenth century, the age structure of the slave population also changed. The number of adult male slaves (over 16 years) fell from 15,513 in 1806 to 13,012 in 1825. In 1824 there were more adult male freemen than slaves for the first time since the seventeenth century. By contrast, the average number of children per female slave rose, as did the percentage of children in the slave population. There is some evidence that the fertility level of locally-born slave women at the Cape was higher than that of imported females.[110] This may explain the rising fertility levels during the nineteenth century when an increasingly high proportion of the female slave population was born in the colony. Nevertheless, even during this period, the total number of children and the number per adult female slave still lagged behind those in the free population.

Although many masters, especially after 1808, encouraged their female slaves to breed, it appears that their fertility was lowered by the conditions of life and labour which they endured. One informed commentator, W.S. van Ryneveld, stated in 1797 that, 'Procreation in proportion to number is amazingly small . . . For the small number of fertile women slaves there is a very large number of them who are entirely sterile or do not bring forth more than one or two children during their whole lives.' Van Ryneveld partially attributed this to 'their continual labour, a circumstance very prejudicial to procreation'. This, together with poor living conditions and diet, as well as the practice of using slave women as wet-nurses for their owners' children, and thus extending their lactation period, may have reduced their capacity for childbirth.[111]

A further cause of the lack of a self-reproducing slave population was its high mortality rate. As in all pre-industrial populations, infant mortality was especially high. Several epidemics have already been noted which affected the slave population with particular severity. Van Ryneveld commented in 1797 that, 'a very considerable number of slaves are lost by continual disorders, especially by bile and putrid fevers to which they are very subject', possibly a reference to typhus.[112] Conditions of life and labour must also have led to a higher mortality rate amongst the slaves than the freemen. In 1825, for example, the death rate amongst slaves was 2.1 per cent, while that amongst the burghers was 1.6 per cent.[113]

Another major difference between the slave and free populations of the Cape was their geographical distribution. The farming settlers were spread rather evenly throughout the colony, but the majority of slaves were held in Cape Town and its hinterland and the southwestern regions of Stellenbosch and Drakenstein which were developed for arable agriculture (Table 3.6).

Table 3.6   Percentages of freeburgher slave force in each district[114]

	Cape District	Stellenbosch	Drakenstein	Swellendam
1701	69%	22%	9%	–
1750	60%	14%	21%	5%
1773	55%	11%	26%	7%

Few slaves lived in Swellendam district. This confirms what travellers' accounts suggest, namely that slaves were found in far fewer numbers on pastoral than on arable farms. Swellendam district, unlike Stellenbosch and Drakenstein had no sizeable region of cultivation. Stellenbosch district included the northern pastoral regions occupied by burghers in the course of the eighteenth century; thus the lower proportion of slaves there than in Drakenstein in 1750. As late as 1834, as Table 3.7 indicates, the majority of slaves were still in Cape Town and the western arable districts (Cape District, Stellenbosch and Worcester, which incorporated the former district of Drakenstein). A slightly higher proportion were found in Swellendam and George (created in 1811 from parts of Swellendam district) than in the VOC period, a change which reflects the development of grain farming in the region, but only a few lived in the eastern pastoral districts of Graaff-Reinet, Uitenhage, Albany and Somerset. The new British settlers who made up a large proportion of the farmers in Albany and Somerset were forbidden to own slaves, and were entirely dependent upon the labour of the Khoisan.

Table 3.7 Numbers and percentages of slaves in various districts in 1834[115]

	Number of slaves	Percentage of total
Cape Town and Cape District	10,343	28.6%
Stellenbosch and Worcester	14,365	39.7%
Swellendam and George	5,661	15.7%
Graaff-Reinet	2,809	7.8%
Uitenhage, Albany and Somerset	2,981	8.2%

The census records also give some indication of the distribution of slaves among the free burghers. In 1750 almost exactly half of the male burghers in the colony were slaveowners.[116] Among burghers who farmed and owned land, the proportion of slaveowners was higher. By 1773, as Table 3.8 shows, almost all farmers in the Cape district and a high proportion in Stellenbosch and Drakenstein were slaveowners. Even in pastoral Swellendam, just over half of the farmers owned at least one slave.

Table 3.8 Percentage of farming burghers with at least one slave in 1773[117]

Cape District	96.5%
Stellenbosch	69.3%
Drakenstein	72.1%
Swellendam	51.4%

In Cape Town, where by 1773, 23.8 per cent of slaves in the colony were owned, the incidence of slave ownership among the freeburghers was also high, although less than in its immediate rural hinterland. Records were not kept separately for the town, but a partial listing survives from 1800 which shows that 754 out of the 1213 recorded urban freeburghers (62 per cent) were slaveowners. This excludes Free Blacks, of whom only 15 per cent (57 out of 370) owned slaves in 1797.

During the VOC period, Company officials also held privately-owned slaves; 27 per cent of them (134 out of 504) were slaveowners in 1797.[118]

Although these figures show a remarkably high incidence of slaveholding at the Cape in comparison with other colonial slave societies of the period, the average number of slaves owned by Cape slaveowners was considerably lower than that of, for example, the slave plantations of the New World. Table 3.9 shows the pattern in 1750.

Table 3.9   Numbers of slave-owners grouped according to number of slaves owned in 1750[119]

Slaves	Cape District	Stellenbosch	Drakenstein	Swellendam	Total owners
1–5	171	39	109	66	385
6–10	74	22	43	8	147
11–25	71	16	29	1	117
26–50	19	5	0	1	25
Over 50	6	1	0	0	7
Total owners	341	83	181	76	681

It is clear that small-scale slaveholding predominated. In 1750, 57 per cent of owners had only one to five slaves, 22 per cent had six to ten. Analysis of slave-holding patterns for other years reveal similar percentages.

The census records thus show that the number of slaves at the Cape increased steadily during the VOC period when growth was dependent on imports, but levelled out after the slave trade was ended in 1808. Most colonists, especially those who were farmers, owned slaves but many of them had only a small number and the majority of the slaves were concentrated in Cape Town and the surrounding arable regions of the western districts. These features of Cape slaveholding reflected the role which slavery played in the economy of the colony and had a significant impact on the forces shaping the nature of Cape slave society.

Slavery and the economy

The numbers and distribution of slaves were derived from the demand for their labour in differing sectors of the economy. They were concentrated in the western districts because they were needed as domestic servants and artisans in Cape Town and as labourers on wheat and wine farms nearby. In the predominently pastoral regions further east they were less in demand, although some were employed as shepherds and herders. The degree to which they were used was dependent both on their suitability for differing economic activities and on the cost of purchasing and maintaining them.

The economy of the Cape differed from that of the slave plantation societies of the Americas. Although there was an important growth of internal trade and some specialisation of production, the colony did not develop a monoculture system dependent upon an external market and based on large-scale production units (ch. 5, p. 255). Farms varied considerably in size, and by the middle of the eighteenth century stratification had developed amongst the arable producers (ch. 2, p. 84).[120] However the largest farmers producing wine or grain rarely owned more than fifty slaves, and holdings of over a hundred were very exceptional. The largest slave holdings were found among the grain farmers of the Tijgerberg and the Hottentots-Holland areas near Cape Town and, from the early decades of the eighteenth century, among the wine farmers of Stellenbosch and the Franschhoek valley. In the 1690s a small group of even larger slaveowners emerged, with over fifty slaves each; they were mostly colonists who had obtained monopoly *pacht* contracts to provide meat and wine to the Company. The scale of the larger farms increased steadily throughout the VOC period as did the number of slaves they employed. By the British period, some of the wine and grain farmers had amassed large estates in these areas and were the wealthiest members and principal slaveowners of the colony. By contrast the smaller arable and mixed farms with less wealthy owners kept only a few slaves and were dependent in part on the labour of their own families, and on Khoikhoi hired workers.

It is clear that slaves provided the backbone of the arable labour force. During the first few decades of colonial settlement, arable farming was uncertain and slave numbers few. However during the early eighteenth century there developed a close correlation between the number of adult male slaves owned and the output of arable farms. This was especially marked in the Cape District, but also in Stellenbosch, where the development of wine cultivation led to intensive use of slave labour. By the 1740s, the correlation in Drakenstein was also high. Although there were fluctuations, depending on the success of the annual crop as well as the accuracy of census recording, it is apparent that farmers producing both wine and grain had the closest correlations, and hence were the most efficient in exploiting their slaves largely because they made more intensive use of them throughout the year.[121]

After the 1740s the correlation between slave numbers and crop output dropped. This was partly because the uncertainties of the slave trade meant that supplies could not always perfectly match demand but also because of the increasing use of forms of labour not recorded in the census, notably the Khoikhoi and the *Bastaard Hottentots* (children of Khoikhoi mothers and slave fathers). However, the farmers of the western districts continued to be dependent upon slavery as their main labour source. In a survey of Stellenbosch and Drakenstein farmers taken in 1806, 39.8 per cent employed only slaves, 54.2 per cent had both slave and Khoikhoi workers and only 6.0 per cent were entirely dependent on Khoikhoi labour.[122] In 1798 a petition of farmers to the Burgher Senate stressed that 'slaves cannot be dispensed with in this settlement'.[123]

The most dramatic growth of production during the period of slavery came after the Second British Occupation with the opening up of the British market to Cape wines. Expansion of vineyards was encouraged by a proclamation of 1811, and British tariffs on Cape wines were lowered in 1813. This created a boom in wine farming until the reduction of British protective tariffs against continental wines in 1825. As a result, slaves from Cape Town and elsewhere in the colony were sold to the wine farmers at high prices. Slave women and children were used more intensively alongside the men in field labour. The number of such slaves on the wine farms increased but there was also a considerable increase in the work load of each slave.[124] Slave labour remained the mainstay of the colony's arable farming sector.

Amongst pastoralist farmers, by contrast, slavery was much less important. Fewer pastoralists were slave owners; between 1688 and 1783, the percentage of slaveowning pastoral farmers in Stellenbosch and Drakenstein was only 46.25 per cent, a figure which compares with 66.7 per cent for all farmers and 90.3 per cent for arable and mixed producers.[125] Some of those pastoralists who did own slaves kept only a handful for domestic work, as well as herders, shepherds and drivers, and slave women also were involved in the production of tallow and butter for the market.[126] As Table 3.9 (p. 136) indicates, the large majority of Swellendam farmers in 1750, all of them pastoralists, had fewer than five slaves. Control over slaves in the more isolated frontier regions was difficult and the availability of skilled Khoikhoi and 'Bushmen' herders reduced the need for them. There was thus little correlation between herd sizes and numbers of slaves owned.

The urban sector of the Cape economy was more dependent on slave labour. During the VOC period an increasingly high proportion of slaves was located in Cape Town: almost one quarter by the 1760s and 31.4 per cent in 1806, figures which reflect the growing significance of the town in the economy of the colony.[127] Although this proportion fell during the British period when slaves were in higher demand on the farms, 15.4 per cent were still living in Cape Town at the time of emancipation in 1834.[128] The main function of privately-owned slaves in Cape Town was domestic labour: cooking, cleaning, and hauling water and firewood for the household. However a number were also hired out by their owners and worked alongside the Company slaves as unskilled labourers, primarily as porters at the harbour. Others acquired skills and were used as drivers, bricklayers, carpenters and tailors. In addition slaves sold and bartered goods on their masters' behalf in the town. One visitor describing his arrival in Table Bay in 1772 commented that, 'we were hardly come to anchor before a crowd of black slaves and Chinese came in their small boats to sell and barter clothes and other goods, fresh meat, vegetables and fruit, all of which our crew were eager to procure'.[129] The mention of slaves in boats also indicates that some of them may have been fishermen, an occupation that was widespread amongst the Free Blacks of the town.

A further factor explaining the distribution of slaves in the economy was the level of profit that could be obtained from their labour. Although slaves were paid no wages, an initial outlay of capital was required to purchase them. Thus only established farmers or town dwellers could afford to have more than one or two slaves. The first arable farmers received slaves from the Company on credit, and in 1677 slaves were sold to ten able but needy farmers at a special concessionary price. Towards the end of the VOC period at a time when demand was high and prices were rising sharply, a number of colonists obtained slaves on credit. Normally, however, they could buy them at auctions of newly-landed slaves in Cape Town or inland where the property of deceased farmers was sold for division among heirs. Since the slave population was not self-reproducing, the colonists were dependent on such sales to supplement or replace their slave labourers, and slaves formed a major item in their capital investment. Guelke has estimated that in the period 1731–80, slaves formed between 13 and 17 per cent of the total value of arable farms in the colony.[130]

There was considerable variation in the price of slaves. Male slaves were preferred to female for the heavy duty labour on the farms and as porters in Cape Town. Children fetched lower prices since they could not be immediately used at full advantage, but amongst adult slaves, younger ones cost more than older ones. Often slaves born in the colony fetched higher prices than new arrivals, who were deemed likely to be troublesome before they had been 'seasoned'. Slaves with special skills were particularly valuable.

As well as these variables, some broad changes took place over time. Table 3.10 indicates the average prices of adult male slaves at differing years of the VOC period.

Table 3.10   Average sale prices of adult male slaves (in rixdollars), 1658–1795[131]

1662–74	100
1692–1715	103
1730–37	134
1748–56	192
1765–72	163
1773–79	195
1785–90	305
1791–95	345

This table reveals the general upward trend of prices noted by many contemporary observers. Prices rose steadily during the period of economic expansion prior to the mid-eighteenth century, reaching a peak in the 1740s, a decade of slave shortages. Although prices declined somewhat during the 1760s, they had recovered by the 1770s. In the last few decades of the eighteenth century, they rose much more steeply, partly because of the general price inflation of the 1780s and 1790s, but also because of an acute shortage of slave labour.

After the Second British Occupation, slave prices increased still further. A report to the Advisory Council of 1826 stated that the average slave price was £150, an increase of 50 per cent from the average of £60 before the abolition of the slave trade in 1808.[132] Clearly the ending of the trade was a major cause of the shortage and high cost of slaves, but so was the demand for labour created by the wine-farming boom. Prices however dropped after the ending of the boom in the mid-1820s.[133] There was a further drop in the late 1820s and early 1830s caused by the knowledge that general emancipation was approaching. Nevertheless, the rates fixed by the Compensation Commissioners in 1836 of £54.11.0 for field labourers and £35.17.1 for 'inferior' field labourers were still far less than their market value in 1830.[134]

Cost largely determined the use that colonists made of slaves. During the late eighteenth century the annual rate of return on each slave was highest on farms where there were many slaves, such as the grain farms of Cape District or the wine farms of Stellenbosch. On the Constantia wine estate of Johannes Colijn in 1789, for example, the 52 slaves each produced an annual rate of return of 10.8 per cent of the capital costs required for his or her purchase and maintenance; a figure which compares favourably with those calculated for the American South and Jamaican slave plantations.[135]

On average-sized farms, by contrast, the profitability of slave labour was lower, although still adequate. Slave ownership was a more risky proposition for owners of the smallest farms, largely because it tied up a great deal of available capital, which could be lost if a slave fell sick, escaped or died. Prosperous farmers, however, could cover the costs of slave ownership more readily and were able to exploit slave labour most profitably. Slavery thus provided the basis of the economic expansion and stratification of the arable farming regions.

Recent research has shown that this situation changed dramatically in the nineteenth century. By the 1820s, wine farmers were not obtaining a satisfactory rate of return on the capital they invested in slaves. A combination of inflated costs of slaves and of goods needed for production together with lower wine prices led to falling profits. During the wine boom of the 1810s and early 1820s, many farmers had mortagaged land and their slaves to expand their production. When it ended, some became insolvent. Slavery in the wine regions had become an economic liability by the late 1820s.[136]

Profits could be made by masters who hired out their slaves or who used them to sell produce in Cape Town. Thunberg observed in 1773 that every slave selling wood in the town was 'obliged to earn for his master two skellings daily, which makes about 80 rixdollars in a year; so that in a few years the master gets his purchase-money back again'.[137] The Company also hired privately-owned urban slaves for special projects, such as quarrying and work on the fortifications in the late 1780s, when it spent 67,145 guilders (22,382 rixdollars) on slave hire in 1787–88 alone.[138] An estimate was made in 1826 that slave artisans in Cape Town could bring in a return of 18 per cent per annum, a figure which was higher than that obtained by rural colonists from their slaves.[139]

Some farmers hired their slaves to the local landdrosts on almost a permanent basis, while others did so only occasionally. The rate was 4 rixdollars a month, plus food and tobacco; this was increased to 6 rixdollars in 1783 at a time when slave purchase prices were rising. Considerable profit could be made by the owner; for example Jan Nel, a wine farmer in Stellenbosch district, obtained a total of 255 rixdollars for hiring two of his slaves to the landdrost over the period between March 1730 and November 1737, an amount which would have covered the cost of replacing them at current auction prices.[140] Farmers also hired their slaves to other colonists; this was especially true of wine farmers who could hire them to grain producers during the harvesting period before they were needed to pick the grapes on their owners' estates.

A further source of profit to some colonists was speculation in slave purchases. The Company and its officials were the beneficiaries of profits made from the slave trade and from sales in Table Bay from foreign slavers. However, some colonists, especially in Cape Town, could make a profit from the re-sale of a slave up-country. This took place from the earliest years of the colony and especially at times of rural slave shortages, most strikingly during the 1810s and early 1820s.[141]

Some contemporaries perceived economic disadvantages in the colony's use of slave labour. D.M. Pasques de Chavonnes, the only member of the Council of Policy who opposed the principle of using slave labour when the issue was debated in 1717, prophesied that slavery would inhibit economic development since 'the money spent on slavery is dead money'.[142] During the period between 1770 and 1800 slave prices increased three- to four-fold while agrarian prices only rose gradually, and the Company administration became very concerned at the large amounts of capital which the colonists had tied up in slaves.[143]

It is apparent that slavery provided a major source of profit to many colonists at the Cape up until the 1820s. As we have seen, it was particularly well suited to the larger arable grain and wine farms, but slaves were also used in other sectors of the economy. Most colonists thought that there was no alternative system of labour which would be as feasible or as profitable. Estimates made in 1717 of the cost of European immigration showed that wage labour would be considerably more expensive. Moreover, as Van Ryneveld pointed out at the end of the eighteenth century, once a system of slave labour was established wages for free labour were drawn down and it was difficult to obtain immigrants willing to perform the labour required.[144]

The Khoikhoi and 'Bushmen' were used extensively by pastoral farmers and increasingly as workers on the arable farms, especially as seasonal hired labour, but could not be so readily coerced to labour as slaves. Initially the Company discouraged the use of Khoikhoi labour by colonists because it wanted to preserve indigenous cattle supplies, and after the 1713 smallpox epidemic and the destruction of indigenous social structure by colonial expansion, the numbers of Khoikhoi in the western arable districts were severely reduced (ch. 1, pp. 18–21).

There was therefore little challenge to the dominant position of slavery in the colonial economy. As J.W. Janssens, the governor of the colony during the Batavian period pointed out in 1804, although the abolition of slavery might have been morally desirable,

> it would destroy all property and plunge the colony into misery (perhaps for good) . . . the whole industry of this country is based on the existence of slaves

> . . . Those who possess many slaves can easily be recognised by the condition of their farms; everything looks better and more prosperous than with those who have to work with scanty means.[145]

Although some opposition to this sentiment developed in the course of the 1820s and early 1830s, it is clear that slavery did contribute to building much of the wealth of the colony in its early stages of development. However, as in all colonial slave societies, these advantages were gained at the cost of the exploitation of human labour and the creation of a coercive and divided social system.

The slave experience

It is difficult to reconstruct the experience of slaves at the Cape. There are very few extensive plantation records or diaries, and slaves left almost no writings or records of their own. The main sources of information must therefore be the occasional records left by slaveowners and the accounts of travellers. Inevitably owners and visitors rarely penetrated far into the lives of slaves. Only occasionally did they record relevant snippets of conversation or events, and then usually with little empathy for the slaves' point of view. The extensively preserved court records provide an alternative source, and the social conditions and experiences of slaves are sometimes revealed in testimonies and evidence.

Slave life was dominated by work. 'I am always working; I need to rest sometimes', grumbled one farm slave in 1759.[146] Although there was seasonal variation in rural labour, hours were generally long, especially during peak periods. A proclamation of 1823 specified that slaves employed in field labour were not to work more than ten hours a day in winter and twelve in summer, 'except during the ploughing or harvest seasons or on extraordinary occasions when a remuneration shall be made to them in money or by additional proportion of food', which suggests that prior to this at least some owners had been demanding even more lengthy hours of labour.[147] Hours could also be long for domestic slaves both in rural areas and in Cape Town, although they were less subject to the intense demands of seasonal work than field hands.

Farm slaves performed a number of tasks throughout the year. Most rural work was unskilled, although some tasks, such as vine-dressing did require special expertise. Farm work was highly seasonal, but farms producing both grain and wine provided work steadily throughout the year. On grain farms the major tasks were sowing and ploughing between May and July and harvesting between December and February.

In the vineyards, cutting and pruning took place in July and August, weeding in October and November and grape-picking in late February and March. Often farmers hired extra slaves or Khoikhoi labourers during the peak periods, and although most farm labourers were men, slave women and children were used for harvesting grain and grapes, as well as for weeding and sometimes for sowing. In addition rural slaves performed a number of non-seasonal tasks such as herding, collecting fuel, driving wagons and doing work in the farmhouse.

There was no mechanisation on the farms, and some tasks were back-breaking, such as the harvesting of grain with sickles, the picking of low-hanging grapes or winnowing with sieves. In the Cape Town hinterland harvesting had to be performed swiftly, between the ripening of grain and its flattening by the onset of strong southeasterly winds. Women also reaped and slave children were occupied in 'following the reapers and gathering the wheat into piles, ready for tying into sheaves.'[148] Work began at dawn and continued until midday when the heat caused the grain to fall out of the husks as it was reaped. It was resumed in mid-afternoon and lasted until dusk at about 8 p.m. After dark the labourers took sheaves to the threshing floors and laid them out ready for trampling by horses and winnowing the next day.

On wine farms the picking and pressing of grapes was also an intensive task. Thunberg, a Swedish botanist who visited several vineyards in the 1770s, noted that slaves

> gather the grapes and put them in a large vessel . . . the sides of which are bored full of holes. [When the grapes are] heaped up to the brim, three or four slaves, after having previously washed their feet very clean in a tub of water standing at the side, get into the vessel that contains the fruit, and holding themselves fast by a rope fixed to the ceiling, trample upon the grapes and squeeze out the fruit as long as they are able.[149]

The slaves then poured the juice into vats ready for fermenting, a process which could continue until late in the evening.

At other times of the year, slaves performed a variety of tasks. Field labour included the seasonal occupations of sowing and ploughing, pruning vine stocks and weeding, as well as herding livestock. Domestic farm slaves also tended vegetable gardens and made butter. Such tasks were normally performed by women, although occasionally males milked the cows and worked in the farmstead house. Other regular chores included the collection of wood, 'an arduous and daily task' as forests became denuded in the arable farming regions.[150] Slave women were also used to wet-nurse their masters' children, and slave children scared birds and animals from the crops, weeded and did other field tasks during the peak seasons. Older farm slaves often worked as shepherds or as ox-drivers in the ploughing season.

This work was largely unskilled; only on the largest farmsteads were slave craftsmen in permanent residence. Rather farmers hired slave carpenters, smiths and builders as required, either from Cape Town or from the villages of the rural districts such as Stellenbosch, Tulbagh, Swellendam and Graaff-Reinet. Slaves were commonly sent to work on other farms, either as hired labour during the harvesting season, or to work for other members of their owners' families. On occasion, privately-owned slaves were ordered by the government to assist in public works such as banking up rivers, building drifts (fordable points in a river), maintaining roads, and clearing mountain passes.

Despite this variety of occupation, most farms were not large enough to produce occupational hierarchies amongst slaves. On a few of the largest farms there were privileged slave overseers or *mandoors*.[151] Some of them were also used as supervisors of hired Khoikhoi labourers when the farmer had pasturage separate from the main farm.[152] More frequent references to mandoors occur during the late VOC and British periods when there were larger farms and more Cape-born slaves able to obtain a position of relative privilege. There were, however, still only a small number altogether in the colony.

On most farms the slaves were supervised either by the farmer and members of his family or, less commonly, by hired white employees known as knechts. During the VOC period, the knechts did not have burgher status and were hired from the Company on annual renewable contracts. They were hired primarily on the larger estates near to Cape Town or on farms where the master was frequently absent and needed a supervisor. As such they were often hated and feared by the slaves and were not infrequently the victims of assault by them.[153]

Living conditions varied greatly. On the larger farms special slave living quarters were provided. On the extensive farm of Martin Melck each of his two hundred slaves 'had a separate brick building to sleep in' but this was very exceptional and most 'slave houses', as they were described in farm inventories, were rudimentary rooms in which all of the slaves lived together and slept on wooden bunks.[154] On smaller farms there were no special living quarters for the slaves; they slept in kitchens, attics, and barns or out of doors in the summer. Slave shepherds and herders often slept with their flocks in sheep and cattle-pens.[155]

Rural slaves were fed with the produce of the farm itself. A visitor in 1751 commented that on most farms, 'masters and slaves eat the same bread . . . although there are a few of the farmers who make good bread for their own table.'[156] This fare was supplemented with vegetables, which on some farms the slaves grew on plots of their own, and also rations of meat and sometimes fish and rice. On larger estates, some owners slaughtered sheep, and even oxen, for their labourers. Some slaves were poorly fed; one visitor commented that 'black bread, half sand, and the offal of sheep and oxen are their general fare'.[157] Tobacco rations were often supplied and on wine farms the tot system, by which slaves were given regular portions of wine throughout the day, was well established by at least the eighteenth century.[158] There was no legislative control over the feeding of slaves until 1823, and slaves sometimes complained that they were inadequately fed and had to steal food.[159]

Circumstances in Cape Town were very different. There were variations between slaves who worked entirely as domestic servants and those who were hired out, as well as a variety of occupational specialisations and skills. The organisation of labour was much less rigidly controlled than on the farms. The majority of urban slaves were not concentrated in large numbers and there are no records of knechts or mandoors supervising them. Domestic slaves were much more directly under the supervision of the master and his family and slept on their owners' premises. There was a greater measure of mobility among them than was the case with rural slaves, especially for those who were employed selling provisions, although the profits of their trading had to be returned to the masters and were closely checked by them. Some Cape Town slaves were better provided with clothing than their rural counterparts, who normally had only a shirt and coarse cloth or leather trousers or sheepskins. By the nineteenth century, some urban domestic slaves were dressed in rich livery.[160] However this was not an invariable rule, since one Russian visitor to the town noted in 1808 that, 'the slaves in this colony are kept very poorly – they are dressed in rags, even those who serve at the table of their masters'.[161]

Historians of other societies have shown that despite the coercive and exploitative nature of slavery, slaves created their own traditions and cultural identity which provided them with some solidarity and protection from the full onslaught of the slave experience.[162] Work on these aspects of Cape slavery is little developed, although some tentative suggestions can be made.

At the Cape there were impediments to the full development of a distinctive and unifying slave culture. One was the extreme diversity of origins, ranging from Mozambique and Madagascar to the Indian coast and the East Indies (see pp. 120–21). Slaves brought with them a wide variety of languages, belief systems and cultural traditions.

Colonists and visitors to the Cape developed stereotypes of individual ethnic groups, particularly regarding their capacity for different kinds of labour. Malagasy slaves, at first only a handful, had a poor reputation initially, but by the 1670s it was appreciated that they were skilled and industrious agriculturalists. Thereafter references to them were usually very favourable and they were frequently assigned by the Company to its outposts and to the Company's garden.[163] The slaves from Delagoa Bay, by contrast, were held in low esteem.[164] 'Negro' slaves from Angola, and during the eighteenth century from Mozambique, were thought to be more suited to heavy labour and field work whilst East Indians were used more for domestic or semi-skilled work.[165]

Variations in the ethnic composition of the slave labour force resulted from variations in the main sources of supply at any one period. During much of the eighteenth century, 'Negro' slaves on the farms were outnumbered by those of East Asian and Indian origin. From the 1780s newly-imported slaves were mainly from Mozambique and Madagascar and these predominated as field labourers in the nineteenth century. After the ending of the slave trade a higher proportion of slaves was born in the colony. These tended to be more highly valued than imported slaves and were more frequently used as domestic workers, artisans and skilled labourers.[166] Most farmers had both imported and Cape-born slaves. This diversity of origin amongst slaves living together could be a source of tension, and in the criminal records there are several cases of assault resulting from ethnic insults. Moreover, among newly arrived slaves the lack of a common slave language sometimes led to misunderstandings and division of interests.[167]

The geographical dispersal of the rural slave population of the colony also inhibited the development of a thriving slave culture. Many slaves lived in small groups on the farms where contact was more frequent with colonists, knechts and Khoikhoi labourers than with other slaves. One outcome of this was the infrequency of stable unions between slaves and the absence of a strong family of the kind identified by historians of North American slave plantations.[168] The sexual imbalance of the slave population, especially in the rural districts, meant that very few male slaves were able to find slave partners, and there could be much jealousy and competition amongst them over the women that were available; at least one farmer would not keep any female slaves because it would 'cause jealousy'.[169] Those slave families that were formed were given little protection. It was not until 1823 that slave marriage was recognised by law, marriage being considered 'incompatible with slavery', and the frequency of auctions of estates at the death of an owner could split any informal unions that were made.[170] Only in 1782 was a ban imposed on selling young slave children separately from their mothers. As late as 1830 the Protector of Slaves, an official of the British colonial administration, reported that slave children who remained with their mothers 'to a later period than ten years are in no respect benefited by it but far otherwise.'[171]

It was thus difficult for slaves at the Cape to build up a strongly cohesive 'world of their own' in a society where they were divided by origin, atomised into a large number of small-scale holdings and unable to develop a pattern of family life or continuity over the generations. They tended rather to be overwhelmed by the cultural patterns of other inhabitants of the colony with whom they came into contact, primarily the colonists and also the Khoikhoi (ch. 4, pp. 225–30).

However in some circumstances these inhibitions were lessened. Cape Town and its immediate hinterland provided an area in which a large concentration of slaves had the opportunity to make contact and to forge some patterns of existence which were not immediately subject to the direct control of the masters. During the eighteenth and nineteenth centuries there developed an urban sub-culture which included the Free Blacks, political exiles from the East, Chinese traders and visiting soldiers and sailors as well as Company and privately-owned slaves. Largely centred on the many taverns of the town, it revolved around not only drinking, but also gambling and dagga smoking and the exchange of stolen, or illicitly traded, goods. Urban slaves were joined by rural slaves who went into the town on Sundays and holidays and stayed in the houses of the 'Chinese' or with other urban slaves.[172] There were also some drinking houses in Stellenbosch village and in the False Bay and Hottentots-Holland area. There were legislative attempts to control slaves gambling or buying liquor and in 1766 for example, slaves were forbidden to leave farms on Sundays since they were 'meeting up together in remote places and there perpetuating many rowdy actions' but this prohibition was largely ineffectual.[173] The growth of this urban sub-culture was characteristic of a marginalised group alienated from the culture of the dominating classes and was strongly resistant to the attempts of the 'respectable' in the colony to suppress it. It provided the basis of working-class culture in nineteenth-century Cape Town.[174]

Another feature of a developing slave culture and identity in Cape Town was the growth of Islam (see ch. 4, pp. 191–94). This was introduced to the Cape by Muslim political exiles and slaves from the East Indies and increasingly gained adherents from other slaves, especially in Cape Town, in the eighteenth and early nineteenth centuries.[175] Slaves had been largely excluded from the beliefs and religious practices of their owners and only from the end of the eighteenth century was any concerted attempt made to convert them to Christianity. In 1831 one missionary commented that 'vast numbers of slaves profess no religion whatsoever: the vast majority of those who do are followers of the doctrine of Mohammed; few, very few, make any profession of Christianity'.[176]

There are signs that the growth of Islam amongst the slaves was more than a passive acceptance of the only religious system available to them. Its teachings were attractive because, as a government report of 1831 stated, 'As it is contrary to the precepts of the Koran that a slave shall be a Mahomedan [sic], the priests endeavour to make the slaves believe that although their bodies are held in slavery, yet that their souls are free, and that they must trust God to make them free when they die'.[177] Moreover, many of the Free Blacks of the colony were also Muslims and Islam provided a linkage with them in a social and ideological system which was distinct from that of the slaveowners. Certainly the authorities perceived Islam as a threat not only to Christian proselytising but also to control over the slave, Prize Negro and Black population. Muslims in Cape Town were subjected to greater interferences from the police because of their association with the slave sub-culture. As one commentator wrote of the colony in 1822:

> . . . the prevalence of Muhammadanism [sic] among the slaves of Christian masters, must be deemed a political evil. The difference of colour furnishes already but too broad a line of distinction. Add the difference of religion, and the line of demarcation becomes yet wider and deeper. A hostile feeling, nursed by religious animosity, may excite the slave against the master; and the colonist of South Africa may ere long, find himself . . . surrounded by domestic foes.[178]

Islam and the sub-culture of Cape Town thus provided sources of a distinctive slave culture, and both were feared by the authorities. Their impact outside the town was limited, however, and in general Cape slaves had little protection from the full effect of the society which their masters had created.

Control and response

The means by which the colonists kept their slaves in subordination was critical for the nature and development of Cape slave society. All slave societies were by definition coercive in structure, as one writer on the Cape in 1803 recognised. 'It is self-evident that the comfort and happiness of the slave must necessarily depend upon the temper, habits and character of the master. We need not cite examples to demonstrate that cruelty is the necessary and inseparable concomitant of slavery, even in its mildest form'.[179]

Cape slavery has sometimes been described both by contemporaries and later historians as 'mild' in nature.[180] These assessments are, however, often based on erroneous assumptions. One was that domestic slaves in Cape Town were typical of the whole colony. Clearly this was not the case, and as several writers of the time noted, 'the treatment of the different classes of slaves at the Cape is by no means the same . . . the people of Cape Town universally treat them well in comparison to the farmers and planters of the country parts'.[181] Another assumption was that slave manumission and intermarriage with freemen were relatively frequent: in fact recent research has shown that the opposite was the case (ch. 4, pp. 204–14). Writers have also stressed the paternalistic relationship between master and slaves which could develop in a society like the Cape where slaves were held in small groups unlike the plantations of other slave societies. Also often cited is the protection that the VOC and British administration offered to slaves against abuse by their owners. These arguments require closer examination.

Clearly there could be variations in the master-slave relationship. Uprooted from their own communities and background, slaves were at least partially assimilated into the world of their masters. Domestic slaves had an ambivalent relationship with the family of their owners with whom they lived in close contact. There is evidence in the court records of some slaves taking a keen interest in the affairs of the family or protecting them from attack by outsiders. Favoured slaves, especially women, were sometimes given bequests in wills and in exceptional cases manumitted (ch. 4, p. 209). As in all slave societies, the relationship between master and slave was more subtle than one of constant and overt coercion, although the essence of such paternalism was an underlying subordination of the slave to his or her owner.

This subordination was made evident by the fact that slaves were items of property over which masters had absolute possession and authority. Masters' rights were established by law; slaves, like material possessions, could be bought and sold, were described and evaluated alongside cattle and sheep in inventories and bequeathed in wills. This could lead to extreme callousness. For example, Johannes Kuuhn, asked by his nephew if he could hit one of Kuuhn's slaves with a spade, said, 'Go right ahead, since I bought him with my money. If he dies from the blow all I need to do is buy another one.'[182]

This was clearly an exceptional circumstance, but it demonstrates that small scale slaveholdings did not necessarily lead to a close paternalistic relationship of master and slave. Indeed there were several features of Cape slave soceity that tended to inhibit such a development. It has been noted in a comparative study of several American slave societies that, 'so long as the slave trade remained open, slaves were greatly abused in all systems.'[183] The openness of the Cape slave system during the seventeenth and eighteenth centuries, when slaves were being imported into the colony and sold internally at auctions may have discouraged careful treatment by owners. After the closing of the slave trade in 1808, the potential for better slave treatment was counter-acted by the boom in wine production and by the heavier labour demands which this created. As in the Americas, rapid economic expansion tended to worsen the living and working conditions of slaves.[184]

A further feature of Cape slave society was the isolation of many rural slaveowners and their fears of their numerically preponderent slaves. Sparrman, visiting a farm in the Paarl region in the early 1770s and seeing the domestic slaves who served him 'in such good humour and so kindly and familiarly treated', observed to the knecht who was left in control of them that, 'his mildness and kindness was the best pledge for their good behaviour, and the surest preservative against their attacks.' However, the knecht responded that the isolation of the farm, the fear of attack by marauding runaways and 'instances of the blacks becoming furious at night, and committing murder, more particularly on the person of their masters; but sometimes, if they cannot get at them, on some of their comrades, or else upon themselves,' required the exertion of a strict discipline; 'I am here in the place of a master to them, and am obliged to punish them whenever they behave ill to me or to each other'.[185] The knecht's attitude may have differed from that of his employer, but the incident indicates that behind a facade of apparent benevolence could lie a darker picture. His reasoning was significant. Although the farm lay well within the settled regions of the colony, inhabitants lived in fear of attack from their own and runaway slaves. On another occasion, Sparrman, visiting a farm whose owner was away, slept in the open rather than in a farmhouse because, 'everybody in this country is obliged to bolt the door of his chamber at night, and keep loaded firearms by him, for fear of the revengeful disposition of the slaves.'[186] One court prosecutor noted in a case in which a slave was accused of attacking his owner, that, 'in this country, everyone is daily placed in great danger by the presence of the slaves.'[187]

Fear of the slaves rose to hysteria when plots were unearthed or suspected. But it also was an underlying factor of the whole slave system. On the larger farms, slaves were locked up in their quarters at night; in Cape Town the Company slave lodge was locked at 8 p.m. and a roll call taken. Measures were taken against the movement of slaves at night, and in 1754 a curfew was imposed upon them in Cape Town.[188] Towards the end of the eighteenth century, a pass system was introduced: slaves who were found walking without a letter or pass from their owner could be apprehended and shot on sight.[189]

Such fears were at one extreme of the response produced in Cape slaveholding society. The daily contact of slaves and owners within the farm or the household involved a degree of co-operation which could not be entirely dominated by fear or mistrust. Nevertheless, proximity between master and slave made it necessary for owners to emphasise their authority constantly. In 1794 for example, the son of one colonist met one of his father's slaves in the farmyard and asked him why he did not say 'Good evening'. The slave replied, 'If I do my work during the day and come home in the evening that is enough.' It was not enough; deference was also required. The slave was beaten for his 'insolence', an offence which included any objection to the orders of the master or his family or any action which appeared to threaten their absolute authority.[190]

Underlying this authority was the threat, either actual or concealed, of physical punishment. When authority and deference broke down, the owner's only resort was to punish the slave by deprivation of food or clothing or, more frequently, by corporal punishment. Whipping was a favoured punishment, often with the rhinoceros hide *sjambok*. It inflicted considerable pain, provided a striking demonstration of the master's authority and yet did not significantly reduce the slave's output in labour. During a whipping other slaves were often ordered to watch or to hold the victim down. The fear of punishment was well engrained amongst the slaves. When in 1752, a slave shepherd was encouraged by runaways to join them, he replied that he had done that once before and been punished for it, and he did not want to repeat the experience.[191] Another slave in 1760 who had been caught stealing hanged himself from a beam in the barn, 'for fear that he would be punished.'[192]

In a society where power was so unevenly divided, such punishment could be limitless. Summing up the case against Johannes Kuuhn in 1770, the Prosecutor of the Council of Justice stated:

It is indisputable, and pitiful findings indicate all too well, that in the lands where slavery exists there will be plenty of people who call themselves Christians, who are in fact no Christians but rather inhumane creatures. It is a great misfortune for those who come under their authority, since these men hardly think that the slaves . . . being paid for with money, are also human beings.[193]

Excessively brutal punishments were likely to occur when knecht overseers were in control of the slaves. Although invested with the authority of the slaveowner, their position was less secure; slaves sometimes refused to obey their orders when the master was away.[194] Moreover, the knechts had no concern for the value or productivity of slaves, whom they did not own, and since most knechts were hired on short-term contracts they had little vested interest in the welfare of the farm. Although there were examples of knechts who tried to restrain an owner intent on maltreating his slaves, in general punishments administered by knechts tended to be the most severe. A Swellendam farmer in 1770 praised the knecht who had been working for him because he 'kept a good control over the slaves', although he admitted that he was inclined to be 'rather strict' with them, a concession made after it was found that the knecht had clubbed to death a slave who had allowed a cow to get loose.[195]

Many slaveowners did not employ knechts, especially in the outlying areas. However, several of the worst cases of maltreatment came from newly and sparsely settled areas of the colony, remote from government authority. During the VOC period, the Bokkeveld and Roggeveld regions were especially notorious and the threat of selling a slave 'up-country' or 'over the mountains' was used by owners in Cape Town and the more settled arable regions.[196] The need for owners to maintain authority in isolated areas led, in the words of the Protector of Slaves in 1827, to many farmers 'taking the law into their own hands.'[197]

Control over the slaves was not entirely confined to the authority and punishments administered by the owners. In Cape Town, and occasionally in the hinterland, owners handed over slaves to the authorities for punishment by the kaffirs, assistants to the fiscaal, who themselves were usually Company slaves.[198] In extreme cases when masters had lost control over their slaves, they sometimes ceded them to the authorities. In 1780, for example the Council of Policy agreed to take over ownership of Geduld van Bougies, whose owner, a widow, claimed that he 'has some evil set in his mind', and that she greatly feared he would murder her; Geduld was placed on Robben Island.[199]

The master's appeal to the authorities was only one aspect of the interaction between domestic slave control and the colony's administrative and legal system. There were also legal controls over masters. Batavian law, which also applied to the Cape, forbade owners to keep slaves in leg-irons or to torture them; it also gave slaves the right to report abuses to the authorities, although it added that slaves who could not give 'major and wholly convincing' proof were to be punished and returned to their owners.[200] This law was reinforced by several decrees at the Cape throughout the eighteenth century. In addition a permit was required from the authorities to bury a slave, and two witnesses were required to testify that death had not been caused by maltreatment. In rural districts during the eighteenth century, one of the local heemraden and a surgeon usually visited the farm to inspect the body.

Some slaveowners were convicted of maltreating their slaves, usually in cases where the slave died and the evidence against them was overwhelming. In 1729, for example, the Landdrost of Stellenbosch successfully prosecuted two farmers who had ordered their slaves to be flogged so severely that they died; the one was fined 100 rixdollars and the other 50 rixdollars.[201] Fines were the normal punishment, although in some cases additional stipulations were made that the slaves who had testified against the colonist were to be sold or that the convicted person was not to be permitted to own slaves in future.[202]

In spite of these convictions, the effectiveness of such legislation was limited. Proof was often difficult to obtain, and it took considerable courage for slaves to give testimony against their own owners, especially since unproven accusations were punished severely.[203] Corroborating evidence was often difficult to obtain in a community which supported the interests of slaveowners rather than the slaves, and since the heemraden and landdrosts were themselves slaveowners they were hardly impartial. Moreover, the remoteness of some farms and the weakness of local authorities meant that the landdrosts and the Council of Justice had only limited ability to summon a colonist to trial. In 1798 the wife of one Swellendam burgher laughed in the face of a representative of the court sent to summon her husband who was accused of murdering his slave and said, 'I will no more listen to the landdrost than to my slave.'[204] In short, as Le Vaillant commented after his visit to the Cape in the early 1780s, 'these wise laws do honour to the Dutch government, but how many ways there are to elude them!'[205]

Towards the end of the eighteenth century the government attempted to increase its control over domestic slave punishment. Instructions given in 1793 by the visiting commissioners from the Netherlands to the landdrost and heemraden of the Stellenbosch and Drakenstein district included 'the oversight of all domestic punishment of slaves' and the institution of an enquiry if maltreatment was suspected.[206] Under the Batavian administration, each landdrost was ordered to 'count it for one of his highest duties to watch over the lot of these unfortunates'.[207] It was not until the 1820s, in response to anti-slavery sentiments in Britain, that new legislation was passed. A proclamation by Governor Somerset in 1823, repeated in an ordinance of 1826, restricted domestic punishment of slaves to a maximum of twenty-five strokes 'with rods and other instruments of domestic punishment', a number reduced to fifteen in 1831. The flogging of female slaves was forbidden in 1830. Moreover, punishments had to be witnessed by another colonist or three adult slaves. Alternative punishments, such as imprisonment, a reduction of diet or placing in stocks were recommended in orders-in-council of 1830 and 1832 for such offences as 'disobedience', 'insolence', and 'absence from work'. The emphasis on protecting females was at least in part an attempt to encourage their fertility.[208]

More severe punishments were given for slave maltreatment in the nineteenth century. In 1801, a farmer who had beaten his slave to death was himself flogged and exiled from the colony.[209] In 1822, an unprecedented death sentence was passed on a colonist, Johann Gebhart, who had one of his father's slaves beaten to death. About the same time courts began to accept slave testimony without the corroborating evidence of colonists. However, the introduction of the jury system in 1827 meant that few juries of colonists were prepared to condemn fellow slaveowners.[210] In 1830, an order-in-council specified that all slaveowners were to keep a 'Punishment Record Book' which was to be inspected by the Protector of Slaves, but this caused considerable hostility among the slaveowners and in 1831 led to a minor riot in Stellenbosch.[211] The slaves were still only partially protected by the law at the time of emancipation in 1834.

In addition to being controlled by their masters, slaves were also subject to a number of government laws and proclamations. Batavian laws as codified in the Statutes of India (*Statuten van Indië*) of 1642 and 1766 and their amendments, were implemented at the Cape and local ordinances or plakkaten were issued to remedy specific problems.[212] These were collected and promulgated in 1754 during the governorship of Rijk Tulbagh.[213] It is questionable how widely the various provisions of these codes were known and observed. Some of the Statutes were relevant only to the Indies and were a dead letter at the Cape. As for the Cape ordinances, they were frequently reissued, which suggests that observance of them tended to wane.

Most of these regulations were concerned with the control of slaves within the colony. Slaves on errands were required to carry a signed and dated letter from their masters. Slave shepherds and herders had to carry a lead medal with their master's name on it, and in 1805 all slaves were required to wear an identification tag. Slaves also had to carry lighted torches at night and to observe curfews in the villages and in Cape Town. They were forbidden from carrying firearms or possessing knives. The 1754 code controlled the meeting of slaves in groups, especially in the potentially dangerous circumstances of Cape Town streets or taverns, or in rural districts on holidays. The need for the law to maintain masters' control over slaves was emphasised by the first article of the code which stated that any slave who should 'calumniate, affront or treat his master without respect, or accuse him falsely with any disgraceful act should be scourged and put in irons or punished according to the circumstances of the case', and the second article that a slave who 'laid hands upon his master or mistress, with or without a weapon', should be punished by death.[214] A similar punishment was decreed for any slave who made sexual advances to his master's wife or daughter.[215]

In the Company period, torture could be used by the authorities to extract confessions both from slaves and freemen, although in practice it was more often applied to the slaves.[216] There was also a wide disparity between punishments given to slaves and freemen. Required by the new British governor in 1796 to justify this discrepancy, the Council of Justice stated that, 'Experience has taught that gentle means are inadequate, even amongst free persons, to maintain law and order . . . consequently altho' strongly actuated by motives of humanity, and viewing the slaves in the most favourable light, it becomes necessary to adopt severe measures to deter them from revolting against their masters and taking advantage of their superior strength.'[217] Escapees were punished by whipping, mutilation or branding. By a resolution of 1711, runaway Company slaves were to be whipped and branded on one cheek for the first offence, and on the other if the offence was repeated. At the third offence they were to be whipped and to have their nose and ears cut off. From 1715 such slaves were also chained in pairs while working.[218] By 1727 there were so many mutilated and disfigured slaves that the law was changed out of consideration for the feelings of colonists, particularly pregnant women who might encounter them; thereafter escaped slaves were to be branded on the back.[219]

The nature of punishment was directly linked to the degree to which the offence had threatened the social order. Attacks on the persons of colonists or their property by arson were the most severely punished. Visitors to the Cape in the Company period were horrified by the barbarity of some punishments in an age not noted for its leniency. Mentzel described the breaking of slaves alive on the wheel, whilst other sentences included the pulling out of flesh with red-hot tongs, mutilation, impaling, burning alive and slow strangulation.[220]

Such severity served to demonstrate the power of the authorities representing the slaveowners and to illustrate the folly of resistance. Bodies of executed slaves were left hanging on gibbets or exposed after mutilation in Cape Town or on farmsteads. During the nineteenth century, the most gruesome forms of punishment were abolished, although whippings, branding and the death penalty were still regularly administered by the courts. A visitor to the Cape Town jail in 1825 witnessed slaves receiving whippings and punishment on the treadmill.[221]

The response of slaves to this sytem of control was diverse. The most common form of resistance was escape. The first recorded slave escape at the Cape was in March 1655 when Anthony of Madagascar ran away and was never seen again.[222] In 1658, soon after the Angolan and Guinean slaves arrived, slave escapes began in earnest, and the freeburghers returned about half of their slaves to the Company, regarding them as more trouble than they were worth.[223]

Thereafter slave escapes were a regular feature of life at the Cape. At certain periods alarm at the number of *drosters* (runaway slaves) was increased, such as in the late 1670s when the rural sector of the colony was rapidly expanding, in 1714 at the time of the smallpox epidemic, in the 1740s and in the 1810s and early 1820s when there was an increasing demand for labour.[224] More apparent than broad chronological variations, however, was the pattern of escapes during the course of each year. Pasques de Chavonnes commented in 1717 that slaves generally ran away at harvest time 'and leave their masters in the lurch' and over a century later, in 1827, the Protector of Slaves noted that, 'in the harvest and sowing times when the services of the slaves are most required, frequent desertions take place'.[225]

Some escapes were clearly planned in advance, comprising large groups of ten or more slaves from differing farmsteads and even from Cape Town who aimed to escape from the colony. Such rejection of slave status was most often carried out by newly-arrived slaves. Malagasy slaves were particularly prone to escape as they are reported to have believed that they could reach Madagascar by travelling overland.[226] In 1751, a group of sixteen Eastern slaves who had been sentenced to imprisonment on Robben Island, plotted to murder the colonists on the way to Madagascar and then sail the ship back to their home in

Batavia.[227] Little is known about the leaders of large slave escapes. They came from different backgrounds but were most frequently from Asia, particularly Indonesia, and led parties whose ethnic composition was often extremely diverse. One notable escape in 1688 was led by a Free Black, Sante of Sant Jago (Cape Verdes) and another in 1712 by a Javanese exile.[228]

Most escapes however were mounted by individuals or groups of two or three. Often they were not pre-meditated but were resorted to in the aftermath of committing a crime or enduring punishment. Cape-born slaves were as likely as new arrivals to make such flights, and such drosters often remained near the farm or town rather than trying to escape from the colony altogether.

The pattern of escapes in the southwestern Cape was strongly influenced by topography. Table Mountain and the other mountains on the Cape Peninsula, the Hottentots-Holland range and the Drakenstein mountains all offered an immediate refuge, within a few hours' journey for most slaves, with good visibility of pursuers and free of dangerous animals. In most places, however, lengthy concealment was difficult.

The want of food curtailed many escapes as slaves were forced to steal supplies from farms and were thus detected and caught. Sometimes drosters obtained food from other slaves or Khoisan in the area. In 1738, for example, four slaves ran away from a Constantia farm after one of them had been beaten, and hid for almost a month in the surrounding hills, feeding on vegetables which they took with them and food brought to them by other slaves at the farm.[229] Mentzel recorded a 'troop' of escaped slaves on Table Mountain in the 1770s who had worked out a silent barter system, exchanging firewood for food with slave woodcutters from Cape Town.[230]

Firearms were also essential for drosters to resist capture. The census lists recorded that all burgher families owned at least one, and their presence was always a temptation for drosters. A decree of 1688 endeavoured to thwart such slaves by ordering all slaveowners' guns to be partially dismantled when not in use.[231] This regulation had little effect. Moreover, trusted slaves, particularly herders, were sometimes given the use of firearms.[232] This was risky for them, however; they might be mistaken for drosters and shot, as happened in 1690 when an armed slave was killed in error when pursuing some escaped slaves.[233]

The authorities organised a regular system of patrolling for drosters and developed an alarm system by which tolling bells and a blue signal flag at the Castle and on hilltops warned the public of an escape. Slaveowners were required to report runaways immediately to the local landdrost or heemraden. Horseback parties of soldiers and farmers pursued fugitives into the interior, receiving hospitality at farms on the way. However there were often delays and the government was also dependent on the colonists themselves to recapture slaves. It offered rewards, increasing the amount in the remoter regions of the colony where recapture was more difficult.[234] Khoikhoi were also enlisted as informers and trackers, and slaves who informed on runaways were rewarded, in some cases with manumission.[235] By a decree of 1714, slaves who had been at large for three or more days and who resisted capture could be shot on sight by colonists.[236] Freemen were absolved from all responsibility in such circumstances and killings were sometimes indiscriminate.[237] There were also severe penalties for assisting or hiding escaped slaves. A Cape Town free black woman who had harboured a slave deserter for two nights was sentenced in 1737 to be whipped and to work in chains for the Company for three years.[238]

Some slaves returned to their masters of their own accord, apparently preferring bondage to freedom with the prospect of starvation and unending harassment from Khoikhoi and search parties.[239] These were heavily punished, but less so than captured slaves. In some instances drosters found employment with frontier farmers who were willing to conceal their presence from the authorities – a serious crime.[240] Those slaves who refused to surrender were usually tracked down and their escapes often ended in gunfights and death.[241] Those captured alive were tried and convicted by the Council of Justice and suffered the kinds of punishment already described. Accounts of trials of escaped slaves form a major part of the judicial records of the entire period. Occasionally a captured droster would manage to commit suicide, thus infuriating his owner.[242]

The authorities were not always successful in recapturing runaway slaves. A particular problem in the remoter districts was that escaped slaves could pretend to be *Bastaard-Hottentots* (the name given to the offspring of Khoisan women and slave men, who were thus not themselves slaves). The landdrost of Swellendam complained in 1774 that many slave deserters, by making such claims, were able to 'procure a free passage and obtain employment among the farmers, to the great injury of their owners, who are thus not only deprived of their property and the work of their slaves, but are put to great expense and trouble in vainly endeavouring to find out the same evil-disposed slaves'.[243] To solve the problem the landdrost of Stellenbosch proposed in 1780 that a pass system be adopted for all Bastaard-Hottentots.[244]

Some runaways succeeded in maintaining themselves out of reach of the authorities in the colony. A group of drosters created an organised maroon community at Cape Hangklip, a promontory at the mouth of False Bay. It lasted from at least the 1720s until the nineteenth century. In 1730 eight slave men and a woman were discovered on a remote beach living in a house with several rooms and a garden.[245] Members of the community survived by raiding farms in the Hottentots-Holland area, fishing in False Bay, and by a chain of slave contacts linking it with Cape Town.[246] Travellers on the mountain pass road behind Hangklip were prey to attacks. One visitor in the 1820s commented on the proximity of such gangs to Cape Town.[247] The numerous commandos sent out against them could be seen crossing the Cape Flats and the marooners had time to hide in the caves and shelters of the mountain area.[248] Runaways also lived on Table Mountain and their fires were sometimes seen from Cape Town.

A few slaves succeeded in escaping from the colony altogether. During the seventeenth and early eighteenth centuries some reached the Khoikhoi or 'Bushmen' communities of the northern Cape.[249] Later many fled towards the Eastern Frontier and some found refuge with Xhosa chiefs and were incorporated into Cape Nguni society.[250] Others found their way north of the Orange River and joined the Oorlams and Griquas, although by the nineteenth century the Griquas regularly returned runaways to the colony.[251] A few escaped by sea, either as stowaways or by enlisting as sailors on visiting ships, Company or foreign, which were desperately short of hands because of the ravages of illness among their crews. On several occasions these ships returned to the Cape months or years later and the slaves were recognised and arrested.[252]

The escaped slave was a dangerous and desperate person, frequently armed, who was a symbol of defiance to the existing order and a potential model for other slaves to follow. Colonists feared the possibility of wider resistance in the form of rebellion by their slaves. In 1793 for example, the veldwachtmeester of Stellenbosch reported to the Council of Policy that there was a 'general fear' in the district of an uprising of slaves and Khoikhoi, who planned to 'attack the farms of Christians and murder the inhabitants', although the landdrost of Swellendam stated that this was merely rumour spread by certain 'malevolent persons'.[253] Such fears were generally unfounded. Large-scale uprisings were made difficult by the dispersed settlement pattern, which separated farms (and slaves) and hampered communications amongst plotters. Also the great ethnic heterogeneity of the slave population inhibited easy co-operation amongst slaves and deprived them of a common language unknown to the colonists. In the Americas slave revolts tended to occur in societies where the slaves heavily outnumbered the free population; at the Cape the numbers of slaves and freemen were virtually equal.

Only two slave uprisings occurred at the Cape; both of them involved small numbers and were easily suppressed. In 1808, two Irish sailors met Louis van Mauritius, a Cape Town slave skilled as a tailor, and another locally-born slave, Abraham, in the Cape Town underworld. They plotted to raise the slaves of the hinterland in rebellion, to march on Cape Town and to enforce the freedom of all slaves. Although the sailors defected, Louis and Abraham persuaded over 300 slaves and Khoikhoi from the Koeberg and Tijgerberg grain-producing areas to join them but were swiftly overcome by the militia at Salt River, just outside the town. The uprising never had any chance of success but it revealed the willingness of slaves and proletarianised Khoikhoi labourers to challenge the existing social order. The rebels were encouraged by the news which the Irishmen brought of countries without slavery and by the uncertainties caused in the colony by several changes of government as well as the abolition of the slave trade in the same year.

Rumours of impending emancipation provided the impetus to the second attempted rebellion which took place in the remoter Koue Bokkeveld in 1825, led by a slave named Galant. Like many slaves before him, Galant reacted against the maltreatment and punishments he had received from his owner, but he was also aware of the debate in the colony over emancipation and the farmers' opposition to it. Galant persuaded other slaves on his master's farmstead to join his rebellion, telling that he had heard 'between Christmas Day and New Year's Day, the slaves were to be made free – and that if it should not take place at that time, then their masters must be killed'.[254] Several members of his owner's family died in a skirmish which broke out on the farm. A commando was hastily formed which quickly crushed the rebels, but the aborted attempt caused great alarm throughout the colony.[255]

Both of these attempted slave uprisings took place in somewhat exceptional circumstances and although they greatly alarmed the colonists they actually posed little threat to the established order. Running away was a much more frequent and effective means of escaping from the world the slaveowners made at the Cape. Other means of resistance occur regularly in the court records. Before escaping, slaves sometimes burned standing grains and houses, which were usually thatched. In 1803, much damage was caused in Stellenbosch village by a fire started by slaves who hoped to obtain booty and then escape.[256]

Several slaves also attempted to poison their owners; in one case in 1754, a slave obtained mercury from the Company hospital for the purpose.[257]

Direct attacks on the person of the master or his family were normally spontaneous responses to punishment rather than premeditated murders, although the latter was always a potential threat. Relatively frequently individual slaves, mainly of eastern origin and normally in Cape Town, ran amok in a frenzy of attacks.[258] A number of slave suicides, on average between fifteen to twenty each year in the eighteenth century, were reported to the authorities.[259] Many of them were foreign-born slaves who had memories of a life before enslavement.

Not all slave responses were so dramatic. Refusal to work when ordered, or working slowly or badly were also ways by which slaves could resist, although they ran the risk of punishment for 'insolence'. Some slaves took that risk; in 1759, for example, Slammat van Bougies who had been found lying on the ground smoking a pipe when he should have been planting vegetables told his master that, 'I am always working; I must also rest sometimes. So if the Baas wants to sell me, then go ahead and sell me'.[260]

While many slaves thus resisted their servitude in various ways, others accommodated themselves, willingly or unwillingly, to their station in Cape society. There were many reasons why this was so, chief of which was probably the lack of viable alternatives. To refuse to be a slave, to refuse to carry out a master's bidding, meant punishment and perhaps even death. The alternative of escape or rebellion was equally dangerous and the uncertainty of its outcome too great to offer a temptation to most slaves. The weak, the timid, the aged, could not choose escape. The safest course – except perhaps in a time of epidemic – was to remain within the system and obey orders. That many did so is clear. Testamentary manumissions were granted in some cases in recognition of years of faithful service as a slave. The slave who did not opt to defy his master, to sabotage his property or to escape, became in effect an accomplice in maintaining his slavery. Defiance and flight might be in his heart but his (or her) body and labour belonged to the master. The slave shepherd with his musket offered a symbol of a man who had accepted his condition.

The ending of slavery

During the seventeenth and eighteenth centuries, slavery was the main labour system of the colony and an important determinant of its social structure. As W.S. van Ryneveld noted in 1797, it might have been better 'if slavery had been interdicted at the first settling of the Colony . . . Yet, the business is done. Slavery exists and is now even indispensable'.[261] But less than forty years after this statement, slavery had been abolished. New ideological forces, mainly stemming from Britain but also finding some response within the Cape, led to the general emancipation of slaves in all British colonies in 1834.

During the VOC period slavery was not questioned by Cape colonists. The only recorded opposition to it came in 1717 from one member of the Council of Policy, Dominique Marius Pasques de Chavonnes, in response to the proposal of the Heren XVII that slaves should be replaced by free labourers. His argument was based not on moral but on economic grounds, substantiated with detailed assessments of the costs of slave and free labour. He also stressed the 'dangers, expense and troubles which residents in the country districts have to endure because of their slaves'.[262] Such views were not shared by his colleagues on the Council of Policy nor by other free inhabitants of the colony. The Company introduced slaves to the settlement and continued to import and sell them to the burghers, thus sanctioning their use. Rights of ownership and control were upheld by the law. Although there were no elaborate justifications for slavery on racist grounds such as emerged later, for example, in the American South, it was generally accepted by the colonists that slavery was essential to the economic and social well-being of the Cape.[263] M.D. Teenstra, visiting the colony in 1825, reported that the masters justified slavery by stressing that it was an institution ordained by God and that slaves were well cared for and would starve to death if emancipated. They objected to visitors who brought 'European prejudices against slavery' and claimed that the slaves were well contented unless 'stirred up by false notions of liberty'.[264]

This was the response to challenges to the Cape slave system which had emerged during the first three decades of the nineteenth century. The Batavian government, following the recommendations of Commissioner de Mist, determined that slavery was unnecessary at the Cape and that it should gradually be removed by the emancipation of slave children and the encouragement of immigrant labourers from Europe.[265] Before this could be carried into effect, the Cape was re-occupied by the British and brought into the orbit of a wider imperial system in which the role of slavery was being questioned.

The ending of the slave trade in all British colonies in 1808 and the move towards general emancipation in following years resulted from a complex interaction of forces. The emergence of industrial capitalism and free trade policies in England completed the decline of the mercantilist system and lessened the significance of the West Indian slave colonies to her economy. The influence of the planters at Westminster was reduced, and at the same time a vociferous antislavery movement gained support in Britain. Strongly influenced by nonconformist Christianity, it was carried to the Caribbean by evangelical missionaries. In addition there was growing resistance amongst the slaves, marked by a series of revolts which undermined the confidence of the planter class and persuaded many that emancipation was necessary.[266]

The leaders of the antislavery movement were concerned with the inhumane treatment of slaves and the immorality of forced labour. However, their ideas also reflected nineteenth century British liberalism and the demands of industrial capital at that time. There was no question of overturning the existing social order; rights of property in all but the slaves themselves was to be strictly maintained.[267] Liberals stressed the need for a 'free' labour force encouraged to work by the incentive of wages, and they criticised the economic irrationality of a coerced and immobile body of workers. But great stress was also placed on the need to inculcate habits of 'diligence' amongst the slaves after emancipation, in order that they might remain compliant labourers. Thus a Cape resident writing in 1828 on 'the demoralizing influence of slavery' in a publication of 'The Society for the Mitigation and Gradual Abolition of Slavery throughout the British Dominions', stated that:

> The relation of master and slave gives rise to a continued exercise of skill on each side. The thoughts of the master are perpetually engrossed with the best means of turning the labour of his slaves to advantage and of securing his property against their depredations; while the thoughts of the slave are generally occupied about the most dexterous methods of deceiving their master and robbing him of his property. A slave has, in fact, no character, and the motives which operate upon a free peasantry have no influence in his case . . .[268]

Slaves, the abolitionists argued, lacking 'character' as a result of their bondage, had to be trained for a freedom which still assigned to them the role of a submissive workforce.

In the 1820s, most of the concern of the British antislavery movement was with this process of preparation of slaves rather than their total emancipation. It focussed its attention mainly on the West Indies, but its ideas were also felt at the Cape. Consequently legislation attempted to ameliorate the position of the slaves in the colony. Concern with their physical well-being was reflected in regulations on hours of work, food and clothing. In addition slaves were permitted to marry and owners were forbidden to sell young children separately from their mothers. These measures were at least in part a response to the need to encourage a self-reproducing labour force after the ending of the slave trade. The impact of missionaries and liberals was evident in laws encouraging the evangelisation and education of the slaves.

In addition, restrictions were placed on the ability of masters to punish their slaves, and slaves were encouraged to report abuses to the authorities. Not only did these measures attempt to protect slaves, but they also increased the control of the colonial state over labour relations hitherto in the private domain of the colonists.[269] An official Guardian of Slaves was appointed in 1826 (renamed Protector of Slaves in 1830), with assistants in some of the rural districts, to ensure that these regulations were put into effect. However, it soon became apparent that his sympathies lay as much with the slaveowners as with the slaves, to the dismay of the antislavery lobby in London.[270]

There was little concerted pressure from within the colony for general emancipation. The right of slaves to purchase freedom had been granted by an Ordinance of 1826, and a small group of Cape Town liberals, many of them English merchants, founded the Cape of Good Hope Philanthropic Society in 1828 for 'aiding deserving slaves and slave children to purchase their freedom'. With money obtained from donations and public subscriptions, they purchased and manumitted slave children but by July 1833 only 126 had been freed in this way. However, they were not concerned with the immediate and total emancipation of the slave population and stressed the importance of not antagonising the slaveowners and of protecting rights of property, including property in slaves.[271]

After the 1831 Jamaican slave revolt, the momentum grew towards complete slave emancipation throughout the British colonies. At the Cape, arguments in favour of immediate emancipation were presented by John Fairbairn, editor of the colony's English newspaper, *The South African Commercial Advertiser*, who maintained strong links with the antislavery movement in Britain. Fully imbued with liberal concepts, he stressed not only the humanitarian arguments of the cruelty inherent in forced labour, but also the economic advantages of a free, rate-paying labour force, and a system which released capital invested in slaves. But he also asserted the slave owners' property rights and insisted that they should be adequately compensated for their slaves.[272] In the early 1830s, Fairbairn published extensive articles on the need to ensure a peaceful transition to a society without slaves, but also without loss of labour discipline and order.[273]

These ideas found a measure of support from merchants and commercial interests at the Cape. The missionaries, who had advocated the interests of the Khoikhoi at the time of the passing of Ordinance 50 in 1828, played a less significant role in the movement against slavery at the Cape than did their counterparts in the West Indies. The majority of the colonists, many of them slaveowning farmers, opposed Fairbairn's arguments.[274]

Recent work has shown that Somerset's 1823 proclamation on slave treatment was accepted by many slaveowners because it preserved the essential controls of masters over their slaves and pre-empted more direct intervention by the Colonial Office in London. After Somerset's removal in 1826, this tacit alliance between the Cape administration and the main slaveowners broke down. Subsequent legislation stemming from London threatened the authority of masters over their slaves.[275] In 1830 and 1832 orders-in-council from London legislated that owners had to keep records of punishments meted out to their slaves. In addition they increased the powers of the Protector of Slaves to prosecute colonists who disobeyed ameliorative slave legislation. A minor riot took place in Stellenbosch village in 1831 which effectively nullified the requirement to bring punishment books to the local authorities.[276] About 2,000 slaveowners gathered at a mass meeting in Cape Town in 1832 and expressed resentment that legislation was being promulgated without their consultation. They did not, however, attempt to defend the principle of slavery. They stressed that if some form of local representative government was obtained, they would ameliorate the condition of the slaves themselves and ultimately emancipate them.[277]

Once the Emancipation Act had been passed by the British Parliament in 1833, slave owners were most concerned with the value of compensation and the way in which it was to be distributed.[278] Reports were received by the authorities during 1834 that some colonists in the eastern districts were attempting to move beyond the boundaries of the colony, 'with the view of preventing the liberation of their slaves' but in general, slaveowners accepted the inevitability of abolition.[279]

This resignation was primarily caused by the powerlessness of the colonists in the face of the determination of the British government. The justification and authority for slavery which the VOC had given was gone. But also developments within the Cape during the 1820s had somewhat modified the economic role of slavery. The ending of the wine-farming boom after 1825 led to insolvencies of many slaveowners and to an agricultural and commercial depression in the western districts where slaves had been most intensively used.[280] Although farmers still stressed the importance of slave labour, their confidence in the durability and profitability of the existing labour system had been weakened. In addition, there was clear evidence of an increasing self-assertiveness by the slaves themselves. Although there were no massive slave revolts of the kind that took place in the Caribbean, Cape slave owners were considerably alarmed by the Bokkeveld uprising of 1825 and the spectre of violent resistance which it evoked.[281] A number of escaped slaves in the 1810s and 1820s stated that they believed they were wrongly enslaved, which indicates the influence of new notions of liberty.[282] The legislation of the 1820s and the early 1830s led to the growing awareness by slaves of their legal rights and, in the words of the Protector of Slaves in 1833, to an increase in the number of 'refractory and ill-behaved slaves' sent to him by their owners 'to instil a better line of conduct'.[283] The steps towards emancipation was beginning to erode the internal control system of Cape slave society.

Slavery was formally ended at the Cape on 1 December 1834. However, slaves were to be apprenticed to their owners for a further four years. In theory this transitional period was to allow them to prepare for a 'useful' existence as freedmen, but in practice they continued to work as before. Freedom of movement and the right to demand wages did not come until 1838. During this time, the slaveowners attempted to secure a vagrancy law to enable them to restrict the mobility and bargaining power of the freedmen as labourers. This was rejected by the Governor, in spite of a barrage of petitions demanding that there be some means of legally detaining unemployed labourers and forcing them to work. In part this rejection resulted from the fear that a vagrancy ordinance would negate the effect on the Khoisan of Ordinance 50 (see ch. 1, pp. 47–49). Without such controls the colonists foresaw economic disaster and social chaos.[284]

In the event, such fears were unfounded. Whilst slaveowners were compensated for their loss, albeit at a rate considered inadequate by many colonists, no provision had been made for land or capital for the freedmen. Many slaves left their masters after 1838 and there were problems in obtaining adequate labour for the harvest of 1838–39. Some found a livelihood in and around Cape Town or in the rural villages and others moved to mission stations. Most, however, continued to work either as permanent or as casual seasonal labour on the farmsteads.[285] In 1841 labour contracts were enforced by the Masters and Servants Ordinance, which provided the basis of later and more stringent measures regulating labour relations.[286] After achieving a measure of self-government in 1853, Cape colonists swiftly encoded the 1856 Masters and Servants Act, which increased penalties on labourers for desertion, and made neglect, insubordination, and 'use of abusive or insulting language' criminal offences.[287] Farmers had to adapt to a wage labour force but legal emancipation for slaves was not accompanied by any significant change in the inequalities of their economic or social position. The shadow of slavery still loomed large over the labourers of the western Cape in the mid-nineteenth century.

Chapter Three   Notes

1. The historiography of Cape slavery has in recent years grown beyond the confines of a brief note. However, monographic-length studies in this field remain relatively few. The most important are, in order of date of publication, W. Blommaert, 'Het Invoeren van de Slavernij aan de Kaap', *AYB* I, 1938, pp. 1–29; Isobel E. Edwards, *Towards Emancipation* (Cardiff, 1942); Victor de Kock, *Those in Bondage* (Cape Town, 1950; reprinted 1963); Lewis J. Greenstein, 'Slave and Citizen: the South African Case', *Race* XV (1973), pp. 25–46; Anna J. Böeseken, *Slaves and Free Blacks at the Cape 1658–1700* (Cape Town, 1977), a work criticised in L. Hattingh, 'A.J. Böeseken se addendum van Kaapse slawe-verkooptransaksies: foute en regstellings', *Kronos* IX (1984) pp. 3–21; Frank R. Bradlow and Margaret Cairns, *The Early Cape Muslims* (Cape Town, 1978); Robert Ross *Cape of Torments* (London, 1983); Nigel Worden, *Slavery in Dutch South Africa* (Cambridge, 1985); Robert Shell, 'Slavery at the Cape of Good Hope 1680–1731' (Ph.D Dissertation; Yale University, 1986); and Mary Rayner, 'Wine and slaves: the failures of an export economy and the ending of slavery in the Cape Colony, South Africa, 1806–1834' (Ph.D. Dissertation, Duke University, 1986). A major locus of Cape slavery studies is now the journal *Kronos* published at the University of the Western Cape.
2. Albert van Dantzig's *Het Nederlandse Aandeel in de Slavenhandel* (Bussum, 1968) is a convenient survey.
3. The major study of this traffic is Johannes Postma's unpublished Ph.D. dissertation 'The Dutch participation in the African slave trade: slaving on the Guinea Coast, 1695–1795' (Michigan State University, 1969–70). See also Postma's 'The Dutch slave trade; a quantitative assessment', *La traite des noirs par l'Atlantique; nouvelles approches. The Atlantic slave trade; new approaches* (Paris, 1976), pp. 232–44.
4. The import of slaves into the Dutch-controlled Indies was prohibited by the Constitutional Law of 1816. However, within the Netherlands Indies internal trade in slaves continued until 1855. See 'Slavernij', *Encyclopaedie van Nederlandsch Indië*, III, 621 (The Hague, Leiden, n.d.), and Jean Gelman Taylor, *The Social World of Batavia* (Madison, 1983), p. 125.

5. A recent survey is *Slavery, Bondage and Dependency in Southeast Asia*, ed. A. Reid (St. Lucia, 1983).

6. There is still no comprehensive study of the Dutch experience with slavery in the East Indies. However, several chapters in Reid, *Slavery* illuminate various aspects of this topic.

7. On the use of slaves at Ceylon, see VOC 4032, Thomas van Rhee (Colombo)-Simon van der Stel (Cape), 13 Jan. 1694, p. 449v.

8. A. Reid, 'Introduction: Slavery and Bondage in Southeast Asian History', in *Slavery*, ed. Reid, p. 29.

9. J.C.H. Grobler's unpublished master's thesis 'Die arbeidvraagstuk aan die Kaap, 1652–1662' (University of Stellenbosch, 1968) contains a detailed discussion of Van Riebeeck's attempts to ensure an adequate labour supply for the Cape.

10. Cf. Grobler 'Die Arbeidvraagstuk', pp. 10–50; Blommaert, 'Het Invoeren', pp. 24–25.

11. Van Riebeeck's views on the need for slaves may be seen in his official correspondence with the Heren XVII and the Raad van Indië, and in his journal: C 493, J. van Riebeeck – Raad van Indië, 25 May 1652, p. 25; C 493, J. van Riebeeck – XVII, 14 April 1653, p. 70, and C 493, 16 April 1655, p. 384; C 493, J. van Riebeeck – Raad van Indië, 24 July 1655, p. 435; J. van Riebeeck, *Daghregister*, ed. H.B. Thom (Cape Town, 1952), I, 2 April 1654, p. 212; 8 Aug. 1655, p. 334; 4 Oct. 1655, p. 352.

12. The Dutch settlement on Mauritius (1638–58) and its modest slave trading with Madagascar are described in K. Heeringa, 'De Nederlanders op Mauritius en Madagascar', *De Indische Gids* (1895), 1, 864–92; (1895), II, 1005–36. This settlement has been more recently studied by Gabrielle de Nettancourt, 'Le Peuplement Néerlandais à l'Ile Maurice (1598–1710)' in *Mouvements de Populations dans l'Océan Indien* (Actes du Quatrième Congrès de l'Association Historique Internationale de l'Océan Indien et du Quatorzième Colloque de la Commission Internationale d'Histoire Maritime tenu à Saint-Dénis-de-la-Réunion du 4 au 9 Septembre 1972) (Paris, 1979) pp. 219–29.

13. Van Riebeeck, *Daghregister*, I, 222–23, 225, 248, 446. Also 'Instructie voor d'Opperhoofden van 't Galijot de Rode Vos . . .' (8 May 1654) in *Precis of the Archives of the Cape of Good Hope, Letters Despatched 1652–1662*, ed. H.C.V. Leibbrandt (Cape Town, 1900), I, 300–05.

14. Van Riebeeck, *Daghregister*, I, 235, 268–70.

15. Blommaert, 'Het Invoeren', pp. 5–7.

16. *Ibid.*, pp. 24–27.

17. Van Riebeeck, *Daghregister*, II, 26 March 1658, p. 268. Blommaert, 'Het Invoeren', p. 24.

18. The data summarised from over forty specific sources in this tabulation are primarily drawn from the trade journals of the individual voyages as well as from relevant correspondence from the Cape to the Heren XVII found in the Cape Archives and in the Algemeen Rijksarchief.

19. For a survey of Dutch contact with St. Augustine's Bay, see James C. Armstrong, 'St. Augustine's Bay and the Madagascar slave trade in the seventeenth century' (forthcoming).

20. For a history of the Malagasy slave trade, see James C. Armstrong,

'Madagascar and the slave trade in the seventeenth century', *Omaly sy Anio* nos. 17–20 (1983–84) pp. 211–33.

21. *Ibid*, pp. 213–16.
22. *Ibid*, pp. 216.
23. *Ibid*, pp. 225.
24. The slave trade to the Mascarenes was of far greater scale than that to the Cape. From 1729, when the trade began in earnest, to 1810, approximately 155,000 slaves were imported into Réunion and Mauritius. Of these, some 45 per cent, or about 70,000, were from Madagascar. See J.M. Filliot, *La traite des esclaves vers les Mascareignes au XVIIIe siècle* (Paris, 1974), pp. 54–69.
25. The voyage of the *Leidsman* in 1715 may be taken as representative, although it was briefer than most. Departing 16 June from the Cape, it traded for slaves at Bombetoka Bay, after a detour to the Comoros. In a fortnight's active trading 200 slaves were purchased, of which 179 survived the return voyage. The ship returned on 21 November 1715. The average cost of these slaves, as computed by the Company, was 45.18.12 guilders. C 702B [Instructions for Leidsman] pp. 708–29. South African Library, Dessinian 140 MSD 3 'Journal der Zeetogt naar d'Eijlanden Ansuany en Madagascar . . . door Hendrik Frappe', unpaginated. See also Dessinian 138 MSD 10 for another journal of this same voyage.
26. Journals kept by the VOC trade commissioner on many of these voyages have survived, and provide much information about trading conditions. A few have been published: that of *De Brak* (1741) appears, in French translation, in A. Grandidier et al., *Collection des ouvrages anciens concernant Madagascar*, VI (1913), 52–196. *De Brak's* subsequent voyage has been summarised in M. Boucher, 'The voyage of a Cape slaver in 1742', *Historia* 24, 1 (April 1979), pp. 50–58. The voyages of *De Zon* (1776–77) and the *Jagtrust* (1777–78) have been translated, with copious notes, by Robert Ross, 'The Dutch on the Swahili Coast, 1776–1778: Two Slaving Journals', *International Journal of African Historical Studies*, 19, 2 (1986), pp. 305–59, and 19, 3 (1986), pp. 479–506.
27. The career of 'Sijmon de Arabier' was especially notable. Cf. Armstrong, 'Madagascar and the slave trade', pp. 232–33.
28. For the VOC's brief occupation of Delagoa Bay and the slave trade there, see C.G. Coetzee, 'Die Stryd om Delagoabaai en die Suidooskus 1600–1800' (Ph.D. thesis: Stellenbosch University, 1954), especially pp. 195–99.
29. Heeringa, 'De Nederlanders', pp. 1006, 1011. A temporary settlement was erected by the distressed crew of the *Barneveld*, 5 Sept.–21 Oct. 1719 at 19° 30'S on Madagascar's west coast. This was only incidentally a 'factory', however. *Reyze van het Oostindisch Schip Barneveld*. (3rd edition; Dordrecht, 1764).
30. The final Company voyage was that of the *Meermin* under Captain Duminy which returned to the Cape on 28 February 1786 with 295 slaves from Mozambique, having lost a further 50 en route. VOC 4315, Van de Graaff – XVII, 4 March 1786, pp. 587v–88. A final Council of Policy resolution to abandon the slave trade came only in 1792. C 99, Res 26 Nov. 1792, p. 672.
31. C 472, XVII – Governor and Council, 8 Jan. 1788, pp. 217 ff; C 83, Res

13 June 1788, pp. 690–94.

32. Tutucorin slaves: VOC 4013, P. de Graeuwe – Joan Bax, 25 Jan. 1677, p. 283; VOC 4012, Joan Bax – XVII, 22 May 1677, p. 863v; Jaffnapatnam: C 443, II, Hendrik Becker – Pol. Raad, 14 Dec. 1712; C 510, III, W. Helot – Abraham van Riebeeck, 13 March 1713, pp. 999–1000; Jaffnapatnam: C 338, Attestatien, 17 March 1719, pp. 165–68. An additional twenty-one died en route from Ceylon.

33. Simon van Leeuwen, *Het Roomch-Hollandch-Regt* (10th ed., 1732), p. 2. Nevertheless, domestic slaves were brought to the Netherlands repeatedly in the seventeenth and early eighteenth centuries. Batavian plakkaats during the period 1637–57 repeatedly but ineffectually prohibited the bringing of slaves to the Netherlands. *De Nederlandsch-Indisch Plakkaatboek 1602–1811*, ed. J.A. van der Chijs (The Hague, 1885–91), vols. I and II.

34. C 717, XVII – Generaal en Raaden, 30 Oct. 1713, p. 409.

35. C 120, Plakkaat of 5 Sept. 1716, p. 463. Also *Nederlandsch-Indisch Plakkaatboek*, IV, 84–85.

36. Charles Peter Thunberg, *Travels in Europe, Africa, and Asia performed between the years 1770 and 1779* (London, n.d.), I, 113.

37. In 1735 the Heren XVII, noting that each slave brought to the Netherlands was also accompanied by a sea-chest, limited to four the number of slaves that repatriating officials could bring home. C 445, Extract uyt de Generale Brief, 3 Sept. 1735, p. 503.

38. Cf. R. Shell, 'Slavery at the Cape of Good Hope, 1680 to 1731', pp. 64–68 and 375.

39. C 59, Res 10 March 1767, pp. 143–45.

40. C 168, Bylagen, Ordonnantie, 28 Sept. 1767, p. 477. Batavia had previously, in 1757, prohibited the import into Batavia of 'Oostersche' slaves over the age of fourteen. Batavian Res 25 Feb. 1757, in *Realia* III (The Hague, 1886), p. 209.

41. C 186, Bylagen, 2 Sept. 1784, p. 477. See also Plakkaat of 13 Jan. 1785, in *KP* I–IV (Cape Town, 1944–49), III, 164.

42. One instance of a confiscation of three oriental slaves did occur in 1784, but this was because of their apparent attempt to incite a mutiny on the ship *Java* en route to the Cape. In early 1787 a ship's captain was arrested for slave smuggling and the two slaves were returned to Batavia. C 76, Res 14 April 1784, pp. 217–19; C 81, Res 17 Jan. 1787, pp. 62–63.

43. C 82, Res 19 Dec. 1787, p. 963. C 472, XVII – Cape, 8 Jan. 1788, pp. 252–53. See also A.L. Geyer, *Das wirtschaftliche System der Niederländischen Ostindischen Kompanie am Kap der Guten Hoffnung 1785–95* (Munich, 1923), p. 40.

44. Armstrong, 'Madagascar and the slave trade', pp. 217–22, and M. Boucher, 'The Cape and foreign shipping, 1714–1723', *South African Historical Journal*, 6 (Nov. 1974), pp. 3–29.

45. 'Lightfoot' was the English slavers' name for Andriandahifotsy (d. 1683), the Sakalava leader. Cf. Armstrong, 'Madagascar and the slave trade', pp. 219–20.

46. Though these individual private transactions rarely figure in the official correspondence of the Company, many of them do appear in the 'Transporten' in the Deeds Office, Cape Town. The slave transporten

1658–1700 are transcribed, but not quantitatively analysed, in A. Böeseken, *Slaves and Free Blacks*. The most extensive work to date on the transporten is R. Shell, 'Slavery at the Cape of Hope, 1680–1731', in which 4,076 slave transfers have been analysed, of which 2,622 refer to internal slave transactions.

47. M. Boucher, who has extensively researched the maritime history of the Cape, observes, 'It seems probable that there was a fairly regular trade in slaves at the Cape by captains of British ships, although information on this point is sparse for the period' [i.e., 1735–1755]. M. Boucher, *The Cape of Good Hope and Foreign Contacts 1735–1755* (Pretoria, 1985), p. 96.

48. *Kaapse Archiefstukken* 1782, I (Cape Town, 1931), Res 21 May 1782, p. 172; Res 18 June 1782, p. 207; DR, 3 June 1782, p. 338. Also C 78, Res 11 Oct. 1785, pp. 642–45; C 78, Res 17 Nov. 1785, p. 765.

49. The slaves of *L'Union* were purchased by the Company for 39,532.4 rixdollars and sold for 49,250.4 rixdollars, a profit of 24.6 per cent. Of *L'Estrelle d'Afrique's* 194 slaves, 177 were sold by the Company at a profit of 69 per cent. The remaining 17 were taken over by the Company. *Le Télémacque's* slaves were bought for 9,000 Spanish realen (10,125 rixdollars) and sold for 15,455 rixdollars, a profit for the Company of 53 per cent. VOC 4314, Inkoop en verkoop rekening van sodanige lading slaven als in den Maand October 1785 Ten behoeven der E. Comp. zyn gekogt en wederom vercogt . . ., p. 260. These were in part fictitious profits, as some slaves were purchased on credit and the buyers subsequently defaulted. See C 218, Dec. 1794, p. 959.

50. C 79, Res 19 April 1786, p. 434; VOC 4315, Van de Graaff – XVII, 19 April 1786, p. 433.

51. VOC 4024, Simon van der Stel – XVII, 20 May 1687, p. 703.

52. C 512, M.P. Chavonnes – XVII, 31 July 1719, pp. 519–21.

53. C 443, XVII – J. de la Fontaine, 14 Sept. 1731, pp. 524–25.

54. VOC 4473, 14 July citing a request of 23 March 1745; C 450, XVII – H. Swellengrebel, 10 Sept. 1746, p. 451; VOC 4917[1], DD, J. van Plettenburg – XVII, 20 March 1781, Bylaag 8, Litt. A., p. 37. Eduard Moritz, *Die Deutschen am Kap unter der Holländischen Herrschaft 1652–1806* (Weimar, 1938), p. 181.

55. VOC 4023, pp. 75–81 'Verklaringen van 't nemen van 't Westerwyck'. *Muiterij: oproer en bevechting op schepen van de VOC,* ed J.R. Bruijn and E.S. van Eyck van Heslinga (Haarlem, 1980).

56. Shell, 'Slavery at the Cape of Good Hope, *passim.*

57. J.L. Hattingh, 'Die klagte oor goewerneur W.A. van der Stel se slawebesit — 'n beoordeling met behulp van kwantitatiewe data', *Kronos* 7 (1983), p. 27.

58. Shell, 'Slavery at the Cape of Good Hope', p. 342.

59. The 1718 opgaaf returns show 1885 slave men, 321 slave women, 124 slave boys and 106 slave girls, for a total of 2,436. The equivalent figures for 1729 are: 2,836 slave men, 590 slave women, 244 slave boys and 238 slave girls, the total being 3,908. The net increase of 951 adult male slaves is striking, and itself is almost six times the recorded sales to burghers. Beyers, *Die Kaapse Patriotte*, p. 341; C 519, I, 507.

60. Worden, *Slavery in Dutch South Africa*, pp. 31, 33.

61. H. Giliomee, *Die Kaap tydens die Eerste Britse Bewind 1795–1803* (Cape Town, 1975), p. 183.
62. BO 50, Ross – Burgher Senate, 2 Dec. 1797, p. 355; BO 32, Memorial, 25 Feb. 1799, pp. 54–55; BO 52, Dundas – Burgher Senate, 4 March 1799, n.p.; VC 104, General Description of Cape of Good Hope, I, 30–31.
63. Giliomee, *Die Kaap*, p. 183.
64. *Ibid.*, p. 184.
65. W. Freund, 'Society and Government in Dutch South Africa: The Cape and the Batavians 1803–6', (Ph.D. thesis: Yale University, 1971), p. 249.
66. G.M. Theal, *South Africa* (6th ed.; London, n.d.), p. 181.
67. C. Saunders, 'Liberated Africans in Cape Colony in the First Half of the Nineteenth Century', *International Journal of African Historical Studies*, 18 (1985), p. 224.
68. Cf. J.A. Heese, *Die Herkoms van die Afrikaner 1657–1867* (Cape Town, 1971). H.F. Heese, in *Groep sonder Grense* (Bellville, 1984) pp. 41–75 records over 1000 unions of Europeans with persons of Asian, Indonesian and mixed Cape origin.
69. R. Shell, 'Slavery at the Cape of Good Hope', p. 376.
70. J.L.M. Franken's *Taalhistoriese Bydraes* (Amsterdam, 1953) cites many of the typically fragmentary archival traces of spoken Portuguese found in the Cape judicial records. M.F. Valkoff in his *Studies in Creole and Portuguese* (Johannesburg, 1966) offers a spirited but tendentious review of the arguments for Portuguese at the Cape.
71. M.F. Valkhoff's *New Light on Afrikaans and 'Malayo-Portuguese'* (Louvain, 1972) is a summary of the debate by one of the debaters.
72. Eugene Genovese, *Roll, Jordan Roll* (New York, 1974), p. 432. For a discussion of other aspects of Cape slave culture, see below, pp. 147–49.
73. J.C. Armstrong, 'Malagasy Slave Names in the Seventeenth Century', *Omaly sy Anio* nos. 17–20 (1983–84), pp. 43–59.
74. Figures taken from twenty Company documents in the Cape Archives and the Rijksarchief.
75. VOC 4000, 'Extraordinaire Oncosten', 1665, p. 502.
76. VOC 4014, DR, 9 Dec. 1678, pp. 481v–82v; *Res*, II, 270 (30 Nov. 1678); VOC 4017, DR, 27 Nov. 1681, pp. 218–19; *Res*, III, 28 (26 Nov. 1681); Charles Lockyer, *An Account of the Trade in India* . . . (London, 1711), p. 297; Nicolas Louis de la Caille, *Journal Historique du Voyage fait au Cap de Bonne-Espérance* (Paris, 1763), pp. 309–12; J. Hoge, 'Rassenmischung in Südafrika im 17 and 18. Jahrhundert', *Zeitschrift für Rassenkunde*, VIII (1938), pp. 138–51.
77. For an early instance of infanticide, see the sentence of Susanna of Bengal, who strangled her 'misties' (mestizo) daughter, CJ 780, Sententiën, 1652–97, no. 112, pp. 333–36. Her punishment was to be drowned in Table Bay, in view of the other slaves.
78. Peter Kolbe, *Naaukeurige en Uitvoerige Beschryving van de Kaap de Goede Hoop* (Amsterdam, 1727), I, 389.
79. J. Hoge's 'Personalia of the Germans at the Cape, 1652–1804', *AYB*, IX (1946), *passim*, documents some of these relationships.
80. H.P. Cruse identified nineteen instances of Company slave children manumitted through purchase by whites in the period 1715–92, *Die*

Opheffing van die Kleurling-bevolking (Stellenbosch, 1947), p. 253. The actual number may have been somewhat higher and may have included some of those twenty-nine children whose freedom was nominally purchased by their (slave) mothers.

81. Data from Company records in Cape Archives and Rijksarchief.
82. Data from various Company records.
83. VOC 4010, Isbrant Goske – XVII, 20 May 1674, p. 23; VOC 4012, Joan Bax – XVII, 14 March 1677, pp. 25v–26; VOC 4038, Simon van der Stel – XVII, 8 March 1698, p. 79.
84. Its predecessor had been burnt down through the carelessness of a slave; VOC 4015, Simon van der Stel – XVII, 23 Dec. 1679, p. 18. The new lodge was repaired and enlarged several times. In 1729 it was so dilapidated that there were many places in it where the slaves could not escape the wind and rain; C 519, I, P.G. Noodt – XVII, 15 March 1729, p. 301.
85. O. Geyser, *Die Ou Hooggeregshofgebou* (Cape Town, 1958), pp. 7–8.
86. VOC 4038, Regelement . . . voor het Hospitaal . . ., 3 May 1697, p. 508v.
87. Kolbe, *Beschryving*, I, 397.
88. VOC 4022, DR, 9 July 1685, pp. 277–77v.
89. C 800, Burger Besware en Kommissies van ondersoek, 1742–96, [Item 5] No. 30, 'Antwoord . . . nopens der slaven de E. Compagnie . . .', 16 Aug. 1789.
90. C 214, Generale lyst van alle 's Compagnies Slaven . . . 31 Dec. 1793, pp. 151–53.
91. C 72, Res, 1780, pp. 245–47; C 80, Res, 1 Nov. 1786, pp. 1112–14; VOC 4353, Van de Graaff-Willem Arnold Alting (Batavia), 29 Feb. 1790, n.p.
92. VOC 4000, Extraordinaire Oncosten, 1664, p. 501; VOC 4008, Extraordinaire Oncosten, 1670, p. 433; VOC 4024, Cassa Boeck, 30 Nov. 1686, p. 1156; *Res*, III, 179 (22 Dec. 1687).
93. VOC 4037, Instructie voor de opperhoffden van het freguat de Soldaat, 31 Oct. 1696, pp. 1070–82.
94. Average cost obtained by dividing figures for Company slave expenses by reported number of slaves for selected years. For example, in 1784/85, 856 slaves and convicts cost the Company 41,536.7.8 guilders, or an average of 44 guilders per slave. The Company's slave expenses were 3.2 per cent of the overall Cape expense of 1,284,912.3.8 guilders. VOC 4320, Van de Graaff – XVII, 24 April 1787, p. 654; C 402, Attestatien, 1785, p. 483.
95. Company slave expenses were reported annually in the Cape outgoing correspondence, C 83, Res, 4 April 1788, p. 423.
96. Giliomee, *Die Kaap*, p. 16.
97. O. Geyser, *The History of the Old Supreme Court Building*, p. 45, citing BR, Bijlagen tot Resolutien, Rapport of Höhne to the Political Council, 9 March 1803, pp. 219–24. On Höhne and other German personnel of the slave lodge in this period see E. Moritz, *Die Deutschen am Kap*, pp. 141, 146, 149, and J. Hoge, 'Personalia of the Germans at the Cape, 1652–1806', *AYB* (1946), *passim*.
98. *Ibid*, p. 57. J.S. Marais, *The Cape Coloured People, 1652–1937* (London, 1939), p. 172.
99. Geyser, *History*, p. 57, citing G. M. Theal, *History of South Africa (1795–1834)*, p. 136.

100. Geyser, *History,* p. 57.
101. W. Bird, *State of the Cape of Good Hope in 1822* (reprint; Cape Town 1966), pp. 79–80.
102. Marais, *The Cape Coloured People*, p. 172, citing *RCC*, XXVI, pp. 494–506; XXXIV, p. 141.
103. The opgaaf rolls were compiled anew each year and changes in the status of individuals known from other sources tend to be reasonably well shown in them. Their accuracy on the returns made of taxable produce, such as wheat or livestock holdings, is dubious, but the figures for burghers and their slaves (who were not taxed) were a reasonably fair reflection of reality. On the whole, they are internally consistent over many decades. A large under-representation of population could have been achieved by very extensive misreporting over many years, but the Company would clearly have become aware of it. There appears to be no evidence that Company officials were concerned about slave under-reporting until 1776 when a plakkaat was issued against it.
104. R. Ross, 'Smallpox at the Cape of Good Hope in the eighteenth century' in *African historical demography,* ed. C. Fyfe and D. McMaster (Centre of African Studies, University of Edinburgh, 1977), p. 421.
105. *KP,* II, 223.
106. *KP,* V, 202–03.
107. SO 15/2, Extract from the Proceedings of the Committee of Enquiry into the Illicit Traffic of Slaves, 4 May 1808; SO 3/1, p. 9, Report of the Guardian of Slaves, 30 June 1827.
108. SO 7/34, Collected lists and returns of slaves. Return of slaves of different ages, 1833.
109. Figures from opgaaf rolls for 1738 (VOC 4136) and 1768 (VOC 4256); CO 6135, Statements of the Population and Quantity of Lands at the Cape of Good Hope, 1806–1825; CO 5976, Cape of Good Hope Blue Book and Statistical Register, 1834, p. 139.
110. Worden, *Slavery in Dutch South Africa,* p. 55–56; M. Rayner, '"Labourers in the vineyard": work and resistance to servitude during the years of the wine-farming boom in the Cape Colony, 1806–1824', paper presented to Third History Workshop, University of the Witwatersrand, 1984, p. 5.
111. CA Accessions 455, W.S. van Ryneveld, Replies to the questions on the importation etc. of slaves into the colony proposed by his Excellency the Earl of Macartney, etc., dated 29 Nov. 1797; Henry Dundas papers, file 107, article 5. S. Newton-King, 'The labour market of the Cape Colony, 1807–28', *Economy and society in pre-industrial South Africa*, ed. S. Marks and A. Atmores, (London, 1980), p. 180.
112. Van Ryneveld, Replies, article 4.
113. CO 5968, Cape of Good Hope Blue Book and Statistical Register, 1826, p. 151a.
114. Figures from opgaaf rolls, VOC 4045 (1701), 4180 (1750), 4276 (1773).
115. CO 5976, Cape of Good Hope Blue Book and Statistical Register, 1834, p. 139. The changes in the boundaries of the administrative districts between the eighteenth and nineteenth centuries are indicated in Figure 1.2 (p. 23).
116. VOC 4180, Opgaaf return for 1750.

117. VOC 4276, Opgaaf return for 1773.
118. J. 37, Kaapstad opgaaf return for 1800; J.443, opgaaf return of Vryzwarten and Compagnie Dienaren, 1797.
119. VOC 4180, Opgaaf return for 1750.
120. R. Ross, 'The rise of the Cape gentry', *Journal of Southern African Studies*, II (1983), pp. 193–217; L. Guelke and R. Shell, 'An early colonial landed gentry: land and wealth in the Cape Colony, 1682–1731', *Journal of Historical Geography* (1983), 265–86.
121. N. Worden, 'Rural slavery in the western districts of Cape Colony during the nineteenth century', (Ph.D. thesis, Cambridge, 1982), pp. 86–90.
122. J. 233, Census return for Stellenbosch district (including Drakenstein), 1806.
123. 1/STB 10/6, Memorial of Stellenbosch and Drakenstein burghers to the Commissioner-General of the Indies, May 1793; BO 19, Memorial to the Burgher Senate, 1798, pp. 18–19.
124. Details of the wine boom and its impact on slaves is given in Rayner, 'Wine and Slaves', esp. ch. 1 and 'Labourers in the vineyard'.
125. The years chosen were 1688, 1692, 1705, 1723, 1731, 1741, 1752, 1761, 1773 and 1783. Data obtained from the computer files of the census records, Instituut vir Historiese Navorsing, University of the Western Cape.
126. V.C. Malherbe, 'Diversification and mobility of Khoikhoi labour in the eastern districts of Cape Colony prior to the labour law of 1 November 1809' (M.A. thesis, University of Cape Town, 1978), pp. 44–50.
127. Worden, *Slavery*, p. 16. Figures for urban slaves in the census returns of the VOC period are only distinguishable from those in the surrounding rural areas of Cape District by the absence of declared produce or livestock, and can thus only be approximate. After 1806 a distinction was made between Cape Town and the rest of the district. Figures for 1806 from CO 6135, Statements of the population and the quantity of lands at the Cape of Good Hope, 1806–25, unpaginated.
128. CO 5976, Cape of Good Hope Blue Book and Statistical Register, 1834, p. 139.
129. Thunberg, *Travels* (2nd. ed.; London, 1795) I, 99. Details of urban slave occupations are provided in R. Ross, 'The occupation of slaves in eighteenth century Cape Town', *Studies in the History of Cape Town* (Cape Town, 1980), II, 1–14.
130. L. Guelke, 'The early European settlement of South Africa' (Ph.D. thesis, University of Toronto, 1974), p. 277. Details of the internal slave market are given in Worden, *Slavery*, pp. 49–51.
131. Prices for the seventeenth century are taken from the *transporten* or deeds of sale which only survive for the seventeenth and early eighteenth centuries. Figures for later periods are from *vendurollen*, the estate auction records for the rural districts of Stellenbosch and Drakenstein. Further details of prices for the seventeeth century are given in J.L. Hattingh, ''n Ontleding van sekere aspekte van slawerny aan die Kaap in die sewentiende eeu', *Kronos* I (1979), pp. 34–78, and distributions of auction slave prices in the eighteenth century in Worden, *Slavery*, p. 74.
132. Proceedings of the Council on the Subject of the Tax on Slaves, proposed

by H.M. Commissioners of Enquiry, 15 Dec. 1826, cited in Newton-King, 'The labour market', p. 180.

133. M. Rayner, 'Labourers in the vineyard', p. 37, fn. 43.
134. For values of slaves assessed by the Compensation Commissioners, see E. Hengherr, 'Emancipation – and after: a study of Cape slavery and the issues arising from it, 1830–1843' (M.A. thesis, University of Cape Town, 1953), pp. 51–71. It appears that the values allocated did not take account of the reports that had been received in London of sale prices in the colony.
135. The calculations on which this figure is based are taken from C 184, Res, Memorial of Johannes Colijn to the Council of Policy, 27 Nov. 1789, p. 230. Details of other estimates of the rate of return on slave labour in differing sectors of the Cape economy during the VOC period are given in Worden, *Slavery*, pp. 64–85.
136. Rayner, 'Wine and Slaves', pp. 204–21.
137. C.P. Thunberg, *Travels*, 1, 233.
138. AR, Aanwinsten, No. LX 117, O.W. Falck *et al.*, Memorie van Consideratie over het beloop der lasten van het Gouvernement van de Kaap de Goede Hoop en aanwijzing van middelen tot dezelver vermindering, 3 May 1790.
139. Minutes of Council, 16 Dec. 1826, *RCC*, XXIX, 495.
140. O. Mentzel, *Description of the Cape of Good Hope* (Cape Town, 1944), II, 90; C 164, pp. 390–91, *Res*, 21 April 1783; figures obtained from CA C 650, Stellenbosch Dagregister, 1729–37.
141. J.L. Hattingh, ''n Ontleding', pp. 34–78; M. Rayner, 'Labourers in the vineyard'.
142. *Reports of De Chavonnes and his council and of Van Imhoff, on the Cape* VRS 1 (Cape Town, 1918), pp. 105–06.
143. C 171, *Res*, 19 April 1786, p. 159.
144. W.S. van Ryneveld, Replies, Articles 4 and 6.
145. P. Idenburgh, *De Kaap de Goede Hoop gedurende de laatste jaren van het Nederlandsch bewind* (Leiden, 1946), pp. 102–03.
146. 1/STB 3/11, unpaginated, testimony of Andries Nolte, reporting statement of the slave Slammat van Boegies, 14 Oct. 1759. Nolte then hit Slammat with a spade for 'daring to speak like that to me' and in the ensuing struggle Slammat attemped to stab him and then to set the farmhouse on fire.
147. *RCC*, XV, Proclamation of 18 March 1823, p. 340.
148. O.F. Mentzel, *A Geographical and Topographical Description of the Cape of Good Hope* (Cape Town, 1944), III, 165.
149. Thunberg, *Travels*, I, 244–45.
150. J. Barrow, *An account of travels into the interior of Southern Africa between the years 1770 and 1779* (London, 1801; reprint New York, 1968), I, 44.
151. For example, a slave *mandoor* worked on the farm of Martin Melck, one of the largest slaveowners in the VOC period. See R. Ross, 'Oppression, sexuality and slavery at the Cape of Good Hope', *Historical Reflections/ Réflexions Historiques* VI (1979), pp. 429–30.
152. 1/STB 3/12, unpaginated, testimony of Titus van de Caab, 1 May 1790; 1/ STB 3/12, unpaginated, testimony of Piet Claas, 12 April 1793.
153. Details of *knecht* numbers and periods of service in the eighteenth century are given in CJ 2870–2913, Council of Justice, Contracts, 1692–1790. For

analysis of some of them, see Worden, *Slavery*, p. 89.

154. J.S. Stavorinus, *Voyages to the East Indies* (London, 1798), II, 62.
155. For example, 1/STB 3/12, unpaginated, testimony of Johann Stegmann, 28 Nov. 1791.
156. N.L. de la Caille, *Travels at the Cape, 1751–3* (Cape Town and Rotterdam, 1976), p. 31.
157. R. Percival, *An account of the Cape of Good Hope* (London, 1804), p. 292.
158. For example, 1/STB 3/10, unpaginated, testimony of Joseph Borsz van Kippinge, July 1750.
159. *RCC,XV*, Proclamation of 18 March 1823, p. 340. An example of a slave who attempted to escape because he had 'obtained no food but much work from his master' was that of Augustus van Batavia, CJ 785, case 17, Dec. 1728.
160. *RCC, XXXV*, J.T. Bigge, Report upon the slaves and the state of slavery at the Cape of Good Hope, 5 April 1830, pp. 373–74; R.C.H. Shell, *De Meillon's people of colour: some notes on their dress and occupations* (Johannesburg, 1978), pp. 6–10.
161. V.M. Golovnin, *Detained in Simon's Bay* (Cape Town, 1964), p. 60.
162. The most notable of these studies being E. Genovese, *Roll, Jordan, Roll*.
163. VOC 4000, Isbrant Goske – XVII, 31 Aug. 1665, pp. 776v–77; C 412, XVII – Joan Bax, 21 Oct. 1676, p. 1260; VOC 4021, R. van Goens – XVII, 24 March 1685, p. 985v; C 83, Res, 14 Feb. 1788, pp. 216–17; VOC 4013, DR, 30 Aug. 1677, pp. 369v–70; VOC 4013, DR, 19 Dec. 1677, pp. 414–14v.
164. C 524, Hendrik Swellengrebel – XVII, 6 May 1739, pp. 309–10; Mentzel, *Description*, II, 125.
165. VOC 4006, P. Hackius – XVII, 22 Feb. 1671, p. 21; *Suid-Afrikaanse Argiefstukke, Belangrike Kaapse Dokumente, Memoriën en Instructiën, 1657–1699*, ed. A.J. Böeseken (Cape Town, 1966), Memorie van Matthias van den Brouch, 14 March 1670, p. 93.
166. For data from differing samples see F.R. Bradlow and M. Cairns, *The early Cape Muslims*, pp. 95–96. The importance of Cape-born slaves and those from Mozambique on the nineteenth century farms is indicated in Rayner, 'Wine and slaves', pp. 63–66.
167. For example, CJ 789, case 11, case of Baatjoe van Mandhaar, 3 Nov. 1757 and 1/STB 3/12, unpaginated, testimony of Jeptha van Madagascar, May 1791.
168. Most notably H.G. Gutman, *The black family in slavery and freedom, 1750–1925* (New York, 1977).
169. A. Sparrman, *A Voyage to the Cape of Good Hope*, VRS, 2nd series, vols. 6 and 7 (Cape Town, 1975, 1977), I, 102. Analysis of the tensions caused by the sexual disbalance of the slave population is given in Ross, 'Oppression', pp. 421–33.
170. W. Wright, *Slavery at the Cape of Good Hope* (London, 1831), pp. 15–16.
171. SO 3/20A, Article 51, Observations of the Protector of Slaves for the Report between June and December 1830.
172. For example, CJ 788, case 4, case of Julij van Boegies, 5 Feb. 1750.
173. Decree of 29 April/1 May 1766, *KP*, III, 64.
174. K. Elks, 'Crime and social control in Cape Town, 1830–1850',

unpublished paper, Fifth Workshop on the History of Cape Town, University of Cape Town, December 1985.

175. R. Shell, 'Establishment and spread of Islam at the Cape, 1652–1838', (BA Hons. thesis, University of Cape Town, 1974) and 'Rites and rebellion: Islamic conversion at the Cape, 1808–1915', *Studies in the History of Cape Town*, V (1984), 1–46.

176. Wright, *Slavery*, p. 4.

177. *RCC*, XXXV, p. 367.

178. *RCC*, XXV, 138; W. Bird, *State of the Cape of Good Hope in 1822*, p. 349, cited in Rayner, 'Labourers in the Vineyard', pp. 31–32.

179. W. Somerville, 'Cape of Good Hope', article in unknown encyclopedia ca. 1803/4, p. 405 (African Studies Library, University of Cape Town).

180. For example, E. Stockenstrom, *Vrystelling van die slawe* (Stellenbosch 1934), pp. 15–66; M.W. Spilhaus, *The First South Africans* (Cape Town and Johannesburg, n.d.), pp. 123–24; *500 Years*, ed. C.F.J. Muller (Pretoria and Cape Town, 1969), pp. 32, 58; De Kock, *Those in Bondage*.

181. Percival, *Account*, p. 292.

182. VOC 4264, Case of Johannes Kuuhn, Case 25, Oct. 1770.

183. E. Genovese, 'The treatment of slaves in different countries: problems in the applications of the comparative method' in *Slavery in the New World: a reader in comparative history*, ed. L. Foner and E.D. Genovese (Englewood Cliffs, 1969), p. 208.

184. Rayner, 'Labourers in the vineyard', pp. 20–21.

185. Sparrman, *Voyage*, I, 102.

186. *Ibid.*, I, 73.

187. VOC 4264, p. 4, Case of Thomas van Totocorijn, 28 Dec. 1769.

188. Percival, *Account*, pp. 284–85; Mentzel, *Description*, I, 116; Plakkaat of 3/5 Sept. 1754, *KP* III, 3.

189. C 650, Stellenbosch Dagregister, 6 Aug. 1736, pp. 774–75; CJ 2491, pp. 112–14, Bletterman to Council of Justice, 6 Sept. 1791; W.J. Burchell, *Travels in the interior of Africa* I (London, 1822–24), p. 34.

190. 1/STB 3/13, Case 11, Testimony of Dirk Hoffman, 24 Jan. 1794.

191. 1/STB 3/10, Testimony of April van Malabar, Dec. 1752, unpaginated.

192. CJ 3173, pp. 56–58, Report of the Council of Justice on the suicide of October van Ambon, Nov. 1760.

193. VOC 4264, Case of Johannes Kuuhn, Case 25, Oct. 1770.

194. Worden, *Slavery*, p. 108.

195. VOC 4264, Case of Jan Harmen Tome, Case 2, Jan. 1770.

196. For example, CJ 795, Case of Damon van Bougies *et. al.*, Nov. 1786, p. 38; 1/STB 3/8, Testimony of Manika van Bengal, 9 Jan. 1749, unpaginated; *RCC*, XXXV, Bigge, Report on Slavery, 374. A study of the severe maltreatment of labourers that could occur in the Bokkeveld is N. Penn, 'Anarchy and authority in the Koue Bokkeveld, 1739–1779: the banishing of Carel Buijtendag', *Kleio* XVII (1985), 24–43.

197. SO 3/1, Report of the Proceedings of the Registrar and Guardian of Slaves at the Cape of Good Hope during the half year ending 24 June 1827, unpaginated.

198. R. Ross, *Cape of Torments*, pp. 33–35.

199. Res, 21 March 1780, *Kaapse archiefstukken lopende over het jaar 1780*, ed. K.

Jeffreys (Cape Town 1928), pp. 33–35.
200. Batavian decree of 5–8 July 1642, *Nederlandsch-Indisch Plakkaatboek*, I, 573.
201. CJ 333, Documents in the criminal cases of Jan Botma and Jan Steenkamp, pp. 265–84; CJ 11, pp. 48–50, Minutes of the Council of Justice, 25 Aug. 1729.
202. For example, CJ 107, Copy of Minutes of the Council of Justice (Criminal), 24 Sept. 1767, pp. 178–79; VOC 4264, Case of Johannes Kuuhn, Case 16, Oct. 1770.
203. For example, CJ 784, Case of Antony van Malabar, Case 11, 1 Dec. 1718.
204. CJ 80, pp. 130–33, Minutes of the Council of Justice, 3 May 1798.
205. F. le Vaillant, *Travels from the Cape of Good Hope into the interior parts of Africa* (London, 1790), p. 102.
206. VOC 4365, Verslag der commissarissen-generaal, bijlagen 405–06.
207. W. Freund, 'Society and government in Dutch South Africa', p. 247.
208. M. Rayner, 'Slaves, slave owners and the British state: the Cape Colony, 1806–34', *The societies of Southern Africa in the 19th and 20th centuries* (University of London, Institute of Commonwealth Studies, XII (1981), p. 19.
209. CJ 799, Case of Carel Hendrik Lewald, Case 25, 24 Sept. 1801.
210. Rayner, 'Slaves, slave owners and the British state', pp. 26–27.
211. J. Mason, 'Slaveholder resistance to the amelioration of slavery at the Cape' (unpublished paper, Western Cape: Roots and Realities Conference, University of Cape Town: July 1986).
212. *Nederlandsch-Indisch Plakkaatboek*, I, 572–76 and IX, 572–92.
213. *KP*, III, 1–6.
214. *KP*, III, 2.
215. Van Ryneveld, Replies, Article 3.
216. R. Ross, 'The rule of law at the Cape of Good Hope in the eighteenth century', *Journal of Imperial and Commonwealth History* IX (1980), p. 13.
217. *RCC*, I, Council of Justice to Craig, 14 Jan. 1796, p. 304.
218. *Res* IV, 227 (1 June 1711); *Res* IV, 452 (16 July 1715).
219. *Res* VII, 333 (4 March 1727).
220. Mentzel, *Description*, II, 133.
221. Sparrman, *Voyage* I, 49; BO 222, p. 33, Sketches of the political and commercial history of the Cape of Good Hope; A 681, letter 16, letter of Mrs. Kindersley, Feb. 1765, p. 4; CJ 10, pp. 42–44, Minutes of the Council of Justice, 22 July 1728; CJ 2569, Council of Justice to Landdrost of Stellenbosch, 5 June 1738, p. 41; M.D. Teenstra, *De vruchten mijner werkzaamheden gedurende mijne reize over de Kaap de Goede Hoop* . . . VRS 24 (Cape Town, 1943), p. 194–96.
222. Van Riebeeck, *Daghregister* II, 294, 295, 370.
223. *Ibid*, II, 281 ff. and 371.
224. Moodie, *Record*, I, 374; *KP*, II, 38–39; BRD 12, 197–198, Petition of Cape farmers to Burgerraad, 1744; Rayner, 'Wine and Slaves', pp. 139–43.
225. *Reports of De Chavonnes*, p. 104; SO 3/1, Report of the Proceedings of the Registrar and Guardian of Slaves at the Cape of Good Hope during the half year ending 24 June 1827, unpaginated.
226. VOC 4013, DR, 8 Feb. 1677, p. 256.

227. CJ 2487, pp. 100–01, Landdrost of Stellenbosch to Council of Justice, 16 July 1778.
228. *Res*, III, 188–89; C 510, W. Helot to XVII, 4 April 1713, pp. 1059–63.
229. CJ 786, 34, Case of Moses van Balij, 18 Dec. 1738.
230. Sparrman, *Voyage*, I, 73.
231. *Res*, III, 184; *KP*, I, 246–47.
232. This was forbidden by various plakkaaten, as in 1687: VOC 4025, DR, 2 Jan. 1687, p. 138v; VOC 4014, Criminele Rollen, 1 Sept. 1678, p. 537v.
233. *Res*, III, 239.
234. *KP*, II, 209.
235. C 52, pp. 383–86, Res, 19 Aug. 1760.
236. C 22, pp. 101–02, Res, 4 March 1727.
237. *KP*, II, 54, 192; 1/STB 3/11, Testimony of Gerrit Marits, 8 June 1775, unpaginated; CJ 2491, Landdrost of Stellenbosch to Council of Justice, 6 Sept. 1791, pp. 112–14.
238. *KP*, I, 120–21 and III, 2; VOC 4135, Case of Clara Tant, Case 27, 7 July 1737.
239. For an early example of hunger forcing slaves to return, VOC 4013, DR, 15 July 1677, p. 341.
240. CJ 333, Criminele Process Stukken, 1729, Case of Jan Bronkhorst, p. 5, 19b, 25–29.
241. A notable instance occurred in 1688: VOC 4025, Simon van der Stel to XVII, 26 April 1688, pp. 26v–28.
242. A typical example is recounted in C 442, Landdrost of Stellenbosch to P.G. Noodt, 12 Feb. 1729, pp. 61–62.
243. Landdrost and heemraden of Swellendam to Governor Plettenberg, 25 October, 1774, Moodie, *Record*, III, 34.
244. C 656, pp. 388–96, Stellenbosch Dagregister, 7 Aug. 1780.
245. C 442, C. van Roeje *et. al.* to Landdrost of Stellenbosch, 25 Sept. 1730, pp. 1029–30.
246. Ross, *Cape of Torments*, pp. 54–72.
247. Teenstra, *Vruchten*, p. 89.
248. For example, C 652, pp. 197–98, Stellenbosch Daghregister, 25 July 1741.
249. Ross, *Cape of Torments*, pp. 38–53.
250. *Ibid*, pp. 81–88.
251. *Ibid*, pp. 88–95.
252. *Ibid*, pp. 73–80.
253. C 218, Resolutions of the Council of Policy, 24 Sept. 1793, pp. 271–75; 1/STB 10/7, Landdrost of Swellendam to Council of Policy, 12 July [?] 1793, unpaginated.
254. CJ 819, p 167, Case of Galant *et. al.*, 21 March 1825.
255. The descriptions of these rebellions are based on the full accounts in Teenstra, *Vruchten*, p. 197–215 and Ross, *Cape of Torments*, pp. 97–116. An evocative portrayal of the Bokkeveld uprising based on the archival sources is given in André Brink's novel, *Chain of Voices* (London, 1982).
256. Worden, *Slavery*, pp. 132–33; Mentzel, *Description*, I, 134–35; M.K.M. Lichtenstein, *Travels in Southern Africa in the years 1803–1806*, VRS, vols. 10–11 (Cape Town, 1928)
257. CJ 788, Case of Rachel van de Caab, Case 22, 31 Jan. 1754.

258. De Kock, *Those in Bondage*, pp. 195–97.
259. Worden, *Slavery*, pp. 134–36. The figures are drawn from CJ 3172–3175, Annotatie boeken en dokumente re verongelukktes en zelf-moorden, 1705–92.
260. 1/STB 3/11, Testimony of Andries Nolte, 14 Oct. 1759, unpaginated.
261. Van Ryneveld, Replies, Article 6.
262. *Reports of de Chavonnes*, pp. 103–07.
263. *Afrikaner political thought: analysis and documents, 1780–1850*, ed. A. du Toit and H. Giliomee (Cape Town 1983), pp. 31–34.
264. Teenstra, *Vruchten*, p. 196–97.
265. J.A. de Mist, *Memorandum concerning recommendations for the form and administration of government at the Cape of Good Hope, 1802*, VRS III (Cape Town, 1920), pp. 251–53. J.P. van der Merwe, *Die Kaap onder die Bataafse Republiek, 1803–1806*, (Amsterdam, 1926), pp. 272–82.
266. D.B. Davis, *Slavery and human progress* (New York and Oxford 1984), part two; M. Craton, 'Slave culture, resistance and the achievement of emancipation in the British West Indies, 1783–1838', *Slavery and British society, 1776–1846*, ed. J. Walvin (London,1982); M. Turner, *Slaves and missionaries: the disintegration of Jamaican slave society, 1787–1834* (Urbana, 1982).
267. M. Rayner, 'Slave worker and free worker': an analysis of the content and significance of British antislavery ideology and legislation, 1816–1834', unpub. paper.
268. *Remarks on the demoralizing influence of slavery, by a resident at the Cape of Good Hope* (London Society for the Mitigation and Gradual Abolition of Slavery throughout the British Dominions, 1828), p. 10.
269. M. Rayner, 'Wine and Slaves', pp. 274–94.
270. For examples of cases in which the Guardian of Slaves ignored illegal punishment of slaves by their owners, see I. Edwards, *Towards emancipation*. p. 127; J. Mason, 'The amelioration of slavery and slaveholder resistance at the Cape', unpub. paper, South African Research Seminar, Yale, rev. ed., Feb. 1986, pp. 35–36.
271. H.C. Botha, *John Fairbairn in South Africa* (Cape Town, 1984), pp. 83–84; R.L. Watson, 'Slavery and ideology: the South African case', *International Journal of African Historical Studies*, XX (1987), pp. 27–43.
272. Botha, *John Fairbairn*, pp. 84–85.
273. J. Fairbairn, *Five papers on the slave question* (Cape Town, 1831).
274. R.L. Watson, 'Religion and anti-slavery at the Cape of Good Hope', *Discovering the African past: Studies in honor of Daniel McCall* (Boston, forthcoming); Du Toit and Giliomee, *Afrikaner political thought*, pp. 34–35.
275. Rayner, 'Wine and Slaves', pp. 161–66, 260–74.
276. SO 1/6, Bergh – Rogers, 14 April 1831. J.Mason, 'The amelioration of slavery' assesses the significance of this resistance in the context of ameliorative legislation and slaveowner responses in the late 1820s and early 1830s.
277. E. Hengherr, 'Emancipation – and after', p. 31; *De Zuid-Afrikaan*, 21 and 28 Sept. 1832; *South African Commerical Advertiser*, 19–29 Sept. 1832.
278. Report of meeting held in Cape Town, *De Zuid-Afrikaan*, 28 March 1834.

279. I/CT 11/16, Colonial Office, Cape Town – Civil Commissioner for the Cape district, 21 Feb. 1834.
280. Rayner, 'Wine and Slaves', pp. 190–221.
281. Ross, *Cape of Torments*, pp. 115–116; Rayner, 'Wine and Slaves', pp. 156–68.
282. Rayner, 'Wine and Slaves', pp. 151–60.
283. Rayner, 'Slaves, slaveowners and the British state', p. 24.
284. N. Worden, 'Adjusting to emancipation: freed slaves and farmers in the Western Cape', *Essays in the social and economic history of the Western Cape*, ed. M. Simons and W.G. James (Cape Town, 1989); A. Ross, *John Philip (1775–1851): Missions, race and politics in South Africa* (Aberdeen, 1986), pp. 111–15.
285. This much neglected area of research has recently been analysed for the grain areas by John Marincowitz, 'Rural production and labour in the Western Cape, 1838–88, with special reference to the wheat growing districts' (Ph.D, thesis: University of London, 1985).
286. C. Bundy, 'The abolition of the Masters and Servants Act', *South African Labour Bulletin*, II (1975), pp. 37–46. R. Ross, 'Pre-industrial and industrial racial stratification in South Africa', *Racism and colonialism: essays on ideology and social structure*, ed. R. Ross (Leiden, 1982), pp. 85–88.
287. Act to amend the laws regulating rights and duties of masters, servants and apprentices, 4 June 1856, Statutes of the Cape of Good Hope passed by the First Parliament during the sessions 1854–1858 (Cape Town, 1863), pp. 148–73.

CHAPTER FOUR

Intergroup relations: Khoikhoi, settlers, slaves and free blacks, 1652–1795*

Richard Elphick and Robert Shell

In the first decades of the colony's history three groups, Khoikhoi, European settlers and slaves, were quite distinct from one another in religion, culture and physical appearance. Moreover, they differed in legal status: the slaves were unlike the European settlers and Khoikhoi in that they were the property of others; the Khoikhoi differed from both Europeans and slaves in being subject to their traditional authorities rather than to the laws and government of the Dutch East India Company.[1] But by 1795 a number of processes had eroded these boundaries. The most important of these were: (1) the incorporation of the Khoikhoi into the European-dominated society as wage-labourers subject to Dutch law, (2) the conversion of slaves and free blacks to Christianity or Islam, (3) miscegenation and intermarriage among groups, (4) the manumission of slaves and the consequent emergence of an important new group – the free blacks,† (5) cultural exchanges among groups. Chapter one of this book dealt with the incorporation of Khoikhoi. The present chapter covers the remaining four processes.

*   We are grateful to James Armstrong, Stanley Engerman, Anna Böeseken, Hermann Giliomee, Keith Gottshalk, Martin Legassick, Robert Ross, Kenneth Hughes and Michael Whisson, whose comments on earlier drafts have greatly improved this chapter. We are also indebted to J.A. Heese for his careful critique of parts of the chapter and his generosity in sharing his data with us.
†   By 'free blacks' we mean all free persons wholly or partially of African (but not Khoikhoi) or Asian descent. This was roughly what the term meant in the Company period, though its boundaries were shifting and imprecise. Apparently the VOC never applied the term 'free black' to either the Khoikhoi or the Bastaards, the other major categories of free people of colour. It was, however, applied to Chinese. A.J. Böeseken has found the first usage of the term 'free black' at the Cape in 1671, though the status which it denoted existed much earlier: 'The Free Blacks during the 17th Century' (unpublished paper), p. 9.

We shall try to determine how far these processes increased or decreased the access of Khoikhoi, slaves and free blacks to the legal and socio-economic benefits of the colonial system. In other words, we shall attempt to measure the 'openness'‡ or fluidity of early Cape society. In this inquiry we shall be concerned not only with significant changes that occurred in the course of time, but also with geographical variations. We shall develop the notion, by no means original with us, that intergroup relations increasingly diverged in three distinct regions of the Cape Colony. These were the port city of Cape Town and its immediate environs, tied to the vicissitudes of international trade and the fortunes of the *VOC*; the settled, arable, slaveowning area of the southwestern Cape; and the pastoral trekboer region. These regions with their distinctive, although interconnected, economies developed substantially different social structures and cultures.

Religion

Until recently, I.D. MacCrone's *Race Attitudes in South Africa*, which first appeared in 1937, has dominated the interpretation of intergroup relations in the VOC period. Through textbooks and popular histories his views have molded the impressions many South Africans have of their country's early history. MacCrone stated that, at first Cape society was divided along religious lines (i.e., Christian vs non-Christian, either Muslim or 'heathen') and that in the eighteenth century this cleavage was increasingly associated in the colonists' minds with a cleavage by race (i.e., 'whites' vs 'non-whites'). In time the racial cleavage overshadowed its religious counterpart, largely because of the isolated and embattled position of colonists on the frontier.

MacCrone was not denying that seventeenth-century Europeans at the Cape were prejudiced against other groups. Rather, he was asserting that they imposed legal disabilities on other groups because of their religion, not because of their race. This proposition led naturally to the

‡   Frank Tannenbaum's pioneering comparative work, *Slave and Citizen* (New York, 1947) was the first attempt to apply the sociological concept of 'openness' to slave societies. Comparing Brazilian and North American slavery, Tannenbaum concluded that Brazilian slaves had much greater opportunities for legal freedom and upward mobility than their counterparts in the American South. We have combined Tannenbaum's concept of 'openess' with I.D. MacCrone's observations about the extent of fluidity or 'flux' in early Cape society. See his *Race Attitudes in South Africa: Historical, Experimental and Psychological Studies* (Johannesburg, 1937), pp. 70 and 73.

corollary that if one changed one's religion one could change one's legal and social position in society. As MacCrone put it: 'a non-European at the Cape, once he had been baptized, was immediately accepted as a member of the Christian community and, as such, was entitled to his freedom, if a slave.'[2] This is a crucial characterisation of Cape society, one which suggests that it was comparatively 'open' in the earlier decades. This would especially be the case if, as G.M. Theal (but not MacCrone) asserted, 'in those days [i.e. the seventeenth century] nearly every one believed it his duty to have his slave children baptized, and hence those who were born in this colony usually became free.'[3]

Our first task, then, is to assess how easy it was for a slave or Khoikhoi to be baptised. Adult candidates for baptism had to show some formal knowledge of the doctrines of the Christian faith. Knowledge sufficient to satisfy the clergy would not be likely to spread spontaneously. Hence the speed at which Christianity grew at the Cape was largely dependent on the zeal of Europeans. However, other than the Moravian Georg Schmidt, who won a few converts in the interior at Genadendal between 1737 and 1744,[4] there were no fulltime missionaries independent of the congregational structure of the Dutch Reformed Church before the 1790s. Some strands of Calvinist theology were indifferent or even hostile to missions, and the Reformed churches had no tradition of clerical orders independent of local congregations, such as those from which mission societies had developed in Roman Catholicism. Nevertheless, the Dutch Reformed Church did conduct successful missions in this period; for example, in Formosa, Ceylon and Amboina. It did so, however, at the request and expense of the VOC, which wanted to combat Islam and Roman Catholicism in these regions.[5] These geopolitical motives did not apply to the Cape.

Despite the absence of funds for proselytisation a number of early Company officials and *predikanten* (ministers), influenced by precedents in Portuguese and Dutch spheres of the Indies, hoped that the Khoikhoi would adopt both Christianity and the Dutch language and culture. The first commander at the Cape, Jan van Riebeeck, promoted these ends by raising Khoikhoi children in his own home. One of his protegées, the famous Eva, learned fluent Dutch and Portuguese, adopted western clothes and customs, and became a practising Christian. After Van Riebeeck's departure in 1662 she married the talented Danish surgeon Pieter van Meerhoff in a Christian wedding financed by the Company. On her husband's death a few years later Eva became a prostitute and drunkard. Wandering between two cultures in which she felt equally alien, she abandoned her children to the mercies of the Council of Policy.

The Council imprisoned her at various times on Robben Island where, in 1674, she died.[6]

Along with the very public tragedy of Van Riebeeck's most promising assimilée, there were several other seventeenth-century Khoikhoi who declared their allegiance to Christianity and Dutch culture, but who were not baptised. One committed suicide, and others renounced their new allegiance. These failures discouraged the Company from further ventures of proselytisation and planned assimilation, though several clergy in the seventeenth century tried to learn the Khoikhoi language and engaged in minor, and usually unsuccessful, proselytisation alongside their pastoral duties.[7] By the eighteenth century the inaction of the Dutch Reformed Church had hardened into a tradition. As Anders Sparrman observed in the 1770's:

> There is no doubt, but that the Hottentots might be easily converted to the Christian faith: but it is much to be doubted, whether any body will ever trouble themselves with the conversion of these plain honest people, unless it should appear to have more connexion that it seems to have at present with political advantages.[8]

VOC schools also exposed a tiny handful of Khoikhoi to European culture and religion. These schools, however, were far more influential in the Christianisation of slaves. In the first decade of the colony Van Riebeeck's brother-in-law, Pieter van der Stael, founded a school for slaves, whose primary objects were the teaching of the Dutch language and Christian beliefs. Other spasmodic attempts followed until, in the wake of Commissioner H.A. van Reede's visit to the Cape in 1685, the VOC founded a slave school which lasted to the end of the Company period. In this institution the teachers were often slaves or free blacks. The school, however, affected only Company slaves in or near Cape Town. In the rural area some freeburghers, who often hired knechts to educate their own children, possibly had their knechts teach their slaves as well; but only two contracts have been found in which this duty was specified. By 1779 a total of eight schools in the colony (mostly urban) reported 696 pupils of whom, however, only 82 were slave children.[9] Clearly then, although Christianisation was Company policy, the slave-holders were not overly zealous in educating or Christianising their slaves.

In this light we may now examine the contention that baptism was a passport to freedom and acceptance into European society. As for the Khoikhoi, so far as is now known, Eva was the only full-blooded Khoikhoi baptised into the Reformed faith at the Cape in the Company period.[10] Thus for Khoikhoi the alleged benefits of baptism were purely academic. The more challenging aspect of MacCrone's view relates to the manumission of slaves, namely the proposition, earlier stated by G.M. Theal, that 'even in the case of pure blacks baptism and a profession of Christianity were always at this time [the seventeenth century] considered substantial grounds for claiming emancipation.'[11]

It is doubtless true that the Church's teachings had implications which, if taken seriously, would have made it hard for Christian colonists to hold their fellow Christians in bondage. The authoritative Council of Dort, which in 1618 had laid down basic doctrines and procedures for the Dutch Reformed Church, clearly supported the right of a Christian slave to his or her freedom:

> [It was resolved] that those who had been baptised ought to enjoy equal right of liberty with the other Christians and ought not to be handed over again to the powers of the heathens by their Christian masters either by sale or by any other transfer of possession.[12]

The overlapping principles of Dort (namely that Christian slaves should be freed and not be sold) periodically pricked the consciences of clergy concerned with Cape practice. In a letter received at the Cape in 1683 the Church Council at Batavia stated that slave children baptised at their masters' request were thereby freed and had to be brought up as children of their former owners.

In 1708 the Rev. E.F. Le Boucq roundly criticised the clergy of the colony for baptising as indiscriminately as did Roman Catholic priests, and denounced the colonial authorities for allowing that 'baptised slaves, and their baptised children, even if they are church members, are frequently alienated here and used as slaves, which is contrary to Christian liberty.'[13] However, these clerical pronouncements lacked the force of law. Indeed, it seems that prior to 1770 no regulations or laws endeavoured to implement the Dort principles at the Cape. It is true that two influential commissioners – Goske in 1671 and Van Reede in 1685 – did declare that slave children of European fathers had the right of manumission, and Van Reede laid down regulations that they should be freed, males at age twenty-five and females at age twenty-two. However, these regulations (which in any event put primary emphasis on ancestry and the religion of the slave's father rather than on the slave's own religious profession) were ineffectual.[14]

The effect of the Dort principles – probably the source of Theal's and MacCrone's theories – can best be tested by compiling figures on slave baptisms at the Cape and then comparing them with figures for manumissions. According to one (incomplete) series of data, 2,012 adult and young slaves were baptised between 1665 and 1795,[15] an average of fifteen every year. An analysis of these baptisms may be seen in Table 4.1.

Table 4.1   Baptism of slaves in the Cape district, 1665–1795 *
(*percentage in parentheses*)

Periods	Privately-owned slave children baptised	Government-owned slave children baptised	Privately-owned slave adults baptised	Government owned slave adults baptised	Totals
1665–1678	23(**)	30(**)	2(**)	0(**)	55
1679–1695	49(**)	172(10.1)	11(**)	44(0.65)	276
1696–1712	32(2.4)	102(6.0)	1(**)	2(0.02)	137
1713–1729	82(2.7)	244(14.3)	1(**)	0(**)	327
1730–1746	90(0.9)	352(20.7)	30(0.04)	6(0.09)	478
1747–1763	34(0.3)	231(13.6)	38(0.05)	0(**)	303
1764–1780	1(**)	194(11.4)	33(0.03)	0(**)	228
1781–1795	8(0.3)	192(13.7)	8(**)	0(**)	208
Totals	319	1,517	124	52	2,012

*Double asterisks (**) indicate that figures are unavailable or impossible to compute.

As is apparent from Table 4.1, the overwhelming number of baptisms were of children and need not necessarily have reflected profound inculcation of Christian teaching. The Company took its obligations far more seriously than did the burghers, baptising an average of twelve slaves a year. The rate of Company baptisms remained very high during the eighteenth century. When we consider the size of the Company's slave force (about 600) and the number of slave children (about 100: see ch. 3, p. 124), it seems likely that a majority but certainly not all of the Company's slave children were baptised. The rates for privately owned slaves, by contrast, were extremely low and declined throughout the period, although the absolute number of slaves in the colony was increasing.

Were all baptised slaves manumitted? For the seventeenth century we do not yet have complete statistics. However, A.J. Böeseken, after a search of the Deeds Office, has found records of only about 100 manumissions in the seventeenth century, mostly after 1685. We know, too, that at least 331 slaves were baptised between 1665 and 1695.[16] Thus it is clear that the majority of baptised slaves were not freed in this period, as MacCrone's thesis would suggest. As for the eighteenth century, during the years 1713–95 there were 1,075 manumissions and 1,535 slave baptisms. The close correspondence of these figures is illusory: almost all the baptised slaves belonged to the Company, and almost all the manumitted slaves belonged to private parties. To illustrate further that the same slaves were not both baptised and manumitted, we have undertaken spot checks of specific decades. To take one example, between 1760 and 1769 the Company baptised forty-seven Madagascan slaves, yet manumitted none.

Moreover, not all manumitted slaves had been baptised. For the period 1715–91 we have considerable information on every manumitted slave given in the *requesten* to the Council of Policy, which supervised manumissions. In this period 1,075 slaves were freed and in only 8.4 per cent of these cases was it argued in the slave's favour that he or she had been baptised: a small proportion were in fact Muslim.[17] Thus for the eighteenth century we have a cogent, two-pronged argument against the notion that Christianity was an 'escape hatch' to freedom: most baptised slaves were not freed, most manumitted slaves apparently had not been baptised. As for the seventeenth century, for which data are less precise, MacCrone's and Theal's views now seem questionable, though all relevant evidence has not yet been analysed.

In 1770 the implications of Christian doctrine for a slave society were for the first time realised in legislation affecting the Cape. In that year the government in Batavia ruled, firstly, that Christians were bound to educate their slaves in Christianity and to allow baptism to those who wished it; secondly, that:

> . . . such [slaves] as may have been confirmed in the Christian Religion shall never be sold, but their Master be under the obligation of emancipating them in the event of their departure from this country or at their death, or to give them away or bequeath them to others under the same obligation . . . or, on the other hand to allow all such Slaves to purchase their freedom themselves at prime cost or by taxation if born in the family or presents from others . . .[18]

One should note that this statute did not oblige the colonists to free their slaves immediately after their baptism. Nonetheless, it moved closer to the Synod of Dort's identification of Christianity and freedom. Moreover, it unambiguously stated that owners should not sell their Christian slaves.

The tensions between Christianity and slavery now became stronger at the Cape. In practice this did not result in higher manumission rates, but it did result in lower baptism rates. Slave-owners were now aware that Christianity posed a threat to their property: even though they had never been overly energetic in attending 'to a circumstance of so little consequence in their eyes as the religion of their slaves',[19] they now had added incentive to neglect their slaves' formal Christian instruction. In October of 1772 Anders Sparrman observed in the hinterland:

> About ten o'clock I took shelter from the rain in a farmhouse, where I found the female slaves singing psalms, while they were at their needle work. Their master, being possessed with a zeal for religion quite unusual in this country, had prevailed with them to adopt this godly custom; but with the spirit of oeconomy [sic] which universally prevails among these colonists, he had not permitted them to be initiated into the community of Christians by baptism; since by that means, according to the laws of the land, they would have obtained their freedom and he would have lost them from his service.[20]

By the beginning of the nineteenth century it had become obvious to travellers that the spread of Christianity had been inhibited by the colonists' knowledge that they could not sell their Christian slaves, and by fears that they might lose them altogether.[21] By 1800 the benches in the *Groote Kerk*, which in recent decades had been set aside for Christian slaves, were empty.[22] Twelve years later the Rev. M.C. Vos, an early evangelist among the slaves, complained to the Cape authorities that:

> . . . there is [a] great obstacle in this country to the progress of Christianity . . . that a Slave who is baptised may not be sold. This circumstance is the occasion that the Proprietors of Slaves, who may perhaps possess truly Christian hearts and entertain a desire of them becoming incorporated in the Church of our Lord Jesus Christ, object to their being baptized.[23]

Consequently the British Governor, Sir John Cradock, promptly repealed the 1770 statute which, he observed, 'had not been attended with the desired, but the opposite effect.'[24]

We may conclude, then, that in the Company period the spread of Christianity among privately owned slaves was slow, and among the Khoikhoi negligible, and that its presence at the Cape did not narrow the social and cultural gulf between settlers and officials on the one hand and Khoikhoi and slaves on the other.

The generally Eurocentric historiography of the early Cape has overemphasised the role of Christianity and neglected that of Islam. An Islamic community appeared at the Cape in the seventeenth century, grew slowly in the eighteenth century and spectacularly in the nineteenth. This growth was not solely due to the transplanting of Muslims from Indonesia, as has sometimes been supposed.[25] Rather it resulted chiefly from internal proselytisation at the Cape, especially in Cape Town. Conversion to Islam was encouraged by the slaves' virtual exclusion from Christianity, but was also apparently due to the ministry of the Muslim *imams* who, unlike the Christian clergy, identified with the black population and performed marriages and funerals which the slaves could not obtain in Christian churches.[26]

The earliest mention of Islamic conversion among the slaves comes from the late seventeenth century, when the great leader of Bantamese resistance to the Dutch, Sheikh Yussuf, and his retinue of forty-nine Muslims were interned near modern Faure, twenty-five km from the port. When Yussuf died on 23 May 1699, the local officials observed that, as a result of his stay at the Cape, 'these Mohammedans are multiplying rapidly and increasing in numbers.'[27]

In 1747 another important Muslim leader, Said Alochie of Mocha, was brought to Cape Town and sentenced to work on Robben Island for ten years. Mocha was formerly the chief port of the Yemen, a flourishing export centre of coffee and Islam. According to the *bandiet* (convict) rolls, Said was a 'Mohammedan priest'. He served his sentence on Robben Island before being brought to Cape Town, where he was employed as a policeman; this might explain the pervasive legend among Cape Muslims that he entered the 'locked and guarded' slave quarters at night 'bearing a Koran under his arm'. This and other more anecdotal traditions attest to the considerable religious influence of Said, who was probably the first recognised imam in Cape Town.[28]

A further important figure in the establishment of Islam was Abdullah Kadi Abdu Salaam, 'a prince of Tidore'. Tidore was an intensively Islamised sultanate in the Moluccas. Exiled to the Cape in 1767, Abdullah became known as Tuan Guru (a Malay-Hindi combination of 'Lord' and 'Teacher'). One of his first accomplishments was writing a copy of the Koran from memory, a volume still in the possession of the Cape Muslim community.[29] In 1781 Tuan Guru completed a further work dealing with Islamic law, customs and mystical rites. This illuminated book, written in Malay with Arabic characters, should, once translated, provide a useful insight into the embryonic Muslim community in the eighteenth century. Tuan Guru clearly assumed leadership of the Cape Muslims: in his will, dated 1801, he calls himself 'Kadi' (judge or leader).[30]

In 1772 Charles Thunberg attended a Muslim ceremony in Cape Town. His description of the 'Prince from Java' might well be of Tuan Guru:

> On the 28th June, the Javanese here celebrated their new year. For this purpose they had decorated an apartment in a house with carpets, that covered the cieling, [sic] walls, and floor. At some distance from the farthest wall an altar was raised . . . The women, who were all standing or sitting near the door were neatly dressed, and the men wore nightgowns of silk or cotton. Frankincense was burned. The men sat cross-legged on the floor, dispersed all

over the room. Several yellow wax candles were lighted up. Many of the assembly had fans . . . Two priests were distinguished by a small conical cap from the rest, who wore hankerchiefs tied round their heads in the form of a turban. About eight in the evening the service commenced, when they began to sing loud and soft alternately, sometimes the priests alone, at other times the whole congregation. After this a priest read out of the great book that lay on the cusion [sic] before the altar, the congregation at times reading aloud after him. I observed them reading after the oriental manner, from right to left, and imagined it to be the Alcoran that they were reading, the Javanese being mostly Mahometans. Between the singing and reciting, coffee was served up in cups, and the principal man of the congregation at intervals accompanied their singing on the violin. I understood afterwards, that this was a prince from Java, who had opposed the interests of the Dutch East India Company, and for that reason had been brought from his native country to the Cape, where he lives at the Company's expense.[31]

By 1799 the Muslim community felt large enough to require a mosque, and petitioned the authorities for permission to build one.[32] The same year Mirzu Abu Taleb Khan, a Persian visitor to Cape Town, provided a further tantalising glimpse of this growing group:

Among them [the free blacks] I met with many pious good Mussulmans, several of whom possessed considerable property. I had the pleasure of forming an acquaintance here with Sheikh Abdulla, the son of Abd al Aziz, a native of Mecca, who having come to the Cape on some commercial adventure, married the daughter of one of the Malays and settled here. He was very civil, introduced me to all his friends and anticipated all my wishes.[33]

By the turn of the nineteenth century, then, there was a flourishing Muslim community in Cape Town which included both slaves and free blacks (with wealthier members of the latter forming the leadership), and which enjoyed some contacts with the great centres of Islam. Unfortunately we cannot determine the size of this community before 1825, when it numbered 2,167.[34] But long before this the authorities were concerned about the spread of Islam. In the same regulations which forbade the sale of Christian slaves there was also an article which outlawed the Muslim imams' practice of circumcising slaves – suggestive evidence that conversion was already fairly widespread.[35]

Thus between 1652 and 1795 two great world religions appeared at the Cape. Among rural slaves the impact of Christianity was superficial, that of Islam negligible. Neither religion profoundly affected the Khoikhoi, if we may ignore Schmidt's short-lived mission. Both religions had their greatest impact in Cape Town. There Christianity, the classical religion of slaves, made some progress, particularly among the Company's slaves, but the converts' understanding and commitment were possibly quite shallow: only a handful of slaves appear on the communion rolls of the Cape Church.[36] The spread of Islam was more spontaneous, arguably more profound, but also limited to the urban slaves and free blacks.

Yet, for all its limitations, the proselytisation of the monotheistic religions contributed greatly to the regionalisation of the Cape Colony: it distanced the port town from its hinterland and enhanced its character as a residency city, whose culture was closer in spirit to Dutch Asia than to the African continent on which it stood.

Miscegenation and intermarriage

A second possible avenue of advancement for slaves and Khoikhoi was miscegenation or intermarriage with the dominant European settlers and officials; theoretically such sexual unions might result in greater rights or opportunities for the black partners or their offspring. This theme of intermixture has caused several painful debates in the race-conscious historiography of South Africa, particularly where it has probed the 'purity' of the Afrikaners' ancestry. We must get beyond the simplistic question of whether there was miscegenation in the Cape Colony – there was – and determine as accurately as possible when, where and between which groups it occurred. The rates of miscegenation and intermarriage can help us identify the development of self-conscious groups and measure their sense of social distance from other groups.

From the beginning, concubinage was illegal in the colony under the general Statutes of India. Moreover, in 1678 the Company issued a proclamation forbidding all kinds of concubinage on pain of penalties varying from a 50 rixdollar fine to thrashing and three years of hard labour on Robben Island. In 1681 the VOC issued prohibitions forbidding Europeans to attend parties with slave women or to enter the Company's slave lodge. The VOC reissued both these regulations in subsequent decades,[37] but there is little evidence that they were enforced.

On one occasion – an inland expedition – a special regulation was issued forbidding sexual relations between Europeans and female Khoikhoi. Such liaisons were, however, comparatively rare in the seventeenth century. Eva was the only full-blooded Khoikhoi to marry a European, and among prostitutes who hung around the docks, slaves vastly outnumbered the few Khoikhoi. The Khoikhoi women, except for a few outcasts without family, were still subject to the disciplines of their fathers and husbands and to the stringent traditional penalties (often death) for adultery. In the seventeenth century, Khoikhoi women were much less available and much less coercible than slave women. Moreover, the European male colonists preferred the Asian and 'mixed-race' women and looked upon the Khoikhoi, with their animal skins and grease, with distaste.[38]

When historians discuss miscegenation at the Cape, they are usually referring to the Company slave lodge which, according to numerous travellers, was the leading brothel in Cape Town in the seventeenth and eighteenth centuries. Otto Mentzel wrote that each evening European soldiers and sailors publicly entered the slave lodge; at 8 p.m. the VOC officials locked the gates and counted the slaves, and by 9 p.m. all European visitors had to leave. The men entertained the slave women in the taverns of the town in return for their favours and sometimes gave them hammocks and clothes superior to the Company issue. Even when semi-permanent unions existed between male and female slaves, the men often encouraged their women to take a European lover to augment the couples' income.[39]

Company officials often provided statistical evidence of miscegenation among Company slaves. In 1671 Commissioner Isbrand Goske reported that fully three-quarters of the children born to the Company slave women were of mixed parentage. In 1685 Commissioner van Reede took an exact census which revealed only slightly less sensational results: of ninety-two Company slave children under twelve years, forty-four (or almost half) apparently had European fathers. So appalled was Van Reede that he issued a number of instructions to stop further miscegenation (even through marriage) and at the same time to foster the rapid manumission and Christianisation of the existing mixed-bloods and their absorption into the European community.[40] Historians have paid much attention to his guidelines, but the Cape authorities seem never to have seriously implemented them. Indeed, Company officialdom was so lax in enforcing its regulations that visitors often believed it was conniving in the general licentiousness.[41] A complete muster of Company slaves was taken on 1 January 1693 and revealed that Van Reede's regulations had accomplished little. Though the pure-bloods outnumbered the mixed-bloods by 237 to 85, among school children 29 were mixed and 32 pure; among infants under 3 years old the mixed-bloods outnumbered the pure-bloods 23 to 15.[42]

A number of cautionary points must be raised lest we exaggerate the significance of this evidence. Firstly, we must remember that the slaves in the lodge comprised an ever diminishing proportion of Cape slaves, equalling only 3 per cent of the private slave force by 1795. Secondly, the slave lodge was also unrepresentative in that so many slaves were housed there in close proximity. Moreover, because of its central location in Cape Town, it naturally drew the attention of travellers and colonists. One cannot conclude from the travellers' evidence that there was widespread prostitution in the lodge in all eras, nor may we extrapolate from the slave lodge in Cape Town to the slave population at large.

It is usually assumed that the high male to female ratios among the European settlers caused widespread miscegenation and intermarriage at the Cape. In assessing this view we must make a clear distinction between the Company and freeburgher sectors of the European community. Company servants rarely brought their wives to the Cape: in 1664 only 6 of 178 employees resident at the Cape had done so.[43] Furthermore, thousands of single Company soldiers and sailors disembarked each year at Cape Town for ten days to three weeks of recreation. For example, from 1701 to 1710 an average of 68 ships visited per year, in the 1780s an everage of 133. On each of these ships were 70 to 300 or more sailors, most of them with money in their pockets and only a brief time to spend it.[44] Accordingly, much of Cape miscegenation took place among the overwhelmingly male Company employees, both resident and transient, in Cape Town. The situation among the burghers was more complicated, as Table 4.2 will show.

Table 4.2   Sex ratios: Adult freeburgher population by districts[45]
(*Figures indicate number of men per 100 women, rounded to the nearest ten*)

Year	Cape district	Stellenbosch	Drakenstein	Swellendam	Entire colony
1660	290	–	–	–	–
1679	160	–	–	–	–
1690	220	280	350	–	260
1711	140	190	180	–	160
1730	130	170	160	–	150
1750	130	170	160	180	150
1770	120	180	140	160	140

The ratios in Table 4.2 show clear regional variation. In each newly settled district males predominated heavily, but these high sex ratios settled down in the course of time, although never reaching parity. Only in the Cape district did the ratios seem to approach parity by 1770, but we should remember that Cape Town had many male Company servants whose numbers were not recorded.

In general the male to female ratios were not very high for a colony of settlement, somewhat closer to those of New England (about 120 in the seventeenth century) than to colonial Virginia (beween 300 and 400 in its first hundred years.)[46] Robert Ross has estimated that 11 per cent of the European males at the Cape could not possibly have found European wives and thus must have found sexual expression elsewhere. But 11 per cent of surplus males is not high, even for non-colonial regions: John Hajnal calculated a 10 per cent celibacy rate as the average norm for early modern Europe.[47] Ross's figures, then, do not allow us to assume high rates of miscegenation in all parts of the colony at all times. They do, however, confirm what common sense suggests: that in any period the highest sex ratios among Europeans would be in the most remote and newly settled districts and (largely because of the anomalous Company sector) in Cape Town itself.

Our findings for Cape Town are confirmed by analyses of the literary sources on miscegenation compiled by Hoge and Franken.[48] Their seventeenth- and eighteenth-century evidence makes it abundantly clear that in Cape Town some burghers as well as Company servants consorted with black prostitutes and concubines. In the eighteenth century, according to Mentzel, it was common for teenage sons of wealthy, respectable Cape families to 'get entangled with a handsome slave girl belonging to the household' and get her pregnant. In such cases the girl 'is sternly rebuked for her wantonness', but as for the boy 'the offence is venial in the public estimation. It does not hurt [his] prospects; his escapade is a source of amusement, and he is dubbed a young fellow who has shown the stuff he is made of.'[49]

Closely related to miscegenation was intermarriage between European men and black women. Such marriages were very rare, and in some cases illegal, in colonies in the Americas.[50] The Cape authorities, however, did not discourage them and they took place steadily throughout the period. Three of the first interracial marriages (1656, 1658 and 1669) were between white men and Bengali women. Bengalis continued to be the favourite pure-blood marriage partners in the seventeenth century, but Cape-born women, many of whom were likely of mixed ancestry, rapidly overtook their Asian counterparts. On the basis of Hoge's *Personalia*, Heese has found 191 Germans who, between 1660 and 1705, married or lived with women who were not pure-blood Europeans; of the 191 women, 114 were Cape-born, 29 were Bengali, 43 were from other Asian regions, and only 5 were Madagascans or Africans.

One of the first burghers to marry a black woman, Arnoldus Willemsz Basson of Wessel, was among the prosperous farmers of the early colony, in 1686 reporting 40 head of cattle, 600 sheep and 16,000 grape vines. Once the authorities opened up the Stellenbosch and Drakenstein districts, a few of the new settlers took black wives with them so that in 1695, of twelve obviously mixed marriages listed on the rolls, ten were in the new districts. However, early in the eighteenth century a new pattern emerged which would last to the end of the Company period; namely, that almost all men whose wives were readily identifiable as black lived in the Cape district, were very poor, and had Cape-born wives, some of whom were probably of mixed descent. By 1770, for example, the opgaaf recorded eighteen such couples: sixteen of them lived in the Cape district, all but one were relatively poor (though many still owned slaves), and all but four of the men had wives designated 'van de Kaap'. Of the four without Cape-born wives, two had wives from Bengal, two from Batavia.[51]

While it is important to note that the authorities tolerated mixed marriages at the Cape, one should not exaggerate the frequency of such unions. Hoge argued that they were 'very numerous' and 'increased markedly' in the eighteenth century, and a much-quoted 'anonymous researcher' estimated that 10 per cent of all Cape marriages between 1700 and 1795 were mixed.[52] A final calculation of the correct figure must await more thorough research than has yet been done. But even if later investigators should support a figure as high as 10 per cent, this would probably include not only marriages with pure-blood Asians and Africans, but also the (arguably more numerous) marriages of Europeans with women themselves of mixed blood. Marriages with pure-blood blacks are easiest to spot in the marriage records because such women tended to have toponyms (e.g., van Bengalen, van Batavia) in addition to, or instead of, 'European' names. A preliminary survey of selected years in the Cape church records suggests that the number of marriages with pure-blood Asians and Africans was far lower than 10 per cent (see Table 4.3).

The European males involved in marriages with blacks originated partly in the Company sector. We do not have information on all of them, but nine or possibly ten were Company servants. Among these were one merchant, one widowed clerk, one messenger of the Council of Justice, one sailor, four soldiers, and two unspecified Company servants. Among the others were seven Cape district burghers (three widowed) and two burghers from the Stellenbosch district.

Table 4.3   Marriages at the Cape Church[53]
(percentage of total marriages in parenthesis)

Periods	Obviously mixed marriages	Marriages between free blacks	Marriages between persons with 'European' names	Totals
1665–1695	5(2.3)	12(5.5)	202(92.2)	219
1696–1712	6(2.9)	19(9.0)	185(88.1)	210
1713–1744	15(2.4)	37(5.9)	571(91.7)	623
1780–1784	7(1.8)	9(0.2)	370(95.9)	386
Totals	33(2.3)	77(5.4)	1,328(92.4)	1,438

It may be significant that these Stellenbosch burghers chose to get married in Cape Town. A spot check of the Stellenbosch church records (1700–09, 1740–49, 1780–88) revealed no obviously interracial marriages at all.[54] If this is typical of rural areas, as seems likely, the low percentages cited in Table 4.3 should be even lower for the colony as a whole. The low rates of intermarriage in agricultural areas parallel our impressions that miscegenation and concubinage in these areas were comparatively rare. Hoge cites a number of examples from Stellenbosch,[55] and there were doubtless many others. But travellers paid less attention to miscegenation and intermarriage in the rural southwestern Cape than in Cape Town and the more remote districts. It is possible that in the settled agricultural regions near Cape Town white family structure was stable, and that moral attitudes against concubinage consequently stiffened, distancing burghers of these areas from the sexual habits of the port dwellers and the rougher morality of some of the trekboers (ch. 2, p. 98). It is of course very difficult to build an argument on silence; but this hypothesis would fit in well with our regional breakdown of the sex ratios among Europeans and with comparative surveys of miscegenation in New World societies.[56]

There was apparently little sexual activity in any district between black males and European females. Heese has found references to only six such unions,[57] and the authorities ruthlessly punished this sort of concubinage. In 1695 Jan of Batavia, a manumitted slave, had sexual relations with Adriana van Jaarsveld, a girl of fourteen living at the home of Jan's employer in Drakenstein. Though there was evidence of the girl's general promiscuity, the court sentenced Jan to be scourged and sent in chains to Mauritius for twenty years' hard labour. In 1713 Anthony of Mozambique was convicted of raping the fourteen-year-old daughter of his master. 'This being an execrable enormity and godless deed committed by the prisoner, a heathen on a European girl,' . . . the court sentenced Anthony to be bound to a cross and to have his flesh pinched from his body by hot irons; his body was then to be broken without *coup de grâce*, decapitated, and finally exposed to the birds; his head was to be affixed to a pole where he had first insulted the girl. In 1732 a similar sentence was inflicted on another slave, Hendrik of Nias.[58] The barbarity of these sentences was totally inconsistent with the mild, and rarely enforced, penalties against concubinage or rape between European males and black females.

What, then, was the sexual outlet for black males? The male-female ratio among blacks was even more unbalanced than among Europeans, and for the same reason: most new arrivals in the community were male. Figures in Table 4.4 illustrate the regional and chronological pattern among burghers' slaves.

Table 4.4   Sex ratios: Adult slaves owned by colonists[59]
(*Figures indicate number of men per 100 women, rounded to the neaest ten*)

	Cape	Stellenbosch	Drakenstein	Swellendam	Entire colony
1660	110	–	–	–	–
1670	280	No women	–	–	–
1690	430	480	No women	–	460
1711	420	340	720	–	420
1730	400	620	700	–	480
1750	400	450	390	440	400
1770	380	430	330	310	360

As with the Europeans, the highest sex ratios among slaves are found in the country districts shortly after their founding: the overall trend is toward stabilisation, but even in 1770 the ratio for the whole colony was still 360, a high figure compared to those in other slave societies. Apparently Cape slaves were not reproducing themselves, and imports constantly had to replenish their numbers (see ch. 3, pp. 133–34). Among the always anomalous Company slaves, however, there seems to have been a surplus of women, at least in some periods. For example, in 1693 slave women outnumbered the males 125 to 98.[60]

Outside their own community almost the only possible sexual partners for black men were Khoikhoi. However, such opportunities were limited in the early years, except perhaps among the small group of urban Khoikhoi. In the seventeenth century there are hardly any references to black-Khoikhoi miscegenation. Of course European observers might have been unaware of such unions because the children would accompany their Khoikhoi mothers back to their communities. The greatest opportunity and (in the light of the black sex ratios) the greatest need for black-Khoikhoi miscegenation occurred on the European-owned farms where, after the 1670s, the two groups began to work and live together. Even here there were inhibitions which would only slowly be overcome – the early pattern of Khoikhoi husbands and wives living together in huts separate from the master's house, and the frequently bitter hostility between Khoikhoi and slaves.

An early indication of black-Khoikhoi miscegenation occurs in a letter of 1721 from several farmers to the Council of Policy. The colonists complained that the mixed children born to Khoikhoi women on their farms were, by virtue of their mother's status, not slaves; yet these children had to be brought up at the farmer's expense, after which they deserted to other employers. The petitioners asked that such children be compelled to work for them for a stipulated number of years.[61] This suggestion, which would have created a form of indentured servitude for the black-Khoikhoi children, was not acted on, though a similar proposal was implemented in 1775 in Stellenbosch (see ch. 1, p. 33).

De la Caille, Le Vaillant and Mentzel all confirm that black-Khoikhoi miscegenation was common on the farms throughout the eighteenth century. Some such unions were so permanent that some observers regarded the slave male as a 'husband'. Yet Le Vaillant claimed that black-Khoikhoi miscegenation was far less common than European-Khoikhoi miscegenation because Khoikhoi were proud to be associated with Europeans.[62] We have scarcely any way of assessing the claim of this often imaginative traveller. We do know that European-Khoikhoi *Bastaards* are mentioned more frequently in travel accounts than their black-Khoikhoi counterparts, but this might only reflect the travellers' greater interest in such unions.

European-Khoikhoi mixing occurred chiefly in the eighteenth century, on isolated farms, especially in the northwest. Sparrman argued that Khoikhoi women were not promiscuous by inclination, but once working on a European farm they could not resist the promises, presents or threats of their masters. It is impossible to estimate the number of trekboers who kept Khoikhoi women, but probably most of them were farmers in remote regions, and possibly some were wandering soldiers and sailors to whom respectable farmers refused to marry their daughters (ch. 2, pp. 99–100). In Houteniquasland in 1768 Jan Willem Cloppenberg found one European man with a Bastaard, another with a Khoikhoi, partner. In Little Namaqualand, north of the Groen River, Robert Gordon reported that there were nineteen cattle farmers among which were 'five married farmers', the rest having 'mostly a Hottentot woman or two, whom they marry in their fashion . . .'[63] Le Vaillant even claimed that on rare occasions a Khoikhoi male might sleep with a European woman (we know of one such case in 1811), and a case of homosexuality between a European sailor and a Khoikhoi on Robben Island appears in the judicial records.[64]

The offspring of European-Khoikhoi miscegenation were of course free. They were known as Bastaards, sometimes distinguished from Bastaard-Hottentots, who were offspring of black-Khoikhoi unions. Both these mixed groups were so numerous that Le Vaillant estimated in 1781–82 that they numbered one sixth of the total Khoikhoi population of the colony[65] (see also ch. 9, p. 454).

Thus there emerged two groups of partially European ancestry: (1) some of the slaves and free blacks, mainly in and near Cape Town and (2) the Bastaards, mainly in remote trekboer regions. How many of these would become members of the 'white' settler community is a vexed and controversial question which cannot be fully answered by our present evidence. It is especially difficult to estimate how many Bastaards or children of European-Bastaard unions passed into the European group, for the social structure of the trekboer regions was fluid, locally differentiated, and largely beyond the knowledge or control of the government. For the southwestern Cape a fairly accurate estimate is in principle possible and, as indicated earlier, calculations from the colony's marriage and baptismal records have periodically been made by historians and genealogists trying to determine the ethnic antecedents of the modern Afrikaner. In 1902 H.T. Colenbrander published an influential study which put the percentage of 'non-white blood' in the Afrikaner at scarcely 1 per cent. Recently J.A. Hesse, in a work which far surpasses Colenbrander's in sophistication, depth and precision, has revised the estimate up to approximately 7.2 per cent.[66]

Heese's calculation rests on the assumption that almost all children of extra-marital unions between Europeans and blacks became 'Coloureds' rather than Europeans. (Indeed, he argues that even some offspring of legal marriages became 'Coloureds'). Broadly speaking, Heese is correct. Offspring of slave women were all legally illegitimate (slaves could not legally marry) and of course remained slaves; illegitimate offspring of free black women would normally (but not always) stay with their mothers and filter into the black community.

It is true that in many comparable societies of this period (including Dutch Batavia) it was very common for European fathers to legitimate their halfcaste children and to manumit them if they were slaves.

However, we know that this rarely happened at the Cape. Of 1,075 manumissions between 1715 and 1791 only 68 (6.3%) were of this type (see Fig. 4.4, p. 213).

If it was rare for Europeans to manumit their offspring, it was a great deal rarer for them to re-enact the ancient Roman *manumissio censu* (whereby the slave, once freed, became a citizen).[67] In only two of the 1,075 manumission cases was such a request for burghership made. On 1 August 1723 the Council of Policy was informed that Christiaan, the slave son of a wealthy deceased burgher, Jacobus Victor, and a slave girl, had reached his majority and wished to claim his freedom and burgher status. The long request ended by stating that 'Christiaan had made good progress as an apprentice blacksmith, and since January last had assisted in making iron work for the mills.' The Council agreed, on the grounds 'that such tradesmen are of the greatest service to the public and that therefore . . . he may be enrolled as a burgher.' The second such request occurred almost seventy years later, in 1790. The memorialist wished that his son, born of a slave woman, might be freed and enrolled on the burgher lists. He went on to quote three cases of European men whose sons, born of slave women, had achieved the status of burghers. He could cite more cases but did not want to waste the Council's precious time 'with the genealogical registers of those who are of humbler birth than his own children and yet [who] have been entrusted with burgher posts and duties'. This application circulated among officials for some years, apparently without their taking any action.[68]

Thus, unlike in Iberian America, miscegenation and intermarriage at the Cape did not enable large numbers of blacks and Khoikhoi to obtain the privileges of the European citizens. For a black woman at the Cape, free-born or recently freed, there was a possibility of marrying a European and also a chance that her children would be regarded as 'white'. Few, however, were able to contract such marriages. The great bulk of intermixture was extra-marital and involved slaves. Neither mother nor child gained permanent social advantages from such liaisons: comparatively few of them obtained their freedom and a negligible number, as far as we can tell, achieved burgher status. Outside Cape Town the mixing of races was limited – far below what one would expect if there were no preference among Europeans for racial endogamy. Miscegenation and intermarriage scarcely ever threatened European dominance at the Cape. There was no 'mulatto escape hatch' such as that which, according to Carl Degler, made Brazilian slave society comparatively fluid.[69]

Patterns of miscegenation and intermarriage seem to have varied markedly from region to region. In Cape Town the rate of European-black concubinage was higher than in the settled agricultural regions, mainly because of the many Company bachelors and sailors on the outward- or homeward-bound fleets. In addition, there were more interracial marriages in the port than elsewhere in the colony. In the cultivating regions of the southwestern Cape the near equal sex ratios among Europeans reinforced stable family patterns and probably kept frequencies of miscegenation low. In the newly settled pastoral regions European sex ratios were very high, and considerable miscegenation, but not intermarriage, occurred.

Manumission

The rate at which slaves became free is another useful, but in itself incomplete, index of the openness of a slave society.[70] The rates must be combined with an analysis of the quality of the ex-slaves' freedom, a subject to which we shall return in our discussion of free blacks. For now, however, we shall examine the manumissions themselves – their frequency, distribution and social function – and draw comparisons with other slave societies.

Throughout the Company period the Cape government constantly tightened manumission regulations. Between 1652 and 1708 owners could manumit their slaves without Company approval. In 1708 Commissioner Joan Simons ruled that owners could manumit their slaves only upon guaranteeing that for ten years their freed slaves would not become charges of the church's poor fund. In 1722 the Council of Policy forbade owners to free their slaves without its permission, and extended the requirement of a guarantee to testamentary manumissions. In 1767 the high government in Batavia stipulated that the owner must place 20 rixdollars in the poor fund before each manumission. The authorities increased this sum to 50 rixdollars in 1777, and in 1783 they extended the bond period to twenty years.[71]

Our analysis of Cape manumissions is based on the applications submitted to the Council of Policy for the freeing of a slave or slaves. Fortunately almost all of these are preserved in the Company requesten: only four years are missing between 1715 and 1791. Spot checks in the resolutions of the Council of Policy suggest that all these requests were granted. Since manumissions for almost all of this period required Company approval, we may assume that the number of requests roughly equals the total number of manumissions. The requests vary greatly in

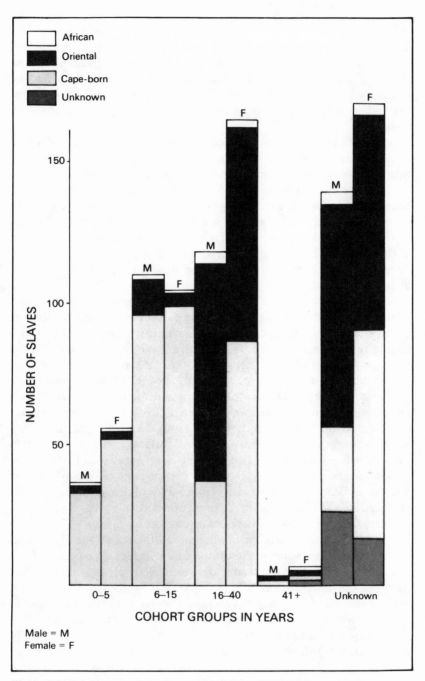

Figure 4.1 Origin, age and sex of manumitted slaves, 1715–1791 (n = 1075)

length. Even the most terse indicate the owner's sex, origin and occupation as well as the sex and origin of the slave. In addition, the longer requests dwell on other topics such as the reasons for the manumission, the marital status of the owner, the family ancestry and age of the slave, and so on. This information has been coded and analysed by computer.[72]

From 1715 to 1791 the Council of Policy received a total of 1,075 manumission requests, of which only 81 involved Company slaves. If we turn these manumissions into percentages of the slave force per year, we find that the manumission rate in South Africa was low and remained so. Indeed, the average rate per year was 0.165 per cent of the slave force. In colonial Brazil and Peru approximately 1 per cent of the slaves could expect their freedom each year, a figure about six times higher than that at the Cape.[73] The low rate at the Cape is one reason why the colony developed only a small free black population compared to those in Spanish and Portuguese America.

Some scholars of American slavery have claimed that many slave-owners manumitted old slaves who were past their productive years and that, in view of this fact, such manumission rates may be as much an index of cruelty as of benevolence. This practice was indeed a problem at the Cape, as an early plakkaat against manumitting *uitgeleefdes* (worn-out slaves) bears out.[74] However, it seems that this callous procedure gradually declined at the Cape, perhaps because of the government's vigilance. For whatever reason, between 1715 and 1791 owners rarely manumitted old slaves (see Fig. 4.1): only 12 (1.1%) of the 1,075 requests concern slaves 41 years or older. Moreover, none of these slaves were casually abandoned. Nine of the twelve were freed through the efforts, not of their owners, but of their own families, who doubtless wished to bring them into their households. Former owners amply provided for the remaining three slaves; one widow even gave her newly manumitted slave a slave of her own to support her.[75]

Of course some owners may have omitted the slave's age in order to circumvent the law against manumitting uitgeleefdes. Indeed, in 33 per cent of the requesten the writer did not specify an age: these slaves comprise the 'unknown' cohort in Figure 4.1. We may assume that few in this unknown cohort were very young: owners would not suppress the age of a young slave, since manumission of children was ostensibly encouraged by the authorities. Thus the question is whether members of the unknown cohort were mainly sixteen to forty years of age (productive adults), or older. The question can be answered if we assume that old slaves would have a lower proportion of Cape-born among their numbers than would younger slaves. Yet a comparison of the unknown cohort with the cohort aged sixteen to forty (Fig. 4.1) shows that the proportion of Cape-born is only slightly smaller in the unknown cohort. Indeed, the two cohorts match almost exactly, not only in origin but in their sex ratios as well. It seems unlikely that the omission of age in the requesten was a camouflage for massive manumission of old slaves.

Hence the old age thesis of manumission remains unproven for the Cape. In Bahia (Brazil) children were 'probably a far more important element of the manumission process . . . than were the old and the infirm.'[76] Similarly, at the Cape fully 27.5 per cent of the male and 30.9 per cent of the female slaves manumitted were under fifteen years of age. This high number of child manumissions was partly due to the practice of manumitting children along with their mothers or other kin.

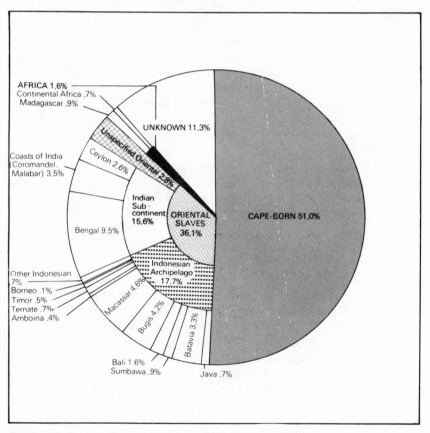

Figure 4.2 Origins of manumitted slaves, 1715–1791 (n = 1075)

Another commonly held view of manumission is that certain slaves, because of their physical appearance, had 'somatic' advantages in obtaining freedom: broadly speaking, the closer in skin colour and physical appearance to their masters', the greater were their chances of freedom. We have already noted (p. 188) that Van Reede favoured slaves with European fathers in his manumission regulations of 1685. Moreover, an analysis of the origins of slaves manumitted between 1715 and 1791 seems – at first glance at least – to sustain the somatic thesis (see Fig. 4.2). Not only did Cape-born slaves (who were more likely than imported slaves to be mixed-bloods) account for more than half the manumissions, but the Indian and Indonesian slaves were manumitted in numbers far exceeding their proportions in the slave community. Madagascan and African slaves, who least resembled their European masters, together accounted for less than 2 per cent of the manumitted slaves, even though they comprised a large proportion of the Cape slaves.

However, these dramatic figures do not necessarily confirm the somatic theory of manumission. One may argue, for example, that it was not so much the appearance as the culture of the Asians which drew them close to their European masters and created a bond which culminated in manumission. Even more likely is an economic explanation. The bulk of the rural slave force was probably Madagascan or African while almost all skilled artisan slaves in the city and on the large farms of the southwestern Cape were certainly Asian. Thus the low manumission rates for Madagascans might be rooted in the labour-intensive nature of Cape farming. It is impossible, on the basis of statistical enquiry alone, to disentangle the relative importance of the somatic, cultural and economic forces which favoured Cape-born and Asian slaves in manumission.

We have noted that the manumission rate at the Cape was much lower than in Iberian America. When one examines the identity of manumitting owners, (see Fig. 4.3), the Cape figure seems even lower: fully a quarter of manumitting owners were free blacks (if institutional owners like the Company and the Church be ignored). In Brazil, by contrast, only 2 per cent of manumitting owners were black. When we consider that the free black population at the Cape was very small – in 1770 there were only 352 free blacks in a total freeburgher population of 8,088[77] – we must conclude that free blacks liberated their slaves many, many times more frequently than did the Europeans.

Of the 609 private owners manumitting slaves between 1715 and 1791, 28 per cent were women, and at least half of these were widows. The high proportion of women and widows may be partly explained by

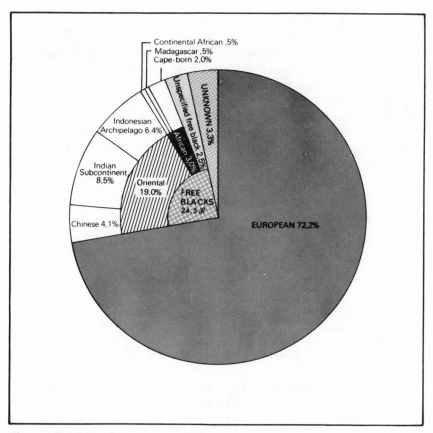

Figure 4.3 Origins of owners manumitting slaves, 1715–1791 (n = 611)

a mistress's affection for her domestic slaves, whom she would free when she could, after her husband's death. Of particular interest is the relationship between the sex of owners and the sex of manumitted slaves. Women owners manumitted roughly the same number of slaves of each sex (131 men and 135 women). Male owners, by contrast, manumitted 267 men and 368 women. This predilection of male owners for freeing females suggests amorous attachments between owner and slave. The texts of the requesten rarely support this hypothesis, except in the case of Chinese owners, who often specified that they were going to marry their manumitted slaves. But of course the requesten were not necessarily candid on such intimate details.

Students of comparative slavery have long debated whether slave owners freed their slaves because they could no longer afford their upkeep. We have attempted an answer for the Cape by dividing manumitting owners into three categories: wealthy, middle-income and poor. The criteria for selection were admittedly subjective, since no readily quantifiable evidence of wealth is found in the requesten. However, we used no information that was not absolutely incontrovertible; consequently fully 70.3 per cent of the cases fell into the 'unknown' category. Nevertheless, enough information survived to make up Table 4.5.

Table 4.5   Wealth of owners of manumitted slaves, 1715–1791[78]

	Number	Percentage of total	Adjusted percentage of private owners for whom inference of wealth is possible
Wealthy	46	7.5	25.4
Middle-income	127	20.8	70.2
Poor	8	1.3	4.4
No inference possible	429	70.3	–
Totals	610	100	100

From the admittedly incomplete analysis in Table 4.5 one may suggest that slave owners who manumitted slaves were not indigent to any great degree. Moreover, further regression analysis shows almost no correlation between the wealth of owners and the numbers of slaves manumitted.

This argument can be pursued further by asking whether the owner imposed any service conditions on the freed slaves. One might reasonably expect that if owners were indigent they would insist on a service contract after manumission. This happened, but not as frequently as might be expected if the owners were extremely hard pressed. Fully 84 per cent of all slaves who obtained their freedom were under no restrictions, while only one slave was offered his freedom on condition that he spend the rest of his life working for his master. Forty-three slaves (4 per cent) were subject to a limited service contract of a few years, while twenty slaves (1.9 per cent) had to work for their owners until they (the owners) died. In a further sixty-three cases (5.9 per cent) there was some misunderstanding about service conditions which prompted the slave to appeal to the authorities. Finally, forty-six slaves

(4.3 per cent) obtained their freedom by promising to accompany their masters as servants on their voyages to Holland or the Indies. In most cases, then, freed slaves did not become thinly disguised indentured servants, but were in reality free. This was so whether the owners were black or European, rich or poor.

Anna Böeseken's material for the seventeenth-century manumissions parallels nearly all our findings for the eighteenth century, with two exceptions. Firstly, in the earlier period manumissions as often as not had service conditions. Secondly, privately owned slaves were more frequently manumitted by governors and high officials of the VOC then by burghers.[79]

In the eighteenth century the Company and not private owners imposed the harshest conditions on freed slaves. Many Company slaves who wanted their freedom had to provide a substitute slave. About half the requests concerning these slaves were in the following form:

> Cecilia, daughter of Angora, a slave in the lodge asks for the manumission of her daughter, Cecilia . . . 14 years old, offers in exchange a slave boy named Malda of Timor. [Attached to this request was the surgeon's report.] The chief surgeon V. Schoor declares that he has examined the boy, who is about 11 or 12 years old and finds him healthy and fairly strong.[80]

On the other hand, the Company manumitted twelve times as many slaves (in proportion to its total holdings) as did the private owners at the Cape. Indeed, the VOC manumitted proportionately twice as many slaves as Brazilian owners, even though its total from 1715 to 1791 was only eighty-one (see Table 4.6).

Table 4.6   Slaves freed by the Company, 1715–1791

1715–24	6	1755–64	15
1725–34	2	1765–74	13
1735–44	11	1775–84	12
1745–54	16	1785–91	6
		Total	81

The regularity of Company manumissions in the mid-eighteenth century strikes a suspicious note. The VOC may well have used manumission as an incentive for its slave force, but we found no evidence for this.

Another form of manumission in which the owner's sacrifice was not very great was testamentary manumission. In these cases, which account for 17.5 per cent of the total manumissions by private parties, the owner had the best of both worlds: he continued to enjoy the services of his slaves until his own death, but still had the satisfaction of knowing he had freed them.

Slaveowners sometimes used a fraudulent promise of manumission as an incentive. For example, in 1778 Johan Adolph Khuul told the Council of Policy that his aunt had bequeathed him certain slaves, including the elderly Manuel of Bengal. Manuel had always been under the impression that at his mistress's death he would be manumitted. Having learned that this was not to be the case, he became bitter and often treated Khuul and his wife 'in a most insolent manner', endeavouring thus to force his new owners to free him. Finally he threatened to commit suicide if he were not manumitted. Khuul, fearing for his own safety, had Manuel incarcerated. So much did he fear the slave's release that he begged the Council of Policy to take the slave over from him and banish him for life on Robben Island. The Council acceded to this request.[81]

In approximately half of the recorded manumissions the cause or occasion of the manumission is evident. These show that the largest categories were testamentary manumissions (17.5 per cent) and manumissions caused by the owners' departure from the Cape (13.1 per cent). Manumissions for purely humanitarian reasons – and one would expect the documents to overemphasise the humanitarian aspect – were comparatively rare, accounting for only 7.6 per cent of total manumissions. A larger number (12.2 per cent) were cases of blacks buying their own freedom or that of their children, spouses or parents (see Fig. 4.4, p. 213).

In discussing religious change and miscegenation, we found dramatically different patterns between Cape Town and the arable southwestern Cape. A similar but even more startling regional pattern emerges from the manumission figures. There are flaws in our data; for instance, only 80 per cent of the requests mention the owner's place of residence, and some which specify the Cape district do not distinguish between town and country. Moreover, some distinctions are blurred by Company administrators and rich burghers who owned both a town house and a large farm. Yet, with all these problems, it is quite clear that manumissions in the Cape Colony were predominantly urban.

To begin with, the Company's manumissions were, by the nature of its economic enterprises, mainly in Cape Town. Moreover, of the 609 private slave-owners who manumitted slaves, only 29 lived outside the Cape district. And not all these rural owners were farmers: some were magistrates or Company officials in inland villages. A striking feature of these rural manumissions is that nearly as many men as women slaves were manumitted. By contrast, urban owners manumitted more women

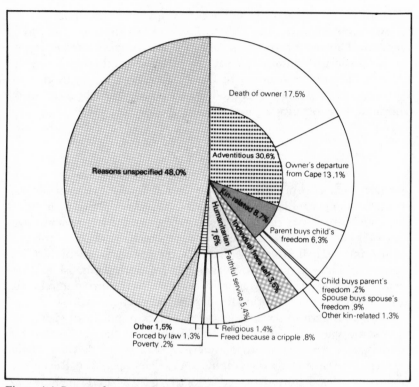

Figure 4.4 Reasons for manumissions, 1715–1791
(Subject to rounding error, ±1 per cent.)

slaves than men. Perhaps many of these rural manumitted slaves were favoured domestic servants whose wives and children were also freed: 54 per cent of those rural slaves were under fifteen years of age.

It is generally and probably correctly believed that rural owners preferred Madagascan and African slaves as fieldhands. These were far cheaper than skilled Asian slaves, whom urban owners imported from great distances at great cost. Yet 75 per cent of the slaves manumitted in the rural areas were Cape-born, 8 per cent were Bengali, 4.3 per cent were from other coastal areas of India, and the rest from the Indonesian Archipelago. Not one Madagascan fieldhand obtained his freedom. Evidently rural slave-owners did not use manumission as an incentive for their labourers. Although they owned the majority of slaves in the colony, they freed only a tiny proportion. In 1793, for example, only about .09 per cent of the rural slave force obtained its freedom.

Thus Indonesian and Indian slaves in Cape Town had much greater access than rural slaves, not only to Islam and Christianity but also to freedom. The imperatives of the labour-intensive agricultural economy and its associated culture may have formed the main obstacles to the manumission of the majority of Cape slaves. As a result, by the late eighteenth century the Cape Colony had become one of the most closed and rigid slave societies so far analysed by historians.

The Free Blacks §

Neither separately nor together did conversion, miscegenation and manumission permit large numbers of blacks, Khoikhoi, or their mixed descendants to obtain the status and privileges of the European settlers and officials. However, as we have seen, each process contributed significantly to regional variation in the culture and society of the Cape Colony. In addition, each process helped form a small but visible status group – the free blacks.[82] Manumission brought the group into being: conversion and miscegenation further shaped its character.

In many American slave societies, free black populations sprang up against the will of the authorities. This was not so at the Cape, where the models were Asian rather than American. Consequently three of the greatest names of the early colony – Van Riebeeck, Van Reede and Simon van der Stel – advocated a society partly based on free black labour. Van Riebeeck continually urged his Batavian superiors to send Mardijkers (roughly the equivalent of free blacks) and Chinese to the Cape to introduce agricultural and fishing skills. Van der Stel, on the other hand, recommended freeing African (but not Asian) slaves who, 'by nature accustomed to hard labour', would expand the colony and cause no trouble. Still more ambitious was the vision of Commissioner van Reede, who wished eventually to entrust colonial agriculture to freed slaves of mixed blood, thinking that the Company 'could have no better subjects.'[83]

The positive attitude of these high officials derived from the European experience with Eastern colonies, where free blacks frequently played an important role. In the Indies the Dutch, drawing on Portuguese precedent, did not generally discriminate against free blacks in law (though they often paid free black employees less than their European counterparts). The Dutch also encouraged some residential

§   See footnote † (P. 184) for our definition of 'free black'.

segregation. The same patterns of mild discrimination and segregation were the practice in the first century of European colonisation at the Cape. On the one hand the colonial authorities provided free blacks with land which they were free to buy and sell; they gave them responsibilities by organising them in a citizen firefighting brigade (a dubious privilege); free blacks were entitled to the services of the Church in baptism, communion and marriage; they could borrow from the Church council; they initiated cases in court; they owned livestock and slaves; they were free to return to Asia if they asked permission and paid costs; they apparently could carry weapons; and in 1722 they were given their own militia company (together with the Chinese) under free black officers.[84] By 1806 this company had developed into two important artillery companies which vigorously defended the colony against the British. Free blacks also paid taxes, a custom which was justified in a proclamation of 1752 on the grounds that they 'enjoy[ed] all privileges and rights of burghers'.[85]

On the other hand, however, the Company, and, more importantly, the burghers, did not always view free blacks as the complete equals of Europeans, at least in the eighteenth century. For instance, the authorities infrequently applied the term 'burgher' (or freeburgher) to the free blacks after the turn of the eighteenth century, and in the requesten from 1715 to 1795 there are no petitions from free blacks asking for burgher papers; Europeans, however, appear on every other page. We still need a thorough investigation of criminal and civil sentences to determine if free blacks received unfair treatment from the courts. One suspects discrimination in several cases; for example, in 1738 three free blacks and three slaves received equal punishment (a beating and costs) for being on the streets after curfew;[86] burghers were free to ignore curfew.

By the second half of the eighteenth century the laws had ceased to be colour-blind. In 1765 the government took notice of free black women who, by their dress, placed 'themselves not only on a par with other respectable burghers' wives, but often push[ed] themselves above them'. The Council of Policy deemed such behaviour 'unseemly and vexing to the public'; henceforth no free black women were to appear in public in coloured silk clothing, hoopskirts, fine laces, adorned bonnets, curled hair or ear-rings. In 1771 there was another instance of discrimination in a plakkaat against the purchase of clothing from Company slaves. The authorities laid down that Europeans were to pay fines on the first two offences and to be punished on the third: free blacks were to be treated as slaves, i.e., to be thrashed and set to work in chains for ten years.[87] By the 1790s there were other more disturbing practices. For example, free blacks now had to carry passes if they wished to leave town.[88] The evolution of the official attitudes to free blacks still awaits thorough investigation, but it would seem that the Dutch at the Cape followed the Roman precedent and developed a distinction between freeborn citizens and freedmen.

The vast majority of the free blacks were ex-slaves or their descendants. However, a sizeable number had other origins. Firstly, there was a handful of Asian settlers such as Abdol Garisch, who came to the Cape in 1790 '*a free man*' (emphasis in the original document.) Abdol Garisch had left his native land, Amboina, in an English merchant vessel bound for various ports in the Indian Ocean. The ship was captured by a French privateer, only to be re-taken by an English man-of-war and brought to the Cape. Abdol Garisch decided to stay on and eventually became a court interpreter and administrator of oaths to Muslim witnesses.[89] Another free immigrant was Abdol Wasie, who arrived at the Cape in the late eighteenth century 'as a free servant of his Batavian master', but elected to stay when his master returned to the East.[90] Though such settlers appear infrequently in the sources, their existence even in small numbers suggests that the Cape had some attractions for free persons of colour.

More influential than voluntary settlers, however, were Asian political figures banished by the Company from the Indies. Several of these exiles were eminent Indonesian princes who lived out their lives, often with a small retinue of family and servants, either on Robben Island or on farms largely isolated from the colony's life. Sometimes their children returned to the East on their parents' death; more often they stayed on. We have come across the names of approximately thirty such exiles, but possibly there were more.[91] With their retinues (De Rottij was reputed to have 100 slaves)[92] their total could not have amounted to much more than 250 in the period 1652–1795. At times the exiles exercised leadership among free blacks, but because of their isolation from the port and colonial life they seem not to have formed a permanent and recognised free black elite.[93]

A much larger number of Asians came to the Cape as convicts (bandieten). A particularly sizeable group arrived in 1743 to work on the breakwater, though most of them died shortly afterwards. On the basis of the bandiet rolls we have estimated that the VOC landed perhaps 200 or 300 convicts at the Cape in the eighteenth century. The authorities treated the convicts more or less as slaves.[94] However, they became free on the expiry of their sentences and trickled into the free black community. The numbers of ex-convicts among free blacks could not have been inconsequential, as the following irate resolution of the Council of Policy in 1749 bears out:

> Considering that this place is so full of Eastern convicts, sent hither from India [i.e., the East], who after the term of their imprisonment has expired, become free and remain free, competing with the poor whites of European descent in procuring their livelihood, and consequently very injurious to the latter . . . the council deem it necessary to take steps, in time, and write by first opportunity to Batavia for permission to send such convicts after the expiration of their terms of banishment back to the place whence they came.[95]

This correspondence to Batavia was apparently unsuccessful, as we have found no indication that convicts left the Cape in increasing numbers after this date.[96]

It is clear that all or virtually all of the Chinese in the free black community were ex-convicts. By 1750 persons with obviously Chinese names numbered at least twenty-two, although in 1770 identifiable Chinese had fallen to seven.[97] This drop was perhaps due to their higher rate of return to Asia than other free blacks, perhaps also to their increasing intermarriage with other blacks. Such assimilation was not characteristic of the early eighteenth century, when Chinese apparently lived apart from other free blacks and even had their own cemetery. In the opgaaf rolls the Chinese nearly always appear as unmarried males, although Mentzel claimed that 'they practice[d] polygamy and obtain[ed] their wives by the purchase of female slaves'.[98]

The only systematic source for the size and make-up of the free black community is the annual opgaaf roll. James Armstrong has convincingly argued that we need not be unduly suspicious of these rolls as far as free blacks are concerned.[99] However, there are always a number of names which the researcher will find hard to identify as black or European. Tables 4.7A and B are based on a preliminary study of the rolls which, to the extent that it errs, does so in underestimating the number of free blacks.

The figures in Tables 4.7A and B show that free blacks were a small group, one whose numerical significance declined even further as both the European and slave populations outgrew it. In 1670 free blacks numbered 7.4 per cent of the total freeburgher community, but by 1770 only 4.4 per cent. Seen as a percentage of the total non-Company sector (including privately owned slaves and knechts but not Company servants and Company slaves), these figures are of course even lower: 5.7 per cent and 2.1 per cent respectively. These proportions are very low when compared to those of free black communities in contemporary Spanish and Portuguese colonies, but in the same range or only slightly lower than those of French and British colonies in the Caribbean and North America. However, in the Cape district free blacks formed a significant and visible part of the population, representing, for example in 1730, 16.3 per cent of the free population. In Cape Town itself, where most free blacks lived, the percentage was doubtless much higher. Unfortunately we have no figures for the town alone in the Company period, but we do know that by 1827 free blacks comprised at least about 25 per cent of the free urban population, excluding troops.[100]

Table 4.7(A)   Free blacks: Entire colony[101]

	Men	Women	Boys	Girls	Total	As percentage of free population
1670	2	2	9*		13	7.4
1679	7	4	8	11	30	10.4
1690	15	13	20*		48	5.7
1701	16	16	8	11	51	4.0
1711	25	20	10	8	63	3.6
1719	47	46	26	17	136	6.6
1730	56	62	52	51	221	8.0
1740	60	92	85	80	317	8.4
1750	94	98	69	88	349	7.2
1760	93	118	51	51	313	5.1
1770	98	141	53	60	352	4.4

*Not known whether boys or girls

Table 4.7(B)   Free blacks: Cape district only

	Men	Women	Boys	Girls	Total	As percentage of free population
1685	4	2	6	2	14	7.6
1711	18	18	1	5	42	6.0
1730	55	61	52	51	219	16.3
1750	94	98	69	88	349	15.8
1770	97	139	51	58	345	12.8

The free black group was unique at the Cape in having a sex ratio below 100. Despite this preponderance of women over men – a result of manumission practices (discussed on p. 209) – the free blacks had a very low fertility rate. In 1760 the ratio of European children to European women in the colony was 2.7:1; among free blacks this ratio was 0.86:1 – that is, considerably below replacement rates. Although the numbers of free blacks were increasing through manumission and, much less importantly, through the freeing of convicts and exiles, their natural increase was too small for them to survive as a community. This may have been due to high infant mortality, itself a result of poverty. Or the free blacks, who were a far more urbanised group than the Europeans, may have undergone the decline in birth rates which normally accompanies urbanisation. However, the subtle psychological mechanisms whereby a group controls its population rarely rise to historical visibility. The other indications we have of low fertility are celibacy and nuptial rates, which at best are only suggestive. Despite the nearly equal numbers of free black men and women, the number of stable unions in the community – if we can trust the opgaaf rolls – was small and declining in the eighteenth century. In 1705 the opgaaf listed 41 free black adults, 20 (48.8%) of them in couples; by 1735 only 24 of 130 adults (18.5%) were listed in this way; and in 1770 the returns recorded only 44 of 239 (18.4%) as being together. Moreover, the admittedly incomplete figures in Table 4.3 (p. 199) suggest that the number of marriages among free blacks, although reasonably high at the beginning, may also have declined in the eighteenth century.

In the early decades, when there were few free blacks and comparatively numerous stable unions among them, most unions were formed between persons of similar ethnic background. In time, cultural cleavages among the free blacks tended to dissolve and the opgaaf shows that few stable unions were contracted within ethnic groups. For example, of the twenty-two stable unions recorded in the opgaaf of 1770, only two were between partners with the same toponym, and only three more were between partners from the same region (e.g. modern India or Indonesia). Fully sixteen were between persons born in different regions.

The opgaaf rolls give a picture of the ethnic origins of free blacks which is almost fully in accord with what we would expect from the manumission figures; i.e., an overwhelming number of Asians divided about equally between persons from modern India (chiefly Bengalis) and persons from modern Indonesia (largely Macassarese/Buginese), with only a smattering of Africans, Madagascans and Chinese ex-convicts.

Figure 4.5 illustrates the increasing incidence from 1705 to 1770 of European names among free blacks, who apparently took these names from masters, protectors, employers and putative fathers, or simply from the European master culture. Most of these blacks would be Cape-born, and could probably be bracketed with the 'van de Kaaps'. Together these groups numbered 22 per cent of the free black population in 1705, 34

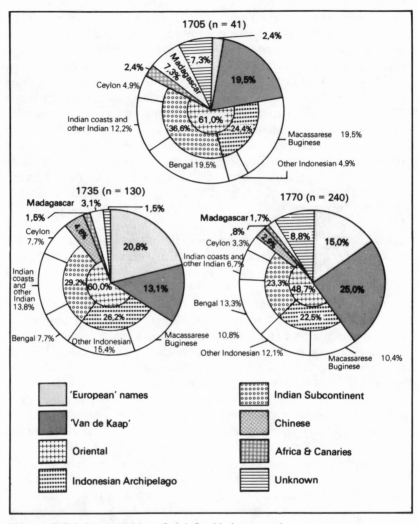

Figure 4.5 Ethnic composition of adult free black community
(As reflected in their names and toponyms recorded in opgaaf rolls in selected years)

per cent in 1735 and 40 per cent in 1770. Thus, as would be expected, the Cape-born component grew proportionately over time.

In the seventeenth century the free blacks did not all live in the Cape district, nor were they all poor. Indeed, after the founding of Stellenbosch (1679) the larger part of the tiny group set up farming in the new region. By 1688 there were six free black households in

Stellenbosch listed as owning livestock, planting crops, or both. Only two or three free black farmers continued to prosper (for example, Anthony of Angola and Jan of Ceylon), and by 1690 almost all were back in the Cape district. By 1714 the pattern for the coming century had been set: there were then only six free blacks in Stellenbosch-Drakenstein, of whom only one had livestock property, and of whom none planted. Even in the Cape district, where thirty-two free blacks lived, most had no property entered on the rolls, except for six who owned slaves and three who had a horse or two.

But one cannot conclude from these figures[102] alone that free blacks had become an under-class separated from Europeans by their poverty. Firstly, free blacks comprised only a minority – though a significant one – of persons listed without property on the rolls. Secondly, since most lived in Cape Town, they may have possessed other types of property (including cash) which the opgaaf did not enumerate. The one form of registered property which free blacks did possess in increasing numbers was slaves; for example, in 1735 the 132 free black adults owned 139 slaves (adults and children). Since most had neither land nor a large home, their purely economic need for manual labour must have been limited. It seems likely that some blacks purchased their own children or aged parents and brought them into their households, perhaps as a prelude to manumission. We have already noted (p. 208) that free blacks manumitted far more slaves in relation to their own numbers than did Europeans. However, since fully 69 of the 139 slaves owned by free blacks in 1735 were adult males, it is likely that the free blacks held some slaves, at least, for their labour or as a form of investment. Also there is evidence in the court records that free black owners, like Europeans, sometimes chained their slaves.[103]

Important information on the occupations of free blacks is found in the court records, which unfortunately by their nature depict a community living illegally. To moderate this impression we must recall that the Company's economic regulations were so severe that they forced many Europeans, as well as blacks, to live constantly beyond the law. Thus we find free blacks, like other burghers, charged with stealing goods washed ashore from shipwrecks, with shooting game beyond permitted borders, and with selling wine illegally.[104] This was not surprising as the majority of Cape Town's inhabitants, European and black, were engaged in the associated occupations of housing and entertaining the transitory population from the ships. Many free blacks worked in the numerous hostels, wine outlets, coffee shops and brothels which came constantly under the Company's changing regulations.

Others actually operated such establishments. In 1729 the burgher Hendrik Thomasz lodged a request 'to establish a branch tap at the place 'Varietas Delectus' at Rondebosch under the charge of Anthony Valentyn, a free black'.[105] By the 1740s Mentzel could report favourably on the apparently extensive restaurant facilities run by Chinese:

> Some of these Chinese are . . . good cooks. Fried or pickled fish with boiled rice is well-favoured by soldiers, sailors and slaves. When the fierce North-Westers blow, crayfish, crabs, seaspiders and 'granelen' [small crabs] are cast ashore. They are jealously collected by these Orientals, cooked and sold . . . These Asiatics likewise keep small eating houses where tea and coffee is always to be had; they specialise in the making of kerri-kerri. One need not be squeamish in patronising their cookshops since they keep the places scrupulously clean and do not touch the food with their fingers.[106]

Later travellers' accounts seldom mentioned these eating houses, an almost certain indication that they did not flourish. Only a few scattered entries in the nineteenth-century street directories suggest that they survived at all.[107]

Other sources indicate that the free blacks had a substantial hold on the artisanry. Many were tailors and shoemakers in Cape Town, probably because of the great number of military and naval personnel needing uniforms. Business prospered so much that in the winter months, when the only secure anchorage was in Simonstown, many free black tailors and haberdashers shuttled across the peninsula to set up shop and swell the village population. There were so many free black Muslims in Simonstown by the middle of the nineteenth century that the butcher there would not sell pork 'for fear of giving offence to his Mohammaden customers'.[108]

Cape Dutch architecture was fundamentally influenced by the 'Malay' masons (presumably free blacks as well as slaves), who were responsible for the many stylish gables which are seen on old Cape homes and farms. Indonesian craftsmen also influenced Cape carpentry and cabinet-making. As L.E. van Onselen comments:

> [the Malays] were probably the first real furniture-makers to arrive at the Cape. The furniture they made would, undoubtedly, have incorporated designs of Eastern origin. Their influence can be seen in the cane and ratan used in some Cape antique furniture and they were probably responsible for the ball and claw foot which was originally a dragon's foot clutching a pearl. The cabriole leg which graces some Cape furniture is Eastern in origin and was, probably, first introduced by them. They would [also] have introduced the marquetry and lacquer work which is Eastern in conception and which was to be universally adopted in Europe during the eighteenth century.[109]

Free black coopers, saddlers, basketmakers and hatmakers are also mentioned in the travellers' accounts and secondary sources.[110]

Fishing was one of the many occupations in which free blacks early established themselves and in which they remain today, as the 'Coloured' fishing communities around the Cape bear witness. Free black fishing began at least as early as 1722, when we have a memorial requesting fishing rights signed by both European and black fishermen. Among them was one Chinese, Sobinko, and two Indonesians, Jacob of Bugis and Jonker of Macassar.[111] Fishing was organised collectively because of the large outlay of labour and capital; as Mentzel indicates:

> No single person or boat-owner is in a position to engage in fishing on a large scale because the co-operative labour of several persons, boats and a net is essential for success. The usual practice at the Cape is as follows. Two men provide a boat each, another supplies the net, and various other people the slaves to man the boats. Each boat requires five persons.[112]

Free blacks were engaged in the retail trades as well. Very early on there were complaints about their competition. For instance, in 1727 several European bakers submitted to the authorities that 'certain burghers and Chinese were in the habit of sending their boys about the streets to sell different sorts of cakes, and pray that this should be forbidden as it causes the memorialists great injury'. Mentzel also noted that the Chinese made money 'by the sale of vegetables cultivated on their private plots of land'. Nor did these traders disappear. Thunberg noted their zeal in 1772 when he arrived in the port: 'We were hardly come to an anchor, before a crowd of black slaves and Chinese came in their small boats to sell and barter, for clothes and other goods, fresh meat, vegetables, and fruit, all of which our crews were eager to procure.'[113] Cape paintings of the period depict numbers of Chinese and Malay traders (easily identified by their conical straw hats or *toerangs*) busily serving the ships' needs in the roadstead.

By 1745 the colonists had convinced themselves that these incipient free black traders were not only 'injuring them' but also corrupting 'the slaves by purchasing from them stolen property, and thus [inciting] them to rob and pilfer'. They even convinced the French traveller Abbé de la Caille, who duly noted their views. Mentzel tried to refute this charge. He admitted that some 'East Indian hucksters are as sharp as needles and will cheat the Devil himself', but argued that they received stolen goods, not from slaves, but from European sailors who smuggled them from the ships. Moreover, he said about the Cape Chinese traders:

> . . . it is dangerous to generalize, and condemn them all as rogues. Some of them will show more consideration to those who owe them money than

Europeans do. I have met people to whom Asiatic dealers had given various commodities such as tea, chinaware and Eastern fabrics on long credit, even until their return from Holland. On the whole, these Chinese live a humble, quiet and orderly life at the Cape.[114]

A profitable trade which the Chinese free blacks monopolised was chandlering. They obtained waste fat from the Cape butchers at a nominal price and then made it into shapely candles much in demand at the Cape. Mentzel remarked: 'The Chinese are the only candlemakers at the Cape, for though the homemade farm candle is serviceable, it cannot be compared in appearance with the handiwork of the Chinamen [sic]. Though made of mutton fat [these candles] are as white and well-shaped as wax candles'.[115]

Thus some free blacks, particularly the Chinese, flourished in the small-scale trades and crafts of the port city. However, the free blacks did not succeed in agriculture, despite their promising start in Stellenbosch. Perhaps part of the problem was lack of capital or credit. Unlike Chinese, Lebanese and Indian traders in nineteenth- and twentieth-century colonies, they did not arrive with an extended family structure in which capital could be accumulated, nor did they have close financial links with their homelands. The colonists and officials could very easily stop the free blacks from rising beyond a certain point by not extending credit, by not granting them licenses to become butchers or bakers, and so on. However, no evidence for such discrimination has yet been found, except that in the requesten (1715–91) no free black ever applied for a license to practice any of the more lucrative trades, whereas European burghers' applications appear throughout the series.

Whatever the reaons, the retreat of the free blacks to Cape Town, and their failure to participate in the town's leading wholesale trades, was of crucial importance in the shaping of the entire colony. For the free blacks were left behind in a society where agriculture and intercontinental commerce provided the only avenues to great wealth. The free blacks' only means of livelihood were handicrafts and pretty retailing, and their fortunes must have oscillated wildly with the presence or absence of ships in the bay. Their slow demographic growth ensured that they never posed a political threat to the ever-burgeoning European settler population. They always appear as a marginal group whose legal status – like the freedman in Roman law – was ambiguous and, as the power of the colonists waxed and that of the VOC waned, increasingly subject to local (European) interpretation.

Changes in culture

Earlier in this chapter we discussed religious proselytisation. We must now turn to more spontaneous aspects of cultural change, by-products of the incorporation of Khoikhoi and slaves into a colony whose dominant members were European in culture. Cape historians have written a great deal on the culture of Europeans, very little on that of slaves, free blacks and colonial Khoikhoi. Hence our analysis will be very sketchy.

The most obvious features of Cape cultural history were the borrowing of cultural traits among groups and the emergence of syncretic cultural complexes. But borrowing was not simply a matter of European culture being transferred to Asians and Africans. It is in any event imprecise to speak simply of 'European' culture: many Company servants arrived at the Cape after a long sojourn – or even a lifetime – in the East Indies, where they had been affected by the mores of the *Indische* (Eurasian) culture in the Company's holdings.[116] Many of these were high Company officials who would have been influential cultural models, particularly in Cape Town. We can discern evidence of the importance of Indische culture in the wide use of Low Portuguese (the 'lingua franca') among Europeans at the Cape,[117] in Cape Dutch architecture, and in Cape cuisine. On the other hand, the Cape was much closer to Europe than was Batavia, and it received a considerable influx of new settlers directly from the Netherlands, Germany, France, etc. These immigrants probably diluted Indische influences in the Cape Colony, particularly in agricultural regions beyond Cape Town. Moreover, just as the mixed Indische culture testified to the cultural impact of subjects on their masters in the Orient, so at the Cape cultural transfer was also mutual. In Cape Town the impress of various Indian and Indonesian cultures continued to be felt on Europeans, particularly through the agency of the Eastern slaves and free blacks working as artisans and domestics.

In the arable regions of the southwestern Cape, slaves probably accepted European culture rather more rapidly. We cannot yet support this assertion with detailed evidence, but we base our opinion on an analysis of the social and demographic framework of slavery in this region. With the possible exception of the Madagascans, there was never a large group of slaves at the Cape with a single cultural heritage, and no ethnic group was intentionally concentrated in one locale (ch. 3, pp. 147–48). The only common and visible culture for slaves to acquire was a creole culture.

Moreover, Cape slaves, unlike plantation slaves, were rather evenly distributed among the burgher population, more than half of them (in 1750) being in groups of five or fewer. Many of these slaves were domestic servants in close contact with Europeans; in poorer locales many lived in the same quarters with their masters; some, as we have seen, had permanent or semi-permanent sexual liaisons with Europeans. All these conditions must have accelerated the acquisition of the hegemonic European culture among the rural slaves. At the same time they encouraged the development of Dutch, and the preservation of Low Portuguese, as a means of communication among slaves and between slaves and masters.

The Khoikhoi in arable areas adopted their rulers' culture more slowly and more selectively than did the slaves.[118] This was partly because they, unlike the slaves, were only gradually incorporated into the colonial economy and society. In the seventeenth century few Khoikhoi spent all of their time on European farms, and even in the eighteenth century, after the collapse of the strong Khoikhoi chiefdoms, opportunities for periodic withdrawal from the colony abounded. Moreover, the Khoikhoi, much more than the slaves, possessed a homogeneous culture and a family structure, undamaged by slavery, to transfer to their young: independent domicile and family solidarity often continued undisturbed even among Khoikhoi on the European-owned farms.

Khoikhoi came into contact with Western culture only as servants. Not surprisingly, their main acquisitions tended to be useful skills or items of material culture. This pattern first appeared among the Strandlopers, the core of the growing population of Khoikhoi in Cape Town from the 1650s onward. But it soon reappeared among the more numerous Khoikhoi who, after the 1670s, came into contact with European culture by spending part of their year on the farms of the southwestern Cape. These Khoikhoi, like their urban counterparts, were attracted by European products, which rapidly became part of their own culture – green vegetables, bread, rice, tobacco, brandy and arak (an East Indian liquor). They learned various forms of pidgin Dutch (one of which was also spoken by slaves and which in some respects resembled modern Afrikaans); on Huguenot farms they learned French.[119] Unlike many of the urban Khoikhoi, their family life persisted in the traditional mat huts which they brought on to the farms: they continued to dress in traditional skins, greased their bodies, and carried *assegais* in the colony. Presumably other, undocumented, aspects of their culture also changed only slowly, particularly their mythology, music and religion.

The smallpox epidemic of 1713 drastically altered the patterns of cultural exchange. It eliminated the majority of Khoikhoi in both Cape Town and the southwestern Cape and destroyed the remnants of their traditional social structure in these areas. It thus impelled the few survivors to more rapid adaptation of European culture and determined that, as a few Khoikhoi filtered back into the region in the eighteenth century, they would find themselves vastly outnumbered by slaves and Europeans, whose culture was now clearly dominant.

Very different was the vast region occupied by trekboers and their slaves after the 1690s. For here the arid climate, rough terrain, and distance from markets encouraged the abandonment of intensive cultivation and favoured the traditional pastoral economy of the Khoikhoi and its associated cultural patterns. Furthermore, in regions remote from Cape Town, the population density of both Europeans and slaves declined, as did the material wealth of the farmers and their opportunity for regular contact with Cape Town and Europe. Such circumstances stimulated the rise of a composite culture in which Khoikhoi influence was apparent, and also completed the submergence of the Asian slave cultures which – apart from the lingua franca – could not survive when few compatriots lived in regular contact with one another.

During the eighteenth century the rise of this composite culture provoked fears that European trekboers would sink to the level of the despised Khoikhoi, losing their culture and, even worse, their religion. Inhabitants of Cape Town conventionally informed overseas visitors that the European colonists in the interior 'both in their manners and appearance more resembled Hottentots than Christians.' Influential officials who had travelled widely in the interior endorsed these views. For example, in 1768 the secunde Jan W. Cloppenburg, noting that Europeans were becoming 'unmannerly and unchristian', advanced a scheme to separate Europeans from contamination by depriving them of Khoikhoi and slave labour. Similar views were expressed for the rest of the century.[120]

At the root of this phenomenon was the adoption by colonists (and their slaves) of a pastoral and hunting economy formerly monopolised by Khoikhoi. The Europeans modified certain aspects of this economy by introducing the controlled breeding of sheep, extensive slaughter of animals for regular human consumption, and a more intensive grazing which ultimately led to soil erosion.[121] They were also more inclined than Khoikhoi to sell their livestock for slaughter in Cape Town. However, all these innovations did not fundamentally alter the isolation, semi-nomadism and comparative self-reliance of the inland pastoralist.

Thus the values and aesthetic standards of the trekboers tended to centre, as Sparrman noted even of the wealthiest trekboers, on 'the number and beauty of their herds and flocks.' Trekboers exchanged livestock at births and marriages and created bonds of clientage by pasturing out sheep and cattle with their neighbours.[122] In these respects trekboer culture resembled Khoikhoi culture, but the extent to which it derived from Khoikhoi culture cannot be determined.

It is only on comparatively superficial matters of material culture that our sources are abundant and easily interpreted. These show a remarkable convergence of the material culture of Europeans, slaves and Khoikhoi, and suggest a considerable influence of the Khoikhoi on the other groups. In some more settled pastoral locales, Europeans had built stone houses; but the typical dwelling seems to have had one or two rooms with clay walls, a straw roof, mere holes for windows, and a door made of reed mats. The water-resistant reed mats were derived from Khoikhoi culture and were also used under tarpaulins as covering for the farmers' wagons.[123] On farms like these, Khoikhoi servants either lived in their own huts with their families, or pell-mell with slaves and Europeans in the main house. Many Europeans, however, lived more simply than this in mat huts, which travellers found indistinguishable from those of Khoikhoi. Perhaps many of these were temporary buildings of new settlers, or a result of the shortage of timber, but there were several remote regions where Europeans used mat houses, tents or wagons as dwellings – or simply slept under a tree – because their lives were as nomadic as those of the Khoikhoi.[124]

Europeans and slaves adopted other aspects of the Khoikhoi cattle culture. Early in the eighteenth century they began to burn the veld, just as the Khoikhoi did, to improve pasture. Thunberg noted poor colonists who stored milk in skin sacks made like those of Khoikhoi, and Sparrman saw Europeans dry strips of game (later called *biltong*) on trees and bushes like Khoikhoi hunters. Generally the trekboers did not adopt Khoikhoi dress; however, sometimes their children ran about in sheepskins, and an occasional farmer like Willem van Wijk, who married the daughter of a Nama chief in a Khoikhoi ceremony, dressed and bore himself as a Khoikhoi. Travellers frequently remarked on the widespread adoption of veldschoenen (Khoikhoi sandals made of cattle hide or animal skin) which were to be found even in Cape Town.[125]

As the colony expanded throughout the eighteenth century, this composite culture spread and consolidated itself in new regions. Khoikhoi who were newly incorporated into the colony had to adapt to it to a far lesser extent than did the Europeans who came to the trekboer regions from Cape Town. Indeed, because the bearers of European culture were few, the alteration of Khoikhoi culture was probably even slower than it had been in the southwestern Cape in the seventeenth century. Again our evidence suggests changes mainly in consumption patterns – the adoption of European food, drink and tobacco. Khoikhoi on farms smoked tobacco in pipes which they made themselves from wood or the horns of gazelle or antelope, though they preferred European pipes when they could obtain them. They continued to adorn themselves in the traditional skins and grease, even near Company posts or on farms as close to Cape Town as Paarl.[126] When hunting, herding, or travelling long distances, they wore veldschoenen, but otherwise went barefoot. In this they differed from the Bastaard offspring of European-Khoikhoi unions, who favoured European clothes, and also from the few Khoikhoi in wealthy homes in and near Cape Town who were sometimes clad in the costume of domestic slaves.[127]

On the more complex aspects of culture our sources are less helpful. However, travellers in the second half of the eighteenth century often noted that Khoikhoi observed their traditional festivals and dances on the farms (though these were sometimes modified by contacts with Europeans), and that they continued to practice customs which were either abhorrent or strange to the travellers, like burying a child alive whose mother had died in childbirth, or feeling compelled to move from a farm where someone had recently died.[128]

A major exception to Khoikhoi cultural conservatism was language. The languages of the immigrants (Dutch among Europeans and Portuguese among slaves) rather than that of the indigenous Khoikhoi became the means of communication in trekboer society. This was due largely to the extraordinary difficulty of the Khoikhoi language; in the seventeenth century the Dutch, famed for their linguistic ability in the Orient, failed to produce one fluent speaker of Khoikhoi although, according to Anna Böeseken, at least two officials, G.F. Wrede and J.W. de Grevenbroek, had a working knowledge of the Khoikhoi langauge.[129] In the trekboer regions of the eighteenth century, white children often learned Khoikhoi (along with Malay and Portuguese) from their playmates, but there is little evidence that they used it later as adults in talking to Khoikhoi labourers on their farms, who normally spoke Dutch and often Portuguese. Travellers give different accounts of the quality of their Dutch, some finding it as good as that of the colonists – though they did not intend this as a compliment – others finding it just passable. Khoikhoi, of course, for a long time continued to speak their own language among themselves, although they took into it many words of Dutch derivation (like the words for wagon, bread and wheat) and coined words, sometimes by onomatopoeia, to describe new cultural items (such as firelock and gunpowder). In 1772 Thunberg heard Khoikhoi spoken in Paarl. However, the language slowly died out, and by the turn of the nineteenth century the well-travelled Lichtenstein heard it only on the colony's borders, and even then with a heavy European admixture.[130]

The prevailing trend in the cultural history of the period we are discussing was towards homogeneity within regions. Various European cultures (Dutch, French, etc.) and various slave cultures (Bengali, Indonesian, Madagascan, etc.) were merging with one another and with the culture of the Khoikhoi. By the late eighteenth century the main cultural cleavages were no longer between ethnic or status groups (European versus non-European, or slave versus Khoikhoi) but between regions. In Cape Town a mixed European and Asian culture was shared by Company officials, some burghers, and slaves, though some of the latter managed to retain more traditionally Asian traits, especially through conversion to Islam. In the agrarian southwestern Cape, slaves and Europeans seem to have shared in a culture which was predominantly of European origin. In the trekboer regions the prevailing languages were Dutch and Portuguese, but otherwise the culture of slaves and colonists was a composite of European and Khoikhoi influences, appropriate to a livestock economy. Here the remaining cultural cleavages were between Europeans, slaves, Bastaards and a few acculturated Khoikhoi on the one hand, and the more traditional Khoikhoi on the other.

Conclusion

We have seen distinct regional variations in our study of conversion, miscegenation, manumission, the history of the free blacks, and cultural change. These regional differentials are hard to quantify, largely because the 'districts' in the Company's statistics did not neatly correspond with our regions: the Cape district was both rural and urban; the Stellenbosch district included both arable and pastoral sections; and the trekboer region was divided among two (later three) districts and one subdistrict. Nevertheless, evidence of regional variations intrudes on all sides, and the cumulative case for a regional analysis is compelling.

Cape Town was a seaward-looking community, a caravanserai on the periphery of the global spice trade. European and Asian cultures flourished in the port; so, too, did Christianity and Islam, though the former had only superficial success among people of colour, being largely confined to the Company's slave lodge. Manumissions, too, were more frequent in Cape Town, partly because some of the slave-owning population was in transit, but mainly because the seasonal fluctuations in economic activity made wage labour a flexible alternative to slavery. Moreover, there were fairly high rates of miscegenation in Cape Town, necessitated by the numerous Company sailors and soldiers who lived or visited there. And, finally, Cape Town was the home of a significant population of free blacks, many of whom were Muslim and a handful Christian. A few of the former were modestly prosperous.

In contrast to Cape Town, the arable lands of the southwestern Cape were more insulated from the influx of new people and ideas, and more dominated by a labour-intensive economy. Here the European settlers soon achieved comparatively balanced sex ratios and the formation of stable European families was possible. Consequently there was little pressure toward miscegenation, and hostility to concubinage intensified. There was also little manumission, even though most of the colony's slaves lived in these areas. Without the ginger group of free blacks who gave Cape Town its rather cosmopolitan air, this region was soon characterised by the assimilation of blacks to European culture, but not by their incorporation into the church or freeburgher society. A clear social distinction between Europeans and blacks was established soon after settlement. Prestige and local power became associated with land-holding, and almost all land-holders were European.

The trekboer pastoralists required a less extensive labour force and, because of their comparative poverty, they relied less on slaves than on Khoikhoi, who were subject to informal labour controls. Their farms were even further from Cape Town, and among them Asian (and to some extent European) culture soon became diluted. Because of a shortage of manufactured goods, a new material culture arose based on the products of pastoralism and the immediate environment. European women were few, and the consequent miscegenation produced a new group, the Bastaards. However, the Bastaards, even if baptised, found it hard to become full-fledged burghers; and ultimately, as the frontier closed (see ch. 9, p. 447–58), they were squeezed out of the colony.

Our emphasis on regionalism should not obscure important features common to the whole colony. Cape colonial society was rigid, even by some contemporary standards. The position of the lower status groups did not improve. Slaves had comparatively little opportunity to become free, even in Cape Town. Khoikhoi never enjoyed the rights of burghers, and free blacks and baptised Bastaards gradually lost the privileges they once had. These latter groups lived in a twilight world, neither slave nor wholly free. Mobility of individuals into the dominant European settler group was quite uncommon. For free blacks, Khoikhoi and their descendants the era 1652 to 1795 – at the end no less than at the beginning – was no golden age.

Chapter Four   Notes

1. On the rule of law at the Cape see Robert Ross, 'The Rule of Law at the Cape in the Eighteenth Century' (mimeo, 1977).
2. I.D. MacCrone, *Race Attitudes in South Africa: Historical, Experimental and Psychological Studies* (Johannesburg, 1937), p. 41; see also pp. 7, 40–46, 76–78, 129 fn. 1, 134–35.
3. George McCall Theal, *History of South Africa* (reprinted, Cape Town, 1964), III, 272; cf. V, 268.
4. See Bernhard Krüger, *The Pear Tree Blossoms. A History of the Moravian Mission Stations in South Africa, 1737–1869* (Genadenal, 1966), pp. 18–44.
5. C.R. Boxer, *The Dutch Seaborne Empire, 1600–1800* (New York, 1965), pp. 138–49.
6. Richard Elphick, *Kraal and Castle: Khoikhoi and the Founding of White South Africa* (New Haven and London, 1977), pp. 106–08, 201–03.
7. *Ibid.*, pp. 203–07. For an early scheme for evangelising Khoikhoi which in some ways foreshadowed nineteenth-century missions see VC 168, Simond – XVII, 1298 ff. We are indebted to Dr. Pieter Coertzen for a copy of this document.
8. Anders Sparrman, *A Voyage to the Cape of Good Hope towards the Antarctic Polar Circle Round the World and to the Country of the Hottentots and the Caffres from the year 1772–1776* (reprinted; Cape Town, 1975), I, 208; cf. I, 263–64.
9. H.P. Cruse, *Die Opheffing van die Kleurlingbevolking: Aanvangsjare, 1652–1795* (Stellenbosch, 1947), I, 83, 101, 106; Res 2 Sept. 1779. We are indebted to James Armstrong for this last reference.
10. One Khoikhoi was baptised in the Netherlands by the Rev. Petrus Kalden.
11. Theal, *History*, III, 150. See also III, 59–60: 'A hundred years later very different views were held, but in the middle of the seventeenth century no distinction whatever appears to have been made between people on account of colour. A profession of Christianity placed black and white upon the same level. The possessions of the heathens were the inheritance of God's people, and could be taken from them without sin. The heathen themselves could be enslaved, but Christians could not be kept in bondage. The archives of the Cape Colony contain numerous illustrations of this doctrine.'

12. Cruse, *Opheffing*, I, 224 (Robin Whiteford translated the Latin citation).
13. Adriaan Moorees, *Die Nederduitse Gereformeerde Kerk in Suid-Afrika, 1652–1873* (Cape Town, 1937), pp. 36–38; MacCrone, *Race Attitudes*, pp. 77–78; Cruse, *Opheffing*, p. 226. The quotation is in Moorees, *Kerk*, p. 38.
14. Donald Moodie, *The Record* (Amsterdam and Cape Town, 1960), p. 309; MacCrone, *Race Attitudes*, p. 76.
15. Dutch Reformed Church Archives (Cape Town), Gl 4/34, Lyst aanweizende hoe veel slavenkinderen . . . gedoopt zyn geworden . . . A copy of this document was kindly provided to us by James Armstrong. We have not had an opportunity to check all of these figures against the original baptismal records: spot checks suggest that in some periods these figures are exact, in some periods too low. Because of strange recording procedures in the original, we have had to use seventeen-year intervals except for the first and last intervals: the mean percentages have been adjusted accordingly.
16. On manumissions see Anna J. Böeseken, *Slaves and Free Blacks at the Cape 1658–1700* (Cape Town, 1977), appendices *passim*. The figure for baptisms are based on Table 4.1. However, this series' figures for this era may be far too low: a spot check of the church records shows 143 privately owned slave children baptised between 1695 and 1712, while the series on which Table 4.1 is based gives only 32.
17. For information on manumissions see pp. 204–14.
18. *RCC*, IX, 131–32.
19. George Forster, *A Voyage round the World . . . in his Britannic Majesty's Sloop, Resolution*, (2 vols.; London, 1777), I, 60.
20. Sparrman, *Voyage*, I, 90; cf. O.F. Mentzel, *A Complete and Authentic Geographical and Topographical Description of the . . . Cape of Good Hope* (Cape Town, 1921, 1925, 1944), II, 130–31.
21. Robert Percival, *An Account of the Cape of Good Hope* (London, 1804), pp. 274–75.
22. Johannes Stephanus Marais, *The Cape Coloured People: 1652–1937* (Johannesburg, 1957), p. 168.
23. *RCC*, IX, 133.
24. *Select Constitutional Documents Illustrating South African History*, G.W. Eybers ed. (London, 1918), p. 18.
25. I.D. du Plessis, *The Cape Malays: History, Religion, Traditions, Folk Tales, The Malay Quarter* (Cape Town, 1972), pp. 1–2. Du Plessis does admit that there was conversion, but seems to emphasise the theory of transplanting of Muslims from the Indonesian Archipelago.
26. In reference to conversion to Islam at Batavia, see Sparrman, *Voyage*, I, 264–65.
27. Robert C.-H. Shell, 'The Establishment and Spread of Islam at the Cape from the Beginning of Company Rule to 1838' (Honours thesis; University of Cape Town, 1974), p. 20.
28. *Ibid.*, p. 32.
29. *Ibid.*, p. 33.
30. MOOC 7/1/53, no. 66 and no. 66½.
31. Charles Thunberg, *Travels in Europe, Africa and Asia performed between the years 1770 and 1779* (London, 1795), I, 132–34.

32. Burgherraad, Incoming Letters, 17, Barnard/1st Feb. 1800; British Occupation 154, Item 236; Samuel Abraham Rochlin, 'The first mosque at the Cape', *South African Journal of Science*, XXXIII (1937), pp. 1100–03.
33. Mirza Abu Taleb Khan, *The Travels of Mirza Abu Taleb Khan in Asia, Africa and Europe in the years 1799, 1800, 1801, 1802 and 1803, written by himself in the Persian language and translated by Charles Stewart* (London, 1810), pp. 72–73; we probably would have learnt more about this group of Muslims had the translator not decided to curtail 'the long list of his friends at the principal places he visited', see preface, p. viii.
34. Shell, 'Establishment', p. 41; *RCC*, XXXV, 367.
35. *RCC*, IX, 131–32, article II, p.147.
36. Dutch Reformed Church Archives, Cape Town, G1:1/1, 8/1, 13/1, 12a/4.
37. Anna J. Böeseken, 'Die verhouding tussen blank en nie-blank in Suid-Afrika aan die hand van die vroegste dokumente', *South African Historical Journal*, II (1970), p. 14; *KP*, I, 152 (1678), 179 (1681), 266 (1692), 331 (1704); *KP*, II, 73 (1718).
38. Elphick, *Kraal and Castle*, pp. 204–05.
39. Mentzel, *Description*, I, 116; II, 81, 124, 130.
40. Theal, *History*, III, 273; A. Hulshof, 'H.A. van Reede tot Drakenstein, Journaal van zijn Verblijf aan die Kaap', *Bijdragen en Mededeelingen van het Historisch Genootschap*, LXII (1941) p. 213; Cruse, *Opheffing*, pp. 91–101; MacCrone, *Race Attitudes*, pp. 76–78.
41. E.g., Charles Lockyer, *An Account of the Trade in India* (London, 1711), p. 297; Capt. Daniel Beeckman, 'A Voyage to Borneo in 1714', *Collectanea* (Cape Town, 1924), p. 114; Böeseken, *Slaves and Free Blacks*, p. 45 and n. 38.
42. KA 4007, Generale Opneming en monster rolle van 's Comp. soo slaven als bandieten, 1 Jan. 1693, pp. 359–68.
43. KA 3976, Muster of 1664, n.p.
44. Numbers of ships determined from annual port records in KA. Numbers of men per ship derived from KA 3996, Oncostboeck van verstreckte ververssingen en scheeps nootwendigheden . . ., 1683, pp. 689–708.
45. Table based on opgaaf rolls of designated years.
46. Herbert Moller, 'Sex Composition and Correlated Culture Patterns of Colonial America', *William and Mary Quarterly*, II (1945), pp. 113–53.
47. Robert Ross, 'The "white" population of South Africa in the eighteenth century', *Population Studies*, XXIX (1975), p. 230; John Hajnal, 'European marriage patterns in perspective' in *Population in History: Essays in Historical Demography*, ed. D.V. Glass and D.E.C. Eversley (London, 1965), Table 2, p. 102 and *passim*.
48. J. Hoge, 'Miscegenation in South Africa in the seventeenth and eighteenth centuries'; Marius V. Valkhoff ed., *New Light on Afrikaans and 'Malayo-Portuguese'* (Louvain, 1972), pp. 99–118; J.L.M. Franken, *Taalhistoriese Bydraes* (Amsterdam and Cape Town, 1953), pp. 16–26.
49. Mentzel, *Description*, II, 109–10.
50. David W. Cohen and Jack P. Greene, *Neither Slave nor Free: The Freedman of African Descent in the Slave Societies of the New World* (Baltimore and London, 1972), pp. 55, 78, 142–43, 154–55, 210, 262, 322.
51. Böeseken, 'Verhouding', pp. 12, 17; opgaafs of 1686 (KA 3999), 1695

(KA 4013), 1730 (KA 4901), 1770 (KA 4240); personal communication from J.A. Heese.

52. Hoge, 'Miscegenation', pp. 110–11; [Anon.], 'The origin and incidence of miscegenation at the Cape during the Dutch East India Company's regime, 1652–1795', *Race Relations Journal*, XX (1953), p. 27.

53. Based on Dutch Reformed Church Archives (Cape Town), G1 1/1, 8/1 13/1, 13/2. We have considered as free blacks (1) those so identifiable by toponym, (2) those identified as free blacks in the documents, (3) those known to be free blacks by prior knowledge. As we have indicated in the text, these crude methods doubtless miss many Cape-born free blacks.

54. Dutch Reformed Church Archives, G2 7/1.

55. Hoge, 'Miscegenation', p. 109.

56. Moller, 'Sex composition', pp. 113–53.

57. Personal communication.

58. KA 4013, DR, 1 June 1695, pp. 745–48; KA 4048, DR, 4 July 1713, pp. 192–205; KA 4098, Landdrost vs. Hendrik van Nias, 2 Oct. 1732, p. 958.

59. As in n. 45.

60. KA 4007, Generale opneming en monster rolle van 's Comp. soo slaven als bandieten, 1 Jan. 1693, pp. 359–68.

61. C 228, pp. 291–92, Requesten, no. 73, 9 Sept. 1721; *Res*, VI, 128 (2 Sept. 1721).

62. Abbé de la Caille, *Journal Historique du Voyage fait au Cap de Bonne-Espérance* (Paris, 1763), p. 324; François le Vaillant, *Voyage de Monsieur le Vaillant dans l'Intérieur de l'Afrique* (Paris, 1790), II, 133–41; Mentzel, *Description*, II, 126. See also KA 4146, Prosecution of Jephta van Sambouwa *et al.*, 5 May 1746, p. 963v.

63. Anders Sparrman, *Voyage*, I, 262–63; AR, Aanwinsten 1881, A viii, Kol. Aanw. 242, [Jan Willem Cloppenburg] Journaal, p. 8; Staf D 593/U/4/3/3, Journaal van de vierde reyse van Captein R.J. Gordon . . ., 23 Sept. 1779, n.p.

64. Le Vaillant, *Voyage*, II, 141; KA 4106, Prosecution of Rijkaart Jacobse and Hottentot Claas Blank, 18 Aug. 1735, pp. 770–76. A Khoikhoi named Cobus eloped with the daughter of Pieter Terblans and went to an abandoned loan farm on the upper Elands River. The couple were met by a raiding Xhosa group who killed the man and left the woman for dead. Uitenhage 15/1, Cuyler-Truter, 6 Feb. 1811. We are indebted to John Hopper for information on this incident.

65. Le Vaillant, *Voyage*, II, 140.

66. H.T. Colenbrander, *De Afkomst der Boeren*, (2nd edn.; Cape Town, 1946). p. 121; J.A. Heese, *Die Herkoms van die Afrikaner 1657–1867* (Cape Town, 1971), p. 21.

67. Paul van Warmelo, *An Introduction to the Principles of Roman Law* (Cape Town, 1976), p. 39, para. 95.

68. C 231. pp. 132–33, Requesten no. 69, 1 Aug. 1724. H.C.V. Leibbrandt erroneously numbered this as 64 and dated it 1723 in his *Requesten* (Cape Town, 1905–06), I, 57; C 287, pp. 1139–45, Requesten no. 22, 19 Nov. 1790.

69. Carl N. Degler, *Neither Black nor White: Slavery and Race Relations in Brazil and the United States* (New York and London, 1971), pp. 223–45 and *passim*.

70. This debate began when Frank Tannenbaum claimed that 'the attitude toward manumission is the crucial element in slavery: it implies the judgement of the moral status of the slave, and foreshadows his role in case of freedom'; see *Slave and Citizen, The Negro in the Americas* (New York, 1947), p. 69 ff. For attacks on Tannenbaum see Marvin Harris, *Patterns of Race in the Americas* (New York, 1974), p. 86 ff. and Harmannus Hoetink, *Caribbean Race Relations: A Study in Two Variants* (New York, 1971), *passim*, and his *Slavery and Race Relations in the Americas* (New York, 1973), pp. 192–210; for an incisive commentary on the ensuing historiography, see Eugene Genovese, 'The treatment of slaves in different countries: Problems in the application of the comparative method', *Slavery in the New World: A Reader in Comparative History*, ed. Laura Foner and Eugene Genovese (Englewood Cliffs, New Jersey, 1969) pp. 202–11.

71. Isobel Edwards, *Towards Emancipation: A Study in South African Slavery* (Cardiff, 1942), p. 29; James C. Armstrong, 'The Free Black Community at the Cape of Good Hope in the Seventeenth and Eighteenth Centuries' (unpublished paper, 1973), pp. 8–9.

72. The material on manumission was found in H.C.V. Leibbrandt's summarised and published *Requesten* I and II, and the summarised but unpublished typescript manuscripts, LM 15, LM 16 and LM 17 (LM = Leibbrandt's manuscript). Where we quoted a manumission request, we referred to the original archival volume and cited it, but we also retained the Leibbrandt reference in the footnote. The archival series is complete except for a few years (1717, 1722, 1777 and 1788), which are not serious flaws. The breaks in 1717 and 1722 are at the beginning of the series, when manumission frequencies were very low. The later missing years could mean that our total of 1,075 manumitted slaves represents a slight (1–2%) underestimation. If a request appeared in one year but referred to another year in which the slave would obtain his or her freedom, we dated the manumission to the latter date. We counted 1,075 manumitted slaves in the period 1715–1791; each slave had 52 variables, all coded in SPSS format.

73. Stuart B. Schwartz, 'The manumission of slaves in colonial Brazil, 1684–1745', *Hispanic American Historical Review*, LIV (1974) p. 604, n. 4. Robert Wayne Selenes in his Ph.D. dissertation 'The Demography and Economics of Brazilian Slavery 1850–1888' (Stanford, 1975), has calculated even higher rates of manumission for this later period. See pp. 484–573.

74. *Res*, III, 40 (8 April 1682); *PB*, I, 184 (8 April 1682).

75. C 265, pp. 184–85, Requesten no. 44, 1766, LM 16, p. 1087.

76. Schwartz, 'Manumission', p. 619.

77. KA 4240, Opgaaf of 1770.

78. 'Wealthy' owners were those who were known to be 'rich', either as Company administrators or as farmers, e.g., Martin Melck, the plantation owner: see John Splinter Stavorinus, *Voyage to the East Indies . . .*, 2 vols. (London, 1798), II, 61–62. For Company servants we approximated eighteenth-century wage scales by using C. Boxer's *The Dutch Seaborne Empire*, pp. 300–03, appendix II, 'Some Salary Scales of Sea-faring and Overseas Personnel.' Thus Michiel Brik, a quartermaster, who wished to emancipate two slaves (Leibbrandt, *Requesten*, II, 173 [no. 44 of 1787])

would have received 14 guilders a month (*Dutch Seaborne Empire*, p. 300). Sailors, who received half this salary and who were the second lowest paid personnel, were regarded as 'poor'. Sometimes the requesten themselves provided evidence of indigence; for example, an owner might ask to be excused from paying the guarantee, on grounds of poverty. Admittedly these are coarse, subjective approximations only. A more severe test would be to compare the wealth of manumitting owners with that of non-manumitting owners, but this was beyond the scope of this chapter.

79. Böeseken, *Slaves and Free Blacks*, appendices.
80. C 241, pp. 121–23 and surgeon's report p.125, Requesten no. 33, 1742. Leibbrandt has made a small mistake here; although listed under 1741 in his *Requesten* (I, p. 245), the numerical sequence of the other Requesten clearly indicates that this item belongs to 1742.
81. C 276, pp. 309–11, Requesten no. 91, 1779; *Requesten* II, 643.
82. On free blacks see Victor de Kock, *Those in Bondage* (Cape Town, 1950), pp. 198–223; MacCrone, *Race Attitudes*, pp. 70–80; Sheila Patterson, 'Some Speculations on the Status and Role of the Free People of Colour in the Western Cape', *Studies in African Social Anthropology*, ed. Meyer Fortes and Sheila Patterson (London, 1975), pp. 159–205; Armstrong, 'Free Black Community'; Shell, 'Establishment'; and Böeseken, *Slaves and Free Blacks*.
83. KA 3969, Van Riebeeck – Batavia, 14 Aug. 1656, p. 41v; KA 3993, S. van der Stel – XVII, 20 March 1681, pp. 11v–12; Hulshof, 'H.A. van Reede . . . Journaal', p. 204.
84. Böeseken, 'Verhouding', pp. 15–16; *KP*, II, 93 (29 Sept./13 Oct. 1722), 116 (1 Feb. 1727), 182 (11 Oct. 1740); *RCC*, XXXV, 191; KA 4039, Church Council vs. Louis of Bengal, 18 Oct. 1708, p. 623; *Res*, V, 282 (10 May 1718), 348 (20 June 1719); *Res*, VI, 211 (13 Oct. 1722).
85. Theal, *History of South Africa*, V, 189–90; Brian Aldridge, 'Cape Malays in action', *Quarterly Bulletin of the South African Library* XXVII (1972), p. 26; the quotation is in *KP*, II, 239 (1 Feb. 1752).
86. KA 4116, Interim Fiscal vs. Three Slaves and Three Free Blacks, 2 Jan., 1738, p. 799–99v. The prosecutor justified the punishment by noting that 'from that sort of people at such an hour [after 11 p.m.] nothing is to be expected but roguery'. But this observation is not necessarily 'racist'. Company servants were also subject to curfew (see KA 4116, Dictum ter Rolle, 2 Jan. 1738, p. 859).
87. *KP*, III, 62 (12 Nov. 1765); 80 (19/20 June 1771).
88. *RCC*, XXXV, 146–47.
89. CO 3956, item 111. We are indebted to Shirley Judges for this and the following reference.
90. CO 3949, item 344.
91. Shell, 'Establishment', pp. 15–28.
92. De Kock, *Those in Bondage*, p. 194.
93. Shell, 'Establishment', p. 28.
94. They were housed together with slaves in the slave lodge and were often indistinguishable from slaves: see Cruse's enumeration in *Opheffing*, I, 221 ff.
95. LM 7, pp. 75–76, Res, 16 Sept. 1749, s.v. 'convicts'.

96. CJ 3321; cf. CJ 3318.
97. KA 4158, opgaaf 1750; KA 4240, opgaaf 1770.
98. Mentzel, *Description*, II, 149.
99. Armstrong, 'Free Black Community', pp. 4–6.
100. Cohen and Greene, *Neither Slave nor Free*, p. 4; Shirley Judges, personal communication.
101. The figures in this Table are probably more complete than those in Table 4.3, because the opgaaf, unlike the marriage records, sometimes listed free blacks (other than those married to Europeans) separately. In 1725 their names were explicitly set apart under the heading 'free blacks'. As a result of this feature one can spot free blacks whose names give no hint that they are not Europeans.
102. This and the previous four paragraphs are based on the opgaaf rolls for the years cited.
103. KA 4095, Independent Fiscal vs. Robbert Schot of Bengal, 27 Dec. 1731, pp. 686v–87.
104. E.g., KA 4069, 19 June 1722, pp. 1312 ff; KA 4010, Landdrost vs. Hans Henske *et al.*, 4 Dec. 1692, p. 239v; KA 4039, Provisional Landdrost vs. Willem Carelsz van de Caab, 18 Oct. 1708, p. 623; KA 4075, Provisional Fiscal vs. Susanna van Gildenhuysen (vryswartin), 12 Oct. 1724, p. 1049.
105. C 235, pp. 215–16, Requesten, no. 50, 1729–32.
106. Mentzel, *Description*, II, 92.
107. *Cape of Good Hope Almanacs 1812–1838, passim.*
108. Karl Scherzer, *Narrative of the Circumnavigation of the Globe by the Austrian frigate Novara in the years 1857, 1858 and 1859*, 3 vols.; (London, 1861), I, 198–99.
109. L.E. van Onselen, *Cape Antique Furniture* (Cape Town, 1959), p. 7.
110. W. Burchell, *Travels in the interior of Southern Africa* (London, 1822–24), I, 27–28; David Lewis, 'Malay Arts and Crafts', *Handbook on Race Relations in South Africa*, ed. Ellen Hellmann (Cape Town, 1949), pp. 646–50.
111. C 229, p. 149, *Requesten*, II, 444 (no. 86, 1722).
112. Mentzel, *Description*, II, 88–89.
113. C 234, p. 17, *Requesten*, I, 60 (no. 4, 1727); Mentzel, *Description*, II, 92; Charles Peter Thunberg, *Travels in Europe, Africa and Asia performed between the years 1770 and 1779* (London, 1795), I, 99.
114. Mentzel, *Description*, II, 149–50; see also 91, 92; Mentzel mentions *Journal Historique du Voyage au Cap de Bonne Espérance* (1763), but does not cite the page on which Abbé de la Caille repeats this story.
115. Mentzel, *Description*, II, 92.
116. On this culture see Pauline Dublin Milone, 'Indische culture, and its relationship to urban life', *Comparative Studies in Society and History*, IX (1966–67), pp. 407–26.
117. Marius F. Valkhoff, *Studies in Portuguese and Creole, with Special Reference to South Africa* (Johannesburg, 1966), pp. 146–91.
118. The following two paragraphs are based on Elphick, *Kraal and Castle*, pp. 207–14.
119. KA 4037, Vraagpoincten . . . Pieter Cronje, 3 March 1707, p. 781v.
120. Quotations are from John Splinter Stavorinus, *Voyages to the East Indies by the late John Splinter Stavorinus* (London, 1798), II, 57; and AR,

Aanwinsten 188, A viii, Kol. Aanw. 242, Cloppenburg Journal, p. 12. But see also Mentzel, *Description*, III, 115 and Henry Lichtenstein, *Travels in Southern Africa in the Years 1803, 1804, 1805, and 1806* (reprinted; Cape Town, 1928, 1930), I, 448.

121. Mentzel, *Description*, I, 56; André Sparrman, *Voyage au Cap de Bonne-Espérance et autour du Monde* (Paris, 1787), I, 269–73.

122. Mentzel, *Description*, III, 112; KA 4119, Res 21 July 1739, pp. 313–14v; The quotation is from Sparrman, *Voyage au Cap*, II, 182: 'Ce n'est pas, à la verité, sur la parure que tombe l'émulation des colons; c'est par le nombre et la beauté de leurs troupeaux, et surtout par la force de leurs boeufs de trait, qu'ils [the trekboers] ambitionnent de se surpasser.'

123. Sparrman, *Voyage*, I, 137–93; Vernon S. Forbes, *Pioneer Travellers in South Africa* (Cape Town and Amsterdam, 1965), p. 68; *RZA*, II, 'Dagverhaal, Plettenberg', p. 74.

124. KZ, Dag register . . . Jan de la Fontaine, 20 July 1734, n.p.; Staf D 593/4/1/3, Vierde Reyse . . . Gordon, 25 July 1779, n.p.; William Paterson, *A Narrative of Four Journeys into the Country of the Hottentots* . . . (London, 1790), pp. 47, 58; Lichtenstein, *Travels*, II, 83.

125. C.P. Thunberg, *Voyages de C.P. Thunberg au Japon par le Cap de Bonne-Espérance* (Paris, 1796), I, 143; Sparrman, *Voyage*, I, 98 and note, 251, 288; II, 21; Jacob Haafner, *Lotgevallen en Vroegere Zeereizen van Jacob Haafner* (Amsterdam, 1820), pp. 68–69; KA 4119, Res 13 March 1739, p. 241v.

126. Mentzel, *Description*, III, 307; Thunberg, *Voyage*, I, 98, 128; AR, Aanwinsten 1881, A viii, Kol. Aanw. 242, Cloppenburg Journal, p. 11.

127. Mentzel *Description*, III, 318; De la Caille, *Journal Historique*, p. 326; L. Degrandpré, *Voyage à la côte occidentale d'Afrique* . . . (Paris, 1801), II, 189; Sparrman, *Voyage*, II, 68; Lichtenstein, *Travels*, I, 193.

128. Sparrman, *Voyage*, I, 277, 283; Lichtenstein, II, 291–92. Lichtenstein commented on Khoikhoi festivities that 'these pastimes, however, had not much of national character, since the present generation of Hottentots in the interior of the colony have, in this respect, very much adopted the European customs'. However, several features of the activities described by Lichtenstein are traditional: e.g. mock combats, and dancing by the full moon.

129. Personal communication.

130. Sparrman, *Voyage*, I, 202; II, 328; Thunberg, *Voyage*, I, 98, 131, 234; Le Vaillant, *Voyage*, II, 144–54; AR, Aanwinsten 1881, A viii, Kol. Aanw. 242, Cloppenburg Journal, p. 11; Mentzel, *Description*, I, 49, 56; III, 302; Lichtenstein, *Travels*, II, 463.

PART II

The Cape economy

CHAPTER FIVE

The Cape of Good Hope and the world economy, 1652–1835

Robert Ross

In 1651, on the advice of two of their officers who had been shipwrecked in Table Bay and had spent a year there, the Directors of the Dutch East India Company (VOC) decided to found a small permanent station at the Cape of Good Hope. In doing so they did not hope for commercial gains in South Africa itself, and indeed the Cape station was run at a very considerable loss throughout the 143 years of its existence. Rather, as their instructions to their first commander, Jan van Riebeeck, made plain, the Heren XVII saw the Cape as a refreshment station and 'general rendezvous' for the large fleets which they sent every year from Europe to the East. It was therefore essential that the ships find there 'the means of procuring vegetables, meat, water and other needful refreshments and by this means restore the health of their sick'.[1] The settlement which grew up around the VOC's station, later known as Cape Town, was thus at first a port of call on the oceanic shipping routes, and this function it long maintained, initially for the VOC exclusively and later for all ships on the sea route between Europe and Asia.

The VOC establishment was generally able to fulfil many of its fleets' requirements itself. The fort was sited at one of the few points on the south-west coast where fresh water was always available, and the Company controlled land alienation and irrigation rights. Vegetables for the ships' crews were grown, largely by slaves, in the Company's gardens in Table Valley. Firewood was cut from the Company's closely guarded preserves on the slopes of Table Mountain and later further inland by the large force of slaves and European employees of the Company.[2] The dockyard, too, was manned by a combined slave and European workforce.[3] The hospital was not a wonder of medical efficiency, even by the standards of the seventeenth and eighteenth centuries, but it probably provided better conditions for the sick – and certainly better rations – than an East India ship would have done. Moreover, Cape Town was undoubtedly far superior as a place for recuperation than a ship's deck could be.[4] Nevertheless, very soon after Van Riebeeck established the Cape station, it became clear that the VOC could not itself profitably produce the bread and meat needed by the fleets, nor could it achieve a sufficient supply of wine, which was necessary for the sailors, both to keep them contented and as a preservable anti-scorbutic. Nor could the VOC acquire what it needed by trade with the Khoikhoi.[5] From 1657, therefore, servants of the Company were encouraged to leave its employment at Cape Town and to set up as farmers. It took thirty years, and the extension of settlement beyond the slopes of Table Mountain, before agriculture was sufficiently well established for the cereal requirements of even the Company itself to be met. But, even before 1700 Europeans had learned, in a somewhat rudimentary way, how to exploit the virgin soils of the Cape, and further expansion of both arable and pastoral activities was limited only by the necessity of conquering the land and by the feasibility of establishing viable farms in the territory so conquered.[6]

More or less simultaneously with the first agricultural freeburghers, men (and a few women) began to settle at the Cape to engage in a whole range of other occupations. Most importantly, they became keepers of drinking and lodging houses, serving the needs of the passing ships. From the earliest days, though, they began to fulfil a much wider range of urban functions, as shopkeepers and general traders, as bakers and brewers, as builders and carpenters, as smiths, coopers and potters and even as silversmiths.[7] With an increasingly large Company establishment, Cape Town quickly grew into a modest town.

By around 1700, then, the economic basis for the colony's continued existence had been laid. The port, its town, and its agricultural and pastoral hinterland had become firmly rooted; their existence was never seriously threatened by attack from within the colony. Slaves had already been imported in fair numbers as the basis for the Colony's labour force. The first Africans, in this case Khoisan, had been at least semi-proletarianised in European service. Nevertheless, the Cape Colony in 1700 was still minuscule. By the 1830s its population had risen from around 2,000 to about 150,000,[8] and stretched, no longer just to the Berg river, but rather to the Orange and the upper Kei. Cape Town was no longer a village of some 70 houses.[9] It had grown to a town with more than 1,500 dwellings, nearly 20,000 inhabitants and the full range of urban attributes.[10] Moreover, although it was still by far the largest settlement in the Cape, it was no longer the only one which could reasonably be called a town. Stellenbosch, Paarl, Worcester, Genadendal, Swellendam, Port Elizabeth, Graaff-Reinet and Grahamstown were all, at the very least, substantial villages. Though by no means at the end of its development, the colony of the 1830s was close enough to maturity for its settlers to begin to agitate for a Parliament.

In general, historians have tended to consider this qualitative and quantitative change as natural and self-explanatory, and as puny in comparison with the socio-economic revolution which followed on the mineral discoveries of the late nineteenth century. After all, such growth was characteristic of colonies of white settlement and of slave societies – and the Cape was both. Indeed, the Cape's success story was far less spectacular than those of, for instance, British North America or the West Indies. All the same, the economic history of the pre-industrial Cape Colony needs to be written in terms which are comparable to those of other colonies, concentrating on the increase of production, the development of export crops, and the establishment of instruments of trade and commerce. These are the important issues in the economic history of the Cape, rather than the much discussed trekboers, and the alleged subsistence economy.[11]

The VOC and the economy

The position of the Dutch East India Company, as both government and commerical company, had elements of contradiction. Obviously, the main task of the high officials was to keep the costs of the Cape as low as possible, since there was never any hope that the station would make a profit for the VOC. At the same time, however, they had to develop the economy to fulfil the role set for it by the Heren XVII, namely the victualling of the Company's ships and the supply of various products, above all wheat to Batavia. In addition, like all eighteenth century officials, whether of commercial companies or European governments, they saw no reason why they should not exploit their offices for personal gain, the prohibitions of the Heren XVII notwithstanding. After the dismissal of Governor Willem Adriaan van der Stel (see ch. 6, pp. 303 – 07), officials could no longer engage directly in production, but they retained privileged access to the import trade in particular.

The VOC had the legal right to impose monopolies over the sale of goods from outside the Cape, over shipping and over the purchase of the produce of Cape farms.* In the event, it did all of these things only in

---

* This last should more strictly be described as a monopsony.

part. As regards the sale of imports, the VOC had certain advantages, which, however, fell far short of total control of the colony's economic life. The large number of ships that it sent annually from Europe to the East invariably had a certain amount of unused cargo space, so that it could import bulk, low-value goods, including iron and coal, without transport costs; hence it dominated the trade in these items.[12] It was also, naturally, the sole importer of those goods whose production it monopolised at source – the spices of the Moluccas, Banda, and Sri Lanka, cloves, nutmeg, mace and cinnamon.[13] In addition, it also tried to enforce by ordinance a monopoly on tobacco imports in the late seventeenth and early eighteenth centuries and on coffee imports towards the end of its rule.[14] Nevertheless, the former monopoly died a natural death, as the Company itself developed no great trade in tobacco, which was not yet produced to any extent within the area of its charter. Rather, the Company focussed increasingly on the importation of Asian goods into Europe,[15] but, even so, it made no attempt to acquire a monopoly in products such as Indian textiles, which did form a major component of its imports to Europe. Thus as the number of non-Dutch ships putting into Cape Town harbour increased in the latter half of the eighteenth century, the VOC's share of the importation to the Cape apparently declined.

As to shipping, the VOC, even had it wished, could not have isolated the Colony from the world's traffic putting into Cape Town harbour. Even its most arbitrary measure along these lines, prohibiting the Cape colonists from chartering or outfitting their own ships for the trade in Eastern waters, probably had little effect on the colony's economy;[16] after the prohibition was lifted in 1792, the colonists sent out only a few ships.[17] Even in the favourable conditions of the early nineteenth century, Cape-based international shipping got no further than working the route between South Africa and Mauritius, Réunion and Madagascar. In other cases it was generally more advantageous for merchants to hire cargo space in ships which were sailing between Europe and Asia.

Although it never monopolised the purchase of the colony's wine, wheat and meat, the VOC considerably affected how these three main agricultural products were marketed. Its income from the retail sale of wine was one of its main sources of revenue at the Cape. As was usual in the Netherlands, each year the Company auctioned the franchise to sell wine in Cape Town's taverns. The franchise holder or *pachter* thus gained a strong, and sometimes excessive, grip on the wine market.[18]

However, the Company as such did not directly control the buying and selling of wine. Indeed, it could not even control the sales of the one product in which it was particularly interested, namely wine from the two Constantia estates, which had become one of the first 'chateau' wines to receive recognition in Europe. The company was able to sell around *f*.25,000's worth a year in Europe in the second half of the eighteenth century[19], but it could only acquire the product on the basis of its contracts with the Constantia owners. These contracts were regularly open for negotiation, both as regards price and quantity, and the owners were not required to sell exclusively to the VOC. Indeed they could use the presence of the VOC's competitors, notably the Danes and the Swedes, to drive up the price.[20] Rather than have the Company monopolise the purchase of the wine, local officials of the VOC preferred to use Constantia wine to attract foreigners to the Cape.[21]

As the sole exporter of grain, the Company was the largest buyer from the farmers. The price it set for its purchases remained constant for long periods, immune to annual fluctuations. This had the effect of ensuring the farmers a guaranteed minimum price for their produce, on which they could base their calculations. This was because the free market price in Cape Town did not drop much below the VOC's figure even in years of abundant harvests, but could rise well above it in years of scarcity, despite the best efforts of the VOC and the Cape Town *Burgerraad* (which in this represented the consumers) to hold it steady. Indeed the sharp rise in the free market price during the Fourth Anglo-Dutch War of the 1780s forced the VOC, too, to buy wheat for nearly double the sum it had paid previously.[22]

The meat market was more complicated. The VOC secured its own supplies by putting a contract out to tender for five years, in general to three people. These contractors acquired certain privileges, notably to use the Company's shambles in Cape Town and the Groen Kloof farms north of the city where the stock driven from the interior could recuperate and put on weight before being slaughtered. However, by the end of the century, the VOC bought only a part of the colony's meat, probably no more than a quarter, and there were alternative uses for cattle in particular, notably as draught oxen and producers of butter. In the face of these competing buyers, contracted butchers could not drive down the purchase price and harm the Cape farmers.[23] The VOC did require all foreign ships visiting Cape Town to buy their meat from the contracted butchers, who could charge the foreigners monopolistic prices and so recoup the losses they suffered in their sales to the VOC. Evidently, then, the more foreign ships that put into Table Bay, the lower the Company's own expenses, and the local officials did what they could to foster these visits.[24] On the other hand, the game could only be played so far, since Cape Town could price itself out of the market of victualling the fleets of Europe's other trading nations.[25] In this, as in so many of its activities, the Company could only seal off the colony to a very limited extent from the world market.

Production

Since the Dutch East India Company was not an effective monopolist, the economy of the Cape Colony can be analysed, much as any other, by discussing the factors of supply and demand.

The production levels of the various agricultural commodities has to be estimated from the annual tax returns, known as the *opgaaf*. Unfortunately, these were subject to very considerable underrecording, especially during the VOC period. This unreliability was least pronounced in the case of wine production, because after 1744 the VOC no longer taxed wine production on the basis of the opgaaf, but rather charged $f.7.4$ † for each barrel that entered Cape Town. This new impost could not be evaded and was thus much more favourable to the VOC. It also removed any motive to underreport wine production. As shown in Figure 5.1, production rose rather regularly through the eighteenth and early nineteenth centuries. For instance, in 1725 1,133 *leggers* (about 660,000 litres) of wine were produced, in 1775, 5,528 (nearly 3-¼ million litres) and in 1806, 9,643 leggers (over 5-½ million). The only major discontinuity was the sharp rise in the 1820s, during the minor boom caused by the temporary preference given Cape wine on the British market.[26]

It is far less easy to provide figures for grain production or for stock holding, where underreporting was rife. For example, between the opgaafs of 1795 and 1798 the colony's wheat production is recorded as having increased by 419 per cent, its cattle herd by 351 per cent and its sheep flock by 346 per cent – an unbelievable rate of growth. The dramatic rise in figures was due to the farmers' fears after 1795 that the new British government would punish evasion more severely than the Company had done. Nevertheless, it is possible to make rough estimates of the level of evasion for both grain and stock.[27]

---

† The two main units of currency in the Netherlands and its empire were the guilder ($f.$) worth 20 stuivers and the rijksdaalder (rixdollar) worth 48. In 1795 the rixdollar was worth £0.20 sterling.

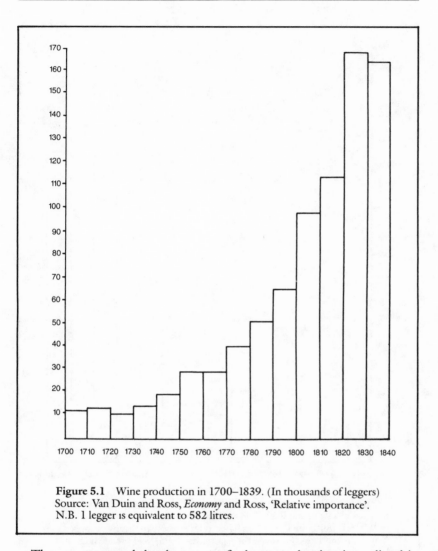

Figure 5.1 Wine production in 1700–1839. (In thousands of leggers)
Source: Van Duin and Ross, *Economy* and Ross, 'Relative importance'.
N.B. 1 legger is equivalent to 582 litres.

The reconstructed development of wheat production is outlined in Figure 5.2. As with wine, it shows the steady rise in production levels throughout the period; from perhaps 15,000 hectolitres in the 1720s to over 50,000 by the 1770s and over 130,000 by 1806. There was only one decade, the 1740s, when production seemed temporarily to be running ahead of consumption, but this was shortly solved by a combination of inferior harvests and an increase in the foreign shipping in Table Bay, because of the outbreak of war.[28] Later, from the 1780s on, the danger

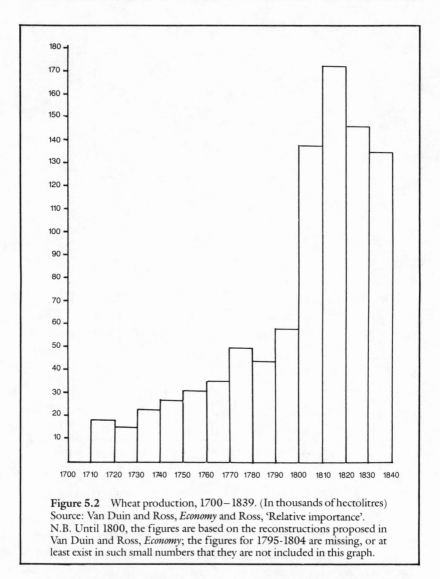

Figure 5.2   Wheat production, 1700–1839. (In thousands of hectolitres)
Source: Van Duin and Ross, *Economy* and Ross, 'Relative importance'.
N.B. Until 1800, the figures are based on the reconstructions proposed in
Van Duin and Ross, *Economy*; the figures for 1795-1804 are missing, or at
least exist in such small numbers that they are not included in this graph.

was that the Cape would be short of grain – and on one occasion it even
had to import one million pounds from the United States to avert a
potential shortfall.[29] This was probably because the Cape's poor roads
restricted the economic cultivation of grain to those areas from where
the market could be reached without crossing a major mountain pass.
Only toward the end of the eighteenth century were any attempts made

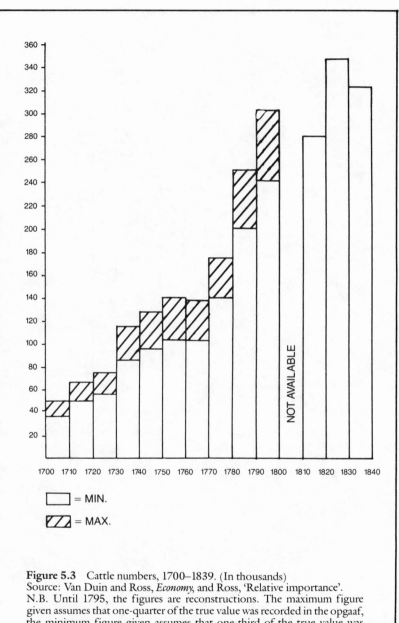

Figure 5.3   Cattle numbers, 1700–1839. (In thousands)
Source: Van Duin and Ross, *Economy*, and Ross, 'Relative importance'.
N.B. Until 1795, the figures are reconstructions. The maximum figure
given assumes that one-quarter of the true value was recorded in the opgaaf,
the minimum figure given assumes that one-third of the true value was
recorded.

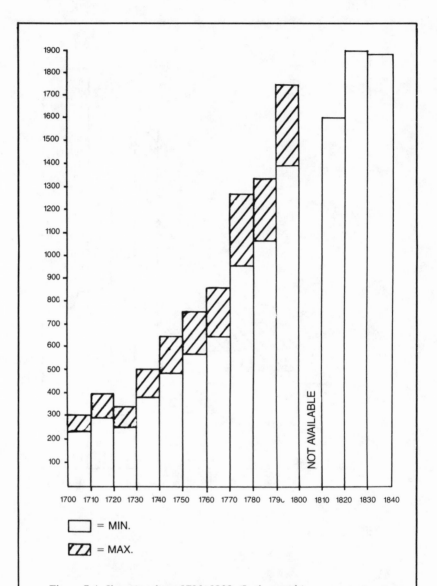

Figure 5.4 Sheep numbers, 1700–1839. (In thousands)
Source: Van Duin and Ross, *Economy* and Ross, 'Relative importance'.
N.B. Until 1795, the figures are reconstructions. The maximum figure
given assumes that only one-quarter of the true value was recorded in the
opgaaf, the minimum figure given assumes that one-third of the true value
was recorded.

to extend the area of potential arable land by developing coastal shipping. The initial experiment, in the Mossel Bay area in the 1780s, failed because of a temporary decline in the market following the end of the Fourth Anglo-Dutch War.[30] After the British take-over, this project was revitalised and the plains from Caledon to Mossel Bay, and also around St. Helena Bay to the north, became growing centres for grain production.[31]

In Figures 5.3 and 5.4 the reconstructed totals for the colonial cattle herd and sheep flock are given. In the 1720s the colony had rather more than 250,000 sheep and rather under 100,000 cattle. In the 1770s there were more than a million sheep and around 250,000 cattle, and the numbers continued to grow thereafter, to over 1-¾ million sheep and over 300,000 cattle by the 1820s. This was of course the result of the steady *trekboer* expansion into the Cape's interior, which was conquered from the Khoisan and later the Xhosa. Although the most distant trekboers were initially not as closely tied to the market as the farmers of the southwestern Cape, in time the butchers would make their presence felt in each successive region, usually within a few years of its initial settlement by whites. In the early years, and in the western Karoo until deep in the nineteenth century,[32] the butchers drove the stock to Cape Town on the hoof. For this reason, Cape hairy sheep, which keep their weight well under such conditions, were for a long time raised in preference to European sheep in such areas. Nevertheless the establishment of small harbours along the southern coast, and especially of Port Elizabeth, was to reorient much of the livestock trade and to provide for the first time a satisfactory outlet for the hides, horns and skins that were previously a discarded by-product of the stock industry. These outlets would then provide the commercial basis for the shift to wool production in the eastern Cape, which was just getting under way in 1835 and which in the later nineteenth century would lead to Port Elizabeth becoming the most dynamic financial and commercial centre in the Cape.[33] It had begun earlier in a few areas of the better capitalised west, but even there, serious expansion had to wait for the importation of the first merino sheep, which unlike the Dutch animals with which the VOC had made a few abortive attempts, were suited to the arid environment of the Cape Colony.[34]

The steady expansion of all sectors of the agricultural economy during the eighteenth and nineteenth centuries demonstrates that South African farmers' actions were not limited by anything other than the availability of capital and markets. When new transport facilities or new markets opened, they responded quickly, at least when they could raise the capital required. Their expansion, particularly of arable crops, was determined by the possibilities they saw of selling their produce, however imperfect these forecasts may have been. In other words, their actions can be explained more in terms of economic rationality, than in terms of Afrikaner 'cultural lag',[35] or other theories which would see their economic behaviour as irrational 'overproduction.' Had there really been chronic 'overproduction' at the Cape, as some historians have argued, there would necessarily have been a decline in prices and widespread bankruptcies among farmers. Neither in fact occurred – at least not until the 1820s when the market for Cape wine contracted sharply with the abolition of preferential tariffs on the British market.[36]

The market for Cape products

The steady growth of production was a response to a continual increase in the size of the market for agricultural products, both at the Cape and overseas. Notwithstanding the intermittent complaints of the farmers, which have led historians to believe that they generally produced more than they could sell, in fact normally Cape agricultural produce found a ready market. Exports never played the predominant role that they did in the frequently export-led economies of the New World. With the exception of elephant hunting, which contributed considerably to the colonists' knowledge of the Cape's interior but little to the economy as a whole, there was no sector which produced exclusively, or even predominantly, for the overseas market. The early exports consisted largely of wheat to the Asian factories (trading sites) of the VOC, where it was made into bread for European traders, and also of butter and wine.[37] For a time in the 1770s, too, Cape wheat production was sufficient to allow considerable shipments to Amsterdam, to compete with Polish grain.[38] Nevertheless, this trade did not produce such great profits, either for the VOC or for the Cape grain farmers, that the Cape wheat production expanded explosively. A series of bad harvests, coupled with the growth of the local market during the Fourth Anglo-Dutch War of the 1780s, curtailed the trade to Europe. Thereafter, grain production was never again sufficient for more than a trickle of exports, although it expanded sufficiently to keep abreast of local demand.[39]

Wine exports, particularly to Europe, were at a much lower level during the eighteenth century because Cape wines – the Constantia vintages excepted – were too inferior or too expensive to find large markets overseas. After the British conquest, by contrast, a new market opened up in England, as a result of imperial preferential tariffs. A very considerable increase in production resulted, until the abolition of the tariff advantages ended the boom. Substitute markets were found after 1830, largely in Australia and South America, but they were insufficient to absorb the temporary glut. A large number of bankruptcies ensued among wine farmers in this single, rather mild, example at the Cape of the boom-and-bust pattern so characteristic of slave economies everywhere.[40]

In the days before refrigeration, direct export of livestock products was necessarily limited. However, some tallow was sent to Europe, and salted Cape butter was sent to Batavia,[41] while the early commercial development of what was to become Port Elizabeth was based on the salting of meat for Mauritius.[42]. Surprisingly, there is no indication of eighteenth-century export of hides, which later became important in the mid-nineteenth century. Wool exports were beginning in the 1820s and 1830s, a period which saw the acclimatisation of merino sheep to South African conditions and the heyday of the colony's largest sheep estate owned by Van Breda, Reitz, Joubert and Co. near Cape Agulhas;[43] wool did not, however, become a major export until the 1840s.

In all cases, except perhaps that of wine production during the early nineteenth century, the local market considerably exceeded foreign markets as an outlet for the Cape's agricultural produce. This can be demonstrated by comparing the amounts brought into Cape Town, or the amounts said to be required by the urban population, with the quantities sent overseas.[44] These figures are not always available before the late eighteenth century, but on the reasonable assumption that the consumption patterns of Capetonians and visiting ships did not change drastically over the eighteenth century, a sufficiently accurate reconstruction can be made of the earlier period to support this conclusion.[45] It must be noted, however, that Cape Town did not comprise the entire local market for wine and grains. There was also a regular exchange of produce between the wheat and wine farms.

Stock production was, by contrast, somewhat less oriented to the market. A considerable proportion of the natural increase of herds and flocks was used by farmers both to build up viable breeding stocks and for their own needs. They also sold stock to the agrarian districts which needed only meat and, more importantly, draft oxen, which were frequently in short supply and without which crops could not have been grown, harvested, or transported to town.[46] In the late eighteenth century only about three to five per cent of the colony's cattle and sheep was butchered annually in Cape Town. This seemingly meagre figure obviously does not represent the totality of the pastoralists' involvement with the market. Virtually all farmers maintained links of varying strengths with the Cape Town market and responded to the pressures which emanated from it. These pressures became steadily greater as, in any given district, European settlement became more firmly established. Moreover, from the beginning, it was often the most active of the colony's entrepreneurs who invested in the opening up of even the most distant areas of the colony; their goals were to supply their own farms with oxen, to ensure deliveries of meat to the Cape market and, later to pioneer wool production. In this they operated alongside those who went to the frontier because they hoped to build up a good estate on the basis of relatively little capital.[47]

Imports

Before 1807 the most important imports of the Cape Colony were slaves, without whom the economy could not have functioned. The total must have been several tens of thousands, spread over the 155 years of the traffic. While the VOC organised a fair number of expeditions to provide slaves for its own use, much of the trade was privately organised, with slaves imported in small numbers, either as part of the illegal, but tolerated, perquisites of VOC sailors and officers or off-loaded from the slavers rounding the Cape of Good Hope en route from Madagascar or Mozambique to the Americas[48] (see ch. 3, pp. 112–19).

The remaining imports to the Cape comprised cotton and other textiles, largely from India; a whole range of consumer goods, led by tropical products such as coffee, tea, sugar and spices but eventually including a wide range of European manufactures as the white Cape community became more established and its tastes more developed; and finally, agricultural and other implements and materials, such as iron, for fabricating them. Significantly, the import business of the Van Reenen family during the 1780s, then the most diversified, enterprising and successful entrepreneurs in the colony, centred on the import of agricultural tools.[49]

As was pointed out above, the VOC did not attempt to impose a monopoly over imports to the colony, except for spices, coffee and, ineffectually, sugar. Other goods were imported quite legally, both from Europe and the East, either by individual sailors using space allowed to them on VOC ships,[50] or by foreigners. Nor did the VOC levy duties on these imports, this being a personal perquisite of the fiscaal. As a result, we do not have figures on imports, except for those goods sold by the VOC, which, in all probability, formed a relatively small proportion of total imports. Some indication of the level of private trading can be gathered from the quantities of money that individuals transferred to Europe via the VOC to pay for imports. Such transfers ran at about *f*.425,000 per annum in the 1750s, rising to *f*.600,000 by the late 1780s.[51] After the arrival of the British, exact figures for imports were produced. During the First British Occupation (1795–1802), they amounted to on average £280,000 (or 1,120,000 rixdollars) per year. Information is again unavailable during the Batavian period, but after 1806, until the end of the Napoleonic wars in 1815, imports were low, consistently under £ 100,000 annually. Since this was also a time of high military expenditure in Cape Town there was probably a build-up of cash in the colony, so that, as trade became easier after 1813, the annual value of imports grew quickly, and only dropped below £ 300,000 four times before 1835, when they stood at an all-time high of £534,000 per annum.

The pattern of exports paralleled that of imports, though consistently at a much lower level. For the VOC period precise figures are not available, but nevertheless the speed with which silver coinage drained out of the colony would seem to indicate a very considerable excess of imports over exports.[52] During the Napoleonic wars, exports were almost always under £100,000 a year, but after 1813 they rose steadily to reach a value of £370,000 in 1834. Of these exports, a proportion ranging between 92 per cent (in 1824) and 77 per cent (in 1822) were of Cape products, the rest being re-exports from Asia and Europe, mainly to Mauritius and Réunion.[53] Thus the balance of Cape trade was conspicuously negative. Between 1807 and 1835, when there are definite figures, there were only three years in which exports exceeded imports and indeed the deficit was often larger than the volume of exports itself. In part this deficit would have been counterbalanced by such invisible exports as the victualling of ships in the harbour, but this activity would not have been nearly adequate to achieve anything approaching a balance of payments.

Nevertheless, the colony's trade imbalance was somewhat rectified over the long term by the transfers of money, first from the Netherlands and then from Great Britain, for the government administration, the army and the navy. Clearly Cape agriculture was kept in business, and its economy allowed to expand, even during the wine and wool export booms, above all by the absorptive qualities of the military and governmental sectors of the colony's economy. W.S. van Ryneveld was quite correct to see the commercial prosperity of the Cape as dependent on the size of its garrison,[54] and indeed the economy's growth in the first half of the nineteenth century was largely financed by British military remittances.[55]

Recognition of the importance of the Cape's internal market for agricultural producers is nonetheless a recognition of the strength of the economy's links to the world economy. The ships and the garrisons were not only very considerable consumers in their own right but also they provided the opportunities on which the non-rural population of the colony could subsist. The income they generated was spent within the colony and thus led to the creation of more income. [‡] Large proportions of the non-agrarian population of the colony were either the direct agents first of the Dutch East India Company and later of the British state, or acquired their living by providing them with services, though naturally the rural economic growth also brought into being numerous merchants and artisans, who in their own turn became consumers of bread, meat and wine. In this way the effect of the world economy penetrated far deeper into Cape society than might appear from an analysis of direct purchases by outsiders.

Currency, credit and banking

As we have seen, the Cape's economy increasingly became commercialised and hence dependent on money and credit arrangements. In the eighteenth century, such facilities were informal but by no means absent. The Cape was linked to the monetary system of the Dutch Empire and the Indian Ocean. As a result, a large variety of coins were in circulation, all in silver, and hence all easily convertible. The Spanish reals (or pieces-of-eight) were the most popular, because their purity was most trusted, Spanish America being the greatest source of the world's silver. The Company's annual shipments of coin to the Cape, which provided a large proportion of the Cape's money, therefore always contained a certain number of reals, although increasingly the Company attempted to replace them with Dutch guilders, to keep the profits from minting coin in the Dutch Republic.[56] The British too, found it necessary to pay their troops in Spanish dollars.[57]

‡ This is of course the multiplier effect of economic theory. For a useful exposition, see G.R. Hawke, *Economics for Historians* (Cambridge, 1980), pp. 63–74.

Credit arrangements in the eighteenth century were also largely informal. Individuals with capital lent it out, particularly to those beginning an agricultural enterprise, generally at 5 per cent interest. Many of the creditors were the Company officials, who had better opportunities than freeburghers to accumulate wealth and fewer avenues for investment, since they were forbidden to directly engage in agriculture.[58] Thus, at his death in 1761, Joachim von Dessin, longtime head of the Orphan Chamber and founder of the South African Library, held *f.* 25,919 in interest-bearing loans made to 33 different people, many of them farmers.[59]

A number of burghers also engaged in lending, and it seems that some of them retired from farm ownership to become rentiers at the end of their life.[60] In addition, the funds of the church were used to provide mortgages[61] and the *Wees- en Boedelkamer* (the Orphan Chamber) acted as a fairly large-scale provider of credit, since it administered the estates of those who died without heirs in South Africa, at least until the heirs could be found. Since there were many single, uprooted men in the service of the VOC, this fund could grow rapidly. In 1720 it stood at over 200,000 rixdollars; by 1780 it had risen to nearly 400,000, in 1800 to over a million and by 1830 to just about three million (admittedly devalued) rixdollars.[62]

The Orphan Chamber and the church were involved largely in financing long-term mortgages. There was also a need for short-term commercial credit, to enable tradespeople to pay for their wholesale purchases before they could resell them. This need was fulfilled in part by private lenders, but even more by the licensed auctioneers. Public sales, for instance of imported goods, were controlled by these people, and they were assured of first claim on the assets of any of their creditors who went bankrupt. As a result, they were willing to provide credit to the purchasers of goods at auctions, to which they were empowered to admit only merchants whose credit they trusted. They were also allowed to charge the high interest rate of 10 per cent.[63]

Between 1782 and 1808, considerable changes occurred in all these matters. First, the metallic basis of the currency was abandoned. In 1782, confronted with a disruption of silver supplies during the Fourth Anglo-Dutch War (1780–84), the Cape government found it necessary to issue money on stamped parchment, in denominations running from an eighth of a rixdollar (six stuivers) to sixty rixdollars. The proclamation of the new currency was accompanied by a promise that it would be redeemed by the Company, when sufficient hard money became available, and by a strict prohibition on the export of precious metal from the colony.[64] The latter provision proved a complete dead letter, and the inconvertibility of the Cape currency led to an increased haemorrhage of silver from the colony.[§] On the other hand, the Company did honour its commitment to buy back the notes it had issued,[65] redeeming most of them until the shortage of currency at the Cape again became acute in 1792 and paper money once again had to be issued. Thus by the time the British first captured the Cape in 1795, there was a total of 1,291,276 rixdollars and 42 stuivers in paper money in circulation.[66]

Thereafter, paper currency was employed in the Cape until 1825, theoretically backed by government land and buildings, not by silver.[67] Therefore, the steady drain of metallic currency from the colony continued, ordinances to the contrary notwithstanding.[68] At the same time, the buying power of the rixdollar fluctuated considerably, although the trend was steadily downwards. Thus by 1803, it stood at 30 per cent below its original value of 4 British shillings[¶] and with the outbreak of war in 1805 it declined very sharply, since the opportunities for money transfers to the Netherlands were few.[69] After regaining par value in 1806, it devalued steadily until by 1821 it was worth only about one shilling and six pence, or three-eighths of its face value.[70]

In 1825, the British Treasury decided that all the currencies of the Empire, including rixdollars, should be made dependent on sterling. The estimated 3,108,000 rixdollars then in circulation were thus to be made convertible into sterling at a fixed (no longer a floating) rate of one shilling and sixpence each, minus a small premium which was reckoned to cover the costs of transporting British coins to South Africa. As a result, the rixdollar slowly faded out of existence, being replaced by British coinage and promissory notes, until on 31 March 1841 it ceased to be legal tender.[71] The measure, which was in effect devaluation, led to vigorous protests in the Cape Colony. A petition signed by 2,115 people was sent to London requesting that the ordinance be rescinded, and their representations were supported by a group of leading merchants and by the board of the Orphan Chamber. The Orphan Masters argued that capitalists would pass on their losses by raising rents and interest rates, causing suffering among debtors, tenants, and in general, the colony's poor.[72] In the event, the devaluation caused considerable losses to those who had borrowed money in sterling to invest in South Africa and who thus needed many more rixdollars to repay their loans.[73]

§This is a classic example of the workings of Gresham's Law, which states that bad money always drives out good.
¶ Until 1970 there were 20 shillings, each consisting of twelve pence, to the pound.

Nevertheless, the effect on the Cape's economy as a whole seems to have been minor, since the colony's inhabitants had long taken account of the diminished value of the rixdollar in their transactions.[74]

It was a matter of considerable contemporary controversy why the rixdollar devalued so fast.[75] John Trotter, commissioned by the Cape Chamber of Commerce to investigate the matter, argued that the negative balance of payments was to blame, but his reasoning was attacked by P.W. Grant, his superior in the Indian revenue service. In general Grant's position has been supported by later investigators. Grant claimed that the excessive issues of money had driven down the value of the rixdollar. The increase in the Cape's money supply, with its unwanted devaluatory consequences, derived from the government's financing public works by printing more money, but also, and probably above all, by its repeated augmentation of the capital of the government-owned *Bank van Lening* (known after 1795 as the Loan or Lombard Bank).[76]

The Loan Bank was set up by the Commissioners-General Nederburgh and Frijkenius in 1793.[77] Their stated motive was to stem the haemorrhage of specie out of the colony, but the effect of their actions, which they probably foresaw, was to give the government a very substantial stake in the lucrative credit business. The Bank did not accept deposits, but rather functioned as a combination of mortgage institution and pawn-broker, lending money against the security of fixed property and valuables, such as precious metal and jewellery. In 1822, however, it began to accept small deposits, but not at a rate of interest likely to attract large sums of capital. The great proportion of its capital was provided by the government, and this was augmented in 1802 by another 165,000 rixdollars, and rose steadily over two million rixdollars.[78] The government profited from interest on the money it loaned to the Bank, which, less the costs, amounted to 25,000 rixdollars in the 1790s rising to over 90,000 rixdollars in 1824.[79]

In addition to the Lombard Bank, a Discount Bank was set up at the Cape in 1808. The two institutions were closely linked, and had the same chairman, but their functions were clearly distinct. The directors of the bank hoped to put an end to the practice whereby money lent on the security of real estate was re-lent at a higher rate of interest to those who required short-term credit.[80] Therefore the Discount Bank provided short-term loans,[81] but it also solicited deposits from Cape Town's inhabitants. Although after 1814 it no longer provided interest on such money, the convenience the bank provided for mercantile transactions induced many people to make deposits. Some depositors wished to remain in good standing with the bank, which was frequently forced to refuse its loan services to the public for want of funds.[82] At any event, by 1824 there were 214 accounts at the bank, with a total of more than one and a half million rixdollars.[83] Of these, 29 were said to belong to Government officials, two to the English East India Company, 34 to merchants and the rest to 'tradesmen and other individuals'. Clearly the Discount Bank had penetrated fairly well into Cape Town's commercial community.

In general, the two government banks did not run great risks by providing credit to the merchants. In a small community like Cape Town, accurate information was available on the financial position of all merchants. In 1812 the president of the two banks commented that no one was astonished when a merchant went bankrupt, because his affairs were perfectly known in advance.[84] His attitude may have hastened the merchant's bankruptcy, but it was certainly a sufficient defence for the financial institutions. The banks were perhaps somewhat less conservative in their dealings with the farmers, and the Lombard bank was badly hit in the late 1820s after the crisis in the wine industry caused a fall in the value of agricultural property.[85]

At first these banking and credit arrangements were limited to Cape Town and its immediate environs (although of course the mortgages on agricultural property spread further up country). It would not have been possible, declared the president of the Discount Bank as late as 1825, to provide the same services in Graaff-Reinet or Grahamstown.[86] Indeed, the great bulk of the colony's currency also remained in the southwestern Cape. This fact does not indicate a lack of commercialisation amongst eastern farmers, who were certainly concerned with the state of the currency, and indeed petitioned against the introduction of paper money immediately on its introduction.[87] Moreover, an alternative form of money (and for that matter of commercial credit) came into existence in the east, namely the so-called *slagters briefjes*, which were promissory notes issued by the travelling butchers.[88] These performed the function of a circulating medium in the country districts but could be cashed only in Cape Town, either by a farmer during his regular but infrequent visits there or, probably increasingly, by the *smousen*, or travelling pedlars. Consequently, the bankruptcy of a major butcher would have widespread repercussions deep into the *platteland*, as those caught with his *briefjes* might not be able to meet their obligations.[89]

Credit provided by farmers to butchers was not the only form of private lending after the founding of the Loan and Discount banks. A goodly proportion of the credit market continued to operate outside the aegis of the government banking system, which could not meet the demands made on it, simply for lack of funds. As the colony's economy expanded in the first third of the nineteenth century, it was natural that attempts should be made to set up private banks, but nevertheless the government blocked the first attempt, by J.B. Ebden in 1826, largely in order to safeguard the revenue it acquired from the state institutions.[90] Such a policy, however, could not last in the laissez-faire climate of the nineteenth century. Pressure for the establishment of a private banking system grew sharply, with the Cape Town Chamber of Commerce, for instance, attributing the bankruptcy of several of its members to temporary cash-flow problems which the Discount Bank could not alleviate.[91] As a result, the first private Cape bank was founded in 1837, the joint stock Cape of Good Hope Bank, and it was rapidly followed by many others, not merely in Cape Town but also in the interior of the colony. In 1843, the government banks abandoned their normal banking operations and became mere adjuncts of the colonial treasury.[92]

The structure of commerce

Although almost from the beginning of the colony's history a number of colonists had engaged in the import trade, particularly in slaves,[93] only in the last third of the eighteenth century did large-scale merchants begin to acquire the leading positions they would maintain throughout the pre-industrial period. Previously, the richest burghers had acquired their wealth through farming, butchering, large-scale fishing, exploiting of liquor franchises, and supplying building materials.[94] By the 1770s, though, major import houses first emerged of the type that would be characteristic later. The first two were La Fèbre and Co. and Cruywagen and Co., both consortia headed by Company officials. These companies were to be among the major targets of the Cape Patriots' complaints (see ch. 6, pp. 309–15). This was not surprising since they were the major competitors of certain leading Patriots, notably the Van Reenens, and enjoyed what were seen as unfair advantages, such as prior access to incoming ships, first claim on the transfer of money to the Netherlands and preference in acquiring cargo space in the VOC ships.[95] The last service was arranged by their agents in Holland, who contracted VOC sailors to fill their sea-chests with the goods ordered by the Cape merchants.[96] Perhaps as a result of the Patriot agitation, the partnerships of Cruywagen and Co. and La Fèbre and Co. seemingly lost importance after 1780 and faded out of existence, although a number of participants remained important Cape businessmen.[97]

About the same time, the economic boom at the Cape during the Fourth Anglo-Dutch War (1780–84) stimulated the development of private mercantile activity, as can be seen most clearly in the activities of the Van Reenen family. Previously engaged in importation, they decided in 1781 to re-enter this business, reckoning both on the discomforture of the officials as a result of Patriot agitation, and on the improvement of economic conditions which would result from the Anglo-Dutch War, and the consequent presence of a large French force at the Cape. The development of their business was made easier by the presence of Jacobus van Reenen in the Patriot delegation that had gone to the Netherlands in 1779. Unfortunately, however, relations between Jacobus and his son Johannes Gysbertus, in charge of the Cape Town operation, became strained and led to a major court case between them.[98] The younger Van Reenen was almost certainly the major importer to the Cape in the 1780s. In three years, his father spent *f*.136,252 on his behalf buying goods in Europe and sending them to the Cape. Apparently these imports yielded a reasonable profit for his son.[99] After 1784, details even of the younger Van Reenen's activities are missing, except for occasional glimpses, such as the bill of lading for about *f*.30,000 worth of ironware (largely agricultural implements), wine, hops and clothing that he had shipped to the Cape via Jan and Willem Willink of Amsterdam in 1787.[100] On the activities of other merchants, nothing is yet known.

In 1792, the Commissioners-General Nederburgh and Frijkenius simultaneously tightened up payment of freight charges and import duties on goods sent to the Cape in Company ships and, for the first time, allowed Cape burghers to own their own ships and to import almost all goods both from Europe and from Asia.[101] In the first years after 1792, probably in part as a result of the outbreak of the French Revolutionary Wars, the Cape was temporarily starved of imported goods. When the British took over in 1795, J.F. Kirsten wrote that 'at present the inhabitants are in great want of Iron, which is not to be procured for money, as well of Cloath, Coals, Timber etc.'.[102] The problem was so great that the British were forced to suspend the Navigation Acts with respect to the Cape, an unprecedented step in their imperial history, and numerous American, Danish and Swedish ships arrived in Cape Town.[103] Nevertheless the shortage of imported goods was so desperate that Henry Dundas, Secretary for War and Colonies, had to prevail upon a London trader to send a consignment of agricultural equipment to the Cape in 1798.[104]

During the period of the First British Occupation and the Batavian

Republic, the conditions of war and uncertainty about the future discouraged the establishment of a settled merchant class. Considerable profits were made, both in the slave trade and in other activities, but the dealings were in general somewhat shady. The most successful individual, Michael Hogan, found it expedient to depart to the United States with his profits after a few years in Cape Town.[105] In addition, under the British, the East India Company attempted to impose a monopoly on the importation of Asiatic goods to the Cape.[106] Nevertheless, very considerable quantities of goods were imported during the First British Occupation, nearly six million rixdollars worth during the four years 1799–1802, excluding smuggled goods.[107] Of these 28 per cent came from the East, the rest from Europe and America. The majority of goods came in English ships. However, both these goods and those that came in American, Danish and Swedish ships were sent by overseas speculators, not on the order of Cape merchants.

In the Batavian period (1803–06) trade suffered as a consequence of war. Goods were up to four times as expensive at the Cape as in the Netherlands, a reflection of the difficulties of transport.[108] Nevertheless, Commissioner-General J.A. de Mist developed plans in this period to turn the Cape into a staple port where Asiatic goods could be stored and resold to European merchants who would thus not have to journey all the way to India or the East Indies archipelago. However, the Dutch government had made no decision on how to re-organise the economics of its colonial empire – the VOC had collapsed in 1795 – when the British reoccupied the Cape in 1806.[109]

In the Second British Occupation, the channels of commerce had to be re-established. In 1812, the president of the Bank commented that there were no more than half a dozen merchants in the colony who imported from England.[110] These would almost certainly not have included members of the old VOC commercial elite, and it has therefore been supposed that the new merchants were all British traders with better access to British business circles than their Dutch predecessors and competitors.[111] This is only partially true. For instance, Constant van Nuldt Onkruijdt, who had been landdrost of Swellendam under the VOC, was nevertheless President of the Cape Town Chamber of Commerce in 1808.[112] To succeed in commerce at the Cape in the early years of British rule, one needed, not just sufficient capital, acumen and good fortune, but also the ability to straddle the worlds of old and new Cape Town. Significantly, several of the most successful British merchants married into established Cape families, notably Hamilton Ross (a former British army officer who was fluent in Dutch by his death), J.B. Ebden and, somewhat later, all three of the partners in the firm of Barry and Nephews, who all married Van Reenens.[113]

During these early years Ebden and Ross established their positions as two of Cape Town's leading merchants, which they were to hold until mid-century. Their activities included not only importation to the Cape, but also provisioning Réunion and Mauritius, where the Cape had been a major supplier since the 1770s.[114] At the same time they and other merchants had to contend with the monopoly on Eastern goods jealously guarded by the English East India Company.[115] Nevertheless, even after the Company's charter was revised in 1813, reducing its monopoly privileges effectively only to tea,[116] the position of Cape Town's merchant community remained parlous. There were numerous bankruptcies among the British settlers in the town.[117] Only in the 1820s, despite the abolition of the preferential tariff for Cape wine, did matters improve, perhaps because of the establishment in London of the Cape of Good Hope Trade Society and the foundation of firms there specifically concerned with Cape trade, notably Abraham Borrodaile and Co.[118]

This stabilisation can be seen not just among the major merchants and mercantile houses but more generally in the structure of the colony's distribution and retail system, both in Cape Town and in the countryside. In the eighteenth century, it was generally reported that every householder in Cape Town was a merchant, either full or part-time.[119] The irregularity with which commodities arrived at the Cape led to rapid price shifts and thus encouraged speculation, which was particularly rife at the auctions.[120] Only by putting a heavy mark-up on the goods acquired at such sales before they were sold to rural customers, could traders protect themselves against the losses inherent in this system. There was little to encourage merchants to specialise in a particular line of goods. As Edward Hanbury noted as late as 1819, 'In this place ship chandlers and storekeepers deal in anything'. To get the business of the shops, Hanbury had to keep 'a general store of goods calculated to retail to the town as well', a combination which was eventually to lead to his bankruptcy.[121] By the 1820s, general merchants and chandlers continued to do business in Cape Town, but there was a steady move towards specialisation: business was no longer conducted from private houses, and there was a steady trend towards the establishment of definite shops, albeit without shopwindows for the display of goods.[122]

The sale of foodstuffs was organised in a number of ways. The retailing of wine was closely contracted and there were also licensing systems for butchers and bakers. However, the retail sale of cakes and biscuits, fish, fruits and vegetables was largely in the hands of the slaves.[123] Initially, retailing by slaves had been organised by the owners of the bakeries, the market gardens in Table Valley and, perhaps, the fishing smacks, but increasingly the slaves themselves came to act as petty entrepreneurs, agreeing to turn over a fixed sum to their master or mistress at the end of the week. If they failed, they risked a flogging, especially as it was believed (generally erroneously) that slave entrepreneurs gambled their proceeds away.[124] A few of the successful slaves were able to use this system to build up their own capital, and thus to purchase their own emancipation. For this reason, there were considerable numbers of fruit-sellers and small retailers among the Free Blacks, who also owned Cape Town's first 'chop-houses' or cheap restaurants, usually in the vicinity of the harbour.[125]

In the country districts a similar process of specialisation occurred, although the continuing expansion of the colony meant that it had to be repeated regularly in district after district. The first persons who commercially penetrated a given district were the smousen. As early as 1774, the Council of Policy had reason to complain of those persons who 'for some time back . . . have made it their business to wander about everywhere in the Interior, from one District to another, with goods and merchandise, conveyed on wagons, horses or pack oxen, thus causing many irregularities in the said districts.'[126] Therefore it decided to forbid this trade, which was being practiced not only among the European settlers but also already among the Xhosa. Nevertheless, this prohibition was neither observed nor enforced, probably in part because Cape Town merchants, including officials, were already providing the financial backing for such trading trips.[127] From then on, until at least the 1930s, these travelling smousen were a regular feature of the Cape Colony's countryside. They also penetrated into Xhosa territory, north to the Tswana and the Ndebele and, after the Great Trek, into the Orange Free State and the Transvaal.[128] Often Dutch, and later, British young men made a number of trips as smousen in the hope, often illusory, of building up the capital they required for more permanent and settled business. To do this, they began with funds borrowed from major Cape Town or Grahamstown merchants.[129]

Trade across the frontier, both with the Xhosa in the east and with the Griqua in the north, required substantially more regulation by the colonial authorities than did the activities of the smousen within the colony. Otherwise, the risks to the traders themselves, on the one hand, and of the sale of firearms, on the other, were too great. In addition, the main source of red ochre, a substance of considerable ritual importance within Xhosa society, was from 1820 within colonial territory, so that many Xhosa would now enter the colony purely to acquire the clay. For this reason, regular fairs were set up, first at the clay pits in the Coombs river valley to the east of Grahamstown and then, from 1824, weekly at Fort Willshire on the Keiskamma. From 1819 annual fairs for Griqua from the northern border were held at Beaufort West. In the beginning, a wide spectrum of colonists traded at these fairs, but quickly the business came to be concentrated in the hands of a small number of professional traders.[130]

Within the colony itself, at least from the early nineteenth century onwards, the smousen had to compete with settled traders in the increasing number of small towns. For example, in the 1790s, when John Barrow visited Graaff-Reinet, he commented that virtually nothing could be bought there.[131] Nevertheless, by 1811 the Circuit Commission reported that there were 25 tradesmen settled in Graaff-Reinet,[132] and two years later it reported that the local shopkeepers were complaining that they had to pay a licence fee to trade while the 'country pedlars' were exempt from such an exaction, an anomaly that was removed shortly thereafter.[133] By the 1830s, Graaff-Reinet had become a sizeable commercial centre, visited by many farmers from further north who thus were spared the annual trek to Cape Town.[134]

The development of the country towns ran parallel with the establishment of larger merchant houses outside Cape Town. This, in turn, was facilitated by the opening of the various bays from the Berg river mouth to Port Elizabeth (as the settlement at Algoa Bay was named in 1820).[135] The pioneer in this coasting traffic was Frederik Korsten, who in 1811 took on a contract to supply Mauritius with salt meat from Algoa Bay. His raw materials were cattle from the Zuurveld and other eastern Cape regions and salt from the Uitenhage pans. From this base he was later able to diversify into sealing, whaling and, later, wool farming.[136] As an Eastern Province entrepreneur, he was followed above all by certain of the 1820 Settlers (ch. 10, pp. 472–74).[137]

The most significant example of the merchant penetration of the Cape countryside was further west, in the commercial empire built up around Swellendam by the firm of Barry and Nephews.[138] Joseph Barry, the senior partner, arrived in South Africa in 1819 and soon began in the coasting trade. He was primarily responsible for opening up Port Beaufort, at the mouth of the Breede River, as an outlet for the produce (above all wheat and wool) of the Swellendam plains. This was a business full of risks, above all that of shipwreck, and Barry went bankrupt in 1827.

Nevertheless, he was able to remain in business and two years later cleared his debts. Thereafter in partnership with his two nephews, and aided by the marriages into the Van Reenen family which all three of them made, he was able to engross a considerable proportion of the business between Swellendam and Port Beaufort. In time the Barrys were able to open ten stores from Worcester to Mossel Bay and at least in this area to drive the smousen into insignificance.[139]

In 1835, the growth of Cape merchant houses was still in its early stages. Nevertheless, the Barrys' success, along with those of other, less prominent, merchants throughout the Cape, illustrates the steady thickening of the Cape's commercial network through the early nineteenth century.

The world economy and the structure of Cape society

This chapter has so far been strictly concerned with economic, and where possible measurable, matters. It has demonstrated that the colony's incorporation in the world economic system resulted in a steady and cumulative increase in commodity production and exchange, both during the Dutch and early British periods. Wine, wheat and livestock production steadily increased. Imports and, to a lesser extent, exports expanded greatly. The Cape's monetary and credit systems became at once less chaotic, more sophisticated and more closely tied to those of the imperial motherland. These interlocking economic processes, in turn, shaped the social structure of the colony, not directly by fostering racial attitudes, but by aiding the establishment of structures of white domination from which racial attitudes were, at least in part, derived and for which they were used as justification.

What were these social effects? First, and most fundamentally, the very existence of the colony and the immigration to South Africa of two of the major population groups, the white settlers and the slaves, was a direct result of the world economy. Without the commercial requirements of the Dutch East India Company the Cape would not have been colonised in 1652; without its networks in the East, and without the slaving routes from East Africa and Madagascar to the New World, it would not have acquired the major component of its labour force; and without the needs of the British imperial system it would not have changed colonial masters around 1800.

Secondly, it was their differing positions in the world economy which gave rise to the sharply divergent worlds of Cape Town and the countryside, a contrast which would long endure. Cape Town was the commercial and, increasingly, the financial centre of the colony, the seat of government and by far the major port; it was thus the sluice through which passed all the colony's contacts with the outside world. The wide range of urban requirements brought into being a substantial skilled artisanate, both free and slave. There were builders, carpenters, smiths, tailors, dressmakers, and cobblers in addition to the small army of slaves who fetched Cape Town's water, cut and hauled its firewood, disposed of its rubbish and shifted its goods about.[140] The skilled slaves, unwilling to submit to the strict discipline of manual labourers, frequently worked on their own, paying their owners a fixed sum (known as *koeliegeld*) at the end of the day or week, as did the slave retail traders. It was not necessarily a humane system, but nevertheless it did give considerable opportunity to the slaves, and encouraged the development of an urban slave culture impossible elsewhere. Moreover, the multiplicity of economic functions meant that contrasts of status between slave and free were not necessarily absolute. Thus the employment opportunities of Cape Town, its pre-emancipation slave culture and the relatively fluid social structure of urban life – all indirectly products of Cape Town's position in the world economic system – led to a relatively more open society for brown and black people after the emancipation of the slaves in the 1830s.

The contrast with the countryside is stark. There, the requirements of wheat, wine and meat production led both to the atomisation of the slave population on isolated farms and to the brutal exploitation of both slaves and the Khoisan.[141] The regular needs of grain growing and wine farming meant that slaves were continually driven, and were shifted from one farm to another to cover the peak periods of two sectors' production cycles. Slaves were worked till they dropped, and if they survived but were worn out, they were likely to be sold up-country as shepherds.[142] In general, the worse the economic conditions, the worse their treatment. Moreover, there was always the danger that they would be flogged to death for alleged misdemeanours.[143]

Thirdly, links between Cape agriculture and the world economy enabled the Cape's merchant community to gain prominence. In the eighteenth century, of course, the merchants were the rulers, and at least in Cape Town everyone traded in whatever commodity seemed likely to offer the best profits. The British traditions of government were somewhat different. An aristocrat like Lord Charles Somerset, son of the Duke of Beaufort, Major-General in the British Army and, perhaps even more significantly, ex-lieutenant-colonel of the highly prestigious

Coldstream Guards, would not have dreamed of trading openly. Nevertheless the British government came to rely on the merchant elite whose own links were with the City of London, together with the larger landowners, particularly in the southwestern Cape. In the 1820s, for example, the governor was ordered by the Colonial Office in London to appoint a legislative council, whose unofficial members were to be chosen from 'the chief landed proprietors and principal merchants of the colony'.[144]

Finally, the nature of economic contacts with Cape Town, and through Cape Town with the rest of the world, did much to determine the course of social developments on the frontier. In the early years of European settlement, for instance in the Graaff-Reinet district, the brutality of relations with the Khoikhoi may well have been the result of the district's comparatively weak links with the market. The farmers' desperate attempts to create a cash income and a desirable life-style led them to acquire labour by the most vicious measures (ch. 1, pp. 31–33). In the first decades of the nineteenth century, as commercial ties became firmer and the district prospered, such excesses were no longer necessary or tolerated.[145] Commercial development, in turn, gave impetus to further expansion. Simultaneously, the Cape's incorporation into the British empire finally provided a military force on the frontier sufficient to ensure eventual European hegemony over the Xhosa (see ch. 10, pp. 478–88). The rise in land values which preceded and followed the introduction of merino sheep led not only to the demand for territory newly conquered from the Xhosa,[146] but also for the extension of colonial settlement into new areas, particularly north of the Orange.[147]

These varying social and geographical developments were, then, products of the steady expansion and diversification of the Cape Colony's economy. From the small beginnings of Van Riebeeck's post in 1652, this economy had grown enormously, largely as a result of its position within the world of the Dutch and, later, the British imperial systems. In comparison with the economies of other colonies and ex-colonies, notably the United States of America, the Cape economy was in all respects still puny. Nevertheless, it had laid the foundation upon which South Africa would later build after the mining of diamonds and gold began later in the nineteenth century.

Chapter Five   Notes

1. D. Moodie, *The Record* (reprinted Amsterdam and Cape Town, 1960), pt. I, p. 7.
2. A. Appel, 'Die Geskiedenis van Houtvoorsiening aan die Kaap, 1652–1795', (MA thesis: University of Stellenbosch, 1966).
3. M.P. de Chavonnes and Baron van Imhoff, *The Reports of De Chavonnes and his council and van Imhoff on the Cape* (Cape Town, 1918), p. 130; O.F. Mentzel, *A Geographical and Topographical Description of the Cape of Good Hope*, 3 vols. (Cape Town, 1921–44), I, 152.
4. Anna Böeseken, 'Die Nederlandse Kommissarisse en die 18de eeuse samelewing aan die Kaap', *AYB* (1944), pp. 145 ff.
5. Richard Elphick, *Kraal and Castle, Khoikhoi and the Founding of White South Africa* (New Haven and London, 1977), esp. ch. 5.
6. On the establishment of settlement, see above ch. 2, pp. 69–73.
7. G.C. de Wet, *Die Vryliede en Vryswartes in die Kaapse Nedersetting 1657–1707* (Cape Town, 1981), chs. 6–10.
8. The figure for 1700 refers to those who were incorporated into the colony, and thus not to the Khoikhoi who still inhabited the great majority of what was to become the Cape Colony.
9. R. Raven-Hart, *Cape of Good Hope, 1652–1702: The first 50 years of Dutch colonization as seen by callers*, 2 vols. (Cape Town, 1971), II, 402, citing Christoffel Langhansz, who was in Cape Town in 1694.
10. In 1822 there were 1468 houses: W. Bird, *State of the Cape of Good Hope in 1822* (reprinted Cape Town, 1966), p. 338. For further statistical information see the *Cape of Good Hope Blue Book and Statistical Register*, in manuscript in the PRO until 1837, thereafter printed.
11. For this tendency see S.D. Neumark, *Economic Influences on the South African Frontier, 1652–1836* (Stanford, 1957); Guelke, above ch. 2, pp. 87–92, and Robert Ross, 'Capitalism, Expansion and Incorporation on the South African frontier', *The Frontier in History: North America and Southern Africa Compared*, ed. Howard Lamar and Leonard Thompson (New Haven and London, 1981), pp. 212–16.
12. This is based on an examination of the *Rendementen*, annual lists of VOC sales in Cape Town which are held in the Algemene Rijksarchief. There are extant lists for 26 years in the eighteenth century, covering the period 1747–77.
13. The best survey of the VOC's activities is F.S. Gaastra, *De Geschiedenis van de VOC* (Haarlem, 1982) and F.S. Gaastra, 'The Shifting Balance of Trade of the Dutch East India Company', *Companies and Trade; Essays on Overseas Trading Companies during the Ancien Régime*, ed. L. Blussé and F.S. Gaastra (Leiden, 1981), pp. 47–70. For the establishment of the monopoly of cloves in the Moluccas, see G.J. Knaap, 'Kruidnagelen en Christenen: De Verenigde Oost-Indische Compagnie en de bevolking van Ambon, 1656–1696,' (Ph.D. thesis: University of Utrecht, 1985). For Dutch Sri Lanka see above all D.A. Kotalawele, 'Agrarian Policies of the Dutch in South-West Ceylon', *A.A.G. Bijdragen*, XIV (1967), pp. 3–33. Dutch Banda awaits its modern historian, but for an indication of the process of conquest, see John Villiers, 'Trade and Society in the Banda islands in the

sixteenth century', *Modern Asian Studies*, XV (1981), pp. 723–50.

14. There were numerous *plakkaten* against the sale of tobacco. The last seems to have been issued in 1740. *KP* II, 188. For coffee, see *ibid.*, IV, 85.
15. See Gaastra, *Geschiedenis van de VOC*; J.J. Steur, *Herstel of Ondergang: De Voorstellen tot redding van de V.O.C. 1740–1795* (Utrecht, 1984), esp. pp. 237–46 and J.P. de Korte, *De jaarlijkse financiële verantwoording in de Verenigde Oost-Indische Compagnie* (Leiden, 1984).
16. A request to this effect was made on 18 July 1719: H.C.V. Leibbrandt, *Precis of the Archives of the Cape of Good Hope: Requesten (Memorials)*, 2 vols. (Cape Town, 1905), I, 49, but was refused. It was repeated at intervals through the eighteenth century.
17. *KP*, IV, Plakkaat of 21 Nov. 1792, pp. 141–55; Gerard Wagenaar, 'Johannes Gysbertus van Reenen: Sy aandeel in die Kaapse Geskiedenis tot 1806' (M.A. thesis: University of Pretoria, 1976), pp. 145–50; A. Böeseken, 'Kommissarisse', pp. 177–78; On the case of the *Herstelder*, owned by the whaling company Fehrzen & Co., which was captured by the British during its voyage to the Netherlands, see PRO, HCA 32/668/82 and *RCC*, O.G. de Wet *et. al.* to General Craig, July 1796, I, 408–10.
18. E.g. VOC 4278, *Resolutiën van de Politieke Raad*, 6 Dec. 1774.
19. Steur, *Herstel of Ondergang*, p. 244.
20. G.J. Jooste, 'Die Geskiedenis van Wynbou en Wynhandel in die Kaap Kolonie, 1753–1795' (M.A. thesis: University of Stellenbosch, 1973), pp. 132 ff.
21. VOC 4319, Governor and Council to XVII, 1 July 1786, pp. 22 ff.
22. For grain prices, see Leonard Guelke, 'The Early European Settlement of South Africa', (Ph.D. thesis: University of Toronto, 1974), p. 264; A.J. du Plessis, 'Die Geskiedenis van die Graankultuur tydens die Eerste Eeu, 1652–1752,' *Annale van die Universiteit van Stellenbosch*, (Cape Town, 1933), II, 80; J.H.D. Schreuder, 'Die geskiedenis van ons graanbou (1752–1795)' (M.A. thesis: University of Stellenbosch, 1948), pp. 42–67. For complaints, see e.g. Leibbrandt, *Requesten*, I, 135, 154–55, 160–67.
23. For the conditions of the meat *pacht*, see the *Resolutiën van de Politieke Raad* for 1 February at, usually, five-yearly intervals. From 1749 this was in the years four and nine of each decade. For the best analysis of the meat market in the last decades of Company rule, see Wagenaar, 'Johannes Gysbertus van Reenen', chs. II and III. See also Pieter van Duin and Robert Ross, *The Economy of the Cape Colony in the Eighteenth Century*, Intercontinent No. VII, (Leiden, 1987).
24. See their concerns on the sales of Constantia wine, cited above in note 21.
25. Wagenaar, 'Johannes Gysbertus van Reenen', p. 82; C.F.J. Muller, *Johannes Frederik Kirsten oor die toestand van de Kaapkolonie in 1795*, (Pretoria, 1960), pp. 85–86. It was possible for a ship to travel from Europe to Asia (or the reverse trip) without putting into port, and St. Helena was always available to allow rewatering.
26. See J.J. Janse van Rensburg, 'Die Geskiedenis van die wingerdkultuur in Suid-Afrika, 1652–1752', *AYB* (1954), p. 2; Jooste, 'Geskiedenis van Wynbou en Wynhandel'; D.J. Van Zyl, *Kaapse Wyn en Brandewyn, 1795–1806* (Cape Town and Pretoria, 1975); Van Duin and Ross, *Economy*, ch. IV.
27. With regard to livestock ownership, this could be done by comparing

individual farmers' *opgaaf* returns with inventories of their estates taken shortly afterwards. See A.J.H. van der Walt, *Die Ausdehnung der Kolonie am Kap der Guten Hoffnung (1770–1779)*, (Berlin, 1928), p. 77; Guelke, 'Early European Settlement', p. 259. The same procedure has been used, e.g. by Du Plessis, *Geskiedenis van die Graankultuur*, to establish the level of evasion with regard to grain, but this is highly suspect, since any grain marketed between the harvest and the making of the inventory would not appear in the latter, while conversely any grain held for longer than one year would reduce the apparent level of evasion. Since a far smaller proportion of stock would have been marketed, the distortions caused by this problem would have been far lower in this case. Levels of wheat evasion were determined, very approximately, by estimating level of consumption in those years when it is known that supply and demand were in equilibrium and comparing that to the opgaaf. For a detailed explication of this, see Van Duin and Ross, *Economy*, ch. III.

28. Van Duin and Ross, *Economy*, ch. III.
29. VOC 4315, p. 576.
30. Muller, *Kirsten*, p. 61; *Belangrijke Historische Dokumenten over Zuid-Afrika*, ed. G.M. Theal (London, 1911), III, 36–38; D.G. van Reenen, *Die joernaal van Dirk Gysbert van Reenen*, ed. W. Blommaert and J.A. Wiid (Cape Town, 1937), p. 285.
31. John Marincowitz, 'Rural Production and Labour in the Western Cape, 1838–1888, with special reference to the wheat growing districts', (Ph.D. thesis: University of London, 1985), p. 18; Edmund H. Burrows, *Overberg Outspan: A Chronicle of People and Places in the South Western Districts of the Cape*, (Cape Town, 1952), p. 233; H.L.G. Swart, 'Die ontwikkeling van handel aan die Kaap tussen die jare 1795 en 1806', (M.A.: University of Cape Town; 1949), pp. 89–93.
32. See Cape of Good Hope, *Statistical Blue Book of the Colony* (1860), JJ4, 7.
33. Alan Mabin, 'The Rise and Decline of Port Elizabeth, 1850–1900', *International Journal of African Historical Studies* XIX (1986), pp. 275–303.
34. VOC 4202, Res, 4 Sept. 1756, p. 374; H.B. Thom, *Die Geskiedenis van Skaapboerdery in Suid-Afrika* (Amsterdam, 1936); R.S. Lopez, 'The Origins of the Merino Sheep', *The Joseph Starr Memorial Volume* (New York, 1953).
35. Cf. Randall G. Stokes, 'Afrikaner Calvinism and Economic Action: The Weberian Thesis in South Afriaca', *American Journal of Sociology* LXXXI, (1981), pp. 62–81. The apparent dynamism of British settlers in agriculture in the nineteenth century probably derived from their greater access to capital, either personal or as a result of banking policy. See William Beinart and Peter Delius, 'Introduction,' *Putting a Plough to the Ground: Accumulation and Dispossession in rural South Africa, 1850–1930*, ed. W. Beinart, P. Delius and S. Trapido (Johannesburg, 1986), p. 28.
36. Eighteenth century records of bankrupticies can be found in the series CJ 2928–2948. In the period 1728–92, there were 155 cases of people going bankrupt or dying insolvent. For the nineteenth century boom-and-bust cycles see Van Zyl, D.J., *Kaapse Wyn en Brandewyn*, pp. 123–36; Mary Rayner, 'Wine and Slaves: the failure of an export economy and the ending

of slavery in the Cape Colony, South Africa, 1806–1834' (Ph.D. thesis: Duke University, 1986), ch. 4.

37. On these exports, see Van Duin and Ross, *Economy*, ch. II.
38. 'Plan om den handel van tarwe van de Caab bij aanhoudendheid te kunnen drijven', *Kroniek van het Historisch Genootschap gevestigd te Utrecht*, XXVI (1872), pp. 203–05.
39. D.J. van Zyl, 'Die Geskiedenis van Graanbou aan die Kaap, 1795–1826', *AYB* (1968), I, 222–33.
40. Rayner, 'Wine and Slaves', p. 218.
41. See Van Duin and Ross, *Economy*, ch. II; F. de Haan, *Oud Batavia: Gedenkboek*, 2 vols. (Jakarta,1922), II, 542.
42. See, e.g., reports of the Commission of Circuit for 1812, *RCC*, IX. 89 and for 1813, *RCC*, X, 98.
43. E.H. Burrows, *Overberg Outspan* (Cape Town, 1952), ch. 4.
44. When these figures are available for the eighteenth century, they are given in Van Duin and Ross, *Economy*, ch. III; for the nineteenth century see Van Zyl, 'Graanbou', p. 273 and D.J. van Zyl, *Kaapse Wyn en Brandewyn, 1795– 1860* (Cape Town and Pretoria, 1975), pp. 104–05.
45. For an attempt to do this, see Van Duin and Ross, *Economy*, ch. III.
46. E.g. *RCC*, IV, 195.
47. On the first group see Leonard Guelke and Robert Shell, 'An early colonial landed gentry: land and wealth in the Cape Colony, 1682–1731', *Journal of Historical Geography*, (1983), p. 272; Wagenaar, 'Johannes Gysbertus van Reenen', p. 12. In general on the problem, see Guelke, above ch. 2, pp. 84– 93 and 'The making of two frontier communities: Cape colony in the eighteenth century', *Historical Reflections/Réflexions Historiques*, XII (1985); Susan Newton-King, 'Some thoughts about the Political Economy of Graaff-Reinet in the Late Eighteenth Century', unpublished paper (1984); Robert Ross, 'The Origins of Capitalist Agriculture in the Cape Colony: a survey', in Beinart, Delius and Trapido, *Putting a Plough to the Ground*, pp. 62–63.
48. On the slave trade, see Robert Ross, *Cape of Torments: Slavery and Resistance in South Africa*, (London, 1983), pp. 3–14; Nigel Worden, *Slavery in Dutch South Africa*, (Cambridge, 1985), pp. 42–48; Robert C-H. Shell, 'Slavery at the Cape of Good Hope, 1680–1731' (Ph.D. thesis: Yale University, 1986), ch. 2 and above ch. 3, pp. 110–22.
49. Wagenaar, 'Johannes Gysbertus van Reenen', pp. 137–39.
50. The estate papers in the archive of the Orphan Chamber, Cape Archives, contain numerous printed forms which record the contact by which a sailor was to deliver his chest to a named merchant in Cape Town.
51. Van Duin and Ross, *Economy*, ch. VI.
52. See below, p. 261.
53. Robert Ross, 'The Relative Importance of Exports and the Internal Market for the Cape Colony', *Figuring African Trade*, ed. G. Liesegang, H. Pasch and A. Jones (Cologne, 1985) pp. 2–54.
54. *Willem Stephanus van Ryneveld se Aanmerkingen over de Verbetering van het vee aan de Kaap de Goede Hoop, 1804*, ed. H.B. Thom (Cape Town, 1942), p. 41.
55. Ross. 'Relative Importance', pp. 248–60.

56. F.S. Gaastra, 'De Verenigde Oost-Indische Compagnie in de zeventiende en achttiende eeuw: de groei van een bedrijf. Geld tegen goederen. Een structurele verandering in het Nederlands-Aziatisch handelsverkeer', *Bijdragen en Mededelingen betreffende de Geschiedenis der Nederlanden*, XCI (1976), p. 254; K P, 111, 136; *RCC*, Proclamation by Sir David Baird, 23 Jan. 1806, V, 305–06.

57. Brian Kantor, 'The Rixdollar and Foreign Exchange', *South African Journal of Economics*, XXXVIII (1970), p. 70.

58. For the operations of J.H. Blankenburg in this respect, see MOOC 14/36/ ii.

59. J.L.M. Franken, ''n Kaapse Huishoue in die 18e Eeu uit Von Dessin se Briefboek en Memoriaal', *AYB* (1940), I, 53.

60. See, e.g., the estates of P.J. Coetse (deceased 1776), MOOC 14/59/14, Johan Smith (deceased 1776), MOOC 13/17/24 and Andries van Sittert, (deceased 1786), MOOC 14/68/4.

61. 'Report of the Commissioners of Enquiry to Earl Bathurst on the Finances', *RCC*, XXVII, p. 459.

62. 'Geschiedkundig Tafereel der Weeskamer', *Het Nederduitsch Zuid-Afrikaansch Tijdschrift*, IX (1832), pp. 310–11.

63. 'Report of the Commissioners of Enquiry . . . on the Finances', *RCC*, XXVII, 459.

64. *KP*, III, 135–36.

65. *Ibid*, III, 161–62. Indeed the Company was forced to mint guilders, a denomination that had never previously been sent overseas, in order to meet this debt. See *Resolutiën van de Staten Generaal*, 12 Dec. 1785. Under the Batavian Republic, coins were also struck specifically for the Cape, but when they arrived De Mist considered the situation too precarious and ordered that they be sent on to Batavia, to avoid capture by the British: C. Scholten, *De Munten van de Nederlandsche Gebiedsdeelen Overzee, 1601–1948* (Amsterdam, 1951), p. 66. I owe this information to my colleague F.S. Gaastra.

66. H.L.G. Swart, 'Developments in Currency and Banking at the Cape between 1782 and 1825, with an account of contemporary controversies' (Ph.D. thesis: University of Cape Town, 1953), pp. 19–21.

67. *RCC*, Macartney to Dundas, 20 Oct. 1797, I, pp. 189–90.

68. A.L. Geyer, *Das Wirtschaftliche System der Niederländischen Ost-Indischen Kompanie am Kap der Guten Hoffnung, 1785–1795*, (Munich and Berlin, 1923), p. 80.

69. Swart, 'Developments in Currency and Banking', p. 69.

70. Kantor, 'Rixdollar', p. 89, citing British Parliamentary Paper 438 of 1826, papers respecting a British Metallic Circulation at the Cape of Good Hope', p. 28. The figures were calculated on the basis of the premiums which had to be paid for the various bills on England, particularly for the army and navy commissariats. Since the military expenditures at the Cape provided the main channels for the transfer of funds from the Cape to England, and as a merchant could pay into the army account in Cape Town, and have his agent draw an equivalent amount from the army's account at the exchequer in London, these premiums provide an index of the real value of the Cape rixdollar, at least in relation to sterling.

71. Kantor, 'Rixdollar', pp. 86–88.
72. BPP 438 of 1826, pp. 50–59.
73. E.g. Memorial of Thomas Rowles, 15 June 1826, BPP 438 of 1826, p. 46.
74. Kantor, 'Rixdollar', p. 86.
75. The main contestants were John Trotter, *A letter addressed to W. Robertson Esq. and the other members of a committee nominated on the part of the mercantile body of the Cape of Good Hope to draw up a report on the state of the commerce, finances and agriculture of that colony for the consideration of His Majesty's commissioners of enquiry* (Calcutta, 1825) and P.W. Grant, *Considerations on the State of the Colonial Currency at the Cape of Good Hope* (Cape Town, 1825). For a handy summary of the controversy see Swart, 'Developments in Currency and Banking', pp. 379–536.
76. The British Colonial Secretary once described the Loan Bank as 'one of the most ingenious expedients ever hit upon for introducing paper currency into a colony and raising a permanent revenue on that circulation', *RCC*, Castlereagh to Caledon, 12 May 1809, VI, 499.
77. *KP*, VI, 284–94. It is a significant comment on the so-called monopolistic position of the VOC that such a measure was instituted so late in the period of Company rule.
78. *RCC*, Statement prepared by H. Grocus, 30 Nov. 1824, XIX, 184–86.
79. Swart, 'Developments in Currency and Banking', pp. 730–31.
80. *RCC*, Evidence given by Mr. Francis Dashwood to the Commissioners of Enquiry, 12 Feb. 1825, XX, 22; Report to the Commissioners of Enquiry on the Finances, *ibid*. XXVII, 461.
81. On the workings of discount banks, see J.G. van Dillen, *Van Rijkdom en Regenten: Handboek tot de Economische en Sociale Geschiedenis van Nederland Tijdens de Republiek* (The Hague, 1970), pp. 439–60.
82. *RCC*, Evidence given by Mr. John Marshall to the Commissioners of Enquiry, 28 Dec. 1824, XIX, 428.
83. BPP 496 of 1827, Documents referred to in the Report of the Commissioners of Inquiry upon the Cape of Good Hope, p. 13.
84. CO 36, Dashwood to Cradock, 6 Aug. 1812, cited in Swart, 'Developments in Currency and Banking', p. 251.
85. Rayner, 'Wine and Slaves', pp. 214–15.
86. *RCC*, Evidence of John Marshall, XIX, 414.
87. Jan Smook et al. to Governor and *Raad*, 15 July 1783, *Kaapse Archiefstukkem, 1783*, ed. M.K. Jeffreys, (Cape Town, 1932), I, 164; Susan Newton-King, 'Commerce and Material Culture on the Eastern Cape Frontier, 1784–1812', Unpublished Seminar Paper, Institute of Commonwealth Studies, London (1985).
88. *RCC*, Report of the Commissioners of Enquiry on Finances, XXVII, 471. 471.
89. See the cases of Jonas Albertus van der Poel (Butcher), CJ 2944/377, 11 Sept. 1788; Johannes Davel, Aug. 1789, and Jan Hendrik Stroebel, CJ 2945/393, Aug. 1789.
90. Marian George, 'John Bardwell Ebden; His business and political career at the Cape, 1806–1849' (MA thesis: University of Cape Town, 1980), pp. 40–64.
91. See the annual report of the Commercial Exchange for 1834, cited in

R.F.M. Immelman, *Men of Good Hope: The Romantic Story of the Cape Town Chamber of Commerce, 1804–1954* (Cape Town, 1955), p. 114.

92. Kantor, 'Rixdollar', p. 88.

93. J.L. Hatting, '°n Ontleding van sekere aspekte van slawerny aan die Kaap in die sewentiende eeu', *Kronos*, I (1979).

94. For the Van Reenens, see Wagenaar, 'Johannes Gysbertus van Reenen'; for Melck, see J.H. Hoge 'Martin Melck', *Tydskrif vir Wetenskap en Kuns*, XII (1934); for H.O. Eksteen, see J. Hoge 'Personalia of the Germans at the Cape, 1652–1806', *AYB* (1946), p. 86; and Mentzel, *Description*, II, 76; *Res*, VIII, 310–311.

95. C. Beyers, *Die Kaapse Patriotte gedurende die laaste kwart van die agtiende eeu en die voortlewing van hul denkbeelde* (2nd edition; Pretoria, 1967), esp. pp. 156–58.

96. See above, note 50.

97. For instance, Christoffel Brand, posthouder of Simon's Town See. C. de Jong, 'Walvisvangst bij de Kaap de Goede Hoop tijdens de Bataafse Republiek' *Historia*, XII (1967), pp. 171–98; *RCC*, Fehrzen & Co. to Craig, July 1796, I, 408–10.

98. Wagenaar, 'Johannes Gysbertus van Reenen', pp. 130–40. It is to this case that we owe our information on these trading activities, since the papers of the case fill a whole volume of the Court of Justice Civil *Processtukken* in the Cape Archives (CJ 2169). No doubt, if others among the circa 1000 volumes of the Civil processtukken were examined, much more would be discovered about the trading activities, and economic life in general, of the Cape citizens.

99. Wagenaar, 'Johannes Gysbertus van Reenen', pp. 136–38.

100. *Ibid*.

101. *KP*, IV, 141–62.

102. Muller, *Kirsten*, p. 64.

103. Judith B. Williams, *British Commercial Policy and Trade Expansion, 1750–1850* (Oxford, 1972), p. 31.

104. Hermann Giliomee, *Die Kaap tydens die Eerste Britse Bewind, 1795–1803*, (Cape Town 1975), p. 147.

105. R.C.-H. Shell, 'The Impact of the Cape Slave Trade and its Abolition on the Demography, Regional Distribution and Ethnic Composition of the Cape Slave Population, 1652–1825', unpublished seminar paper, Yale University, 1979; Peter Philip, *British Residents at the Cape, 1795–1819* (Cape Town, 1981), pp. 182–83.

106. On this, see the various works of Marcus Arkin: 'John Company at the Cape: A history of the Agency under Pringle, 1795–1815', *AYB*, II, (1960); 'Supplies for Napoleon's Gaolers: John Company and the St. Helena Trade during the Captivity, 1815–1821', *AYB*, I, (1964); 'Agency and Island: John Company and the Twilight years of the Cape – St. Helena Trade, 1822–1836', *AYB*, I, (1965) and *Storm in a Teacup, the Later Years of John Company at the Cape, 1815–1836* (Cape Town, 1973).

107. Swart, 'Ontwikkeling van handel', pp. 112–17.

108. J.P. van der Merwe, *Die Kaap onder die Bataafse Republiek, 1803–1806* (Amsterdam, 1926), p. 377; Theal, (ed) *Belangrijke Historische Dokumenten*, p. 277.

109. *Ibid*. p. 329.
110. CO 36, Dashwood to Cradock, 6 Aug. 1812, cited in Swart, 'Developments in currency and banking', p. 253.
111. E.g. Muller, *Oorsprong*, pp. 148–49.
112. Giliomee, *Kaap tydens die Eerste Britse Bewind*, pp.201–04; John Campbell, *Travels in South Africa, undertaken at the Request of the Missionary Society*, (London, 1815), pp. 3, 13–15.
113. George, 'Ebden', p. 3; *Dictionary of South African Biography*, II (Cape Town and Johannesburg, 1972) pp. 606–07; A.P. Buirski, 'The Barrys and the Overberg' (M.A. thesis: University of Stellenbosch, 1952), pp. 7–9.
114. George, 'Ebden', pp. 7–40; *Dictionary of South African Biography*, II, 606–07.
116. This privilege was itself to be abolished in 1834, after a sharp struggle with, among others, Cape merchants. See Arkin, *Storm in a Teacup*, pp. 3–125.
117. Roger Beck, 'Edward Hanbury: Cape Town ship chandler and merchant, 1819–1825', *Quarterly Bulletin of the South African Library*, 39 (1984–85); P.H. Philip, 'The vicissitudes of the early British settlers at the Cape', *idem*, 40–41 (1986).
118. George, 'Ebden', pp. 74 ff.; Immelman, *Men of Good Hope*, pp. 59–70.
119. For descriptions, see e.g. Mentzel, *Description*, II, 75–80; C.P. Thunberg, *Travels in Europe, Asia and Africa performed in the years 1770 to 1779*, 4 vols. (London, 1793), II, 117.
120. Mentzel, *Description*, II, 76–77; 'Auctions – their good and evil tendencies', ed. Robert Shell, *Quarterly Bulletin of the South African Library*, 39–40 (1985).
121. Beck, 'Edward Hanbury'. The citation is from p. 27.
122. Immelman, *Men of Good Hope*, p. 26, P.W. Laidler, *The Growth and Government of Cape Town*, (Cape Town, 1939), pp. 203–09.
123. Robert Ross, 'The Occupations of Slaves in Eighteenth Century Cape Town', *Studies in the History of Cape Town*, II, 11.
124. For examples of this see cases against Talima van Soping, VOC 4253, 4 Oct. 1770; VOC 4182, Robo van Bouton et al., 1 Oct. 1750; and VOC 10984, Alexander van de Kust et al., 13 Sept. 1785. In 1794 the belief that these activities gave such great opportunities for slaves to dispose of stolen goods caused them to be forbidden: *KP*, IV, 248. However, this proved unworkable and in 1805 the prohibition was rescinded: *KP*, VI, 241.
125. See, for instance, *The African Court Calendar for 1814*, (reprinted, Cape Town, 1982), entries for Amarelia van Bougies, Fura van Batavia, Lys, Maart van Bengalen and Thomas van de Kaap.
126. *KP*, III, 93. I have followed the translation in Moodie, *Record*, pt. III, 24.
127. Moodie, *Record*, pt. III, 1, pp. 21–34. Newton-King, 'Commerce and Material Culture' describes the goods which the various trekboers acquired. See also J.B. Peires, *The House of Phalo: A History of the Xhosa People in the Days of their Independence* (Johannesburg, 1981), p. 98.
128. Peires, *House of Phalo*; C.F.J. Muller, 'Robert Scoon, vriend van die Afrikaner en die Matabele', in his *Leiers na die Noorde: Studies oor die Groot Trek* (Cape Town, 1976).
129. See, e.g., the letter by Mr. Crout cited in Neumark, *Economic Influences*, p. 147 and *The Reminiscences of Thomas Stubbs*, ed. W.A. Maxwell and R.T.

McGeogh, (Cape Town, 1978), p. 100.

130. Roger B. Beck, 'The Legalisation and development of trade on the Cape Frontier, 1817–1830', (Ph.D. thesis: University of Indiana, 1987), chs. 4–6.

131. John Barrow, *An Account of Travels into the Interior of Southern Africa*, 2 vols. (London, 1801–1803) I, 112–14.

132. *RCC*, VII, 299.

133. *RCC*, X, 98.

134. Andrew Steedman, *Wanderings and Adventures in the Interior of Africa*, 2 vols. (London, 1835), I, 124.

135. For a survey, made by the Commissioners of Enquiry, see *RCC*, XXXV, 275 ff.

136. *RCC*, Reports of the Commissioners of Circuit for 1813, IX, 89; for 1814 *RCC*, X, 98; *Dictionary of South African Biography*, II, 371–72, Basil A. le Cordeur, *The Politics of Eastern Cape Separatism 1820–1854* (Cape Town, 1981), p. 39.

137. Le Cordeur, *Eastern Cape Separatism*, pp. 40, 123–29.

138. The Dutch name for this firm gave rise to one of the Cape's first advertising slogans: 'Als jij lekker wilt leven, koop bij Barry en Neven'; see Burrow, *Overberg Outspan*, p. 255.

139. Buirski, 'Barrys', p. 94.

140. Ross, 'Occupations'.

141. This is argued in Ross, *Cape of Torments* and Worden, *Slavery in Dutch South Africa*. For a divergent point of view, see Shell, 'Slavery at the Cape of Good Hope', esp. p. 227; on the Khoikhoi, see Henry Bredekamp and Susan Newton-King, 'The subjugation of the Khoisan during the 17th and the 18th centuries', Conference on Economic Development and Racial Domination, Bellville, (1984) and Susan Newton-King, 'Background to the Khoikhoi rebellion of 1799–1803', Collected Seminar Papers of the Institute of Commonwealth Studies, London: The Societies of Southern Africa in the nineteenth and twentieth centuries, X (1981).

142. Robert Shell, personal communication based on an analysis of slave sales from the 1820s.

143. Worden, *Slavery in Dutch South Africa*, pp. 101–13.

144. Cited in T.R.H. Davenport, 'The consolidation of a new society: The Cape Colony', in *The Oxford History of South Africa*, ed. Monica Wilson and Leonard Thompson, 2 vols. (Oxford 1968–1971), I, 320. For more on this alliance, see Rayner, 'Wine and Slaves', ch. 2.

145. On this, see D. van Arkel, G.C. Quispel and R.J. Ross, *De Wijngaard des Heeren? Een onderzoek naar de wortels van 'die blanke baasskap' in Zuid-Afrika*, (Leiden, 1983), pp. 55–60.

146. See for instance, Peires, *House of Phalo*, p. 123.

147. The standard work on this is still P.J. van der Merwe, *Die Noordwaartse Beweging van die Boere voor die Groot Trek (1770–1842)*, (The Hague, 1937).

PART III

Government and society

Company and colonists at the Cape, 1652–1795 *

Gerrit Schutte

Any attempt to describe relations between freeburghers and the Dutch East India Company yields, at first, more questions than answers. True, the broad outlines are known. Much has been written on the Cape burghers' conflict with Governor Willem Adriaan van der Stel, the Cape Patriot movement, and the evolution of the trekboer. By contrast, only slight attention has been paid to socio-economic conditions among the freeburghers in and around Cape Town, who have on occasion been dismissed as unimportant,[1] or at least as lacking a character of their own. The same holds for social stratification and its development during the first 150 years of settlement, population growth and expansion. We also know little about the history of ideas at the Cape: political, religious, racial and social.[2]

Equally serious is the scant attention paid to the colonial character of the Cape community. What place did the Cape have in the global strategy of the *VOC*? How did its colonial character make it different from contemporary European states? Is anything to be gained by comparing it with North and South American colonies or with similar Dutch settlements like Ceylon, Batavia, Surinam, Curaçao, etc.? Or was C.R. Boxer correct in calling the Cape a colony *sui generis*?[3]

Curiously, we lack information even on the VOC establishment at the Cape. Apart from some scattered generalisations and a number of studies on specific persons, there seems to be nothing on the composition of the official group – its recruitment, training, social character and behaviour – and little on the personal and official relations that VOC servants had with one another, with the residents of the Cape[4] or with the *Heren XVII* in the fatherland. Similarly, there is no detailed economic history of the Cape, despite historians' repeated criticisms of the Company's economic policies there.[5]

* Translated from Dutch by Henry Snyders and Richard Elphick.

In this chapter I shall explore some of these more neglected themes and reconsider some of the less neglected. This is a big undertaking, particularly when so many essential preparatory studies are lacking. Hence this must be regarded only as a first attempt. I shall describe the social structures of Cape society and the place of the colony in the VOC system. This will provide a background for a more detailed consideration of three specific episodes: the campaign against Willem Adriaan van der Stel (1705–07), Barbier's rebellion (1739), and the Patriot movement (1778–87). I shall try to demonstrate the similarity of these conflicts between ruler and ruled at the Cape, a similarity which was rooted in the striking continuities in the internal structure and external relations of Cape society.

The Heren XVII and their subordinates

Historians often forget that the Cape settlement was only a part of the extensive interests of the East India Company, and thus divorce it from the overall structure to which it belonged: the world of the VOC and the policies of its directors.[6]

It should be grasped at the outset that the VOC was a private commercial undertaking, owned by a number of shareholders (*actionarissen, participanten*) and managed by an executive council (Heren XVII or Lords XVII). Day-to-day affairs were managed by the First Advocate (*Eerste Advocaat*) and his staff of officials.

The VOC (*Verenigde Oostindische Compagnie*) had been formed in 1602 by uniting a number of commercial undertakings, each of which retained a measure of autonomy. These so-called *kamers* (chambers) were each managed by a number of shareholding directors (*bewindhebbers*) – Amsterdam had twenty; Zeeland twelve; Delft, Rotterdam, Enkhuizen and Hoorn seven each – who were nominated by the incumbent directors and then appointed by provincial or municipal governments. A number of them (eight from Amsterdam, four from Zeeland, two from Rotterdam/Delft, two from Hoorn/Enkhuizen, and the seventeenth by rotation from the Chambers outside Amsterdam) formed the Heren XVII, the central policy-making body. The directors almost invariably came from the ranks of the local governing patriciate of the chamber cities.

Abroad the Company's affairs were managed by the Governor-General and Council of India (sitting in Batavia, on Java) and the corps of officials under their command. In theory the Indian authorities were entirely bound by the many and often detailed instructions sent from the fatherland; in practice slow communications and the need for expeditious and energetic management gave them considerable autonomy. Until 1732 the Cape was governed by instructions both from the Heren XVII and from Batavia, but after that date instructions came from the fatherland alone. A measure of inspection and control over the Cape was also exercised by passing admirals of the return fleets, acting as commissioners. However, their activities were restricted by the brief duration of their visits and by their need to co-operate with Cape officials. In addition, special Commissioners-General (e.g., Van Reede, 1685; Nederburgh and Frykenius, 1792–93) were occasionally sent to introduce really significant measures, mostly on specific instructions from the Heren XVII.

As with any commercial firm, the object of the VOC was to make a profit. Since the shareholders' capital was kept low, a large part of the profits went towards financing investments internally. The ownership of overseas territories was by no means the primary object of VOC policy; it simply was, in places, the solution to problems of security posed by competitors. Even when, in the eighteenth century, the Company became more and more the de facto sovereign of diverse territories, it hesitated to acknowledge its sovereignty openly.[7]

The VOC at first brought only comparatively small, though profitable, quantities of luxury products into the European market. It had a monopoly on the sale of products originating in its own possessions; but this monopoly was naturally valid only for sales in the Netherlands, where it could anyway be fairly easily evaded. The only way to obtain a larger share of the European market for colonial goods was to supply these cheaply. To this end overheads had to be kept as low as possible, and consequently the directorate of the Company showed scant enthusiasm for expensive settlements.

It was of course an important aim of the Company to thwart competitors at the sources of production overseas: hence it strove to obtain monopolistic contracts with Asiatic rulers. At times it even tried to control production, but succeeded in this aim with only a few products of decreasing importance. To achieve and maintain its trading advantages, the Company had to establish itself as an Asian power; such political authority was also crucial to support its inter-Asiatic trade. The profits were used by the Company to finance much of its operation and to purchase return freight. There was very little direct exchange of products between Europe and Asia, since Europe could offer Asia little except precious metals.[8]

In 1602 the States-General had conferred upon the VOC a charter 'in order to promote the welfare of the United Netherlands, to secure and develop trade, and to operate for the profit of the Company and the inhabitants of the Country.'[9] It was, above all, the Company's contribution to the Dutch staple market economy and its share in the struggle against the Republic's competitors (Spain, Portugal, England and France) that made the VOC important to the Dutch government. It is true that contemporaries overestimated the contribution of the VOC to the Dutch economy. Still, it amounted to about 15 per cent, and became relatively larger toward the end of the eighteenth century. Moreover, the Company contributed directly to the state by paying for its charter and its licences, by paying import and export duties (*convooi-en licentgelden*), and by providing ships and sailors in time of war.[10]

Dutch statesmen – themselves merchants and steeped in the merchant tradition[11] – were perfectly aware of how much the VOC could contribute to the power of the Republic. In their merchant world, power was mainly identified with economic and maritime prosperity. It is no wonder, then, that they adopted mercantilist measures (such as tariffs, monopoly and the exploitation of overseas territories) to entrench the VOC.

An understanding of the VOC must begin with the decentralised structure of the Republic of the United Netherlands. The Republic was by no means a unitary state but rather an alliance of provinces composed, in their turn, of cities and rural districts strongly concerned with their own interests and liberties. It was to placate regional sentiments that the VOC remained divided into six chambers, an arrangement that fitted in well with the form of commercial concerns of the time. The Company was subject to little direction from the state. True, the States-General (the central deliberative body, charged with defence and foreign policy) was responsible for extending the Company's charter and received regular reports from it.

In practice, however, its supervision did not amount to much and was exercised in a somewhat unusual manner by combining the functions of Company directors and local regents in the same hands. By virtue of their wealth and prestige, the regents formed an elite in the Republic, holding local power and maintaining it by co-option. From this local power base some of them were sent to the provincial States and the States-General, and were appointed to various executive posts. Although the Republic had a less centralistic, absolutistic character than neighbouring countries, it was no democracy. The regents jealously guarded their position and tolerated no popular infringements of it. Politically, socially and economically their status and power were virtually absolute; even the judiciary and the church were under their control.[12]

Just as the regents governed their cities or provinces in virtual autonomy, so the regent-directors governed their company. However, in comparison with the Dutch Republic, the VOC was much more centralised, bureaucratic and hierarchic. The Heren XVII and their confidants had immense power. By the terms of its charter the VOC had sovereign rights in its territories; for instance, it could enter into international agreements, issue edicts, execute justice, and exercise any governmental authority it deemed necessary. The contract setting out the legal position of VOC officials (*artikelbrief*) bound them to absolute loyalty to the Heren XVII and restricted their liberty in many spheres.

The community of freeburghers at the Cape was created for the Company's benefit. They could produce, more efficiently and more cheaply than the personnel of the Company, the commodities needed by the Cape settlement and by passing ships. It is true that there was a second motive as well, namely to provide a livelihood for the poor, but this was a very minor consideration. Commissioner van Reede stated quite clearly in 1685: 'The Company's interest . . . above all, must be the first and foremost object of this settlement.'[13] And a century later fiscal W.C. Boers explained that

One would be greatly mistaken if one were to draw a comparison between the inhabitants of a colony such as this and the privileged citizens of our large cities in the Republic.[14]

Like the settlement itself the colony's inhabitants were, in accordance with mercantilistic thinking, subservient to the interests of the mother country (in this case the Company). Theirs was a second-class citizenship. It was official VOC policy that the freeburghers, like the officials of the Company, had to take an oath of loyalty not only to the States-General, but also to the VOC directors and their servants abroad. So, too, people born in the colonies, on moving to the Netherlands, had to secure their civil rights by obtaining letters of naturalisation.[15] The proposal in 1786 that the confusing term 'civil rights' (*burgerregten*) be deleted from the letters conferring freeburgher status was fully in accord with Company views.[16] The clause, in the same letters, that freeburghers who misbehaved could be brought back under direct VOC discipline, underlines the limited nature of their freedom. The Company in fact exercised this right. The best known example was the banishment of the freeburgher Carel Hendrik Buytendagh to Batavia in 1779; but one of Willem Adriaan van der Stel's adversaries, the ex-burgher councillor

Johannes Rotterdam, had suffered the same fate.[17] For the rest, however, the VOC allowed the freeburghers as much practical liberty and autonomy as was reconcilable with its own interests.

Understandably the freeburghers themselves saw their position differently. Why did the VOC charter call the States-General their sovereign, or why did their letters of freeburgher status speak of civil rights, if the Company could act arbitrarily and treat them as slaves?[18] They naturally considered themselves 'free-born men and subjects of Their High Mightinesses' (i.e., the States-General).[19] By the end of the eighteenth century, moreover, Enlightenment concepts of the rights of subjects were coming into conflict with a political order which many were ready to label 'feudal'.[20]

The modern observer is likely to sympathise with the views of the freeburghers. But one should bear in mind that the VOC was in a strong position in terms of contemporary law. Furthermore, it is hard to imagine what concrete meaning free citizenship under the States-General could have had at the time. In practice the burghers in the Netherlands itself were not the subjects of the States-General but of the local and regional authorities. The law differed from place to place, as did the degree of political influence exerted by the inhabitants. But in all fields of life there were so many repressive regulations and discriminatory privileges that in the Republic itself 'free citizenship' was an aspiration rather than a reality.

The Cape in the VOC system

The Cape occupied a somewhat peculiar position among the settlements of the VOC: its founding derived not from any direct commercial interest, but from the need for a refreshment station and harbour. During the eighteenth century the settlement's value as the 'gateway to the East' increased enormously as the maritime power of the Republic and the Company steadily declined[21] and that of their competitors grew. Consequently in the eighteenth century, the loss of the Cape would have been regarded as a disaster; only the spice-producing and directly governed territories (Ceylon, Java, the Moluccas) were considered more important for the prosperity of the Company.[22]

No matter how important the Cape Colony may have been as a refreshment station and seaport, the Company never lost its commercial attitude towards it. The Cape was an expensive undertaking; therefore the cheaper the produce it supplied to the ships, and the lower the costs of its administration and defence, the better. Numerous attempts were made to increase the revenues at the Cape: there were experiments with all kinds of crops, and repeated attempts to find ores and timber and to develop fishing, seal hunting, etc. On the whole the results were disappointing.

It transpired that the Cape had little to offer apart from some agricultural produce; even this was not very promising considering its quality, its prices, and the distance to possible markets. The authorities could see no way to contain the ever-rising costs, except to buy produce at low prices, to transport and sell imports at the highest possible profits, and to keep administrative costs at a minimum. This explains why, shortly after 1652, production of refreshment foodstuffs was shifted on to the freeburghers who, in addition, were given military obligations; their free labour seemed to be cheaper than that of Company personnel or slaves, and in this fashion the size of the garrison could be restricted. The freeburghers would have to pay import, export and excise duties and various other taxes such as pachtgeld, stamp duty and a tithe on wheat. Thus they would make good the costs which the Company incurred in settling and governing them.[23]

The freeburghers did not live up to the Company's military expectations. They were of little use in defence against attacks from the sea, because they lived too far inland and were reluctant to leave their homes and occupations to perform poorly paid military service for a Company they did not love. They were required to participate in regular drills, but military officers considered them undisciplined, inadequately trained, and rebellious. As the eighteenth century progressed the officials became more and more gloomy about the freeburghers, and during the troublesome final decades they scarcely trusted them at all. Thus it became necessary to spend more on defence, especially fortifications, and correspondingly less on economic experiments.[24]

The Cape was neither the first nor the only VOC territory that had freeburghers; other concentrations were at Batavia, Ceylon and the Moluccas. The directors had hoped that the freeburghers would form a core of reliable subjects among the native populations and thus permit a retrenchment of the company's garrisons. They also thought that the burghers, like the nutmeg planters on Banda, would regularly supply certain products needed by the Company. In the seventeenth century, then, both inside and outside Company circles there were those who advocated the colonisation of non-European territories by European settlers. The principal motives were relief of poverty at home and the expansion of Dutch economic, political and religious spheres of influence.

But experiences in the VOC territories were not very encouraging. Many of the freeburghers in the East were not colonists in the true sense of the word but people who hoped that they would quickly accumulate enough riches to be able to return to the fatherland. Furthermore, many freeburghers survived on the peripheries of the Company's activity, as purveyors of liquor, food and lodging; as shopkeepers and merchants in produce that did not particularly interest the Company; and as smugglers and participants in illicit trade. The instability and lawlessness of the freeburgher groups, as well as their meagre economic achievements, scarcely confirmed the high hopes the Company had had for them. Although the Company was prepared to assist freeburghers in cases of extreme need, it did little to improve their position and kept them excluded from certain territories and certain enterprises; occasionally, they were forcibly re-enlisted by the Company or banned from its territory.

At the Cape the burghers also felt powerless in political matters. The only policy-making body of any importance, the Council of Policy, consisted entirely of officials, as did three-quarters of the highest judicial body, the Council of Justice. It is true that the three burgher councillors on the Council of Justice could also be consulted on matters of government, but this was not obligatory. It was only in 1783 that the numbers of freeburghers and officials were made equal on the Council of Justice (six members each), provided that the thirteenth member – the chairman – was an official. There was a similar division in the Court of Petty Cases (*Hof voor kleine Zaken*), the Court of Marital Cases (*Hof voor Huwelijkse Zaken*), the Orphan Chamber (*Weeskamer*), and the board of directors of the Bank, founded in 1793. The freeburgher members were chosen from a double list by the Council of Policy, which also had to approve the elected members of the Civil Defence Council (*Burgerkrijgsraad*).

Even members of the Church Council were nominated by the governor and Council of Policy. In Cape Town, as also for example in Batavia, many seats on the Church Council were filled by men from the VOC hierarchy. In the territories of the VOC, even more so than in the Netherlands, the Reformed Church was controlled by the authorities. The ministers were in fact officials in the service of the Company which, until the second half of the eighteenth century, allowed no other denomination in its territories.

In the rural districts of the Cape Colony, government was in the hands of the landdrost and heemraden. They acted as the local government, as a court of law in minor civil matters, and as executive officers for decisions taken in Cape Town. The landdrost functioned as chief police officer as well as commander of the militia. In the wards, the landdrost was represented by fieldcornets, who combined the originally distinct offices of policeman (*veldwachter*) and sergeant of the militia (*wachtmeester*); they were influential people, especially as leaders of *commandos*. The landdrost was a full-time official; the others were burghers, nominated by the heemraden and appointed by the Council of Policy.

Until a closer study has been made it is difficult to assess what influence the freeburghers actually had on the government of the Cape.[25] It is clear that the Company's authority was not very effective in the interior; there, colonists decided on their own day-to-day affairs, and the field-cornet – a farmer among farmers – was a man of authority.[26] But in important matters (border conflicts, legal matters, wars, etc.) the landdrost played an active role: a high Company official, and usually a stranger to the district, he was assisted by a secretary, a messenger, and a number of soldiers, who were all equally foreign. It seems significant that quite a few landdrosts clashed with the citizenry of their districts – not only Maynier and Bresler but, even earlier, Starrenburg and Marthinus Bergh (before he became a Patriot). Moreover, in judging the influence of all the burgher functionaries we should remember that the Company reserved the rights of supervision and veto; and that in all matters of policy it could make its will effective, in Cape Town at least, through the large majorities it commanded on all the councils.

To what extent did the office-holding burghers consider themselves as representatives of their fellow citizens? Caution should be observed in answering this question, but is does seem that the heemraden and burgher councillors saw themselves in this light: they were, at least occasionally, at the head of protest movements, especially so in the second half of the eighteenth century. It is clear that the position of the freeburghers at the Cape was in accordance with the general pattern of the VOC, except that at the Cape the burghers were relatively more numerous and hence perhaps more selfconscious and self-assertive than freeburghers elsewhere. In other territories, where the numerical proportion was more favourable to the officials and where the burghers were mostly concerned with trading in commodities, they may have been more directly dependent upon the VOC than were most freeburghers at the Cape; their closest counterparts at the Cape were the burghers in Cape Town itself.

Inevitably the mercantilist views of the directors led to economic conflicts with the Cape freeburghers. The burgers were dependent upon the Company not only for an outlet for their produce, but also for the delivery of numerous commodities and services. Moreover, the Cape economy was regulated strictly for the benefit of the Company and left little scope for private initiative. Within the framework of the eighteenth century much of this must be accepted as normal. To condemn the VOC economy as the epitome of heartlessness and selfishness, as writers such as Scholtz[27] have done from their twentieth-century viewpoint, is to ignore the values and presuppositions of the time.

The attitude of the VOC to indigenous peoples was also strongly determined by its character as a commercial firm. In general it tried to maintain good relations with the peoples with whom it traded, preferring to draw up treaties with them in terms of western international law. Even where the Company exercised authority over indigenous peoples, it preferred indirect rule: the Khoikhoi in southern Africa were, like the natives of Java, governed as much as possible through their own chiefs. This policy was founded on practical considerations (the need for economy, and lack of power), but was also a logical consequence of the VOC's commercial character: empire-building was contrary to the mentality of the Dutch merchant-regents.

Thus the Company treated the Khoikhoi (and later the 'Bushmen') with a mixture of goodwill and a hardness born of the determination to achieve its own objectives. This was clearly stated in 1685 by Commissioner Van Reede, who emphasised the Company's goals but also praised Simon van der Stel's treatment of the Khoikhoi because it 'served very well to gain us their goodwill and friendship, mainly because they were not handled contemptuously or unjustly but were heard and treated courteously and patiently'.[28] In Van Reede's words one still perceives a tone of respect for other peoples and a Christian sense of responsibility, to which the Enlightenment would later add a nuance of its own. It is not surprising that in relations with the indigenes, the VOC officials and the freeburghers would clash sharply, the frontier farmer having been brought to a harsher view by his circumstances. It should be borne in mind that the VOC, whose interests lay in and about Cape Town, paid little attention to the interior; if it did so it usually acted unobtrusively and correctively. The white population could hardly have prized either the neglect or the correction, even if this scant supervision meant that they were often free to go their own way.

This freedom applied not least of all to the occupation of new land. As we have shown, the VOC did not like expansion, elsewhere or at the Cape. Van Riebeeck's hedge and Van Goens's proposed canal were graphic symbols of the Company's insularism.[29] At the outset a measure of expansion proved inevitable for military purposes, to make the Cape self-supporting and to enable it to serve as a refreshment station. When both objectives were achieved in the time of W.A. van der Stel, the Heren XVII considered further immigration unnecessary.[30]

Nevertheless, the Cape population grew and expanded into new regions. P.J. van der Merwe has noted that the limitations of the Cape market stimulated the expansion of stock farming, which was fairly independent of the market (see ch. 2, pp. 84–93).[31] But the VOC accepted the expansion reluctantly. It is characteristic of VOC policy that the granting of freehold was replaced by the granting of grazing rights, which were of course intended to be temporary.[32] The stock farmers had to pay taxes on their land, yet they had no legal security of tenure. Obviously such inconsistency would irritate them. Once the Cape settlement had grown into a colony in spite of the VOC, the Company was faced with problems it could not solve without prejudice to its own commercial character. This irreconcilable conflict of interests – the essential dualism of a commercial company with extensive territorial possessions – gave birth to tragedy not only in Dutch colonies but in those of other European powers as well.

The Company's personnel

It will now be clear that the structure of the Company had certain consequences for social relations in its territories. Before dealing with these consequences, we need to consider two major social groupings: in this section the officials, in the next the citizenry.

A study of the officials of the Company produces conflicting impressions.[33] On the one hand there were many complaints about their poor qualities and bad behaviour; on the other hand it is clear that a rather small number of them conducted the very extensive and varied activities of the Company with considerable success.[34] Let us remember that the limited population of the Netherlands could find employment elsewhere than in the East, which was popularly regarded as a man-eating Moloch. The Dutch were not very willing to enter the service of the VOC – even ex-Company employees such as Mentzel advised against it.[35] Those who did join often did so out of need. The large percentage of foreigners in the Company's personnel, which grew steadily during the eighteenth century (57 per cent in 1700, 80 per cent in 1779),[36] is explicable in terms of the poverty and over-population of their countries of origin (Germany, Scandinavia, Switzerland, etc.). In the stable, stratified society of the eighteenth century the VOC provided not only an escape from unpleasant circumstances and the pleasure of adventure, but real opportunities for financial gain and social advancement. Those who were capable (and who survived) could make a decent career.[37]

Apart from certain specialised fields (military, technical and legal), a career with the VOC usually started at the bottom of the ladder. A man who had enlisted as a soldier could 'take up the pen' and rise, via all sorts of activities, to assistant, under-merchant (*onderkoopman*), merchant, chief merchant (*opperkoopman*), Councillor of India. The rapidity of promotion naturally depended on training and ability, but personal and family ties undoubtedly played a large part too, as they did everywhere in eighteenth-century society. It is known, for example, that Governor-General van Diemen's fellow-Culemborgians (amongst them Jan van Riebeeck) did well in the service of the Company, as did officials from Groningen under the late eighteenth-century Governor-General Alting. Similarly, a marriage with the daughter of one's superior was usually a promising start to a successful career.

But having the right ancestors and relatives was not everything. The VOC never lost sight of its profit motive, and profit-making demands capable and efficient employees. The Heren XVII made stringent demands on their servants, in practice as well as in theory. Every promotion had to be approved in the fatherland, and promotion was by no means automatic, particularly to the higher ranks.

Given the comparative independence which the Indian government had attained from the fatherland, it was the local hierarchy of officials that was of most direct importance to the career-conscious. This led to untiring efforts to gain the favour of superiors and to score over competitors. Since VOC officials usually lived in small white enclaves in the midst of foreign peoples, it is not surprising that they engaged in so much petty politics and quarrelling, so many betrayals and cover-ups.

The salaries of VOC officials have often aroused astonishment. A soldier, for example, earned 9 guilders a month, an assistant about twice that, an under-merchant some 60 guilders, and a chief merchant about 100 guilders. Only one half of these salaries was paid abroad. But nobody, not even the directors, reckoned with the nominal salary alone. Apart from their monthly salaries, Company officials received board and numerous other emoluments. Thus the fiscaal (prosecutor) kept certain fines he imposed, the victualling officer and the auctioneer certain surtaxes, etc. In 1710 the Cape governor received a nominal salary of 2,400 guilders per annum. But Valentyn calculated that subsistence allowances and payments in kind quadrupled this amount.[38] By the end of the eighteenth century the tithe on the wheat planted at the Cape ensured the governor of a tidy supplementary income, and by that time his nominal salary, too, was much higher.

Similar augmentations of salary occurred in the lower ranks. For example, no clerk at the Cape copied a document without claiming sixpence in payment.[39] Both Mentzel and the petitioning Patriots could report many anecdotes of extortions committed by officials. Those who travelled to the fatherland were burdened with other people's letters, bills of exchange and parcels – the sea chest which was transported free of charge seems to have been rather elastic.

No doubt the VOC winked at such practices as were deemed marginal to its business, and applied its prohibitions flexibly. But in a situation where everyone, from high to low, tried to enrich himself by more or less permissible means, excesses easily occurred. These were vigorously attacked from time to time, but not the system as such; towards the end of its existence the Company in fact gave legal sanction to this system by introducing a levy on real rather than nominal incomes (1791)[40].

Under the *ancien régime*, when norms for official behaviour differed totally from modern ones, such a system of payment was by no means rare. The manner in which officials systematically abused their offices was in accordance with custom and had long enjoyed social tolerance. It should be emphasised that such practices had to observe reasonable limits; especially in time of crisis, those hurt by the system would resist it. And conflict became almost inevitable when, towards the end of the eighteenth century, radically new notions about the character and the performance of official duties gained influence.

At the Cape the number of officials was fairly large: for example, in the second half of the eighteenth century only Batavia, Ceylon and the district of the northeast coast of Java had more. The Cape official establishment rose from approximately 120 in 1660 to 545 in 1700 and some 2,000 by 1795.[41] Until far into the eighteenth century there were more VOC officials than adult male freeburghers at the Cape: 545 as against 487 in 1700, 1,016 as against 717 in 1732.[42] It was only around 1755 that the number of male adult freeburghers exceeded the number of officials; in 1795 the proportion was still about two to one. A comparison with the total freeburgher population (men, women and children) shows that the numbers were roughly even in 1660, but in 1700 there were already 1,334 freeburghers as against 545 officials; in 1795 the proportion was 15 to 2, and if the slaves were added, 15 to 1.

VOC officials could be roughly divided into four groups according to function. Those employed in administration fell from 10 per cent of the

total in 1670[43] to 8 per cent in 1700 and 6 per cent in 1779. In 1670 the artisans accounted for 14 per cent, in 1779 for 15 per cent. In the agrarian sector (gardeners, herdsmen) there was a reduction from 19 per cent in 1670 to 5 per cent in the eighteenth century. In reality this decrease was not as large as it seems, because many soldiers later did the work of herdsmen at outlying posts (whether or not assisted by Company slaves). In the light of the Cape's strategic value there was naturally a sizeable garrison at all times; it accounted for 50 per cent of the Company's establishment in 1670, 70 per cent in 1700 and almost as much in 1779. In accordance with its priorities the Company often sent governors to the Cape who had a military background: four of the ten eighteenth-century governors were professional military men.†
Frequent contacts with the passing subjects of foreign powers demanded an official corps at the Cape that could cope socially, diplomatically and militarily. Thus among the high officials there were quite a few who had a patrician background or whose fathers had reached a responsible position in the Company's service.

Probably the increase in the rank and status of the governors at the Cape was related not only to the expansion of the settlement, but to this need for a show of power. Van Riebeeck was only a chief merchant, as were most of his successors.‡ It was only in 1690 that Simon van der Stel was given the title of governor, and in the next year the rank of councillor-extraordinary of India. The eighteenth-century governors were almost all councillors of India – a rank shared only by the governors of Ceylon, Coromandel, the Moluccas, Macassar and Java.

There were great differences in rank and social standing among the officials at the Cape. The gap between a councillor of India and a bookkeeper was enormous, and perhaps even greater was that between a colonel and a surgeon, even though they all had the prestige of having their names on the exclusive Roll of the Qualified (*Rolle der Gequalificeerden*) which included only 2.5 to 5 per cent of the total number of VOC servants.[44] In times of class consciousness and preoccupation with protocol, such differences gave ample opportunity for friction.[45] Quarrels among government factions were normal phenomena during the *ancien régime*, and they were not lacking at the Cape.[46]

---

† Van Assenburg (1708–11), De Chavonnnes (1714–24), Noodt (1722–29), Van de Graaff (1785–91). Commissioner-General Frykenius (1792–93) was a naval officer.
‡ Goske (1672–76) and Bax (1676–78) were exceptions.

Family relationships played a part in the officials' careers – and in their factional conflicts, at the Cape as elsewhere. It was because of the support of friends and relations that Willem Adriaan van der Stel could take over the governorship from his father in 1699. Governor Hendrik Swellengrebel (1740–51) had a very extensive network of blood relationships at the Cape, which his brother-in-law and successor, Rijk Tulbagh (1751–71), inherited from him. Like the regents of the fatherland, the elite at the Cape built up a clientele behind each faction; thus the phenomenon penetrated to the lower ranks as well, as may be observed in numerous appointments.

Officials generally considered their stay at the Cape as merely a temporary phase in their careers or a means of gaining enough wealth to be able to return to the fatherland (or even, as in the case of H. Swellengrebel, who was born and raised at the Cape, to settle there for the first time.) The faction system tended to exclude permanent residents of the Cape from office. Sons of freeburghers did not readily gain entrance to the official stronghold. Of the ninety-four officials employed in the central administration in Cape Town in 1779, forty-eight were of Cape birth; however, they were all sons of VOC officials. Even when certain official families had settled at the Cape, sometimes for generations, they retained the stamp of belonging to the Company rather than to the citizenry. This was particularly true of officials in higher ranks; among the lower ranks there seems to have been a stronger inclination to settle.

In all these respects Cape officialdom was by no means exceptional, not even in the world of the VOC: the nepotistic government in Batavia, where the principal functions were in the hands of a small coterie, tightly linked by blood and friendship, became virtually proverbial. But the high Cape officials were more vulnerable to criticism than similar groups elsewhere, perhaps because of the small size of the Cape settlement. Cape Town was like a gossipy village where the burgher population kept a close watch on the officials. Here pomp and luxury could not be defended, as they were in Batavia, by the claim that a large indigenous population needed to be impressed. The richer and more educated freeburghers were the ones that most readily and frequently took umbrage at the actions of officials who, owing to the structure of government and the legal position of the freeburghers, exercised authority in the somewhat arrogant manner of the regents in the Netherlands.

The freeburghers at the Cape

The first deeds of freeburgher status were issued to nine men in 1657. By 1660 the burghers, with women, children and servants, numbered 105. Their population had grown to 1,334 by 1700, and by the end of the VOC period (1795) to some 15,000.

The increase was at first sluggish in the seventeenth century, but the arrival of some 180 Huguenots in the 1680s provided a considerable boost. In the first half of the eighteenth century the rate of increase rose from an average of 400 in the first decade to about twice as much in the fifth. After only a slight rise during the 1750s (smallpox struck during this period) there was a strong surge in the second half of the century.[47] New settlers had accounted for the bulk of the increase in the seventeenth century, but increase by birth was most important in the eighteenth. The colonists tended to marry young and had large families. In the eighteenth century the median age for first marriages among women, just over 17 years around 1700, slightly increased but stayed well under 20. This increase was due to a narrowing of the disparity between the numbers of males and females. During the whole century, however, men by far outnumbered women. As a result, nearly every female married (and remarried when widowed) but a relatively high percentage of men had to stay legally unmarried (the effects of the imbalanced sex ratio on unofficial relationships will be clear; see ch. 4, pp. 192–204) while their median age of first marriage was higher too. The median number of children per married woman was at least six, frontier families tending to be even bigger. The average life expectancy for adults was well over 55 years.[48]

Little concrete information is as yet available on the social origins of the settlers, except that the bulk of them apparently originated among the lower strata of European society: the urban proletariat, minor tradesmen and farmers. The growth of the Cape population brought increasing differentiation among the settlers, not only geographically but socially. This was so despite the rather similar origins of the burghers in Europe, and despite the fact that less attention was paid to social background at the Cape than was the case in the older and more stable societies of Europe.

The natural character of the country, and the need for good land for planting and grazing, soon drove the settlers further and further away from Cape Town. In 1679 (when there were only about 100 male freeburghers) Stellenbosch was founded, in 1687, Drakenstein. The Cape district had 393 freeburgher inhabitants in 1691,[49] 615 in 1700, and ten times as many in 1795. The 'Cape hamlet', as the mother city was called until late in the eighteenth century, grew slowly and steadily, although for a long time it remained no more than a thriving village. In 1710 there were about 155 houses which, together with the Company buildings, served to house some 500 VOC servants and about the same number of freeburghers and their slaves.[50] According to Stavorinus[51] there were approximately 500 houses by about 1770, most of these still single-storeyed.

The district of Stellenbosch had a freeburgher population of 464 in 1706 and 957 in 1783, and Drakenstein had 525 and 4,081 in the same years respectively. In 1795 their combined population was 4,654, the decline in the number of inhabitants being due to the administrative separation of Graaff-Reinet. In 1795, nine years after the first magistrate had been appointed to the district of Graaff-Reinet, it already had 3,079 freeburgher inhabitants. There had been a similar decline in the population of Drakenstein after the founding of Swellendam (1743), which had 551 freeburghers in 1748 and 2,247 in 1795.

In the Cape Colony, agriculture and stock breeding were the most important economic activities, and many (particularly tradesmen) were directly or indirectly dependent upon these activities. But this phenomenon must be more closely examined. Although in theory they were permitted hardly any trading, many Capetonians lived by some form of craft, enterprise or service: according to passing seamen every house in Cape Town was a public house or inn. Even in 1660 only twenty of the thirty-five independent freeburghers were directly involved in the agrarian sector (agriculture, horticulture and stock breeding); of the rest three were boatmen, two fishermen, three carpenters, and two masons; the remaining five consisted of a barber, tailor, miller, thatcher and messenger. Three-quarters of a century later roughly the same percentage (i.e., 57 per cent) were engaged in agriculture.

Thanks to Governor de la Fontaine[52] we know the professions of most of the freeburghers in 1732 (see Table 6.1). In de la Fontaine's survey the agrarian character of the Cape community shows up clearly: the figures for Stellenbosch and Drakenstein leave no doubt as to the predominance of stock breeding and, particularly in Stellenbosch, of cultivation. In Drakenstein the artisans were restricted to a cobbler, a tailor, a carpenter, a saddler and a mason. In Stellenbosch there were, in addition, a smith, two thatchers and two wagon-makers (but no carpenter or saddler). In the Cape district, however, three-quarters of the freeburghers were in non-agrarian employment. One is also struck by the high number of people involved in inn-keeping (often linked with wine-selling) as a primary source of income. One should not overlook the 20 per cent who were tradesmen (divided among sixteen trades) and the 12 per cent in services and 'middle-class' professions.

Table 6.1　Freeburghers' occupations by district, 1732

Profession	Cape District	Stellenbosch	Drakenstein
unknown	7	7	3
retired	21	–	1
poor, indigent, decrepit	55	33	26
bachelor, employed by parents	29	32	58
agriculture, stockbreeding	66	48	193
gardener	24	5	–
fisherman	4	–	–
monopoly operator (*pachter*)	13	1	–
brewer	1	–	–
vintner	1	–	–
inn-keeper, vintner	26	–	–
shopkeeper	7	–	–
miller	1	2	1
butcher	6	1	–
baker	11	–	–
surgeon	1	–	–
wagoner	5	1	–
barber	4	–	–
midwife	1	–	–
nurse	1	–	–
bellringer	1	–	–
nightwatchman	1	–	–
messenger	1	–	–
beadle	–	1	1
teacher	3	–	–
artisan	72	8	5
free black, ex-convict	54	–	–
Company employee	–	2	–
Total	416	141	288

It is clear that the various economic activities would give rise to social distinctions. These were most evident in Cape Town's internationally oriented community of sailors, soldiers, artisans, tradespeople and administrators – some 7 000 people at the end of the eighteenth century, with widely varying backgrounds of race, wealth and education. Roughly speaking, the Cape Town population may be divided into a labouring class, a modest middle class and a well-established haute bourgeoisie. The slaves – about half the city's eighteenth-century population – constituted the mass of the labouring class, to which also belonged the majority of the free blacks and some burghers, as indicated by de la Fontaine's description of them as 'indigent', 'poorer than poor', etc.

As Cape Town grew, so did its distance from its rural environs. Farms in the southwestern Cape were worked with the assistance of European and non-European labourers, and especially slaves (whose numbers soon exceeded those of the whites). As with their counterparts in Cape Town, settlers in this region cannot simply be classed under one heading. In the early eighteenth century, a small group of wealthy, economically active landowners emerged. They possessed large profitable estates (partly the result of 'dynastic' marriages – Martin Melck is the most conspicuous example) with relatively large slave workforces. These estates invite comparison with the holdings of the gentleman farmers and lesser landed gentry in Europe[53]. These settlers lived in the vicinity of the city, with which numerous economic and social contacts were retained. They met with one another as well as with outsiders, including a fair number of passengers from ships. Not isolated like the migrant farmers of the far interior, they enjoyed social contacts, education and literature. The naval officer Cornelius de Jong noted the external aspects of their cosmopolitanism: 'In the vicinity of the Cape the country people are dressed like first citizens, their wives like ladies; many even have coiffures.' Further evidence is found in the diary of Adam Tas and the comments by many visitors on the open court that Hendrik Cloete kept at Constantia.[54] All this, however, should not obscure the fact that the majority of the southwestern Cape farmers owned middle-sized farms with varying degrees of profitability. Since the first quarter of the eighteenth century, the increasing amounts of capital demanded by wheat and wine farming obviously made it more difficult for them to compete with the small group of dominant gentlemen-farmers.

Moreover, as the colony grew, more and more distinctions arose – geographically, socially and culturally – between the wheat and wine farmers of the southwestern Cape and the stock farmers further to the north and east. Like the arable farmers, stock farmers were by no means all equally rich (even if one ignores the servants and retainers). Many of them had originated in the southwestern Cape. Unable to start farming there because of the high capital investment needed, they settled in the frontier area. Others, lacking even the modest capital to settle as stock farmers, nevertheless tried to make a living there, by hunting, working for others, etc. (see ch. 2, pp. 84–93). In the eyes of the people of the southwestern Cape, they shared a rather homogeneous culture and set of customs: those of a more or less nomadic migrant farmer community, poor economically, socially and culturally. They lived far from Cape Town and were very isolated. Under the circumstances they had to shed their European background and adapt themselves to African conditions; their frontier existence gave few opportunities for refined cultural expression. The Bible and a few other devotional works were their only literature, hunting their main recreation. They lived a patriarchal life, austere and adapted to the demands of nature, which led some observers to fear that they might sink to the level of their Khoikhoi neighbours – with whom some of them indeed had very close connections.

The various groups of whites at the Cape did not live in impenetrable compartments; on the contrary, in such a small community there were all kinds of contacts – both commercial and personal – between various classes of burghers and officials. Marriage, in particular, was an institution that bridged all divisions although, especially in the rural areas, marriages within an extended family were common.[55] Younger sons of freeburghers sometimes entered the service of the Company, while many of the Company's officials became burghers. Sometimes they did so after scouting out the field as a *pasganger* or knecht (Company servant temporarily hired by a burgher), sometimes by settling with their accumulated savings, and sometimes when, having married, they were driven to it by the expenses of keeping a family. In general, however, it was the sons of established farmers, and not ex-officials, who, forced by lack of land, moved to the northeast and became trekboers.

Naturally there was also some upward mobility: VOC officials were promoted and thus moved into higher social classes, or freeburghers succeeded in their undertakings. Thus Henning Husing, Johannes Swellengrebel, Martin Melck, Joachim von Dessin and Rijk Tulbagh all arrived at the Cape as soldiers and ended in high positions or became very rich. Visitors from overseas tended to complain about the parvenu character and behaviour of the Cape citizenry. 'Here no one loves anything but money', wrote Valentyn in 1726. Half a century later Stavorinus stated that avarice was the dominant characteristic of people at the Cape and condemned their laziness. According to Cornelius de Jong, the Capetonians' 'high opinions of themselves' made them despise manual labour as being work for slaves.[56] This was, however, a typical complaint about colonists, by no means peculiar to the Cape.

The various groupings among the Cape population had conceptions of one another that clearly underlined the differences between them. Both the Western Cape gentry and the high officials considered the migrant stock farmers as the worst sector of the population: degenerate, uncultured and lazy, almost less civilised than the 'Hottentots'.[57]

Conversely, these so-called 'canaille' held no very high opinion of the urban merchant,[58] not to mention the vain and avaricious official.

Among the population groups of the Western Cape, prejudices were no less severe. In general, the higher officials had the same attitudes to the Cape citizens as those of overseas visitors, namely that they were greedy for wealth and comfort but unwilling to work or make an intellectual effort. This reproach was directed not so much at the common people as at the higher classes: it was brought against both Van der Stel's adversaries and the Cape Patriots. On their side, the burghers of means and status – including many of the Patriots – did not deem themselves less than the highest officials, and they indulged in considerable prejudices against commoners. A well-established and prosperous farmer such as Adam Tas did not consider attending the funeral of his poor white servant; he and his friends looked down upon the 'common' people in the Cape who signed the petition in favour of Van der Stel and who included so many 'blacks'.[59] Hendrik Cloete of Constantia wrote arrogant remarks about less successful neighbours, while an aristocrat such as Hendrik Swellengrebel, the younger son of a governor, did not deem it necessary to mention the name of the common soldier who illustrated his travel diaries.[60]

It will be obvious that these entrenched prejudices between Cape citizens and officials, and among the burghers themselves, would intensify the repeated conflicts which broke out in Cape society. We must now pay closer attention to these conflicts themselves, firstly by examining three specific episodes in detail, and then by considering the features which lay at the root of them all.

The struggle against Willem Adriaan van der Stel

This is not the place for a detailed account of the well-known conflict between Governor van der Stel (1699–1707) and a group of self-conscious freeburghers during the years 1705–07. Here we shall merely draw attention to some important events and the issues surrounding them. Some years before Van der Stel took over the government from his father in 1699, there had been complaints that food production was inadequate for the needs of the ships and of the Cape itself. Willem Adriaan therefore knew what the Heren XVII expected of him. Like his father before him, he took up his task energetically. In order to obtain a good supply of slaughtering stock, he issued licences allowing farmers to graze in the Land of Waveren, and even suspended the prohibition on stock bartering with the Khoikhoi. He also stimulated grain and wine farming.

In all this Willem Adriaan did not forget his own interests. Since Van Riebeeck's time the Cape governors had done their own farming, mostly on a considerable scale. Van der Stel, too, farmed in the grand manner, and also favoured his friends with grants of land. Secundus Elsevier owned 110 morgen; the Rev. Petrus Kalden 100 morgen; the surgeon Ten Damme, the quartermaster Jacobus de Wet and Landdrost Starrenburg, 60 morgen each. But all these properties were insignificant compared with the Van der Stels' own: Willem Adriaan owned 613 morgen and his father, Simon, 891 morgen; their estates at Vergelegen and Constantia respectively were planned like country estates in the tradition of the Dutch regents. In addition, Willem Adriaan's brother Frans had 240 morgen, and each of the three had extensive grazing grounds at his disposal. The Van der Stels' power and status, moreover, granted them an easy and cheap access to the labour market, buying slaves at low prices and using Company personnel as their workforce.[61]

The policy of stimulating agricultural production bore results. In these years the Cape reached a stage of overproduction, but in the meantime the Company had failed to provide a single new outlet. The various groups of producers – freeburgher farmers and farming officials – consequently waged a desperate battle for the available market. Van der Stel himself, true to the VOC tradition, exploited his official power in this conflict of business rivals; because the Van der Stel faction was fairly small they formed a compact marketing cartel. In 1702 the governor, after receiving complaints about abuses, withdrew the rights of burghers to trade with Khoikhoi. In August 1705 he inaugurated a new variant of the wine concession, which he defended as more advantageous to both the small consumer and the Company, but which in any event secured him a market for his own produce.

The issue of the wine concession goaded into action a group of freeburgher entrepreneurs who had long observed the activities of the governor and his friends with dissatisfaction. They drafted a petition and started collecting evidence against their adversaries. Their leader was Henning Husing, a former soldier who had worked himself up to being the richest man in Cape Town. His wealth had been obtained, for the most part, from a typical institution of the VOC system, the meat monopoly. Husing's principal allies were the Stellenbosch burghers Jacob van der Heijden (a very rich farmer, money-lender and livestock dealer), Jan van Meerland, Pieter van der Bijl, Ferdinand Appel and Adam Tas – also by no means poor men.[62] Tas, for instance, owned 184 morgen. These men gained a following among their neighbours and friends and also obtained support from the Huguenots in Franschhoek.

Thus two groups were contending for control of the monopoly. But there was a social conflict as well. Van der Stel had lost sight of the limits on official behaviour which custom would tolerate. Given his social background, this is perhaps not incomprehensible: why should an Amsterdam regent and former city magistrate such as Willem Adriaan pay any attention to a huddle of Cape freeburghers? Was he not the supreme authority in the land? As the conflict developed, Willem Adriaan abused his position in typical Dutch regent style. Alluding to the fate of the Amsterdamers who had rebelled against the regents some years before, he threatened to string up his adversaries, and in fact had the former burgher councillor Johannes Rotterdam, who had clearly shown his contempt for the governor, banished to Batavia by the Council of Justice.

Once it became clear to Van der Stel that his adversaries' complaints had reached the Council of India and the Heren XVII, he obtained signatures for a counter-petition or 'testimonial'. Among the 240 Cape inhabitants who signed this petition there appeared – by no means fortuitously – the governor's favourites and protégés, such as the gardener Jan Hartog, and Jan Mahieu, the secretary of the heemraden in Stellenbosch. It was normal for Dutch regents to build up a following by bestowing favours, positions and presents, and to call upon it in times of need. In explaining Van der Stel's behaviour, including his browbeating of arrested opponents, it is of course nonsense to indulge, as historians sometimes have, in fantasies about his 'Oriental character' or 'slavish following'. What showed itself here was his recent past as a regent in Amsterdam and not his remote Eastern origins (his great-grandmother had been an Indian).[63]

On the other hand, the actions of his adversaries were by no means free from self-interest. Henning Husing was, after all, as eager to obtain monopolies as was Van der Stel. Before the two quarrelled, Husing had had no objection to close and profitable co-operation with the governor, and had paid him liberally for services rendered. Nor did the obstinate Van der Heyden endure his many months of imprisonment purely for universal liberty or the public weal.[64] He had been willing to pay high prices to obtain a great deal of land from the governor. Probably his anger at being robbed of the profitable barter with Khoikhoi was one of his strongest incentives to revolt.[65] None of these people objected to cheating the Company when they reported their taxable assets – in his diary Tas merely records, sourly, that compared with others he was still reporting too high a percentage of his wealth. Tas, by birth a member of the occasionally anti-regent middle class, cleverly publicised the idea that he had joined battle against Van der Stel for the sake of freedom – the new name of his farm, Liber-tas, could be translated either as 'freedom' or as 'Tas is free'.

Thus this was not a conflict in which the freedom-loving Afrikaners obtained justice against tyrannical, oppressive officials. Nor was it a frontier rebellion, as Eric Walker supposed, for it was mainly men from the western Cape who were involved.[66] The burghers' petition was cleverly drafted to gain the favour of the directors; it represented Van der Stel and his group as incompetent officials who robbed the Company. The impression was created that only the interest of the Company led the plaintiffs to draw up their petition; only in passing did they point out the harmful economic consequences which the behaviour of the officials had had for the freeburghers, and in this regard they appealed to the fatherly sentiments of the Heren XVII. Their lamentations, in which they represented themselves as sorely tried victims of official caprice and contempt, concluded with a warning, wrapped in velvet, but clear nonetheless: they threatened disruption.

In his *Korte Deductie* (Brief Statement) Van der Stel naturally concentrated on the weak points in the accusations. He attempted to cast doubts on the characters of his adversaries, pointing out that they had misrepresented themselves as being concerned solely for the interests of the Company. He also tried to minimise the force of the complaints and to defend his own actions by comparing them to practices permitted in the past. Significantly he elaborated on the aversion of the Cape burghers to law and order. The freeburghers had accused Van der Stel of dictatorial action; he hit back by complaining of their anarchic behaviour and virtually democratic aspirations. This was not simply the obvious retort to make; it seems that he wanted the Heren XVII to draw comparisons between the Cape unrest and similar movements (the *Aansprekers* riot and the *Plooierijen*) that had some years previously disturbed the peace of the regents in the fatherland.

It seems unlikely that the Heren XVII recalled Van der Stel because they were fully convinced of his despotic behaviour or of the harm he had allegedly done to the Company. They discharged him and summoned him home, but they allowed him to retain his salary during the homeward passage and otherwise hardly bothered him. Rev. Kalden, who had been as violently attacked as the governor, later obtained a good post with the Company as rector of the seminary on Ceylon. Bergh, Blesius, Ten Damme, De Wet and Starrenburg simply retained their posts.

It may be that the directors merely wanted quiet at the Cape during those times of war (the War of the Spanish Succession, 1701-14), or that they genuinely felt the governor had overstepped the bounds of propriety. Or, alternatively, Van der Stel may have been the victim of a typical eighteenth-century feud. Of the seventeen Amsterdam directors who were responsible for his discharge, half had assumed their posts after Willem Adriaan's appointment in 1697: the same applied to the Company's Advocate, Everard Scott. Most of the new incumbents belonged to the following of Joan Corver (a director since 1688), who was the most powerful man in the Amsterdam regents' circles after 1702. Because of Corver, Van der Stel's patron, Nicolas Witsen, had lost much of his influence. A number of other men who had been prominent in 1697 had died by 1706. It was not unusual for such a shift of power in the Amsterdam government to have far-reaching effects on the followers of the factions concerned.[67]

Van der Stel's discharge was naturally an important victory for the freeburghers, though hardly an occasion for unrestrained rejoicing. The final settlement of the dispute – including the sale of the property of the accused – took years and did not always work out to the advantage of the petitioners. After 1707 monopoly contracts remained; officials continued to farm extensive lands and engage in trading; and cattle bartering was still forbidden to the colonists.

Some officials had disappeared, but not the VOC system itself. The real problems had not been solved: the discrepancy between production and marketing outlets, the mercantilist restrictions on trade, the competition between the Company (and its servants in their official as well as private capacities) and the citizens. The Heren XVII did try to do something about these problems by stopping further immigration (1705) and by creating some further possibilities for marketing. But the VOC system was not abandoned.

The absence of major conflicts in the following decades was due to several more or less fortuitous circumstances that dissipated tensions. Thus, for instance, grain harvests in this period were just as irregular as the marketing possibilities; the latter, moreover, in general tended to expand.[68] More importantly, the position of the freeburghers changed: the expansion by the trekboers gathered momentum, and the stock farmer was temporarily less concerned with the problems of marketing than his counterpart in the southwestern Cape. Furthermore, this expansion was not seriously hampered either by the Company or by the indigenous population. The migration of the white freeburghers to the interior prevented the simmering economic and political conflict at the Cape from reaching boiling point.

The Barbier Rebellion

The Van der Stel episode was an internal dispute in the white community; apart from the question of barter with the Khoikhoi, policy toward native peoples played no part.[69] But in the rebellion of 1795 on the Eastern Frontier (see ch. 9, pp. 438–39), and repeatedly later in South African history, this issue would be at the heart of settlers' disputes with the government.

That the problem had existed even earlier is apparent from the episode of 1738-39 in which Estienne Barbier played the principal part: here the policy of the Company, which was founded on good relations with the independent Khoikhoi, quite clearly clashed with the interests of white stock farmers. In the 1730s younger, and as yet unsettled, freeburghers were doing what had long been customary: crossing the borders of the colony to hunt, to 'barter' cattle, and to find pasture.[70] In general the Company was opposed to these movements and took sporadic action to control them, as in 1738, when it again prohibited stock bartering after receiving complaints about the misdeeds of barterers.

In 1739 a group of frontier farmers rebelled against this prohibition, incited by Estienne Barbier, a French-born sergeant in the service of the Company.[71] Barbier had served at the Cape since 1735 and does not seem to have been a very co-operative character: he was unwise enough to publicly attack one of his highest superiors, Ensign R.S. Alleman, with complaints about malpractice. When Barbier brought these charges a second time, he was imprisoned in the Castle.

On 24 March, 1738, he managed to escape from the Castle and made his way to the interior, where he found refuge in the Drakenstein Valley. His tales of the iniquities of high Company officials were eagerly accepted, especially since a number of frontier farmers had recently suffered legal action following the complaints of Nama victims of a stock-bartering expedition. At the head of about ten young frontier farmers Barbier began his rebellion. At the Paarl church he and his followers' ripped down the Company notice against stock-bartering (1 March, 1739); they then incited others to disobedience, and threatened violence. Barbier, whose leadership abilities seem to have been meagre, managed to gather only a small number of desperados behind him.

But the Council of Policy itself acknowledged the broad sympathy in the colony for Barbier's action, and hence acted cautiously.[72] They even granted amnesty to his followers and at the same time sent – perhaps as a distraction and a token of goodwill – a punitive commando against the

Khoisan; the pardoned men and some who had been accused of raiding the Khoikhoi were ordered to take part! Barbier himself managed to stay free for another six months, but was executed on 14 November, 1739, after conviction of charges of *lèse-majesté* and rebellion.

The importance of Barbier's rebellion lies not in his rather inconsequential actions, but in the wide sympathy he elicited among the local population – a sympathy that allowed him to elude justice for one and a half years. The two-fold complaint that Barbier voiced was widely shared: firstly, that the Company paid too much attention to 'the word of unbaptised Hottentots, who know neither salvation nor damnation',[73] and secondly, that by illegal and semi-legal means the officials made economic enterprise nearly impossible for the burghers of the Cape. With regard to the second point, they charged that officials traded and farmed illicitly and demanded presents from those who wanted to have loan farms registered in their names (the same charge had been brought against Van der Stel). All these practices made life expensive, as did excessive taxes for people with low incomes. These complaints contain clear echoes of those of 1705 and 1779, and it is not surprising that half a century later the Patriots would pass favourable judgement on Barbier.[74] The complaint that heathenish Hottentots were protected and advanced above Christians would also be frequently voiced in the future.[75]

The Cape Patriot movement[76]

In May 1778 a number of secret meetings were convened in and around Cape Town. At about the same time a pamphlet was circulated, mainly by night. In this pamphlet 'the powers and freedoms of a society of citizens' were 'defended by the opinions of the foremost lawyers, and dedicated to the judgement of the Cape citizenry'.[77] The 'power' of the burghers was the freedom – in fact, the duty – to change the form of government by violence if necessary, should the authorities no longer perform their natural task of 'standing for the people, and defending their lives, property, and liberty.'

This pamphlet was clearly a theoretical justification of the right of revolt: it was intended as a preamble to a request that the governor redress grievances – or so one can deduce from its wording – but no such request was ever made. What did happen, almost a year later, was that the burgher Carel Hendrik Buytendagh was arrested, forcibly re-enlisted in the Company's service, and sent to Batavia.

The freeburghers now felt that their rights and liberties were truly at stake, and 400 of them signed a petition to the governor asking

permission to send a delegation to lay complaints before the Heren
XVII. This request was naturally refused by the governor: if there were
complaints he, the governor, was the one to whom they should be
addressed. The burghers calmly proceeded to designate Barend Jacob
Artoys, Nicolaas Godfried Heyns, Tielman Roos and Jacobus van
Reenen 'as joint representatives of the entire citizenry' (7 May 1779).
The four men left for Europe, and on 9 October 1779 submitted an
elaborate petition to the Heren XVII. This petition, the so-called
Memorandum of 1779, consisted of three sections. The first set out the
bad economic circumstances of the Cape freeburghers. The second
showed how these were aggravated by the actions of officials, whose
selfish and tyrannical character was illustrated with numerous examples.
The third section contained a number of economic proposals: that
burghers be permitted to trade freely with foreign ships in the harbour,
and that they obtain better prices for goods they sold to and bought
from the Company. There were also some political requests: the
petitioners wanted half the members of the Council of Policy to be
freeburghers, who would also have the right to report to the Heren
XVII. In addition, they called for the codification of laws and
delineation of the powers of officials and, of course, for a strict
prohibition on their private economic activity.

In keeping with Company practice, the accused officials were called
upon to explain their actions. The wording of their defence was
strikingly reminiscent of that adopted by Willem Adriaan van der Stel. In
his 'Considerations' (submitted on 20 March 1782) Governor van
Plettenberg declared that the signatories of the Memorandum were by
no means representative of all freeburghers, but merely a small and
insignificant group. The economic privation of which they complained
could not be squared with the facts: great prosperity and luxury prevailed
at the Cape. It was because the Cape burghers were lazy and refused to
exert themselves that they did not prosper. The complainants were
merely jealous of the hard-won success of officials, whose private trading
activities remained well within the bounds of established custom. Fiscal
Willem Cornelis Boers, who had been sharply attacked in the
Memorandum for his extortionate actions, defended himself with a
frontal assault on the political pretensions of the signatories.
Government at the Cape, he held, was the sole prerogative of the
officials; it was, after all, solely for the Company's benefit that the Cape
settlement had been founded and maintained.

The mills of the VOC could grind very slowly. The Heren XVII gave
their judgement only in December 1783, and then for the most part they

exonerated the officials. This could not be a definitive judgement, however, for in 1782 the Cape representatives had submitted a Further Memorandum, repeating and augmenting earlier complaints. But it was not only the Heren XVII who had to deal with the complaints of the Cape citizenry. Having become wiser about affairs in the fatherland, where the Patriots were embroiled in an intense struggle with the Orangist establishment, the burghers also appealed to the States-General and to the States of Holland (in addresses dated December 1784, but submitted in 1785).

Events in the fatherland (where the Prince of Orange and his faction were losing ground), as well as those in North America, were closely followed at the Cape; and their echoes were noticeable. In 1784 the dissidents at the Cape showed signs of organising themselves. A representative body ('Commissioned Representatives of the People') was chosen to co-ordinate activities, which consisted mainly of drafting the above-mentioned appeals to the States-General and of electing and briefing four new delegates to the Netherlands (Martinus Adrianus Bergh, Johannes Roos, Johannes Henricus Redelinghuys, and Johannes Augustus Bresler). After this, few new developments appear to have taken place at the Cape. The Patriots apparently fell out among themselves.

Meanwhile the second delegation to the Netherlands, having gained legal advice, submitted their petition to the States-General, and in April 1786 yet another. Moreover, they tried, through a number of publications, to influence public opinion, and especially to persuade the Dutch Patriots that the two movements were similar. In temperament, revolutionary intentions, and methods the four delegates differed widely. Bergh even distanced himself publicly from his co-delegates. They did not achieve much, although the postponement of the appointment of a new fiscaal in 1785 was perhaps due to their efforts. Compelled by the States-General, which demanded information, the directors of the VOC closely examined Cape affairs in 1785. In the end, however, they upheld their judgements of December 1783. The most important concessions they were prepared to allow were free trade with foreign ships and the purchase of surplus produce at fixed prices – all this, of course, after the normal demand of the Company had been met. One could hardly call these radical solutions to the marketing problems of the Cape producers – many uninvolved observers recognised this – but within the framework of the VOC they were probably realistic.

In general the directors were determined to protect their servants, even when the States-General became involved. The strategy of the Cape

Patriots in publicising their grievances and seeking contacts with the
Dutch Patriots probably turned the directors against them. In these years
the Company was facing growing financial problems as well as increasing
attacks on its privileged position, its structure and its mode of operation.
One must not, of course, assume that these attacks came entirely from
theorists questioning the value of all monopoly companies like the
VOC; many who called for greater supervision of the VOC by the state
were self-interested.

Since the directors were Orangists and supporters of the status quo,
one could hardly expect them to be sympathetic to the Cape petitioners,
who were so patently supported by their political opponents. In
September 1787 the Prince of Orange, backed by British diplomacy and
a Prussian army, resumed full powers; his Patriot opponents were chased
out of their offices and the country. This meant that the Cape Patriots
could gain no further hearing. Indeed, their representatives in the
Netherlands were even obstructed when they tried to return to the Cape.
As is shown by the VOC's decisions, including the reforms made by
Commissioners-General Nederburgh and Frykenius during their stay at
the Cape in 1792–93, the achievements of the Cape Patriot movement
were meagre indeed.

As in the movement against Van der Stel at the beginning of the
eighteenth century, the local economic and social situation formed the
background to the Patriot movement. But in the three-quarters of a
century between the two conflicts the population of the Cape had
expanded considerably, society had become more stratified, and
problems of the economy had become more severe and complex. The
Cape burghers had become more deeply rooted in the colony, and hence
more alienated from the governing class. There was also, on both sides,
a stronger urge to express complaints and demands in theoretical terms.

At the end of the eighteenth century certain centuries-old institutions
were under strong attack from ideas associated with the Enlightenment.
Many thinkers, proceeding from the idea of equality, were rejecting all
forms of aristocracy and group privilege, and advocating government for
and by the people instead of by remote ruling bodies like the VOC. They
were also demanding the abolition of monopolies, nepotistic politics,
and secretive procedures in government – all of which made it difficult
for popular policies to prevail.

It is still too early to assess the degree to which Cape leaders were
influenced by the Enlightenment. For instance, we hardly know what
literature reached the Cape – a good deal it seems – nor, more
importantly, who read it. It would seem, however, that the closer one

lived to Cape Town, the greater one's chances were of being influenced by Enlightenment thinking. It has been proved, for example, that the events of the American Revolution and the conflict between Patriots and Orangists in the Netherlands were followed closely in the southwestern Cape. Even more, of course, those Cape citizens who went to Europe would imbibe new ideas. The most radical and explicitly Enlightenment pronouncements of the Patriot movement came from those who had visited the Netherlands: their statements should not be uncritically regarded as products of the intellectual climate at the Cape.[78]

One should also note that the Patriots need not have derived their ideas solely from Enlightenment thinkers, but that they may have been drawing on a long Dutch tradition of revolt. Among the 'gentry' and bourgeoisie of the southwestern Cape there were men with administrative experience – not only officials who had formerly been burghers, but also field-cornets, heemraden, militia officers, and burgher councillors. Such people were likely to find some inspiration in the 'democratic' tendencies which had cropped up from time to time in Dutch history: e.g., during the war of 1672, in the decade after the death of William III in 1702 (the 'Plooierijen'), and in 1747-48 when broad layers of the population revolted against the economic and political dominance of the regent classes (the tax farmer riots and Doelisten movement).[79]

However, the main inspiration for the Patriots' ideas was neither the Enlightenment nor Dutch history, but the situation at the Cape. In fact their grievances, as reflected in their Memorandum of 1779, hardly differed from those of Van der Stel's opponents: a precarious economic situation aggravated by the actions of officials who abused their position for private purposes, and high-handed action by officials against freeburghers who had no rights. Their recommendations to improve the situation were mainly economic and did little more than demand affirmation in practice of what already existed in theory. All that struck a new note was the request for a clearer definition of the rights of the burghers, and for more burgher councillors with greater powers. This, too, was by no means revolutionary.

Once again, it seems as if the background of the Cape Patriot movement was the structure of society and economy at the Cape. The mercantilist policy of the VOC, the discrepancy between production and marketing, the role of the officials in both government and economy, all collided with the interests of the colonists.[80] The avaricious actions of the officials above all affected those who were economically weak; but strong and active entrepreneurs were also annoyed with the restrictions imposed by the officials on their undertakings.

The leaders among the Cape Patriots were clearly inhabitants of the city and of the western Cape. Among the former one notices a number of more or less intellectually trained men (Artoys, Heyns, Redelinghuys) and a fairly large number of ambitious bourgeoisie: entrepreneurs, merchants (the Van Reenens, Roos, Verweij, J. Smith Jurriaansz), and people who had savoured participation in government and who wanted more, such as burgher councillors Meyer, Van der Poel, Maasdorp and Bergh. This was a kind of colonial elite that came into conflict with officials from abroad and that could gain influence by exploiting feelings of dissatisfaction in wider circles.

The relationship between the urban and the rural members of the Patriot movement did not remain good for very long: Redelinghuys later complained [81] that the rural leaders had left him in the lurch. In fact, the western Cape gentry were not undivided in their support of the Memorandum. It is significant that a number of the most prominent western Cape farmers submitted a separate request (1784) in which better economic arrangements were called for, but which contained none of the political and social acrimony of the Memorandum. [82]

During the last five years of Company rule, relations between burghers and government became even worse. In 1789 the Heren XVII recalled the free-spending Governor C.J. van de Graaff and withdrew a large part of the garrison from the Cape. [83] In 1792-93 Commissioners Nederburgh and Frykenius visited the Cape and attempted to grapple with the distressing state of the Company's finances by curtailing government spending, tightening the collection of existing taxes, and levying new ones.

At the same time the export economy was suffering from a decline in the number of foreign ships which visited the Cape as a result of the war which had broken out in Europe in 1792. Nederburgh and Frykenius made some concessions to the burghers, such as allowing them to export colonial products with their own ships, and to engage in the slave trade on the East African coast and at Madagascar. But these measures, being adaptations rather than reforms, were too little and too late to revive the economy. Great discontent arose among the burghers about economic matters, particularly the declining value of the rixdollar. With a weakened garrison, Company authority seemed insubstantial. Burghers expressed contempt for the government and openly defied its authority. Nederburgh spoke of 'a spirit of confusion and insubordination toward all authority without exception.' [84] J.F. Kirsten said 'Government had lost its respect . . . Everybody would command here and nobody would obey.'[85] Among the burghers, revolutionary voices were increasingly heard. Some wanted the Cape to be governed directly by the States-General, others wanted total independence.[86]

In the eastern districts the settlers became more and more aware that the Company could neither protect them against their indigenous enemies nor punish them for insubordination. In 1795 the burghers of Graaff-Reinet and Swellendam rose in rebellion.

The world of the VOC was breaking up.

Conclusion: The framework of conflict

The conflicts between freeburghers and VOC officials at the Cape were largely rooted in the social, economic and administrative structures of the Cape settlement. Since these structures remained essentially unchanged, there was a constant element in the various conflicts: from the freeburghers who in 1658 complained to Van Riebeeck about their economic subservience to Company interest, to the Memorandum of the Cape Patriots in 1779, or – to give another example – Hendrik Cloete's attempts in the 1780s to find better marketing outlets for his famous Constantia wines.

In the interior, most conflicts between stock farmers and officials concerned land policies, taxes and relations with the indigenous peoples. Stock trading with the Khoikhoi was a point of contention virtually from the beginning of the settlement, as were hunting and grazing beyond the borders. Why could grazing concessions or loan farms not be obtained more readily and cheaply? Why was stock bartering prohibited when the Company itself engaged in it? Why were boundaries which were recognised by the government always years behind the actual ones? Why must farmers pay high prices and high taxes on goods from the Company's stores when their own produce could be sold only at fixed, low prices? Why were taxes not used for better defence of the borders or to establish churches and administrative centres deeper in the interior?

A second set of grievances held by stock farmers centred on the different attitudes which officials often had to the threat from Khoisan and later Xhosa. In brief, the farmers wanted to know why Cape Town and its agents paid serious attention to complaints from native spokesmen, yet left the people of the frontier to fight their battles alone. Grievances regarding native policy rankled throughout the century, coming into brief prominence in Barbier's rebellion, but not giving rise to a major revolt until the frontier uprisings of 1795.

Clearly the conflict between officials and stock farmers owed a great
deal to the social and cultural differences between them. While the gap
was smaller in Cape Town and surrounding districts, it still existed,
however, and was aggravated by the constant contact between the two
groups which took place there. It was the city-dweller who knew the
officials best, and it was he who was most dependent upon them for
jobs, favours, commodities and services. And, as we have seen, the city-
dweller played a significant part in the conflict with officials and, by
extension, in the formation of the Afrikaner people.[87] While social and
administrative contacts between officials and freeburghers produced
ample occasion for conflicts, it was the economic structure of the Cape
that made such conflicts virtually inevitable. By about the beginning of
the eighteenth century the Cape could produce enough for its own
needs, for the passing VOC ships, and even for export. The VOC
realised this and allowed exports, but only on its own conditions. Its
claims always had to be satisfied first, at fixed and low prices, and even
then the producers were tied hand and foot to the Company. The
production of the Cape occasionally was too large for the local market.
But chance circumstances such as failed harvests, unusually large
numbers of passing ships, expanded garrisons, or temporary measures by
the Company could solve this problem from time to time. The
importation of many products also fluctuated, owing to all kinds of
circumstances, but here, too, the freeburghers remained dependent
upon bodies and persons who were primarily serving other interests.
Although the Company tried from time to time to reconcile these
opposed interests by a variety of measures (supplying import goods by
order, free auctions, buying up surpluses, fixing prices), such measures
remained no more than patchwork as long as their execution was
organised in such a way that officials had every opportunity for
profiteering, nepotism and bribery.

If, as we have argued, the constitution of the Cape was structurally
unsound, we will no longer need to explain the endemic conflict with
stereotypes of either the lazy, self-opinionated and uncultured Afrikaner
or the vain, avaricious and tyrannical VOC official. While some
members of both groups clearly deserved these labels, the stereotypes
were created in the struggle itself and have no value as historical
explanations. Nor need we be misled into exaggerating the role of
ideology among the burghers. 'Freedom', 'national sentiment',
'democratic liberalism' and such characterisations seem to have had little
bearing on the realities of these conflicts. Those, for example, who treat
the Cape Patriots too ideologically and who see in the Great Trek, in Paul

Kruger, and in the declaration of the Republic (1961) 'the continuation of their [the Patriots'] ideas'[88] are guilty of facile simplification by hindsight.

But to say that the conflict was rooted in the specific conditions of the Cape's society and economy is not necessarily to say that such conditions were unique. The settlement at the Cape was, after all, only one of the territories of the VOC, and the VOC formed part of the Republic of the United Netherlands. This means that Cape structures and events should be seen in the context of the Netherlands and of common Dutch colonial patterns, which in turn reveal certain similarities with the general and colonial history of the time.

Chapter Six Notes

1. This is implied by Leo Fouché, *Dagboek van Adam Tas 1705–1706* (Cape Town, 1970), p. 390 and Gert D. Scholtz, *Die Ontwikkeling van die politieke denke van die Afrikaner* (Johannesburg, 1967), I, 176.
2. But on social stratification see titles cited in note 53 below. On the intellectual history of the late eighteenth century see *Afrikaner political thought: Analysis and documents*, ed. André du Toit and Hermann Giliomee (Vol. I; Berkeley, 1983).
3. Cited in M.F. Katzen, 'White Settlers and the Origin of a New Society', *The Oxford History of South Africa*, ed. Monica Wilson and Leonard Thompson (Oxford, 1969), I, 231. For information on the social system of other Dutch colonies see H. Hoetink, *Het patroon van de oude Curaçaose samenleving* (Assen, 1958); R.A.J. van Lier, *Frontier Society: A Social Analysis of the History of Surinam* (The Hague, 1971); J.G. Taylor, *The social world of Batavia. European and Eurasian in Dutch Asia* (Madison, 1983). Recent comparative studies such as *White supremacy. A comparative study in American and South African history*, ed. George M. Fredrickson (New York 1981) and *The Frontier in history. North America and Southern Africa compared*, ed. Howard Lamar and Leonard Thomspon (New Haven 1981) pay only limited attention to the structure of the dominant white groups and their relations to the colonial empires to which they belonged.
4. Anna J. Böeseken, 'Die Nederlandse Kommissarisse en die 18e eeuse samelewing aan die Kaap', *AYB*, VII (1944), p. 25 states that only a few traces can be found of co-operation between officials and freeburghers, but does not explain this phenomenon.
5. Scholtz, *Ontwikkeling*, I, ch. 5 and Katzen, 'New Society', pp. 189–190, 202, 217.
6. Still indispensable for a study of the Company is a work completed around 1700 by the Company's advocate, Pieter van Dam, *Beschrijvinge van de Oost-Indische Compagnie*, ed. F.W. Stapel and C.W. Th. van Boetzelaer (7 vols.; The Hague, 1927–54). For a brief overview see F.S. Gaastra, *De geschiedenis van de VOC* (Haarlem 1982). See also W.M.F. Mansvelt, *Rechtsvorm en*

geldelijk beheer bij de Oost-Indische Compagnie (Amsterdam, 1922); C. de Heer, *Bijdrage tot de financiele geschiedenis der Oost-Indische Compagnie* (The Hague, 1929); J.J. Steur, *Herstel of ondergang. De voorstellen tot redres van de V.O.C. 1740–1795* (Utrecht 1984).

7. Leslie H. Palmier, 'The Javanese Nobility under the Dutch', *Comparative Studies in Society and History,* II (1959–60), p. 208.

8. Kristof Glamann, *Dutch-Asiatic Trade, 1620–1740* (Copenhagen, 1958), ch. 3; F.S. Gaastra, 'De VOC in de zeventiende en achttiende eeuw: de groei van een bedrijf; geld tegen goederen', *Bijdragen en Mededelingen betreffende de Geschiedenis der Nederlanden*, XCI (1976), pp. 249–72.

9. Van Dam, *Beschrijvinge*, I, 78.

10. I.J. Brugmans, 'De Oost-Indische Compagnie en de welvaart in de Republiek', *Welvaart en Historie*, ed. I.J. Brugmans (The Hague, 1950), pp. 28–37; Johan de Vries, *De economische achteruitgang der Republiek in de achttiende eeuw* (Leiden, 1968).

11. Johannes C. Boogman, 'Die holländische Tradition in der niederländischen Geschichte', *Westfälische Forschungen*, XV (1962), pp. 96–105.

12. Van Dam, *Beschrijvinge*, I, 80. Toward the end of the eighteenth century attempts were made to put the VOC under the supervision of the state; see Gerrit J. Schutte, *De Nederlandse Patriotten en de koloniën. Een onderzoek naar hun denkbeelden en optreden, 1770–1800* (Groningen, 1974), chs. 3, 5; Steur, *Herstel of ondergang*.

13. H.A. van Reede tot Drakenstein, 'Journaal van zijn verblijf aan de Kaap', ed. A. Hulshof, *Bijdragen en Mededelingen van het Historisch Genootschap te Utrecht*, LXII (1941), p. 123.

14. AR, Nederburgh Collection, no. 143, Kaapsche Stukken 1785, III, 136.

15. Eduard van Zurck, *Codex Batavus* (Delft, 1711), pp. 413, 565.

16. AR, Nederburgh Collection, no 149, Van de Graaff – Heren XVII, 19 April 1786, p. 70.

17. Banishment also occurred at Batavia: Abraham Bogaert, *Historische Reizen door d'oostersche Deelen van Asia . . .* (Amsterdam, 1711), pp. 129 – 30.

18. This phrase was already used in 1658. See Foort C. Dominicus, *Het ontslag van Wilhem Adriaen van der Stel* (Rotterdam, 1928), p. 12.

19. Bogaert, *Reizen*, p. 495.

20. C.W. de Kiewiet's use of this term is an unjustifiable concession to eighteenth-century sentiment: see his *A History of South Africa – Social and Economic* (Oxford, 1946), p. 5. The same objection can be made to Katzen, 'New Society', pp. 213ff.

21. Taco H. Milo, *De invloed van de zeemacht op de geschiedenis der VOC* (The Hague, 1946).

22. This was still the opinion in 1802: Schutte, *Nederlandse Patriotten*, p. 211.

23. After 1740 the annual losses of the Cape settlement averaged 300,000 guilders (*Nieuwe Nederlandsche Jaarboeken*, 1790, p. 1014; AR, Nederburgh Collection, no. 106). There is a need for closer study of the taxes imposed at the Cape to compensate for expenses, and for a comparison of these with taxes in other colonies and in the Netherlands itself. On the politics behind the settlement of burghers, see Van Dam, *Beschrijvinge*, Book II, part 3, 500ff; *The Reports of De Chavonnes and his Council, and of Van Imhoff, on the Cape* (Cape Town, 1918), pp. 25–32.

24. Van Reede, 'Journaal', p. 125; O.F. Mentzel, *Life at the Cape in Mid-Eighteenth Century, being the Biography of Rudolf Siegfried Alleman* (Cape Town, 1920), p. 151. In the 1780s and 1790s the VOC increasingly based the security of the Cape on Anglo-French rivalry: *Nieuwe Nederlandsche Jaarboeken*, 1790, pp. 1011–64.
25. We still lack a thorough study of the governmental and judicial structure of the colony. Scattered data on the burghers' role in government are found in Böeseken, 'Kommissarisse', ch. 4; P.J. Venter, 'Landdros en Heemrade', *AYB*, III (1940); *Bepalingen en Instructiën voor het bestuur van de buitendistricten van de Kaap de Goede Hoop*, ed. G.W. Eybers (Amsterdam, 1922); J.C. Visagie, 'Die ontstaan van die Burgerraad', *Kleio: Bulletin of the Department of History of the University of South Africa*, V (1973), pp. 33–36; Scholtz, *Ontwikkeling*, I, 143. Scholtz's comments are rather confused. On the one hand he gives the impression that Cape colonists, like the Netherlanders, had little political influence at the time (I, 145), that they did not desire it (I, 220) and that their behaviour always had an economic motivation (I, 221). On the other hand he emphasises the political significance of 1706 and 1779 (I, 234–35, 243–44, 256ff) and speaks of the colonists' burgeoning political activity (I, 220ff).
26. Still the farmers sometimes mistrusted the field-cornets. See J.S. Marais, *Maynier and the First Boer Republic* (Cape Town, 1944), pp. 10ff, and L.C. van Oordt, 'Die Kaapse Taalargief 10: Een-en-dertig Afrikaans-Hollandse briewe uit die jare 1712–1795, hoofsaaklik afkomstig van veldwagmeesters', *Tydskrif vir Wetenskap en Kuns*, XVI (1956), no. 303.
27. Scholtz, *Ontwikkeling*, I, 85.
28. Van Reede, 'Journaal', pp. 202–03. Compare his 'Instructie voor Simon van der Stel', *Belangrijke Historische Dokumenten*, ed. George McCall Theal (Cape Town, 1896), Vol. I. On frontier mentality see the remarks made by Governor van Plettenberg in his letters to Hendrik Swellengrebel Junior: *Briefwisseling van Hendrik Swellengrebel Jr oor Kaapse sake 1778–1792*, ed. G.J. Schutte (Cape Town, 1982) pp. 62, 107, 119.
29. The renowned political publicist Pieter de la Court had recommended such insularism for Holland in a book of 1669: see Boogman, 'Holländische Tradition'.
30. Plans for colonisation in the East Indies by Governor-General J.P. Coen had earlier been rejected and the West India Company had given up Brazil. See also Van Dam, *Beschrijvinge*, II (3), pp. 500ff; for the decision to stop immigration to the Cape, see Theal, *Belangrijke Dokumenten*, III, 2, 4, 6. Scholtz's jeremiads about this decision totally ignore contemporary values (*Ontwikkeling*, I, 62).
31. P.J. van der Merwe, *Die Trekboer in die Geskiedenis van die Kaapkolonie* (Cape Town, 1938), ch. 2.
32. *Ibid*. See also P.J. van der Merwe, 'Van Verversingspos tot Landbou-Kolonie', *Geskiedenis van Suid-Afrika*, ed. A.J.H. van der Walt, J.A. Wiid and A.L. Geyer (Cape Town, 1965), pp. 88–89.
33. An authoritative study of the recruitment, backgrounds, qualifications and performances of the personnel of the VOC, based on the Company's archives, pamphlets and travel journals, is not available. F. Lequin, *Het personeel van de Verenigde Oost-Indische Compagnie in Azië in de achttiende*

eeuw, meer in het bijzonder in de vestiging Bengalen (Leiden, 1982) provides an introductory survey with useful data on quantitative aspects. For the late eighteenth century see Schutte, *Nederlandse Patriotten*. The qualities of officials can be deduced from their reports to their successors; those for the Cape before 1700 are found in *Memoriën en Instructiën*, ed. Anna J. Böeseken (Cape Town, 1966).

34. The Generale Monsterrolle (list of employees) of 1700 (KA 8518) gives a total of 13,204, though this omits a few minor factories. The rolls of 1779 (KA 9314) give a total of 17,267; those of 1789 (KA 9314), 19,006. (Europeans only; the total number of VOC servants – European and Asian – was only 17,387, 18,410 and 20,706 respectively: Lequin, *Personeel*, appendix 4, table 3 A).

35. Mentzel, *The Cape*, p. 162.

36. Generale Monsterrollen, see n. 34.

37. Schutte, *Nederlandse Patriotten*, pp. 32–38.

38. François Valentyn, *Beschryvinge van de Kaap der Goede Hoope* (Cape Town, 1973), II, 250.

39. Böeseken, 'Kommissarisse', p. 33. Many other forms of income are discussed by Mentzel.

40. Schutte, *Nederlandse Patriotten*, p. 50. The proclamation of 25 Oct. 1791 is in J.A. van der Chijs, *Nederlandsch-Indisch Plakkaatboek* (Batavia, 1893), XI, 358.

41. KA 3973 and KA 4022. During the 1780s the actual numbers were temporarily increased (up to 1789) by the stationing of extra troops (Lequin, *Personeel*, appendix 4, table A. 26.4).

42. Katzen, 'New Society', p. 217. Figures on the burgher population after 1700 are in Coenraad Beyers, *Die Kaapse Patriotte gedurende die laaste kwart van die agtiende eeu en die voortlewing van hul denkbeelde* (Pretoria, 1967), appendix H.

43. KA 3983. See Lequin, *Personeel*, appendix 4 for comparable data elsewhere.

44. Based on a sample of the years 1700 to 1769.

45. Already noted by J.S. Stavorinus in his *Reize van Zeeland over de Kaap de Goede Hoop, . . . in de jaaren 1768 tot 1771...* (Leiden, 1793), I, 243. For excellent introductions to the factional character of the Ancien Régime, see Lewis B. Namier, *The Structure of Politics at the Accession of George III* (London, 1961); Daniel J. Roorda, *Partij en Factie* (Groningen, 1961); M. van der Bijl, *Idee en interest. Voorgeschiedenis, verloop en achtergronden, van de politieke twisten in Zeeland en vooral in Middelburg tussen 1702–1715* (Groningen, 1981). Factional conflicts in the VOC factory of Bengal are described by Lequin, *Personeel*, pp. 171–76.

46. The faction of Van der Stel, Elsevier, Starrenburg and Kalden was opposed by one led by Johannes Swellengrebel (nicknamed Zwelling Rebel) and Oortmans. Factional disputes were rife under Govenors d'Ableing (1707–08), Van Assenburgh (1708–11) and Pasques de Chavonnes (1714–24); See *Res*, IV, 79, 400; D.B. Bosman, *Briewe van Johanna Maria van Riebeeck en ander Riebeeckiana* (Amsterdam, 1952), pp. 78, 110–11, 115. A vehement conflict arose in the late 1730s about the successor to Governor van Kervel between the fiscaal Van den Henghel and the secunde Hendrik Swellengrebel, *Res* IX, 143–46, 195, 263–65; R.P.J. Tutein Nolthenius, *Het*

geslacht Nolthenius (Tutein Nolthenius) (Haarlem, 1914), pp. 459, 1039 ff, 1055 ff; Governor van de Graaff was opposed by a faction too: see AR, Admiraliteiten, Aanhangsel 39, Van der Hoop no. 80; H.C.V. Leibbrandt and J.E. Heeres, 'Memoriën van den Gouverneur van de Graaff over de gebeurtenissen aan de Kaap de Goede Hoop in 1780 - 1806', *Bijdragen en Mededelingen van het Historisch Genootschap te Utrecht*, XV (1894), pp. 180 - 256.

47. H.T. Colenbrander, *De afkomst der Boeren* (Cape Town, 1964); Beyers, Patriotte, appendix H; J.A. Heese, *Die herkoms van die Afrikaner* (Cape Town, 1971); Robert Ross, 'The "White" Population of South Africa in the Eighteenth Century', *Population Studies*, XXIX (1975), pp. 217 - 30, G.C. de Wet, *Die vryliede en vryswartes in die Kaapse nedersetting 1657–1707* (Cape Town, 1981). Figures for burghers include free blacks.

48. Ross, ' "White" Population', pp. 224–28. Leonard Guelke, 'The Anatomy of Colonial Settler Population: Cape Colony, 1657–1750' (unpublished paper).

49. KA 4005.

50. Valentyn, *Beschryvinge*, II, 238.

51. Stavorinus, *Reize 1768*, II, 127.

52. AR, Radermacher collection, no. 507, Letter of Jan de la Fontaine, 30 Jan. 1732, and appendices. De Wet, *Vryliede* provides data on the various categories of professions before 1707.

53. Leonard Guelke and Robert Shell, 'An early colonial landed gentry: land and wealth in the Cape Colony 1682–1731,' *Journal of Historical Geography*, IX (1983), pp. 265–86; Robert Ross, 'The Rise of the Cape Gentry', *Journal of Southern African Studies*, IX (1983), pp. 193–217; Nigel Worden, *Slavery in Dutch South Africa* (Cambridge, 1985); Leonard Guelke, 'The making of two Frontier Communities: Cape Colony in the Eighteenth Century,' *Historical Reflections/Réflexions Historiques* XII (1985), pp.419–48.

54. Cornelius de Jong, *Reizen naar de Kaap de Goede Hoop, Ierland en Noorwegen, in de jaren 1791 tot 1797* (Haarlem, 1802), I, 79–84, 99. See also Schutte, *Briefwisseling Hendrik Swellengrebel Jr.*

55. This is the impression one gets from travel journals and from C.C. de Villiers and C. Pama, *Geslagsregisters van die ou Kaapse families* (Cape Town, 1966).

56. Valentyn, *Beschryvinge*, I, 134; J.S. Stavorinus, *Reize van Ierland over de Kaap de Goede Hoop . . . in de jaaren 1774 tot 1778 . . .* (Leiden, 1798), II, 309–11; De Jong, *Reizen*, I, 134.

57. Van Reede, 'Journaal', p. 149; Bogaert *Reizen*, p. 565; Fouché, *Dagboek Adam Tas*, I, 2, 4; Fiscaal Cloppenburg cited in Van der Merwe, *Trekboer*, p. 139; *Journal of Hendrik Swellengrebel Jr* (in preparation).

58. Fouché, *Dagboek Adam Tas*, p. 138; Bogaert, *Reizen*, p. 468.

59. Fouché, *Dagboek Adam Tas*, p. 122; Bogaert, *Reizen*, p. 501–02; Anna J. Böeseken, *Simon van der Stel en sy kinders* (Cape Town, 1964), p. 183.

60. Schutte, *Briefwisseling Hendrik Swellengrebel Jr.*, p. 282; *Journal of Hendrik Swellengrebel Jr.* (in preparation).

61. J.L. Hattingh, 'Die Klagte oor Goewerneur W.A. van der Stel se slawebesit – 'n beoordeling met behulp van kwantitatiewe data, *Kronos*, VII (1983), pp. 13–41.

62. KA 4022, Generale Opneeminge der Vryluiden Gedoente en Effecten, 1700.
63. Fouché, *Dagboek Adam Tas*, p. 10, 12; George McCall Theal, *History of South Africa before 1795* (Cape Town, 1964), III, 384, 386, 414.
64. Husing paid 10,300 guilders for the meat monopoly: Bogaert, *Reizen*, p. 478; Fouché, *Dagboek Adam Tas*, p. 154. On Van der Heyden see Dominicus, *Het Ontslag*, p. 68.
65. It is going quite too far to say, as Fouché does (*Dagboek Adam Tas*, pp. 8–9), that the resistance to Van der Stel was rooted in 'the most extreme hardship' suffered by his opponents. The behaviour of, for example, Van der Heyden in later years suggests other motives: *Res*, VII, 127.
66. Eric Walker, *The Frontier Tradition in South Africa* (London, 1930), p. 8; S.F.N. Gie, *Geskiedenis van Suid-Afrika of ons Verlede* (Stellenbosch, 1924), p. 137, formulated better: the rebels wanted no constitutional changes; their main demands were economic. Theal (in *History of South Africa*, III, 451) supports Gie's view, but elsewhere contradicts him (*ibid.*, 444–45) by stating that this was a struggle for freedom.
67. It is not certain whether Corver's main opponent, Jeronimus de Haze, was related to Willem Adriaan's wife, Maria de Haze. See Johan E. Elias, *De vroedschap van Amsterdam* (Amsterdam, 1923); A. Porta, *Joan en Gerrit Corver* (Assen, 1975).
68. The middle decades of the eighteenth century–roughly the Swellengrebel and Tulbagh period – have been inadequately investigated. It is possible that the many wars of the time benefitted the Cape economy: 'Father Tulbagh' might owe his nickname to these benefits.
69. Fouché (*Dagboek Adam Tas*, pp. 364ff) correctly argues that Van der Stel was not a victim of his protective policies toward the Khoikhoi. It was not protection of Khoikhoi that was in contention, but the question of who would conduct the profitable trade with them.
70. There is no reason to separate such trekkers and hunters from the general population by labelling them 'riff-raff': Fouché, *Dagboek Adam Tas*, p. 244; Theal, *History of South Africa*, III, 416–17. See also Nigel Penn, 'The Frontier in the Western Cape, 1700–1740' (unpublished paper: Workshop Spatial Archaeology Research Unit, University of Cape Town, 1984).
71. KA 4118, 4119, 4120; Theal, *Dokumenten*, I. For Barbier see also bibliography in *Suid-Afrikaanse biografiese Woordeboek*, I, 54–55 and R.H. Pheiffer, 'Hernuwde aandag vir 'n verloopte Fransman: Tekste in gebroke Nederlands van Estienne Barbier', *Tydskrif vir Geesteswetenskappe*, XV (1975), pp. 34–93.
72. KA 4119, Governor and Council, 21 March 1739, p. 252v.
73. Theal, *Dokumenten*, I, 2.
74. Schutte, *Nederlandse Patriotten*, pp. 77, 84.
75. Investigation is needed into such complaints for the period up to and including the Great Trek.
76. Schutte, *Nederlandse Patriotten*, ch. 4, where primary and secondary sources are cited and information is given on the interest shown towards the Cape Patriots in the Netherlands. See also Schutte, *Briefwisseling Hendrik Swellengrebel Jr*; Beyers, *Patriotte*; and *Kaapsche Stukken* (4 vols., VOC publication, 1785).

77. Schutte, *Nederlandse Patriotten*, pp. 61–62; I.L. Leeb, *The Ideological Origins of the Batavian Revolution* (The Hague, 1973).
78. See e.g. anon., *L'Afrique Hollandaise* (n.p., 1783); Schutte, *Nederlandse Patriotten*, pp. 78–82; Gerrit J. Schutte, 'Johannes Henricus Redelinghuys: een Revolutionair Kapenaar', *South African Historical Journal*, III (1971), pp. 49–62.
79. Pieter Geyl, 'Democratische tendenties in 1672', *Pennestrijd over staat en historie*, ed. Pieter Geyl (Groningen, 1971); Leeb, *Ideological Origins*; H.A. Wertheim-Gijse Weenink, *Democratische bewegingen in Gelderland* (Amsterdam, 1973); Pieter Geyl, *Revolutiedagen te Amsterdam, Aug. – Sept. 1748* (The Hague, 1936); Rudolf Dekker, *Holland in beroering. Oproeren in 17de en 18de eeuw* (Baarn, 1982).
80. Contemporary data and analysis of the Cape economy are to be found in Schutte, *Briefwisseling Hendrik Swellengrebel Jr.*
81. Schutte, 'Redelinghuys'.
82. Beyers, *Patriotte*, appendix E. Details on the origins of this petition are given in Schutte, *Briefwisseling Hendrik Swellengrebel Jr.*, pp. 196–202.
83. On the costs of the Cape during Van de Graaff's governorship see *Nieuwe Nederlandsche Jaarboeken*, 'Memorial of Falck, Craeyvanger and Scholten', pp. 1011–64.
84. AR, Nederburgh Collection, no. 531.
85. C.F.J. Muller, *Johannes Frederick Kirsten oor die toestand van die Kaapkolonie in 1795* (Pretoria, 1960), pp. 54–55.
86. Hermann B. Giliomee, *Die Kaap tydens die eerste Britse Bewind* (Cape Town, 1975), p. 31.
87. Leo Fouché, *Die Evolusie van die Trekboer* (Pretoria, 1909), p. 1; Scholtz, *Ontwikkeling*, p. 176.
88. Beyers, *Patriotte*, pp. 281–95.

CHAPTER SEVEN

The Cape under the transitional governments, 1795–1814[*]

William M. Freund

The transitional years, 1795–1814: An introduction

In September 1795 a British force took command at the Castle and put an end to almost 150 years of VOC rule. The Cape Colony was not in a position to defend itself against European invaders from overseas and perhaps not even from the Xhosa chiefdoms that lay to the east; yet despite its weakness and small population it had developed into a society with its own characteristic social forces. The development of the colony was only in part a direct result of the policies and wishes of the *Heren XVII*; the successor regimes would find, often to their disgust or to their cost, that the Cape social structure was sufficiently resilient and deeply rooted to defy administrative attempts at change.

The VOC regime, because of its venality and inability to provide the colonists with security or scope for enterprise, had no deep hold on their loyalties. Its weakness in the last years opened the possibility for revolt; yet, if the freeburghers had much to dispute with the VOC, it was also true that the VOC had endorsed their internal position as masters of thousands of slaves and landless servants. This fact would continue to lie at the heart of the relationship of the Cape freeburghers with the colonial regimes.

Between 1795 and 1814 the Cape Colony changed hands three times, finally coming permanently under the control of the British. These years may be conveniently considered as a transitional period divided into three phases: the first British occupation lasting from 1795 to 1803; the

* While writing my dissertation, on which part of this chapter is based, I worked in the Algemeen Rijksarchief (The Hague), the Cape Archives (Cape Town), the Kerkargief (Cape Town), the London Missionary Society Archives (London) and the South African Public Library (Cape Town). I wish especially to thank the editors of this work for their painstaking and valuable criticisms of this chapter.

Batavian interlude when the Cape fell under the rule of the Batavian Republic that had been established in the Netherlands; and the second British occupation resulting from the reconquest of 1806. The transitional period ended when the Dutch permanently ceded the Cape at the London Convention of 13 August 1814.

The first British occupation was a time of convulsive disorder at the Cape.[1] The frontier Khoikhoi rose in conjunction with the Xhosa (1799 to 1803) while the frontier settlers, already in revolt when the British took over, challenged the authority of the government again in 1799 and 1801 (see ch.9). Considerable hostility towards the British, marked by passive resistance, existed in the west as well. Consequently the British regime was authoritarian, in fact much more effectively so than the VOC had been in its final days. At the same time the British were not interested in transforming the Cape. British official opinion was divided on the question of retaining the colony, and ultimately the anti-retention party negotiated the return of the Cape to the Dutch by the treaty of Amiens.[2]

The Batavian interlude between 1803 and 1806 appears superficially to present a striking contrast to the first British occupation. Batavian policy aimed at making a real and permanent impact at the Cape. After the treaty of Amiens a specially appointed commisioner-general, J.A. de Mist, was sent out to the Cape to implement a memorandum, which he himself had written, proposing reforms that would make the colony both prosperous and orderly.[3] In fact, however, De Mist was prevented from accomplishing much, both by a lack of resources and by his need to preserve the shaky social order.

Many historians have extolled the Batavians.[4] De Mist has been seen as everything from an enlightened innovator to an inventor of apartheid. These writers have ignored both the extent to which the Batavian reform ideas were a continuation of the ideas expressed during the first British occupation and VOC times, and how little change the Batavians actually succeeded in bringing about at the Cape. George McCall Theal wrote that the Batavian school and church ordinances awoke a storm of protest at the Cape which was not yet ready for radical notions, but all evidence indicates that, to the extent that these ordinances were new, they were rather popular.[5] Both De Mist and Janssens were quickly disillusioned with the Cape and especially with its economic prospects. Neither advocated that the Dutch recover it after it fell to the British in 1806.

The years after 1806 were marked by a consolidation of British authority at the Cape. Although little structural change, even of the administration, could be envisaged until a formal treaty recognised

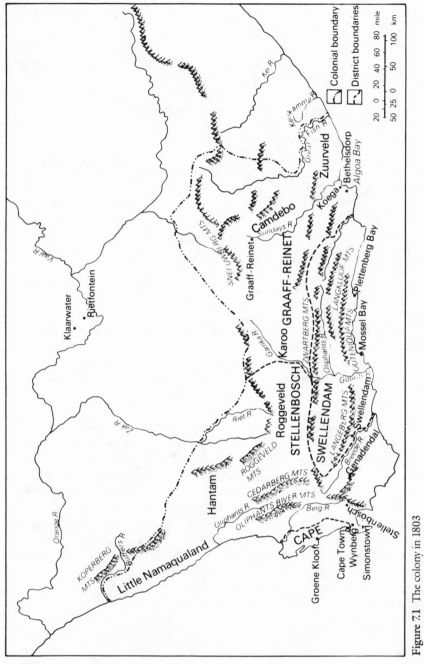

Figure 7.1 The colony in 1803

Source: Hermann Giliomee, *Die Kaap tydens die Eerste Britse Bewind, 1795–1803* (HAUM, 1975).

British rule, home opposition to the retention of the Cape had dwindled. On the whole the post-1806 period was more stable and less conflict-ridden. Despite its importance for economic and social change, historians have generally paid much less attention to this phase than to its predecessors.[6]

If all three periods have their special characteristics, the transitional era as a whole exhibits considerable unity. In the problems they faced as well as in the solutions they considered, the early British governors and Batavians had much in common, and there is remarkable continuity in economic, social and administrative concerns throughout the period.

This continuity resulted from the essentially similar aims of the Cape's rulers: prosperity and order. The Cape, undercapitalised, sparsely populated and lacking decent transport, produced little for international trade. The colonial accounts were unbalanced and the currency unstable, yet in Europe the hope remained that successful policies could transform the Cape economy.

The proposed remedies of the era, taken up and passed on from one administration to the next, were diverse. Yet the limited resources or commitments of the regimes did not allow for much innovation, and the economic problems of the Cape remained similar in 1814 to what they had been twenty years earlier.

In maintaining order the governments of the transitional era were more successful than the VOC had been in its last years. This was a period of consolidation of white control in the countryside. In the master-servant relationship the British and the Batavians intervened with increasing decisiveness on the side of the masters. Social control was also served by increased bureaucratisation of an administration, the basic structure of which, however, was only gradually altered.

If one can regard this period as a whole from the vantage point of the rulers of the Cape, there is an even stronger justification for doing so from the perspective of the people of the Cape. Because of uncertainty about retaining the Cape (on the part of the British) and because of their limited financial resources, the colonial authorities did not succeed in dramatically altering the lives of South Africans. The larger social developments of the turn of the nineteenth century, notably the mission movement, developed at their own pace and not at one imposed from the Castle.

Our analysis will focus on broad themes covering the entire transitional period: firstly economic policy and economic change at the Cape; secondly, relations among masters, slaves and servants; thirdly, the impact of the missionaries on Cape society; and finally, the relationship between rulers and ruled.

Economic policy and economic change at the Cape

The economic structure of Cape life changed in some important respects during the era of transition, partly as the result of internal developments and partly of new administrative policies. Consequently by 1814 the Cape was ready to receive new impulses – notably the development of the wool trade – which would greatly increase its importance in world commerce.

As for the international linkages of the Cape economy, the most obvious change after 1795 was the development of a British trade connection. During the first British occupation, British shipping bearing British and Eastern manufactures quickly came to dominate Cape commerce.[7] After the Batavian interlude British merchants and shipping became even more important than before. Traders such as Alexander Tennant, Michael Hogan and John Murray had settled at the Cape after 1795 and gained ascendancy over foreign trade, largely because they had the commercial and financial connections in England and with British officials at the Cape that the older Cape merchants lacked. Those older entrepreneurs whose careers have been most carefully documented, D.G. van Reenen, J.F. Kirsten and W.S. van Ryneveld, all fared poorly under British rule.[8] There was a greater distance between officials and merchants in this period; the educated and wealthy Cape officials continued to serve in important positions because of their knowledge of local law, customs and language while a new, relatively small, group of British immigrants achieved commercial mastery. By the early 1820s, W.W. Bird described the Cape traders as mainly agents for British firms.[9]

This was only one aspect of the incorporation of the Cape into the British imperial system, vastly larger and more dynamic than that of the VOC. The scale of trade increased greatly, although before 1814 the continued role of monopolist companies and restrictions on external and internal trade prevented any important development of local private enterprise. Under the first British occupation imports rose and a sharp inflation set in. In 1798 over one million rixdollars worth of British goods were brought to the Cape.[10] Thereafter, with the Cape market sated, trade took a downturn. These slow years were followed by the depressed Batavian period when the Cape was partially closed off to world commerce by the resumption of the Napoleonic wars.

Through its monopoly over Eastern trade and over the arms traffic, the English East India Company in many ways fulfilled the part which the VOC had played in the commercial field until 1795. During the first

British occupation one governor, Lord Macartney, sought to give it political power over the Cape as well. In actual fact the East India Company had little interest in the Cape apart from its fear of smugglers cutting into its monopolistic profits. It proved so ineffective at supplying the Cape with foodstuffs during bad harvests that the Cape government was henceforth obliged to contact authorities directly in India to ship badly needed rice to the Cape.[11] During the Batavian period most of the Eastern trade was officially in the hands of a monopoly run by the *Aziatische Raad*, a government agency that had both political and economic authority. However in practice, as a result of wartime conditions, neutral ships, particularly from Denmark and the United States, did most of the carrying trade.

After 1806 there was again a large increase in trade, notably in re-exported goods. According to Kantor's calculations, exports (together with re-exports) rose in value from 180,000 rixdollars in 1807 to 630,000 in 1811 and 1,320,000 in 1815, and imports increased correspondingly.[12] The increase in imports reflected the swollen size of the garrison, at its peak numbering 6,407 men – more than were stationed at Gibraltar or Malta[13] – and the presence of a growing number of highly paid British officials demanding British goods. British cotton manufactures were by far the most important imported item by 1813 while British iron and steel goods were increasing in value.[14]

The British had begun to free internal trade in 1795, but all the transitional governments continued to set the prices of staples and to tax produce entering Cape Town. Moreover, the *pachten*, or monopolistic farms – whose owners purchased from the government the sole rights to distribute valuable commodities, notably spirits – although under attack from the Batavian period onwards, were only very slowly replaced by licensing arrangements.[15] During the second occupation legislation gradually brought the Cape into the system of British imperial preferences, even though the English East India Company held on to most of its old prerogatives, only losing its Eastern trade monopoly (excluding tea) in 1815. By far the most important of these measures was the reduction of duty on Cape wines entering Britain in 1813. As a result the Cape could for the first time compete effectively with continental wine-growers in a foreign market. There followed a large increase in the production and export of wine. By 1822 Cape wine represented 10.4 per cent of the wine consumed in Britain.[16] Government revenues, devoted largely to official salaries and administrative expenses, grew rapidly in consequence.

The significance of these changing trade patterns emerges only in an analysis of the productive forces in Cape society. The Cape population grew rather substantially over this period, but overall increases mask two important shifts: the declining proportion of slaves and the declining proportion of people in the capital. That category of people labelled 'inhabitants' or 'Christians' in the census, which included free blacks as well as whites, grew from 22,000 in the relatively accurate count of 1798 to 37,000 in 1815. These figures are not exact but they indicate the general scale of growth. The number of 'Hottentots', by the same set of figures, grew from 14,000 to 17,000, but these are certainly underestimates and too inaccurate for the historian to formulate any conclusions from them. The slave population is recorded as growing from 25,000 to 30,000 between 1798 and 1815, although the last figure is definitely too low. Almost all the increase among slaves took place before the abolition of the slave trade in 1807 (see also ch. 3,pp. 119–20).

Population trends were not uniform throughout the colony. In particular Cape Town grew far more slowly than outlying rural districts. Its population was estimated at 15,500 in 1798 and 15,600 in 1815. This was in part because so many slaves were sold to the country districts after 1807, but even the free population experienced only a moderate increase. By far the biggest population growth occurred in the east, especially in the Graaff-Reinet district. In 1798 the 'Christian' population there was counted as 4,262; in 1815, together with the now detached Uitenhage district, that total was 11,650. In the other rural districts it increased at rates of 25 to 50 per cent per decade.

In general, agricultural production seems to have increased, but not as rapidly as the population. Between 1795 and 1804 wine production doubled from 6,000 to 12,000 leaguers, doubtless affected by the demands of fleet and garrison; but thereafter decline set in. In 1813, an especially poor year, wine production was again below 7,000 leaguers. However, from this date there was a rapid increase.[17]

There was an overall, if uneven, increase in quantities of cereals grown at the Cape. In 1798, a good year for grain production, 138,000 muiden of wheat were grown and 44,000 brought to market; 186,000 muiden were grown in an excellent harvest in 1815 and 63,000 muiden brought to market. The remainder of the increase was absorbed by the expanding rural population. To compare good years, however, is to ignore the bad years when so little grain was brought to Cape Town that imports were required; this continued to happen throughout the transitional era and after. Grain was no more reliable as an export crop than it had been in earlier times. Shortages dashed the hopes – both of the British in 1795 and the Batavians in 1803 – that the Cape could be a granary for the East. Part of the increase in production which did occur took place in the eastern districts of Graaff-Reinet and Uitenhage, which grew only about 5 per cent of the colonial wheat in 1795 but about 15 per cent twenty years later.[18]

The census rolls show still greater variations in the livestock population, concentrated in the north and the east. Between 1798 and 1806, largely because of frontier wars, the number of cattle decreased considerably at the Cape, by perhaps 25 per cent overall. Thereafter the totals rose, surpassing the 1798 figures by 1815. Nevertheless this meant an overall decline in the number of cattle per household. By contrast the 1807 census roll indicated a considerable increase in the number of sheep over the preceding decade,[19] with the increase occurring in the eastern rather than the northern pastoral zones. The number of colonial sheep peaked in 1811, on the eve of the expulsion of the Xhosa from the Zuurveld, and thereafter declined as a result of losses in the Graaff-Reinet district. By 1815 there were somewhat fewer sheep per farmer than there had been twenty years before. Whether the quality of stock altered is difficult to ascertain.

Population growth was not coupled with significant expansion of colonial territory. The result was increasing pressure on land, a phenomenon that P.J. van der Merwe has dated to the end of the eastward movement of the trekboers around 1780[20] Over the entire period the census rolls show an increasing ratio of farmers to registered farms. It is not clear whether this had a severe effect on living standards. Farms could often provide a living for more than one family and were frequently subdivided informally, since loan farms could not legally be partitioned. There were definitely some areas where land-hunger was especially severe and an impoverishment of the population resulted. Such an area was the Baviaans River section where the Slachtersnek rebellion took place in 1815. This area was more populous at that date than 150 years later.[21] By 1813 some 2,000 applications for new loan farms had collected in the Castle, as many loan farms as were then in existence.

The loan farm system, the characteristic form of land tenure in outlying areas, was itself under attack during the transitional era. Critics of the system believed that it had encouraged the population to spread out so widely that the remoter countryside was ungovernable and prone to rebellion. They also feared that the cheapness of loan farm land discouraged capital investment and the development of a more productive agriculture. Finally there was the nagging issue of the annual rents which were invariably badly in arrears. Government attempts to improve collection played an important role in provoking the rebellions of 1795 and 1799.

But the loan farm system survived. Until 1806 both Governors Dundas and Janssens recognised that despite its flaws it functioned reasonably efficiently, especially on the cattle and sheep farms and in arid country. More commercially productive land tended to be converted to freehold voluntarily.

The second British occupation saw a renewed attack on the loan farm. On 6 August 1813 Governor Cradock issued a proclamation prohibiting the further granting of land in loan and created a mechanism to speed conversion into quitrent tenure which would prove more profitable to the government. Though the loan farms survived for a long period thereafter, the decree gradually had its effect; it became far more expensive for cattle boers to acquire new land and discriminated against the large number of squatters who were unable to apply for the purchase of land on which they were squatting. The 1813 proclamation contributed to the origins of the Slachtersnek rebellion and to an overall land squeeze that played a major role in bringing about the Great Trek. In the agrarian southwestern Cape the new policy had no effect as land had generally already been converted to other forms of tenure, suitable to more intensive land use.[22]

Though the end of the loan farm system caused some hardship, this was perhaps mitigated by the increasing prosperity of the eastern part of the colony. Despite the insecurity caused by war and rebellion, the east experienced a striking growth of population, grain production and ownership of slaves. Qualitative change was noticed by officials and visitors after 1806. In the northeast, especially in the Sneeuwberg, Tarka and Nieuwveld, farmers benefitted from the establishment of better relations with the 'Bushmen', increasing numbers of whom came to work on their farms.[23] Further south, travellers reported the growing wealth of the Camdebo and the resulting transformation of Graaff-Reinet after 1806 into a prosperous-looking village.[24] In the southeast colonial policy culminating in the 1811–12 war did not succeed in reducing Xhosa raids or repopulating the Zuurveld with whites, but the war itself, by bringing a large garrison to the east, considerably stimulated agriculture and trade.[25] In 1812 the firm of Pohl and Company began direct exports from Algoa Bay: this was the beginning of improvements in transport and the general economic growth of the east that laid the foundations for the wool economy to come.

The export of wool was one of several administrators' dreams that did not achieve much substance before 1814. Merino sheep had first been introduced in VOC times. The Batavian Agricultural Commission tried to force farmers to pure-breed their sheep, but to little avail. Caledon's attempts to encourage the breeding of wool-bearing sheep also failed. The meat and fat products of the Cape sheep continued to be surer market commodities for the farmer than wool. Efforts to encourage the development of other potential exports at best met with indifferent success. The whale fisheries had many unproductive years and provided little scope for entrepreneurs, despite government attention and assistance. Somewhat more important was the increasing export of aloes for medicinal purposes, of hides and skins and of ivory. However, none of these commodities remotely rivalled wine as an export. Nor did new, planned European settlements develop at the Cape despite a number of schemes suggested to this end.[26] During the transitional era, immigration from Europe continued as a steady trickle with a preponderance of ex-soldiers from the garrison.

The undercapitalised Cape economy rested upon the insecure foundation of the inconvertible rixdollar. The financial and monetary weakness of the Cape continued throughout the whole transitional era. Despite ensuing inflation, all the transitional adminstrations found it easiest to increase the supply of paper rixdollars and thus to encourage commerce and finance extraordinary government expenditure. When the regime was stable and the economy expanding, the reign of the rixdollar was in some ways advantageous. There is some evidence that prices for produce kept abreast of inflation in better times.[27] However, when the economy stagnated, lack of confidence in the currency, which lost half its exchange value over twenty years, continued to provoke serious crises (see ch. 5, pp. 259–61).

The transitional economy, then, was characterised by certain changes of considerable significance: the development of the British connection, the gradual dismantling of monopolies, the increasing prosperity of the eastern districts, the growth of population, the smaller growth of agricultural production and (at the close of the period) the reduction of duties on wine imported to Britain, and the land tenure legislation of 1813. These changes were not sweeping or sudden; they came singly without building up to a quantum leap or visibly changing the overall economic pattern. The Cape was not yet transformed from an entrepot, essentially dependent on its marginal role in the Europe-Asia trade, to a colonial export economy. However, it was moving in this direction. It was perhaps indicative of the intensification of commercial activity that after 1806 the all-purpose Cape Town inn-emporia were gradually replaced by specialised hotels and shops.[28] By 1814 the Cape was far more ready than twenty years before to be engaged to new productive forces.

Masters, servants, and slaves

Traditional conceptions of early Cape society have emphasised the existence of distinct racial groups which took on the character of castes from their separate, virtually endogamous nature. This view ignores certain aspects of Cape society.[29] Racial lines remained somewhat flexible during this era, as they had been much earlier. Legal distinctions between races were not clearly formulated or systematically applied: for example, such terms as 'free black' were not well delineated. Intermarriages continued in this period as they had throughout the eighteenth century; such marriages affected the social structure, particularly in Cape Town. Moreover, there were prominent members of Cape society who transparently were not entirely of European ancestry (see ch. 11, p. 547). Evidence that racism intensified and that racial delineation sharpened is only quite modest in reference to the eighteenth century, though stronger for the nineteenth. There was nothing in Cape society to suggest a race consciousness stronger than in many, perhaps most, colonial societies of the day nor anything that particularly prefigured the later elaboration of apartheid (see ch.11, pp. 540–48 for a different view).

Nor was 'white' South African society homogeneous or egalitarian. A caste society assumes the determining role of a fairly coherent white 'group'. In practice 'white' South African society was neither egalitarian nor homogeneous. The concept of class based on wealth and control over property has been applied to colonial society as a whole in consequence. Numerous white individuals, particularly demissioned soldiers and sailors, owned no property and had little claim to be reckoned as burghers. It was they who typically married women of colour. At the other end of the social spectrum, a relatively small minority of the landholding population owned a disproportionately large share of valuable property, including slaves. Robert Ross calls this group the 'Cape gentry'.[30] According to Ross, for generations the same families occupied commanding positions of wealth and influence in the agricultural southwestern Cape, typically after establishing themselves in the final quarter of the eighteenth century. The closest thing to a ruling class in colonial Cape society was this gentry. However, the crucial social relationship that lay at the heart of Cape society was between the free population at large and a subordinate majority of slaves and servants.

Slavery had become inseparable from productive activity at the Cape, above all in arable farming.[31] The indigenous population of the Cape, although not enslaved, had, in losing their lands and herds, effectively lost their freedom. It was they rather than the slave population who posed a crisis of order for the transitional regimes, a crisis which focused in the border regions of the colony (see ch. 1, pp. 33–35). The British, in order to forge some sort of peace that would restore the cattle and sheep economy, were obliged to come to grips with the master-servant relationship in the colony. For the next decade the evolution of a policy governing this relationship was a major administrative priority.

By contrast the slaves remained a docile force in Cape society. The one slave rising of the era, which took place in 1808, was not sufficiently serious to challenge colonial authority. The most important change came in the increasing European criticism of the slave trade, leading to its abolition in 1807 (see ch. 3, pp. 162–68). The institution of slavery, however, survived intact throughout the period.

European administrators and those Cape officials who worked for them during this period (Van Ryneveld, Van Reenen, Stockenstrom, Maynier) had mixed and often contradictory feelings about the conditions of slaves and servants. On the one hand the complaints of the servants were clearly not without justification, and slavery increasingly seemed a socially noxious and economically deleterious institution. On the other hand the colonial order rested on an economic basis of rigid labour subordination and on the political co-operation of the white masters who effectively controlled the means of production. The solution was to find a balanced policy between master and servant; but as the threat of rebellion gradually diminished on all sides, the ideal balance in the official mind increasingly lay in strong support for the white farmer with some protection for the servant and some mitigation of abuses for the slave.

However, there was an increasing contradiction between the continued need for state-authorised control over the movements and contractual employment of workers, particularly in agriculture, and the principle of free labour that the triumph of British imperialism enshrined, symbolised by the abolition of the slave trade in 1807. Abolition was part of a broad movement towards the creation of a new and it was hoped, more efficient and self-motivated working class advocated by the ideology of industrial capitalism formulated in Britain, the workshop of the world.[32] Susan Newton-King, who assessed the history of the Cape in the early nineteenth century in terms of the transition to free labour, believes that freedom of movement and absence of contracts and other legal constraints on their working lives permitted white artisans to earn wages up to 50 per cent higher than free men of colour working at the same trade.[33] In the Cape, the abolition of the slave trade began to cause labour shortages, given the level of wages and working conditions that property owners were prepared to provide. The shortage of slaves enhanced the employers' desire to defend slavery itself and other forms of coerced labour and substantially slowed the broad movement toward freer conditions of employment stimulated by events overseas.

The servants offered the government their most powerful argument for better treatment in the rebellion of 1799 (ch. 1, pp. 33–35). General Dundas negotiated a truce with the rebels which did not oblige them to return to work for the farmers and which granted land to several of their leaders, including the famous Stuurman brothers. At the same time, in order to encourage the re-establishment of the eastern farms, returning servants were offered a contractual system of employment. The contract had to be signed by both employer and employee in the presence of the landdrost and it could not be fixed for a period of over a year.[34]

The Batavian government was more hostile than Dundas to the maintenance of any autonomy by the Khoikhoi. It stressed the need to get the Khoikhoi back to the farms. The Batavian contract system, established in 1803, was more weighted towards masters as opposed to servants than its British predecessor. Surviving contracts show that there were violations of the one-year maximum on labour contracts; moreover field-cornets, themselves local employers, were now authorised to approve contracts.

During the second British occupation, government policy was further refined and developed. Memories of rebellion began to recede and, once the French had been driven from Mauritius in 1810 and a large garrison sat idle in Cape Town, the government acted with more energy and force on the frontier than before. The new British authorities stood for a policy of rigidly subordinating the servants while also protecting them against contractual abuses; this policy was epitomised in the Hottentot Proclamation of 1809, the institution of circuit courts in 1811, and the apprenticeship legislation of 1812 (ch. 1, pp. 40–41). Caledon and Cradock also moved against the last remaining independent communities at the Cape, turning several of them into mission stations.

The new legislation enabled fair-minded magistrates like the Stockenstroms to eliminate the most brutal abuses of the labour system, but it entrenched the position of the servants as landless labourers with no opportunity for independence or advancement.[35] Travellers in the second and third decades of the nineteenth century, such as Campbell, Latrobe and Burchell, all recorded the continued frequency of contract abuse. The judicial and administrative organisation of the colony could hardly alter this, for it consisted of white officials, judges and advocates who condoned the use of corporal punishment by employers and strongly disliked imposing harsh sentences on whites in disputes involving slaves or Khoikhoi. Furthermore its effectiveness was limited by its reliance on the pivotal role of the field-cornets.[36]

A special feature of the government's policy towards masters and servants was the maintenance throughout the transitional period of the Hottentot Corps (ch. 1, pp. 35–38). The Corps, founded in the last days of the VOC, was expanded and strengthened after 1795 with the specific intention of posing a counterweight to the suspect freeburgher population.[37] The Batavians wished at first to dismantle it, but after the outbreak of war in Europe in 1803 they recruited so actively that the Corps resembled a forced labour venture. There was renewed expansion and contraction after the British reconquest. Although loyal both to the Batavians in 1806 and to the British in 1811–12, the Khoikhoi soldiers disliked army service when it entailed separation from their families, and there is some evidence that they resented recruitment.[38] The white farmers opposed the Corps because it cut into their labour supply and because it was potentially a stick which the British and Batavians could use to beat them. Yet from 1803 the Corps was increasingly intended for use not against rebellious whites but against Khoikhoi and Xhosa as well as potential foreign foes. The Corps was thus no real escape from the master-servant nexus at the Cape and served rather to reinforce it.

Slavery was an essential feature of Cape society in 1795, slaves forming the largest sector of the population. The transitional era witnessed an increasing outcry in Europe against the slave trade and the social effects of slavery which posed a challenge to its continued existence. Yet colonial administrators on the whole agreed with Governor Janssens that 'the abolition of slavery in South Africa would overturn all property and leave the colony [in misery], possibly irredeemably.'[39] Pressure to end the slave trade came from outside. Both during the first British occupation and the Batavian period the home authorities weighed the future of the trade and put temporary or partial checks on it (ch. 3, pp. 163–67).

During the first decade after 1795 perhaps only 3,000 slaves were imported to the Cape (2,000 during the first British occupation, more than 1,000 during the Batavian period) mainly from Mozambique, and the price of slaves consequently climbed steeply.[40] In 1808 the abolition of the slave trade in the British Empire took effect at the Cape. The slave population, heavily unbalanced in favour of adult males, had according to the census rolls climbed from 25,000 in 1798 to nearly 30,000 in 1806. After abolition of the trade it grew very slightly, if at all, in the next decade. (The 1817 count of 32,046 seems not far from accurate.) Slaves ceased to be the largest element in the population from 1810 and ceased to form a majority in Cape Town from 1815.

Slave labour declined in the non-agricultural sector of the economy. In the capital, where slaves were often owned for speculative purposes, hired out as artisans, or used for exclusively domestic tasks, their population shrank by some 2,000 (or more than 20 per cent) between 1806 and 1815. Slaves were increasingly sold up-country to farmers, where their numbers increased especially in the more outlying areas, although the bulk continued to live in the southwestern Cape.[41] By this means the labouring population in the agricultural economy continued to grow reasonably rapidly and the Cape economy managed to weather the new situation.

After 1808 labour needs in town were partly filled by the prize Negroes brought to the Cape from slave vessels captured by the Royal Navy.[42] Prize Negroes could be apprenticed to employers for fourteen years although the government was supposed to ensure their decent treatment. With the growth of the apprentice and free black population, especially in Cape Town, the overall trend in the west, even before 1815, was away from slavery to free labour: in 1806 the slaves had constituted about 85 per cent of the population considered non-European in Cape Town; in 1817 perhaps only 70 per cent. Most manumissions also took place in Cape Town (92 per cent of the 1,245 manumissions between 1815 and 1830).[43]

In 1812, on the advice of the Rev. M.C. Vos, Governor Cradock abolished the VOC statute forbidding the sale of Christian slaves. This was done largely to facilitate the conversion of more slaves to Christianity, which the statute had hindered. The following year the government limited to thirty-nine the number of lashes a slave could receive in punishment; this was the beginning of ameliorative legislation for slaves that would continue until the final abolition of slavery twenty years later. In 1797 the British eliminated the more brutal forms of torture used on suspected and convicted criminals; this reform, which was introduced despite opposition from local officials, was probably for slaves the most beneficial consequence of British rule before 1815.[44]

The one slave rising of consequence during the transitional period came in response to the hopes that were aroused among slaves by the abolition of the slave trade. The 1808 rising began in the Zwartland where its leader, Louis, had contacts. Louis was a Cape Town slave born in Mauritius, light enough to pass for white. He led a band of slaves south towards Cape Town where they hoped the governor would announce their freedom. After they had caused some damage to property but little physical harm, they were met by a government force and disarmed. Severe punishments and the execution of five leaders followed. The remainder of the slaves were returned to their masters. Unlike the handful of original plotters, who genuinely hoped to overthrow the social order, most of the slaves had expected a benign government to confirm the rumours of coming freedom. The initial conspiracy had involved two Irishmen, both of whom abandoned the slaves before the rising had begun and one of whom became a witness for the prosecution; several 'Hottentot' servants also participated (see also ch. 3, p. 161).

During the 1795–1814 era the inequities of the Cape social system were sharply attacked not only by missionaries and private travellers but by high officials. Yet the colonial order had become reliant over a century on the strict subordination of labour. The British achievement of gaining the support of the white population by 1815 was an enormous one, and suppressing qualms about the inequities of the system seemed a moderate price to pay for it. As long as the servants and the slaves could not themselves challenge their treatment, retention of the status quo was certainly the cheapest and easiest way for the colonial regime to function. As a result the transitional era, which began with a severe crisis of master-servant relations, ended in powerfully confirming the existing order.

The coming of the missionary

The transitional era marked the beginning of the age of the missionary at the Cape. In 1795 mission activity consisted of the newly refounded Moravian settlement at Baviaanskloof and some local preaching. Over the next two decades the mission field vastly expanded. The London Missionary Society (LMS) began work in 1799 and in 1803 established its first permanent settlement at Bethelsdorp on the Eastern Frontier. Under the guidance of Johannes Theodorus van der Kemp, a Dutchman, Bethelsdorp served as a focal point for mission protest against government policies towards the Khoikhoi and the Xhosa. Other LMS missionaries – British, German and Dutch – worked beyond the

Northern Frontier and established settlements in the colony at Zuurbraak (1812), Hoogekraal (1813) and Theopolis (1814).[45] Cape colonists themselves organised the South African Missionary Society in 1799 with the assistance of Van der Kemp and J.J. Kicherer. As a result of secessions, separate mission societies were later formed in Stellenbosch and Paarl. The South African society had gained a membership of several hundred within a few years and supported a wide range of mission activities, mainly within the colonial borders, founding no special settlements. Finally, the Moravian Brethren continued to direct the establishment at Baviaanskloof (renamed Genadendal in 1805), the largest colonial institution, and founded a second station at Groene Kloof in 1808. By 1815 more than 2,500 Khoikhoi and others were affiliated to missionary settlements while thousands of servants and slaves had come into contact with them.

To the extent that they created new communities, the missionaries represented a threat to Cape employers that their labourers would desert them and find champions for their grievances. As a result, despite widespread belief that Christians must work for the conversion of the heathen, the mission stations evoked much opposition among employers. Moreover the government, increasingly anxious to support the farmers, came into conflict with the missionaries. At the same time both government and employers could appreciate the advantage for the colony if the mission stations could add to the stability of the social order. As a result of these ambiguous attitudes, phases of co-operation between government and missionaries were juxtaposed with phases of conflict.

The missionaries themselves differed in their attitudes towards politics. The Moravians were not insensitive to the difficulties faced by the Khoikhoi and indeed met with enormous hostility from local farmers in the first decade after they returned to the Cape in 1792. Yet they had a tradition of quietism towards secular power and an authoritarian, paternalistic attitude to their flock that enabled them to settle down within the confines of Cape society and government policy. H.R. van Lier, the Cape pastor who really inspired the local mission movement, and his influential associate, M.C. Vos, believed that the concern of missionaries was exclusively with the spiritual life and not the social condition of the slaves to whom they preached. Even among the LMS missionaries most, like J.J. Kicherer or the Englishman, William Anderson, were hardly social critics. By contrast, Van der Kemp and Read fought against administrative demands for unpaid corvée and military labour, for the right to preach to whom they willed, and against the enforcement of contractual obligations made under duress or false pretences. Van der Kemp championed the cause of the Khoikhoi on the Eastern Frontier and strongly opposed slavery. He married the daughter of a Malagasy slave woman in the belief that a missionary should throw in his lot with the people he was trying to convert.[46] Van der Kemp's opposition to the master-servant system was further developed by John Philip and continued as a critical tradition into the twentieth century.

Officials of the first British occupation originally favoured the missionaries in the hope that they could prove effective intermediaries with the Xhosa and the rebel Khoikhoi. Van der Kemp played a major role in this capacity. Support for him diminished towards the end of the period as he became more hostile to the labour system in the east, although no real confrontation took place before 1803. At the same time the neat Moravian settlement of Genadendal, with a more co-operative attitude toward the authorities, won official approbation.

The Batavians held similar hopes that missionaries would support their politics of stability and made the grant of Bethelsdorp to Van der Kemp. However, they soon turned sharply against the missions, partly because of their mistrust of the LMS link to Britain, partly because of the hostility of the established Reformed ministers to 'enthusiastic' preaching and, above all, because they resented resistance to their labour policies. Van der Kemp was forced to leave Bethelsdorp in 1805 and Janssens hoped to ban mission activity, including that of colonists, entirely. Again, however, the Moravians were exempted from government disapproval.

After 1806 clashes between the British administration and the missions continued. Acrimonious relations between Colonel Jacob Glen Cuyler, the landdrost of Uitenhage, and Van der Kemp led the Bethelsdorp missionaries to appeal over the heads of the Cape administration to Britain for help in ensuring juster treatment for their charges. As a result the Cape government instituted the so-called Black Circuit of 1812, which vindicated many of the accused colonists but showed the potential influence which missionaries could wield in a colonial cause. Other signs of hostility during the second British occupation were the continually voiced suspicion that the Orange River missionaries harboured runaway slaves and servants, and the opposition by Cradock and Lord Charles Somerset to the Groene Kloof mission, which they would have preferred as a country residence for themselves.

At the same time British government officials to an increasing extent saw the value of the mission institutions as fixed locations from which the Khoikhoi could emerge to work for farmers. They also valued them as a means of blunting the disaffection of servants, at least as long as the missionaries did not overtly challenge the administration. Government priorities became central to the planning of new mission stations. Groene Kloof was founded in 1808 by the Moravians on the invitation of Lord Caledon despite the opposition of Hans Klapmuts, the still independent captain and Hottentot Corps veteran on whose kraal the institution was established.[47] Zuurbraak and Hoogekraal were also founded on the sites of some of the last surviving independent kraals in the colony; Hoogekraal especially was intended by the government as a labour reserve to serve farmers in a poor stretch of countryside.[48] Theopolis was placed near the eastern border in order to establish colonial security at a strategic point where white farmers feared to settle. By 1815 the mission stations were surviving and, despite some underlying tensions, had come to terms with the colonial government.

The mission stations and the mission movement had a profound influence on Khoikhoi society. Between 1795 and 1815 thousands became Christians. During this period conversions at Bethelsdorp, at first on a small scale, became numerous, while most residents of Genadendal, the oldest institution, were baptised by 1815. The intensity of the converts' zeal was often striking. Bethelsdorp in particular spawned numerous preachers from an early date.

Christianisation went hand in hand with the destruction of the older Khoikhoi culture. William Burchell's travels, published in the 1820s, described baptised Khoikhoi who refused to eat zebra meat – a prejudice he believed derived from Europeans – and others who looked down on the 'Hottentotten'. Burchell also noted adult Khoikhoi (not 'Bastaards') in the Graaff-Reinet district who could speak no language but Dutch.[49] This new class that despised its 'Hottentot' roots was on its way to becoming what would later be called the Cape Coloured people. As the last Khoikhoi settlements were replaced by mission stations or broken up, the remains of Khoikhoi political and cultural independence dissolved.

The South African Society (SAS) worked primarily with slaves and free blacks. Their work flourished, but on a smaller scale than that in the mission settlements. The administration supported the SAS partly because it feared the spread of Islam. Increasing numbers of slaves and free blacks were baptised in the Reformed and Lutheran churches, and their conversion facilitated their adoption of the dominant European culture of the colony.

The conversion of slaves and servants to both European religion and European ways did not provide them with a higher status at the Cape.

Despite the efforts of Van der Kemp and Read, the missionaries were rather ineffective at challenging the treatment of labourers in Cape society. None of the mission stations in the colony was big enough or productive enough to provide its inhabitants with much of a livelihood. Genadendal was fairly fertile but small; the Moravians favoured communal labour under the supervision of the missionaries, thus discouraging any initiative from the people. Moreover, their land was unsuitable for livestock. Bethelsdorp was far poorer; cattle and sheep only flourished in the better years, while cultivation was impossible.

In general, adult male inhabitants of the mission stations had to support themselves and their families by going to work for the colonial farmers: for example, the census of 1 April 1813 recorded only 94 adult males among Bethelsdorp's 608 residents.[50] The principal alternative lay in the practice of crafts or some other kind of enterprise. At Genadendal the Khoikhoi made high-quality knives which were widely used in the colony, but this enterprise was entirely under mission direction. Bethelsdorp, despite its less prepossessing appearance, was a far more active centre for artisans and transporters, especially after the establishment of a large garrison at nearby Fort Frederick.[51]

The really new features in the mission movement for Cape society were the incentive provided to Khoisan cultural assimilation and the thread of articulate protest first picked up by Van der Kemp. Yet the mission establishments also served to mute protest. Unable to alter the course of labour relations at the Cape, the mission stations became palliatives that sweetened the bitter pill of social subordination for the Khoikhoi. On the station a family could live in domestic peace, somewhat sheltered from the harsh conditions of life outside, while it acquired cultural attributes of the dominant colonial society. On a small and crude scale, the mission Khoikhoi were anticipating the lives of millions of Africans in the reserve system of a future industrialised South Africa.

Ruler and ruled at the Cape

After a fairly detailed examination of the attitude of the transitional administrations to economic development and labour relations at the Cape, we should now consider their general philosophy of colonial rule. British as well as Batavian governors were influenced by Enlightenment thinking which, above all, favoured the formation of a new sense of community and the destruction of ancient barriers of caste and estate. Linked to this was the new secularism, the cult of the energetic and enlightened ruler, a growing concern with technical efficiency in economic and administrative activities, and the ideal of an informed and loyal citizenry. Two factors modified the application of Enlightenment ideas at the Cape: the inherently extractive nature of the colonial relationship in which the colony existed for the benefit of the European government, and the inhibiting influence of the counter-revolution of the 1790s, concerned with combating the pull of revolutions in France, the United States and Haiti.

At the Cape the means at hand for altering the nature of society were limited. The government had little money to spend on economic improvements or education. Above all, and especially while the war continued in Europe, the social order was too delicately poised for administrators to dare to initiate sweeping, perhaps unpopular, changes. Their very first priority was to preserve tranquility and so avoid any large expenditure of money and effort on South African affairs. The Batavians were especially hampered by limited funds as well as a fear, ultimately justified, of renewed attack from the sea. De Mist was the most explicitly reforming administrator at the Cape during the transitional era and for this reason his quick retreat into an acceptance of local conditions was especially striking. Particularly before 1803 the British did not act decisively because their legal control over the colony remained uncertain and their commitment to retaining it was not yet total. Even after the reconquest the home government urged avoidance of fundamental changes for this reason. Anglicisation of the law and the official use of the English language had hardly begun before 1814, although General Grey and Govenor Cradock had started to talk about changes along these lines.

Moreover, during the second occupation civil peace, the quickening economic tempo, and increasing closeness of view between the British and the white farmers on master-servant relations and frontier security, greatly blunted the critical acuity that had earlier characterised administrators' attitudes to the colony and the VOC system. By 1814 administrative dispatches had become self-satisfied and conventional compared to the crisis-ridden hand-wringings of the first occupation and Batavian times.

On the whole, administrative forms did not alter greatly between 1795 and 1814. Two tendencies, however, stand out: a growth of professionalism in government and continuing adamant opposition to a greater representative role for colonists. The first tendency resulted in a significant but measured advance before 1814; the second accorded perfectly with the administrators' authoritarian inclinations and their fear of radical ideas originating in the French Revolution.

In 1797 the British raised official salaries and created some where none had existed before; they also suppressed certain perquisites which had formerly been the principal income of officials. These important innovations were designed to stamp out the corruption associated with the VOC administration. Officials brought out from England were paid handsomely in pounds rather than in rixdollars; henceforth official salaries became by far the largest item in government expenditures. During the first British occupation there was a major scandal involving favouritism which in 1801 led to the recall of Governor Yonge. In the long run, however, the calibre of officials improved; most of the major transitional administrators such as De Mist, Janssens, Cradock and Caledon were honest and set an example for improving standards.

In his memorandum De Mist promised a further advance in professionalism and greater inclusion of colonists in the administration. His most lasting reform in the first direction was the introduction of several Dutch graduate lawyers into the Council of Justice. He also created a central accounting office, the *Rekenkamer*, which was however eliminated by Janssens in 1805. De Mist's second promise was not kept. The number of Cape-born officials tended to decrease rather than increase during the Batavian period, and De Mist's original intention of making the Burgher Council or Burgerraad elective was quietly dropped.

After 1806 the number of British civil servants at the Cape increased steadily, perhaps somewhat at the expense of the old official class. Yet the official class, because of its command of Dutch and knowledge of local conditions, continued to play a crucial role before 1815. Its most prominent member until his death in 1812 was Willem Stephanus van Ryneveld, who served the British as fiscaal. Van Ryneveld's reports on social and economic conditions still read impressively today. Local officials continued to monopolise other offices, but as we have seen above, their economic position was in good part usurped by a new group of British merchants.

The Burgher Senate remained an appointive body, and the governments, both British and Batavian, sought to reduce its functions more or less to those of a municipal council. Members continued to petition the government in the name of the colonial population and thus claimed for the Senate a representative role. Their petitions, however, tended to be turned down with the advice that senators should confine themselves to narrower tasks which lay within their legitimate sphere.[52]

In the transitional era the power of the governors over the colonists expanded beyond what it had been in VOC times. Under the British and the Batavians there was no longer a *secunde* (lieutenant-governor) nor a fiscaal (prosecutor) independent of the governor and his council. (The fiscaal's independence had in any event been largely curtailed after the Nederburgh-Frykenius mission to the Cape in 1792–93.) Furthermore, the VOC officials in Batavia no longer remained as countervalent influences to the governor and the Company regime in Holland. The Council of Policy was abolished by the first British occupation; the Batavians restored it, but for most of their administration its members consisted entirely of Hollanders. There were numerous limitations on the power of British governors, notably the division of civil and military jurisdictions before 1811 and the possibility that colonists could exert influence on the Colonial Office in Britain, as the missionaries attempted to do. Yet for most Cape colonists, who had no friends or associates in Britain, these avenues were not of much use. Nor was the Batavian period a democratic interval. Between 1804 and 1806 Governor Janssens moved in a more and more authoritarian and centralising direction, regarding his role as that of a viceroy with responsibility exclusively to his home office and with no check on his will in the colony. The British governors were content that local influences, if present at all, should be mediated through a few trusted officials such as Van Ryneveld.

In the countryside the administrative system changed even less. There was a striking continuity of office-holders, particularly at the level of the field-cornets. The landdrosts continued to be selected from the Cape Town elite while the local farmers played their crucial role as heemraden and as field-cornets. Before 1814 no British officials served in these offices, apart from the landdrost of Uitenhage, Colónel Cuyler, a Dutch-speaking military officer born in New York. However, the formal duties of local officials were codified with increasing precision, notably in the 1797 ordinanᵔe for veldwachtmeesters and in the 1805 ordinance for the administration of outlying areas.

There was some intensification of central authority through the creation of new districts and sub-districts. In 1804 the Batavian regime formed two districts to encompass the northwestern and southwestern frontier zones, with headquarters at Tulbagh and Uitenhage respectively. In 1808 a new district was created in eastern Swellendam, centred on George. During the second British occupation five subdistricts were established by 1814. In the countryside there were as a result more administrators directly responsible to the Castle, which thus gained a closer control over local circumstances. The churches and schools which were built in the new drostdies also spread commercial and 'civilising' influences which the government viewed with favour. Another reform that had the same tendency was the institution of the circuit court in 1811. This deepening of central government influence played a role in the apparent extinction of the rebellious embers that had flared up between 1795 and 1801.

The British were slow to introduce legal changes at the Cape. They made only a beginning at modifying Cape law to conform to imperial models.[53] The growing British community, however, was subject to British law, an inconsistency which occasioned nagging disputes. This legal continuity further retarded social change during the transitional period.

The governments of the transitional period were concerned with transforming the population into a more orderly, more loyal, more enlightened citizenry: this was to be done by means of formal education. In 1795 the Cape educational system was weak. Though there were numerous small schools in Cape Town, they were quite unco-ordinated with each other, and there was no secondary education outside the feeble Latin School. In the countryside, education was largely in the hands of wandering tutors, often demissioned soldiers. There were virtually no schools, and illiteracy was fairly common among whites and the norm among slaves and servants. From the first British occupation onwards the administration became increasingly concerned about improving the quality of education. This was especially true of the Batavians, who frequently wrote about the problem and promulgated the *Schoolorde* of 1805. The Schoolorde attempted to systematise the colonial education structure and created a school commission consisting of officials and ministers to preside over education matters. The second British occupation saw further advances, notably the establishment in 1812 of local Bible and school committees that began to further education in the countryside.

According to Theal the Schoolorde was deeply resented at the Cape, because it was seen as an attempt to dragoon the pious citizenry into secular schools which emitted unwelcome Enlightenment propaganda. Actually there is no record of such resentment. Advances in formal education were welcomed by the local population, even in remote areas, and the Schoolorde largely continued the tradition of church-state collaboration which was typical of education under the VOC and in contemporary Dutch society generally. The principal brake on educational improvements was financial: the colonial governments were unable or unwilling to set aside much money for schools. The second part of the Schoolorde, dealing with financial regulations, was never issued: the Batavian government had learned through various protests that new taxes for education would be most unwelcome.

Yet education moved forward in fits and starts with general government approbation. During this era the 'Tot Nut van het Algemeen' school, the first good private school in Cape Town, was established and supported by well-to-do Cape officials and merchants. The real inspiration behind the 'Tot Nut' society was H.A. Vermaak who, as a Patriot, spent the years of the first British occupation in Holland and was much impressed with the work of the Dutch parent society, an important Enlightenment institution. In 1813 the Cape Town Free School for the needy was founded, and before the end of 1814 it was educating over 200 students of both sexes and all races.[54] Outside the capital little schools sprang up in the country villages while missionaries had an educational impact on slaves and other brown and black peoples. In 1803 the Batavians, afraid of this impact, had forbidden mission stations to teach reading and writing; however, this decree, which remained in force after the British re-conquest, was in practice ignored.

Even as late as 1814 formal education at the Cape was unimpressive. Facilities for rural children were still rare and the population mostly lived far from any urban centre. More crucially, given the hopes of the colonial regimes, no elite institutions had been created that functioned effectively as socialising agents. De Mist's model of such an institution, a secondary school for the training of teachers and officials, firmly reflecting Batavian ideals and prerogatives, was reluctantly dismissed by the school commission as an impossibly expensive and visionary proposal, at least at the time. Certain British officials of the second occupation, notably General Grey and Governor Cradock, wanted to further the use of English by means of the school. Yet they had not progressed very far before 1814. By that time British children attended separate English-medium schools; to an increasing extent the other schools taught English as a subject, but they were not yet seriously used as instruments for Anglicisation.[55]

The Cape press was created during the transitional era to serve an educative purpose. The *Cape Gazette*, a government organ, was founded in 1800 and continued to operate throughout the period as the only Cape newspaper. It was a dull sheet which, apart from commercial advertisements, consisted mainly of government exhortations and announcements. Both the British and the Batavians were hostile to the notion of a free press and thus banned private printing. Their attitude to the press sharply reflected the view that education should set youth on a road that led in but one direction – towards loyalty and better performance of duty within the colonial order.

How successful were the transitional administrations in transforming the Cape population into the desired loyal citizenry? Administrative priorities and limited finances would obviously prevent ambitious schemes for social reformation from getting very far. At the same time, however,there was a strong evolution between 1795 and 1814 of a more positive feeling on the part of the authorities towards the dominant freeburgher class. During the first British occupation the regime feared rebellion, and officials such as Barrow had a low opinion of all but the most distinguished and Anglophile civil servants at the Cape. This antagonism dwindled considerably during the Batavian period and virtually disappeared during the second British occupation. Contrasting with Barrow's hostile view is the far more sympathetic commentary of Hinrich Lichtenstein, the most distinguished official traveller and commentator of Batavian times, and the even more pro-colonist views of Colonel Collins, perhaps the most influential British official of the first decade of the second occupation.

The colonists, although disaffected with the VOC, did not greet the British with much warmth in 1795. During the first British occupation there remained a large number of Dutch sympathisers in the colony, including pockets of Patriot supporters who were labelled Jacobins by the British and their colonial opponents. There were incidents of sabotage, refusal or reluctance to take the British oath of loyalty and other acts of passive resistance. That acute observer, Lady Anne Barnard, saw little loyalty to the British developing before 1803. During the same period rebellion broke out on the Eastern Frontier on three occasions. However, the British proved more able and determined than the VOC in stifling protest and enforcing compliance.

Relations between the Batavians and the colonists were better. In the southwest, resistance to Batavian rule was insignificant and no further rebellions took place in the east. At the same time the regime kept a tight grip on the population and was suspicious of popular loyalties.

The first decade of renewed British rule was even more placid. Little resistance took place; the Patriot flames had apparently died down and the last of the eastern rebellions, that of Slachtersnek in 1815, was by far the least serious and the most easily contained.[56] Part of this conciliation came about because the British ever more clearly espoused the cause of employers and slave-owners and because they were won over to the views of frontier farmers on Xhosa policy. Partly, too, it was the result of British strength. Throughout the transitional era thousands of European troops were stationed at the Cape, a very formidable force to the small colonial population of the day. Serious military action against the British was not feasible, especially once the possibility of a French attack on the Cape was removed by the British conquest of the Mascarene islands (Mauritius and Réunion) in 1810. The greater prosperity of the period after 1806 also soothed rebellious spirits. So, too, did the fact that while the British brought to the Cape new ways, a new language and a new church, their policy before 1815 was quite conciliatory on cultural matters and they showed little inclination to impose change beyond the purview of the Castle.

Helping to adjust the population to the changes in rule were the high officials and prominent merchants of Cape Town. A few, such as H.A. Vermaak or the Van Reenen family, were genuinely Patriot and anti-British but, in general, partisan divisions merely reflected family feuds and rivalries. These citizens gave their loyalty either to the British or Dutch in their role as keepers of order, holders of economic privilege and employers of bureaucrats. As J.J. Oberholster has written about the reaction of the Burgher Senate to the British re-conquest of 1806:

> So complete was the continuity of the Burgher Senate, that no interruption took place in its sessions. From the arrival of the British fleet on January 4 to January 10, the day Cape Town was occupied, the Burgher Senate sat day after day to support Janssens in his war operations; from January 10 to January 18, the day Janssens capitulated, they held daily sessions to help provide the necessary wagons and horses for the English.[57]

During the transitional period a growing alienation between church and state took place. The British interfered very little with the Reformed church during their first occupation. By contrast the Batavians were much concerned with church organisation and reorganisation. They extended toleration for Christians outside the Reformed church and in the *Kerkorde* of 1804 provided for a new and more self-supporting church administration. Despite assertions by Theal and others, contemporary evidence shows a great deal of support by church boards and ministers for the Kerkorde. In fact the new role of the state in education and the solemnisation of marriages did not signally differ from VOC tradition, and ministers welcomed Batavian financial assistance. After 1806, however, the continued role of the government in church affairs was resented because the government was no longer in the hands of Reformed church members. Extensive controversy developed over British insistence on helping to select deacons (despite the fact that this was no longer required by the Batavian Kerkorde), and over the interference of the *Commissaris-politiek*, the government representative in church affairs.[58]

To the majority of the colonial population, the slaves and servants, the various transfers of power meant relatively little. The Khoikhoi responded positively to the rather open policies of General Dundas towards the rebels of 1799 and to British attempts to use the Khoikhoi as a lever against whites. There are a few indications that Khoikhoi regretted the Batavian take-over in 1803 and that they had high hopes when the British returned in 1806; however, these hopes were dashed when the British sided increasingly with white farmers. What is known of the slave rebellion of 1808 hints at the expectations the British must have aroused among slaves by abolishing the slave trade. On the whole, however, the increasing tendency of the transitional administrations to maintain the status quo prevented any change in role for the slaves or servants.

By 1815 the relationship of ruler to ruled had once more settled into a stable pattern. Part of the special interest of the earlier years of the transitional period lies in the instability of this relationship: the British and the Batavians were initially suspicious of the existing order. Critical reports questioned, or at least discussed from an outsider's point of view, fundamental social institutions, while the regimes seemed to require substantial reforms in order to meet their goals. Yet without important reforms the new colonial administrations were able to cement a firm working arrangement with the dominant class at the Cape and to reaffirm the essentials of the Cape social structure as it had developed before 1795.

Conclusion

The era of transition began in a time of crisis and conflict in Cape society; gradually the crisis dissipated and calm was restored. On the whole the recreated order was not the result of bold reforms by the government nor of dramatic social transformation. The reformist impulse which figured in the schemes of Governor Yonge and Sir John Barrow, or of De Mist and officials such as Alberti or Van Ryneveld, declined markedly after 1806. Changes in Cape institutions, whether educational, administrative or legal, came slowly.

On the whole the next twenty years of Cape history, which would encompass the beginnings of the Great Trek, the coming of the 1820 settlers, the rise of the wool industry, Ordinance 50, the abolition of slavery, the full onslaught of Anglicisation and the build-up of conflict with Xhosas on the far side of the Fish River, is both a more dramatic era and one that made a far more emphatic break with the past (see ch. 10, pp. 470–509). Nevertheless, the transitional period was not without change, and important trends that can be observed before 1814 point to later events. Foremost among these were economic changes: the gradual dismantling of monopoly, increasing economic growth dramatised by the expansion of wine exports towards the end of the period, and the rapid rise of British traders and British trade. One may also regard the abolition of the slave trade and the increasing importance of tightly controlled but free labour as early steps away from the slave system. The expulsion of the Xhosa across the Fish River in 1811–12 was decisive in putting an end to the longstanding power-vacuum on the Eastern Frontier and in throwing the weight of the British army on the side of the colonists. Finally, the expanding mission movement, which would dramatically affect the culture and society of brown and black peoples at the Cape, was perhaps the most striking new social phenomenon of the period, and the one with the greatest long-range significance.

Chronology

1795	16 Sept.	British take possession of Cape Town. General James Craig, acting governor.
1797	January	Conclusion of the Graaff-Reinet rebellion.
	5 May	Arrival of Lord Macartney, governor.
1798	20 Nov.	Departure of Lord Macartney; Major-General Francis Dundas, acting governor.
1799	Jan.–April	'Van Jaarsveld' rebellion.
	April–Oct.	Khoikhoi rising.
	31 March	Arrival of the first LMS missionaries.
	10 Dec.	Sir George Yonge, governor.
1801	20 April	Resignation of Yonge; Dundas, acting governor.
	April	General introduction of the contract system for farm labourers.
	October	Graaff-Reinet rebellion.
	December	Resumption of hostilities on the frontier.
1802	1 April	J.A. de Mist appointed Commissioner-General.
	23 Dec.	Arrival of De Mist and Governor Jan Willem Janssens at the Cape.

1803	1 March	Batavian rule proclaimed.
	2 June	Van der Kemp takes possession of Bethelsdorp.
	25 July	*Kerkorde*.
1804	11 Sept.	*Schoolorde*.
	25 Sept.	Resignation of De Mist.
1805	23 April	Expulsion of Van der Kemp from Bethelsdorp
1806	18 Jan.	Capitulation of Janssens to the British. Major General David Baird, acting governor.
1807	17 Jan.	Lieutenant-General Sir Henry George Grey, acting governor.
	22 May	Du Pré Alexander, Earl of Caledon, governor.
1808	29 April	End of the slave trade proclaimed at the Cape.
	October	Slave rising in the Zwartland. Introduction of first apprentices to the Cape from among Prize Negroes.
1809	1 Nov.	Hottentot Proclamation.
1811	4 July	Departure of Caledon.
	6 Sept.	Sir John Cradock, governor.
	Oct. – March 1812	Attack on the Zuurveld Xhosa; their expulsion across the Fish.
	December	Death of Van der Kemp.
1812	23 April	Apprenticeship of Servants law.
	23 Sept.	Black circuit initiated.
1813		Reduction of duties on Cape wine.
	6 August	Land tenure proclamation.
1814	6 April	Lord Charles Somerset, governor.
	13 August	London convention, whereby the Netherlands acknowledges British right to the Cape.
1815	November	Slachtersnek Rebellion.

Chapter Seven   Notes

1. A major work on the first British occupation is Hermann Giliomee, *Die Kaap Tydens die Eerste Britse Bewind 1795–1803* (Cape Town, 1975).
2. A good discussion of the debate in British government circles can be found in Vincent Harlow, 'The British Occupations 1795–1806', *Cambridge*

History of the British Empire, VIII (Cambridge, 1936). See also L.C.F. Turner, 'The Cape of Good Hope and the Anglo-French Conflict 1797–1806', *Historical Studies of Australia and New Zealand*, IX (1961).

3. J.A. de Mist, *The Memorandum of Commissary J.A. de Mist*, trans. K.M. Jeffreys (Cape Town, 1920).

4. A.H. Murray, *The Political Philosophy of J.A. de Mist* (Cape Town, n.d.) and Harlow, 'British Occupations'. A detailed work on the period, basically in the conservative camp, is J.P. van der Merwe, *Die Kaap onder die Bataafse Republiek 1803–06* (Amsterdam, 1926). The historiography of the period is discussed in William M. Freund, 'Society and Government in Dutch South Africa, The Cape and the Batavians 1803–06' (Unpublished Ph. D. thesis; Yale University, 1971).

5. George McCall Theal, *A History of South africa since 1795* (London, 1906), I, 121.

6. The principal exception is Hermann Giliomee, 'Die Administrasietydperk van Lord Caledon 1807–11', *AYB*, XXIX (2), 1966.

7. Giliomee, *Eerste Britse Bewind*, p.202, gives pertinent figures. Apart from coasters, of 742 vessels calling at the Cape between 1795 and 1800, 458 were British: Theal, *History*, I, 41.

8. C.F.J. Muller, *Johannes Frederik Kirsten oor die Toestand van die Kaapkolonie in 1795* (Pretoria, 1960); H.B. Thom, introduction and notes to W.S. van Ryneveld, *Aanmerking over de Verbetering van het Vee aan het Kaap de Goede Hoop* (Cape Town, 1942); W. Blommaert, Biographical sketch in Dirk Gysbert van Reenen, *Die Joernaal van Dirk Gysbert van Reenen* (Cape Town, 1937).

9. [W.W. Bird], *State of the Cape in 1822 by a Civil Servant* (Cape Town, 1966), p.147. See the list of wine merchants in D.J. van Zyl, *Kaapse Wyn en Brandewyn 1795–1860* (Cape Town, 1975), 126–27.

10. Giliomee, *Eerste Britse Bewind*, p.147.

11. *RCC*, II, General Fraser – Clive, 12 Feb. 1799, pp. 504–05.

12. Brian Kantor, 'The Rixdollar and the Foreign Exchange', *South African Journal of Economics*, XXXVIII (1970). The value of exports rose to over 3,000,000 rixdollars in 1817, declining thereafter. Imports rose above 2,000,000 in 1813 and reached almost 5,000,000 in 1817 and 1818.

13. *RCC*, VII, Gordon-Harrison, 4 April 1810, p.274.

14. *RCC*, XI, Account of Imports from and Exports to Cape of Good Hope, 1813–1817, pp.293–94.

15. Bird, *State of the Cape*, pp.41–43, for a discussion of the pachten as they were in the early 1820s.

16. René F.M. Immelman, *Men of Good Hope: The Romantic Story of the Cape Town Chamber of Commerce 1804–1954* (Cape Town, 1955), p.72. See also Van Zyl, *Kaapse Wyn en Brandewyn*.

17. Between 1811 and 1819 some 9,000,000 vines were planted and in 1815, a record year, production already exceeded 14,000 leaguers. Figures are from annual returns in the volumes of *RCC* and Immelman, *Men of Good Hope*, which discusses the rise of wine export and production.

18. Figures are from *RCC* and Dirk Jacobus van Zyl, 'Die Geskiedenis van Graanbou aan die Kaap 1795–1826', *AYB* XXXI (1), 1968, p.275.

19. The 1806 figures are so low as to fit no rational sequence.

20. The most important source on the land question at this time remains P.J. van der Merwe, *Die Trekboer in die Geskiedenis van die Kaapkolonie* (Cape Town, 1938). See also Freund, 'Society and Government', pp.70–71.
21. J.A. Heese, *Slagtersnek en sy Mense* (Cape Town, 1973), pp.67–71.
22. RCC, IX, Proclamation by Cradock, 6 Aug. 1813, pp.204–08. The best discussion of Cape government land policy is Leslie C. Duly, *British Land Policy at the Cape 1795–1844: A Study of Administrative Procedures in the Empire* (Durham, 1968).
23. For the 1808 turn in colonist – 'Bushman' relations in the northeast, see Giliomee, 'Caledon', pp.267–69. There is an important discussion in chapter five of P.J. van der Merwe, *Die Noordwaartse Beweging van die Boere voor die Groot Trek (1770–1842)* (The Hague, 1937). A crucial contemporary account is the report of Richard Collins in RCC, VII, 201.
24. See RCC, VIII, Report of the Circuit Court Commission, 28 Jan. 1812, p.299; William J. Burchell, *Travels in the Interior of Southern Africa* (Cape Town, 1967), II, 143–46 and the enclosed reprint of Burchell, 'Hints on Emigration', I, 38.
25. For the career of one later famous trekker who went east to seek his fortune as an entrepreneur at this time, see J.L.M. Franken, *Piet Retief se Lewe in die Kolonie* (Pretoria, 1949).
26. The considerable and controversial literature about the failure of the Van Hogendorp scheme during the Batavian period is reviewed in Freund, 'Society and Government', pp.415–30.
27. Van Zyl, 'Graanbou', pp.271–72.
28. Immelman, *Men of Good Hope*, p.25.
29. I have further elaborated these points in W.M. Freund, 'Race and the Social Structure of South Africa 1652–1836', *Race and Class*, XVIII (1976).
30. Robert Ross, 'The Rise of the Cape Gentry', *Journal of Southern African Studies*, IX (1983).
31. Nigel Worden, *Slavery in Dutch South Africa* (Cambridge, 1985).
32. The local consequences are explored by Mary Rayner in 'Slaves, Slave Owners and the British State: The Cape Colony 1806–34', Societies of Southern Africa in the 19th and 20th Centuries postgraduate seminar, Institute of Commonwealth Studies, University of London, 1980.
33. Susan Newton-King, 'The Labour Market of the Cape Colony 1807–28', *Economy and Society in Pre-Industrial South Africa*, ed. Shula Marks and Anthony Atmore (London, 1980), p. 182.
34. See the crucial report prepared for Dundas by Van Ryneveld, RCC, IV, 88 - 96.
35. For discussion of labour policies with special relevance to the Eastern Frontier, see chapter 9 in this volume.
36. For the strong comments by the generally conservative Governor Cradock on the light sentences passed on whites in such crimes, see RCC, X, Cradock-Bathurst, 15 April 1814, pp.1–5.
37. RCC, I, Craig-Henry Dundas, 12 April 1796, pp.353–56.
38. Collins-Caledon, 6 Aug. 1809, in *The Record; or a series of official papers relative to the conditions and treatment of the native tribes of South Africa*, ed. Donald Moodie (Amsterdam and Cape Town, 1960), p. 22; George

Thompson, *Travels and Adventures in South Africa* (Cape Town, 1967), II, 74.

39. AR, Inventory Aziatische Raad, 311, Janssens-Staats-Bewind, 21 Dec. 1804, p.171.

40. Before 1795, 600 slave arrivals a year was a normal figure: Giliomee, *Eerste Britse Bewind*, p.182.

41. In 1798 there were 964 slaves in Graaff-Reinet district. The figure rose to 1,905 in 1806 and 2,874 for the combined districts of Graaff-Reinet and Uitenhage. These figures are taken from the census rolls in *RCC*.

42. Some 2,000 arrived at the Cape Town between 1808 and 1816: J.S. Marais, *The Cape Coloured People 1652–1937* (Johannesburg, 1957), p.161.

43. *Ibid*, p.167.

44. *RCC*, I, Court of Justice-Craig, 14 Jan. 1796, pp.302–09.

45. The first two were later renamed Caledon Institute and Pacaltsdorp.

46. For Van der Kemp, see W.M. Freund, 'The Career of Johannes Theodorus van der Kemp and his role in the history of South Africa', *Tijdschrift voor Geschiedenis*, LXXXVI (1973), pp.376–90 and the sources quoted there.

47. Christian I. Latrobe, *Journal of a Visit to South Africa in 1815 and 1816 with some Account of the Missionary Settlements of the United Brethren Near the Cape of Good Hope* (New York, 1969), p.47; Bernhard Krüger, *The Pear Tree Blossoms, a History of the Moravian Mission Stations in South Africa 1737–1869* (Genadendal, 1966), pp.102–03.

48. *RCC*, IX, Report of the circuit commissioners for Graaff-Reinet, Uitenhage and George, 1812, pp.76–77.

49. Burchell, *Travels*, II, 179, 238, 286.

50. For evidence on the economy of Genadendal see, among others, Van Reenen, *VRS* 18, p.23 and *Periodical Accounts Relating to the Mission of the Church of the United Brethren 1795–1834* (translated typescript, South African Public Library), 2.39. For Bethelsdorp see John Campbell, *Travels in South Africa undertaken at the request of the London Missionary Society* (London, 1812), pp.84, 90–93. Campbell wrote (p. 90) that '... those who have obtained most property, are such as have remained most constantly at the settlement, while those who have been much in the service of the boors, have gained little.'

51. Important and sympathetic accounts of the missions at the close of the transitional era are Latrobe on the Moravians and Campbell on the LMS. An interesting comparison of the two mission traditions by H.T. Colebrooke is to be found in Bird, *State of the Cape*, p.350.

52. The best sources on this institution is J.J. Oberholster, 'Die Burger-Senaat 1795–1828' (unpublished M.A. thesis, University of Stellenbosch, 1936).

53. C. Graham Botha, 'The Early Inferior Courts of Justice at the Cape', *South African Law Journal*, XXXVIII (1921), pp.406–23.

54. W.S. van der Westhuyzen, 'Onderwys onder die Algemen Skoolkommissie: Die Periode 1804–30', *AYB*, XVI (2),1953, p. 40.

55. For education during the transitional era, see Giliomee, *Eerste Britse Bewind*, pp. 231–33 and Freund, 'Society and Government', pp. 227–39. This subject has covered in depth in Van Der Westhuyzen, 'Onderwys', and in several works by P.S. du Toit, especially *Onderwys aan die Kaap onder die Bataafse Republiek 1803–06* (Pretoria, 1944).

56. The most recent account of Slachtersnek is Heese, *Slagtersnek*.
57. Oberholster, 'Burger-Senaat', p.36.
58. The conflict is documented in *Boustowwe vir die Geskiedenis van die Nederduits-Gereformeerde Kerke in Suid-Africa*, ed. A. Dreyer (Cape Town, 1936), III, 88–135.

CHAPTER EIGHT

The Northern Frontier to c.1840: The rise and decline of the Griqua people*

Martin Legassick

Introduction

This chapter is concerned with the peoples who inhabited Namaqualand,[†] Bushmanland,[‡] and central Transorangia[§] during the eighteenth and early nineteenth centuries. At that time this region had long been occupied by a variety of communities. The major theme of this chapter is the increasing domination of these communities by the social relationships emanating from the VOC (and, later, Batavian and British) colony at the Cape. Its minor theme is the emergence of the Griqua, a new community with a way of life distinct from that of the settled Cape Colony and from those of earlier peoples in this region.

The social relationships characteristic of the Cape Colony, and the history of their expansion and consequent domination over the pre-existing communities of southern Africa, have been viewed in a number of different ways. Most frequently domination and conflict have been analysed in 'racial' terms, and assumed to have developed historically

* This is a revision of parts of my Ph.D. thesis (University of California, Los Angeles, 1969) entitled 'The Griqua, the Sotho-Tswana, and the Missionaries, 1780–1840: The Politics of a Frontier Zone.' I am much indebted to Professor L.M. Thompson both for supervising my thesis and for comments on an earlier draft of this chapter. The chapter has also benefitted from extensive comments on the thesis by Professor Jeffrey Butler, and on various drafts by the editors of this volume. I am grateful also to Bill Freund and Christopher Saunders who at different times provided material.

† The mountainous and rugged granite terrain along the escarpment south of the lower Orange was regarded as Little Namaqualand; the area extending from the Orange River to Rehoboth in the north and from the great escarpment to the Kalahari sands was called Great Namaqualand.

‡ Bushmanland is the dry plain east of Little Namaqualand and south of the Lower Orange. Orange.

§ This was the region to the north of the middle Orange River mainly comprising Griqualand West and what was once called British Bechuanaland.

along unambiguously 'racial' lines. Thus, in discussing the expansion of the Cape Colony, there was a tendency among historians, from Theal and Cory to Macmillan, to focus on the 'remorseless advance of white agricultural colonisation'[1] establishing domination over the indigenous population of South Africa. A significant alternative explanation of these phenomena has been that offered by the liberal school of South African historiography of which Macmillan was, ambivalently, a founder, and whose major insights were presented in the *Oxford History of South Africa*. A central theme of this school has been how expansion of the trade established 'co-operative' relationships between the Cape Colony and indigenous societies, forming a 'new' South African society. The task of this school, therefore, has been to explain how the harmony generated by trade has become 'distorted' into historic and contemporary forms of racial conflict.[2] This they have achieved with various measures of empirical success, but on the basis of theoretical deficiencies.[3]

The concept of 'white agricultural colonisation' confuses a number of processes which must be disentangled and examined separately. What, in the Cape, was the relationship between the expansion of the territorial authority of the ruling power and the expansion of white settlement? What was the relationship between the extension of trade, and the expansion of white settlement? Were all European immigrants who moved away from the Cape Peninsula agriculturalists? Were all European immigrant agriculturalists bearers of 'colonial' political and economic relationships? Did not some of the indigenous population come to perform 'colonial' political and economic roles? And, if trade was the 'co-operative' act assumed by the liberal historians, what then were the factors which led to domination and conflict, whether in class or racial forms? Who were the bearers of this trade? And, to the extent that the trade created relationships of exploitation and domination, were these not class relationships?

The first of the settlers were the freeburghers, a social category created in the seventeenth century by the Dutch East India Company (VOC) regime. As the freeburghers moved inland from the Western Cape heartland in the late seventeenth century, they were not initially agriculturalists, but traders and hunters. Earlier, the trade in cattle and other goods to Cape Town had been by Company officials through direct purchase from Khoikhoi suppliers or middlemen: the mercantile VOC had thus been the initial agency of expansion of trade. Freeburghers began to usurp this middleman role, by trading cattle and other products of pastoralism or the hunt. There was no reason why this trade had to lead to political domination. Trading or hunting could be carried out with the permission of the political leadership (such as it was) of the Khoikhoi. But in practice the bearers of trade came to be the bearers of *de jure* or *de facto* political authority. In the same way (but under different conditions) missionaries, bearers of ideology, also came to be bearers of trade and political domination.

Thus settlers might appropriate the products of the hunt without reference to the political authority of the community on whose territory they hunted. Equally, simple trading could develop into coerced exchange, into raiding, and into pure robbery. In 1738, on what may have been the first trading expedition from the Cape Colony to reach the Orange River, a simple exchange of cattle was supplemented by theft. 'A few colonists, well armed, assemble together: then, falling suddenly on some solitary horde [of Khoisan], they compel those who compose it to bring them all their cattle, from which they select such as may suit them, and give in return what they think proper'.[4] After departing, the colonists on the following day sent their Khoisan dependents to seize further cattle. In no single instance was the transformation of a trading relationship into one of coercion inevitable or necessary; its occurrence indicated the ultimate relationship between European metropolis and indigenous community, mediated only by the settlers. This raiding of cattle and other goods could also lead to the seizure of people as captives, to be subordinated as dependants, or distributed or sold.

The possibility of such developments reflected the fact that the VOC had established the Cape Colony on a basis of slave production. In the eighteenth century, the VOC progressively lost control of land allocation in the regions of freeburgher expansion.[5] Although it claimed to rule the entire domain into which freeburghers and other immigrants (*knechts*, deserters, escaped sailors, etc.) were moving, it could not exert a uniformly effective authority. In other parts of the colonial world of the period the colonial regime abandoned all pretence of authority: the settlers were left to 'go native' and to integrate themselves into roles in the indigenous society. But in the Cape Colony this did not occur. The reasons for this resolute, if ineffective, legalism of the VOC and the reasons for freeburghers clinging to the lifeline – these are among the fundamental problems of this period of South African history.[6] They can be described, though not explained, through the concept of the 'frontier zone'.[7] The freeburghers (and their dependents) lived in a 'frontier zone', a fluid region of social transition, relatively autonomous from both colonial base and the indigenous social systems, but dependent on both. For three generations, the frontier zone of the eighteenth century Cape remained in limbo. Only at the turn of the nineteenth century as industrial capitalism came to displace mercantile capitalism in Europe, and as Britain displaced the VOC and Batavians in South Africa, were the processes set in motion for the reincorporation of the frontier zone into the Cape colonial system. In Giliomee's terms, what had been an 'open frontier' became a 'closed frontier' (see ch. 9, pp. 424–28).

The major institution of the open frontier zone was the commando. Its tasks were simultaneously political and economic. It drew from both the indigenous and colonial systems but, as a band of armed retainers, had feudal characteristics which distinguished it from each. Dependent for its existence on firearms and (more crucial in the short term) on a constant supply of powder, the commando, like the frontier zone itself, was ultimately subordinate to its colonial base. For the freeburghers on the frontier the commando was the military form of the hunting and trading party. The VOC's attempt to preserve a trade monopoly by declaring *all* intercourse between colonists and the indigenous population illegal, encouraged the former to maximise their illegal gains by the most coercive means. Raiding, which was the result, exacerbated social conflict and confirmed the VOC's decision to prevent contacts. But at the same time, from about 1715, the strafkommando replaced the VOC soldiery as the main agency for the defence of the colonial interior against attack. Coerced trade, unregulated hunting and raiding bred resistance by the Khoisan peoples in the eighteenth century; and the VOC was compelled to depend on the commando to defeat them.[8] Thus, for political reasons, the VOC was forced to permit the supply of firearms and powder to an institution to which it was economically opposed. Only in 1795, when Eastern Frontier settlers rebelled against the colony, was the powder-supply actually suspended as a sanction.

These separate political and economic tasks of the commando became reunited in the appropriation of land. It is true that there was no one-to-one relationship between military conquest and seizure of land. On the other hand, in the absence of an effective legal power, it was the commando system which enabled the replacement of an indigenous system of usufruct of common land by a system of private land-holding. This transformation was, for the most part, initially effected on the spot by *de facto* occupation; only thereafter would the land-owners seek to guarantee their occupation in perpetuity through registration of a land title with the colonial government. Strictly speaking it is only such land-owners who turned to agricultural production on colonially registered land who can be regarded as agricultural colonisers. Nor, as will be seen,

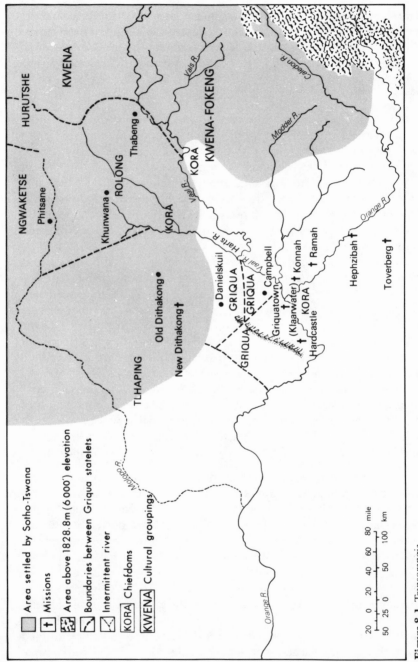

Figure 8.1 Transorangia

It is probable that Sotho-Tswana settlement between the Vaal and the Modder was overlaid by a northeast thrust of the Kora between 1800 and 1820.

were they uniformly white. Moreover, to the extent that such production became the most important aspect of their subsistence, they tended to delegate the tasks of trading and hunting and the *de facto* extension of land appropriation to their family and their dependents. Colonisation in this sense was a form of closing the frontier zone, not of extending its openness.

There were, broadly speaking, two main northward thrusts in the eighteenth-century expansion of the open frontier of the commando. The first of these was along the plains near the west coast, over the Oliphants River, to the Khamiesberg, to Little Namaqualand and into present-day Namibia. The particular significance of this thrust was – as Marais pointed out in his classic though dated study – that it was pioneered largely by people who were not white.[9] Marais, concentrating on a particular period, exaggerated: until the 1730s whites predominated in this thrust. Only as whites moved across the mountains south of Bushmanland was a space created for frontier settlers of mixed racial descent.

A second northward thrust came much further to the east. From about 1810 the frontier north of Graaff-Reinet and the Sneeuwberg began to open as the resistance of 'Bushmen' hunters crumbled; the descendants of those settlers who had turned east across the mountains south of Bushmanland in the 1730s now began to push to the north. In the meantime the northward penetration along the west coast had turned eastwards along the valley of the Orange River. By 1820 the two streams were meeting in central Transorangia. Here again there was a predominant, though not exclusive role played by people who were not white (see Fig. 8.1).

The minor theme of this chapter, we have said, is the rise and decline of a distinctive new community. This Griqua community was formed in the crucible of the frontier zone and shaped by the institutions of the commando. To say that the Griqua people were not 'white' is at least partially anachronistic in reference to the eighteenth century: the economic and political conditions in which racial categories could become established did not as yet firmly exist. The eighteenth-century colour line, at least in Cape Town and some frontier areas, was a blurred one in which the criteria of legal and social status by no means always coincided with those of ethnic origin (see ch. 11, pp. 546- 48). Many who later became assimilated into the white side of the South African colour line descended from a biological and cultural mixture in the eighteenth century. At the same time there emerged in the eighteenth century a social category denominated *'Bastaards'*. Though these

originated as dependents or commando-members in the open frontier
zone, they could also become property owners under colonial law. Like
the freeburghers, they initially aspired to Christianity and to citizenship
of the colony. From this Bastaard nucleus there emerged in the early
nineteenth century a series of communities (along and north of the valley
of the Orange, from Namibia to central Transorangia) with a social
identity which is most conveniently denoted as 'Griqua'.[10]

This chapter begins with a description of the indigenous communities
which occupied the Northern Frontier prior to its 'opening' from the
Cape. There follow sections on the open frontier of the commando, and
on the forms of stabilisation of the frontier zone through land claims and
territorial rights. The main body of the chapter discusses the abortive
attempts by the post-1800 colonial government and the bearers of its
authority, the missionaries, to close the frontier zone, and the
consequent emergence of new forms of domination and exploitation
(not along racial lines), especially the attempt of the Griqua to establish
their political authority over the other peoples of central Transorangia.
The last parts describe the processes which, after 1836, sealed the fate of
the Griqua and secured the 'closing' of the Northern Frontier in terms
which began to entrench the ideology of race and the power of white
colonists.

The indigenous communities: Bantu-speakers and Khoisan

The eighteenth-century commando frontier impinged on regions
inhabited by Bantu-speakers and Khoisan. ('Khoisan' includes both the
pastoral Khoikhoi and groups of hunter-gatherers whom Khoikhoi
called 'San' and whom the colonists called 'Bushmen'). In central
Namibia, south of the Ovambo peoples, were the Bantu-speaking
Herero, cattle-keepers par excellence.[11] East of the Kalahari (which may
not have been as extensive then as it is now) the Highveld and central and
eastern Transorangia were dominated by the Bantu-speaking Sotho-
Tswana peoples, who were cultivators as well as pastoralists. The
southernmost of these in the eighteenth century were the Rolong (south
of the Molopo) and, to their east, the Fokeng, Ghoya and Taung spread
as far south as the Caledon River (see Fig. 8.1, p. 362).[12]

South of the Bantu-speakers, and interspersed among them, were the
Khoisan.[13] Prior to the eighteenth century there is evidence that cattle-
keeping Khoikhoi were living adjacent to Bantu-speaking communities,
at least in Namibia and along the middle Orange.[14] By the early

nineteenth century these Khoikhoi north and south of the lower Orange were known generically as 'Nama', and those north and south of the middle Orange as 'Kora'. In contrast, the region of eastern Transorangia (roughly the present-day Orange Free State) was, in the eighteenth century, occupied only by Khoisan hunter-gatherers alongside Bantu-speakers.[15] In all these cases, and specifically regarding Nama and Kora, it is almost impossible to disentangle which elements were long-established inhabitants of the area, and which had retreated from the Cape during the seventeenth or eighteenth centuries, though there is fragmented evidence of both situations.[16] The resulting tangle of social relationships, exacerbated in the frontier zone period, makes it well-nigh impossible to link Khoisan political groupings in the nineteenth century to any earlier Khoisan political history.[17]

The obsession in the historiography of South Africa with the analysis of society in 'racial' terms produces endless attempts to differentiate Bantu-speakers from Khoisan, Khoikhoi and 'San', Sotho from Nguni, and, within each, sub-tribes from sub-tribes, and so on. It is only through an analysis which begins from the social relations of production that this tendency can be overcome.[18] Indeed, for the purposes of this chapter, the fundamental proposition concerning the societies being discussed here is their similarity. All were small-scale societies in which persons were dependent on forces of nature over which they had but little control. Some communities gathered for subsistence, others hunted, others kept cattle or grew crops. Some engaged in more than one, or all of these practices.

The social relations of production in such communities have been inadequately explored. Certainly there was a sexual division of labour, although this was more pronounced among agriculturalists and mixed-production communities than among pure pastoralists or hunter-gatherers. There were also craft specialisations (blacksmiths, herbalists, rainmakers), mostly in Bantu-speaking communities. Mining was carried on, both of metals and of a decorative yellow ochre called 'sibello': we do not know who did the mining, nor under what compulsions or incentives.[19]

Relationships in all communities were expressed, neither economically nor politically, but in terms of kinship. Kinship was the language of social interaction, disguising the relations of production. The only potential for class relationships existed in societies where there was chieftainship. This office was inherited through lineage descent, and could therefore emerge or disappear in kin-based communities without any basic alteration in social structure. Where it became institutionalised, it was surrounded by a structure of government based on leading lineages: lineage-members were the counsellors of the chief. The officers of government had the obligation to redistribute resources for the benefit of the community, but these obligations obviously required the appropriation of resources to redistribute.[20]

These forms of appropriation have been inadequately investigated. Clearly they involve the appropriation either of labour-time, or of products, or of both. The prerogative of chiefs to receive tribute labour was well established in many Bantu-speaking societies by the nineteenth century (though this practice may have post-dated the upheavals of the Mfecane in the 1820s and 1830s). Equally, the presence of mining products, handicrafts and cattle provided a potential basis for appropriation and for either redistribution or private accumulation.

If redistribution to provide social insurance and attract new members was the main form of 'internal' recycling of goods, a limited amount of trading was the main form of 'external' recycling of goods. By the late eighteenth century, trade was already conditioned by merchant capital: Khoisan traded cattle southward to the Cape; Bantu-speakers exported metals, karosses (hides), finished furs and, increasingly, ivory to the Portuguese settlements of the East Coast.[21] This trade was not carried out by long-distance traders but through a series of relays. It seems likely, therefore, that it grew out of local circulation rather than the reverse. Exchanges of goods customarily took place either at the neutral frontier between communities or at the *kgotla* (forum) in the town centre of the community. Where a chiefly structure existed, the chief attempted to monopolise this trade. Trading disputes may well have been the main cause of the occasional inter-community warfare which took place, warfare which was clearly (as will be seen) exacerbated by the impact of the frontier. Disputes over succession, or over access to limited resources such as water, would also have led to conflict.

Chiefs, and the heads of lineages, would gather around them 'as many Men as their wealth would admit, to each of which they assign the milk of one or two cows which, together with the efforts of the Man's wife in gathering roots, wild fruit, locusts, and the cultivation of a Garden, is generally sufficient to enable him to maintain his family'.[22] At one level this relationship of clientage was simply one of the major ways through which communities could grow on a non- or quasi-kin basis. At another level it was a protofeudal relationship of personal dependence which acquired the name of the *fhisa* or *mafisa* system among Sotho-Tswana in the nineteenth century. It clearly provided the basis for the emergence of a class differentiation between property-owners and serfs. Powerful communities might, through their chief, also hold as tributaries not only single individuals or families, but also internally coherent (kin-based) groups of herders or cultivators. Hunter-gatherers might also become dependents, acquiring dogs, old iron weapons or tobacco from their patrons in return for supplying karosses.[23]

Many of these forms of dependence became possible only to the extent that an export trade existed; equally, the development of an export trade, dominated by the chief and his associated lineage-heads, encouraged such forms of dependence. It is, however, important to emphasise that class relationships remained fluid. Dependent groups or individuals could leave a particular dependency relationship, either for autonomy or for a different relationship with another community. Previously autonomous groups or individuals could become dependent. Overall, mobility was possible. But to the extent that all communities tended towards the development of chieftainship or absorption into a chieftainship, and to the extent that trade was expanding, the situation was ripe for the overall emergence of a class society.

In the eighteenth century this process was interrupted in southern Namibia and central Transorangia by the arrival of Khoisan pastoralists and hunter-gatherers. Their pressure was one of the factors in the demise, south of the Molopo, of the hegemony of the Rolong clan ruled by Tau, whose sway, one source relates, 'extended from the Bahurutsian mountains to the Hamhanna hills, a distance of two hundred miles' (and a considerable sway it was, considering the conditions of communication of the time).[24] Another factor in the Rolong demise was probably the emergence, north of the Molopo, of the Ngwaketse, who competed with the Rolong for the ivory and pelts of the Kalahari borderlands.[25] The Rolong disintegrated into five smaller chiefdoms, some of them moving north and eastwards. Some Rolong tributaries (whether as a group or as fragments is unclear) asserted their autonomy and became known as the Tlhaping. Central Transorangia, as a result, came under the sway of Khoikhoi named the Kora, of the Tlhaping, and of lesser Sotho-Tswana groups.[26]

Of these the most important were the Tlhaping. In 1801 their chief settlement had a population of some 16,000 and was described as being 'in circumference as large as Cape Town'.[27] The hegemony of the Tlhaping extended from the Langeberg in the west to the Harts River in the east, a substantial area (see Fig. 8.1, p. 362).[28] This state was 'multi-ethnic' even in the origins of its rulers. Molehabangwe, then Tlhaping chief, was probably the son of a Kora woman and had at least one Kora wife. His half-Kora son, Mothibi, who succeeded him, married a Kora woman (like others of the ruling lineage), and later confided to a missionary that having 'grown up among the Corannas', he was sceptical of many Tlhaping customs.[29] This state, embracing Sotho-Tswana and Kora, testifies to the irrelevance of the ethnic characterisations of South African historical pseudo-anthropology. The Tlhaping state had, it was later claimed, never been 'so rich or so numerous as in the late eighteenth century'.[30]

Trading, hunting and raiding

From the 1730s the northward thrust of colonial expansion, defined in terms of the registration of farms, turned eastwards from the Oliphants River across the mountains. Apart from an occasional official expediton, the area north of the Oliphants River was left predominantly for the trading, hunting and raiding dimensions of frontier expansion. Until the last two decades of the eighteenth century it is difficult, however, to trace either the chronology of geographic extension of the frontier or much about the activities of frontier settlers.[31] The emergence of the commando-like band, which was the vehicle for the hunting, trading and raiding of the frontier zone, depended on access to firearms, horses and gunpowder. Underlying much of the politics of the frontier zone was a struggle to gain access to arms. The 'opening up' of the Northern Frontier zone and the long persistence of its 'openness' was partly rooted in the multiplicity of channels for the diffusion of arms. Much of the colonial governments' struggle to 'close' the frontier zone was the attempt to exert control over the firearms trade.[32]

Some leaders of the commando-like bands of the Northern Frontier zone were white; others were not. But at first it was colonial subjects who could control and distribute the crucial resources of arms and powder. As they moved out to tap new trade routes or new hunting-grounds, they would have found Khoikhoi eager to accept arms and powder in return for serving as guides. Such a relationship could become transformed into the pattern of the commando band in two overlapping ways. In the first place, Khoikhoi who had lost their cattle and pasture land would attach themselves to frontiersmen and would probably be given the use of a cow or two, hoping to acquire more cattle, a horse and a gun. By the end of the eighteenth century this class of Khoikhoi dependents, some of them having regained autonomy, had become sufficiently numerous to become known as Oorlams, 'that is, Hottentots who come from the upper country [i.e. beyond the 'frontier'] and are born and bred with the farmers; most of whom understand and speak the low Dutch language.'[33]

In the second place, colonists might be invited to intervene in a dispute between indigenous groups. Although also coercive, such intervention differed from raiding. Both forms of coercion, however, involved the risks of detection by the colonial authorities and consequent deprivation of access to arms. Thus veldwachtmeester Adriaan van Zyl, who led a commando to participate in a Kora dispute on the middle Orange, probably in 1786, was banished from the colony.[34] In the 1790s Guilliam Visagie had his grant of a farm at present-day Keetmanshoop in Namibia revoked for leading a band of 'half-breed and Hottentot' raiders, and was brought back to the colony by an Oorlam-led colonial commando.[35] It was somewhat less risky for those with official positions or titles to land to trade in arms and powder, though even here their actions could bring punishment.[36] To avoid difficulties with the colonial government, some 'respectable' frontierspeople retained the services of trustworthy commando leaders whom they recruited either from deserters or from among the Oorlams.[37]

A case in point was veldwachtmeester·Petrus Pienaar, a man well respected among his fellows.[38] The owner of several farms in the northwest, he turned his attention in the 1780s to the valley of the middle Orange. There he met Jan Bloem, a German from Thuringia who had deserted from a ship in Cape Town in 1780, murdered his wife, and fled to the Orange.[39] Pienaar established Bloem on his farm on the Orange, provided him with powder, and sold the cattle which Bloem was able to capture. Bloem acquired a following of Kora and raided not only the other Kora communities but Sotho-Tswana as well, moving his base of operations further into central Transorangia. This 'firearm frontier' furthered the Kora thrust, to roll back the area of Sotho-Tswana hegemony. As Bloem moved towards central Transorangia, Pienaar acquired another commando leader, an Oorlam named Klaas Afrikaner, who had earned a reputation for his role in large colonially-authorised straf commandos against the Khoisan in 1792. After refusing to be conscripted into military service in Cape Town, he settled at Pienaar's farm on the Orange and began to raid. Afrikaner made south Namibia his sphere of operations.[40]

Besides white frontierspeople and their Khoikhoi-Oorlam dependents, the so-called Bastaards began to play an increasingly important role in the Northern Frontier zone. The word 'bastaard' of course indicates illegitimate birth, but within the social system of the Cape Colony it acquired two further meanings. In the first place it came to specifically denote the children of mixed parentage, particularly white and Khoikhoi, but also slave and Khoikhoi.[41] Initially such persons acquired a stigma because of their illegitimacy as much as their colour; indeed, children of inter-ethnic marriages could be more readily absorbed into the white community. Moreover, the term Bastaard apparently denoted an economic category as much as a social status of illegitimacy or colour. Thus Maynier described the Bastaards as 'such Hottentots, *particularly* [i.e. not only] of the mixed race, who possessed some property, who were more civilised'.[42]

Partly, no doubt, because of their descent from higher status groups, the 'Bastaards' gravitated to less menial jobs than hired farm labour or domestic service. They were transport riders, day labourers, small farmers, or craftspeople. Or they were 'a superior and confidential type of servant', trusted to take charge of a farm during the owner's absence, or to act as overseers on loan farms. Lichtenstein wrote that when a master died, such a servant would often assume his name, 'and not infrequently sought himself some little spot, to which he retired with all belonging to him, and gained a subsistence for himself and his family by the breeding of cattle.'[43]

Their colonial affiliations through descent encouraged the Bastaards to acquire other forms of colonial status. Lichtenstein noted that they 'were educated in Christianity: they learnt to sing psalms, and to read: and were, even to receiving the sacrament of baptism, as good Christians as the offspring of Europeans'.[44] At the turn of the century the Bastaards of the Orange River valley saw themselves as 'swarthy Hollanders' and 'in their behaviour there was a certain good-natured ostentation, a sort of vanity, which seemed to show that they considered themselves as much superior to the rude Hottentots'.[45] Others who were not illegitimate or of part-white descent might aspire to Bastaard status. Among them were slaves and Khoikhoi as well as people of mixed descent who were trusted as overseers or who acquired the independence of small property-owners. Colonial officials claimed that runaway slaves, particularly those of part-Khoikhoi descent, found it easy to pass themselves off as Bastaards in the interior.[46] It is significant that both the two most wealthy and powerful Bastaard families of the Orange appear to have had slave origins. One of these was the Koks: Adam Kok and his sons Cornelius and Salomon. Adam Kok was a manumitted slave who acquired a farm at Piketberg in the mid-eighteenth century.[47] The other was the Berends family, including the brothers Klaas and Piet, though whether they were by origin slaves or 'mixed' Bastaards is not so clear.[48] Oorlams and other Khoikhoi may also have aspired to the status of Bastaards.[49]

Bastaards certainly participated, along with whites, Oorlams and Khoikhoi, in the raiding expeditions of the Northern Frontier zone.[50] But apparently some leading Bastaard families were attempting towards the end of the eighteenth century to create, or recreate, more stable patterns of trading. This attempt may well have been associated with the emergence of an ivory trade on the frontier which complemented the cattle trading that had dominated throughout the eighteenth century. In 1780 Klaas Berends and his followers probably formed the vanguard of the trading frontier among Khoikhoi in southern Namibia and even higher up on the Orange.[51] Within two decades both the Kok and the Berends families had begun to establish relationships with the Tlhaping, and Cornelius Kok and a follower had even ventured further on at least one trading expedition to the Rolong.[52]

Two factors may have contributed toward the stabilisation of trade with the Sotho-Tswana. The Sotho-Tswana were less easily raided than the Khoisan communities. Secondly, the dwindling number of elephants in the Orange River valley[53] forced traders to tap the north-easterly trade routes controlled by the Sotho-Tswana. A desire to sell ivory directly to Cape Town,[54] instead of through white farmers acting as agents, probably also encouraged the Bastaards to build a stable order and trading relationships in the frontier zone. For, by assisting the colonial authorities in the establishment of stability, they could hope to have their rights and privileges of access protected by the colonial government.[55]

Between 1800 and 1820 Bastaard-Tlhaping trade relationships became firmly institutionalised.[56] However, the Bastaards were not able to significantly extend their trading hinterland beyond the Tlhaping. This was partly a result of Tlhaping success in defending their monopoly by blocking the movements of white and Bastaard traders. The Tlhaping, moreover, were very selective about what they would accept in exchange for cattle or ivory. They sold ivory for sheep, which they did not possess, or for tobacco or dagga, which they did not grow but which the Bastaards did. Cattle were sold for carefully selected beads, for raw iron, or for cloth.[57] In 1801 the Tlhaping were unimpressed by the looking-glasses, linen handkerchiefs, tinderboxes and knives brought by an official colonial expedition, regarding their own knives as superior; indeed, they were at the time selling knives, hatchets and other metalware to the Bastaards.[58] Nevertheless, trading with the Tlhaping and hunting in their territory proved fairly profitable for the Bastaards and others. A profit of some 8 rixdollars (nearly 100 per cent) could be made on a cow sold in the colony, and considerably higher profits on a tusk of ivory.[59]. Certainly the first missionaries on the Orange, who engaged in ivory trading, did well.[60]

Stable ivory hunting and trading, controlled by the leading Bastaard families, overlaid but by no means supplanted illegal raiding of cattle in the Northern Frontier zone and their sale, in exchange for arms, to the frontier farmers. This illegal trading dominated on the lower Orange. After 1800 the Bastaard-Tlhaping relationships on the middle Orange seemed to presage a new pattern, the continuation of which, however, depended on the ability of the Bastaards to control the channels for the diffusion of arms. This became a well-nigh impossible task as white colonists with arms to sell registered land titles closer and closer to the Orange.

In particular, a new threat to this more peaceful trade emerged from the extension to the Kora of the illegal arms trading conducted by white frontiersmen like Coenraad Bezuidenhout, Cobus Vry, Gerrit Coetzee and Coenraad de Buys as well as Bastaards from the Eastern Cape.[61] From about the 1820s the illegal trade in arms extended more deeply into central and eastern Transorangia with such people as intermediaries, and led to cattle raiding and the seizure of hunter-gatherer 'apprentices'.[62] 'Such Bastaards', wrote Governor Somerset in 1817, were 'expert in the use of firearms' and subsisted 'in great measure from the game they kill'. However, he continued, 'to procure firearms they must revisit the Colony and bring with them something which will induce the itinerant traders to supply them with these prohibited articles. The consequence is that they plunder the distant tribes and traffic with the booty'.[63] This eruption of the firearms frontier in control of new people, both weaned followers away from the leading Bastaard families and placed firearms in the hands of Kora and Sotho-Tswana groups in Transorangia, something that the Bastaard ivory traders had sought to prevent.[64]

Land claims and territorial rights

On the Eastern Frontier the stabilisation of social relationships was achieved by the colonial government from 1811–12 through the 'closing' of the frontier zone (ch. 9, pp. 447–58). It thereby established effective colonial control and entrenched the domination of a community consisting almost exclusively of white farmers. The initial attempt to normalise relationships in the Northern Frontier zone was, by contrast, undertaken by the leading Bastaard families both with and without colonial co-operation. They tried not only to regularise trade, as we have seen, but also to assert effective claims to territory and political authority.

Whites and others in the frontier zone who formerly claimed land *de facto* through the power of the commando now increasingly had to seek a colonial 'legitimisation' to retain that title. Even a Khoikhoi could retain legitimate title by obtaining colonial recognition of his status as chief, with a staff of office and rights to territory.[65] But, to the extent that there were competing claims to territory, registration of an individual title was a more secure long-term guarantee. For some who were not white, particularly baptised Bastaards, it was possible to register colonial land titles in the same way as whites.[66] Moreover, Bastaards held on to land, whether registered or unregistered, in isolated areas in the Zwartberg, the Cedarberg, De Koup and Nieuwveld, the Zak River and elsewhere.[67]

A good example of Bastaard land ownership was Little Namaqualand. In general, the northward extension of *de jure* settlement was slow north of the Oliphants River,[68] for the area was unsuited to agricultural or pastoral production.[69] In the late eighteenth century Bastaards could still obtain farms here easily, as is apparent from the farms which Kok, Diedericks, Brand, Meyer and other baptised Bastaards received.[70] Of these the most prominant family was undoubtedly the Koks. Adam Kok, the manumitted slave, was granted the farm Stinkfontein between 1751 and 1760 and received 'burgher rights' at apparently the same time.[71] Adam died in 1795, but his son Cornelius had already registered at least four other Namaqualand farms in his name. In 1799 the local veldwachtmeester wrote that Cornelius had become his 'one great help', and contemporary accounts indicate Cornelius's considerable wealth and status. He even had white bijwoners (tenant farmers), and was baptised some time between 1795 and 1803.[72]

Such a concentration of Bastaards in Little Namaqualand may already have been a consequence of their extrusion from less remote areas by white frontier colonists.[73] The later movement, at the turn of the century, of Bastaards, Oorlams and others who were not white from Little Namaqualand to the middle Orange may have partly resulted from the same pressures as well as from the attraction of hunting and trading in Tlhaping territory. It was also caused by new pressures on brown people within the colony, for example, changes in the terms of military service. Throughout the eighteenth century, Bastaards and Khoikhoi were active participants in officially authorised commandos. Indeed, in many instances whites sent such dependents on commando as their substitutes.[74] This in itself may have been seen as a burden: 'All the Hottentots and Bastaards fit for commandos', complained a veldwachtmeester in 1778, 'are going away to Namaqua country to evade serving on commandos . . . [they are] trafficking and bartering with the Namaquas.'[75] The position became worse with the formation of the *Corps Pandoeren* in Cape Town in 1781–82 (see ch.1, pp. 35–38). Not only did this require military service away from the frontier, but for Bastaards it meant enrolling under the lower status of 'Hottentot'. It was the summons to the Corps Pandoeren which induced Klaas Afrikaner to set himself up as a raider in the 1790s and which in 1814 provoked a revolt among Bastaards and Oorlams of the middle Orange.[76]

Regulations governing dependents also began to be tightened towards the end of the eighteenth century and began to impinge more directly on Bastaards. By 1783 some colonists argued that the emergence of the Bastaards must be 'mischievous' since they might produce 'a leader of talent to unite the injured Hottentots, and perhaps the slaves, against the white inhabitants.'[77] In the 1770s there were moves to compel Bastaards to carry passes and to 'apprentice' slave-Khoikhoi offspring, though to what extent these were a result or a cause of the Bastaard movement to the frontier zone is not clear.[78] This movement or 'desertion' was probably encouraged by the more stringent regulation of 'Hottentot' labour in the Caledon and Cradock codes of 1809 and 1812 respectively, following the abolition of the slave trade in 1808[79] (see ch. 1, pp. 40–41). From this time, it would seem, the colonial mind steadily assimilated the Bastaards into the category of a homogeneous 'Hottentot' (Coloured) labouring class. Commissioner Bigge referred to 'the Hottentots . . . in which class is generally included the mixed race of Hottentots and the white and free coloured inhabitants denominated "Bastaards".'[80]

These were the conditions under which leading Bastaard families attempted, after 1800, to establish new claims to land on the middle Orange. In doing so they were not alone. Jan Bloem, a white, in the 1780s and 1790s seemed to have welded together disparate Kora and Khoisan hunter-gatherers into a multi-ethnic unit, taking a wife from each new group. His final venture to construct a wider military alliance against the Ngwaketse failed, and on his return to the middle Orange Bloem died of poisoning.[81]

Petrus Pienaar's other protegé, Klaas Afrikaner, was in the long run more successful in building a new social order in the frontier zone. In the mid-1790s Afrikaner and his sons fell out with Pienaar, killed him at his farm, and from an island base on the Orange began to accumulate a growing following of Khoisan of the lower Orange valley, and even a scattering of Xhosa displaced from the Eastern Frontier. For a short period this political grouping fought against the colony in a war contemporary and perhaps even co-ordinated with the 1799 Khoikhoi rebellion on the Eastern Frontier (see ch. 1, pp. 33–35). Afrikaner was joined by rebellious dependents and opposed by colonial commandos, including both white and leading Bastaard families.[82] A state of mistrustful peace was restored between the colony and Afrikaner at the same time that the Eastern Frontier rebellion died away. For a time some missionaries had hopes of the emergence of an Oorlam-led state on the lower Orange parallel to that of the Bastaards in central Transorangia. But the dependence of Afrikaner's community on raiding militated against such a development. They moved further northwards into Namibia in the 1820s, where both the Afrikaner family and other Oorlam groups came to exert substantial hegemony through much of the nineteenth century.[83]

From shortly after the turn of the century, attempts to consolidate Transorangia politically came from the southeast rather than the southwest. Between 1805 and about 1814 the communities of the middle Orange valley and central Transorangia – Kora, Sotho-Tswana, and Bastaards alike – were harassed by a Xhosa-led raiding community, numbering perhaps three to five hundred, which appears to have been obtaining supplies of firearms from frontier farmers.[84] One of its original leaders was one Danster, a Xhosa who was for a while a follower of Afrikaner. In 1814 he was acting as a guide to the former Eastern Frontier 'rebel', Coenraad de Buys, in Transorangia. Thereafter De Buys built up and led the most prominent Transorangian raiding community. He was able to win supporters from the Xhosa and dissident Bastaards and Oorlams by providing them with arms.[85] His last venture in the Transorangia frontier zone was to construct a military alliance from Tlhaping, Rolong and others against the Kwena or Fokeng chiefdom, the Motlala. His venture was as unsuccessful as Bloem's. Thereafter he decisively separated himself from the trade links to the south and attached himself successively to a number of Sotho-Tswana communities, moving along the lines of trade with the Portuguese settlements on the East Coast.[86]

The firearms frontier, and the commando-like organisation which accompanied it, therefore, had a disruptive effect along the whole length of the Orange River valley. Between 1750 and 1800 the expansion of the northern colonial frontier zone had drastically compressed the belt where Khoisan lived, squeezing them against the southernmost limit of the Sotho-Tswana and intensifying conflict amongst themselves and between them and the Sotho-Tswana. Those who were dispossessed saw few ways to regain their cattle except plundering; those who retained their cattle sought the means to defend them. In both cases the means were greater access, and privileged access, to arms and powder. But obtaining these goods generally meant selling cattle, or selling 'apprentices', along the southward trade routes, and this perpetuated and extended the cycle of raiding and robbery.

Firearms not only caused the breakdown of existing social structures but also transformed them. The forms of political organisation which were re-created on the basis of firearms were, as Moorsom has argued, essentially parasitic.[87] The commando-based bands of the frontier zone became dependent on appropriating the production of others through raiding. As such productive resources became exhausted, the tendency was to seek them further afield rather than to create the conditions for renewed production. The hunting and trading in ivory was different from the trading and raiding of cattle, for the depletion of ivory did not drain the vital resources of the existing communities of the area; by contrast cattle, which were necessary for human subsistence, were depleted to levels where they could not reproduce fast enough to maintain the size of the herds.

The missionaries, who in 1801 came to live among the Bastaards of the middle Orange, dogmatically believed that greater economic and political stability could be achieved by the introduction of agriculture by the Bastaards themselves. But in fact, as a Griqua later argued to Andrew Smith, either pastoralism or agriculture or both would have provided an economic base.[88] More important was the ecological question: which form of production was best for a given area? There was also a political question: under what conditions could the necessary military power and political authority be generated to protect such an economic base?

Missionaries and the Griqua state, 1800–1814

In 1800 the decisive step took place in the migration of the leading Bastaard families from Little Namaqualand towards the middle Orange. At that time Jan Bloem died in central Transorangia, and on the lower Orange Afrikaner's forces were disrupting trade into Namibia.[89] For several years drought and the activities of Afrikaner made the Bastaards uncertain where to establish themselves, but in 1804–05 they planted crops at a number of fountains around Klaarwater (later Griquatown) with good results. In April 1805 they began building houses in stone, and they and their followers, numbering pehaps 400 to 500, took possession of a line of springs running some fifty miles southwest and northeast of Klaarwater. Other more distant fountains – they were to become Campbell and Danielskuil – were also identified at this time, though settled later.[90]

At this time the development of the new Bastaard-dominated political community in Transorangia became inextricably entangled with the London Missionary Society, whose missionaries had started to arrive at the Cape in 1799. The British and Batavian regimes took some time to come to terms with the phenomenon of missionary activity: were its social effects likely to be dangerous or desirable? At the turn of the nineteenth century, missionaries were beginning to establish mission stations inside the Cape Colony for the incipient 'Coloured' community who sought from the missions a measure of economic autonomy which would reduce their dependence on service with colonial farmers (see ch. 1, pp. 38–40). As far as the colonial government was concerned, however, these institutions were to maintain social order and to preach the dignity of wage-labour. Missionaries thus faced pressures exerted by their conflicting socio-political roles, and adopted a variety of responses.[91]

The Bastaards themselves, probably the Berends family, first invited the London Missionary Society (LMS) to move to the middle Orange from the station they had established among Bastaards and Khoisan hunter-gatherers at the Zak River.[92] With the arrival on the middle Orange of William Anderson in 1801, a permanent missionary presence was established in the area.[93]

The Bastaards who invited the missionaries to the middle Orange apparently wanted to retain, and even strengthen, certain kinds of links with the colony at the same time that they were separating themselves from it geographically. They wanted access to the Cape Town market and a legal means of procuring arms and powder. They also wanted to sustain their status as Christians, since, in colonial eyes, church membership had a close correlation with citizenship.[94] In this sense they saw the missionaries as something like representatives of the colonial government, expecting them to ensure their equality of status with colonists. At the same time they were concerned to develop a polity with an autonomous economic base to supplement their trading activities. For this, too, they wanted the missionaries' support, desiring them to represent to the colony their collective rather than their individual interests. These contrary expectations of colonial citizenship and political independence created tensions which were compounded by the colonial authorities' suspicions of missionaries. The Batavian distrust of missions beyond the colony led to the recall of J.T. van der Kemp from among the Xhosa. However, two official colonial expeditions in 1801 and 1805 reported favourably both on the mission at Klaarwater and on the Bastaards.[95]

The 1801 expedition apparently regarded the Bastaard community as autonomous and under the authority of the Kok and Berends families, but favourably disposed towards the colony; it was prepared to allocate to Anderson and the Bastaards a supply of powder for the defence of the mission station.[96] The expedition of 1805, led by the landdrost of the newly-established district of Tulbagh, laid down much firmer regulations for the conduct of the mission, based on Governor Janssens's edict of February 1805. This edict recognised the right of accredited missionaries to teach and promote 'religion and cultivation among the heathen nations' beyond the colonial borders, but far enough away that they had 'no communication with the inhabitants upon these boundaries, much less with those that live within them, either Christians or Heathens'. Moreover, the missionaries had the obligation to teach 'the first ideas of social order such as exists in the mother-country . . . as far as the capacity of the Natives is fit for comprehending [it].' The teaching of writing was forbidden (though this part of the edict may not have been confirmed).[97] The landdrost elaborated on the edict by lecturing to the inhabitants of the Klaarwater settlement on 'obedience' to Anderson as 'one of their first duties; assuring them that the neglect of it would be considered as an offence against government, and would be punished accordingly.'[98]

The terms of this edict attempted a dramatic transformation in the relationship of the Bastaards and their followers with the colony. It expressly precluded them from trading with frontier farmers or with Cape Town, except through the missionaries themselves.[99] By implication it therefore encouraged them to become subsistence agriculturalists and pastoralists. But could such a transformation be effectively implemented? The government could impose direct sanctions against Bastaards who came within the area of effective colonial authority, but not within the frontier zone itself.[100]

It was the missionaries who were ultimately most dependent on their attachments to the colony, logistically, culturally and personally. Thus sanctions could effectively be imposed on them by the colonial authorities and through them on the Bastaards. Indeed, the missionaries were quick to make use of the authority thus bestowed upon them by the colonial authorities. People who refused to help build a mission-house were threatened with government retribution; potential dissidents were warned that leaving the station would mean loss of their guns and of access to the colony. Missionaries distributed powder to ensure the loyalty of those at the settlement and to encourage the adherence of new members. They negotiated with groups hostile to the settlement, allocated and redistributed land and water resources, adjudicated disputes, and punished crimes.[101]

The community over which the missionaries attempted to exert such an authority was a growing one with considerable social stratification and a changing economy. The Berends following, which invited Anderson to the Orange in 1801, may have numbered about 200 people. In 1813 the numbers appear to have increased to 1,266 Bastaards (including 291 adult males) and 1,341 Kora.[102] This increase was partly due to an increasing drift from the lower Orange and the Eastern Frontier, and partly to the incorporation of Khoisan communities on the spot. In these Bastaard-dominated communities there were considerable gradations of wealth and status. At the head were the prominent Bastaard families. Cornelius Kok, who in 1816 moved to the middle Orange with 500 followers, owned perhaps some 45,000 sheep at his various farms.[103] Of the 3,000 cattle estimated at Klaarwater in 1812, Adam J. Kok (son of Cornelius) may have owned as many as 400, besides his 1,000 sheep, 800 goats and 3 teams of oxen. Other 'big men' among the Bastaards might have herds of 50 to 200 cows, while poorer Bastaards and others might have 2 or 3 cattle each.[104] The wealthier families had dependants whose treatment varied widely. While the Koks were noted for their benevolence, others among the Bastaards acted 'with great severity flogging and abusing them like slaves.'[105] Kora dependents were considered indolent and 'Bushmen' dependents were preferred, especially for herding cattle at a distance from where the owner lived. By the 1820s it was very common for Bastaard cattle-owners to contract 'Bushmen' for hire, the men to herd the cattle and the women to guard the fields.[106]

The main form of production was clearly pastoral, and cow's or goat's milk, supplemented by meat, was the basic diet. After 1804 crop cultivation, predominantly of maize and wheat, though with some vegetables, increased. The basic problem was the drying up of the fountains around Klaarwater. In 1812 Anderson stated that the maize crop was insufficient for subsistence needs. In the following decade cultivation by irrigation started at Campbell and Danielskuil.[107]

The political structure of the Klaarwater community resembled three overlapping forms which had already existed in Little Namaqualand. The first was the authority of a Khoikhoi chief sometimes officially recognised by the colony. The second, characteristic of the frontier zone, was the authority of commando band leaders, created through their access to arms and powder and sustained through the distribution of spoils. The third was the power, implicitly reinforced in colonial law, of the head of a colonial family over its members and dependents. Colonial farms, argued Lichtenstein, were almost 'states in miniature'.[108] In all these respects the dominant figure of authority for the Bastaards in 1800 was Cornelius Kok, a wealthy farm-owner, a leading hunter and trader, and possibly already the possessor of a staff of office from the colonial government.[109] In 1801 Cornelius 'appeared not only to command love and respect but also . . . to maintain his directions by the good feeling and co-operation of those about him. His followers . . . bore him willing allegiance from affection: his interests seemed closely connected with theirs, and his superiority as chief or captain was tacitly acknowledged.'[110]

In 1804 or 1805, relates Lichtenstein, 'the persons of most distinction among the Bastaard Hottentots were appointed as magistrates to inspect and take care of the rest.'[111] This new office of magistrate represented, at least potentially, a change in the form of political authority away from the patriarchy of the leading families, the Koks and the Berends. It seems plausible that this innovation was stimulated by the missionaries. Initially, however, the actual appointments (it is not clear how they were made) seem to have confirmed the authority of the leading families. Two of the magistrates, Salomon Kok and 'Kort Adam' Kok, were members of the Kok family and a third, Hans Lucas, was a close Kok associate. Two others, Piet and Klaas Berends, were from the second leading family, and another, Jan Hendrick, was a close Berends associate.[112] At this time the magistrates, in the words of a later *kaptyn* at Griquatown, 'governed . . . in the name of old Cornelius Kok, as his deputies.'[113] But whatever its initial nature, the new office of magistrate created the potential for the development of 'popular' or at least anti-patriarchal power among the Griqua. The stage was set for tensions similar to those between the patriarchal military leader and the 'Volksraad' party which can be traced to as early as the Eastern Frontier 'republics' of the period (see ch. 9, pp. 440–443), and which characterised much frontier politics on the highveld after the Great Trek.[114]

At Klaarwater, the potential tensions involved an additional factor: the missionaries. The Janssens edict of 1805 gave the missionaries a political mandate, potentially in conflict with the patriarchal structure and with the magistrates. At the same time the missionaries were increasingly not 'above and outside' the Klaarwater community, but actively involved in its social nexus, firstly, through marriages (the missionaries married into both the Pienaar and Engelbrecht families)[115] and secondly through the emergence of a church membership at Klaarwater. Baptism commenced in 1807, and within two years the church had twenty-six adult and forty-six child members; by 1813 there were forty-two adults.[116]

The church members formed a cohesive political grouping, subject to the discipline of the missionaries, which could exert a powerful influence on the community either in its own interests or those of the missionaries. Moreover, it offered to less powerful and less wealthy members of the community, those not close to the leading families, a new status which could be used politically to challenge old elites. Early converts included members of the Pienaar, Hendricks and Goeyman families, as well as 'diligent' agriculturalists such as Moses Adam Renoseros or Willem Fortuin.[117] Another early convert was Andries Waterboer, who was to become kaptyn in 1820. Born in 1789, he was of 'Bushman' extraction with apparently no white ancestry and, according to some accounts, came to Klaarwater as a dependent of Adam J. Kok. The missionaries saw him as a 'truly serious young man' who had 'distinguished himself above all our people in receiving instruction,' and he soon became their principal interpreter.[118] Moreover, some of the appointed magistrates soon gravitated to the 'church party' and became church members.

Although the records are obscure on these points, it may have been the growing influence of the missionaries through the church, even to the extent of weaning the magistrates away from their client-like dependence on the leading families, which provoked counter-reaction. Certainly between 1807 and 1809 the original magistrates were dismissed and replaced by Adam J. Kok and Berend Berends. In 1809 Anderson, travelling to Cape Town, obtained the sanction of Governor Caledon for these appointments, but Caledon regarded them as 'chiefs' rather than as 'magistrates' and granted each of them a staff of office. Significantly, in the same memorial Anderson appealed to the colony to grant baptised members of the mission 'common privileges' with other colonial citizens, particularly free access to the colony.[119] The counter-reaction of the leading families against the church party may have won support by pointing out that increased missionary influence had gone along with attempts to regulate the community's previously unrestricted access to the colony rather than with any secular benefits.

Four years later, in 1813, there was a fresh attempt to establish a political structure for the community which could integrate the claims of the leading families with the increasing influence of the church and popular elements, and give a due place to the missionaries. These innovations were introduced by John Campbell, a director of the LMS, on a tour of South African stations.

One of Campbell's proposals was that the Bastaards change their name to 'Griqua' and that Klaarwater be renamed Griquatown, because 'on consulting among themselves they found a majority were descended from a person of the name of Griqua', that is, from the eponymous ancestor of the Khoikhoi clan, the /Karihur ('Chariguriqua').[120] The truth of this contention is less important than the change in reference-point from the colonial origins of the Bastaards to their claims of indigenous ancestry. The name change aimed, therefore, to break down the distinction between those who saw themselves as 'swarthy Hollanders' and those who were Oorlams, Kora or 'Bushmen', and thus to provide a means whereby indigenous Khoisan could become integrated into the polity. However, the old distinction and concomitant tension persisted for some time, being constantly reinforced by those Bastaards who moved to Transorangia from the colony, and by the persistence of aboriginal Khoisan identities. But as early as the 1820s the distinctions between 'descendants of the colonists and of the aboriginal tribes' were reportedly breaking down.[121] And the name 'Griqua' survived into the late nineteenth and early twentieth centuries in nostalgic remembrance of a better past.

Campbell also drew up a constitution. Adam J. Kok and Berend Berends were to remain as chiefs or kaptyns to act as 'commanders in things requiring the public safety' and, jointly with the missionaries, as a court of appeal. Thus was the status of the leading families formally protected. But by this time their influence was further on the wane, extending, it was reported in 1811, 'very little beyond a voluntary submission on the part of the people. It is confined principally to that of ordering out the force of the tribe to attack an enemy, or to take up arms in defence of the settlement …. But in ordinary cases, their power does not seem to be so strong, as the good of their society requires.'[122] Under the Campbell constitution, at the same time, the popular elements secured their representation by electing nine magistrates who would be responsible for enforcing a constitution of thirteen clauses. For the most part this constitution affirmed existing prohibitions, those which had derived from the missionary interpretation of the 1805 edict. It also imposed severe punishments. Murder would be punished by execution; house-breaking, theft or robbery by flogging or hard labour. In 1816 important amendments provided for fines for failing to clear irrigation channels or failing to cultivate land.[123]

The final innovation concerned the church, and was probably the work of the Eastern Frontier missionary, James Read, who accompanied Campbell. At the first LMS station at Bethelsdorp Van der Kemp had sought to involve Khoikhoi converts rapidly as officers of the church and itinerant evangelists. Campbell supported such a 'native agency', because a self-propagating church would release missionaries to begin work in more distant areas of southern Africa.[124] Therefore Campbell's visit was rapidly followed by the election of deacons in the Griquatown church and, in August 1814 at Graaff-Reinet at a meeting, by the appointment of six 'native agents' to work in Transorangia, two from Bethelsdorp and four from Griquatown.[125]

All these innovations together provided the political basis for the strengthening of the Griquatown community, and indeed constructed a 'democratic oligarchy' which, as Ross has argued, formed the basis for most subsequent Griqua captaincies.[126] The native agency also provided a potential basis for the geographical extension of political authority over new territory and peoples. Thus, in the years after 1814, native agents settled themselves above and below Griquatown on the lower Orange and also north and east further into Transorangia.[127] Their immediate purpose was evangelisation. But, aspiring to be leaders of the communities in which they were situated, their latent political role was either to be for or against the Griquatown polity. In some cases individuals explicitly combined political and religious functions. Thus Berend Berends (kaptyn, deacon and native agent) and Peter Davids (magistrate, deacon and native agent) were initially at Kloof (formerly Hardcastle) after 1814, but before 1820 had moved to Danielskuil on the northeastern border of Griqua territory.[128] Equally, members of the Kok family, although some were not so woven into the Griquatown political or church structure, moved from the core of the polity to the settlement of Campbell.[129] Significantly both Danielskuil and Campbell had much greater potential for crop cultivation than did Griquatown itself.

In 1816 James Read, moving to the Tlhaping to re-establish an LMS station there in the wake of abortive attempts earlier in the century, took with him a number of native agents. Read concentrated on attempts to introduce improvements in agriculture and left religious instruction to Jan Hendricks, Griquatown magistrate, deacon and native agent.[130] At the same time native agents from Bethelsdorp were established both among the Kora in the Harts-Vaal area and at several stations for hunter-gatherers along the upper reaches of the Orange.[131]

Thus the native agency after 1814 created a core of Bastaards and Khoisan, exerting religious authority over a wide geographic spread of peoples from the lower Orange in the west to the Tlhaping in the north and across to the Harts-Vaal area in the east. Nominally these people were subject to the religious authority of the LMS. But where did their political allegiances lie? Depending on the character of this political allegiance, they could act as foci for the extension of the hegemony of the Griquatown state, as nuclei for revolt against it, or as centres of autonomous political authority. In fact, in the ensuing years some of them played each of these roles.

Missionaries and central Transorangia, 1814–1820

In January 1814 the colonial government commanded William Anderson to supply twenty youths between the ages of seventeen and twenty from the Griquatown mission for the Cape (Hottentot) Regiment (formerly the Corps Pandoeren;[132] see ch. 1, pp. 35–38). This order was the first serious attempt by the colonial government to 'close' the Northern Frontier zone, at precisely the time when it had successfully completed this task on the Eastern Frontier. Because of the different conditions of the Northern Frontier zone, however, this attempt not only precipitated a rebellion which dislocated such political stability as had been achieved by the Griqua, but also kept the frontier zone in Transorangia 'open' for another three decades.

The colonial government, in a letter to Anderson, defined the relationship between Griquatown and the colony. It stated: 'you may urge that your Institution is without the Colonial Border and therefore not properly subject to the Government of this territory, but it is also to be remarked that you have on every occasion received protection from the Colony . . . . If you then wish that this protection should be continued the Condition imposed must be that, by which every Society is bound, viz. that of contributing to the General Protection.'[133] The colony was now urging the Griqua to seek out and return to the colony any 'deserters' – slaves, Khoikhoi, Bastaards and criminals – along the Orange River valley.[134] This was a new level of intervention by the colonial government, which wished both to tighten its authority and to obtain further labour resources for the colony.[135]

From Anderson's point of view the 'protection' accorded hitherto by the colony had been far from satisfactory. He had had to struggle to secure that access to arms, powder and the colonial market which would foster Bastaard hegemony in central Transorangia. For the Griqua the demand for military service in the colony, made more unpalatable by the low and segregated status of a 'Hottentot' regiment, was the breaking point. It seemed to deny their autonomy, however dependent, guaranteed by the colonial recognition of the kaptyns in 1809, and by Campbell's constitution in 1813. They would serve the colony in their 'native place', they insisted, but they would not furnish recruits. Anderson hastened to the colony to plead with the authorities. They told him that the Griqua could expect no assistance or protection, and they withdrew their support from the kaptyns, insisting that the Griqua were subject to colonial law.[136]

Anderson returned to Griquatown in February 1815 to find, not surprisingly, severe demoralisation and dissension. This soon escalated into actual revolt against the Griquatown polity as many of its subjects moved to the Harts River (some 80 km away) and styled themselves the 'Hartenaars'. In part they were reverting to the trading-raiding patterns that had predominated in the Northern Frontier zone up to 1800. They linked up with the networks of illegal trade in arms and powder and began to raid Khoisan communities for cattle and 'apprentices'.[137] But their rebellion was also the rejection by a frontier zone community of attempts to 'close' the frontier through an extension of effective colonial control. As such it was related to the revolts by white Eastern frontiersmen between 1795 and 1815 (see ch. 9, pp. 438–41 and 450). It was indeed, contemporaneous with the Slachtersnek rebellion, the participants in which, like the Griqua rebels, were known as 'Patriots'.[138] Significantly too, Coenraad de Buys, the former Eastern Frontier rebel who had crossed the Orange in 1814, was among the Hartenaars. He did not instigate the revolt, but he could extend and confirm the participants' perceptions of their grievances.[139]

The revolt was therefore directed ultimately against the colony and the attempt to extend its authority. But since this authority was mediated through both the missionaries and the political structures established by the Campbell constitution of 1813, these, too, became objects of attack. Significantly, however, it was the kaptyns (the bearers of patriarchal authority, now sanctioned by the colonial government in weaker form) rather than the popularly chosen magistrates who were the major focus of hostility.

The dissidents commenced their revolt by refusing to cultivate, and by referring to Campbell's laws as the 'punishments'. Anderson and the kaptyns were blamed for the demand for conscripts, for the lack of gunpowder and for the prohibition on legal entry to the colony. 'You may compel me to stay, but you can't compel me to work' said one leader to Anderson. This hostility to the political role of the missionaries extended to their educational and evangelical activities.[140] 'As to losing their teachers they did very well before they came and could do again as well without them', said another. At the Harts, it was reported, the rebels 'had given up all religious worship' and some went so far as to 'testify their aversion to it.' Anticipating that many still at the station would support them, they planned to attack Griquatown, seize the gunpowder, and shoot Anderson and Kaptyn Kok (but not Berends). The Hartenaars, it was said, 'had bound themselves not to speak Dutch, nor to ask after each other's welfare' (the latter point no doubt being a reference to habits of bourgeois politeness which had been inculcated by the missionaries).[141] Since former pillars of the community and the church (such as Jacob Cloete, church member and elected magistrate) were among the leaders of the revolt, those who remained supporters of the church were also particular foci for hostility.[142]

Anderson's first response to the widespread rebellion was a renewed attempt to win free access to the colony for those authorised by the mission. In return, he said, the Griqua would try to capture and return deserters.[143] The colonial authorities were not interested in this compromise. Anderson then fell back on trying to boost the authority of the leading families, including summoning the patriarch, Cornelius Kok, to move to the Griquatown area from the middle Orange. This, too, was of no avail: the Campbell constitution had reaffirmed a new source of authority (the elected magistrates), and the popular aspirations this aroused could not now be denied.[144] Anderson therefore shifted his position and began to make overtures to the rebels, saying that he would withdraw support from the kaptyns and bolster the authority of the council of magistrates.

On this basis the Hartenaars began to return to Griquatown, and by the middle of 1817 most of them had been pardoned and re-admitted to the church. Berends and Kok, the loyalist leaders, were summoned several times before the newly emboldened council of magistrates (an unprecedented occurrence), and reprimanded for their neglect of duty. They then 'became dissatisfied, went from the presence of the Council, and Captain A. Kok threw away his Captain's Staff and immediately removed from the place, with his whole family, to the Great Orange River. Berend Berends also left the place, with a small following.'[145] In withdrawing, Berends and Kok accused Anderson of unwarranted leniency towards the rebels: 'his system is contrary to the Bible and he wishes to be a terror to them that do well and protect them that do evil.'[146]

Neither the return of the Hartenaars, nor the departure of Kok and

Berends to Campbell and Danielskuil respectively, restored complete tranquillity. Although there was more cultivation of crops and good harvests in 1817 and 1818, gardens were destroyed, cattle were hamstrung and Anderson received additional threats to his life. Anderson himself began to complain increasingly of spiritual and temporal 'backsliding' and 'degeneracy'. Finally, in February 1820, the situation grew too much for him and he left Griquatown, abandoning all his attempts to construct an independent Griqua polity, whether under the leadership of the patriarchs, the magistrates, or a combination of both.[147] In his frustrations he turned against his former protegés. 'Were some measures not adopted to crush the existence of the Bastaard Independency,' he wrote to the colonial authorities, 'it would prove ruinous to them, and most detrimental to the prosperity of the Colony.'[148]

This was exactly what the colonial authorities had been thinking since the Griqua defiance in 1814. Not only were the Bastaards refusing to send conscripts to the colony, but also, the colonial government believed, desertions to the Northern Frontier zone were increasing, along with trading of arms and powder, and raiding of cattle and 'apprentices'.[149] This was all true; white and Bastaard frontiersmen had been, from the time of De Buys, pioneering new trade routes from the Graaff-Reinet area into Transorangia. The response of the government was, however, to act against missionaries rather than such traders. In 1817 it ordered the closure of the upper Orange River out-stations for the Khoisan hunter-gatherers. It also refused to allow four newly-arrived LMS missionaries, including Robert Moffat, to take up their positions at stations outside the colony.[150] It recommended that the Griquatown mission should become directly subject to colonial law under the authority of the magistracy newly created at Beaufort West.[151] In June 1819 Governor Somerset went further, arguing that the Griquatown mission should be broken up and re-established 'either within the Colonial border or at least so close to it as to be considered under the control of the Colonial government.'[152]

This last recommendation was endorsed by Anderson in February 1820. Acting Governor Donkin responded rapidly, ordering Andries Stockenstrom, landdrost of Graaff-Reinet, to take Griquatown by surprise with two companies of Cape Infantry and a burgher commando, to seize the Griqua firearms and cattle, and to return all the Griqua to the colony. Stockenstrom, who had visited Griquatown in 1818 and who had obtained a rather different picture of events from the kaptyns than that presented by Anderson, demurred. An attack on Griquatown, he

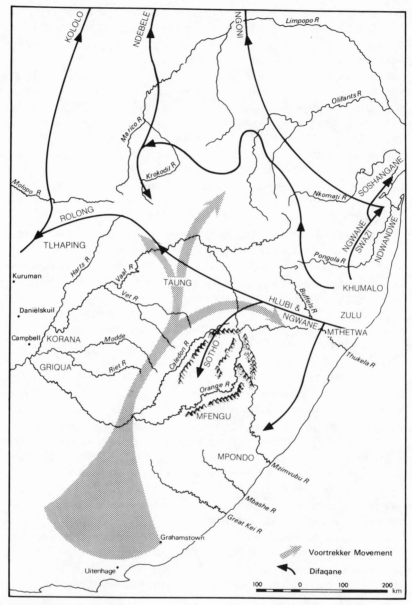

Figure 8.2 The Mfecane

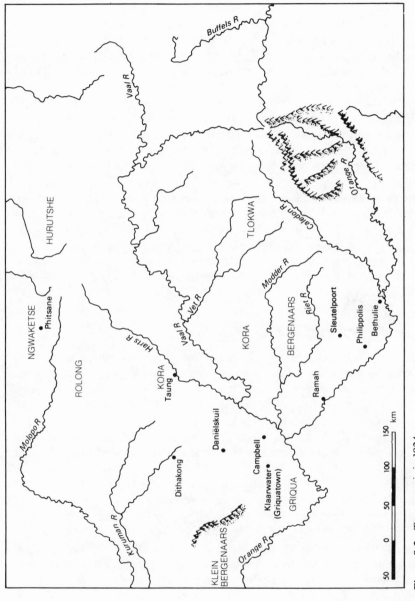

Figure 8.3 Transorangia in 1824

argued, would force the Griqua to flee further into the interior.[153] Stockenstrom recommended rather that the colonial boundary should be extended to include Griquatown, and a magistrate appointed to the settlement. It this was regarded as too expensive, he suggested that the Griqua should be given renewed recognition as an independent community.[154]

Stockenstrom's basis for this second proposal was a novel one. Bringing the Griqua back into the colony, he maintained, would 'generate the entire dissolution of the shadow of restraint which, little as it is, keeps the Corannas [i.e., Kora] from those depredations of which the colony had to complain'. He did not, in other words, present the Griqua as a force essentially hostile and menacing to the colony, nor did he present the missionaries as the only force for stability and 'civilisation' in the Northern Frontier zone. He was, in fact, suggesting that the Griqua should be seen in their own right as potential allies of the colony, as active agents and collaborators in 'closing' the Northern Frontier zone by extending stability in the area.[155] It was this view of the Griqua which began to inform colonial Northern Frontier policy after 1820, although it did not come to full fruition until the 1830s in the treaty-state policy.

Griqua state-building, 1820–1830

In the two decades before the Great Trek, political and social relations went through immense upheavals in much of present-day eastern Botswana, the Free State, Lesotho and the Transvaal. These upheavals were caused not only by the further extension of frontier relationships, but also by the huge dislocation and restabilisation of the *Mfecane*.[156] From early 1822, when the Hlubi erupted across the Drakensberg, there was a period of unprecedentedly intense and bloody warfare – which led not merely to great loss of life and hardship, but to the economic, political, and territorial disruption of almost every community from the valley of the Orange in the south, across to the Kalahari in the west, and over much of the area north of the Vaal.

Meanwhile, the advance of the colonial market, followed by the spread of frontier settlement (white and brown) across the upper Orange, had extended the 'frontier zone'. Here were incentives to raid for cattle and 'apprentices', and exchange them for firearms and horses to make further raids. Writing in 1824 of the 'Bergenaar' Griqua rebels, John Melvill, colonial government agent at Griquatown, said: 'Powder and lead, guns, horses and brandy they get enough from the Bastaards and farmers for cattle and men.'[157]

This pattern, which as we noted began before 1820, now spread in the extended Transorangia frontier zone. The participants were not only Griqua dissidents, but also many Kora communities, and new arrivals, white and brown, from the eastern half of the Colony, who, pushed by land-shortage, and pulled by opportunities, visited or settled semi-legally beyond the colonial boundaries.[158] Many of the new group appear to have been eastern Cape Bastaards, landholders deprived of their land, or they were servants whose relative privilege was being ended. By 1834, 400 such persons were estimated to be near New Platberg (in the Caledon valley), and 'some thousands' of Bastaards dwelt along the valley of the Caledon.[159]

The events of these two decades virtually completed the transformation of the Kora from pre-frontier pastoralists organised largely in kin-groups into frontiersmen banding together under military-style leaders. Visiting one such group in 1825, the LMS missionary John Philip wrote: 'I expected a horde of naked savages and I found a number of smart young men, dressed quite in the style of the most respectable farmers of the colony. The young men had generally white fustian jackets, leather pantaloons, striped waistcoats, white hats with broad edges, shirts, neckcloths, stockings and shoes.'[160] The new developments also increased the anti-colonial strain in Griqua consciousness. 'The strong spirit of independence among the Griquas', wrote Melville, 'with the strong prejudice in the minds of some against the Colony, appears to be occasioned in great measure by their connexion with the 'Bastaards' of the Colony, who live all along the Orange River, and in different parts of the country, and who seem at present to acknowledge no authority whatever.'[161]

On 20 December 1820, Berend Berends was compelled to follow Adam Kok into resigning his office at Griquatown. Andries Waterboer was elected kaptyn in his place. This replacement of the authority of the two Bastaard families by an elected kaptyn of 'Bushman' extraction was a step which initially reinforced the 'popular' party in the state. But, in the turbulent climate of the northern frontier zone – and with contradictory expectations placed on him by government, missionaries, and his subjects – Waterboer proved as incapable as his predecessors of consolidating united Griqua power in Transorangia. His efforts to do so, however, form a central theme of the history of the period.

In 1822 the colonial government appointed John Melvill as its agent to Griquatown. His instructions were to persuade the Griqua to accept a system of laws based on those of the colony. They also contained a 'charter' which was to provide Waterboer with his ambitions virtually throughout his rule: 'Assuming that the limits of the Griqua country and possessions are regularly defined . . . there remains no doubt but that all tribes residing within them should be considered subject to the laws of the Griquas, whether they be Boshuannas, Corannas, or others'.[162] But what were the 'limits' of Griqua country, and how could the subjection be achieved and enforced?

Denied any special assistance from the colonial authorities in the form of arms and ammunition, Waterboer was deprived of one crucial means of building support and checking dissidence.[163] The authorities were, moreover, reluctant to give Waterboer, or any other Griqua kaptyn, authority over white colonial subjects in territory supposedly under Griqua rule. In effect, this limited the power of the kaptyns, also over Kora and dissident Griqua themselves – who could buy firearms from such whites.

Another hindrance to Griqua hegemony was disunity of the leading Griqua. Within months of Kok and Berends resigning their offices at Griquatown, they were reasserting their authority in independent domains: Kok at Campbell, and Berends at Danielskuil. Waterboer never fully reconciled himself to this division of Griqualand. The other chiefs, in turn, were resistant to any unification that gave Waterboer any authority over them. Though a number of attempts were made to restore at the least some agreed modus vivendi, each attempt broke down as the different kaptyns manoeuvred for support among those disaffected with one or other of the leaders.[164]

The high point of co-operation among the three leaders was in June 1823 – in the face of an apparent threat to Griqualand posed by southwards movement of Mfecane groups. They united in a commando, together with Kora and Sotho-Tswana, to beat off an assault by Mfecane groups on the Tlhaping and missionaries at Kuruman.[165] But this unity against external attack could not be sustained in the face of internal upheaval – specifically, the progressive desertion of Griquatown by the 'Bergenaar' rebels, resistant to authority in the manner of the earlier 'Hartenaars', and particularly resistant to Waterboer.

Though on occasion Waterboer offered 'carrots' to the rebels, he acquired a reputation for severity, and even arbitrariness. 'He was without experience, headstrong and fiery to the extreme . . . wherever he thought blame lay he punished without enquiry on just mere belief', said Adam Kok of him later.[166] Perhaps anyone would have been similarly judged who attempted to enforce his authority in the conditions of the time. As one observer wrote, most offences passed without punishment 'not because they are considered as not meriting punishment, but because the government of the country are afraid of the offenders.'[167] But there are specific incidents in which Waterboer did 'rush to judgement', and the memory of these lingered long and hindered his ability to exercise rule unchallenged.[168]

In 1825 John Philip, superintendent of LMS missions, made an attempt to restore harmony by presiding over yet another meeting of Waterboer, Kok, and Berends. 'An agreement was entered into', one participant later related, 'that yearly they should assemble and regulate the general affairs of the nation, hear cases of murder, etc.'[169] Philip congratulated himself on this agreement, but other missionaries were cynical. Melville and Waterboer were outraged.[170] In fact, far from contributing to Griqua unity, the 'agreement' further entrenched the divisions, its provisions for joint regulation of affairs being a dead letter from the start.

Within months, Melvill resigned as government agent, probably principally angered that his own recommendation to government – for the incorporation of Griqualand into the colony – had been rejected. He and Waterboer were also upset that Philip had been persuaded by Andries Stockenstrom to give the 'old chiefs' Kok and Berends equal standing with Waterboer.[171] In January 1826, Adam Kok's authority as kaptyn was renewed by government. According to the Wesleyan missionaries, Berend Berends' position was similarly re-endorsed – though this never gave him the same favour with the colonial authorities as Waterboer and Kok.[172] Philip's agreement involved ceding to Kok and Berends the LMS Philippolis mission. The 'old chiefs' now had a base far enough from Griquatown for them to ward off Waterboer's influence though Berends never took up the offer, settling instead at Boetsap, which was, moreover, on better land, had new lines of access to the colony, and was near new communities among whom to recruit a following.

Two years later Waterboer once again tried severity. In a renewed attempt to crush the Bergenaar rebellion, he tried to expose the tolerance being shown the rebels by the 'old chiefs', and to seek favour from the colony. But by executing six captured Bergenaar leaders, he merely provoked an intensified revolt, which drew in many who had not participated before, and with more arms than previously.[173] Perhaps 1000 were involved in the revolt – and only some 18 families remained at Griquatown. The rebels besieged Griquatown from 7 to 10 July 1827, killing six people, burning down twelve houses including Waterboer's, and seizing 1200 cattle. More damage was averted only because both sides ran out of ammunition.

For about eight months there were fears of the complete collapse of the Griquatown statelet – and of the LMS mission on the Kuruman – with further attacks on both. But the arid Langeberg where the rebels were now based could not sustain prolonged revolt, and by mid-1828 they were in desperate straits, suffering from disease, quarrelling and being raided themselves.[174] This was the nadir in the fortunes of Griquatown, and of Waterboer. Berends at Boetsap and Adam Kok II at Philippolis now emerged as principal foci of Griqua power.

At Boetsap in 1826 Berend Berends gathered around him a following of Griqua, Kora, and Sotho-Tswana.[175] In contemporary and later accounts, his kaptynskap has been overshadowed by Griquatown and Philippolis. But, for a time, it played no less important a role. Berend's closest associates were those Griqua least involved in raiding. He also attracted many disillusioned Bergenaars. Jan Bloem II (son of the frontiersman, a Kora leader, and a Bergenaar) joined him in 1829.[176] Within his 'sphere of influence' were also Sefunelo's Rolong, settled with Wesleyan missionaries at Platberg. The Wesleyans wrote how Berends and his followers, with their 100 guns and 'proportionate number of horses', provided a 'necessary protection from marauding parties from the interior . . . To Platberg this station [Boetsap] is as necessary as the colony to our stations in Caffraria.'[177]

At Philippolis Adam Kok and his followers inherited from the LMS the site of a 'Bushman' mission, whose occupants also included so-called 'old inhabitants' ('Bastaard Hottentots' from Bethelsdorp mission or the colony generally). In 1827 the estimated population was 60 families of Griqua and 'old inhabitants', 20 Kora families, and 180 families of Sotho-Tswana.[178] Additional Kora, San and Sotho-Tswana lived in the area over which the state claimed jurisdiction: from Ramah in the west 'as far as the Caledon' in the north-east, and to the Riet and Modder Rivers in the north. At about the time of Kok's arrival in 1826, white colonists were also beginning to use the area as pasture, and pressing for more permanent settlement rights.

Though Adam Kok and his following brought with them the legacy of pre-1820 Griqua government, they had a task at least as formidable as Waterboer's to secure hegemony over the peoples of this territory. In fact Kok wanted to resign, and continued as kaptyn only because of the premature death of his preferred successor Cornelius II in 1828, and the lack of a suitable alternative. Until 1838 the infant statelet was wracked by division.[179] This division was complex, but its poles were the 'Bastaards' on the one hand and the 'Kora' on the other – with previous Griquatown inhabitants ranged in between. In essence the Bastaards wanted a settled existence (and resented having being made insecure in the colony), while for the Kora the old raiding way of life was preferable. The former hoped for support from the colonial authorities, and saw white colonists as rivals for land. The latter found colonial influence restrictive, and saw white colonists as merely potential trading partners.[180]

Adam Kok was balanced weakly between the factions. His tacking and veering diminished the authority of the state over its subjects and its periphery. By 1834–35, several alternative political poles of attraction, strengthened by new mission stations, had been established within the territory ostensibly under the government of Philippolis. These included Piet Witvoet and his Kora following at Bethany; and the Tlhaping chief Lephoi at Bethulie.[181]

The Sotho-Tswana in the frontier zone before 1830

Before 1820, the impact of the frontier had begun to create divisions among the Tlhaping and weaken the power of their state. The frontier zone posed a set of vexing, inter-related problems for Tlhaping rulers: how to maintain monopoly control of trade in the face of the diffuse pattern of Griqua raiding, hunting and trading; how to secure coveted firearms; what relations to have with missionaries, the Griqua kaptyns, and the colony. To these problems after 1820 were added those of the dislocation of the Mfecane, and the threat of Mzilikazi.

The half-Kora Mothibi had become Tlhaping chief in 1812 on the death of his father. He was keen for firearms – partly with an eye on the powerful Ngwaketse to the north, and partly because Jager Afrikaner was already providing firearms to his Tlharo subjects.[182] This need motivated him to seek close relations with the Griqua and the colony, and to invite a missionary presence in his territory – which effectively began with the arrival of the LMS missionary James Read in 1816. Almost from the start, however, he also had doubts – inspired by the divisions among the Griqua themselves towards the colony and missionaries. Many Tlhaping feared that the missionaries 'would change their old customs like the people at Griqua Town, who once wore a Corass but now wear clothes, once had two wives, but now one. This . . . the Boochuannas will not submit to.' James Read also found 'that on account of the Missionaries at Griqua Town having the chief management I perceived that a great jealousy existed especially among the Chiefs that it would be the same at Lattakoo (Dithakong).'[183]

Tlhaping divisions over missionary presence intensified centrifugal pressures from groups wishing to separate themselves from the authority of Mothibi and to establish their own lines of trade with the Griqua and others. Mothibi could only counteract this separatism by securing, through the missionaries and the colonial authorities, privileged and sole access to firearms as a carrot to his followers. But this access he was continually refused. Matters became more confused when Read, by now winning some trust, was withdrawn from the area by the LMS in 1820, to be replaced by the redoubtable and severe Robert Moffat. By 1822 internal dissent over missionary presence reached a high point, contributing to the centrifugal pressures on the state.[184]

The victory of the Griqua commando over Mfecane bands at Old Dithakong in 1823, with its apparent message of Griqua protection for the Tlhaping, restored missionary prestige – and even induced dissidents to return to the fold. But the re-unification was tentative. Very soon the peoples gathered under Tlhaping rule were being raided by the Bergenaars. Disintegration intensified, as elements of the community searched for the weapons with which to defend themselves – and then were inevitably themselves sucked into the vicious cycle of illegally buying firearms from Griqua or colonial traders and raiding cattle to procure the means to purchase the arms. Those Tlhaping who strove to maintain a settled existence came to believe that the colonial government was attempting to ruin them by 'conniving' in the firearms trade and the raiding.[185]

These new pressures completely fractured the Tlhaping chieftaincy itself. Mothibi moved with a part of the people, to place himself within Waterboer's territory and under his protection. His brother Mahura, on the other hand, moved in another direction with his own following. He refused to look to the Griqua because, as he said, 'of the Griquas beating the Kafirs with ox-whips' and because they 'might expect him to submit to their laws.'[186]

Transorangia in the 1830s

By 1830 Transorangia faced a new threat from the disruptions of the Mfecane. Mzilikazi, at the head of the powerful Ndebele, had established a military state first in the central and then in south-western Transorangia, subjugating several Sotho-Tswana communities and threatening others. At the time Berends' kaptynskap was the most stable Griqua statelet in the area. It was he who took the initiative in mid-1831 by inviting all and sundry to join a commando against Mzilikazi. Waterboer refused the invitation and Adam Kok II was ambivalent. Nevertheless 3600 mounted Griqua and Kora with guns set out (including detachments from Campbell and Philippolis), together with at least 1000 Sotho-Tswana. The commando was successful in seizing large numbers of Ndebele cattle. But this was not enough to secure victory. When the party was encamped on its return, it was set upon by an Ndebele impi of 400 specialising in night-attack. They not only recovered the cattle, but decimated Berends' forces. Between 80 and 100 Griqua and Kora were killed, and larger numbers of Sotho-Tswana, and at least 200 horses and guns lost. Firearms and horses, which had previously provided overwhelming military advantage on the Northern Frontier, were not enough faced with the military sophistication of the Ndebele state. What was needed also was a secure means of defence – later to be developed in the Great Trek in the form of the laager of wagons.[187]

In 1832 the LMS superintendent John Philip, crossing the Orange for the first time since 1825, took note of the continued Griqua schisms, the power of Mzilikazi, and the influx of white colonists in the east, and set about a new attempt to consolidate Griqua hegemony in Transorangia.

Like Stockenstrom and Melville before him, Philip would have preferred that Griqua territory be annexed to the colony – on the same basis as the Kat River settlement on the Eastern Frontier. The terms of Ordinance 50 of 1828, he believed, would guarantee Griqua equality before the law[188] (see ch. 1, pp. 47–50). But he knew the colonial government would not accept such an annexation. Instead he put forward proposals for the relations among the colonial government, the missionaries, and the Griqua kaptyns in the form of a 'charter' for Griqualand, which drew on an only partly-true account of Griqualand's history. His history over-emphasised the role of the LMS, and suppressed the independent roots of the Griqua kaptynskap, regarding it as an essentially delegated authority from the colony.[189] The Griqua, argued Philip, could simultaneously serve as a 'civilising' influence in the frontier zone, and act as a kind of 'frontier militia.' 'I have always considered it important', he wrote, 'to have belts of civilised natives between the colonists and their less civilised neighbours.' Just as they had defended the colony against Mfecane bands, they could now do so against Mzilikazi and also prevent emancipated slaves or white colonists from leaving the colony.[190]

Following the precedent in Melville's Instructions of 1822, Philip envisaged the Griqua as exercising rule over all the peoples of

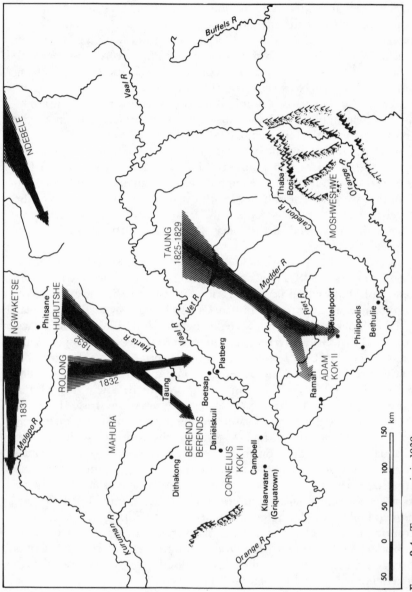

Figure 8.4 Transorangia in 1838

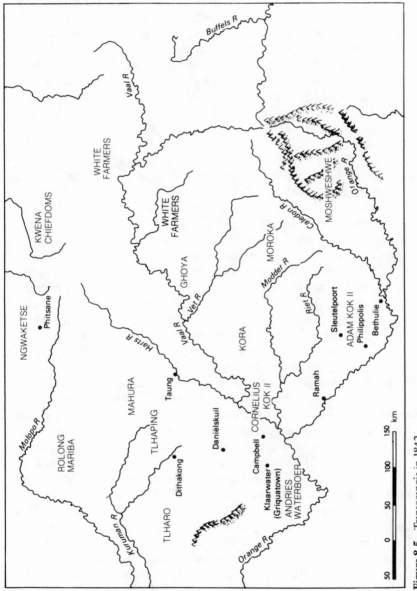

Figure 8.5 Transorangia in 1842

Transorangia – without explicit definition of the northward limits of this rule. His imagination saw a 'new country . . . brought within the pale of Christianity . . . by the labours of the missionaries and in which already we see perhaps 30,000 Bechuanas looking to the Christian chief of Griqua Town, who cannot perhaps muster more than 200 horsemen, as their sole dependence and their only safeguard against the overwhelming and ferocious band of Mzilikazi.'[191] Reversing his position of 1825, Philip now proposed that Waterboer should become commandant of the whole district, with any other Griqua kaptyns subordinated to him.

Philip's 'charter' was for a 'Christian Griqua Republic' with a quasi-feudal oligarchy of armed Griqua exercising sway over subject peoples. Implicit in it was the possibility that political rule would enforce economic subjection. The Griqua way of life was fundamentally based on hunting, pastoralism, trading, and raiding. Only a minority of Griqua had turned, under missionary pressure, to a more settled agricultural life. Now the prospect was opened up for Griqua to secure tribute from the production of Sotho-Tswana agriculture – if they could collect it. In this respect the envisaged Griqua republic was similar to the states that would later be established by Voortrekkers on the highveld.[192] In contrast, however, the Griqua republic was to be bound politically to the colony through the missionaries and kaptyns, rather than in rebellion against it.

On December 11 1834, a treaty was signed between the colony and Andries Waterboer. Its terms derived largely from Philip's proposals. Waterboer was charged with protecting the colonial frontier, sending back fugitives, and warning of possible attacks. To the north, the limits of his territory were undefined. He was to be paid a salary of 100 pounds a year, and to receive a supply of arms and ammunition. The Griquatown school would receive a grant of 50 pounds a year. Moreover, in an unprecedented development, Peter Wright, LMS missionary at Griquatown since 1828, and loyal confidant of both Philip and Waterboer, was appointed a Government Agent *in secret*.[193]

Philip's 'charter', and even a treaty, were one thing. But could this vision be translated into practice? It soon became apparent that Waterboer was no more able than in the 1820s to unite or assert undisputed supremacy over the other Griqua kaptyns. The most he could try for was to freeze them out of favour with the colonial authorities.[194] Partly under pressure from Waterboer, Berend Berends chose, not for the first time, to distance himself from the situation. In 1833–34 he moved with a large part of his following across Transorangia to a string of settlements along the Caledon valley. However Jan Bloem remained in the Harts-Vaal area, with some 2000 well-armed Kora followers, claiming to rule subject to the authority of Berends. Also in this vicinity, around Taung, a new loose polity began to develop in the 1830s with the Tlhaping chief Mahura as the dominant leader, but including an assortment of Sotho-Tswana groupings.[195]

In the Philippolis state of Adam Kok II, the struggle between the 'Bastaard' and 'Kora' factions remained unresolved. This division was the more injurious because of the growing influx across the Orange of white colonists to whom – as has been explained – these factions had different attitudes. By 1838 at least 800 farmer families were across the Orange.[196] Widespread leasing of land by Griqua to whites began – though largely on the northern fringes of the polity, in the valleys of the Riet, Modder and Vet rivers. This took place despite the opposition of Adam Kok II and the 'Bastaard' element – who were concerned, however, not with the presence of white farmers as such, but with whether they would submit to Griqua authority or undermine it by trading with Kora raiders.[197]

In 1832 Waterboer and Philip intervened to try to resolve the factionalism by securing the deposition of Adam Kok II. They failed to impose their candidate – largely because of the opposition of one Hendrick Hendricks, who from this time became the dominant political figure and 'kingmaker' in the statelet. Learning to read and write at Griquatown, becoming a 'Bergenaar' rebel, then marrying Adam Kok's daughter, Hendricks was a figure who impressed contemporary observers with his abilities.[198]

By 1834 Adam Kok declared his willingness to hand over to his second son Adam III. Philip then accepted that 'placing Waterboer over the chief of Phillipolis is no longer necessary.' He reconciled himself even to the political role of Hendrick Hendricks, whom he had earlier denounced as a 'thorough scoundrel.'[199] At Philip's suggestion, Adam II went to sign a separate treaty with the colonial government, but died before this was accomplished. Abraham (the eldest son), and not Adam III, took office and reached an 'agreement' with the colony in January 1837, followed by one between himself and Waterboer, which provided for their joint rule over 'the Griqua country', under 'two separate governments' each 'governed by its own separate laws.'[200]

By the end of 1837, however, Abraham was replaced as kaptyn by Adam Kok, who had organised the commando with Berends and others against Mzilikazi. Adam Kok III was more acceptable to the Waterboer forces, and in November 1838 Waterboer signed a new treaty with him, no longer as 'separate governments' but stating that 'the chiefs and inhabitants of Griqua Town and Philippolis will be considered as one people, and also stand in connection with each other, having one interest.' A treaty between Adam III and the colony followed only in 1843.[201]

This whole series of treaties reinforced Philip's 'charter' for Christian Griqua hegemony over the peoples of Transorangia. From 1834 – but most strongly between 1838 and 1843 in conjunction with Adam III – Waterboer tried to assert this hegemony. The attempt failed, essentially because of the resistance of the Sotho-Tswana. Nevertheless it was of significance. It was the conclusion of a period in which the activities of brown frontiersmen dominated the history of the Northern Frontier.

Waterboer and his loyal missionary Wright painted, from 1834, a rosy picture of Griqua hegemony. The extension of this benevolent protection, they claimed, was welcomed by Sotho-Tswana and merely a continuation of the refuge Griquatown had afforded since the eruption of the Mfecane.[202] Among the symptoms of Sotho-Tswana compliance, they said, were not only the attitude of chiefs, but the increasing rate of conversion of Sotho-Tswana to Christianity – particularly the Tlhaping. The conversions were the result of the resumption of a 'native agency' which led to the growth of the Griqua church and outstations from some 50 in 1832 to 3600 in 1842, of whom 416 were Tlhaping. The converts included, significantly, Mothibi's chief wife, his son Jantje, and other Tlhaping royals.[203]

However, Sotho-Tswana apprehension was soon becoming fuelled by the arrogant manner in which the Griqua began asserting their power, confirming the suspicions also of those – like Mahura – who distanced themselves from Waterboer from the start.[204] Visiting the Tlharo near Kuruman in 1835, for example, Waterboer and his son-in-law Nikolaas Kruger convened the chiefs and 'insisted on them and their people becoming his subjects' on the basis that the territory was his 'by right of conquest' – by which he meant the commando he had led against Mfecane groups in 1823. Griqua field-cornets would be appointed to govern the Tlharo, he said, and, if the chiefs did not submit, he 'threatened them with the deprivation of everything like guns or ammunition or visits of traders.' When the Tlharo responded that they 'liked your friendship but not your sway', and that they had their own chiefs and missionaries, Waterboer replied that their missionaries would be removed if they stood in the way of Griqua rule. Soon afterwards, Sotho-Tswana groups began to complain that the Griqua were trying to restrict their access to arms and ammunition from traders, and in some cases were seizing traders' wagons.[205]

On the basis of these stories, missionaries to the Sotho-Tswana, both LMS and non-LMS, complained against Waterboer to Philip and LMS headquarters. Between 1838 and 1842 both from Griquatown and from Philippolis there was a stepped-up drive to assert Griqua political authority over communities within their orbit, and to remove all missionaries who complained.[206] Bound up with this drive was a new self-confident assertiveness among the Griqua in their collective identity, and the 'mission' that this gave them. This was perhaps most strikingly recorded in the words of Nicholas Kruger to LMS missionary Rogers Edwards in 1838, threatening him with expulsion from the Kuruman. 'Look at the American nation, what a powerful (or able) people they are and if our first teachers had done their duty, we should have been as advanced in civilisation and knowledge as they, for our nation began to receive the Gospel at the very same time the colonisation of America commenced . . . but now we have able teachers who teach us and we also are now able to teach the inhabitants of the whole country including the Bechuana tribes.' When Edwards' wife replied that the Kuruman was not Griqua territory, Kruger significantly asserted 'it is my country. My mother was a Mochuana. I shall go and put them to rights. They are all in ignorance. They must hear or obey me'.[207]

'Formerly', wrote the Paris Evangelical missionary, Prosper Lemue, the Griqua 'were friendly, but now they are haughty to the most people and arrogant with the missionaries. They now pass us by affecting disdain . . . They have threatened to visit the schools of the missionaries in order to convince themselves that the latter have performed their duty'. Griqua preachers were being reported as saying the Kuruman had the 'doctrine of hell', and that those joining the Kuruman church should 'repent'. Is it surprising, wrote the Kuruman missionaries, that the Tlhaping were asking 'A merimo mberi?' ('Are there two gods?'), one for Griquatown and one for the Kuruman.[208]

But, by the early 1840s, Waterboer's Griqua were forced to renounce their pretensions to hegemony – less because of missionary resistance, however, than because of the reassertion by the Sotho-Tswana of their independence. As Moffat wrote, the Sotho-Tswana, 'though unable to defend their country against enemies who possessed both firearms and horse, were nevertheless extremely jealous of every encroachment on the domains of their ancestors'.[209] The departure of Mzilikazi northwards around 1838 lessened the need for Sotho-Tswana to shelter under Griqua guns, and thereafter numbers of them left the Griquatown and Philippolis areas. Formally, the end of the attempt at unrestricted Griqua expansion was signalled by the treaty signed by Waterboer in 1842 which, for the first time, acknowledged northern limits to his rule. Significantly, this was signed not with his closest 'allies' among the Tlhaping royals, but with Mahura, who had always kept his distance from Waterboer, and was now emerging as the Tlhaping ruler with the largest following.[210]

At Phillippolis, Adam Kok III was faced with new problems which diverted attention from the drive for Griqua hegemony. The stream of white settlement now taking place across the Orange was making Philippolis, rather than Griquatown, the key to the fate of the Griqua.[211] After the difficulties of the early 1820s, there was a period of relative peace at Philippolis between white farmers and Griqua. In 1840, in fact, a treaty was signed between the white farmer leader Oberholster and the Philippolis government. Admitting what had become a *fait accompli*, it permitted the leasing of land to whites north of a designated line. On their part, the Griqua promised, 'at all times, when required, to render . . . assistance to the emigrant farmers' and justice on any complaints. 'Servants' who absconded would be returned by both sides. The white farmers acknowledged 'the Government of Philippolis as proprietors and owners as far as our country extends', but reserved the right to retain for themselves colonial law.[212]

With their return from Natal in 1843, 'hard-line' Voortrekkers led by Jan Mocke 'disturbed the peace' by threatening to assume government over sections of Philippolis territory. Almost in the same breath, however, Mocke sought rapprochement with the Griqua on the ground that British intentions were 'to reduce the country under the tyrannical yoke of the British government, and the Griquas and other nations would not be able to bear the oppression of that Government.' But the Philippolis Griqua – especially Hendrick Hendricks – preferred to place their faith in the benevolence of Britain, finally securing a treaty with the colony in 1843.[213] This was the start of conflict between Britain and the Voortrekkers which would lead to the proclamation of the Orange River Sovereignty by Britain in 1848 – and then to the restoration of independence to the Orange Free State in 1854. By then, the Transorangia frontier zone was thoroughly closed.

Conclusion

By the 1830s much of Transorangia had become bound up, economically, politically, and even culturally, with the Cape Colony through the extension of the Northern Frontier. It was brown frontierspeople – the Griqua – who (together with missionaries) had pioneered the establishment of polities which had many similarities with those established by Voortrekkers later in, for example, the Transvaal. Like their white counterparts, the Griqua sought to establish their supremacy, through the force of the commando – and also through the church – over 'Bushmen', Kora, and Sotho-Tswana.

This Griqua role in the Northern Frontier zone – which reached its temporary apogee in the attempt at Christian Griqua hegemony in Transorangia in the 1830s and early 1840s – was inevitably a transitory phenomenon. The formal 'non-racialism' now developing in the Cape could not cloak the fundamental reality – that power, politically and economically, was predominantly in white hands in South Africa, and that British overlordship based itself on this reality.

The establishment of white supremacy in Transorangia, and the marginalisation of the Griqua in the area, followed not so much because of a dramatic increase in the power of white frontiersmen – but more because of economic and political changes in the era of British sovereignty. From the 1840s capital derived from wool and speculation in the Cape began to be invested in Transorangia. The large traders and speculators tended to base themselves in Bloemfontein rather than Philippolis, despite the success of Griqua sheep-farming.[214] It has been cogently argued that it was this 'English party' who were largely responsible for the racially-restrictive franchise and obligations to military service in the Free State constitution, which excluded the Griqua.[215] If, as Hobart Houghton has argued, the 'economic impact of international markets were carried into the interior, not in the wagons of the Voortrekkers, but upon the backs of merino sheep',[216] then it was the effects of that international market, of those merino sheep, which created the Orange Free State in this form and sealed the fate of the Griqua.

The first part of the nineteenth century was the last period when 'brown' people could play a relatively independent role as actors in South Africa's history. Today, as the result of colonial frontier expansion and conquest, and then of capitalist industrialisation based on segregation and apartheid, the real actors in South Africa's history are on the one hand a ruling capitalist class, resting chiefly on white support, and on the other the proletarianised 'brown' and African majority, increasingly demanding democratic rule and socialism.

Chapter Eight   Notes

1. See W.M. Macmillan, *The Cape Colour Question* (Cape Town, 1969), p.11.
2. Among the first to discuss the concept of 'co-operation' was H.M. Robertson, '150 Years of Economic Contact between White and Black', *South African Journal of Economics*, II (1934) and III (1935).
3. For discussion and criticism of the assumptions of this school, see M. Legassick, 'The Frontier Tradition in South African Historiography', *Collected Seminar Papers on the Societies of Southern Africa in the Nineteenth and Twentieth Centuries*, II (London, 1971); 'The Dynamics of Modernization in South Africa,' *JAH*, XIII, (1972), pp. 145–50; *The Analysis of 'Racism' in South Africa,'* Dare-es-Salaam: United Nations/ African Institute for Economic Development and Planning, 1975.'
4. KA 4119, Res, 13 March 1739. (I am grateful to Richard Elphick for this reference.) Those involved were in this instance summoned to a colonial court and instigated a petty and unsuccessful frontier revolt: the government then issued a severe general plakkaat against any trading with the indigenous population. See E.A. Walker, *A History of South Africa* (London, 1928), pp.97–98. The quotation is from F. le Vaillant, *Travels into the Interior Parts of Africa by way of the Cape of Good Hope in the years 1780–1785* (London, 1790), II, 72–73.
5. L. Duly, *British Land Policy at the Cape 1795–1844: A Study of Administrative Procedures in the Empire* (Durban, 1968) discusses the chaos in the land tenure system by the early nineteenth century.
6. The tradition of explanations based on 'trekgeest', which can involve certain philosophical assumptions about humanity's essentially migratory nature, and which stressed the detachment of frontier society from western Cape society, was empirically challenged by S.D. Neumark, *Economic Influences on the South African Frontier, 1652–1836* (Stanford 1957). Neumark emphasises the frontierspeople as bearers of commodity relationships; and his argument is not wholly refuted by W.K. Hancock, 'Trek', *Economic History Review*, 2nd series, X (1958), pp.331–59. There is perceptive discussion of these issues in M. Moerane, 'Towards a Theory of Class Struggle in South Africa: Historical Perspectives', *Maji-Maji* (Dar es Salaam), 21 July 1975.
7. For the concept of a frontier zone see M. Legassick, 'The Griqua, the Sotho-Tswana, and the Missionaries, 1780–1840: the Politics of a Frontier Zone' (Ph.D.; University of California, 1969), pp.1–22. I must acknowledge my debt to W.K. Hancock in thinking through this concept.
8. The commando system has not been adequately treated; but see G. Tylden, 'The Development of the Commando System in South Africa, 1715–1792', *Africana Notes and News*, XII (1959), pp. 303–13; P.E. Roux, 'Die geskiedenis van burger-kommando's in die Kaapkolonie, 1652–1878' (Ph.D.; University of Stellenbosch, 1946). On Khoisan resistance in this period see works of Nigel Penn cited in ch.1 of this volume and S. Marks, 'Khoisan Resistance to the Dutch in the Seventeenth and Eighteenth Centuries', *JAH*, XIII (1972).

9. J.S. Marais, *The Cape Coloured People, 1652–1937* (Johannesburg, 1937), pp.11–12, 26, 32, 74. See also P.J. van der Merwe, *Trek* (Cape Town, 1945), p.207; W.P. Carstens, *The Social Structure of a Cape Coloured Reserve* (Cape Town, 1966), p.19.

10. The specific weighting of the discussion cannot but be influenced by the volume and character of the sources available. For much of the time the indigenous peoples left few literary sources, and usable oral traditions did not generally survive. Moreover, the preoccupations of racist and liberal South African historiographers and anthropologists have pervaded almost all the available subsequent records. For the earlier period travellers' accounts, the Cape Archives and oral tradition recorded in the early nineteenth century are valuable; subsequent notes criticise the interpretation of such sources. From 1800 the almost continuous presence of missionaries provides a systematic, though partisan, eye-witness record of events, supplemented by travellers, the Cape Archives and oral traditions.

11. The standard, though seriously outmoded, account of the indigenous inhabitants of Namibia is H. Vedder, *South West Africa in Early Times* (London, 1938). It is preoccupied with 'origins and movements' on the one hand, and a static ethnic description of social structure in the timeless anthropological present on the other. On Namibian history see R. Moorsom, 'The Political Economy of Namibia until 1945' (M.A.; University of Sussex, 1973). In a truly independent Namibia we may expect a revival of serious scientific historical work.

12. The literature on the Sotho-Tswana is surveyed, and some reinterpretation offered, in M. Legassick, 'The Sotho-Tswana peoples before 1800', *African Societies*, ed. L.M. Thompson (London, 1969), pp.86–125. The furthest expansion of Sotho to the southeast is discussed in PEMS, G.M. Theal – H.M. Dyke, 4 Oct. 1883; H.M. Dyke – G.M. Theal, 23 April 1883; and D.F. Ellenberger, 'Preamble to Third Period of History of the Basutos 1833–1854' (Ellenberger Archives). I am grateful to William Lye for providing these sources.

13. Prior to Elphick (see note 14), the most comprehensive account is I. Schapera, *The Khoisan Peoples of South Africa* (London, 1930), which suffers from defects similar to those in Vedder's account (see note 11).

14. The first documentary evidence supporting the existence of Khoikhoi (herding) communities north of and along the Orange comes, for the coastal areas, from the seventeenth century and, for the middle Orange, from the journeys of Wikar and Gordon. See Richard Elphick, *Kraal and Castle: Khoikhoi and the Founding of White South Africa* (New Haven, 1977), p.20; *The Journal of Hendrik Jakob Wikar (1779) and the Journals of Jacobus Coetsé Jansz (1760) and Willem van Reenen (1791)*, ed. E.E. Mossop VRS 15 (Cape Town, 1935); Staffordshire County Record Office D 593/U/4/1 to 5, Four Journals of Captain R.J. Gordon.

15. The first Kora penetration north of the Orange seems to have occurred after 1800; see *inter alia* John Campbell, *Travels in South Africa . . . Second Journey* (London, 1822), II, 293; MMS, S. Broadbent, 1 June 1823; T. Wangemann, *Geschichte der Berliner Missiongesellschaft und ihrer Arbeiten in Südafrika* (Berlin, 1872), II, 6 ff. However, T.M. O'C Maggs, 'Pastoral

Settlements on the Riet River', *South African Archaeological Bulletin* (1971), p.37–61 posits pre-nineteenth century pastoralism in this area.

16. See Legassick, 'Griqua', p. 62.
17. The problems in such a venture are illustrated by any attempt to use for the purpose Vedder, *South West Africa*; J.A. Engelbrecht, *The Korana* (Cape Town, 1936); and L.F. Maingard, 'The Lost Tribes of the Cape', *South African Journal of Science*, XXVII (1931), pp.487–504; 'Studies in Korana History, Customs, and Language', *Bantu Studies*, VI (1932), pp.103–62. On the other hand, these scholars evinced an interest in the 'peoples discarded by history', such as the Khoikhoi.
18. See, as a recent attempt along these lines, R. Moorsom, 'Political Economy'. *The Oxford History of South Africa* claimed in its introduction to be replacing 'ethnic' by 'economic' categories, but achieved variable success in this respect.
19. For the Tlhaping *sibello* quarry see Campbell, *Second Journey*, II, 194–96.
20. The classic, but dated, accounts of Tswana political structure are by I. Schapera, *Handbook of Tswana Law and Custom* (London, 1938); *Government and Politics in Tribal Societies* (London, 1956) (which deals also with Khoisan). But the brief comments here are confirmed by every early traveller; see Legassick, 'Griqua', pp. 30–39.
21. C. Saunders, 'Early Knowledge of the Sotho: Seventeenth and Eighteenth Century Accounts of the Tswana', *Quarterly Bulletin of the South African Library* (1966), pp.60–70; Legassick, 'Sotho-Tswana', pp.107–10; Alan Smith, 'Delagoa Bay and the Trade of South-Eastern Africa', *Precolonial African Trade*, ed. R. Gray and D. Birmingham (London, 1970), pp.265–89.
22. MMS, Hodgson and Archbell, 31 March 1827. Also Campbell, *Second Journey*, II, 214; W.J. Burchell, *Travels in the Interior of South Africa* (London, 1953), II, 216, 247–48.
23. See Legassick, 'The Griqua', pp.51–55.
24. R. Moffat, *Missionary Labours and Scenes in South Africa* (London, 1842), ch. XXIII.
25. I. Schapera, 'A Short History of the Bangwaketse', *African Studies*, I (1942), pp.1–26.
26. On these events see Legassick, 'Griqua', pp.60–68.
27. *RCC*, IV, 380.
28. Legassick, 'Griqua', pp.69–70, 251–54, 271–72.
29. LMS, Read, 15 March 1817. On the existence of ruling lineage intermarriage and its origins see Legassick, 'Griqua', pp.61, 68–70.
30. LMS, Mothibi, quoted in R. Moffat, 23 Nov. 1836.
31. The trading-raiding expedition of 1738 (see note 4) may have been the first party of frontiersmen to reach the Orange; official expeditions travelled to and across the lower Orange in 1760 and 1761–62. Both these expeditions were accompanied by the Bastaard Klaas Berends who, by the time of the next recorded journeys, had a cattle-kraal near the junction of the Hartebeest and Orange, and appears to have been trading both into Great Namaqualand and up the Orange valley.
32. In 1797 Lord Macartney, for the British administration, reconfirmed the regulations stipulating that gunpowder was to be purchased from the

government alone, and forbidding resale. Official statistics on powder and arms sales thereafter may be found in Great Britain Government Publication 252 of 1835, Wade-Stanley, 14 Jan. 1834, pp.75–84.

33. This, the earliest definition I have traced of a term which became widely used in the nineteenth century (especially in Namibia) is from Albrecht and Seidenfaden, entry 12 Oct. 1805 (LMS Journals).

34. A. Smith, *The Diary of Dr. Andrew Smith* (Cape Town 1939) VRS, I, 203–04. The date is derived by J.A. Engelbrecht, *The Korana: An Account of their Customs and their History* (Cape Town, 1936), p. 20, from documents in the Cape Archives; the dispute was between Kora chiefs named Taaibosch and Philip. For Van Zyl's complaints a few years earlier about Bastaards trading with the Nama (see note 75).

35. *The Journals of Brink and Rhenius*, ed. E.E. Mossop (Cape Town, 1947) (VRS no 28), pp. 114–15. See Moffat's comments in Smith, *Diary*, I, 255–56; Moffat, *Missionary Labours*, ch. 5.

36. See, for example, LMS Journals, Albrecht etc., entry Aug. 1805; Carstens, *Social Structure*, pp. 107–08; Smith, *Diary*, I, 203.

37. For more information on deserters such as the Kruger brothers and Stephanus see Legassick, 'Griqua', pp. 137–38, 140, 147–48.

38. On Pienaar see Legassick, 'Griqua', pp. 133–34, 143.

39. On Bloem see Legassick, 'Griqua', pp. 133–37, 251.

40. For Klaas Afrikaner and his sons see Legassick, 'Griqua', pp. 141–42. Possibly the first mention of Afrikaner is in the Gordon Collection: Staffordshire County Record Office, D593/U/4/1/6, entry of 8 Dec., n.p. (I am indebted to Richard Elphick for this reference.)

41. See also ch. 4, p. 202 in this volume.

42. *RCC*, XXI, Evidence by Maynier, 25 April 1825, p.394.

43. Lichtenstein, *Travels in Southern Africa in the Years 1803, 1804, 1805* (Cape Town, 1930), II, 303. Also I.D. MacCrone, *Race Attitudes in South Africa* (Oxford, 1937), p.98. Contemporary sources, and later research, provide much evidence of both 'white' and 'Bastaard' descendants of late eighteenth-century white frontiersmen: Engelbrechts, Van der Westhuizens, Bloems, Krugers, Pienaars. See Legassick, 'Griqua', pp.115–17, 138–39, 172, 186, 190, 199, 218, 220, 317ff., 356–58, 512, 547, 549ff. Also E. Fischer, *Die Rehobother Bastards und das Bastardierungsproblem beim Menschen* (Jena, 1913); J.A. Heese, 'Onderwys in Namakwaland: 1750–1940' (D. Ed. thesis; University of Stellenbosch, 1943), pp. 79–82.

44. Lichtenstein, *Travels, II, 241*; Heese, 'Onderwys', p. 80.

45. LMS, Anderson, 12 Aug. 1806; Lichtenstein, *Travels*, II, 244.

46. D. Moodie, *The Record* (Amsterdam, 1969), III, 34, 77ff. For such persons managing loan farms, or farming themselves, see for example *Journal of Brink*, pp. 74–75; Lichtenstein, *Travels*, I, 55, 82; W. Paterson, *A Narrative of Four Journeys into the Country of the Hottentots and Caffraria* (London, 1787), pp.46, 102–03.

47. See Campbell, *Second Journey*, II, 359ff; and, for eighteenth-century Cape archival references to Adam Kok (sometimes described as a 'Hottentot'): Heese, 'Onderwys', p.76; R.J. Ross, 'The Griquas of Philippolis and Kokstad, 1826–1879' (Ph.D.; University of Cambridge, 1974), p.21.

48. For origins of the Berends family see Legassick, 'Griqua', pp.112–15; also MacCrone, *Race Attitudes*, p.80. Heese claims that Klaas Berends married a white woman named Cloete, the same to whom Le Vaillant, *Travels*, II, 150–51, refers as the chief of a Little Nama community (personal communication from Hermann Giliomee).

49. Though there is a certain convergence between the terms 'Bastaard' and 'Oorlam', it should be noted that the first originates in a designation applied within the colonial system of social stratification, becoming 'accepted' by those to whom it applied; 'Oorlam' seems to originate in a designation applied by extra-colonial Khoikhoi to those who had been 'in service', becoming 'accepted' by those to whom it applied. In Namibia in the nineteenth century there remained a clear distinction between Oorlam communities and the Bastaard communities who emigrated from the south later; in central Transorangia both terms tended to disappear in favour of 'Griqua'.

50. For an example of a Bastaard-led raiding party, see *Journal of Wikar*, p.47.

51. For subsequent estimates of the date that Bastaards reached (or established cattle-kraals on) the Orange, see Lichtenstein, *Travels*, II, 240, 252; LMS, Anderson, 12 Aug. 1806; Burchell, *Travels*, I, 252; Campbell, *Second Journey*, II, 359–60.

52. For the pre-1800 journey by Cornelius and Hans Luyken (Hans Lucas?) to the Rolong, see Theal, *RCC*, IV, 404; J. Barrow, *Voyage to Cochinchina* (London, 1806).

53. For the growing scarcity of elephants, see Lichtenstein, *Travels*, II, 259; LMS, Anderson, 21 Aug. 1809.

54. Lichtenstein, *Travels*, II, 240, 252, 259. J. Barrow, *An Account of Travels into the Interior of Southern Africa*, II, 305, says that the official figures for the ivory trade over four years (probably c. 1795–98) were 5,981 pounds valued at 6,340 rixdollars. On the profitability and potentialities of the ivory trade see also Neumark, *South African Frontier*, pp.64–67; S. Bannister, *Humane Policy* . . . (London, 1829), pp.110–16.

55. Lichtenstein, *Travels*, II, 259, claimed that 'Individuals among the Bastaard families have sometimes come privately to Cape Town, where they have bought the powder more advantageously; but experience has taught them that it is better to give the higher price, and be spared the fatigue and expense of the journey'. Given the strenuous post–1800 attempts by Bastaards to open up legal access to Cape Town, it would seem more likely that it was other concerns (possibilities of military conscription?) that were hindering them before that time.

56. See Burchell, *Travels*, II, 329, 391; Campbell, *Second Journey*, II, 23, 274; Moffat, *Apprenticeship*, pp.171, 280; LMS, Melville, 2 April 1827; Smith, *Diary*, I, 332, 362, 371, 408–09. The institution of trading *maats* which characterised this trade, involved the sharing of property and of wives.

57. See LMS, Edwards, 27 July 1802; Anderson, 12 Aug. 1806; LMS Journals, Anderson, entries 21 April 1806, 11 May 1807; Burchell, *Travels*, I, 253–54; II, 196, 230, 280ff, 368, 379–80, 414; Campbell, *Second Journey*, II, 216; Moffat, *Apprenticeship*, p.187; Smith, *Diary*, I, 251.

58. Flints, steel knives, European clothing and haberdashery also began to develop a small market. On trade see Barrow, *Cochinchina*, p.403; *RCC*, IV,

380–86; Lichtenstein, *Travels*, II, 308–10; LMS Journals, Anderson entry March 1808; see also Legassick, 'Griqua', pp.254, 273, 535–36.

59. See Burchell, *Travels*, I, 254–54; II, 196, 284, 380; Legassick, 'Griqua', pp.235–37. The Bastaards at Klaarwater were also able to increase their supply of firearms from about 50 in 1801 to perhaps 500 in 1823.

60. In perhaps only two years of hunting, J.M. Kok netted 3,000 rixdollars, and in 1806 William Edwards made 3,200 rixdollars in two journeys to the Cape. See LMS Journals, Anderson entry Nov. 1804; Burchell, *Travels*, II, 283; Campbell, *Travels*, p.317. See also Legassick, 'Griqua', p.236.

61. These frontiersmen were all previously involved with the Xhosa. See R. Wagner, 'Coenraad de Buys in Transorangia', *Collected Seminar Papers on the Societies of Southern Africa in the Nineteenth and Twentieth Centuries*, IV (1974), pp.1–3; Legassick, 'Griqua', pp.244ff.

62. Legassick, 'Griqua', pp.353–55. These activities in western Transorangia contest the description of conditions in G.M. Theal, *Basutoland Records* (Cape Town, 1883), II, 424 that the Afrikaners first crossed this part of the Orange River in 1819, but only to hunt.

63. *RCC*, XI, Somerset-Bathurst, 23 Jan. 1817, pp.252–56. See also *inter alia RCC*, XII, Stockenstrom-C.O., 27 Aug. 1818, pp.34–36; Smith, *Diary*, I, 357–58; Wagner, 'De Buys', p.3 and Legassick, 'Griqua', p.247.

64. Thus, despite desperate efforts directed towards all who visited them, the Tlhaping were unable to evade the Bastaard refusal to sell them firearms until the 1820s; see Legassick, 'Griqua', pp.259–60, 270, 275–76, 363–64, 368–70.

65. A colonially recognised Nama chief named Wildschut was able to have the claims of his community to the Khamiesberg farm of Leliefontein upheld over the white frontiersman Hermanus Engelbrecht: see Moodie, *The Record*, III, 10–11; Le Vaillant, *Travels*, III, 430–37.

66. In Graaff-Reinet a separate roll of Bastaard landowners existed from 1787 until at least 1822. See Marais, *Cape Coloured People*, p.12; MacCrone, *Race Attitudes*, p.121 fn.; J.S. Marais, *Maynier and the First Boer Republic* (Cape Town, 1944), p.31.

67. Marais, *Cape Coloured People*, p.12. See also Lichtenstein, *Travels*, II, 185, 241; Campbell, *Travels*, 258–60; Theal, *RCC*, XII, 111–12; XXVII, 382–83.

68. See *Journal of Wikar*, pp.4, 34 fn.; *Journal of van Reenen*, p.307; P.J. van der Merwe, *Die Noordwaartse Beweging van die Boere voor die Groot Trek* (The Hague, 1937), pp.4–5.

69. See the description of the missionary Sass who remarked that in this region people have 'but mats and bushes, for that they have nothing to build with and they must move from one place to another for to find food for the cattle'. LMS, Sass, 10 April 1812.

70. Heese, 'Onderwys', p.84.

71. The precise meaning of 'burgher rights' is not quite clear. For the legal position see ch. 9, p. 457 fn.

72. See Legassick, 'Griqua', pp. 118, 122, 140–43, 170–71; Heese, 'Onderwys', pp. 76–77.

73. See the (retrospective) statements by Lichtenstein, *Travels*, II, 241–42.

74. See, for example, Moodie, *The Record*, III, 104–05.

75. Moodie, *The Record*, III, 77. The complaint was made by one Van Zyl, almost certainly the person leading an extra-colonial raiding party in 1786; see note 34.
76. LMS, Philip Papers, Anderson-Meynell, 26 March 1814; G.Thomspon, *Travels and Adventures in Southern Africa* (London, 1827), p.301.
77. Quoted by Bannister, *Humane Policy*, p. 211.
78. See MacCrone, *Race Attitudes*, pp.84, 130.
79. LMS, Anderson, 15 Nov. 1814, wrote that 'The restrictions made relative to Hottentots leaving the Colony have been made within a few years, since slavery in the Colony has decreased'. For the interpretation of the codes see Macmillan, *Cape Colour Question*, p.155; Marais, *Cape Coloured People*, p.123. See also in this volume chapters 7 and 9.
80. *RCC*, XI, 252–56; XII, 111–12, 242–48; XXVIII, 37. For evidence on this 'desertion' by slaves, dependents and non-white landholders, see Legassick, 'Griqua', pp.198–200, 247–48, 349–51; Ross, 'Griqua', pp.26–27; Wangemann, *Geschichte*, II, 2, 97.
81. Legassick, 'Griqua', pp.136–37.
82. *Ibid.*, pp.141–48. The relationship of this revolt to that on the Eastern Frontier is suggested not only by their simultaneous existence and comparable recruitment of Khoisan dependents, but by the presence among Afrikaner's following of Xhosa, with whom he maintained connections for a while thereafter.
83. This chapter does not treat the history between 1800 and 1820 of the 'protostate' which Jager Afrikaner, son of Klaas, attempted to establish in southern Namibia (in parallel with the Bastaard attempt at Klaarwater), which was resisted by the dominant 'Bondelswarts' community of the area. Jager died in 1823 and his son, Jonker, resumed raiding activities, subsequently (in the 1830s) moving northwards to the Windhoek area, where his following established a hegemony over both Nama and the Herero: see, for example, Legassick, 'Griqua', pp.216, 257, 260, 444; Vedder, *South West Africa*, pp.179–82, 186–89, 196–281.
84. Legassick, 'Griqua', pp.201, 248–50; Wagner, 'De Buys', pp.1–3.
85. Wagner, 'De Buys', pp.1–3; Legassick, 'Griqua', pp.244–47.
86. See Legassick, 'Griqua', pp.244–47, 270–72; Wagner, 'De Buys', pp.3–5, who argues that it was a Griqua commando set in motion by landdrost Andries Stockenstrom in September/October 1818 which was the decisive event encouraging De Buys to sever his trading links with the colony.
87. Moorsom 'Political Economy of Namibia', p.34.
88. Smith, *Diary*, I, 215. Compare Burchell, *Travels*, II, 525.
89. The Nama then, and for some time to come, identified all 'hatwearers' as raiders: see LMS, Albrecht *et al.*, entry 14 Oct. 1805; Albrecht, entries June-September 1806; Moffat, *Missionary Labours*, ch.8. Both the Kok and the Berends families led commandos against Afrikaner in this period.
90. See Legassick, 'Griqua', pp.116–17, 146–49, 172–75, 179–80, 253.
91. On government relations with missionaries, see Legassick, 'Griqua', chapters 3, 6, 9. See also in this volume chapter 7.
92. Before Berends, requests had come from Kora on the Orange, and links had been established with members of the Bastaard (?), Oorlam (?), Balie and Goeyman families: see LMS, Anderson, 12 Aug. 1806; Campbell, *Travels*, p.228.

93. At about the same time Cornelius Kok persuaded Klaas Afrikaner to allow the establishment of a missionary at his Warmbath headquarters. In the lower Orange area, however, LMS stations never took root, either in Little Namaqualand or across the river in southern Namibia; the extension of missionary activities was the work of other societies at a later time. The Wesleyans established a mission at Leliefontein (Khamiesberg) in 1816. The post-1800 history of the Bastaard communities of Little Namaqualand is not treated in this chapter. For this see Marais, *Cape Coloured People*, ch.3.

94. There is some debate as to whether Dutch Reformed Church ministers would, by the early nineteenth century, baptise Bastaards: Ross claims there was some discrimination ('Speculations') while Giliomee (personal communication) argues that Bastaard children were usually baptised if they met the requirements.

95. The 1801 expedition was principally concerned with the purchase of cattle from the Tlhaping, and only incidentally with the Klaarwater mission. By 1805 the Batavian regime was concerned about the existence of foreign (i.e., British) missionaries outside the colony among the 'equivocal and dangerous . . . Hottentots of the Great River' and this was the reason for sending the expedition: see particularly Lichtenstein, *Travels*, II, 150–52, 257, 260.

96. LMS Journals, Anderson, entry 3 Feb. 1806; the Bastaards had, according to Anderson, 'without knowledge' made use of this powder 'for other purposes'.

97. Imperial Blue Book 50 of 1835, *Papers relative to the condition and treatment of the native inhabitants of South Africa*, Edict of Janssens, 20 Feb. 1805, pp.163–64.

98. Lichtenstein, *Travels*, II, 260 -61. See also LMS Journals, Anderson, entry June 1805.

99. It was Anderson who had to travel to Cape Town in 1806 and 1809 to try to procure supplies of powder for the mission; Legassick, 'Griqua', p.156.

100. See Lichtenstein, *Travels*, II, 150, 240–41.

101. Legassick, 'Griqua', pp.182–88.

102. Besides post-1813 additions from the colony or middle Orange Khoisan, the Klaarwater settlement was joined by perhaps 600 of the Kok following, so that by the early 1820s there may have been some 2,000 to 3,000 in central and western Transorangia who were called 'Bastaards' or 'Griqua'. On population figures see Legassick, 'Griqua', pp.146, 196–200, 380–81. In 1805 H. van de Graaff and H. Lichtenstein conducted a census at the Klaarwater settlement. It should be attached to ART, Janssens Collection, H. van de Graaff, 'Dagverhaal der Rijse van de Drostdye Tulbagh naar de Griquas en terug...', but is not. Anyone who can locate it will have a rich source.

103. P.B. Borcherds, *An Autobiographical Memoir* (Cape Town, 1861), p. 118; LMS, Anderson, 7 Sept. 1802.

104. Burchell, *Travels*, I, 253–54; LMS, Anderson, 12 Aug. 1806; 4 Aug. 1812; Campbell, *Second Journey*, II, 277–78.

105. Borcherds, *Memoir*, pp.117–19. Also Kicherer, LMS *Transactions*, II, 1, p.27; Campbell, *Second Journey*, II, 260, 265–67.

106. Lichtenstein, *Travels*, II, 242, 244–45, 261; Campbell, *Travels*, pp.227–29; LMS, Campbell, 26 July 1813; R. Moffat in Imperial Blue Book 50 of 1835, pp.127–28 and a letter reflecting on his period in the area between 1813 and 1816–20; LMS, Read, 6 Feb. 1850. Some 'Bushmen' also seem to have been landholders.

107. See Legassick, 'Griqua', pp.202, 214–16.

108. Lichtenstein, *Travels*, I, 47.

109. Certainly Adam Kok II acquired a staff of office in 1809 as kaptyn at Klaarwater. Campbell, *Second Journey*, II, 359 (who was in a position to know) originated the story about the grant of a staff of office to Adam Kok I, though Heese can find no record of this in the Cape Archives (personal communication from Hermann Giliomee). Although Adam Kok I, according to Campbell, was a manumitted slave, it is interesting to find that the loan farm was granted to him as a 'Hottentot', and that in 1806 Albrecht *et al.* (LMS Journals, entry 3 Oct. 1805) were told by Adam Kok II that Cornelius was baptised but 'a Hottentot born'. In view of the clear association between the Koks and the Chariguriqua, it may be plausible to assume that the family founder was an escaped slave (and this Khoikhoi community in the seventeenth century was almost the only Cape Khoikhoi group receptive to such persons), who collected a following of Khoikhoi and at a later date was able to pose as a 'Hottentot'. See also R. Ross, 'Assimilation and Collaboration: The Aspirations and Politics of the Griqua Captaincies of Mid-Nineteenth Century South Africa' (unpublished mimeo, n.d.), p. 3.

110. Borcherds, *Memoir*, pp.117–18.

111. Lichtenstein, *Travels*, II, 306.

112. LMS Journals, Anderson, entry 16 May 1807; Legassick, 'Griqua', pp.172, 182. It is unclear to what extent the Berends family saw themselves as autonomous equals of the Koks or subject to their overall authority. There was certainly animosity between Cornelius and the Berends family in 1798–1801: see LMS, Anderson, 12 Aug. 1806, but Berend Berends seems to have been the son of Cornelius Kok's sister (married to Klaas Berends): Andries Waterboer, 'A short account of some of the most particular and important circumstances attending the Government of the Griqua people' (c Nov. 1827). LMS Journals, Anderson and Jansz, entry Oct. 1807.

113. LMS, Waterboer, 'A short account.' This important document, it should be mentioned, was written in a spirit of great antagonism towards the Kok family, and to discredit the character of their rule.

114. E.A. Walker, *The Great Trek* (London, 1960).

115. See LMS Journals, C. Sass, entry Aug. 1815; LMS, Read, 29 July 1813. Lambert Jansz, son of the Jansz-Pienaar marriage, later became an important Griquatown figure.

116. LMS Journals, Anderson and Jansz, entry Oct. 1807-Feb. 1808; LMS, Anderson, 31 Aug. 1809; Campbell, *Travels*, p.239.

117. Legassick, 'Griqua', pp.186–87, 217.

118. LMS Journals, Anderson and Jansz, entries Oct. 1807, Jan. 1808. For his origins see Legassick, 'Griqua', pp.107, 186, 211; Wangemann, *Geschichte*, I, 268; Thompson, *Travels*, p.79.

119. These events are not recorded in contemporary missionary letters, except for the mention in LMS Journals, Jansz, entry 3 June 1810 of 'two captains'. Kok and Berends were certainly the 'captains' at the time of Burchell's visit. See Legassick, 'Griqua', pp.170–71, 187–88.
120. Campbell, *Travels*, pp.235–36.
121. See Legassick, 'Griqua', pp.194–95, chs. 7 to 12; Ross, 'Griqua'.
122. Burchell, *Travels*, I, 253. He instanced a trial before Adam Kok and 'several of the head people, as his council'.
123. Campbell, *Travels*, pp. 236–39, 244, 282; LMS, Campbell, 5 May 1813; LMS, Anderson, 18 Jan. 1816.
124. *RCC*, IX, Campbell-Cradock, 12 Feb. 1814, pp.353–55. On the 'native agency' see also Campbell, *Travels*, pp.239–40.
125. LMS, 'Minutes of conference . . . of missionaries, Graaff-Reinet', Aug. 1814; Report of LMS Directors, 1815 (quoted in D. Arnot and F. Orpen, *The Land Question of Griqualand West* [Cape Town], p.156).
126. R. Ross, 'Griqua Government', *African Studies*, XXIII (1974), pp.25–42.
127. The LMS also established two stations for the 'Bushmen' at and near the present Colesberg in 1815–16 under Erasmus Smit and a black West Indian named William Corner, who were accompanied by a number of Khoikhoi. See LMS 8/3a, 'Ramah Missionary Station', 'Konnah Missionary Station' (established after Tooverberg and Hephziba stations were closed); Campbell, *Second Journey*, II, 244, 289–90, 301–03; Helm, 9 Sept. 1822; Corner, 2 Sept. 1816; LMS, Read, 12 Oct. 1816.
128. See Legassick, 'Griqua', pp.206, 213–17.
129. LMS, Read, 12 Nov. 1816; Legassick, 'Griqua', pp.199, 216.
130. See Legassick, 'Griqua', pp.261–75 *passim*. Read, who was strongly opposed to the degree of political influence exerted by Anderson at Griquatown, was able to win the confidence of the Tlhaping.
131. These included one, Cupido Kakkerlak, who employed revivalist methods of conversion among the Kora, including all-day house-to-house singing parties, which he claimed had been successful at Bethelsdorp. LMS, Anderson, 19 April 1816; Kakkerlak, 29 May 1816.
132. LMS P. Papers, Meynell to Anderson, 3 Jan. 1814.
133. LMS P. Papers, Bird to Anderson, 27 May 1814.
134. *RCC*, IX, 310–12, 318–19, 349–55; Legassick, 'Griqua', p. 197. Until 1813, according to Anderson, there were only three such desertions to Griquatown itself, though desertions to Transorgania in general increased thereafter.
135. See, for example, *RCC*, IX, Cradock – Vicars, 14 Nov. 1812, pp. 7–10.
136. Legassick, 'Griqua', pp. 164, 166–67, 201, 204, 284. Anderson was claiming that the Griqua were not colonial subjects, but 'independent of this settlement and its Government'.
137. See Legassick, 'Griqua', pp. 202ff.
138. See Nicholas Kruger, Jan Pienaar, *Bluebook*, pp. 19–21, 350.
139. Buys told the rebels that they were a free people who ought not to submit themselves 'to laws made by Englishmen.' Campbell's intention from the beginning was to 'betray them by the Government'; he was 'the cause of the late requisitions for their children by the Government.' The purpose of the registration of births was only 'to betray the number of males to the

Government.' (The Griqua refused to register births and deaths until at least 1819). See LMS Journals, Anderson and Helm, entry 23 June 1815; LMS, Anderson, 18 Jan. 1816; see also Legassick, 'Griqua', pp. 204–05, 344ff; Wagner, 'De Buys', pp. 2–3.

140. The mistrust of the role of missionaries at Griquatown spread to other communities like the Tlhaping. Nevertheless a mission was established among the Tlhaping which soon generated lines of conflict parallel to those at Griquatown, and sowed the seeds of the fragmentation of a much more powerful polity than the Griqua had been. See Legassick, 'Griqua', pp. 261–79, 361–71.

141. These quotations may be found in LMS Journals, Anderson and Helm, entry March 1815 – Dec. 1815; LMS, Anderson, 19 April 1816.

142. Hartenaar leaders were Hendrick Hendricks and A. N. Kok, probably the same 'Kort Adam' who had been magistrate before 1808: see Legassick, 'Griqua', pp. 182, 208–10. For Hendricks at Philippolis see Ross, 'Griqua' *passim*.

143. LMS Anderson, 17 Sept. 1816; *RCC*, XI, Anderson-Stockenstrom, 25 Nov. 1816, p. 229.

144. Andries Waterboer, in a partisan account of the rebellion, later showed that the kaptyns could exert no effective power. See LMS, Waterboer, 'A short account . . .'; Legassick, 'Griqua', pp. 206, 208.

145. LMS, Waterboer, 'A short account . . .'; Legassick, 'Griqua', pp. 209, 213–15.

146. LMS, Read, 23 May 1817. Also LMS, Read, 15 March 1817; Anderson, 24 Aug. 1820.

147. LMS, Waterboer, 'A short account . . .'; Legassick, 'Griqua', pp. 219–21, 291.

148. CO 2625/34, Letter of Baird, 21 April 1820.

149. *RCC*, XI, Somerset-Bathurst, 23 Jan. 1817, pp. 252–56.

150. See Legassick, 'Griqua', pp. 159–63, 283–90 and the sources quoted.

151. In the following year, however, some concessions were made to the Griqua. Persons from Griquatown authorised by the missionaries might proceed to the annual fair at Beaufort West in order to trade with the farmers. But although the Griqua acquired wagons, horses, tobacco and brandy, the fair excluded trade in arms and powder. The Griqua were also unable to get cloth, beads and implements for agriculture and carpentry. See *RCC*, XI, 252–56; *RCC*, XII, 62–64, 111–12, 242–48. For the fair and other Griquatown/farmer trade see Legassick, 'Griqua', pp. 132–33, 238–40.

152. *RCC*, XII, Somerset-Bathurst, 30 June 1819, pp. 242–48.

153. Stockenstrom, *Autobiography*, I, 177–83. See also the memorial by Philip, *Researches*, II, 72–75. (The original is in CO 120/32 and was received before 26 May 1820). In this memorial Philip warned that the Griqua might 'disperse themselves in hostile bands among the neighbouring tribes . . . and bring war upon the colony, from the mouth of the Keiskamma to the mouth of the Orange River . . .'.

154. For Stockenstrom's visit, and recommendations, see Imperial Blue Book 50 of 1835, Stockenstrom, 13 Sept. 1820, pp. 129–33.

155. This argument was subsequently adopted very vehemently by John Philip.

See LMS, Philip, 'A brief view . . .'. (c. 1823); Philip in *South African Commercial Advertiser*, 26 Nov. 1825; Legassick, 'Griqua', pp. 449–61.

156. See W.F. Lye, 'The Difaqane: the Mfecane in the Southern Sotho area, 1822–24, *JAH*, VIII, (1967), pp. 107–31; J.D. Omer-Cooper, *The Zulu Aftermath: a Nineteenth-Century Revolution in Bantu Africa* (London, 1966), pp. 86–97; Legassick, 'Griqua', pp. 328–42.

157. Melvill, 17 Dec. 1824 (Imperial Bluebook 50 of 1835), p. 217.

158. See van der Merwe, *Noordwaartse Beweging*, chapters IV, VII; Macmillan, *Bantu, Boer and Briton*, pp. 60–65; Melville in Imperial Bluebook 50 of 1835, pp. 216–17, 219–223; Moffat, *Apprenticeship*, pp. 167–68, 272–74; Legassick, 'Griqua', pp. 346–55. Trade was legalised on a permit system in 1825.

159. MMS, Edwards, 18 July 1834; T. Arbousset and F. Daumas, *Narrative of an Exploratory Tour to the Northeast of the Colony of the Cape of Good Hope* (reprinted, Cape Town, 1968), p. 10.

160. Philip, *Researches*, II, 334. The leader of this group was Abraham Kruger, one of the 'mixed' sons of the early northern white frontiersman Jacob Kruger.

161. Quoted, Macmillan, *Bantu, Boer and Briton*, p. 55.

162. Quoted in J.M. Orpen, *Reminiscences of Life in South Africa from 1846 to the Present Day* (London, 1908), pp. 109–10.

163. Melvill's instructions permitted 'orderly' Griqua to enter the colony with a pass from the Agent, but this system was to hinder, rather than help, in acquiring arms.

164. See, e.g., Legassick, 'Griqua', pp. 298, 302.

165. Legassick, 'Griqua', pp. 333–35.

166. Smith, *Diary*, I, 199–200. For the onset of the Bergenaar rebellion, see Legassick, 'Griqua', p. 299ff.

167. Smith, *Diary*, I, 102.

168. One such occasion was in 1824 when a commando led by Waterboer seized the Rolong chief Sefunelo and fined him 600 head of cattle for engaging in cattle-raiding, when in reality Sefunelo was innocent, and his people were the victims of raiding by Mfecane groups. See Legassick, 'Griqua', pp. 308–10, 331, 337ff, 454–56.

169. Hendrick Hendricks told this to Andrew Smith (Smith, *Diary*, I, 213–14).

170. Waterboer (LMS, 'A short account . . .', 1827) wrote in anger of Philip's intervention that 'Thus were our own People encouraged in their rebellion against us . . . We can well appreciate the good intentions of our friend, Dr. Philip . . . but he was much too ignorant of the real state of things among the Griqua.' By the 1830s, however, the relations between Philip and Waterboer had been transformed into those of close political co-operation. See also Philip, *Researches*, II, 87–100, 103–04; Legassick, 'Griqua', pp. 318–22.

171. See Legassick, 'Griqua', pp. 316, 323–25.

172. Legassick, 'Griqua', pp. 379, 383–85. For Berends, see especially MMS, Hodgson and Archbell, 10 Oct. 1827.

173. Legassick, 'Griqua', pp. 409–16. This was one of the occasions on which Waterboer specifically defied the 1825 agreement among the three kaptyns, which provided for joint trials in cases of murder. See also

Legassick, 'Griqua', pp. 385–86.

174. Legassick, 'Griqua', pp. 415–16.

175. Berends chose to move to Boetsap on the Harts River rather than to Philippolis.

176. On Berends' statelet see Legassick, 'Griqua', pp. 400–06.

177. MMS, Hodgson, 18 Aug. 1829. Before 1830, there was a store at Platberg. See also Legassick, 'Griqua', pp. 374–75.

178. See R. Ross, 'The Griqua of Philippolis . . .', pp. 36–38; Legassick, 'Griqua', pp. 380, 384.

179. See LMS, Melville, 1 Jan. 1829; Legassick, 'Griqua', pp. 388–89.

180. Ross, 'The Griqua of Philippolis', p. 55; Smith, *Diary*, I, 80–81, 122, 148–49, 151, 154, 176, 182, 195–96; Legassick, 'Griqua', pp. 389–92.

181. Legassick, 'Griqua', pp. 391–400.

182. Legassick, 'Griqua', pp. 257–61.

183. LMS, Read, 15 March 1817; LMS, Read, 'A short account of the commencement, progress, and state of the Mission at New Lattakoo with some remarks', 12 July 1820; LMS, Hamilton, Journal, 26 Sept. 1816.

184. See Legassick, 'Griqua', pp. 263–79, 288–89.

185. Legassick, 'Griqua', pp. 361–71.

186. Mahura and Molehabangwe in *Bloemhof Bluebook*, pp. 90, 302–03. See also LMS, Kuruman missionaries, 10 Sept. 1838. Another Tlhaping royal, Lepui, moved with some 2000 followers to Philippolis at the same time.

187. See Legassick, 'Griqua', pp. 421–31; and, for related incidents, *ibid.*, pp. 345–46, 433, 513.

188. See Philip, *Researches*, II, 328–29, 354.

189. See, for example, Colonial Office 1778, Philip, 'Return of Missions belonging to the LMS', 1830, quoted in Macmillan, *Bantu, Boer and Briton*, p. 65 and Van der Merwe, *Noordwaartse Beweging*, p. 275; Philip to Wade, 10 Oct. 1833 (Imperial Bluebook 425 of 1837), pp. 143–51; Legassick, 'Griqua', pp. 456–79.

190. Philip (Imperial Bluebook 538 of 1836), p. 605.

191. Philip to J.B. Purney, May 1833, quoted in *Letters of the American Missionaries, 1835–1838*, ed. D.M. Kotze (Cape Town, 1950), pp. 35–36. In reality, of the Griqua kaptyns, only Berends had dared to challenge Mzilikazi, and then unsuccessfully.

192. On the Griqua economy see Legassick, 'Griqua', pp. 486–92; and especially, LMS, Wright, 25 Sept. 1835. On the character of the Voortrekker states as based not on 'yeoman farmers but on the domination of a class of land-owning notables over lesser whites and, more fundamentally, over Khoisan and African captives and tributary groups', see S. Trapido, 'The South African Republic: class formation and the state', *Collected seminar papers on the societies of Southern Africa in the 19th and 20th centuries*, III (School of Oriental and African Studies; London, 1973), pp. 53–65; 'Aspects in the transition from slavery to serfdom, *ibid.*, pp. 24–31; 'The long apprenticeship; captivity in the Transvaal, 1843–1881' (mimeo, 1976).

193. For the treaty, etc., (Imperial Bluebook 252 of 1835), pp. 114–17. For the change this meant in Waterboer's relationship with the colonial authorities, see Legassick, 'Griqua', pp. 416–20, 481, 493–96.

194. For Waterboer's disputes with Berends and with Cornelius Kok (at Campbell), see Legassick, 'Griqua', pp. 407–09, 418, 487–88, 502–10, 548.

195. Legassick, 'Griqua', pp. 489–90, 510–17. Among the groups at Taung were the Hurutshe, refugees from Mzilikazi. By 1838 a visiting missionary, 'from the centre of Mahura's town . . . could distinguish fifteen villages, spread on the two banks of the Harts. Several of these villages did not have less than 500–600 huts.' (P. Lemue, *Journal des Missions Évangéliques*, 28 Dec. 1838, XIV, 331–32).

196. Van der Merwe, *Noordwaartse Beweging*, pp. 290–91.

197. Ross, 'The Griqua of Philippolis', pp. 51–52, Legassick; 'Griqua', pp. 395–400, 518–20.

198. Ross, 'The Griqua of Philippolis', pp. 58–62, Legassick, 'Griqua', pp. 520–24

199. Philip to D'Urban, 16 July 1834 (Imperial Bluebook 538 of 1836), p. 620. Also Philip to Wade, 10 Oct. 1833 (Imperial Bluebook 425 of 1837), pp. 144–47, 153.

200. For the treaty, see D. Arnot and F. Orpen, *The Land Question of Griqualand West* (Cape Town, 1875), pp. 191–93. Also Legassick, 'Griqua', pp. 526–29.

201. For the treaty, see *Bloemhof Bluebook*, pp. 30–31. Also Legassick, 'Griqua', pp. 551–54; Ross, 'The Griqua of Philippolis . . .', pp. 65–67.

202. See, for example, LMS, Wright, 15 July 1835; 17 Aug. 1835.

203. Legassick, 'Griqua', pp. 532–35, 539–40.

204. Andrew Smith reports that Mahura told the Hurutshe chief that he was moving to Taung 'soon after the news was heard concerning Waterboer's power and which was reported to be so great as to warrant him in interfering with Latakoo (Dithakong) and its inhabitants' (Smith, *Diary*, I, 387; II, 274).

205. For this and similar incidents see LMS, Kuruman Missionaries, 10 Sept. 1838; LMS, Lemue to Wright, 2 July 1840; LMS, Wright to Lemue, 25 Sept. 1840; LMS, Hamilton and Edwards, 18 Dec. 1838; MMS, Boyce, 6 March 1839; Arnot and Orpen, *Land Question*, pp. 242–43.

206. Legassick, 'Griqua', pp. 547–51, 554–56. Waterboer, for example, was reported to have said that now that the Griqua had the *bongaka* (power of healing souls), white missionaries, except for Peter Wright and his associate Isaac Hughes, were not needed: 'This year all old things must be done away and all things must begin anew at the commencement of the year.' (Sources in note 205 and LMS, Edwards, 10 Sept. 1838; 7 Feb. 1839). In attacking Robert Moffat, the Griqua charged him with adultery, a charge with a history of use among missionaries against each other in the course of political or personal disagreements.

207. LMS, Edwards, 'Notes of events at Daniels Kuil', 10 March 1838.

208. LMS, Lemue, 2 July 1840; and other references in note 205. The Kuruman missionaries claimed that when Waterboer signed the treaty with the colony, 'someone (for we leave you to guess) put it into his head to convert his handful of subjects into an empire'; Wright was concerned not just with 'bringing souls to Christ', but with wanting to 'proselyte as many as possible to the Church at Griquatown . . . to enlarge the dominion of Waterboer.'

209. Moffat, *Missionary Labours*, chapters XIII, XXVII. See also LMS, Edwards, 10 Sept. 1838: 'The truth must be told . . . the Bechuana are a rising and numerous people and will eclipse the Griqua who are despised by them as a mere company of Bastards.' For further detail on the missionary reaction to Griqua expansion see Legassick, 'Griqua', pp. 558–63, 569, 572–73, 576–81, 585–97.

210. For versions of the treaty, see *Bloemhof Bluebook*, pp. 27–28, 115–16. Also *ibid.*, 3, 7, 10–11, 193, 351; LMS, Ross, 5 July 1842, 8 March 1843. On the Tlhaping in this period and subsequently, see Legassick, 'Griqua', pp. 563–68, 570–76, 579–83, 626–33, 641–43, 656–58. Mothibi's rule ended at this time, and he died in 1845. He handed his office to a son, Jantje, who settled at Lekatlong, while another son, Gasebonwe, split away and settled at Borigelong. Mahura's Treaty ignored Gasebonwe, and left Jantje in Waterboer's territory. In Mamusa, Mahura's following numbered at least 20,000: the main settlement was 'the largest Bechuana town that is known' (LMS, Ross, 2 June 1846). Ross wrote that Mahura 'seems to be very much respected as a ruler . . . His policy seems to be to copy the example of Mosheshe [sic] the Great Chief of the Basutus [sic] who has called Missionaries among his people; he has embraced many of the customs of the Europeans . . . he uses every strategem to increase his people and gain a name . . .' (LMS, Ross, 17 July 1844; 14 May 1845).

211. Cf LMS, Wright, 1 Feb. 1837. Also Legassick, 'Griqua', pp. 621–22, on Wright's transfer to Philippolis and death there in 1843. Wright's grandson, Samuel Cronwright, was to marry Olive Schreiner, daughter of another former Philippolis missionary.

212. Ross, 'The Griqua of Philippolis', pp. 53–54. For an 1840 Treaty between Oberholzer and Cornelius Kok and Jan Bloem, see Arnot and Orpen, *Land Question*, pp. 254–55.

213. Ross, 'The Griqua of Philippolis', pp. 85, 88–89. For events at Philippolis in this period see also Legassick, 'Griqua', pp. 576–77, 619–23. For the decline of Griquatown from the 1840s, see Legassick, 'Griqua', pp. 611–19.

214. See, *inter alia*, T. Kirk, 'Some Notes on the Financial State of the Eastern Cape, 1840–1850, and the Fate of the Kat River Settlement', *Collected Seminar Papers on the Societies of Southern Africa in the Nineteenth and Twentieth Centuries*, III, (London, 1973), 13–23; Ross, 'Griqua', ch. V.

215. D.J.P. Haasbroek, 'The Origin of Apartheid in South Africa', *Historia*, XV (1970–71), 13–23. On the Cape franchise see also S. Trapido, 'Origins of the Cape Franchise Qualifications of 1853', *JAH*, V (1964).

216. *Oxford History of South Africa*, II, 4. Compare C.W. de Kiewiet, *A History of South Africa* (Oxford, 1942), pp. 57, 67, 89.

The Eastern Frontier, 1770–1812*

Hermann Giliomee

At the end of the seventeenth century the limits of European habitation were only 80 km from Cape Town. During the eighteenth century the line moved more than 800 km further as hunters, traders, raiders and, finally, cattle farmers pushed eastward into the interior. During the same period, along the southeastern coast, the limits of Xhosa settlement were slowly moving westward. In about 1770 the vanguard of white settlement reached the outlying Xhosa chiefdoms, and the so-called Eastern Frontier opened. This was to be the most dramatic of all South African frontiers. Here European and black pastoralists dispossessed and finally subjugated the last of the eastern Khoikhoi ('Hottentot') clans. Here, too, began the process of interaction between white and black which has dominated South African history. For four decades trekboers and Xhosa, both aided at various times by Khoikhoi, jostled each other, neither succeeding in establishing supremacy, until in 1812 a combined colonist-Khoikhoi force under British military leadership finally pushed the Xhosa over the Fish River.

The Eastern Frontier and its inhabitants

The frontier, as the term is used in this chapter, has two dimensions: social and geographical. In the geographical sense, historians in the twentieth century have meant by 'the Eastern Frontier' the coastal belt between the Sundays and the Kei Rivers where armed clashes between European and black took place. In this chapter the term will be used in

---

* I am indebted to Leonard Thompson for opening new perspectives and providing warm encouragement; to Richard Elphick, a hard and therefore invaluable taskmaster as regards style and structure, and to the following scholars who also made incisive and most helpful critical comments on previous drafts: Louis Botha, George Fredrickson, J.A. Heese, John Hopper, Martin Legassick, Shula Marks, Richard Moorsom, Jeffrey Peires and Christopher Saunders.

two geographical senses: in the context of colonist-Khoikhoi relations to correspond to the Graaff-Reinet district established in 1786 (see Fig. 9.1), and in the framework of colonist-Xhosa relations to refer to a smaller part of that district, namely the Zuurveld and adjacent divisions.

The Graaff-Reinet district could be divided into three parts. Most of the southeastern quarter was taken up by the Zuurveld, which stretched about 75 or 100 miles to the east and west of the present day Grahamstown. In the late eighteenth century the Zuurveld was considered to be bound by the Zuurberg and Fish River mountain chains in the north, the Fish River in the east, the Sundays River in the west, and the Indian Ocean in the south.[†] The pastures of the Zuurveld are suitable for both sheep and cattle farming. As the name Zuurveld (sourveld) indicates, its soil is of high acidity; it produces fast-growing vegetation, most of which is harmful, even fatal, to cattle in autumn and winter. As a result, the Zuurveld plains are suitable for pasturage only during certain parts of the year, usually from August/September to December/January. However, the river valleys with their dense, semi-succulent, thorny scrub thickets and sweetveld provide good grazing throughout the year. Thus the early pastoral occupants of the region concentrated themselves in the valleys, using the plains mainly as summer pastures. As the Zuurveld became more densely settled, one of the biggest problems was to achieve the desired rotation of livestock between sourveld in the summer and sweetveld in the winter. Such transhumance often led to territorial disputes between different communities.[1]

The second region was the northeastern part of the Graaff-Reinet district. This included the well-watered Sneeuwberg and the choice division of Bruintjes Hoogte (near the present-day Cradock), and is the best part for stock farming. Large areas are covered by sweet grassveld and shrubs growing on soil with neutral acidity. The veld may therefore be grazed throughout the year.

The third region, i.e., the western half of the district, covered the area between the present-day Prince Albert and the town of Graaff-Reinet and included the Nieuwveld, De Koup and Camdebo divisions. Although dry, its shrubs and succulents offer good pasturage for sheep. In the eighteenth century it provided winter grazing for stock raised in the Zuurveld.

During the course of the eighteenth century Khoikhoi clans, some of

---

[†] During the period under discussion contemporaries also referred to the Zuurveld in a more restricted sense as the area between the Boesmans and the Fish Rivers.

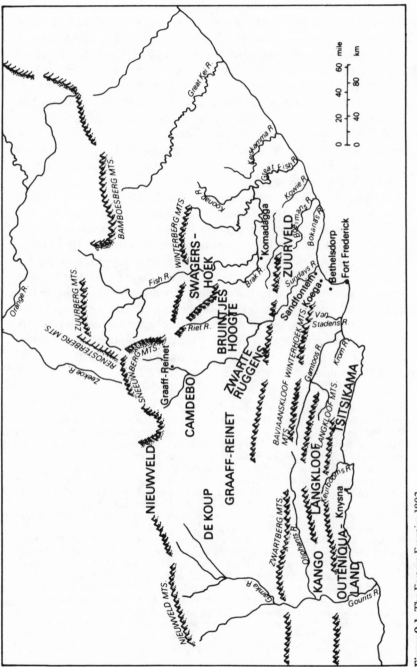

Figure 9.1 The Eastern Frontier 1803.

which had previously lived in the southwestern Cape, retreated in the face of the colonists' expansion until they were east of the Gamtoos River. Xhosa, pushing westward beyond the Kei River, forced other Khoikhoi to withdraw in the direction of the Fish River. In the area between the Fish and the Gamtoos various Khoikhoi clans combined to form chiefdoms, each headed by a chief of limited authority.[2] In the late eighteenth century the most important chiefdoms in the area were those of the Gona, who had incorporated Xhosa on a large scale, and the Hoengeiqua. This latter group had been formed from Khoikhoi remnants by Ruyter, a Khoikhoi fugitive who had killed a fellow Khoikhoi in the Roggeveld.[3]

The trekboers (European colonists who usually called themselves 'Christians') reached the Sneeuwberg mountains, Camdebo and Sundays River by the end of the 1760s.‡ They had gradually colonised the interior by acquiring loan farms from the government (the Dutch East India Company). These farms were on average roughly 6 000 acres (2,420 ha) in size. In densely settled areas the basic social unit was the extended family, which consisted of several related nuclear families living close together under the leadership of the senior male. On their farms there were often one or two bijwoners (Europeans who had no claim to the land but were part of a broader European cultural and kinship network), Khoikhoi servants and their families, and, in the case of wealthy landholders, a slave or two.

---

‡ The discussion of the causes of trekboer expansion has been dominated by P.J. van der Merwe, who concluded that the trekkers consisted predominantly of the surplus population of the settled areas which was unable to find free or cheap land elsewhere: see especially his *Trek* (Cape Town, 1945), pp. 59–60. Subsequently S.D. Neumark in his *Economic Influences on the South African Frontier* (Stanford, 1957) argued that the major force behind the expansion was the better opportunities provided by stock farming and hunting, and that the marketing of certain products like soap, butter and tallow gave the expansion movement an additional impetus. Neumark's work provides valuable insights into the way in which trekboer society was linked to its Cape Town base, but one must question his attempt to relate frontier expansion to market opportunities rather than to population pressure. Apart from the fact that Neumark is obviously wrong to see the marketing of soap and butter as a factor determining expansion beyond Swellendam, he exaggerates the degree to which stock farming was geared to the market. Stock farmers did not sell the majority of their stock as Neumark asserts. There is, instead, abundant evidence of overstocking and of the farmers owning more cattle than they could market. There were two reasons for this. Firstly, market prices in Cape Town were never high enough for the farmers to sell the majority of their stock at a profit. Secondly, the stock farmers, with their meagre consumer needs, had little reason to convert cattle into money. Far from being mainly marketable commodities, livestock were predominantly capital and consumption goods. See J. Barrow, *Travels*, II, 302, 332; BO 6, Consideratiën noopens . . . het Slagtvee, 8 Sept. 1799; GR 1/1, Minutes, 1 Nov. 1790, p. 147; GR 1/4, Minutes, 5 Aug. 1805, pp. 22–23.

By 1770 the Xhosa, a branch of the Nguni-speakers, were organised at three levels: patrilineages, consisting of the descendants of a known common ancestor; patriclans, composed of a number of lineages, all claiming descent from a putative common ancestor; and chiefdoms which were political units, each occupying a certain area under a chief. Chiefdoms, which were usually spatially separated, enjoyed a great measure of independence from one another.

Two major splits had occurred in Xhosa society in the hundred years before 1770. At the end of the seventeenth century, while the Xhosa were living west of the Mbashe River, several minor chiefs and their followers had hived off from the nuclear political unit under the paramount, and established separate chiefdoms at a distance. By 1750 these chiefdoms, which included the Ntinde, Gwali, Mbalu, Dange and Gqunukhwebe, were located in the area between the Kei and the Keiskamma Rivers. The westernmost chiefdom, the Gqunukhwebe, was distinct from the others because its members had mixed to a much greater extent with the Gona who, as Khoikhoi, were not initially regarded as equals in the Xhosa chiefdoms into which they had been incorporated.[4] It is conceivable that the Gqunukhwebe, although Xhosa in culture, were regarded as inferior by the Xhosa because of their partly Khoikhoi origin. The Gqunukhwebe chief was scorned by his fellow chiefs because he was not of the royal lineage,[5] but there is no evidence that he was politically subordinate to them in the late eighteenth century.[6]

The second major schism occurred in the middle of the eighteenth century when the Xhosa nucleus split into two sections under the leadership of Gcaleka and Rharhabe, with the Rharhabe moving westward in the direction of the Fish River. In the authority crisis which followed, Rharhabe and Gcaleka each claimed to be a paramount with some authority over other chiefs in his vicinity.

Some scholars believe that all Xhosa chiefdoms which had been established as a result of fission were independent of one another and of the Gcaleka and Rharhabe 'paramounts'.[7] They argue that chiefs did not have to act in unison in external affairs, nor did they have to pay tribute or provide military aid to the paramount. This may have been the position in the nineteenth century. However, the flux of Xhosa society in the eighteenth century makes such a static model inadequate.

In particular, the relationship of the chiefs in the Ciskei with Rharhabe and his successors was vague and shifting. When Rharhabe moved west of the Kei after c. 1760, he claimed authority over the Ntinde, Gwali, Dange, Mbalu and Gqunukhwebe.[8] It is not clear whether he really considered them as rebellious subjects who should be subjugated by force, or whether he made this claim merely to acquire the colonists' support. In any event, these chiefdoms were unwilling to relinquish the degree of independence they had established since the beginning of the eighteenth century, and rejected Rharhabe's claim whenever they felt themselves to be in a strong enough position to do so.[9] It was not genealogical ranking – that is, the seniority of chiefs – but power which was the main determinant of relationships between the Rharhabe and the Gcaleka chiefs, between the Rharhabe and other Ciskei chiefs, and among these chiefs themselves.[10]

The Xhosa were cattle-herders and hoe-farmers who lived on well-watered lands in dispersed village settlements, each of which could supply most of the economic needs of its inhabitants. There was a tendency for each chiefdom to occupy a specific river valley. A chief was forced to expand at the expense of his neighbours if a territory could no longer satisfy the needs of his subjects, who otherwise might join another chief.[11] A corresponding phenomenon occurred in colonial society. Here capital was scarce and extensive land use the norm. When an area became densely settled, the European stock farmers did not attempt to increase the carrying capacity of the land, but expanded further, forcing Khoikhoi out. When expansion beyond the colony was no longer possible, 'forcing in' between the loan farms or expansion into Xhosa territory were seen as the only solutions.[12]

Thus at certain stages in the late eighties and early nineties the Zuurveld was a space where chiefdoms and European farmers competed for land. This competition was exacerbated by the conflicting views about landholding of the colonists, who considered a certain defined area as belonging exclusively to them, and those of the Xhosa, who saw land as communal property, the boundaries of which were hardly ever sharply defined. Conflict over livestock was also important, for in both Xhosa and colonial society, cattle were a major form of capital and a commonly recognised symbol of wealth. Raids to supplement stock and recoup losses were endemic in the frontier struggle.

The open frontier: its characteristics

We noted before that the frontier had not only a geographical but also a social dimension.[13] Unlike a boundary, which evokes the image of a line on a map and demarcates spheres of political control, the frontier is an area where colonisation is taking place. Here two or more ethnic communities co-exist with conflicting claims to the land, and no authority is recognised as legitimate by all the parties or is able to exercise undisputed control over the area. Thus the stress is on coercive power, i.e., the ability to realise aims forcibly in the face of opposition from others. In this sense the Cape Eastern Frontier calls to mind W.K. Hancock's reference to the frontier which once existed between England and Scotland: '[It] was not a line but a district where thieving Scot and thieving Englishman had sufficient liberty for roving forays'.[14]

One of the major characteristics of the frontier zone, then, is that it is a disputed area, claimed at one stage or other by the various peoples living there. Some time between 1750 and 1780 the Gqunukhwebe penetrated that part of the Zuurveld lying between the Boesmans and Fish Rivers. They were followed by the Mbalu under Langa and his sons Umlawu (also known as Nqeno) and Thole; the Gwali under Tsatsu; the Dange; and the Ntinde. During the 1700s the colonists started occupying the land between the Sundays and the Fish Rivers. Hemmed in by Xhosa and colonists, the Khoikhoi chiefdoms, whose survival depended on a large territory in which they could hunt and pasture stock, disintegrated.

The Zuurveld became an area where various attempts were made to legitimise conflicting claims to the land. Ruyter's Hoengeiqua chiefdom, now consisting mainly of the Gona, claimed prior occupation; but the Gqunukhwebe insisted that their chief, Tshaka, had purchased the land between the Fish and the Kowie Rivers from Ruyter. This was denied by Ruyter's grandchildren. The colony's claim was based on the boundary settlement concluded by Governor van Plettenberg in 1778, when he had persuaded some Gwali chiefs to recognise as the boundary of the colony the upper reaches of the Great Fish River and the Boesmans River mountains. Two years later this claim expanded when the Council of Policy proclaimed the Fish River along its entire length as the boundary.[15] Thus the land between the Boesmans and the Fish was now also regarded as colonial territory. Some Xhosa and Khoikhoi disputed this; however, nobody waited for the disputes to be resolved at a higher level. Europeans, Khoikhoi and Africans settled down close to one another: from the beginning 'kraals and [European] habitations were mixed.'[16]

Another characteristic of a frontier is the lack of a single government able to exercise undisputed authority over all individuals in the frontier zone. On the frontier there were of course various authorities exercising some control over their respective communities. But while they were considered legitimate by probably the majority of their subjects, they were often too weak to prevent challenges which ranged from unauthorised action to rebellion.

No Xhosa authority was able to fill this authority vacuum. There was no political leader – not even a paramount – who could make decisions and agreements without the consent of the various Xhosa chiefdoms which would be affected. The colonial officials failed to understand this. From the beginning they attempted to find a supreme chief with whom an agreement could be made which would be binding on Xhosa on both sides of the Fish River. Eventually they attempted to establish peace between the Rharhabe chief, whom they regarded as a paramount, and the Zuurveld chiefs, who claimed that they were at war with him and therefore afraid to return over the Fish.[17]

Secondly, the Zuurveld chiefs, who were indeed recognised as legitimate authorities by their subjects, could only to a limited extent control them or bind them in negotiations. In normal times chiefs were able to punish thieves, but in unsettled frontier conditions they would hardly risk losing their following by punishing a large number of their subjects who had enriched themselves in a raid. The rationale of serving a chief was, after all, the security which he provided for the accumulation of cattle.[18]

Lastly, the colonial government failed to establish itself as an undisputed authority on the frontier. The colonists, of course, originally accepted the Company's authority, but they were mainly concerned with two aspects of Company rule. Firstly, they wanted to be incorporated into the landholding system of the colony. Under this system the Company would recognise their claim to the land in return for their acknowledgement of Company rule and their agreement, at least in theory, to pay rent (*recognitiepenningen*) for their farms. Secondly, the colonists wanted the government to appoint from their ranks a capable person to be field-commandant.[19] This would set in motion the commando system which was fundamental to the security of colonists on the frontier. Under this system the colonists were obliged to serve on commandos against indigenous enemies while the government would provide ammunition for these expeditions.

The Company's authority was further undermined by the inadequacy of its military and police force. The establishment of the Graaff-Reinet district in 1786 only nominally increased its control over the frontier. The landdrost of Graaff-Reinet was assisted by only four or five *ordonnantie ruiters* (mounted police).[20] In a situation where colonists had almost free access to guns and ammunition and considered it their right to fire on raiders, the landdrost could not remotely claim to monopolise the use of force. His authority and the colonists' respect for colonial laws suffered accordingly. Landdrost Woeke of Graaff-Reinet remarked in a letter to the colonial government that unless he was aided by fifty or sixty soldiers 'the rot will continue . . . and if not suppressed will increase to such an extent that everyone will act arbitrarily and do everything at his own sweet will.'[21]

In these circumstances the landdrost was forced to rely on the *veldwachtmeesters* (later field-cornets) to ensure compliance with the laws in their respective divisions. But the field-cornets were dependent on the support of their fellow colonists and often chose to uphold their interests. Thus the key role in the local administration came to be played by men who were often the agents of the colonists rather than of the colonial government.

Company officials on the frontier were unsuccessful in asserting their authority over the Xhosa in the Zuurveld. Awed at first, the chiefs soon sensed that these officials were unable to make good their threats to expel them forcibly. The officials also exploited the widening rift between the government in Cape Town and the frontier colonists.[22] On the other hand, both the colonial government and the colonists did succeed in establishing their authority over the Khoikhoi, whose political structure had disintegrated under European and Xhosa impact, leaving them no other system of authority around which to rally.

In the fragmented political structure of the frontier it was common for various ethnic communities, or rather groups within these communities, to form alliances to obtain specific ends. Thus there was an alliance against the Zuurveld Xhosa consisting of the Rharhabe leaders, who wished to integrate the various Xhosa chiefdoms in the west under their command, and the colonists in the southeastern part of Graaff-Reinet, who desired the removal of these same chiefdoms.[23] To counter this, the Gqunukhwebe incorporated Khoikhoi and slaves who had absconded from European farms. The conflicts between the colonists and the colonial government also saw both sides attempting to enlist allies across ethnic lines. In the rebellions on the frontier some colonists solicited the help of Xhosa. And as late as 1803 Governor Janssens would tell Graaff-Reinet colonists that if disorder in the district did not cease 'he would have to adopt such measures as would exterminate those who were the cause of the turbulence, even if it were only possible with the assistance of Kafirs and Hottentots.'[24]

During the period 1770–1812 one can distinguish two phases, overlapping one another in time and space, in the evolution of the frontier. These may be called the open and the closing frontier. There was a fluidity on the open frontier which contrasted strongly with the increasingly stratified closing frontier. On the open frontier a low population density allowed Khoikhoi labourers to move freely to and from the farms. It was comparatively easy to desert, and employers were often unable to use coercion effectively. Thus the labourers who had been attracted to their service could be called 'clients' as distinct from the unfree labourers of the closing frontier.

Closely related to this was the complexity of a situation in which the three contending parties (Khoikhoi, Xhosa, and colonists) were each unable to exert coercive power over all inhabitants in the region. Goals were pursued more commonly through negotiations than through violence. There was an uncertainty of status: Europeans were not all masters, non-Europeans were not all servants. This produced the paradox of, on the one hand, a degree of inter-ethnic co-operation and, on the other, bitterness and rivalry as members of different groups attempted to find a footing on which they could base their relationship. In all these respects the open frontier situation was distinct from that which would result after the closing of the frontier.

The open frontier, 1770–1793

Although some Khoikhoi settlements in the 1770s and 1780s were smashed by Xhosa and trekboers, many Khoikhoi were incorporated into these societies peacefully. The Zuurveld was not a safe area. Lions roamed freely[25] and 'Bushman' raiders threatened the security of herding communities. These dangers prompted some Khoikhoi to seek the protection of Xhosa chiefdoms. However, they often found that it was impossible to leave without loss of their cattle. During the first phase of incorporation Khoikhoi were usually simply menial servants.[26]

Khoikhoi who rejected Xhosa domination,[27] but who still desired protection and a chance to build up stock, attached themselves to trekboers, an action facilitated by the existence of a clientship tradition in Khoikhoi society. While there were obviously trekboers who from the beginning used violent methods against Khoikhoi, seizing their cattle and compelling them to stay in their service,[28] there were cases where Khoikhoi and colonists established a symbiotic relationship.[29] In such relationships a Khoikhoi entering a trekboer's service retained his livestock; this livestock was supplemented by payments in kind which he received for tending his master's cattle and accompanying him (or going in his place) on commandos against the 'Bushmen'.[30]

The opgaaf rolls (census lists taken for tax purposes) show that many Khoikhoi in colonial service owned a considerable number of cattle. An opgaaf taken in 1798 lists between 1,300 and 1,400 Khoikhoi heads of households in the Graaff-Reinet district; they owned 140 horses, 7,571 cattle and 30,557 sheep – an average of 5 cattle and and 23 sheep per head of household. However, there were some who owned considerably more. Adriaan, a servant of B.J. Foster, owned 30 cattle and 207 sheep; Adriaan Deerling, in the service of S.J. Burger, owned 58 cattle and 250 sheep; and Clara, in the service of D.P. Liebenberg, owned 33 cattle and 177 sheep. Those Khoikhoi who owned more livestock than average tended to be concentrated on a few farms, a fact which suggests that they were living in traditional community on the farm.[31]

For Khoikhoi the transition from independent herder to client may not have been traumatic, provided they could retain their stock and also maintain the bonds with their clan or kinsmen, perhaps settling with them on a colonist's farm.[32] In fact, Khoikhoi often succeeded in bringing their kinsmen along to the farm. Explaining why some trekboers had so many Khoikhoi in their service while others had so few, Andries Stockenstrom, landdrost of Graaff-Reinet from 1803 to 1811, remarked that Khoikhoi refused to separate from their families.[33]

Thus the frontier was as much a place where disparate groups attempted to maintain existing conditions and institutions as one in which, as some historians have suggested,[34] new modes of life and new institutions originated.[35] In adopting a conservative strategy, the Khoikhoi, especially in the way in which they retained and supplemented their stock, often obtained better economic terms from the colonists than from the Xhosa, who at times seized their stock. However, their social prospects, in the sense of full integration with the new society, were far better with the Xhosa. Because biological mixing with Xhosa occurred freely, Khoikhoi did not develop into a separate caste; rather their descendants became Xhosa. In colonial society, however, they were rarely baptised, seldom married colonists, and never granted burgher status. Despite the degree of miscegenation which took place, it did not take long before the Khoikhoi came to form an inferior caste in colonial society.

In other ways the open frontier also spelled the decline of the Khoikhoi. As they lost land they lost their political leverage in colonial society. They also inevitably became enmeshed in, and often bore the brunt of, hostilities between the Xhosa and colonists. Indeed, Khoikhoi were indispensable to the commandos, and Khoikhoi herdsmen were the first to be killed in Xhosa raids.

The colonists and Xhosa had had an uneasy relationship ever since their advance guards had started to mingle in the 1770s. The high value which each attached to cattle, and the opportunities each saw for supplementing stock through raiding and trading, became both bonds and sources of conflict between two peoples who soon were to find that they could live neither with nor without each other.

Barter was the tie which initially brought colonists and Xhosa together. Many Xhosa were keen to acquire European copper, iron and beads, which they had formerly obtained from Khoikhoi intermediaries. European officials and colonists regarded such trade as an excellent opportunity to acquire cheap livestock. Some tried to barter with the Xhosa, as they had with the Khoikhoi, by cajoling or dragooning them into parting with their cattle. The difference was that the Xhosa could retaliate if duped or dispossessed of their cattle.[36] Collins characterised this process as follows: the Xhosas 'at first gave their cattle and labour without knowing its value; but a little experience having opened their eyes on these points, altercations between them and the farmers were the necessary consequence. These contentions grew into enmities. . .'[37]

It was partly to prevent this that the Company declared it illegal for colonists to barter with Xhosa. Equally important, however, was its desire to secure control of the trade for itself, thereby making the colony less dependent on the colonists for its meat supply.[38] After announcing the Company's plans to barter cattle with the Xhosa, Landdrost Woeke to his dismay discovered that the heemraden of Graaff-Reinet were implacably opposed to such a course, arguing that this would spark off hostilities between colonists and Xhosa. Woeke, however, was convinced that the underlying reason for their opposition was the fear that such a trade would depress the price the Company paid the colonists for their cattle. In the mean time the cattle trade between colonists and Xhosa continued illegally. In 1786 Field-Sergeant H.J. van Rensburg of the Boesmans River division reported that many, if not all, of his fellow-colonists were guilty of bartering with the Xhosa.[39]

Labour was a second tie and source of conflict. Khoikhoi were unevenly distributed among the farms, not only because Khoikhoi families were unwilling to split up, but also because they could not always know about better working conditions elsewhere. Thus many farmers were forced to seek Xhosa labour. To Xhosa, especially those who had suffered misfortune, this was an acceptable opportunity to build up their livestock and earn food.[40] But there were various points of friction in the labour situation. When herdsmen lost cattle through negligence they were punished. Misunderstandings also arose over payment, and colonists withheld wages. As an old coloured man, Brantanje Jantjes, recounted of the early frontier: 'Many of the Caffres served the farmers and there were constant disputes among them. The Caffres when not regularly paid or flogged informed their chief and came and stole cattle from the farmers by way of repaying themselves for the injuries they had sustained.'[41] Both Jantjes and Landdrost Maynier regarded the cycle of maltreatment and reprisals as a cause of the 1793 war.[42]

A third activity in this context was begging – or so colonists regarded it. To the Xhosa this was reciprocal exchange in which a poor man asked for food from someone without offering payment. In traditional Xhosa society this was given unstintingly because the giver saw it as a form of insurance against the day when he himself might experience need.[43] At first the colonists gave food liberally to build up goodwill. Soon, however, this practice became a source of friction. As the Xhosa population in the Zuurveld grew, increasing numbers of Xhosa visited farms to request or even demand food. In some cases it was difficult to distinguish between begging and exacting tribute. Lichtenstein wrote: '. . . in peace the Xhosa expect as a sort of tribute what in war they seize by force. They often come in large bodies, and will stay several days or even weeks . . . Their importunity, their numbers and the fear of quarreling with them . . . commonly secure them good entertainment.'[44]

Thus those Xhosa who had earlier moved into the Zuurveld, mainly as a result of political developments in Xhosa society, were now joined by others seeking pasture and opportunities for barter, labour and begging. Some were fleeing from their home regions after committing a crime or suffering defeat in war. These Xhosa moved in groups, bringing along large numbers of cattle. In this way two cultures, which both valued land as a means of production and cattle as a source of wealth and prestige, were brought together in a single area.

Were ethnic or material factors the most important sources of conflict between the colonists and the Xhosa? The colonists carried with them to the frontier a set of attitudes, most important of which was the notion that as 'Christians' they were culturally superior to the 'heathens' whom they often associated with crudeness, conflict and treachery.[45] Although a few individuals went to live among the Xhosa, the colonists were bent on excluding them from their culture and kinship network, and from their political system. As for the Xhosa, eighteenth-century encounters with colonists were such that many distrusted and feared them.[46] However, partly because they were much more numerous, the Xhosa never dreaded that they would be submerged or dominated by

Europeans. Indeed, their approach to neighbours was in direct contrast ·
to that of the colonists: Xhosa society was basically an open one which,
through intermarriage and other means, incorporated and eventually
integrated non-Nguni speakers. There is evidence that the Xhosa were
inclined to incorporate the colonists in the same way. In this they were
unsuccessful, often being rebuffed by the colonists, who misunderstood
their approaches. Consequently during this period colonists and Xhosa
kept their separate identities, each group to a large extent regarding the
other as standing outside their moral community. Such an attitude helps
to explain wartime atrocities (such as the mutilation of corpses and the
colonists' abduction of Xhosa children) which so embittered relations.[47]

Yet, however important ethnic differences were, it is hard to believe
that the conflict between the colonists and Xhosa would have occurred
on such a large scale had it not been for their opposing material interests.
It is difficult to say which was the most important source of conflict –
land or cattle. The colonists clearly wished to have the Zuurveld to
themselves, most of all because the land could not provide pasture for the
cattle of both themselves and the Zuurveld Xhosa.[48] However, such
was the stalemate in the battle to control the Zuurveld that possession of
cattle became an alternative of equal or even overriding importance.

This phenomenon is illustrated by the events of the First Frontier War
(1779–81). Towards the end of the 1770s the Prinsloos of Agter
Bruintjes Hoogte raided cattle east of the Fish and killed some Xhosa.
Bands of Xhosa retaliated late in 1779, capturing a large number of cattle
(21,000 according to the usually exaggerated estimate of the colonists).
This led to commandos in 1780 and 1781 in which the raiding of cattle
was the main activity. Summing up the events of those early years, Collins
remarked: 'The wars that were at first waged against the Caffres were
carried on exclusively by the settlers, who seem, whenever they have
been unsuccessful, to have failed in a great degree from their having
considered the recovery of stolen cattle as the principal object of
hostility.'[49] Hubert Dirk Campagne, an observer sympathetic to
colonists, offered this explanation: while it was not possible to subjugate
the Xhosa by force of arms, it was easy to capture cattle.[50]

In the case of the Zuurveld Xhosa there was a parallel tendency to
attach prime importance to control over cattle rather than land. When
the First Frontier War broke out their main concern was cattle –
protecting their own and capturing the enemy's. After a skirmish they
were quite prepared to withdraw over the Fish, provided they could keep
their booty.[51] The one exception was the Gqunukhwebe. Not of royal
lineage, and acknowledging the Gcaleka chief rather than the Rharhabe

chief as paramount, the Gqunukhwebe chief, Tshaka, considered his stake in the Zuurveld as crucial. He was, of all the Xhosa chiefs, least inclined to retreat. Beyond the Fish, positioned between him and his paramount, was the Rharhabe chief, who might easily capture his cattle and subjugate or even destroy his chiefdom. If Tshaka were to maintain his autonomy, the Zuurveld was definitely the safest place. The fact that the Gqunukhwebe, to a far greater degree than other Xhosa, had entered the service of colonists and had close links with the Khoikhoi in the colony, also explains their determination to stay.

During the course of the First Frontier War the commandos defeated the Ntinde, Gwali, Mbalu and Dange, thus inducing their chiefs to recognise the Fish as the boundary between themselves and the colonists.[52] This left Tshaka of the Gqunukhwebe as the only important chief in the area with whom no boundary settlement had been concluded. The settlement with the other Xhosa did not last long. It was ignored by Xhosa as well as by some colonists; both crossed the Fish to hunt and to barter cattle, or to graze their own. Nevertheless, the frontier remained comparatively quiet for the next five or six years.[53]

In 1786, in response to requests by Adriaan van Jaarsveld and other leading colonists, the Company established the frontier district of Graaff-Reinet. This decision stemmed from the Company's desire to assert greater administrative control over the colony's outlying regions as well as to prevent another clash between the colonists and the Xhosa.[54] Landdrost Woeke was instructed to prevent colonists from trespassing beyond the Fish, to persuade the Xhosa to settle east of the Fish, and to prevent any contact between colonists and Xhosa. When his request for fifty or sixty soldiers was turned down, Woeke attempted to obtain these objectives through negotiations. He soon discovered that several smaller issues were negotiable. Xhosa chiefs, especially Tshaka, were prepared to punish cattle thieves on representations from the landdrost or veldwachtmeesters in the Zuurveld. On his side Woeke was ready to redress wrongs which the chiefs reported. Thus a degree of communication and understanding developed between European and black as the two societies became increasingly interlocked.[55]

However, Woeke was soon to be faced with an unnegotiable conflict. From 1786 the numbers of the Xhosa in the Zuurveld progressively increased, and colonists demanded that they be expelled. By 1789 a traveller saw several thousand Xhosa with over 16,000 cattle on a farm at Kariega.[56] In the same year Woeke reported that four Xhosa chiefs were west of the Fish with a multitude of followers.[57] One of them was Langa, who in 1781 had been driven from the Zuurveld and had now returned;

another was Tshaka, who had probably never left.

There were two immediate causes of the Xhosa influx into the Zuurveld after 1786. Firstly, there was a severe drought in that year which killed many cattle and almost all game.[58] Many Xhosa came to the Zuurveld for pasture and food and, after the drought had broken, stayed on. Secondly, political disputes in Xhosa society induced many Xhosa to move westward for safety. The death of Rharhabe in c. 1781 brought to the fore an aggressive new leader in the person of his son, Ndlambe. Ndlambe was next in rank to the heir, Mlawu, who had died before his father. Acting as regent while Mlawu's heir, Ngqika, was still a minor, Ndlambe aimed to establish himself as paramount with effective control over both his own chiefdom and the 'rebel' chiefdoms in the west. During the late 1780s and early 1790s Ndlambe, in alliance with Langa, defeated the Gqunukhwebe, who suffered heavy losses and subsequently retreated further westward into the colony. There were now many destitute Xhosa in the Zuurveld, anxious to recoup their losses or simply to find food. It was they who were mainly responsible for cattle thefts in the Zuurveld after 1789; such thefts had rarely occurred during the preceding decade.[59]

It was not only Xhosa numbers and thefts which outraged the colonists; Langa at this time was becoming increasingly self-assertive. Demanding compensation when one of his subjects was killed or injured, he sent word in c. 1788 to Coenraad de Buys that the 'Christians' should not think he was afraid to make war.[60] During this time his people, according to Woeke, roamed the Zuurveld in groups of ten to twenty, 'getting up to all kinds of mischief and troublemaking, raiding cattle and in general refusing to listen to friendly warnings.'[61] 'Mischief' included the looting of houses for copper and iron, destruction of crops, and killing of game on farms.

In response to the colonists' insistence that the Zuurveld Xhosa be driven from the colony, Woeke in 1789 sent out a commando under Captain Kühne to 'goad' them over the Fish. This plan failed because the river was in flood and prevented the commando from expelling those Xhosa whom it had rounded up.[62]

Later in 1789 Woeke set out at the head of a small negotiating party to urge the Xhosa to withdraw from the area west of the Fish. He was under strict orders from the government to avoid violence but to buy off all Xhosa claims to the land in the Zuurveld.[63] He encountered resistance, especially from the Gqunukhwebe, who claimed that they had bought the land between the Kowie and the Fish, and now refused to renounce their claim.[64] Moreover, some Xhosa had come to see the issue as a clash between irreconcilable claims: they insisted that if they had to leave the land, the colonists would have to do the same.[65] In 1792 another commando also failed in an attempt amicably to persuade the Gqunukhwebe and other Xhosa to leave the Zuurveld. Hereafter both parties increasingly turned to force in order to back up their demands and claims.

At the same time numbers of Khoikhoi were absconding from colonists' farms and allying themselves with the Xhosa, especially the Gqunukhwebe. These Khoikhoi were rebelling against the loss of their land, restrictions on their mobility, and maltreatment at the hands of their masters.[66] They enhanced Xhosa military power, since they often brought guns they had taken from their masters, or at least could handle the firearms which Xhosa had bartered from the colonists for cattle.[67] Unlike the Xhosa, some Khoikhoi were superb horsemen and knew the colonists' strategy. The Zuurveld Xhosa valued these allies, while the Khoikhoi welcomed the opportunity for revenge against the colonists. On occasion when the colonists appealed to Xhosa to release their runaway servants, the Xhosa showed their solidarity with these Khoikhoi by refusing. The colonists were also asked why they did not let their other servants go.[68]

Having lost confidence in the government's peaceful policy towards the Xhosa and in its ability or willingness to protect them, the colonists in the southeastern divisions resolved to expel the Xhosa themselves. As Woeke remarked: 'War was not only inevitable but many inhabitants felt very much inclined to do battle.'[69] Several colonists used violence against individual Xhosa, even against chiefs. Langa, for instance was locked up by R. Campher and forced to barter cattle; his wife was seized by Coenraad de Buys and used as a concubine. Chungwa was imprisoned in a mill and forced to work it himself. Some of the chiefs' followers were shot by men like De Buys, the Bezuidenhouts and C. Botha.[70] Apart from these individual acts of violence there is also some evidence of a massive cattle raid by a commando in 1789.[71] This raid, if in fact it did occur, would further explain the increase in cattle raids by the Xhosa after 1789.

Unlike in the 1780s, when they were still awed by the colonists' guns and horses, the Xhosa from the early 1790s started to challenge the colonists' position in the Zuurveld. The colonists in general were unable to accept a situation in which 'heathens' were allowed to lord it over 'Christians'.[72] They were convinced that with a sufficient supply of ammunition they could re-establish 'proper relations'. The Zuurveld Xhosa had a different conception of what proper relations were. The points on which colonists felt superior – literacy, different sexual mores and Christian religious beliefs – had, after all, little meaning for the Xhosa.[73] Unlike the Khoikhoi, the Zuurveld Xhosa retained their traditional culture while the various chiefdoms remained intact. This provided them with strength and self-assurance in their resistance to the colonists. Their strength was bolstered by the guns they had acquired since the opening of the frontier and by the support of Khoikhoi marksmen.[74] It is conceivable that they also derived comfort from the compact way in which they were settled compared to the colonists, who were thinly spread over a vast area.

Some Xhosa were now demanding gifts, raiding farms when their owners were absent, and threatening to attack colonists who had particularly aroused their wrath.[75] Even where no actual violence had taken place there was still constant friction over pasture and water. A colonist echoed the feelings of most Europeans near the Boesmans River when he wrote of the 'nuisance caused me by a Kaffir captain Langa on my farm . . . with his people and his stock he lies between me and Zwaanepoel and not only overgrazes the field and consumes the water supply but also ruins the veld by burning.'[76] What had started as an uneasy co-existence turned into an increasingly aggressive battle for pasture and cattle. There were still colonists like Adriaan van Jaarsveld who proposed that 'for the sake of lasting peace with the Xhosa the Zuurveld [meaning the area between the Fish and the Boesmans], which had been their own land, should be handed back to them.'[77] However, on both sides there was a growing feeling that neither negotiations nor concessions, but only force, would resolve disputes.

Thus the period 1770–92 had given rise to the preconditions of the strife and warfare which would engulf the frontier in the two decades after 1793. In summary they were: conflict over land and cattle; the absence of any force which could impose peace and order; maltreatment of Khoikhoi and Xhosa servants; the transfer of allegiance of some Khoikhoi clients of the colonists; the presence in colonial territory of large numbers of Xhosa whom the colonists perceived as a threat to their lives and property; and mutual suspicion and mistrust which, as the result of individual acts of aggression and violence, grew into bitterness and hate. To take only one example: during the hostilities of 1779–81 Adriaan van Jaarsveld tossed out some tobacco to a band of Xhosa, and then, while the Xhosa were scrambling to pick up the tobacco, fired on them, killing many. He later explained that he had feared treachery. According to the Xhosa historian, J.H. Soga,[78] this incident rankled in the minds of the Ntinde even into the twentieth century.[§] In an atmosphere so pervaded with fear and violence the outbreak of armed hostilities was a distinct possibility.

The frontier crisis, 1793–1812

In 1793 a severe drought made the conflict over pasture much more explosive. Wars between Europeans and Africans, however, did not break out simply because tempers snapped.[79] On this occasion two events on different sides of the Fish River threatened to destroy the balance of power and then triggered a war. Firstly, a number of Xhosa engaged in a feud with Ndlambe fled from him into the colony, prompting some colonists to abandon their farms. Secondly, in May 1793 Barend Lindeque, a militia officer in the Zuurveld, who early in 1792 had given public warnings of his intention to attack the Zuurveld Xhosa, on his own initiative attempted to push them over the Fish. He had already contacted Ndlambe, who was also anxious that all Zuurveld Xhosa be driven back so that he could subjugate these 'rebel' chieftains to his authority.

The Second Frontier War (1793) broke out when Lindeque's commando and Ndlambe's men attacked the Zuurveld Xhosa and captured about 2,000 cattle. Thereupon, as a result of some misunderstanding, the coalition fell apart. The Zuurveld Xhosa, with the Gqunukhwebe in the vanguard, counter-attacked. This sparked off a general panic in which the colonists abandoned the Zuurveld almost completely.[80] In ensuing raids the Xhosa killed forty Khoikhoi servants, burnt twenty homesteads and, according to the colonists' estimate, captured 50 to 60,000 cattle, 11,000 sheep, and 200 horses.

A combined commando from Graaff-Reinet and Swellendam took the field under Landdrosts Maynier and Faure. It had instructions to expel the Xhosa from the Zuurveld and to indemnify the colonists for their losses. Besides capturing 8,000 cattle, the commando forced a considerable number of Xhosa to retreat beyond the Fish, where Ndlambe's forces defeated them, killing Tshaka (the Gqunukhwebe

---

§ A similar event, but with the roles reversed, took place in 1811 when Landdrost Stockenstrom and fourteen of his men were killed by Xhosa. Stockenstrom in good faith had tried to persuade these Xhosa to leave the Zuurveld before they would be attacked by armed forces. This event, like the one noted above, only led to greater distrust between colonists and Xhosa. The next generations of course only remembered the 'massacre' that the other side had perpetrated.

chief) and capturing Langa (the Mbalu chief), who apparently died soon afterwards. The commando found it impossible to clear the Zuurveld of all Xhosa, and after the commando withdrew, those Xhosa beyond the Fish began to return. After the war Maynier, who refused to call out another general commando against the Xhosa, failed to negotiate the withdrawal of the Xhosa in the Zuurveld and the restitution of raided cattle. He limited police action to the apprehension of thieves.[81]

All evidence suggests that the colonists of the Graaff-Reinet southeastern divisions, even with the help of some Swellendam burghers, could not successfully subjugate the Xhosa. Unable to draw on the northern divisions, which were fighting a desperate battle against the 'Bushmen', they were far inferior in numbers to the Xhosa.[82] The advantages provided by their guns and horses were neutralised by the opportunities the Xhosa had for concealment in the bush. And the colonists were hampered by dissension, lack of leadership, and the government's control over the flow of ammunition. It was probably because they sensed their weakness that few of the 150 European families who had formerly inhabited the Zuurveld returned after the war. By the beginning of 1798 Landdrost Bresler reported that no colonists lived between the Fish and the Sundays; by September of that year only a third of the Zuurveld families had returned.[83]

After the war new leaders attempted to seize control of their respective communities. Each apparently realised that an unchallenged, single-leadership structure could more effectively negotiate, wage war and perhaps establish a monopoly in trade with other communities.[84] In 1795, the same year in which the British first occupied the Cape, the colonists of the southeastern divisions seized control of Graaff-Reinet and renounced their allegiance to the government of Cape Town. While there existed widespread dissatisfaction about the Company's stepped-up collection of the loan farm rent, the sectional grievances in the southeastern divisions were decisive. Farmers in these divisions blamed Maynier for the colonists' failure to recapture all their lost cattle and to drive all the Xhosa from the Zuurveld. Maynier had also alienated leading colonists by summoning farmers to appear in court if they were suspected of maltreating Khoikhoi servants. Maynier was less unpopular among burghers of the northern divisions, since the military efforts of these areas were concentrated on the battle against 'Bushmen' raiders who had forced the colonists to evacuate parts of Sneeuwberg and several other northern divisions.

In February 1795 the rebels under the leadership of Marthinus Prinsloo ordered Maynier to leave the district and forced officials who supported the peace policy towards the Xhosa to resign. The rebels, calling themselves Patriots, also expelled a commission sent to investigate the disturbances and they renounced Company rule. Subsequently self-styled *representanten des volks* (representatives of the people) began to attend the meetings of the Board of Heemraden and soon established dominance over the local authority. The representanten claimed to be chosen by the *volkstem* (voice of the people), but there is no evidence that they were democratically elected. Most came from the southeastern divisions, and they were probably all chosen by the rebel leaders.

In 1796 the new British government sent Frans Bresler out as landdrost. Bresler backed the policy of conciliation toward the Xhosa and refused to recognise the representanten. The rebels now threatened to punish all colonists who swore the oath of loyalty to the British king. Shortly afterwards they expelled Bresler with a request to government that future landdrosts be appointed by the burghers.[85]

Across the Fish, Ngqika ousted the regent Ndlambe, who had been reluctant to step down, and then tried to extend his own power by various measures,[86] like deposing councillors and bringing their people directly under him, and by claiming the entire estate of deceased commoners.[87] In the Zuurveld, where chiefdoms like the Mbalu, the Dange and the Ntinde had suffered almost fatal blows in the war of 1793, the new Gqunukhwebe chief, Chungwa, attempted to extend his authority over his weakened neighbours. He realised that power lay in numbers: in 1797, when two small chiefs started to retreat over the Fish, he confiscated their cattle, declaring that if they left he would be too weak to sustain his claim to the land.[88] By 1799 he was claiming the Sundays River as his western boundary.[89]

None of these three attempts was successful. The Graaff-Reinet rebellion petered out because the government cut off the supply of ammunition. Ngqika's attempt to build up his power failed because some councillors resisted him and led their followers over the Fish. They were followed by Ndlambe shortly afterwards. Finally, Chungwa was unsuccessful, since Ndlambe, soon after his arrival in the Zuurveld in 1800, established himself as the most important chief there. Unable to dominate the frontier, the various leaders sought to establish alliances. Ngqika and the colonists enlisted each other's help in their conflict with the Zuurveld Xhosa,[90] while Chungwa did his best to attract Khoikhoi allies to defend himself against a two-pronged attack.

Meanwhile in 1799 another rebellion broke out in Graaff-Reinet (the Van Jaarsveld rebellion), an event which would shortly trigger the Third

Frontier War (1799–1802). Adriaan van Jaarsveld, who had been active in the 1795–96 rebellion, was arrested on a charge of fraud. While being taken to Cape Town he was set free by a party of rebels under Prinsloo. They tried to win general support but received no backing from Sneeuwberg. A force of British and Khoikhoi troops under General Vandeleur was sent to the frontier, where they arrested the rebel leaders. This action caused a frontier upheaval in three ways. Firstly, when Khoikhoi saw a partially Khoikhoi force advancing, some raided their masters and then sought the protection of the army. Secondly, Vandeleur unsuccessfully tried to push the Gqunukhwebe, by now the westernmost chiefdom in the Zuurveld, over the Fish, thus arousing their hostility. Thirdly, having failed to resolve the situation, Vandeleur made arrangements to return to Cape Town. It soon became clear that the Khoikhoi who had flocked to his side would be left behind. A number of these now allied themselves to the Gqunukhwebe and started to raid the entire southern part of Graaff-Reinet, sparking off a large-scale retreat of colonists from these divisions. (See ch. 1, pp. 33–35). The colonists tried to regroup; but a Khoikhoi force, consisting of 700 men with horses and 150 guns, together with Gqunukhwebe and other Zuurveld Xhosa, defeated a commando of 300 men, pinned down Vandeleur and 200 regular troops in Algoa Bay, and forced almost all the colonists to evacuate the southern part of Graaff-Reinet and some of the eastern divisions of Swellendam.

In August 1799 British reinforcements under General Francis Dundas left Cape Town for the interior. Accompanied by Maynier, whose influence among the Khoikhoi and Xhosa was highly rated by the British, Dundas desired to establish peace through conciliation. Toward the end of 1799 Maynier succeeded in ending the war by persuading the Khoikhoi to break off their alliance with the Xhosa. A large number went back to the farms in return for a promise of better protection from their employers. The rest stayed with the Xhosa or lived independently under Klaas Stuurman and other chiefs at the Sundays River. Maynier tried to establish peace in several ways. He induced colonists to return to their original farms. He offered Khoikhoi the protection of labour contracts and acted immediately when he heard that a labourer had been maltreated. He introduced patrols of young colonists, later reinforced with armed Khoikhoi, to follow the spoor of stolen cattle and, if necessary, to shoot the thieves. Finally, he refused to send a large commando against the Zuurveld Xhosa but attempted to negotiate their evacuation of the Zuurveld.

The relative stability started to disintegrate in 1801. Petty thefts committed since the middle of 1800 caused alarm among the colonists. Large numbers of Khoikhoi who feared the wrath of the colonists flocked to the town of Graaff-Reinet where the missionaries J.T. van der Kemp and James Read had started to work. Maynier's decision to allow Khoikhoi to worship in the church caused great dissatisfaction among the colonists, who also objected strongly to his use of armed Khoikhoi troops. Maynier nevertheless believed he could ride out the storm and even refused an offer from Cape Town of a thousand troops. By early 1801, however, alarming rumours were circulating among the colonists that Maynier was planning a joint Khoikhoi-Xhosa attack upon his enemies. These rumours were probably spread by a Zuurveld farmer, H.J. van Rensburg, who wanted to get rid of Maynier before attacking the Xhosa and Khoikhoi in the Zuurveld. As a result of the rumours large numbers of colonists fled from Bruintjes Hoogte and the Zuurveld to the northern divisions. In June 1801 a group of armed men appeared at the outskirts of Graaff-Reinet town, demanding that permission be granted to attack the Xhosa, that labour disputes be settled by burgher officials instead of by the landdrost, and that the church be closed to the Khoikhoi. Maynier conceded only the last demand, and in October the colonists besieged the town. In November 1801 British troops from Cape Town relieved the town and handed Maynier orders for his recall. recall.

The colonists had succeeded in getting rid of Maynier, but their large-scale evacuation of farms had left the district wide open to attacks. From mid-1801 to the end of 1802 bands of Khoikhoi and Xhosa raided large areas of Graaff-Reinet and Swellendam. By the end of 1802 some 470 farms, fully 35 per cent of the farms registered in the two districts, were estimated to have been laid waste. Peace was concluded early in 1803 on the sole condition that each side retain possession of the cattle it had captured. The colonists' losses, according to their own estimate, were approximately 50,000 cattle, 50,000 sheep and 1,000 horses. A quarter to a third of the European population of the southeastern sector of the colony had fled their farms. As in 1793, European settlement in the east had been rolled back.

The Batavian administration (1803–06) decided to maintain the colonial government's claims to the frontier zone and to restore the European-dominated social order.[91] To this end it founded the district of Uitenhage in the Zuurveld and appointed an able man, Ludwig Alberti, as its landdrost. Through persuasion as well as compulsion a large number of colonists were induced to return to their farms in the southeast.[92] The Batavians were also successful in persuading more

Khoikhoi to leave the Zuurveld Xhosa and return to the farms. Already during the war the alliance of Khoikhoi and Xhosa raiders had begun to fall apart as the partners began to dispute the division of booty. Some Xhosa, in fact, killed a Khoikhoi leader, Boezak, although he claimed to have served them loyally.[93] In peace time there was also an irreconcilable conflict between the Zuurveld Xhosa chiefs, who wanted settled conditions in which they could exercise more effective control, and the Khoikhoi chiefs, who wished to continue raiding. Even among the Khoikhoi leaders divisions appeared as some chiefs challenged Klaas Stuurman, who apparently also opposed further raiding and wished to settle down quietly in the Zuurveld. Eventually the government bought off Klaas Stuurman and other Khoikhoi leaders by giving them small plots of land; their followers who had left the Xhosa had no alternative but to return to the farms or join the Cape Regiment (ch. 1, pp. 35 – 38).

However, the Batavians failed to dislodge the Zuurveld Xhosa, establish a firm border,[94] or regulate the relationships between colonists and Xhosa. The British, who again occupied the Cape in 1806, made futile attempts through Captain J.G. Cuyler, Alberti's successor as landdrost of Uitenhage, to persuade the Zuurveld Xhosa to retreat beyond the Fish. They were unwilling to provide the military resources necessary for a forcible expulsion, especially while a major European war was in progress. Government policy was neatly summarised by Governor Caledon's statement that 'it is better to submit to a certain extent of injury than risk a great deal for a prospect of advantage by no means certain.'[95] In these circumstances frontier landdrosts were compelled to establish a makeshift security system which depended on winning the goodwill of the chiefs and securing their co-operation in apprehending thieves. At the same time the colonists were strictly forbidden to do anything which might provoke hostilities. Patrols commanded by field-cornets were established to follow the spoor of stolen cattle to the thief's kraal. There the patrols were amicably to persuade the chief to hand over the cattle.[96]

These measures greatly handicapped the colonists' ability to maintain their interests effectively, and the government's policy was criticised both by contemporaries and by later historians. Some critics, however, assume that the colonists could have given substance to the claim, expressed by three commandants in 1803, that they were 'strong enough to recover [their] belongings at the point of the sword and to provide a peace that would give quiet and security to . . . Government for years to come'.[97] But was this indeed the case? Even if the colonists were to receive from the government 'a good supply of powder and lead', as the commandants requested, it is doubtful whether, in the absence of generally accepted leaders, they could have totally expelled the Zuurveld Xhosa. Still more questionable was their ability to maintain peace by manning a boundary patrol which would prevent the return of Xhosa to the Zuurveld. The colonists showed no great enthusiasm for participating in these patrols; but the colonists also so distrusted the Khoikhoi that they would have opposed any plan to arm themselves in this capacity, unless they were commanded by men in whom they had complete confidence.[98] In these circumstances the colonial government assumed that peace could best be maintained by limiting local confrontations.

During the first decade of the nineteenth century the Zuurveld Xhosa, especially Ndlambe, gained in strength as Ngqika's power decreased. In 1800 it had been different. Ngqika had defeated Hintsa, the Gcaleka chief, and then claimed to be paramount of all the Xhosa. He had also established a sound relationship with the colony, born of a common desire to subjugate the Zuurveld Xhosa. On the other hand, Chungwa and Ndlambe, despite their cattle gains in the Third Frontier War (1799–1802), still lacked confidence and strength. Then in about 1807 Ngqika committed a grave error by ordering the abduction of one of Ndlambe's wives. Capitalising on the general revulsion at this deed, Ndlambe attacked and defeated Ngqika. Although Ngqika subsequently succeeded in recouping some of his losses and honour, it was clear that he had lost the initiative. He realised that his collaboration with the colonists was costing him dearly. In 1809 he lamented that 'the favours [the Christians] had almost exclusively bestowed on him made every Kaffer his enemy.'[99]

In contrast Ndlambe, having returned to the Zuurveld after the battle, steadily gained in power and prestige. Colonial observers were at first sceptical of his claim that he could subdue the other chiefs. In 1805 Alberti reported that if he attempted to do so he would be resisted because each chief wished 'to be his own master.'[100] To some extent Alberti was correct. Not only Chungwa but also some less powerful Xhosa chiefs like Habana and Galata of the Gwali, Nqeno of the Mbalu, and Xasa of the Dange, were still successfully resisting control by Ndlambe, whose interests differed from theirs. He almost certainly disapproved of their raiding and antagonising of the colonists. However, Ndlambe's power was steadily increasing, and by 1809, with 3,000 men under his command, he was undoubtedly the most powerful chief in the Zuurveld. Cuyler even thought that he was head of all Xhosa within the colonial boundaries.[101]

Chungwa, whose strength seems to have declined in inverse proportion to Ndlambe's rise, moved further westward during this period. This could have been due both to his desire to escape Ndlambe's control and to the necessities of transhumance. By 1808 there was a community of Chungwa's followers at Leeugamka, halfway between the Fish River and Cape Town; Chungwa himself was settling in the Langkloof. He was forced to retreat and became increasingly hemmed in by Ndlambe, who threatened his autonomy, and the colonial authorities. The government scorned his attempt to pay for pasture and his expressions of goodwill, and insisted that he should retreat over the Fish, a move which would end his independence.[102]

For Xhosa the opportunities for small-time raiding gradually decreased in the period between the frontier wars of 1801–02 and the year 1809, as important chiefs in the Zuurveld became more powerful. In times of peace, Chungwa, and even more so Ndlambe, tried to curtail cattle-lifting in order to prevent conflict with the colony. These Xhosa chiefs seem to have favoured an equilibrium on the frontier which would allow them to enjoy the benefits of labour and trade with the colonists. To foster stability they sought to increase their control over chiefdoms in their vicinity. Yet despite Ndlambe's growing strength, he could not control all the minor chiefs, especially those in the mountains, who were primarily reponsible for the convulsion of the frontier which started in 1809. In this year the partial accommodation between colonists and Xhosa started to collapse.

The disintegration of the political order manifested itself in various ways. Firstly, Xhosa belonging to minor chiefdoms pushed into Bruintjes Hoogte and as far north as Buffelshoek (the present Cradock), settling among the colonists. They wanted both to pasture their cattle on sweetveld, which had become exhausted in the Zuurveld, and to escape from Ndlambe's control.[103] Secondly, from 1809 minor chiefs like Nqeno, Xasa, Habana and Galata began to raid cattle on a much larger scale than before, causing colonists in the exposed divisions to retreat. Field-cornet reports indicate that in Uitenhage alone more than 2,000 head of cattle were stolen in 1810. It was clear that the pattern of these raids differed from the petty thefts of four or five years before and that an extensive raiding network was in operation. In 1810 Cuyler declared:

'I am convinced that the cause of the intrusion of many of the Kaffir Chiefs so near upon the settlement is to cover or favour the stealing of their people, which booty they more or less share – indeed stealing among the Kaffirs from the inhabitants is become quite a trade. The cattle are stolen and driven to the furthest Kaffirs where they are eagerly exchanged for Kaffir cattle, and the cattle received in exchange are brought back by the thieves.'[104]

Stockenstrom believed that these cattle were bartered to the Tembu and other kraals beyond the Kei River.[105]

The audacity of the raiders, and the resulting loss of heart among the frontier colonists, had much to do with the feeling on both sides that the colonial government was intent on avoiding aggressive measures at all costs. In 1810 the government sent 200 regulars and 360 members of the Cape (Hottentot) Regiment to replace the burgher patrols. Executing a repeatedly issued proclamation against the employment of Xhosa, these troops rounded up the colonists' Xhosa servants, numbering 'some thousand', and brought them to the Sundays River to join the chiefs.[106] Many of these servants then joined the raiders. It soon became obvious that the troops, inhibited by their instructions to avoid hostilities, would not stop the raids. At the same time government regulations made it virtually impossible for the colonists to do so either. Cuyler wrote:

> 'the Caffres already knowing that they cannot be fired at by the Boors except when attempting to kill them, commit their outrages with that degree of confidence and impunity to defy our feeble attempts to take them alive and encourage them to repeat their robberies.'[107]

In 1810 and the first half of 1811 Xhosa scoured the country in groups of four or five to demand gifts or to raid cattle, prompting colonists to evacuate large parts of Graaff-Reinet and Uitenhage. A British officer in 1811 reported from Bruintjes Hoogte:

> 'The country is on every side overrun with Kaffres, and there never was a period when such numerous parties of them were known to have advanced so far in every direction before; the depredations of late committed by them exceed all precedent and . . . unless some decisive and hostile measures are immediately adopted, I solemnly declare I apprehend considerable and most *serious consequences*.'[108]

By the middle of 1811 raiders and Xhosa who wandered around to 'beg' were active at the Sundays River, Bruintjes Hoogte and Buffelshoek. Great numbers of Xhosa turned up in Tarka and Sneeuwberg in the northeast of Graaff-Reinet under the pretence of visiting, which usually entailed 'begging'. Along the entire eastern border colonists were preparing to abandon their farms. Hardly any farms were occupied east of the Uitenhage drostdy, and many colonists had left Bruintjes Hoogte and Buffelshoek. The majority of the Bruintjes Hoogte colonists were reportedly ready to quit the district.[109]

Both the colony and Ndlambe attempted to stabilise the situation. At the initiative of Stockenstrom, patrols of burghers and soldiers gradually pushed most of the Xhosa out of his district (Graaff-Reinet). Ndlambe in turn exerted pressure on the minor chiefs who were mainly responsible for the raids. Before the end of 1811 Habana, Xasa, Galata and Nqeno were all compelled to leave the colony. During the second half of 1811 there was indeed a lull on the frontier, but the situation was far from normal and many colonists refused to return to their farms. In Cape Town the dislocation on the Eastern Frontier was viewed with great concern. Sir John Cradock, who became governor in 1811, was warned that Xhosa might penetrate close to Cape Town. Unlike his predecessor, Caledon, the new governor was a military man who saw the Xhosa as a threat to the security of the hinterland and to the meat supply of Cape Town. Accordingly he instructed Lieutenant-Colonel John Graham to drive all the Xhosa (Chungwa and Ndlambe included) over the Great Fish River, 'the acknowledged boundary of . . . His Majesty's Settlement.'[110]

With the arrival of efficient military men such as Graham a new element was introduced to the frontier scene. Up till then the European and the Xhosa on the frontier had in some respects resembled a couple in a disastrous forced marriage: they would fear and fight each other, but neither would destroy the other – in fact their constant battle to gain the upper hand or stand up against one another was what made their lives meaningful and morbidly filled their daily thoughts. For the colonists the Xhosa were labourers, trading partners, foes – sometimes all in one. For Graham there was none of this: the Xhosa were simply enemies, 'horrid savages'. Plundering parties should be followed to their settlements and there 'every man Kaffer' that could be found, 'if possible the chief', should be 'destroyed'.[111] In the summer of 1811–12 British officers, heading 900 burgher militia and 700 men of the Cape (Hottentot) Regiment, drove roughly 8,000 Xhosa, women and children included, over the Fish while 500 British troops brought up the rear. During the campaign Chungwa was killed. Afterwards Cradock established twenty-seven military posts near the Fish River to prevent the return of the Xhosa.

Thus ended the first phase of intensive contact between colonists and Xhosa. Ties of trade and labour had bound them together in a system which for a long time could survive the ongoing struggle. In times of war no quick and decisive victory had been possible, because the more numerous Zuurveld Xhosa lacked horses, guns and co-ordinated leadership while the colonists had guns and horses but insufficient numbers and inadequate leaders. Eventually the colonists prevailed, but only after their disunity and rebelliousness were overcome by the appearance of a strong imperial power around which they could rally.

Victory was achieved by European and Khoikhoi cavalry under British leadership, and ultimately by the links with Europe which provided indispensable guns and ammunition.[112]

For much of the period 1770–1812 the frontier remained open to the Xhosa. Attempts to dislodge them from the Zuurveld were unsuccessful and chiefdoms rarely faced shortages of pasture severe enough to create irreconcilable conflicts. The frontier was a place to which commoner clans who resisted subordination could escape, and where the poor and destitute could attempt to improve their position. Peace-time cattle raids were generally the work of small groups, evidently attempting to build up stock and power.

The closing of the frontier

We noted earlier that two phases in frontier history can be distinguished: the open and the closing of the frontier. However, one should remember that the closing of the frontier did not start at the same time in all areas: it was always dependent on whether a group could establish its hegemony over others in its immediate vicinity or whether some external power was able to put an end to the relative anarchy of the open frontier. In general one may say that the frontier began to close for the Khoikhoi in the 1780s, gradually for the colonists during the 1790s, and for the Xhosa between 1807 and 1812.

The closing frontier differed from the open frontier above all in the loss of liberty for individuals and groups to assert themselves and maintain their interests. One frontier colonist illuminated the essence of the transition when he reminisced that 'in those old times [c. 1780] when they were robbed they redressed themselves, but now their hands were tied.'[113] Mostly their hands were tied by their dependence on ammunition. In 1795, after the first rebellion had broken out, the government used the grave sanction of suspending ammunition supplies to colonists of the Graaff-Reinet district. The colonists thus knew that they had to win official backing for their attempt to close the frontier through expelling their Xhosa adversaries and asserting their individual (and arbitrary) authority over labour. The government, however, had other ideas – to avoid clashes with the Xhosa and to give Khoikhoi court protection. The rebellions of 1795–96, 1799 and 1801 were thus simultaneously attempts to get the government's support for the closing of the frontier and acts of resistance to the way in which the government preferred to close it.

Ultimately the colonists did have their way. By 1811 the government had come to agree that it was in its interests to have the Xhosa expelled and the Khoikhoi subordinated as a dependable labour force. A coincidence of interest between the government and the wealthy frontier settlers had developed. For this reason the Slachtersnek Rebellion of 1815 was different from its predecessors. Whereas the rebellions of 1795–96, 1799 and 1801 were led by comparatively wealthy farmers keen to increase their hold over land, cattle and servants, the Slachtersnek Rebellion of 1815 was largely the work of poor, landless and desperate colonists. They wished to avenge the death of a colonist who, having assaulted a servant and ignored a court summons, was shot dead while resisting arrest. The Slachtersnek rebels also wished to settle on land beyond the border after reaching an understanding with some Xhosa chiefs. They attracted little support. Wealthier farmers had come to believe that their interests lay in supporting the government and in looking to it to uphold order and defend their claims against those of the Xhosa. They saw little sense in risking their lives and property in support of poverty-stricken colonists who refused to face the fact that the open frontier had passed.

The second way in which the closing of the frontier manifested itself was the distinct change in the ratio of population to land. In contrast to the sparsely populated open frontier, the closing frontier was characterised by pressures on the land caused by the arrival of several new groups of settlers. During the 1770s it was still possible for a young colonist with little or no capital to acquire land and start raising cattle.[114] By 1798, however, only 26 per cent of the colonists owned farms. By 1812 this had shrunk to 18 per cent.[115] (Figures for married men were higher: 39 per cent and 25 per cent respectively.[116]) The Khoikhoi, who during the years of opening the frontier had roamed about freely, were gradually squeezed out of the few remaining unoccupied spaces. In 1797 Barrow reported that there were no independent Khoikhoi settlements in the district of Graaff-Reinet.[117]

Thirdly, the status of non-European labourers deteriorated, and many of them became fixed at the lowest stratum of society. On the open frontier there was some quid pro quo between a master who dealt justly with his clients and protected them, and his client who rendered services in return. On the closing frontier Khoikhoi rapidly lost their land as well as the ability to refuse their labour and exist outside someone's service. One should not, however, think that the status and conditions of labourers changed dramatically. There were various intermediate stages between the master-client relationship at the one extreme and serfdom on the other. The master-client relationship easily evolved into paternalism. This implied that the master had to provide for and dispense justice to his labourers and treat them humanely, while his labourers, who had slowly lost the freedom and status of clients, were bound by the duty to work properly and obey their master's commands.[118] Paternalism again could shade into the more extreme system of labour-repression in which extra-economical devices were employed to ensure an adequate and docile labour force.[119] At the furthest extreme some colonists abducted Khoisan or Xhosa children[120] and sold them or kept them in bondage almost like slaves.[121]

The colonists' institution of labour-repressive practices and involuntary servitude was dependent on the establishment of hegemony over the Khoikhoi and on the realisation among Khoikhoi that colonists had the force to smash any resistance. Under this system the master kept his servant on the farm by withholding his wages, impounding his livestock, or preventing his family from leaving the farm with him (ch. 1, pp. 31–33). Collins, who in general was sympathetic to the colonists reported about conditions in Graaff-Reinet:

> 'A Hottentot can now seldom get away at the expiration of his term. If he should happen not to be in debt to his master . . . he is not allowed to take his children, or he is detained under some frivolous pretence, such as that of cattle having died through his neglect, and he is not permitted to satisfy any demands of this nature otherwise than by personal service.'[122]

Through the landdrosts the colonial government attempted to check some of these practices. Especially under Maynier (1793–95 and 1799–1801) colonists were frequently reprimanded or taken to court when they did not pay their servants or release them when the contracted period expired. However, there were limits to the colonial government's commitment to providing Khoikhoi equal protection under the law. In practice its policy was subservient to two needs: the need for 'order' (which also implied the maintenance of the social hierarchy), and the need for labour, both of which were strongly felt by the last decade of the eighteenth century. Firstly, the colonial government desired that Khoikhoi should not be idle but be constantly employed. If they neglected their duties 'the good order', as Fiscal J.A. Truter put it, demanded that they, like 'children, apprentices and slaves', be punished by their superiors.[123] Secondly, Cape Town's demand for meat greatly increased after the coming of the British in 1795,[124] necessitating a docile and regulated work force. The need was especially great after the abolition of the slave trade in 1808 and the expulsion in 1810 of Xhosa servants working on farms in the eastern districts.

For these two reasons the government increasingly supported or institutionalised some of the labour-repressive methods of the colonists, such as the indenture system which was used to compel Khoisan children to serve farmers up to their twenty-fifth year (see ch. 1, p. 32). For the British the indenture system posed no particular problem, depite the fact that anti-slavery sentiment was beginning to prevail in Britain. Although they opposed plantation slavery, even Britain's reformers seemed to give their approval to coercive forms of labour which did not involve the ownership of one person by another.[125]

Another curb on Khoikhoi mobility and the search for better opportunities was provided by pass and vagrancy regulations designed to prevent Khoikhoi from absconding to Xhosa settlements or other farms where they received better treatment. In 1794 the central government issued a proclamation permitting colonists to arrest as deserters any armed Khoikhoi who were found idle along the roads or in the fields.[126] At the end of the eighteenth century the Swellendam and Graaff-Reinet district authorities prohibited Khoikhoi and slaves from moving from one farm to another or from farm to drostdy without a pass issued by a colonist or official.[127] In his comprehensive Hottentot Proclamation (1809) Caledon retained some of these restrictions (see ch. 1, pp. 40–41).

Thus even a strong central government, deeply concerned about the condition of Khoikhoi labourers, was not prepared to institute any structural changes in their favour. The British, while subscribing to a limited conception of equal justice for all, did not grant Khoikhoi political or social equality with the colonists. And as men of their time they had no intention of removing the vast disparities in wealth and economic opportunity by guaranteeing a minimum wage (Khoikhoi on farms in Graaff-Reinet earned an average of nine to twelve sheep per year), or by supplying them with land. Such was the structure of colonial society that even Ordinance 50 of 1828 failed materially to change the position of the Khoikhoi (see ch. 1, pp. 47–50). As Stockenstrom was to observe in a later period: they were subjected to the same treatment as slaves, except that they could not be sold and were not bound to their master except by contract. Far removed from the magistrate, Stockenstrom went on, they were in a state of moral debasement and physical misery; they were treated even worse than slaves, because a farmer valued his slaves above his servants, who could not be sold.[128]

Khoikhoi reacted in various ways to the closing frontier. There were those living on farms who internalised their servile and inferior status, seeing themselves, as one expressed it, as 'heathens who must obey the commands of our *baas*.'[129] Others resisted. Roving Khoikhoi bands, some of which declared that they would take back their land,[130] operated in Graaff-Reinet as late as 1809. The supreme effort of the Khoikhoi to liberate themselves had been the great revolt of 1799. However, despite its short-term success, it had taken a heavy toll in Khoikhoi lives,[131] and had failed to stop the closing of the frontier.

For one Khoikhoi group, the Gona, there was still a respite as long as the Xhosa remained in the Zuurveld. Both Xhosa and colonists valued the Gona as spies, emissaries and messengers. Moreover, the colonial government made a clear distinction between the Gona living among the Xhosa and the 'Hottentots' who had long been living on farms. Colonists were forbidden to fire on Xhosa or Gona except in self-defence and were instructed to treat all chiefs kindly.[132] Throughout the period of this chapter Xhosa incorporation of Gona continued.

Some Khoikhoi joined Van der Kemp's missionary station at Bethelsdorp (founded in 1803) in an attempt to escape serfdom. Van der Kemp wanted them to be 'perfectly free, upon an equal footing in every respect with the colonists.'[133] However, by offering Khoikhoi a haven, the missionaries blunted the edge of their resistance to conquest and finally induced them to accept their lot as a landless and marginal group in society. In 1812 the missionary James Read wrote that Bethelsdorp had become an asylum for numbers of Khoikhoi 'who otherwise were accustomed to join the Kaffers or unite themselves in the woods to seek redress.'[134]

Bethelsdorp, moreover, was unable to provide the Khoikhoi with a viable economic alternative. They were thus forced to seek employment on neighbouring farms. Furthermore, those who sought to occupy intermediate roles in the economy by hunting, driving wagons, or bartering soap, timber and salt, often found obstacles thrown in their way. They were thwarted by colonists, who saw such activities as falling in the category of 'burgher trades.'[135] They were also hampered by the restrictions imposed by Landdrost Cuyler who refused to provide them with passes for hunting and cutting timber.[136]

Although some of Cuyler's restrictions were the result of the unsettled conditions in the Zuurveld, there was also a fundamental issue at stake: the completely different goals the missionaries and colonial authorities envisaged for Bethelsdorp. The authorities insisted that Bethelsdorp should not, as the missionaries desired, provide an alternative to farm labour – a place where the Khoikhoi were on a par with the colonists on their farms. Instead, the government wanted it to be a receptacle for surplus Khoikhoi – the sick and the unemployable – as well as a training station sending industrious Khoikhoi into society. In the government's view Bethelsdorp also had to provide the colony with recruits for the Hottentot Corps (Cape Regiment) and labour for the construction of roads or buildings at the drostdy.

To the missionaries these views were anathema, since they fatally undermined their insistence that Khoikhoi be accorded the same status and rights as colonists.[137] They fought a running battle against Cuyler on this issue. In the end they decided that they could best help the Khoikhoi by advising them of the laws which protected them, and by informing friends in Cape Town and England of all the allegations of Khoikhoi maltreatment which had come to their notice,[138] thereby becoming, as it were, 'Khoikhoi field-cornets'.

In response to the missionaries' campaign the government appointed a circuit court, the controversial Black Circuit (1812), which investigated charges of cruel treatment of Khoikhoi. Some historians have argued that the court's well-known lambasting of the missionaries proved that their charges were unfounded and that the colonists did not illtreat their servants.[139] They overlook the fact that the missionaries reported *all* allegations of atrocities and maltreatment which had come to their notice; the colonial government, however, decided only to prosecute criminal action allegedly perpetrated after 1806.[140] Cuyler, an observer sympathetic to the colonists, declared: 'I have no hesitation in believing that some years ago, particularly under the first Dutch government's time and perhaps of later date, barbarous cruelties were committed in the distant districts from the capital.'[141] This is borne out by the records of Graaff-Reinet, which contain approximately twenty cases of unnatural deaths of Khoikhoi between 1786 and 1800. In most of these a *prima facie* case of murder or homicide could be made out against colonists. The documents give the impression that the colonists often covered up evidence against accused fellow colonists, with the result that judicial proceedings were not instituted before the Court of Justice.[142]

The question remains whether the missionaries did more harm than good to the Khoikhoi by the methods they used. On the one hand it may be argued that, instead of winning over enlightened colonists to their cause, the missionaries alienated them. They sent their complaints of Khoikhoi maltreatment directly to London and not to the governor in Cape Town; they also created the erroneous impression that the crimes had been recently perpetrated and laid unfounded charges before the court, which earned them a rebuke from the judges.

But two observations are pertinent here. The missionaries decided to appeal directly to London because complaints laid before the colonial government were bound to be referred to Cuyler, who disagreed fundamentally with them on what constituted proper treatment of Khoikhoi. Secondly, the missionaries' strategy was not designed to win the hearts and minds of the dominating class, but to wage war relentlessly against the domination under which the Khoikhoi suffered. They sought maximum publicity for the plight of the Khoikhoi, anticipating that any decisive intervention on their behalf would come only from the imperial authorities, spurred on to action by a public outcry overseas. In this larger struggle the missionaries made progress by spreading a greater awareness of the position of the Khoikhoi and by inducing the government to a broader commitment to equal justice for all classes.[143]

The closing of the frontier deeply affected not only the Khoikhoi but also the 'Christians', among whom there emerged large disparities of wealth. It has already been pointed out that only 26 per cent of the 972 people listed as 'inhabitants' in the 1798 opgaaf[$] (all male burghers or landholding widows) held farms. This 26 per cent owned 75.2 per cent of the slaves, 56.6 per cent of the cattle, 55.8 per cent of the sheep and 51.3 per cent of the horses in the district.[144]

Even within the landholding group there were considerable disparities in wealth. The 1798 opgaaf listed 174 inhabitants who held only one farm each, 63 who held two, 14 who held three and 2 who held four farms.[145] Of the group of landholders approximately 44 per cent owned less than 400 livestock units.

Table 9.1 summarises the differences in livestock wealth among the various categories of 'Christians'.

Table 9.1   Livestock units owned by 'Christians': Graaff-Reinet, 1798
(One livestock unit = 1 head of cattle or 6 sheep

Livestock units	Landholding 'inhabitants'	Landless married 'inhabitants'	Landless unmarried 'inhabitants'	Company servants	Baptised Bastaards
0–11	3	30	109	48	10
12–19	14	118	121	26	22
100–199	25	122	33	6	5
200–399	71	125	13	2	2
400–799	93	33	5	1	–
800–1,199	36	3	–	–	–
1,200+	11	3	–	–	–

§ Opgaaf lists are defective as indices of absolute wealth, since some colonists underreported to diminish their taxes. However, apart from inventories of estates they are the only indices we have. I have chosen the list of 1798 for these calculations, since that opgaaf was the first one to be performed under oath. Moreover, shortly before, soldiers had for the first time been stationed on the frontier and they could make good the government's threat to punish irregularities.

The upper stratum of 'Christian' society consisted of landholders, followed by people living on a kinsman's farm, some of whom could look forward to becoming landholders themselves. Beneath these were the bijwoners, i.e., colonists who lived and farmed on other people's land or eked out an existence as woodcutters. In the face of increasing pressure on the land, the position of the bijwoners, and even of those colonists living with kinsmen, deteriorated. By 1810 many had of necessity become nomads. Stockenstrom reported from Graaff-Reinet that there were 800 to 900 colonists without farms who roamed about, staying some months on one farm before moving to another.[146] Since opgaaf lists did not clearly distinguish between kinsmen and bijwoners, it is not possible to indicate their respective wealth.

Company servants, although considered 'Christians', were mentioned separately in the opgaaf lists. They were persons who had been removed from the Dutch East India Company's payroll while being temporarily employed by farmers as itinerant teachers, farm managers or tradesmen.[147] A few became wealthy after marrying the widow or daughter of an affluent farmer – all nine Company servants owning more than a hundred units of livestock were married – but most remained poor. Only one of the eighty-three Company servants on the 1798 opgaaf roll held a farm; seventy-five lived on someone else's farm and eight lived in Graaff-Reinet town.

Another group officially regarded as 'Christians' but also listed separately were the so-called baptised Bastaards. The 1798 opgaaf lists thirty-eight men, sixteen women, twenty-eight boys and thirty-nine girls in this category. Only one of them held a loan farm.

In the more stratified closing frontier, as distinct from the more egalitarian open frontier, the burden of civil duties fell mainly upon the 'poorer class', as Governor Janssens noted. He also remarked that 'people do not respect the field-cornets as they ought, the rich especially.'[148] Janssens was referring to the self-supporting administrative system of Graaff-Reinet, in which field-cornets and other office holders had the right to command colonists to participate in commandos, provide transportation and relays, forward mail, and help erect public buildings. According to an early historian, these levies formed 'a system of impressment which opened a wide door to favouritism on the one hand, and oppression on the other, in many cases an intolerable burden.'[149] The closing frontier was thus stratified politically as well as socially, for rich people were powerful enough to resist the demands the government made upon them. It also suggests that the closing frontier witnessed increasing domination, not only of masters over servants, but also of rich over poor Europeans and of Europeans over Bastaards, though they all belonged to the official category of 'Christians'. Research covering a longer period would be necessary to test this tentative conclusion, but the following passage in the 1802 journal of William Somerville shows how the strong treated the weak in the absence of institutional controls. Commenting on the docility of the Bastaards on the Orange River who fled the colony, Somerville wrote that 'the circumstances they related of the oppression and tyranny of the wagtmasters [field-cornets] are truly shocking. In a matter of 600 sheep one of them under the former Government told a bastaard: You might have right to the sheep but your adversary is a Christian and you are but a heathen therefore I can't compel him.'[150]

Despite an increasing racial rigidity, the closing frontier was not stratified solely in terms of Europeans' ethnic and racial perceptions, that is, their attitudes towards different cultures and physical types. Rather it consisted of a number of status groups with varying ranks on the social scale. There were many criteria of status, like baptism – regardless of colour, baptised people shared certain privileges[151] – control of land, and possession of livestock. Since almost all independent farmers were European and baptised, these categories largely overlapped. However, outside the group of landholders, their kinsmen and the more affluent bijwoners, there were people who qualified for relatively high status on some grounds but not on others. For example, baptised Bastaards were not white; however, on the 1798 opgaaf rolls they owned on average more livestock units than the European Company servants (fifty-six against thirty-nine units per person). They were also recognised as practitioners of a burgher craft or occupation, while Company servants still had to apply for burgher status.** In both these groups people who thought themselves worthy of respect, but were in fact marginal people, strove to be fully accepted as burghers. For instance, when a Company servant named De Jong accused David Willemzen, a baptised Bastaard, of improper conduct and assaulted his wife, Willemzen exclaimed that he was as good 'a burgher man' as De Jong and beat him up.[152]

The 'racial' groups tended to be endogamous. Of the 689 couples listed in the opgaaf as 'inhabitants' only 5 to 6 per cent can be described

** It is not quite certain what 'burgher status' meant. People wishing to leave the Dutch East India Company service had to apply for burgher status; children of married burgher couples were automatically considered to be burghers. However, in the eyes of the colonists the crucial question seems not to have been one's nominal status, but whether one actually exercised burgher rights, like practising a burgher craft or occupation, or holding office. See *RCC*, IX, Truter – Bird, 7 Jan. 1816, p. 120.

as 'mixed', in that one of the partners had a grandparent who was not European. Barrow remarked that the Bastaards 'generally marry with each other, or with persons of colour, but seldom with Hottentots.'[153] However, a study of the opgaaf lists shows that the percentage of 'mixed' marriages among the lower status groups was not inconsiderable.[154] Of the seventeen married Company servants on the 1798 opgaaf roll, four had non-European wives; and of the seventeen baptised Bastaards five had wives who, judged by their immediate ancestry, were European. Some of the children of 'mixed' parentage eventually emerged as European and others as non-European. The children born out of the liaison between Coenraad de Buys and his concubine, the Bastaard Maria van der Ros (or Horst), went into different groups: one son, Coenraad Wilhelm, married a European woman, most of his descendents becoming Europeans; a daughter, Elizabeth, married a European named Sowietsky and had descendants who became Europeans. De Buys's other seven children and their descendants passed into the non-European fold.[155]

It was partly because racial categories were not yet as rigid as they were to become that some Europeans occasionally sought to overthrow Europeans in power by using non-Europeans as allies. There were, for example, 'skelmbasterkraals' consisting of British deserters, Bastaards and colonists scheming to 'liberate' themselves and conquer part of the colony.[156] And there are indications that in 1795, during the British attack on the Cape, Delport and his Swellendam burghers incited not only the lowly Company servants but also free blacks in Cape Town against Company rule.[157] Lastly, in more remote regions there were always colonists like De Buys and the Bezuidenhouts who had no objection to soliciting the help of non-Europeans in their struggle against the government.[158]

It was not only among the various categories of 'Christians' that there was a distinct measure of stratification. Hunted and hated, the Khoisan hunter-gatherers were considered inferior by the Khoikhoi menial servants,[159] themselves in many respects on a par with slaves and thus despised by Bastaards, who enjoyed greater freedom of movement. All these groups were in turn held in contempt by the socially superior categories of people.[160]

People constantly strove to rise to a higher status group. Khoisan hunter-gatherers became 'tame Hottentots', fugitive slaves tried to pass for Bastaard-Hottentots in order to move about without passes and obtain paid employment,[161] and Khoikhoi and especially Bastaard-Hottentots hoped to enter Christian society through baptism. The converse also occurred: a free Bastaard-Hottentot (the son of a slave father and Khoikhoi mother) might easily be apprehended after having been mistaken for a slave born of a liaison between a female slave and a male Khoikhoi.

However, this analysis should not detract from the key significance of race as an indicator of social and political status. The cross-racial alliances mentioned above were mainly temporary and opportunistic and they disintegrated rapidly. As frontier society evolved, landless European colonists sought the protection of affluent landholders, even though they might have been despised or exploited. As for the lowest strata of society, the formal and informal means of control of the closing frontier compressed 'Bushmen', Khoikhoi and Bastaard-Hottentots into an undifferentiated servile class, none of whose members were European. True, some still tried to acquire status through baptism and marriage. But only at Bethelsdorp were they allowed to participate in these rites and in any event Europeans did not really value these symbols of status. status.

As for the Xhosa, their expulsion in 1811–12 effectively closed the frontier to them. It deprived them not only of extensive grain fields but also of the use of the Zuurveld as an escape hatch. In addition, they had lost a considerable number of cattle, which Graham kept as a guarantee against further Xhosa inroads, and as compensation for European victims of Xhosa raids. By the end of 1812 there was so much hunger among the Xhosa that Graham was compelled to allow some to return to the Zuurveld to reap the harvest.[162] This was a lesson which subsequent administrators would also learn: that to expel the Xhosa was not to rid the colony of its Xhosa 'problem'.

Thus by 1812 the frontier zone was largely closed to members of all three societies. Or to put it differently, the frontier had been colonised. The Xhosa gradually ceased to regard the Zuurveld as a disputed area, one to which their ancestors had once staked a claim.[163] At the same time the colonial government established unquestioned authority in the area. In time the Khoikhoi also recognised its legitimacy, as an ever increasing proportion of Khoikhoi adults knew no other government. The government did not tolerate some of the colonists' labour-repressive practices. However, through the pass laws, it ensured for the farmer a docile work force trapped at the lowest tier of society.

There were still parts west of Graaff-Reinet district, such as the hillier areas of Rivier Zondereind, where officials protected Khoikhoi rights to the land and prevented the frontier from completely closing in on them. However, Xhosa, like the freebooter Danster,[164] Khoikhoi, Bastaards, and burghers such as De Buys were increasingly attracted to the next open frontier of Transorangia in the north, where they could regain their former freedom.[165]

Conclusion

Frontier history between 1770 and 1812 has traditionally been seen as a stark conflict between distinct and hostile 'races'. In the post World War II era, some liberal historians moved away from the 'conflict-between-races' interpretation: instead of emphasising conflict, they had as their central themes co-operation and peaceful interaction between the frontier peoples, and the failure of the colonial government's attempts to limit these processes. Revisionist historians like Martin Legassick, while continuing to see conflict as primary, paid increasing attention to the non-conflictual aspects of the frontier, such as cross-racial alliances or the coalescence of classes across racial lines.

These interpretations have deepened our understanding of the frontier. The open frontier, particularly, is incomprehensible if one does not realise that relationships were formed in a system embracing various peoples and held together by the goods and services they exchanged with one another. Different groups found it to be in their interests to establish and maintain a balance of 'no war – no peace' which allowed this system to survive.

However, at least on the Eastern Frontier, such co-operation and voluntary interaction did not result in the biological, cultural, political or economic integration of separate peoples.[166] Especially on the closing frontier, the prevailing characteristics were withdrawal, exclusion and strife. Thus, far more important than miscegenation between colonists and Khoikhoi (apart from the De Buys case there is hardly any evidence of Xhosa-colonist miscegenation) was the limited degree to which children born out of interracial liaisons were assimilated into the European community. Though there was considerable acculturation, particularly between Europeans and Khoikhoi (see ch. 4, pp. 225–30) it did not lead to the removal of ethnic distinctions. The colonists resisted efforts to instruct Khoikhoi in the more complex aspects of their culture, such as reading, writing and religion, because this would 'put [them] upon an equal footing with the Christians.'[167] As for European-Xhosa acculturation, each group borrowed only minimally from the other. In the sphere of politics it was not the establishment of colonist-Xhosa political alliances that was significant, but rather that these alliances failed to achieve anything substantial.

One must also qualify the second element of the traditional interpretation, i.e., that the frontier was dominated by *racial* conflict. An analysis of class[††] rather than race relations can illuminate important aspects of intergroup contact. In a loose sense one might see the colonists not so much as a race, but as a class dominated by large land-holders on whose farms several landless families lived who helped control the immobile servile class. As the frontier closed, the class divisions between landholders and landless colonists became deeper, assuming serious proportions in the case of the Slachtersnek rebellion (p. 448). The Khoikhoi-colonist relationship can also be interpreted as being increasingly dominated by a class conflict between landowners and a landless labouring class. Yet, even if full weight is given to these views, the fact remains that contemporaries overwhelmingly perceived conflicts in racial terms. The poorer whites vigorously stressed their racial identity, believing that this qualified them for membership in the dominant group. Xhosa and colonists distinguished themselves from others mainly by their perceptions of racial and ethnic differences.[168] They had come to see each other more as racial adversaries as well as economic competitors, and conflict occurred mainly along racial lines. This is not to suggest that prejudice and fantasies about race and culture in themselves gave rise to the struggle on the Eastern Frontier. Tension arising from the struggle to control land, cattle and labour greatly reinforced the racial cleavage and made the conflict much more intense and all-embracing.

Although stable relations and various forms of co-operation existed at times between the various peoples, conflict was pervasive. Because it had both a racial and a class dimension, negotiations were less effective in resolving disputes than is often the case in purely economic conflicts. To realise their objectives, people turned increasingly to forceful means, such as labour-repressive devices, exaction of ransom, raiding and war. The ultimate struggle was, of course, the battle for hegemony on the frontier. This struggle reached a climax in 1812, when the last remnants of peaceful co-operation between colonists and Xhosa in the Zuurveld were destroyed, along with the frontier system which had bound them together.

---

†† 'Class' is used here in the sense of most radical historians, i.e. to denote a group of people with a common relationship to the means of production. This is to be contrasted with the concept 'status group' which denotes a group with a social status conferred by members of a society, according to certain criteria such as physical type, baptism, wealth, achievement, etc.

Chapter Nine Notes

1. J. Barrow, *Travels into the Interior of Southern Africa* (London, 1806), II, 373–76; D.G. van Reenen, *Die Joernaal van Dirk Gysbert van Reenen* (Cape Town, 1937), p. 195; J.P.H. Acocks, *Veld Types of South Africa* (Pretoria, 1953), map I and pp. 76–84, 150, 154.
2. F. Mason, 'An Account of Three Journeys from Cape Town into the Southern parts of Africa', *Philosophical Transactions of the Royal Society*, LXVI (1776), p. 177. See also H. Lichtenstein, *Travels in Southern Africa in the years 1803, 1804, 1805 and 1806* (Cape Town, 1930), II, 319.
3. G. Harinck, 'Interaction between Xhosa and Khoi: emphasis on the period 1620–1750', *African Societies in Southern Africa*, ed. Leonard Thompson (London, 1969), pp. 166–67.
4. C.A. Haupt, 'Joernaal', *RZA*, III, 310–11. For a discussion of Khoikhoi incorporation into Xhosa chiefdoms, see J.B. Peires, 'A History of the Xhosa, c. 1700–1835' (M.A. dissertation, Rhodes University, 1976), pp. 56–60.
5. No eighteenth-century source verifies J. Henderson Soga's statement that the Gqunukhwebe were aliens who never had a place assigned 'within the body of the Xhosa tribe': *The South Eastern Bantu* (Johannesburg, 1930), p. 117.
6. In contrast Hammond-Tooke describes the Gqunukhwebe as a tributary chiefdom. See W.D. Hammond-Tooke, 'Segmentation and Fission in Cape Nguni Political Units', *Africa*, XXXV (1965), p. 146.
7. Anthropologists see segmentation and fission as a regular process in the unstable Cape Nguni political units. Hammond-Tooke in 'Segmentation and Fission', pp. 143–56 and 'The "other side" of frontier history: a model of Cape Nguni political process', *African Societies in Southern Africa*, ed. Leonard Thompson (London, 1969), p. 240 describes a Xhosa chiefdom as structurally unstable since it was divided into a Great House, headed by the Great House wife's eldest son (who is the legal heir), and the Right-Hand House, headed by the eldest son of the Right-Hand wife. The other wives were allocated to either the Great or the Right-Hand Houses. Segmentation and fission frequently occurred along the lines of these two Houses. There was even an expectation of fission: the Right-Hand House had a pre-emptive right to break away. This interpretation has been attacked by the historian J.B. Peires, who argues that there was no fission in the Xhosa paramountcy since the overall authority of the paramount remained unquestioned. Subdividing occurred when junior members of the royal lineage dispersed to conquer new lands and independent Khoikhoi, hunters and Nguni. Rather than setting up independent chiefdoms, they expanded the territory, population and authority of the Xhosa chiefdom: J.B. Peires, 'The Rise of the "Right-Hand House" in the history and historiography of the Xhosa', *History in Africa*, II (1975); and 'Xhosa Expansion before 1800', *Collected Seminar Papers on the Societies of Southern Africa* (Institute of Commonwealth Studies, 1976), vol. VI.
   For the eighteenth century the Hammond-Tooke theory of independent states cannot be accepted. But there is also insufficient proof for the view that there was one paramount who retained overall authority

as the political head of the Xhosa 'nation' and that the Xhosa were a 'state' rather than a 'cluster'. The actual position seems to have fluctuated, according to prevailing power relationships, between the two positions depicted by Hammond-Tooke and Peires. In his M.A. dissertation, written after the articles cited above, Peires is prepared to classify the Xhosa as being organised in a segmentary state in which the centre only exercised limited control over the subordinate authorities on the periphery, provided it is taken into account that there were both centralising and decentralising forces at work. See Peires, 'A History of the Xhosa', pp. 218–26.

8. Stb. 20/2, Report of Van Jaarsveld – Landdrost of Stellenbosch, 22 June 1780. See also Donald Moodie, *The Record* (Cape Town 1960), III, Extract Letters of Landdrost of Stellenbosch, 10 Oct. 1780, p. 96.

9. Technically they were entitled to do this: if they were subject to anyone it was to Gcaleka rather than Rharhabe. In social and ritual matters, at least, they acknowledged the importance of the Gcaleka chief. Chungwa, in fact, once described him as his king.

10. A sentence in the journal of Collins illustrates this: 'Zlambie having taken a fancy . . . to the lands near the Bosjesmans River, occupied by some of the kraals of Konga [Chungwa], and the latter having refused to resign them on his demand, his people were driven from them by force.' Moodie, *The Record*, V, 14.

11. See the figures in Robin Derricourt, 'Settlement in the Transkei and Ciskei before the Mfecane', *Beyond the Cape Frontier*, ed. C. Saunders and R. Derricourt (Cape Town, 1974), pp. 66–68; Basil Sansom, 'Traditional Rulers and Realms', *The Bantu-Speaking Peoples of Southern Africa*, ed. W.D. Hammond-Tooke (London, 1974), pp. 258–59.

12. *RCC*, VIII, Report of the Commission of Circuit, 28 Feb. 1812, p. 298; 'Journal of Swellengrebel's Journey', *Zuid-Afrika*, IX (1932), p. 136.

13. For a suggestive analysis of the frontier concept, see M.C. Legassick, 'The Griqua, the Sotho-Tswana, and the Missionaries, 1780–1840: The Politics of a Frontier Zone' (Ph.D. Thesis, University of California, 1969), pp. 6–19.

14. W.K. Hancock, *Survey of Commonwealth Affairs* (London, 1940), Vol. II, part 1, p. 3. Cf. also the remark of Owen Lattimore in *Inner Asian Frontiers of China* (Clinton, 1940), p. 238, '. . . the concept of a linear boundary could never be established as an absolute geographical fact. That which was politically conceived as a sharp edge was persistently spread by the ebb and flow of history into a relatively broad and vague margin.'

15. P. Cloeten, Journal of Swellengrebel's Journey, 1776, *RZA*, IV, 46–50; Moodie, *The Record*, III, 93, 99.

16. Moodie, *The Record*, Journal of Collins (1809), V, 10. It is not clear whether the Xhosa or the colonists first moved into the territory between the Fish and the Boesmans Rivers. Compare P.J. van der Merwe, *Die Trekboer in die Geskiedenis van die Kaapkolonie* (Cape Town, 1938), p. 266 and J.S. Marais, *Maynier and the First Boer Republic* (Cape Town, 1944), p. 6. In 1794 Adriaan van Jaarsveld declared that the Zuurveld (probably meaning the territory between the Boesmans and Fish Rivers) was formerly the land of the Xhosa (GR 1/9a, Records of Militia Officers, 1794).

17. BO 27, Diary of Du Plessis and Van Rensburg, 27 Aug. 1797, pp. 255–59. The frontier colonists at times seem to have had doubts about the paramountcy of the Rharhabe chief (see note 71).

18. See Ngqika's remarks in Moodie, *The Record*, V, Journal of Collins (1809), p. 48.

19. This is illustrated by a letter of some colonists, living illegally beyond Bruintjes Hoogte who asked the government to extend its authority over them. See Moodie, *The Record*, III, 5, 24; CO 309, Memorial of Willem Prinsloo and others, 10 Nov. 1774, p. 302.

20. GR 8/1, Sluysken – Maynier, 2 Dec. 1794, no. 118. Sometimes there were even fewer mounted police (cf. *RCC*, IX, 62).

21. C 470, Woeke – Governor, 16 Nov. 1786, p. 663 (my translation).

22. Cf. Chungwa's remark to Wagener, a Graaff-Reinet official, that the 'Groot Baas' would not begrudge him the Zuurveld; only his adversaries living in the vicinity did so. (GR 1/1, Minutes, 3 Aug. 1789, pp. 109–10.)

23. GR 1/9, Letter from Lucas Meyer, n.d. (c. 1790); GR 1/9a, Fragment of letter to militia officers, 22 March 1795; *Transactions of the (London) Missionary Society* (London, 1804), I, 388; Moodie, *The Record*, III, 96.

24. Van Reenen, *Joernaal*, p. 209. Examples of other coalitions or proposed coalitions abound. In 1792 Tshaka proposed to field-cornet Hurter that they should attack Langa together; he said Langa and Ndlambe wished to force him across the Boesmans River. In 1792 Langa was reported to have concluded an alliance with a 'Bushman' band to attack the colonists.

25. For a description of the menace from lions, see VC 753–54, Gordon ms., Journal of Third Journey, 28 Aug. 1778–25 Jan. 1779.

26. Moodie, *The Record*, V, Journal of Collins (1809), p. 12; *RCC*, VI, 46; C.A. Haupt, 'Journaal', *RZA*, III, 310–11; CO 2572, Statement by Graham, 1812.

27. Moodie, *The Record*, V, Journal of Collins (1809), p. 12.

28. (Oppenheimer) Kitchingman Papers, vol. 406, Statement by Klaas Klopper (n.d.)

29. For a description of the symbiotic relationship, see M. Banton, *Race Relations* (London, 1967), pp. 77–79.

30. A. Sparrman, *A Voyage to the Cape of Good Hope . . . chiefly into the country of the Hottentots and Caffres from the year 1772 to 1776* (Dublin, 1786), II, 167.

31. J 116, Graaff-Reinet Opgaaf, 1798.

32. For illuminating remarks on this phenomenon, see A.P. Elkin, 'Reaction and Interaction: A Food Gathering People and European Settlement in Australia', *Beyond the Frontier*, ed. P. Bohannen and F. Plog (New York, 1967).

33. GR 16/1, Stockenstrom – Janssens, 7 July 1804.

34. Until the 1970s this was the orthodoxy in South African historiography. Particularly influential has been the work of I.D. MacCrone, 'The Frontier Tradition and Race Attitudes in South Africa', *Race Relations Journal*, XXVII (1961), pp. 19–30, and *Race Attitudes in South Africa* (London, 1937), pp. 98–136. For a critique, see M.C. Legassick, 'The Frontier Tradition in South African Historiography', *Collected Seminar Papers on the*

Societies of Southern Africa Institute of Commonwealth Studies, (London, 1970–71), vol. II.

35. In a general context see the remarks by Stanley Lieberson in 'A Societal Theory of Race and Ethnic Relations', *Racial Conflict*, ed. Gary T. Marx (Boston, 1971), p. 122.

36. C 470, Woeke and Heemraden – Governor and Council of Policy, 4 Nov. 1786, p. 707.

37. Moodie, *The Record*, V, 10.

38. In 1786 O.G. de Wet tried to assuage the colonists' fears in this connection. See GR 8/1, De Wet – Woeke, 16 Dec. 1786, p. 236. See also C 470, Woeke – Governor and Council of Policy, 16 Nov. 1786, pp. 659–66.

39. Moodie Afschriften, Woeke – Council of Policy, 8 Dec. 1786.

40. GR 1/9, Journal of Hurter, 26. Feb. 1792.

41. (Oppenheimer) Kitchingman Papers, vol. 4061, Statement by Brantanje Jantjes, 29 Dec. 1836. (I altered the spelling of 'Caffres').

42. C 196, Report of Maynier, 9 May 1794, pp. 182–90.

43. Basil Sansom, 'Traditional Economic Systems', *The Bantu-Speaking Peoples of Southern Africa*, ed. W.D. Hammond-Tooke (London, 1974), p. 156.

44. H. Lichtenstein, *Travels in Southern Africa . . .* (Cape Town, 1928), I, 268–69. See also Moodie, *The Record*, V, Cuyler – Caledon, 10 Aug. 1810, p. 58.

45. MacCrone, *Race Attitudes*, pp. 123–32 cites various pronouncements in this regard.

46. Moodie Afschriften, Journal of H. Muller, 23 March 1783.

47. For a discussion of the openness of Xhosa society, see O.F. Raum, 'A Topological Analysis of Xhosa Society', *Wort und Religion: Kalima Na Dini*, ed. H.J. Greschat and H. Jungraithmayr (Stuttgart, 1969), pp. 321–32 and Peires, 'History of the Xhosa', pp. 81–84, 105–107. For atrocities, see BO 24, Faure – Dundas, 21 Nov. 1802, no. 156. For abduction of children, see sources quoted in note 120.

48. Stb. 20/2, Report of Van Jaarsveld, 22 June 1780.

49. Moodie, *The Record*, V, 17.

50. VC 76, Campagne: Berigt, 1796, pp. 243–45.

51. GR 1/1, Minutes, 12 Aug. 1793, p. 234; Moodie, *The Record*, III, Report of Van Jaarsveld, 20 July 1781, p. 111.

52. The first time this settlement is mentioned in the records is with reference to the Woeke commission, which in 1789 attempted to negotiate the withdrawal of the Gqunukhwebe. The commission claimed that after the conflict of 1779–81 peace was concluded with 'most of the Xhosa' and in particular with 'Marottie' (Mahote of the Dange), 'Dika' (probably Cika, commander of the Ntinde army), Langa of the Mbalu, and 'Kobe' (probably the Gwali chief). See also Soga, *The South-Eastern Bantu*, pp. 134–35.

53. C 470, Woeke – Governor and Council, Oct. 1786, pp. 680–86.

54. C 79, Resolutiën, Aug. 1786, pp. 601–02.

55. Woeke, for instance, attempted to satisfy Langa's demand for compensation in the case of one of his followers who had been killed by a colonist. A similar dispute sparked off the first hostilities in 1779 (C 470, Woeke – Governor and Council of Policy, 6 Nov. 1786, pp. 683–85.)

56. F(ranz) von W(inkelman), Reisaantekeningen, 1788–89, *RZA*, IV, 74.
57. C 493, Woeke–Governor, 9 Feb. 1789, pp. 39–43.
58. C 470, Woeke–Governor and Council, 6 Nov. 1786, p. 669.
59. Moodie Afschriften, Woeke, 6 Nov. 1787; P.J. van der Merwe, *Die Trekboer*, p. 317.
60. Moodie Afschriften, C. de Buys – Landdrost and Court of Militia, 6 April 1788.
61. C 473, Woeke – Governor and Council of Policy, 9 Feb. 1789, p. 40 (my translation).
62. C 473, Woeke – Governor, 8 March 1789, pp. 65–67.
63. GR 8/1, Governor and Council of Policy, 20 March 1789, no. 33.
64. Van der Merwe incorrectly states that Wägener, an official who was left behind to continue the negotiations, allowed the Gqunukhwebe to return from east of the Fish River to their communities (*Trekboer*, pp. 309–10). Wägener, in fact, remarked that despite all his efforts he could not succeed in getting the Xhosa to leave the 'district of the Kowie' (an area west of the border). See C 321, Wägener – Landdrost, 3 Aug. 1789, p. 963.
65. GR 1/1, Minutes, 13 July 1789, p. 99.
66. GR 1/1, Minutes, Report of Wägener, 5 July 1789, pp. 102–03.
67. VC 66, Proclamation of 23 Oct. 1793, pp. 316–23.
68. GR 12/2, Report of C. van Aardt, 2 Oct. 1787.
69. GR 1/1, Minutes, 13 May 1789, p. 94.
70. There are more details, with references, in Marais, *Maynier*, pp. 24, 28–31. *Boer Republic* (Cape Town, 1944), pp. 24, 28–31.
71. The Kühne commando in 1789 apparently disobeyed its instructions when it acted against the Xhosa. There is no reference to what the commando actually did, but subsequently the landdrost and heemraden sent gifts to Khawuta, the Gcaleka paramount, assuring him that they desired peace despite the 'wrong conduct' of Kühne and the resulting tumult. In 1825 Maynier testified before the Commission of Inquiry that he had witnessed on Kühne's commando the distribution of 30,000 cattle taken in booty (*RCC*, XXI, Evidence by Maynier, 25 April 1825, pp. 386–87). The fact that Maynier arrived in Graaff-Reinet after the commando had returned conflicts with this evidence. On the other hand, it is unlikely that Maynier would make such a statement if nothing of the sort had ever occurred.
72. See the remarkable letter of C. de Buys in Moodie Afschriften, C. de Buys – Landdrost and Militia Officers, 6 April 1788. See also G 1/9, Scheepers – Woeke, 21 Dec. 1789.
73. For a discussion of this in the context of Indian reaction to European settlement in North America, see N.O. Lurie, 'Indian Cultural Adjustments to European Civilization', *Seventeenth Century America*, ed. J.M. Smith (Chapel Hill, 1959), p. 31.
74. In 1792 Chungwa, to whom most of the Khoikhoi had fled, remarked to Hurter even with 'honden [hundreds?] gewaapende mannen' he would not do him much harm. (GR 1/9, Journal of Hurter, 14 Feb. 1792.) Hurter commanded twenty-five men.
75. Some fifty Xhosa once told the wife of a certain Jordaan that if her husband had been at home they would have cut him from end to end since he was

so good at shooting Xhosa. (GR 12/1, Letter of C.J. van Rooyen, 11 Dec. 1796.) See also C 196, Woeke – Rhenius, 9 Feb. 1792, pp. 309–11; GR 1/1, Minutes, Report of Wägener, 5 July 1789.

76. GR 1/9, Scheepers – Woeke, 27 Dec. 1789.
77. GR 1/9a, Combined Meeting of Landdrost, Heemraden and Militia Officers, 26 May 1794.
78. Soga, *The South-Eastern Bantu*, pp. 137–38. G.M. Theal asserts that the Dange were involved (*History of Africa South of the Zambesi from 1505–1795* [London, 1922], III, 279–80.)
79. For a perceptive discussion of the causes of the Xhosa – colonist conflict see Peires, 'History of the Xhosa', pp. 101–06.
80. According to J.L. Maray only three farms in the Zuurveld were still occupied by September 1793 (GR 12/2).
81. The most important documents pertaining to the war are C 104, Joint Report of Maynier and Faure, 27 Nov. 1793; VC 68, Journal of Faure, 10 Dec. 1793; C 106, Maynier's report of 31 March 1794; and VC 76, Campagne's Berigt.
82. Before the war there were approximately 150 families of colonists in the Zuurveld and roughly 4,000 colonists (1,000 adult men) in the entire district of Graaff-Reinet. According to one estimate there were 6,000 Xhosa in the Zuurveld (GR 8/1, Council of Policy – Maynier, 12 Aug. 1793, no. 87).
83. Hermann Giliomee, *Die Kaap tydens die Eerste Britse Bewind* (Cape Town, 1975), p. 274.
84. The colonial authorities wanted to negotiate and trade with a single chief representing all Xhosa (*RCC*, VII, Journal of Collins, 1809, p. 75).
85. For a full discussion of this and the subsequent rebellions see my 'The burgher rebellions on the Eastern Frontier, 1795–1815,' *The Shaping of South African Society 1652–1820* ed. Richard Elphick and Hermann Giliomee (1st edition, Cape Town, 1979), ch. 9.
86. For discussion of the concepts 'scope' (degree of authority) and 'location of command', see Sansom, 'Traditional Rulers', pp. 247–48.
87. *RCC*, VII, Journal of Collins, 1809, pp. 54, 78; L. Alberti, *Account of the Tribal Life and Customs of the Xhosa in 1807* (Cape Town, 1968), p. 81; Peires, 'History of the Xhosa', pp. 98–99.
88. BO 27, Statement by Bresler, 3 Dec. 1797, p. 306.
89. *Transactions of the Missionary Society,* Journal of Van der Kemp, pp. 466–67.
90. In 1799 Ngqika offered to the colonists land between the Kacha Mountains and the Koonap River (*Transactions*, I, 388). Obviously the colonists would have served as a buffer against his Xhosa enemies.
91. William M. Freund, 'The Eastern Frontier of the Cape Colony during the Batavian period (1803–1806)', *JAH*, XIII (1972), pp. 631–45. 631–45.
92. Journal of the Journey of Janssens, 1803, *RZA*, IV, 172.
93. Moodie, *The Record*, V, Journal of Collins (1809), p. 14. See also *RCC*, III, Vandeleur – Dundas, 22 Aug. 1799, p. 475.
94. The Batavians, in fact, accepted the principle that Xhosa who had been in the service of colonists for more than a year could stay. See Van Reenen, *Joernaal*, pp. 132–33.

95. *RCC*, VII, Caledon – Cradock, 1 July 1811, p. 111.
96. For a discussion, see Hermann Giliomee, 'Die Administrasietydperk van Lord Caledon, 1807–1811', *AYB* (1966), no. 2, chapters 10 to12.
97. Van Reenen, *Joernaal*, p. 119.
98. *RCC*, IV, Provisional Justification of Maynier, April 1802, pp. 326–27; Marais, *Maynier*, pp. 120–21.
99. Moodie, *The Record*, V, Journal of Collins, 1809, p. 48.
100. Quoted by W.M. Freund, 'Society and Government in Dutch South Africa: The Cape and the Batavians, 1803–6' (Ph.D. thesis; Yale University, 1972), p. 320. For an assessment of the various chiefs' strengths, see Moodie, *The Record*, V, 50.
101. CO 2575, Cuyler – Bird, 6 May 1811, no. 23. It was probably in c. 1809 that Ndlambe claimed that he had purchased the right to reside in the Zuurveld from a commission consisting of a landdrost and some colonists. For various reports on this, see Moodie, *The Record*, V, Journal of Collins (1809), p. 10; (Cory Library, Grahamstown) Stretch Journal ms., n.p.; A. Stockenstrom, *The Autobiography of the late Sir Andries Stockenstrom* (Cape Town, 1964), I, 50, 52, 58.
102. See Giliomee, 'Lord Caledon', pp. 323–24; Peires, 'History of the Xhosa', pp. 111–12.
103. CO 2572, Stoltz – Cuyler, 23 June 1810. For a further discussion see Peires, 'History of the Xhosa', pp. 6–9, 107–112 and Table 1.
104. CO 2572, Cuyler – Alexander, 18 Dec. 1810, no. 11.
105. CO 2571, Stockenstrom – Caledon, 14 July 1810.
106. CO 2575, Cuyler – Bird, 6 April 1811, no. 23.
107. CO 2566, Cuyler – Colonial Secretary, 4 July 1809, no. 14.
108. CO 2576, Hawkes – Cuyler, 24 June 1811, enclosure to no. 3.
109. CO 2576, Stockenstrom – Bird, 26 July 1811; CO 2577, Stockenstrom – Bird, 7 Aug. 1811.
110. *RCC*, VIII, Cradock – Graham, 6 Oct. 1811, pp. 160–62; *RCC*, IX, Cradock – Bathurst, 18 Nov. 1812, pp. 14–16.
111. CO 2582, Graham – Alexander, 30 Nov. 1812.
112. Graham wrote: 'With the exception of a few artillery and dragoons none of the regular troops are in the field.' (CO 2582, Letter of Graham, 31 Jan. 1812).
113. Quoted by C.F.J. Muller, *Die Oorsprong van die Groot Trek* (Cape Town, 1974), p. 193.
114. Sparrman, *Voyage*, II, 168–69.
115. J 115 and J 138, Opgaaf Graaff-Reinet, 1798 and 1812.
116. Van der Merwe, *Trek*, p. 55.
117. Barrow, *Travels*, I, 93.
118. For an elaboration of the concept of paternalism, see Eugene D. Genovese, *Roll Jordan Roll: The World the Slaves Made* (London, 1975), pp. 133–49. Genovese, of course, uses the concept in the context of the master-slave relationship.
119. For a discussion of labour-repressive systems, see Barrington Moore, *Social Origins of Dictatorship and Democracy: Lord and Peasant in the Making of the Modern World* (Boston, 1966), pp. 433–35.
120. *RCC*, XXI, Evidence of Maynier, 25 April 1825, pp. 387–88;

Lichtenstein, *Travels*, I, 409; BO 24, Faure – Dundas, 21 Nov. 1802. These sources suggest that the abduction of Xhosa children was not uncommon.

121. P.J. van der Merwe, *Die Noordwaartse Beweging van die Boere voor die Groot Trek, 1770–1842* (The Hague, 1937), cites various sources pertaining to traffic in hunter children and concludes that it could only have occurred in exceptional cases (pp. 168–75). The evidence regarding a traffic in indentured Khoikhoi children is ambiguous, but there is a case of a Khoikhoi woman complaining that a colonist had sold five of her children for 176 rixdollars: see BO 53, Barnard – Faure, 28 Feb. 1800, no. 264; W.B.E. Paravicini di Capelli, *Reize in de Binnenlanden van Zuid-Afrika* (Cape Town, 1965), who travelled in the interior at the time of the Batavian administration, wrote that many farmers preferred that the Khoikhoi be forced to serve them like slaves (p. 9).

122. Swm 1/3, Minutes, 4 Dec. 1797, p. 330.

123. Moodie, *The Record*, V, Report of Collins, 1809, p. 22.

124. GR 9/10, J.A. Truter – Stockenstrom, 7 April 1810.

125. Giliomee, *Eerste Britse Bewind*, pp. 157–58.

126. GR 16/1, Stockenstrom – Janssens, 7 July 1804; Freund, 'The Eastern Frontier', p. 640.

127. See D.B. Davis, *The Problem of Slavery in the Age of Revolution, 1770–1823* (Ithaca, 1975), especially pp. 453–68, and a review of it by G.M. Fredrickson, 'The Use of Antislavery', *The New York Review of Books*, 16 Oct. 1975. For a discussion of the unfreedom of workers in England and the views of the English ruling class toward them by the turn of the century, see E.P. Thompson *The Making of the English Working Class* (London, 1968), especially chapter 6.

128. VC 66, Proclamation of 23 Oct. 1793, p. 330.

129. Swm 1/3, Minutes, 4 Dec. 1797, p. 330; GR 1/2, Minutes, 2 Jan. 1798. p. 174.

130. Imperial Bluebook no. 50 (1836), Aborigines Committee Report, question 2310. For an incisive dicussion of the significance of Ordinance 50, see Leslie Clement Duly, 'A Revisit with the Cape's Hottentot Ordinance of 1828', *Studies in Economics and Economic History*, ed. Marcelle Kooy (London, 1972), pp. 26–56.

131. GR 3/18, Deposition of J.H. Otto, 9 Aug. 1784, no. 67.

132. GR 3/19, Depositions of Schutte, Koegelman and Streso, 16 Dec. 1809, 5 Jan. 1810.

133. GR 16/1, Stockenstrom – Commission on Stockbreeding, 13 Jan. 1806.

134. *RCC*, VI, Collins – Cuyler, 6 April 1809, pp. 484–88.

135. *Transactions*, I, 490–91, 494.

136. CO 2582, Read – Cradock, 23 Jan. 1812.

137. CO 2582, Memorandum by Read, n.d.

138. CO 2582, Graham – Bird, 1 Sept. 1812.

139. Stockenstrom recounted the heated disputes between Cuyler and Van der Kemp over the question of equal justice for all (*Autobiography*, I, 84). See also the remarks quoted by Freund, 'The Eastern Frontier', pp. 634, 641–42.

140. See for instance C.R. Kotzé, '\'n Nuwe Bewind, 1806–1834', *Vyfhonderd Jaar Suid-Afrikaanse Geskiedenis*, ed. C.F.J. Muller (Pretoria, 1968), p. 113.

141. *RCC*, VIII, Truter – Cradock, 15 June 1812, pp. 439–41.

142. *RCC*, VII, Cuyler – Caledon, 25 Oct. 1810, p. 399. See also Alberti, *Account of the Xhosa*, p. 101.

143. GR 3/16 and GR 3/18.

144. J 115, Opgaaf Graaff-Reinet, 1798.

145. By 1798 there were 492 registered loan farms in Graaff-Reinet (Barrow, *Travels*, II, 185). When this opgaaf was taken, almost two-thirds of the Zuurveld colonists had not yet returned to the farms which they had abandoned in the war of 1793.

146. GR 16/1, Stockenstrom – Bird, 20 Sept. 1810.

147. Although after 1795 these people were no longer in the employ of the VOC, they were still being described as Company servants in 1798. The 1798 opgaaf lists 43 knechts in Graaff-Reinet. Most of the knechts were Company servants. Sometimes a burgher who lost all his cattle became a knecht. One of them was Andries van der Heyden who in 1798 earned a 'knecht's wage' of 170 rixdollars from one employer and 72 rixdollars from another.

148. LM 37, Janssens – Landdrosts, 26 May 1805, no. 243.

149. G.A. Watermeyer, 'The Rise and Early History of Graaff-Reinet', *The Graaff-Reinet Herald*, 27 July 1861.

150. Journal of William Somerville, entry of 11 March 1802 (Dr Frank Bradlow kindly gave permission to consult his photocopy of this journal).

151. W.J. Burchell, *Travels into the Interior of Southern Africa* (London, 1953), II, wrote of a certain baptised Bastaard, Cornelis Goeïman, that he 'was by his baptism entitled to the same privileges as the Dutch colonists.' Because Goeïman drank too much, the minister and the landdrost prohibited the sale of brandy to him without their permission. When Goeïman discovered this, he indignantly asked 'what right anyone had to restrain him as if he were a Hottentot; was he not a Christian?' It is clear that the theoretical rights of baptised Bastaards could not always be enforced in practice, and there was much room for misconceptions on the one hand and discriminatory practices on the other.

152. GR 3/18, Depositions of Janssens and Nieuwenhuizen, 2 July 1795, no. 74.

153. Barrow, *Travels*, I, 97. When Bastaard children were baptised, other Bastaards usually acted as witnesses.

154. In an important article Robert Ross has recently argued that it was the poorer and less well-connected male members of the Christian community who found their partners among people who were not white. ('The "White" Population of South Africa in the Eighteenth Century', *Population Studies*, XXIX, 230).

155. Except where otherwise indicated this paragraph is based on J.A. Heese, *Die Herkoms van die Afrikaner* (Cape Town 1971), and personal communications by him with respect to the relevant opgaaf rolls.

156. BO 27, Deposition of Du Plessis, 2 April 1798, p. 31.

157. VC 65, Report of Sluysken, p. 201.

158. *RCC*, III, Report of Maynier, 14 Aug. 1800, and Criminal Claim, 14 Aug. 1800, pp. 212–43; BO 27, Vandeleur – Van Rensburg, 24 May 1799, pp. 223–25.

159. On seeing his children tied by their necks to a tree, a Khoikhoi protested to his master that they were not 'Bushman' children. GR 3/16, Deposition of Jacob, 10 Jan. 1791, no. 162.
160. Burchell, *Travels*, I, 128; II, 170, 203–04, 324, 330. See also *RCC*, IX, Bathurst – Cradock, 9 Oct. 1813. Here the defence in a murder trial referred to the prevailing notion that to kill a debased Khoikhoi was less reprehensible than to kill another man.
161. Moodie Afschriften, Extract Dagregister, Landdrost and Heemraden of Stellenbosch, 7 Aug. 1780. Armed Bastaard-Hottentots played a leading role as resisters. See for instance GR 14/1, Extract Resolutie, 13 July 1792.
162. CO 2582, Graham – Alexander, 16 Aug. 1812 and 5 Sept. 1812; *RCC*, VIII, Cradock – Liverpool, 23 Jan. 1812 and 7 March 1812, pp. 254, 354.
163. Like the eastern Ndlambe of today, for instance (personal communication of Louis Botha, who has done extensive fieldwork among them). The fact that Chungwa's grave is in Alexandria district (in the Zuurveld) may serve to keep alive among the Gqunukhwebe the memory of their Zuurveld background and claims.
164. For Danster, see Peires, 'History of the Xhosa', p. 116.
165. For a discussion of this particularly interesting frontier, see Legassick, 'Griqua, Sotho-Tswana and Missionaries'.
166. For illuminating theoretical discussions of the relationship between different ethnic communities, see *Ethnic Groups and Boundaries: the Social Organisation of Cultural Difference*, ed. Fredrik Barth (Boston, 1969), introduction, and William J. Foltz, 'Ethnicity, Status and Conflict', *Ethnicity and Nation Building*, ed. Wendell Bell and Walter E. Freeman (Beverley Hills, 1974), pp. 103–16.
167. *Transactions*, I (Van der Kemp's Journal), pp. 480–83.

The British and the Cape 1814–1834

J.B. Peires

The final transfer of the Cape from Dutch to British rule did not in itself precipitate a revolution in government. As W.M. Freund has pointed out (ch. 7, p. 351) the reformist impulses of the early British and Batavian administrations were soon submerged by the weight of established Cape practice to the extent that by 1814 the transitional governments had simply reaffirmed the essentials of Cape social structure as it had existed prior to 1795.

When Lord Charles Somerset assumed office in 1814 as Governor of the Cape, there was no reason to suppose that any major transformation of Cape society was in prospect. Certainly, Lord Charles himself was very far from wishing any changes at all. It was his misfortune to govern the Cape at the time when the new social forces generated in a rapidly industrialising Great Britain engulfed the colony, sweeping aside not only Somerset but the entrenched power of the local oligarchy and the established rhythms of the local economy. The double explosion of the 1820 settlers at the periphery of the colony and the 'revolution in government' at its centre reverberated far beyond the borders of the Cape, exposing the peoples of the interior to a dual invasion by British settlers, apostles of free enterprise and free trade, and Afrikaner Voortrekkers, bearers of a racial ideology predicated on a system of coerced labour. It is the purpose of this chapter to explore the origins and early history of these momentous innovations.

Lord Charles and the settlers

The royal commission issued for Lord Charles Somerset's guidance upon his appointment as Governor of the Cape stated that 'for the present and until our royal wish be further signified, the temporary administration of Justice and the Peace of the Settlement should, as nearly as circumstances will permit, be exercised by you in conformity to the laws and institutions which subsisted under the Ancient Government.'[1] No instructions could have been more congenial to a man of Lord Charles's upbringing and temperament. Politically the highest of English High Tories, Somerset held views which were coloured by a home environment which prided itself on maintaining 'the best remnant . . . of all that fealty existing in feudal times between the lords of territory and their retainers.'[2] He was the second son of the Duke of Beaufort, inventor of the modern version of the 'sport' of fox-hunting and whose country seat at Badminton boasted 116 rooms and innumerable multitudes of horses, dogs and servants. Blue-blooded connections raised the young Charles to the position of Gentleman of the Bedchamber to the Prince of Wales, found him a seat in Parliament, and purchased him the rank of Major-General before he had so much as seen a shot fired in anger. But as a second son, Somerset's position was always precarious and when his sinecure as Joint Paymaster of the Forces was abolished, the Prime Minister himself intervened to compensate him with the governorship of the Cape.

A man such as Somerset could not have been much inclined to tamper with the existing administrative and legal systems of the Cape, which centralised all relevant powers in the hands of the Governor. Nor did he scorn to make full use of the political and financial patronage which the inherited Dutch system placed at his disposal. Habits of extravagance learned from the Prince Regent at Brighton blotted out the stern injunctions towards financial stringency emanating from the Colonial Office, and Lord Charles did not hesitate to pay himself an unauthorised 45,000 rixdollars in salary, or to spend £28,000 of public money on his country residence at Newlands, or to issue 100,000 new rixdollars instead of cancelling 500,000 old ones according to instructions.[3] Apart from his frontier policy and his patronage of Cape agriculture, Lord Charles's main positive contributions towards Cape history during his first period of governorship (1814–19) were limited to a new constitution for the South African Turf Club and a thoroughgoing reform of the local hunting regulations. It should not be thought that the Governor's pronounced inactivity was in any way distasteful to the Cape establishment. On the contrary, Somerset's conservative disinclination to interfere with the status quo entrenched their local power, and his free-spending policies considerably enhanced their prosperity. Colonel Christopher Bird, the Dutch-speaking strong man of the Cape civil service, encouraged Somerset in his course.[4] In retrospect it is clear that Somerset's first spell of office was a transitional period which largely cushioned the shock attendant on the British decision to retain the Cape after the Treaty of Vienna in 1814.

The first assault on the decaying structures of the old Dutch colony came not from the Governor but from the British settlers of 1820. Though Somerset had asked for British settlers before his departure from Britain, he never once returned to the subject until the Colonial Secretary, Lord Bathurst, proposed the idea in July 1817.[5] The initiative for the settlement scheme thus originated in Britain rather than at the Cape, and it was planned in line with British rather than Cape interests. Theories of 'overpopulation' were gaining ground in England as convenient explanations for the mass unemployment and political riots which racked Britain in the aftermath of the Napoleonic Wars. The Colonial Office had tried Canada but had become disillusioned by the number of emigrants who turned their assisted passages into cheap tickets for the United States. They were still weighing the alternatives when, completely out of the blue, the Chancellor of the Exchequer proposed a grant of £50,000 to send settlers to the Cape. Exaggerated notions of the fertility of the Cape were then current in Britain, and more than 80,000 hopeful Britons applied for assistance to emigrate.[6]

In its origins, the 1820 settlement was nothing but a political manoeuvre by a Tory Government, desperate to demonstrate public concern for the unemployed in order to stave off pressures for more radical reform. But the Colonial Office was quite aware of the real difficulties which the settlers would face and it was not prepared to turn the Cape Colony into a dumping ground for paupers. The ideal settler, in its view, was a small agricultural capitalist at the head of a party of indentured labourers, and the emigration regulations were framed with precisely this class of person in mind.[7] Applications by single individuals were deemed unacceptable, and the Colonial Office declared that it would negotiate exclusively with the heads of prearranged parties, each of whom put down a deposit of £10 per adult male and received in return a land allocation calculated at a rate of 100 acres per man.

Only about twelve parties, the so-called 'proprietary parties,' conformed to the Colonial Office ideal. At the other end of the scale were the parties of paupers sent out at the expense of their English parishes. There were only five of these, even though the ostensible object of the scheme, as understood by the British Parliament, was to assist the unemployed. The vast majority of settlers were neither proprietors nor paupers, but respectable individuals possessed of some financial means but lacking the large capital necessary to support a whole party of employees. Such individuals clubbed together to form 'joint-stock' parties under elected leaders who negotiated with the Colonial Office on their behalf. These joint-stock parties made possible the emigration to the Cape of a very diverse group of people, quite different from the landed gentry proposed by the Colonial Office and expected by Lord Charles Somerset. A recent random survey of 500 successful applicants has shown that fully 50 per cent of them were urban artisans while only 36 per cent described themselves as farmers or unskilled labourers. Even this figure may over-represent the agricultural element, for many emigrants pretended to be farmers in order to get their applications approved at the Colonial Office.[8]

The joint-stock parties began to break up even before they landed in South Africa. Thomas Willson, the nominal head of the largest, was obliged to flee for his life after no more than one night in the promised land. Several immigrants sought employment in the towns as soon as they landed, and within a month of their arrival in Albany district (April 1820), the colonial authorities were faced with a mass exodus of settlers from their prescribed rural locations. Citing the 'vagabondizing' of many immigrants and the 'capricious' attempts of many indentured labourers to quit their masters, the Cape government ordered the local magistrate to apply the full rigour of the act governing master and servant relations to contracted labourers, and to employ the colonial vagrancy laws to check the flight from the land.[9] Nevertheless, by May 1823, only 438 of the original 1004 male grantees remained on the rural locations.[10]

It is clear that the failure of the Albany settlement to develop along the lines anticipated by the Colonial Office and Lord Charles Somerset was due not only to the infertility of the soil, or to the effects of Xhosa raids, or to the three successive seasons of rust, drought and flood so dear to settler legend, but also to the ambitions and capabilities of the settlers themselves. The majority of 1820 settlers were not English country gentlemen seeking merely to replicate their traditional lifestyle, but were themselves products of the new nineteenth-century England, seeking out in a strange land the opportunities which their lack of substantial capital denied them at home.[11] Unwilling rather than unable to make a living off the land, they turned with enthusiasm to the more profitable avenues of trade and manufacture.

Above all, they were a people habituated to the use of money in commercial transactions. Whereas the Afrikaner farmers, dependent on the scarce and depreciating rixdollar (ch. 5, pp. 259–61), still conducted most of their business by barter and direct exchange of services,[12] the British settlers, relatively speaking, were awash with cash, either from the capital which they had brought out with them, or from the half-pay they received in semi-retirement, or from refunded deposits or charity subscriptions raised by their British compatriots, or from the remittances sent by relatives and friends at home. Thoroughly accustomed to evaluating everything in pecuniary terms, the hard-nosed British traders bartered cheap but attractive goods such as cloth and iron utensils to Xhosa and Afrikaner producers in exchange for valuable commodities such as cattle-hides and ivory which fetched high cash prices on the English market.

Notwithstanding the efforts of the country *smouse* (itinerant traders) the three months that it took to travel from Cape Town had severely limited the habitual purchases of most frontier Afrikaners to 'bare necessaries, a few of the conveniences, and none of the comforts of life.'[13] The ease with which the early settlers bartered such minor items as watches, used clothing and Sheffield knives for good livestock is ample proof of this.* The settler John Montgomery, who possessed no capital at all, was able to get a start in business by borrowing the cast-off goods of other traders and hawking them around remote areas which no other pedlar had previously visited.[14] The majority of traders were able to get substantial credit from the wholesale merchants of Cape Town, turning country towns like Graaff-Reinet into entrepots of the new trade.[15] This trade not only enriched several of the settlers, but it inspired the frontier Afrikaner with a whole new range of commercial desires, precisely at the time when the colonial government was planning to strike at the economic root of his productive activities.

Those settlers who stuck to their farms soon came to prefer the woolled merino sheep to the indigenous fat-tailed variety, which provided fine mutton and candle-fat for the subsistence farmer but commanded no price whatsoever on the markets of the world.[16] Wise traders and sheep-farmers put their money into land, to raise more sheep or to sell again when the price was right. Judicious investments and speculations made rich men out of settlers such as Robert Godlonton, George Wood and James Howse, who used their wealth and their newspaper, the *Graham's Town Journal*, to promote their personal interests as if these were those of the Eastern Province as a whole.[17]

---

* This is not the place to enter into the so-called Neumark controversy, but the obvious inference from the 1820 settler evidence is that Neumark greatly overestimated the extent to which *smouse* had penetrated the interior. The settlers were able to take advantage of the fact that trading opportunities in the eastern Cape hinterland had been tremendously underexploited.

For the remainder of the 1820s, however, these economic changes were not nearly as apparent as the tension which soon arose between the authoritarian structure of Lord Charles's government and the democratic practices which the upper strata of the settlers claimed as their right. Even before the settlers arrived, the **Deputy** Colonial Secretary had predicted that 'some modification of the [Cape] Colonial laws will be required, which are in many points founded upon principles abhorrent to the English practice.'[18] On the instructions of the Colonial Minister, Lord Bathurst, Somerset issued a proclamation (July 1822) to the effect that English would gradually replace Dutch over the next four years as the official and judicial language of the Cape. He also recruited some English-speaking clergymen and teachers from Scotland, and financed the establishment of a new English school in Cape Town to counteract the 'most disgusting principles of Republicanism' allegedly taught at a private school run by the liberal settler, Thomas Pringle.[19]

These tentative steps towards Anglicisation were overshadowed by the clash between Somerset and Sir Rufane Donkin, who was appointed Acting Governor (1820–21) during Somerset's absence. Donkin seems to have cherished the hope that his appointment would be prolonged, and he was lavish with his patronage, earning the gratitude of both British settlers and ranking civil servants by strategically generous grants of land. He also went out of his way to humble Lord Charles's eldest son, Henry, temporarily a junior officer under his command. The settlers, who arrived during Donkin's stewardship, were unwittingly drawn into the struggle on the Acting Governor's side.

Incensed by Donkin's attempts to usurp his prerogatives, Somerset lost no time in asserting his authority over the settlers as soon as he returned. A pro-Somerset Landdrost and pro-Somerset Heemraden were installed in Albany in the place of Donkin's nominees, the settler capital was moved from Bathurst to Grahamstown, and Donkin's settlement at Fredericksburg in the Ceded Territory (pp. 483 below) was abandoned. The new Landdrost of Albany brusquely employed his arbitrary powers to put down dissent and withdrew many of the land grants which Donkin had promised to his partisans. These measures aroused the indignation of many middle-class settlers hitherto unaccustomed to such naked exercise of power patronage, and they despatched a stream of complaints and newspaper articles to their influential connections in England. The first of these complaints appeared in the British press in September 1822, just two months after the British Government had decided to appoint a Commission of Inquiry to make detailed recommendations concerning the government of its new acquisitions of the Cape, Mauritius and Ceylon.[20] It was this Commission (see pp. 494–98 below) and not the protests of the settlers which ultimately overthrew the Somerset autocracy. The so-called 'Albany Radicals' were not hostile to the patronage system provided they got their share, and Lord Charles found it surprisingly easy to make peace with them when he visited the frontier during the boom harvest year of 1825.[21]

But the damage was already done.[22] Bishop Burnett, a gentleman farmer bankrupted by his attempts to break into the monopoly of military contracts hitherto enjoyed by the government farm at Somerset East, continued to agitate against the system. Burnett was articulate and litigious and his attempts to obtain legal redress eventually involved him in a host of secondary prosecutions the upshot of which was to thoroughly expose the arbitrary nature of the Cape judicial system and of Roman-Dutch law itself. Another cause célèbre of the time was that of Launcelot Cooke, a wealthy Cape Town merchant who was imprisoned, banished and ultimately bankrupted for his part in exposing a racket operated by the Collector of Customs, who allocated 'prize negroes' (ex-slaves released from captured slave ships) for hire at a profit. The clique around Colonel Bird, deposed in 1822 allegedly for his Catholic faith but in reality for his alliance with Donkin, fed the rumour mill with further allegations, for example that Somerset had issued grants of land to farmers who purchased his privately-owned horses.

Somerset's attempts to stifle the growing scandal resulted in a series of sensational trials, which revealed that under the Cape judicial system the government had unlimited powers of search, detention and banishment; that the accused had no right to summon their own witnesses or cross-examine the witnesses of the prosecution; that the Fiscal, or prosecutor, was also one of the judges and that there was no trial by jury; and that none of the Cape's top judicial officers was fully conversant with the English language. Backed into a legal corner, the Fiscal was forced to declare explicitly that he took his stand on Roman-Dutch law. Bishop Burnett thereupon refused to offer any defence whatsoever on the charges brought against him, maintaining that he was an Englishman in an English colony and that Roman-Dutch law was no more relevant to his situation than 'the laws of the Danes or the Calmuc Tartars.' Further sensations associated with these trials – the revelation that the defendants' fiery attorney William Edwards was an escaped convict on the run, the involvement on the government side of the notorious provocateur known as Oliver the Spy, an anonymous placard hinting at the Governor's sexual misbehaviour with the female transvestite Dr

James Barry – made the Somerset administration a convenient target for the Whig opposition in the British Parliament.

What made all this especially unbearable for Somerset was that detailed reports of these trials were printed in George Greig's *South African Commercial Advertiser*, the first independent newspaper ever published at the Cape (1824). Prior to this, the weekly *Government Gazette* had been the only permitted news medium and the authorities had underlined their opposition to a free flow of information in 1820 by seizing a printing press found aboard a settler ship. Greig's own attempts to start a newspaper were stalled for six months until, having discovered that publication was not in fact illegal, Greig went ahead regardless.

Infuriated by Greig's temerity in printing the court proceedings, Somerset ordered the Fiscal to censor pre-production proofs of the *Advertiser* on a regular basis and to demand a bond of 10,000 rixdollars as a surety for its good behaviour. Greig refused to comply with these conditions and, as a result of his public protestations, was ordered to leave the colony. At the same time Thomas Pringle and John Fairbairn, who edited a small literary journal, were threatened with prosecution. They too suspended publication and joined Greig in his attempts to persuade the Colonial Office in London to overrule Somerset.

Through their unyielding refusal to accept any concessions less than full press freedom and their ruthless exploitation of Somerset's personal unpopularity, Greig and Fairbairn eventually carried their point. Suspended a second time for continuing their attacks on the departed figure of Lord Charles, the *Advertiser* was reinstated in October 1828 and this time there was no turning back. By Ordinance 60 of 1829, the Cape press was finally freed from the executive control of government and allowed to print whatever it liked short of the common law of libel. Fairbairn, now the editor of the *Advertiser*, saw this as only the first victory for democratic rights in South Africa, but his continuing campaign for representative institutions was to be frustrated until 1853.[23]

Far from preparing the Cape for its inevitable assimilation into the British colonial system, Somerset's conservative autocracy nurtured the oligarchic and mercantilist tendencies it had inherited from the Dutch East India Company. Even the few feeble steps which Somerset took towards Anglicisation failed to make much progress. Dutch continued to serve as the de facto medium of communication in the country districts, and attempts to confine jury service to those who spoke English were abandoned in 1834. Attendance at the government schools slumped after Dutch was cut out of the syllabus and more than a third had collapsed by 1832. Education in Cape Town was dominated by the newly-founded South African College and the *Tot Nut van 't Algemeen* private school, both under Afrikaner control.[24]

The political impact of the 1820 settlers outside the district of Albany has been greatly exaggerated. Lord Charles's regime could never have survived the Commission of Inquiry, which was set up without reference to settler grievances. The British settlers were nevertheless responsible for bringing about a profound transformation in the Cape Colony's social and economic structure. Bearers that they were of an urban and commercial culture, the British introduced South Africa to a spirit and practice of enterprise and accumulation which soon carried them far beyond the borders of the Cape. Although the Voortrekkers are usually exclusively credited with the colonisation of the far interior, we should not forget that it was British traders who established Natal and British missionaries who opened up the road to the north. Above all, the British brought with them the new conception, foreign to both African and Afrikaner farmers,† that land was a commodity that could be acquired and sold without ever necessarily being possessed and worked first. Frustrated eventually by the stubborn resistence of the Xhosa, the land speculators turned northwards and, within the short space of forty years (1840–80) gobbled up most of Natal, the Free State, the northern Cape and the eastern Transvaal.[25] But it was on the Cape Colony's Eastern Frontier that the expansionist tendencies of the British settlement first cut its teeth.

An explosion on the Eastern Frontier

Prior to the war of 1811–12 (ch. 9, p. 448) the Xhosa were an aggressive and expanding nation pushing rapidly westwards, driven less by the need for grazing than by the political ambition of each chief's son to establish an autonomous chiefdom.[26] Ndlambe and Chungwa, the two chiefs who effectively occupied most of the territory between the Sundays and the Fish rivers, did not possess more than 2,500 followers between them,[27] yet it is clear from their cavalier treatment of the colonial authorities that they did not view the whites as a serious threat. Colonel John Graham's

† This is not meant to imply that land speculation was unknown under the VOC. Piet Retief (pp. 508–10) is a good example. But in land tenure, as in so many other respects, the capitalism of the VOC was not yet fully mature. Legally speaking, it was not the land itself but the *opstal* (the buildings and improvements) which was being sold, a procedure which assumed at least some personal occupation before sale.

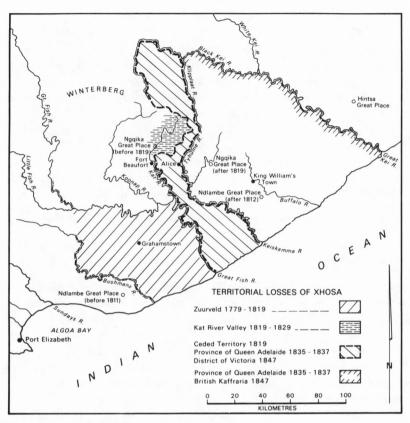

Figure 10.1 Territorial losses of the Xhosa.

brutal and efficient campaign of 1811–12, deliberately designed to inspire the Xhosa with 'a proper degree of terror,' rudely surprised the Xhosa chiefs and forced them into a drastic reassessment of the situation.[28] Whereas they had formerly resisted suggestions that they should keep to their own side of the boundary,[29] they now began to see in a firmly sealed border their only hope of survival as an independent nation.

The years 1812–20 commenced with a Xhosa attempt to reverse the defeat of 1812 and ended with a resounding confirmation of colonial military superiority and another major extension of colonial territory. Though the Xhosa had learned too much from the war of 1811–12 to risk another direct confrontation, they did their best to expel the colonial intruders through the guerilla tactics of house-burning and cattle theft.

By 1820, only 38 of the 145 Zuurveld farms given out after the victory of 1812 were still occupied by white farmers.[30] Somerset and his advisers preferred to see the problem as one of cattle-theft rather than land dispossession, and in 1817 he met the Xhosa chief Ngqika at the Kat River to clarify procedures for the recovery of stolen colonial cattle.

Ngqika was the senior chief of western Xhosaland, but his notorious avarice with regard to the property and even the wives of his subjects had made him deeply unpopular. He had assisted the colonial forces against his uncle and main rival, Ndlambe, and that had made him more unpopular still. Somerset's policy was based on consciously exploiting Ngqika's weakened position to make him a more pliable tool of colonial interests, as this dispatch to the Colonial Office shows:[31]

> The authority of [Ngqika] long considered to be principal [Xhosa] chief had been for some time on the decline . . . I availed myself of this circumstance, and by adopting a line calculated to give him weight with the whole [Xhosa] people I trust I have made it his interest to adopt my views.

Xhosa oral tradition remembers the Governor's proposition to Ngqika as a succinct 'You protect me, and I'll protect you.' Initially reluctant to accept Somerset's offer, Ngqika soon entered fully into the spirit of collaboration and sent peremptory messages to his uncle Ndlambe and other Xhosa chiefs who bucked his authority. Such high-handed behaviour soon provoked an anti-Ngqika coalition headed by Ngqika's nominal superior, the Xhosa king Hintsa, and directed by the celebrated wardoctor Nxele (Makana). After crushing Ngqika's forces at the battle of Amalinde (1818), the victorious Xhosa allies sent Lord Charles Somerset an urgent message asking him for peace and requesting him to keep out of Xhosa domestic politics. Somerset ignored these peaceful overtures, and in the ensuing clash (Fifth Frontier War, 1818–19) the colony once again emerged victorious.

If Somerset had contented himself with this military triumph, he might have been able to secure some kind of durable political rapprochement on the basis of the Fish River boundary. But he was unwilling to leave it at that. Having duly punished Hintsa, Ndlambe and the other chiefs then in arms against the colony, he turned on his supposed ally Ngqika and demanded, as the price of his military assistance, the rich lands between the Fish and the Keiskamma River where Ngqika himself had always resided. The horrified Ngqika protested that although indebted to the English for his existence as a chief, 'When I look at the large extent of fine country taken from me, I am compelled to say that, though protected, I am rather oppressed by my benefactors.'[32] Somerset's treachery immensely broadened the scope of the military struggle on the colonial frontier. The early frontier wars had involved only the relatively minor chiefs of the western outposts of Xhosaland. Ngqika, the most powerful chief west of the Kei, had always tolerated and even encouraged colonial attacks on his rebellious subordinates. But after this betrayal, resistance flickered briefly even in his corrupt and exhausted soul. His sons, Maqoma and Tyhali, uncompromised by their father's double-dealing, became the leaders of the new generation of anti-colonial warriors.

One of the hardy minor myths of South African history is that Somerset intended to create a 'neutral belt' of open territory between colonist and Xhosa. But Somerset's official dispatch on the subject unambiguously refers to the land in question as 'ceded' to Great Britain, describes it as 'as fine a portion of ground as is to be found in any part of the world, and strongly recommends it to the Colonial Secretary as a suitable area for systematic colonisation.' It was only after his rival, Acting Governor Donkin, established a settlement within the Ceded Territory that Somerset began to claim that his policy all along had been to interpose a 'neutral space' between the settlers and the Xhosa. These avowals did not stop the Governor from offering farms in the Ceded Territory to Afrikaner farmers willing to support his embattled cause.[33] Despite all these ambiguities and inconsistencies, the notion of a 'neutral belt' was taken up by Lord Bathurst, the British Colonial Secretary, who ordered Somerset's successor to keep the Ceded Territory empty.[34]

The 'neutral belt' policy, conceived as it was in treachery and dishonesty, could not possibly have worked. Maqoma refused to leave his home in the valley of the ceded Kat River and the colonial authorities, fearing to remove him by force, allowed him to remain there on condition of his 'good behaviour'. Inevitably Maqoma and his brothers clashed with the Afrikaner farmers moving in on the Ceded Territory from the direction of Somerset East. The old story of the Zuurveld, which gave rise to five wars between 1779 and 1819, was re-enacted in the Ceded Territory. The colonial government took its stand on a verbal treaty (the Somerset/Ngqika talks of 1819) which the Xhosa rejected as invalid and unfair. The colonial army, though strong enough to defeat the Xhosa in any open confrontation, was too weak to police an extensive and bushy country against persistent Xhosa cattle-raiding. In the recriminations which followed the outbreak of war in 1834, much was said on the settler side concerning the Xhosa tendency to steal their cattle while the Xhosa had ample reason to complain of military patrols and volunteer commandos which attacked guiltless homesteads and seized the cattle of the innocent as compensation for cattle stolen or allegedly stolen.[35] Although there can be no doubt that the escalating cycle of Xhosa raid and colonial reprisal was a major cause of the war of 1834, it is essential to remember that these raids and reprisals did not take place across a mutually defined border but were a direct consequence of the disputed cession of 1819.

In an attempt to seal the colonial border more effectively, Commissioner-General Andries Stockenstrom ordered the expulsion of Maqoma from the Kat River Valley in 1829, and created an autonomous settlement for landless Khoikhoi to take his place. Stockenstrom was sincerely concerned to 'collect the remnants of the Hottentot race, to save them from extirpation, to civilize and Christianize them,' but an examination of his dispatches shows clearly that the desire for a dense buffer settlement in the Ceded Territory preceded his concern for the Khoikhoi.[36] By 1833, more than 2,000 Khoikhoi had been settled as smallholders in the Kat River Valley.

Maqoma's expulsion was decided on in November 1828, but Stockenström lacked the excuse he needed to justify such a measure until, in January 1829, Maqoma himself supplied the pretext by raiding the Thembu chief Bawana and chasing his followers into colonial territory. Maqoma's motives have not been documented, but it is significant that he acted in concert with his brother-in-law Maphasa, who was Bawana's son.[37] He certainly regarded his attack on Bawana as a purely domestic matter and was genuinely surprised to find that the colonial authorities insisted on regarding it as a hostile act. Bawana, though an inoffensive neighbour, was not a colonial ally and Stockenstrom's indignation against Maqoma rings somewhat hollow in the light of the fact that his decision to expel that chief had been taken some three months previously. Stockenström's decision was wholly in accordance with his belief that strict segregation was the only possible solution to the problems of the frontier, but the expulsion of Maqoma's Xhosa from their natal lands was a fatal blunder which ultimately gave rise to the Frontier War of 1834–35. As one of his fellow-chiefs remarked, 'Macomo's heart was very sore about the land; the subject always set him on fire; he fought in hopes of getting it back.'[38]

Maqoma reacted to his expulsion by stepping up raids on white farms until he was tacitly permitted to return to the Ceded Territory. In 1833 Acting Governor Wade decided to enforce the expulsion order not only on Maqoma but on his brother Tyhali as well. The officer who conveyed Wade's message to Maqoma has left a graphic account of the scene.[39]

He distinctly said, which we found out afterwards to be the case, that he could not make out the cause of his removal, and asked me if I could tell him; and I really could not; I had heard nothing; no cause was ever assigned to me for the removal.

A sympathetic frontier commandant allowed the Xhosa to reoccupy their lands, but this permission was withdrawn and the Xhosa were ordered out for the third time. These rapid shifts of policy and the failure of the new Governor, Sir Benjamin D'Urban, to visit the Xhosa chiefs increased the tension on the frontier to breaking-point. When Chief Xhoxho, a brother of Maqoma and Tyhali, was wounded in the head by a British patrol, the Xhosa decided to go to war. They invaded the colony quite unexpectedly on 21 December 1834.

Though land and retaliatory raids were the prime causes of Xhosa-colonial conflict in 1834, new factors of greater long-term significance also contributed, namely trade, labour migration and missionary influence. These factors ultimately destroyed the social and economic foundations of Xhosa independence and determined the terms on which the Xhosa would eventually become incorporated into colonial society during the post-frontier period. The process was a lengthy one which only reached fruition in 1857, but by 1834 it had already made its first appearance.

The lucrative nature of the ivory and cattle trade had induced some of the British settlers to begin trading with the Xhosa very soon after their arrival. As the colonial authorities feared. not without reason, that firearms and alcohol might be changing hands, they took steps in August 1822 to open a fair for legitimate trade near the colonial border.[40] These carefully supervised fairs failed to prosper, and in July 1824 regular weekly fairs, open to all settlers and Xhosa, were commenced at Fort Willshire in the Ceded Territory. These were immediately successful. Fifty thousand pounds of ivory and fifteen thousand cattle hides were released onto the market within the first seven months. Ivory soon peaked, but the export of hides soared to seemingly infinite heights. Although they had never exceeded 6,000 in any year before 1822, they passed 78,000 in 1827, an increase of over 1200 per cent in just six years. This trade, which averaged £34,000 per annum in the years before the Frontier War, constituted the highlight of a depression-ravaged Cape economy and cracked the official policy of non-intercourse wide open. In September 1826, Lieutenant-Governor Bourke granted permission for licensed traders to start fairs in the interior and in December 1830 Sir Lowry Cole repealed all the regulations prohibiting trading operations beyond the borders of the Cape. Within a few years there were somewhere between 150 and 200 itinerant traders operating deep in the heart of Xhosaland subject to very little control from either their own government or that of the local chief.

The decision to bar all Xhosa from the colony, adopted in 1811–12, when even farmworkers were expelled from the Zuurveld, was likewise overturned by economic necessity. In 1825, the frontier had been breached from the unexpected direction of the northeast as the *Mfecane* (a series of wars set in motion by the Zulu king Shaka) sent waves of Sotho-speaking refugees, collectively known as Mantatees, streaming into the colony. These refugees had been rendered pliable by hardship, and they were snapped up by the labour-hungry settlers who found them excellent servants. This encouraged Lieutenant-Governor Bourke to pass Ordinance 49 of 1828 'to procure such number of useful labourers from the Frontier Tribes as the Colonists may be desirous of engaging and it may be safe and prudent to admit.'[41] Under the provisions of this ordinance, prospective black immigrants were to be granted passes for the sole purpose of seeking work. All employment agreements for more than a month were to be registered as contracts, and no employer was allowed to coerce a worker into entering his employ. Such conditions were unenforceable on the Eastern Frontier, where many farmers had not seen a magistrate for several years. In practice Ordinance 49 was merely a convenient fiction to disguise the fact that the colonial government could not control the black immigration which it had permitted. The farmers, who bitterly regretted the abolition of apprenticeship and other forms of labour coercion, were not appeased by this influx of free and uncontrolled labour. Numerous allegations that Xhosa 'with passes' were responsible for cattle-stealing led Sir Lowry Cole to deny them the right of entry to the colony (1829).[42]

The ranks of black immigrants were, however, greatly swelled by the arrival of a large force of Natal refugees headed by Matiwane, chief of the Ngwane. These were defeated by a combined colonial/Xhosa/Thembu/Mpondo army at the battle of Mbholompho in August 1828. They scattered in all directions and sought food and refuge among their conquerors. A few of them entered the colony where they were given the name of Mfengu ('seekers for service') to distinguish them from the Sotho-speaking Mantatees. The majority of Mfengu, however, settled among the independent Xhosa and Thembu, whom they served as clients and herdsmen.[43]

The period 1820–35 also saw a vast upswing in missionary activity. Joseph Williams of the London Missionary Society arrived in Xhosaland in 1817, and he was soon followed by the Presbyterians of the Glasgow

Society, who concentrated on intensive work among the Ngqika Xhosa. Under the able direction of William Shaw, the Wesleyans staked out a prior claim to most of the Xhosa-speaking world by establishing a chain of stations running all the way from Grahamstown to Port Natal (later Durban). These early missionaries identified the spread of Christianity with that of European culture and colonial domination. William Shaw, for example, maintained that[44]

> While Christianity alone can give us influence with the natives, and excite in them a desire of improvement, yet we ought to connect with inculcation of its principles every judicious plan . . . to raise them to an improved condition . . . [This] plan makes the work of conversion and civilization proceed concurrently, and therefore more efficiently and rapidly.

Shaw gave practical effect to these principles by introducing the Xhosa on his stations to European styles of dress and housing, to the wagon, the plough and the irrigation furrow, and to the trader's shop, where tea, sugar, cloth and European-style iron goods were sold. He also used his influence over the Gqunukhwebe Xhosa chiefs to persuade them to hold back from the Frontier War of 1834–35. Some missionaries explicitly rejected any political stance, but even Dr John Philip, whose London Missionary Society was actively pro-Xhosa, declared that his missionaries were 'everywhere scattering the seeds of civilization, social order, and happiness, [and] they are, by the most exceptional means, extending British interests, British influence and the British empire.'[45]

The penetration of Xhosa society by alien traders and missionaries awakened the fears of the more far-sighted of the Xhosa chiefs. They were alarmed not so much by the way in which colonial traders cheated their people, but by the fact that they had lost control over their own economy. The Fort Willshire fairs had created a considerable class of Xhosa middlemen traders who had enriched themselves by reselling goods purchased there to the African peoples of the far interior and who exerted a considerable degree of control over the kind of goods on offer. The penetration of better-capitalised white traders knocked out this class of Xhosa middlemen. Many of the traders did not even bother to consult the chief of the country they traded in, threatening the locals with commandos of colonial troops if they did not give way. 'Who gave that man the right to go about my country showing the people his goods?' demanded the Xhosa king Hintsa, who was fully alive to the implications of the situation.[46] Hintsa was also extremely worried about the exchange of cattle, his country's productive resource, for unproductive consumer goods.[47]

He said that now their cattle were all sold and also their skins, so they would now have no means of getting what they wanted. He was anxious that there should be introduced cows and that the [Xhosa] would be glad to change oxen for them (one for one).

It was small wonder that many traders were openly robbed, assaulted and even murdered during the tense months which led up to the 1834 Frontier War. 'Tell them I have taken these goods,' remarked Hintsa on one such occasion. 'You need not hide it for they have taken my country from me.'[48]

Missionaries were similarly distrusted, though many aspects of the Christian gospel proved very attractive to the Xhosa. A smallpox epidemic in the late eighteenth century had caused them to abandon their usual burial customs, introducing a disturbing element of uncertainty into the Xhosa conception of the relationship between the material and spiritual worlds.[49] The simple and sympathetic preaching of Dr J.T. van der Kemp and other London missionaries, especially that concerning the resurrection of the dead and the redeeming figure of Jesus Christ, struck a sympathetic chord in many Xhosa hearts. The comprehensive defeat of 1811–12 further weakened Xhosa confidence in the sufficiency of their existing religious beliefs, and made them receptive to the prophecies of Nxele and Ntsikana who flourished between 1816 and 1820. Nxele taught of a black warrior god who would revenge himself on the whites for killing his son. Ntsikana preached of the Broad-chested One, a strong and gentle redeemer who would bring peace to a suffering people.

But the Christian missionaries who entered Xhosaland after 1820 did not pick up any of the threads indicated by Nxele, Ntsikana or even Van der Kemp. One or two of the first missionaries were formally appointed government agents, and the Xhosa never quite shook off the idea that they were spies sent out to undermine and divide the black community. In most cases missionary requests to establish stations were granted only with extreme reluctance, and even then only because it was felt that to refuse would be to offend the colonial authorities. Though some missionaries were able to overcome this initial hostility by providing tangible benefits to the Xhosa and by impressing them with the purely spiritual nature of their interests, others managed to inflame Xhosa suspicion and hostility even further.[50] An important example of the latter case was that of John Ayliff, who espoused the cause of the beaten Mfengu refugees among the Xhosa and protected them against the authority of his host, the Xhosa king Hintsa.

Even the improved access to the colony conferred by Ordinance 49 was disliked by the chiefs who viewed it as a means for stealing their people. Ngqika's prescription for frontier peace was based on the concept of total separation. 'If white man cross the river, black man shouid kill him, and if black man cross, white man should kill him,' the chief proposed.[51]

The Sixth Frontier War of 1834–35 was initiated by the Xhosa to recover their lost lands and to seal their border against the hostile forces which were penetrating their society.[52] They rushed into the colony with fire and sword, destroying 456 farmsteads and sweeping off 276,000 stock. They could not, however, sustain their momentum, and the main Xhosa armies under the leadership of chiefs Maqoma and Tyhali retired to their natural fortress in the thickly wooded Amathole Mountains. Rather than face them there, Governor D'Urban and his military commander, Harry Smith, broadened the scope of the war by marching against the Xhosa king Hintsa, whose role in the war had been limited to passive logistic support for his compatriots rather than active participation. D'Urban demanded 50,000 Xhosa cattle in compensation for the colonial cattle supposedly hidden by Hintsa on Maqoma's behalf. It was a fateful decision. After receiving D'Urban's guarantee of his personal safety, Hintsa entered the British camp to negotiate a settlement and found he was being held a hostage for delivery of the 50,000 cattle. Unwilling to co-operate, the Xhosa king attempted to escape. He was eventually shot dead while lying helpless face down in a pool of water. His ears were cut off as souvenirs, and attempts were made to dig his teeth out with a bayonet.

Meanwhile, the Mfengu refugees in Hintsa's country, encouraged by their missionary John Ayliff, rebelled against their Xhosa hosts and attached themselves to the British army. Seventeen thousand of them were settled in the Ceded Territory at Fort Peddie, where they swore a great oath to accept Christianity, obey the Queen and educate their children. Willy-nilly, the Cape had acquired a substantial resident black population who had espoused European values and could not easily be shut out again.

Maqoma and Tyhali were by no means defeated but they were shaken by the death of Hintsa, and they were deceived into surrender by some unofficial messages promising them lenient terms. Their territory between the Keiskamma and the Kei was annexed to the British Crown under the name of Queen Adelaide Province and Harry Smith set himself up in it as a kind of dictator under martial law.[53] He gave the chiefs the titles of magistrates and proposed to teach them to administer English law and live off salaries rather than fines. He planned to flood Xhosaland with schools, missionaries and trade commodities in order to 'civilise' the Xhosa. Outwardly, the chiefs smiled but inwardly they raged. Oblivious of the fact that peace had officially been declared their followers continued to raid the colony virtually at will.

Only one thing prevented the resumption of open hostilities. Lord Glenelg, the British Colonial Secretary, was deeply unhappy about several aspects of Cape policy and he had growing doubts concerning D'Urban's competence.[54] The brutal mutilation of Hintsa's body settled his mind. He rescinded all D'Urban's measures, and restored to the Xhosa all the lands they had lost, including the right to occupy parts of the Ceded Territory. Andries Stockenström, the liberal Afrikaner protagonist of strict separation between Xhosa and colonist, was appointed Lieutenant-Governor of the Eastern Cape to implement a new system of treaties based on recognition of the mutual independence of the Cape and the Xhosa (1836).

This is not the place to relate the story of Stockenström's downfall and the gradual drift towards the Seventh Frontier War (1846–47). In retrospect, however, the treaty system never had a chance. Trade, mission activity and labour migration had already bound the Xhosa inextricably to the Cape Colony. These links had been compounded during the Sixth Frontier War which saw the large-scale settlement of pro-Christian Mfengu on colonial territory and which had revealed to land-hungry settlers the great potential of Xhosaland as a sheep-farming country. Ten years after Lord Glenelg had abandoned Queen Adelaide Province, Harry Smith returned to it as Governor, ready and determined to implement the same policies as he had formerly contemplated.

The revolution in government

The Dutch East India Company was an archetypal phenomenon of the mercantilist age, which was characterised by the close identification of the interests of the state with the interests of the merchant class. So much attention has been paid to the specific peculiarities of the Cape of Good Hope that it is often forgotten that the essential structures of Cape society – a close association between government and commercial enterprise, coupled with a poorly capitalised productive sector reliant on coerced labour – were typical of an economic era in which the transition to a fully-blown capitalist system, based on free trade and free labour, was still in progress.

The death of the VOC did nothing to eliminate the fundamental assumption of the Cape public officials that financial profit was a legitimate goal of administrative activity. Ironically enough, the Cape Dutch found that British rule suited their interests far better than the monopolistic regime of the VOC whose economic interests sometimes conflicted diametrically with their own. The decision of the Cape Council of Policy to secretly share the contents of the Batavian Military Treasury among themselves on the eve of the British takeover in 1806 bears ample witness to their general attitude towards public funds and the public service.[55]

Cape officials habitually made up their incomes by holding a number of incompatible offices simultaneously. They collected the greater part of their salaries directly from the public in the form of fees for services rendered. Many officials ran private businesses on the side, and they did not scruple to grant themselves substantial loans and contracts. The case of Sir John Truter, one of the treasury looters of 1806, is instructive. Sir John was the President of the Orphan Chamber, a body with considerable funds at its disposal. In this capacity, he agreed to lend himself and his family some 51,000 rixdollars though he must have known that he never could – and, indeed, never did – repay them. Any anxiety which Sir John might have felt on this score was, no doubt, considerably alleviated by the thought that he was also President of the Court of Justice and thus empowered to deliver the final judgement on any case that might be brought against himself! We have already (p. 478) seen the extent to which the Cape Court of Justice forsook its supposed judicial neutrality to uphold the political authority of Lord Charles Somerset. Its partiality in civil cases was even more notorious. Truter and his colleagues were not in the habit of giving any reasons or explanations for the decisions which they made, and this practice, together with what the Commission of Inquiry (below, p. 495) called 'the spread of local influences and the infinite extent and obligation of family connexions,' led civil litigants to believe that their cases depended more on the personal feelings of the judges than on the uniform and impartial application of the law.[56]

Given the pervasive spirit of private accumulation among public officials, and given the opportunities for graft which existed when a single individual held a multiplicity of offices, it is not surprising that numbers of civil servants followed Truter's example. F.R. Bresler, the Deputy Receiver-General, got away with 36,000 rixdollars in 1813, while Colonial Treasurer and Landdrost J.W. Stoll acquired some £15,000 of government money during his 15 years in office. The Vendue Master of Albany, finding himself short of ready cash to pay his creditors, satisfied them with funds from the sequestered estates under his control. It is important that we should view these peculations not as the isolated acts of individual criminals but as the inevitable consequence of the institutional arrangements inherited from the VOC, which confused the business of government with the business of private gain. British officials were far from immune from the temptations of such a system. The British government auditor participated in the Bresler fraud and Governor Cradock, who seems to have been aware of the whole transaction, did nothing to stop it.[57]

Just as Cape government was unduly involved in commerce, so was Cape commerce unduly involved in government. Government control of commercial credit and government licensing of trade and production through the system of pachts and other monopolies created a tight oligarchy of businessmen closely linked to their official patrons through ties of friendship, family and reciprocal financial obligations. In 1793, for instance, VOC Commissioners established the Lombard Bank for the purpose of encouraging economic enterprise by providing government-guaranteed loans at a low rate of interest (see ch. 5, pp. 261–62). But very few of the bank's funds were used to sponsor genuine economic entrepreneurs. The bank commissioners overlooked many reasonable requests for credit, preferring to lend out most of the bank's capital in long-term loans to their particular friends, who then re-lent it, at usurious rates, to those outside the magical circle of power and influence. The Orphan Chamber, a body created for the purpose of taking care of the estates of orphans and absent heirs, deliberately delayed the payments due to legitimate claimants and invested the money in property and in cheap loans to favoured individuals. The Vendue Department, which supervised all public auctions in Cape Town, likewise entrenched and enriched the Cape oligarchy. Only those persons deemed creditworthy by the Vendue Department were allowed to bid at such sales. These lucky individuals received three months credit, and before they had so much as paid for the goods they purchased, they had already resold them to the poorer, supposedly less creditworthy people who had been excluded from the auction. The Burgher Senate, a self-perpetuating body of four members administering the affairs of Cape Town, were fairly representative of this dominant group. They controlled the collection of taxes, which they assessed to their own advantage and that of their friends, and they also disposed of various other privileges such as the licensing of butchers and bakers. The Commissioners of Inquiry declared that 'great abuses and irregularities have prevailed' on the Burgher Senate 'from which the indigent classes of the inhabitants have suffered considerably.' Corrupt officials were occasionally replaced, but the system was more powerful than any individual, and the Commissioners concluded that there was no hope of ensuring the financial probity of the Senate as long as 'persons engaged in trade' controlled its affairs.[58]

The network of patronage and influence which determined the patterns of social and economic behaviour in Cape Town was replicated on a smaller scale in the country districts. The Landdrosts who administered these districts were appointed by the central government but they soon became enmeshed in the local networks of their districts. 'Some of the Landdrosts . . . are so overwhelmed with debt and so involved in their circumstances as to render them anything but respectable,' the Colonial Secretary reported in 1825.[59] In each district the Landdrost was assisted by a Board of Heemraden chosen by the Governor from a list of local notables submitted by the existing Board. The District Secretaries, who performed most of the executive tasks of the Board, were 'constantly exposed to the influence of local partialities, of hereditary prejudices and of family connections.'[60] The Boards of Landdrost and Heemraden possessed considerable administrative powers in respect of finance, taxation and labour allocation, all of which they exercised selectively in favour of their chosen clients. District Boards freely loaned money to their friends and their power to assess taxes frequently led to 'undue severity in some cases, and to lenity in others.' In the allocation of lands and the calculation of quitrents, the Commissioners of Inquiry found the boards guilty of 'a sacrifice of the public revenue, either in subservience to their own views, or to the interests of their neighbours.' Landdrosts acted as sequestrators in cases of bankruptcy and often used these powers to connive at the evasion of responsibility by select debtors.[61]

Caledon's 'Hottentot Proclamation' of 1809 entrusted the Landdrosts with the responsibility of granting passes to Khoikhoi workseekers, a power which effectively enabled these officials to distribute Khoikhoi labour to anyone they chose. Landdrosts and Field-Cornets arbitrarily extended the provisions of Cradock's apprenticeship regulations of 1812 (ch. 1, p. 41) to coerce the labour of children and young adults who were legally entitled to their freedom. Since the Boards of Landdrosts and Heemraden acted both as prosecutors and judges, the clauses of Caledon's proclamation which were designed to protect the labourer were usually not applied.[62]

These conditions would have drawn the disapprobation of the Commissioners of Inquiry at the best of times, but the prolonged depression which began in the year 1825 made the matter infinitely more urgent. Revenue at the Cape was notoriously unable to keep pace with government expenditure, and the early governors had resorted to massive injections of paper money to keep the local economy afloat.[63] Over one million new rixdollars (nearly 50 percent of all currency in circulation) were issued between 1806 and 1822, and even so the spendthrift Somerset had been obliged to raise an extra quarter-million via a loan from the English East India Company. Galloping inflation slashed the real value of the rixdollar, and when the time came to convert it into British silver (1825), it was done at the going rate of one shilling and sixpence per rixdollar rather than the nominal value of four shillings. This abrupt deflation halved the value of assets estimated in rixdollars, multiplied bad debts and outright insolvencies, and sent the whole colony spinning into depression.

To make matters worse, the removal of British preferential tariffs on Cape wine severely cut back the colony's most important export, and the death of Napoleon reduced the demand for Cape produce at St Helena. The internal market at the Cape was artificially depressed by the monopoly system, while sinecurist officials performing no useful functions weighed down the civil service payroll. 'As to our finances, we are perfect bankrupts, and it is needless to conceal it, as we have not enough to pay our own salaries,' the Cape Colonial Secretary reported in 1825, while the newly appointed Acting Governor Bourke added that 'we have no manufactures and commerce and agriculture are on the brink of ruin.' Neither was exaggerating.[64]

The Commission of Eastern Inquiry, appointed in 1822, was given the widest possible brief to investigate all aspects of Cape administration and to make specific recommendations 'for the purpose of prospective regulation and practical improvement.'[65] Although appointed about the same time as the 1820 settlers began to protest against the Somerset autocracy, the Commission owed its origins to the spirit of liberal economic reform associated with William Huskisson, the President of the British Board of Trade, whose chief object was to root out the remnants of mercantilism and direct the emerging British empire towards free trade. The Commission of Inquiry, which was also to investigate conditions in Mauritius and Ceylon, was part of this thrust.

R.W. Horton, the British Under-Secretary of State for the Colonies who was instrumental in appointing the Commission, took care to appoint a man of strong reformist sympathies to succeed Somerset. This was Richard Bourke whose modest rank of Lieutenant-Governor belies the important role he played in Cape history. Bourke was a Whig

(Liberal), a rare political tendency among Cape Governors, and his firm personal commitment to liberal ideals was undeniably important in implementing the decisive measures which destroyed the 'old corruption' of Somerset's government. But Bourke's personal convictions, strong though they were, were not in themselves responsible for these reforms. Reform began in Somerset's time and continued well after Bourke's departure, despite the extremely conservative orientation of his successor, Sir Lowry Cole. The traumatic changes at the Cape were not the work of a single individual but the consequence of the inevitable dismantling of the old Dutch mercantilist system and the integration of the colony into the liberal political and economic order of the nineteenth-century British Empire. The fact that the Commissioners of Inquiry consciously de-emphasised their own personalities, and deliberately presented themselves as faceless and impartial servants of the British Crown has usually misled the personality-minded historians of South Africa to underestimate their significance. But it was these cautious and bureaucratic officials who were responsible for initiating one of the biggest upheavals which Cape society ever experienced. As Bourke put it, describing the changes which took place during his administration, it was 'a kind of revolution . . . casting off our old skin and proposing to appear on 1st January next [1828] as bright as Virgil's snake.'[66]

The major recommendations of the Commissioners of Inquiry fell roughly under three headings. First, they sought to create an independent legal system which could guard against both arbitrary misuse of power and corruption within the ranks of the administration. Second, they sought to create an efficient civil service capable of withstanding the temptations and inequities associated with the patronage system. Third, they sought to remove the last of the economic restraints associated with the old mercantile system, and to stimulate prosperity through free enterprise. Their recommendations towards the anglicisation of the colony were strongly linked to the first two of these objectives, and their recommendations with regard to the Khoikhoi (ch. 1, pp. 44–46) were linked with the third.

The power of the Governor had already been circumscribed by the decision of Lord Bathurst in 1825 to establish a Council of Advice before which the Governor was obliged to lay all matters of importance. In practice, members of the Council of Advice were unwilling to contradict the Governor, even after two unofficial nominated members were added to it in 1828. However, the Commissioners felt that fully representative institutions were out of the question until the question of slavery had been finally settled.[67] Emphasis was therefore placed not so much on changes in the executive and legislative branches as on the reconstitution of the judiciary.

A new Supreme Court was to be created for the Cape, headed by a Chief Justice who would be the third-ranking official in the Colony. This Supreme Court would take over the role previously performed by the Governor as a Court of Final Appeal. Sir John Truter, the president of the existing Court of Justice, and David Denyssen, the fiscal, were to be retired immediately, and their places were to be taken by a Chief Justice and Attorney-General sent out directly from England. All future judges were to be chosen from the British bar, and all future Cape lawyers were required to take their degrees in England, as Commissioner J.T. Bigge was convinced that local bias and colour prejudice made the Cape Afrikaners incapable of attaining the degree of judicial impartiality which 'constitutes the brightest excellence of the English Judicial Character'.[68] The language of the courts was to be changed to English, and the jury system was to be introduced to inspire confidence in all parties of the neutrality of the law. The effect of this was somewhat spoiled by Bigge's insistence that all jurors should be able to speak English, but this stipulation was dropped in 1834. Bigge stopped short of recommending the immediate abolition of Roman-Dutch law, but he did urge that the 'forms of Process ... be assimilated to those of England.' Lest anyone remain unaware of the magnitude of these suggested changes, the Commissioner suggested that they be proclaimed in the form of a 'Charter of Justice'.[69]

The Commissioners sought to limit the autocratic powers of the Governor by creating an autonomous Eastern Province under its own Lieutenant-Governor and by reserving the more important civil appointments, formerly the prerogative of the Governor, directly to the British Crown.[70] The Burgher Senate, that stronghold of the Cape oligarchy, was abolished and the Orphan Chamber was to be forced to pay all unclaimed inheritances directly into the Colonial Treasury. Public officials were no longer allowed to hold several conflicting offices at once, nor to collect their salaries in the form of cash fees for services rendered.

Financial considerations blocked some of these measures, such as the plan for an autonomous Eastern Province. But the reforms which the Commissioners proposed for local government in the outlying districts were accepted with far-reaching effects. The Commissioners condemned the extent to which the 'self-elected Boards' of Landdrosts and Heemraden had encroached on and virtually superseded 'the powers and just influence' of the colonial government.[71] Resident Magistrates, trained in British jurisprudence, were to take over the judicial duties of the Landdrosts; and Civil Commissioners, likewise British, were to take over executive duties such as the collection of taxes, the keeping of accounts and the allocation of lands. The Commissioners' original intention of completely separating the offices of Resident Magistrate and Civil Commissioner proved impractical on financial grounds, but the besetting sin of the old system, namely the confusion of executive, judicial and personal interests, was effectively done away with. By Ordinance 33 of December 1827, the old Boards of Landdrosts and Heemraden were abolished and with them went the chief means by which the Cape Afrikaners had influenced and manipulated the government which ruled them. The vague promises of the Commissioners that, after they had learned some English and liberated their slaves, the Afrikaners might conceivably be granted some small measure of representative government, were hardly adequate compensation.

But then, the Commission of Inquiry was frankly prejudiced against Afrikaners, whom they saw as supporters of the Somerset regime and resistant to any change. Not one Afrikaner came forward voluntarily to give evidence to the Commission and those that were summoned disclosed the minimum of information sullenly and evasively.[72] Commissioner Bigge condemned what he called the 'indolence and indifference' of the Cape Afrikaners, and he described them as 'a people devoted to agricultural pursuits; and whose views in life have hitherto rarely exceeded the attainment of decent maintenance for their families, and the establishment of their sons in situations and conditions as nearly analagous as possible to their own.' This Afrikaner 'indolence' was largely due, the Commissioners thought, to the presence of slave and Khoikhoi labour, which they regarded as 'a great obstacle to the improvement of the Colony.' They suggested a tax on servants as a means to stimulate the industry of the Afrikaners and render their families more productive. The views of the Commissioners were indeed somewhat extreme, but it should not be forgotten that even progressive Afrikaners such as the influential Stockenström considered that the traditional methods of Cape agriculture were wasteful and economically ineffective.[73]

The Commissioners considered that the servile condition of Khoikhoi and free blacks further inhibited productivity by discouraging the black working class and misdirecting their energies towards frivolous pursuits. It was believed that the inability of Khoikhoi to gain access to private property in land was the main obstacle to their general progress, and the success of one Khoikhoi who had managed to obtain a farm near Clanwillian was cited as an example of the potential productivity of the Khoikhoi once this disability had been removed. The efficiency of Khoikhoi artisans when engaged in properly remunerated employment was also noted. Ordinance 50 of 1828 (see ch. 1, pp. 47–50), though a broadly conceived measure designed to grant equality before the law to every free inhabitant of the Cape, should also be seen, therefore, in the context of the attempts of the Commissioners and the colonial authorities to stimulate the depressed economy of the Cape. Given personal liberty and security of property, it was hoped that the Khoikhoi would eventually become 'industrious farmers and respectable members of the community.'[74]

The judicial reforms were explicitly designed to infuse a 'spirit of active industry and intelligence' into Afrikaner life, and the economic and financial measures proposed at the same time were geared to a similar end. The Commissioners reviewed, with distaste, the piecemeal system of rents, tithes and taxes from which the civil revenue of the Colony was generated; the array of licences, concessions and monopolies granted by the VOC which had long outlived their usefulness; and the clammy hand of state regulation which necessarily plunged any commercial transaction into the morass of official patronage networks. They concluded that, by restraining free competition, the existing system drove up the price of provisions and prevented the growth of the internal market, limited the economic demand of the colonists 'to the acquirement of a few articles of the first necessity,' and deprived the Cape of 'the solid prosperity of a thriving and industrious population.'[75]

The Commissioners proposed to abolish this motley crew of taxes and to make up the revenue by increasing the slave tax and by instituting a more uniform and effective tax on land. These proposals aroused opposition, even from Bourke, on the grounds that new taxes were sure to be resisted whereas the old ones had acquired the legitimacy of custom. Nevertheless, the Commissioners' commitment to free trade precipitated a veritable St Bartholomew's Eve Massacre of monopolies, *pachts* and other special concessions in 1827 and 1828.[76] Out went the monopolies enjoyed by the butchers, the bakers, the wine traders and the vendue masters. Local taxes and tithes were abolished, and internal trade was promoted by new roads and improved postal services. The Land Board was revamped and the increasingly efficient and rapid surveying of farms hastened the spread of quitrent tenure, introduced by Governor Cradock in 1813 but hardly effective.[77]

The appointment of Resident Magistrates and Civil Commissioners in the place of Landdrosts and Heemraden marked a decisive shift in the locus of power throughout the Cape's country districts. The local notables might still be able to obstruct and resist unpopular new laws, but they had forever lost their capacity to exploit the machinery of administration in the service of their own interests. By the early 1830s the new land and labour regulations, imperfectly enforced though they may have been, were already beginning to bite, and the more far-sighted among the frontier Afrikaners were already able to predict the consequences of their loss of control. As one frontier farmer complained in 1830:[78]

> Now we have a Civil Commissioner to receive our money for Government and for Land Surveyors, a Magistrate to punish us, a clerk of the Peace to prosecute us, and get us in the Tronk [prison], but no Heemraad to tell us whether things are right or wrong . . . The Englishman is very learned . . . They and the Hottentots will squeeze us all out by degrees.

Out of such sentiments was the Great Trek born.

The origins of the Great Trek

The Great Trek is the name conventionally given to the deliberate emigration from the Cape of some 15,000 Afrikaners, almost all of them from the eastern districts, in search of a place where they could govern themselves according to the 'old Burgher [citizen] regulations and duties'[79] and generally reconstitute the way of life of which the 'revolution in government' had stripped them. The central causes of this emigration are commonly agreed on by most historians, but so far little has been done to assign an order of priority to these causes or to situate them in their historical context.[80] Even the most recent historians stress the consequences of the 1834–35 Frontier War, although the first hints of premeditated emigration date back to 1832 and the first organised trek parties left the colony nearly a full year before the unexpected Xhosa invasion of December 1834. The fact of a radical shift in colonial policy between 1824 and 1828 has not however received the emphasis it deserves. It will be argued that most of the causes of the Trek can be referred directly back to the recommendations of the Commissioners of Inquiry. For there can be no doubt that the emigration was a response to certain specific policies of the colonial government rather than an Afrikaner nationalist reaction to British rule or a response to the breakdown of black-white relations on the Eastern Frontier.

In spite of the Slagters Nek rebellion of 1815 (which was poorly supported), the Cape Afrikaners had shown themselves remarkably satisfied with English government prior to 1827–28. They were accustomed to authoritarian behaviour, and they were inclined to defend Somerset at a time when most of the British settlers were busily engaged in pulling him down. There was no shortage of Afrikaner signatures on pro-Somerset petitions, whereas not a single Afrikaner was prepared to come forward and testify to the Commission of Inquiry. Even if, as Somerset's opponents alleged, Lord Charles had bribed some Afrikaners with offers of free land, this only goes to show that the governor spoke a language which they understood.[81] But after 1828, in the three critical fields of labour, land and local administration, the 'revolution in government' overturned Somerset's practices and installed a new system inimical to the needs of the Afrikaner.

One of the first priorities of the Voortrekkers, as their spokesman Piet Retief promised in his published Manifesto, was 'to preserve the proper relations between master and servant.'[82] The proposed emancipation of the slaves hit the frontier farmers harder than conservative historians such as Theal are prepared to admit. In 1828, there were 6,598 slaves in the eastern districts, almost all of them the property of Afrikaner farmers. The 147 applicants for land in the Ceded Territory possessed 459 slaves between them, a critical factor in Lord Bathurst's decision to deny them the land grants they expected. Farmers such as Louis Tregardt were thus forced to choose between getting their land and keeping their slaves, clearly an intolerable position.[83] As far as other kinds of labour were concerned, farmers complained that as a result of Ordinance 50 they were 'not being allowed to chastise a bad or insolent servant, but compelled to ride a great distance to a magistrate' for a punishment that was inadequate and uncertain in their eyes.[84] The 'despotic and barbarous treatment' which the farmers meted out to unwilling servants was not the product of wanton cruelty but it was 'inherent in the nature of the forced labour system.'[85] That system was itself the result of an inadequately capitalised rural economy which was so short of money that it conducted most of its commercial transactions by barter and had no coppers to spare for cash wages (above, p. 475). Precisely at the very time when farmers – squeezed by the economic depression and tempted by the new goods offered by settler traders – had most need of their labourers, the colonial authorities intervened to free these from their involuntary servitude.

As we have seen, Lieutenant-Governor Bourke and the Commissioners of Inquiry condemned forced labour not only for moral reasons but because they believed it was economically inefficient and led, in the Commissioners' words, to 'indolence and indifference.' They hoped that measures such as Ordinance 50 would stimulate the Cape's feeble economy by increasing the productivity of both the labouring classes (now given the incentive of the profit motive) and the former master class (now deprived of indolence-inducing coerced labour). The installation of Magistrates and Commissioners in place of Landdrosts and Heemraden, though primarily intended to destroy the patronage networks of the 'old corruption', incidentally destroyed a judicial system which had tolerantly closed its eyes to the violent measures occasionally necessary to coerce unfree labour into the farmers' service. It seemed blatantly unfair to the frontierspeople that the British might so casually liberate servants 'whom the Boers at the risk of their lives had ventured to capture among rugged rocks and civilise.'[86]

Bourke realised that an immediate labour crisis might arise from the proclamation of Ordinance 50, but he thought he had pre-empted this by Ordinance 49 which permitted Africans to cross the colonial border to enter into service contracts, The Afrikaner farmers were, however, unwilling to allow the new Magistrates any part in determining the proper relationship between master and servant. Knowing that they could not express their complaints in terms of their demand for labour and their regret for the passing of slavery, they phrased their grievances around the problem of 'vagrancy', which conveniently represented their demands for labour as if they were legitimate necessities of self-defence. The uncontrolled influx of black refugees from the Mfecane furnished an inexhaustible pool of potential labourers, but so long as the colonial government lacked the means or the will to coerce or control them, these were more of a danger than a benefit to the hard-pressed farmers.[87]

The principal motivation behind the farmers' clamour for vagrancy laws was not self-defence but, as one western Cape farmer candidly phrased it, 'for the purpose of stimulating the Negroes to more industry, befitting them for Christian society and inducing them to become field labourers.'[88] Encouraged by the vaguely conservative administration of Governor Cole (1828–33) many frontierspeople lived in hopes that such a vagrancy law might be enacted. It was only in 1834 when the final abolition of slavery coincided with a British government veto of vagrancy legislation approved by Cole that they realised there was no turning back. Field-cornets who tried to enforce vetoed vagrancy regulations were dismissed. Afrikaners complained that the consequent labour shortage induced them to work like 'slaves,' and that even their wives and daughters were condemned to perform menial tasks. Observers of the early Voortrekkers commented on the 'heart-rending scenes' of 'young and tender females' driving sheep and cattle in the absence of their fathers' slaves and servants. It was the disruption of the farm economy rather than any form of cowardice which led Afrikaners such as J.H. Hatting to object to compulsory military service.[89]

> It was not only that one didn't know what would become of these children, but who would undertake the farming? Who would look after the cattle, horses and sheep?

'The Boers were completely deprived of labourers,' he added, 'and together with their children, had to do all the work and tend the livestock.' But that, surely, was precisely what the Commissioners of Inquiry had intended!

Side by side with the 1828 revolution in labour relations, though more gradual in its inception and its effects, was the revolution in land tenure which sought to turn land from a free gift of nature into a taxable and marketable commodity. Under the original VOC system of loan-places land was carelessly granted by the Boards of Landdrosts and Heemraden to the first person who applied. Casually erected beacons and inaccurately drawn boundaries acquired the semi-legitimacy of custom among neighbours. Land rents were claimed by the VOC but the Heemraden who fixed the assessments did not care to squeeze their neighbours and allowed them to run up large arrears. The consequent effect on the colonial revenue prompted Governor Cradock to introduce the new system of quitrent in 1813. This was strenuously opposed by Afrikaner landholders, who saw no need for change, 'Every proprietor of land in this District,' wrote the sworn surveyor of Stellenbosch, 'claims his ancient boundaries, keeps his money in his pocket, and possesses the Government Ground in the same manner as if he had a title Deed.' Numbers of farmers, objecting to the prospect of rent payments in cash, wrote to Cradock, declaring inter alia that 'we do assure Your Excellency that six cattle farmers are not able, between them, to procure fifty rixdollars.'[90]

Farmers were, however, protected from Cradock's land reforms by the colonial government's inability to implement them. Charles D'Escury, the Inspector of Lands and Woods during the Somerset administration, was unqualified and overworked and never left Cape Town. Effective disposal of unoccupied land remained in the hands of Landdrosts and Heemraden, who continued to grant land and assess land taxes with the same latitude as before. Because no further land titles were allowed to be issued on the old loanplace system and because the colonial administration was too inefficient to pursue its policy of quitrent effectively, a new type of provisional occupation known as 'request-places' became the predominant form of land tenure in the eastern districts. As soon as a farmer had sent in a 'request' for a piece of land, he proceeded to occupy it as if it were already his property. By 1824, there were 1,000 farms held as request-places in the Graaff-Reinet district, but not a single farm on quitrent.

The cash-starved farmers preferred request-place occupation to quitrent tenure,[91] but they felt insecure about their lack of official title. This insecurity was greatly heightened by the decision of Lord Bathurst to withdraw the permission granted by Somerset to 120 Afrikaner families to settle in the East Riet River portion of the Ceded Territory.[92] It is significant that the farmers of this district provided a high proportion of the first Voortrekkers including their leader, Provisional Field-Cornet Louis Tregardt. The prohibition also served notice to the frontierspeople that the colonial government, having obstructed their access to fresh lands north of the Orange,[93] would likewise block their expansion further east. This policy was all the more offensive inasmuch as the same government had just granted extensive lands gratis to recent settlers of British and Khoikhoi extraction.

The movement to replace traditional Afrikaner land tenure gained further momentum with the recommendations of the Commissioners of Inquiry which speeded up the tempo of land-surveying and hastened the spread of the quitrent system.[94] The first proper Cape Land Board served by the Cape's first qualified surveyors was appointed in 1828. The efficiency of this Land Board was improved even further by Governor D'Urban's reforms of 1834, which included measures designed to force landowners to pay off their rent arrears.

Such innovations were hardly welcome to the frontierspeople, whose numbers were increasing much faster than the land available to them, as the Resident Magistrate of Albany explained:[95]

> The early marriages contracted by the [Afrikaner] people, the consequent rapid increase in population, their disinclination to procure any other mode of subsistence than that which is obtained by the possession of land, the degradation which is attached to servitude . . . these combined causes rendered a movement such as is now contemplated inevitable when land could no longer be found within the colony to satisfy the demands of increased population.

In the frontier district of Graaff-Reinet in 1812, only 18 per cent of burghers were legal holders of land although available water resources were so utilised that 'where there was a puddle, there was an occupant'.[96]

By 1832, there were 162 families permanently settled over the colonial boundary in the Stormberg region alone. If it was difficult even for a prosperous farmer like Karel Landman to get a legal grant of land, it was virtually impossible for a poorer person. It was not government policy to make land grants to undercapitalised applicants, and government awards always went to the richer claimant. The high fees payable in cash for inspection and survey which had to accompany every application were a further source of distress and anger to the more indigent Afrikaner farmers:[97]

> We were compelled to have our farms expensively surveyed, and for a small farm we had to pay from 40 to 200 rixdollars.

> [The Voortrekkers] say that their farms are too expensively taxed. For small little weak fountains, Rd 200 must be paid to get the title deed.

It is small wonder that a man found among the Voortrekkers with surveying tools was almost killed as a government spy.[98]

The third major complaint of the emigrant Afrikaners related to the changes in local government following the replacement of the Boards of Landdrosts and Heemraden. Some historians have argued that the financial parsimony of the British government left the frontier lawless and unpoliced,[99] but it was the presence rather than the absence of the supposedly one-sided British law to which the farmers objected. Statements such as 'of the government we know nothing except when we have money to pay, and the law never reaches us except to fine or otherwise punish, often for acts we did not know to be wrong' should be read as a protest against existing laws rather than as a plea for law itself. 'There is no longer any justice for the burghers, but only for blacks,' was a typical complaint, engendered by such events as the dismissal of Provisional Field-Cornets Potgieter and Smit for going on an old-fashioned commando, described by an unsympathetic government as the 'barbarious shedding of human blood.'[100]

What the Afrikaners missed in the old Boards was not so much an element of political representation but the influence which they had exerted through the Boards on the essential determinants of their material prosperity: control of labour, allocation of land, assessment of taxes. The oft-repeated complaints of the frontier Afrikaners that the British government deliberately denied them access to the gunpowder they required were simply manifestations of the deep-seated conviction that an unpredictable and basically malevolent power had usurped control over their destiny.[101]

Of the other Voortrekker grievances, the most interesting is their indignation concerning the British devaluation of the rixdollar.[102] This is a curious complaint when we remember that most rural Afrikaners did not contract their business in paper money, and that those who did were liable to be debtors rather than creditors. As the future President Boshoff of the Orange Free State pointed out, when raising the issue, few of the farmers were directly affected by the issue but they thought it unjust. Further research is needed into this matter, but the most likely explanation of the grievance is that, unaware of the causes of the general depression which began in 1825, the farmers not unnaturally blamed it on the depreciation of the rixdollar. The Voortrekkers also complained of the losses they had incurred when the British government decided to pay out the slave compensation money in Britain rather than in South Africa. This caused slaveowners to lose up to four-fifths of the market value of their slaves. The Voortrekker leader Gerrit Maritz lost £908 by this arrangement.[103]

These various discontents stimulated Afrikaner exploration of the far South African interior. The first party, which included at least one of the stepsons of Piet Retief, set out in 1831 and returned with encouraging reports of abundant land containing 'a plentiful supply of water, grass of excellent quality, and an abundance of timber.' Over one hundred frontiersmen expressed the desire to trek when they received this news, but they eventually decided against it. In August 1832, Retief hinted at the idea of a trek when he told his magistrate that the Afrikaners would 'rather go and live in a desert land' than quarrel openly with the British government. As the final abolition of slavery approached and the possibility of a vagrant law receded, the pace of Afrikaner preparations for the Trek increased. The first to leave was Louis Tregardt, who crossed the colonial border in February 1834. Shortly thereafter, in September 1834, Piet Uys set off to investigate the possibility of a Voortrekker settlement in Natal.[104]

These dates are important because they demonstrate conclusively that the Great Trek was already well under way when the Sixth Frontier War commenced in December 1834. The grievances associated with this war can only therefore be seen as a secondary cause of the Trek. Similarly, the return to South Africa in July 1836 of the newly appointed Lieutenant-Governor Stockenström with his declared policy of 'equal rights to all,' and the acrimonious correspondence with Retief which followed, only confirmed a trend to emigration which already existed.[105] The most that can be said of the Frontier War as a cause of the Great Trek is that, by burning down their houses and driving off their cattle, the Xhosa unknowingly severed the material links which bound many Afrikaners to the Cape and made it easier for them to commit themselves to a dangerous and risky enterprise. Even so, relatively few Afrikaners did decide to go on Trek – no more than 15,000 altogether, almost all of them from the eastern districts.[106]

The specific effects of these general causes can best be illustrated by examining the early careers of the Voortrekker leaders, Louis Tregardt and Piet Retief. Neither was a typical figure, but both were important leaders and an examination of their experiences in the Cape Colony prior to the Trek will help us to understand the impact that the broad trends of British policy outlined above could have on individual Afrikaners.

Louis Tregardt's father was prominent in the Graaff-Reinet uprisings of 1795 and 1799 (ch. 9, pp. 440–443) and he grew up in the frontier district of the Tarka.[107] He was a skilled, respected and highly successful farmer, and by 1825 he had amassed some 16 horses, 323 cattle and 1791 small stock. To sustain and expand farming activities on such a scale, Tregardt required easier access to land and labour than the circumstances of Cape Colony permitted. He already owned ten slaves, and in 1825 he thought he had secured the land he needed when he took possession of two farms totalling 2,675 morgen just east of the Great Fish River. These farmer, and by 1825 he had amassed some 16 horses, 323 cattle and 1,791 Charles Somerset had allocated to the Afrikaners in order to secure their political support (p. 483), but the Colonial Office refused to approve the grants because they did not want slaveowners within 48 kilometres of the Xhosa border. The fact that the British government was unwilling to make land grants to Afrikaners whereas it was more than generous to British settlers and Khoikhoi caused widespread resentment in the district, and the practical steps towards slave emancipation proved the last straw for Tregardt. In January 1834, he and thirty families of his district sold up their property and left the colony intending never to return.

All this is perfectly in accordance with our general impression of the Voortrekkers, but Tregardt's next move will surely startle all those brought up on the conventional image of the 'true' (*rasegte*) Afrikaner.[108] Instead of heading for the wide open spaces of Natal, Tregardt proceded no further than the upper reaches of the White Kei, where he was given a substantial farm of 12,000 morgen by his new overlord, the Xhosa king Hintsa. There is every indication that the relationship between the king and the Voortrekker was a close one. Karel Tregardt, Louis's son, recalled many years later that if it had not been for the Sixth Frontier War, 'the Tregardt family would probably have established itself [in Xhosa country] forever.'[109] It is possible that Tregardt supplied Hintsa with firearms and there can be no doubt that he imbued him with his fierce hatred of all things British. 'Louis Strickard [Tregardt] had great weight with Hintsa,' according to one British source. Early in 1835 the Xhosa king responded in a positive manner to a private appeal for peace from an Afrikaner named Christiaan Muller, and suggested that the Boers should 'remain on one side, and allow the [Xhosa] to drive the English from the frontiers,' adding that 'the Boers should have restitution for their [raided] cattle in three days if they wished to receive it.'[110]

This offer was never taken up, but Tregardt did not wait around long enough to see the climax of the war or the tragic death of his Xhosa patron. Instead, he trekked north accompanied by one of Maqoma's uncles, the old frontier chief Mnyaluza. A fragment of information from a Xhosa spy gives us a brief insight into the relationship between Afrikaner and Xhosa trekkers:[111]

These Boers abused the English very much, [and] said 'We have no powder yet, but we shall have; tell your chiefs to come to us; the English will seize them as they have done others before and will make servants of the whole of you. Do not trust the English.' The [Xhosa] said 'We cannot go back now, it is too late; our chiefs are over, and so are our cattle. Umyalousie is to cross three more rivers; we then come to a large bush where we are to live, Boers and all together. Louis Trichard and Umjaloosie are our chiefs: we cannot come back.'

What are we to make of this information, and, in particular, how does it affect our view of the racial attitudes of the Voortrekkers? For it has been generally accepted that race prejudice was one of the chief causes of the Great Trek. The very same Karel Tregardt who declared that the Tregardt family would have been happy to remain forever the subjects of a Xhosa king also said that the main objection of the emigrant Afrikaners 'to the coming new order of things was the equalisation of the coloureds with the whites.' Piet Retief stated on one occasion that the Afrikaners were 'neither willing nor able to change our colour for the sake of temporary happiness,' and his niece, Anna Steenkamp, declared that placing slaves on an equal footing with 'Christians' was 'contrary to the laws of God and the natural distinction of race and religion.' The constitution of the later South African Republic [Transvaal] roundly proclaimed that 'The people desire to permit no equality between coloured people and the white inhabitants either in church or state.'[112]

One cannot dismiss the racial implications of these and other similar statements, but nor should one dismiss Tregardt's close association with Hintsa and Mnyaluza as some kind of aberration. There was a general perception among Afrikaners that Hintsa was their friend and it was even considered that by invading his country the British government had triggered off an unnecessary additional war. The idea of a Xhosa-Afrikaner alliance against the British is a constant theme in early Afrikaner history, appearing in both the Graaff-Reinet rebellion of 1799 and the Slagters Nek revolt of 1815.[113] The same Mnyaluza who joined Louis Tregardt in 1835 had hoped to assist Faber and Bezuidenhout at Slagters Nek. Many Afrikaners seem to have believed that as native born Africans themselves, they were better equipped to make satisfactory arrangements with black Africans then were the alien British. This belief seems to have underpinned Retief's rather naive conviction that he could reach a mutually beneficial agreement with the Zulu king Dingane. Nor did Hendrik Potgieter scruple to make use of the Pedi King Sekwati in an attack on his fellow-Afrikaners at Ohrighstad.[114]

The solution to this apparent contradiction in Afrikaner thinking seems to lie in the argument first put forward by Martin Legassick that the origins of racial prejudice lay not in external cross-border conflict but in the internal labour relations of master and servant. The very same Afrikaners who developed a racial ideology to legitimate the coercive labour system were quite prepared to concede equality to the independent African nations living in their vicinity. The ideal relationship envisaged by the Voortrekkers seems to have been that proposed by Hendrik Potgieter to the Griqua leader, Adam Kok: 'We are emigrants together with you . . . who together with you dwell in the same strange land and we desire to be regarded as neither more nor less than your fellow-emigrants, inhabitants of the country, enjoying the same privileges with you.'[115]

Unlike Louis Tregardt, Piet Retief was a farmer only by necessity; by avocation, he was a businessman.[116] He grew up in the western Cape, the son of a wealthy farmer who set him up as a young adult with a wine farm of his own. Losing all his property as the result of a disastrous speculation, he came east in 1812 to escape his creditors. Establishing himself in Grahamstown as a contractor for government supplies, Retief again overreached himself, losing his government contract after getting heavily into debt and failing to meet his obligations. Engaged by government in 1822 to build a new barracks and a new drostdy for Grahamstown, he again failed to meet his commitments and was forced to sell almost all his possessions in order to stave off insolvency. The remainder of his years in the colony were spent dodging the accumulated debts of former speculations, and his property was more than once attached by bailiffs. Temporary expedients such as bootlegging liquor could not redeem the situation, and, after a brief spell in the debtors' prison, he was finally declared officially bankrupt in June 1836. Eight months later, he left the colony. His decision to trek was not motivated by financial factors alone, but it is probable that these played some part.

The reasons for Retief's business failure have not been clearly understood. His biographers have blamed greedy British officials, unreliable black and white labourers, and even Retief's own 'restless' disposition, but ultimately they have confessed themselves baffled. 'In these and other cases . . . we cannot but wonder at Retief's attitude,' write Eily and Jack Gledhill with reference to his financial lapses.[117] The mystery is solved however if we withdraw our gaze from the contemplation of Retief's personality and direct it towards a consideration of the nature of government contracts.

The first fact to consider is that Retief secured the contracts by bidding for them at prices well below the cost of the goods which he was expected to supply. In the case of the 1813 contract, for instance, he tendered exactly half the price of the next highest bidder.[118] How could he tender so low and still hope to make a profit? The answer is obvious to anyone who realises that this was standard practice during the VOC period. Let us consider the example of the Van Reenen brothers who obtained the VOC contract for the supply of meat during the 1780s. It was well worth the Van Reenens' while to incur a loss on the meat contract itself because their status as government contractors gave them access to highly lucrative business opportunities which would otherwise have been closed to them.[119] Everything about Retief's business practices indicates that he was attempting to implement a similar arrangement, that is to make up the unavoidable losses incurred on government contracts by using his position as government contractor to set up other, more profitable business deals.

The details of these transactions do not, naturally enough, appear in the written records, but the overall pattern is clear. Retief's first government contract in 1813–14 was disastrous both for the British troops who never got a proper supply of provisions and for Retief's creditors, who were left holding debts of up to 30,000 rixdollars. Retief blamed the weather, but it is more probable that he went deliberately into debt in order to speculate in land.[120] His knowledge of local conditions, his influence at the drostdy of Uitenhage and the capital acquired via unpaid debts enabled Retief to obtain grants of no less than seven deserted farms totalling more than 120,000 morgen and to purchase more than 30 erven in Grahamstown plus several in Uitenhage and Port Elizabeth. When the 1820 settlers arrived, he made use of his local contacts to monopolise the supply of corn and flour, buying it at no higher than 16 rixdollars per muid and selling it at 30 rixdollars per muid. By 1823 Retief, who had arrived virtually penniless on the frontier ten years previously, was possessed of more than 1200 cattle, nearly 4,000 sheep and goats and 92 horses in addition to the landed property just mentioned.[121]

He had also run up innumerable major debts which he juggled and deferred, making full use of his influential friends and his knowledge of the innumerable loopholes in the Cape's judicial machinery in order to stay out of trouble. Ever in search of another financial windfall, Retief tendered a ridiculously low quote for the construction of the new barracks and the new drostdy.[122] The logic was the same: get the government contract at a loss, and then make use of the facilities that accompanied it to make up a profit on the side. After six weeks of exemplary contracting, he began to put these intentions into operation: using military labour and military storehouses for private building contracts elsewhere, making surreptitious use of inferior building materials, securing double payments from an unwary commissariat, pestering his superiors for advances on work not done, and, above all, obtaining further credit throughout the Eastern Province on the basis of his government connections. In the old days of inefficient accounting, corrupt officials and the general perception that the government was there to be robbed, Retief might have got away with it. But those days were over. Commandant Scott and Landdrost Rivers held Retief strictly to the letter of his agreement, not without difficulty; as Scott remarked, 'I have had more difficulty and irritation from this contract [with Retief] than from the whole of the frontier command.'[123] Blocked in his hidden agenda, Retief's debts came home to roost, and in 1824 he was forced to sell up all his possessions. It is from this period that his first thoughts of trek emerged.[124]

Conclusion

The changes of 1824–28 shook the entire colony. The establishment of an independent judiciary and an impersonal and bureaucratic civil service destroyed the power base of the Cape oligarchy which had regarded government primarily as a convenient means to its own enrichment. The diminution of direct administrative involvement in the economy, the abolition of special concessions and monopolies, the adoption of sound money and fair credit, the freeing of labour, and the proper registration of private property in land, were all essential preconditions for the development of a fully capitalist free market. That these changes were not as successful or far-reaching as the British Board of Trade and the Commissioners of Inquiry might have liked does not in any way detract from their significance. The Cape was thrust, greatly hesitating and dragging its feet, towards participation in the great Victorian empire of free trade and private enterprise.

Meanwhile, at the fringes of the colony, new forces of aggressive expansionism were let loose. The territories north of the Orange and the Vaal rivers were settled by Cape Afrikaners determined to perpetuate their threatened precapitalist social order. At the same time, other regions such as the eastern Cape, the northern Cape and Natal were penetrated by British traders, missionaries and speculators, who bore on their shoulders precisely the very same new way of life which the Voortrekkers were trying to escape.

Lieutenant-Governor Bourke spoke truly indeed when he described the changes he had authorised as 'a kind of revolution.' Perhaps it was not as complete as he would have liked, for it failed to thoroughly rid South Africa of the old system of labour relations, or of the racial stereotypes with which these were associated. Nor was the new society which now emerged ever 'as bright as Virgil's snake.' A new society, the hybrid offspring of Afrikaner social structure and British economic enterprise, was indeed in the process of being born, but the nature of the beast had not yet become apparent.

Chapter Ten Notes

1. Quoted by A. Millar, *Plantagenet in South Africa* (Cape Town, 1965), p. 60.
2. Millar, *Plantagenet*, p. 13.
3. G. Cory, *The Rise of South Africa* (1910–40; repr. Cape Town, 1965), II, 242–312; M. Donaldson, 'The Council of Advice at the Cape of Good Hope, 1825–1834,' (Ph.D. thesis; Rhodes University, 1974), pp. 136–37. It is unfortunate that Millar's book, still the only full-length study of Somerset's administration, is so uncritically partisan as to be virtually useless.
4. H.J.M. Johnston, *British Emigration Policy, 1815–1830* (Oxford, 1972), p. 45.
5. Johnston, *Emigration Policy*, pp. 27, 33.
6. On the origins of the 1820 settlement, see Johnston, *Emigration Policy*, ch. III and M.D. Nash, *Bailie's Party of 1820 Settlers* (Cape Town, 1982), ch. I. This section is heavily indebted to Nash, whose book has revolutionised 1820 settler historiography.

7. Nash, *Bailie's Party*, ch. I.

8. The urban and commercial orientation of the settlers is emphasised in Nash, *Bailie's Party*, ch. II. The figures quoted are taken from L. Bryer and K.S. Hunt, *The 1820 Settlers* (Cape Town, 1984), pp. 41–42.

9. W. Bird, *State of the Cape of Good Hope in 1822* (1823; repr. Cape Town, 1966), pp. 198–201.

10. A.C.M. Webb, 'The Agricultural Development of the 1820 Settlement down to 1846.' (M.A. thesis; Rhodes University, 1975), p. 57.

11. Nash, *Bailie's Party, passim*, especially pp. 99–100, and the short biographies, for example of Adams, Anderson, Biddulph, Hewson, Hoole, Plowman and Reed, pp. 129–56.

12. On this important point which is often glossed over by S.D. Neumark, *Economic Influences on the South African Frontier: 1652–1836* (Stanford, 1957), and others in their generally correct attempts to show that the rural Afrikaner *was* tied to the market, see especially the Examination of C.H. Olivier, 11 Dec. 1826, in *RCC*, XXIX, 476–79. See also E.H.D. Arndt, *Banking and Currency Development in South Africa* (Cape Town, 1928), p. 30.

13. Cory Library, MS 7288, J. Ayliff, 'Memorials of James Howse'. I have modified my original position somewhat to take account of an excellent recent paper by S. Newton-King. 'Commerce and Material Culture on the Eastern Cape Frontier, 1784–1812,' (paper presented to the History Workshop, University of the Witwatersrand, Feb. 1987). Newton-King shows that the Graaff-Reinet farmers were inextricably linked to the market, and that many of them were unduly impoverished due to the unfavourable terms of trade imposed on them by licensed butchers and others. My own arguments do not contradict these propositions, but simply affirm that the activities of the settler traders stimulated new wants among the already severely undercapitalised farmers of the eastern districts.

14. J. Montgomery, *The Reminiscences of John Montgomery*, ed. A. Giffard (Cape Town, 1981), p. 90.

15. R. Godlonton, *Introductory Remarks to . . . the Irruption of the Kaffir Hordes* (1835; repr. Cape Town, 1965), p. 198. For more on the impact of settler trade, see B. le Cordeur, *The Politics of Eastern Cape Separatism* (Cape Town, 1981), pp. 40–43; Webb, 'Agricultural Development,' pp. 29–30.

16. On the rise of sheep-farming, see Webb, 'Agricultural Development,' pp. 116–37.

17. J.B. Peires, *The House of Phalo* (Johannesburg, 1981), pp. 121–24; Le Cordeur, *Eastern Cape Separatism*, pp. 40–43.

18. Millar, *Plantagenet*, p. 122.

19. On Anglicisation at the Cape, see the useful summary by J. Sturgis, 'Anglicisation at the Cape of Good Hope in the early nineteenth century,' *Journal of Imperial and Commonwealth Studies* XI (1982).

20. It is important to stress that the Commission of Inquiry was the product of the tendency towards colonial economic reform originating in Great Britain, and was decided on *before* the complaints of the 1820 settlers reached London: Millar, *Plantagenet*, pp. 146–48.

21. Nash, *Bailie's Party*, ch. V.

22. The best summary of the events leading to Somerset's downfall is still Cory, *Rise*, II, ch. VII.
23. On the freedom of the press, see Donaldson, 'Council of Advice,' ch. X; H. King, *Richard Bourke* (Melbourne, 1971), ch. V, VIII.
24. Sturgis, 'Anglicisation,' pp. 16–25; C.F.J. Muller, *Die Oorsprong van die Groot Trek* (Cape Town, 1974), pp. 181–83.
25. Land speculation in South Africa is still badly under-researched. See, however, H. Slater, 'Land, Labour and Capital in Natal,' *Journal of African History* (1975); K. Shillington, *The Colonisation of the Southern Tswana* (Johannesburg, 1985); P. Delius, *The Land Belongs to Us* (Johannesburg, 1983), esp. pp. 127–36. The role of the land speculator in Sir Harry Smith's grab for the Orange River Sovereignty and in the dispossession of the Philippolis Griqua awaits its historian.
26. Peires, *Phalo*, pp. 19–22.
27. H. Lichtenstein, *Travels in Southern Africa* (1812–15; repr. Cape Town, 1928–30), I, 347.
28. J. Cradock – Lord Liverpool, 7 March 1812, quoted in B. Maclennan, *A Proper Degree of Terror* (Johannesburg, 1985), p. 128.
29. Lichtenstein, *Travels*, I, 386.
30. Webb, 'Agricultural Development,' pp. 13–14.
31. *RCC*, XI, C. Somerset-Lord Bathurst, 24 April 1817, p. 306.
32. J. Brownlee, 'Account of the Amakosae or Southern Caffers,' in G. Thompson, *Travels and Adventures in Southern Africa*, ed. V. Forbes (1827; repr. Cape Town, 1967–68), II, 200.
33. For Somerset's first dispatch on the 'Ceded Territory,' see *RCC*, c. Somerset-Lord Bathurst, 15 Oct. 1819, XII, 337–45. For his later denial that he intended to settle Europeans there, *RCC*, Report of Commissioners of Inquiry, 24 Dec. 1825, XXIV, 159. For his subsequent decision to settle Afrikaner farmers in the Ceded Territory, 'Afer' [pseudonym], 'The Caffer Frontier,' *Oriental Herald* (1827), p. 10.
34. *RCC*, Lord Bathurst-R. Bourke, 23 Aug. 1826, XXVII, 279; *RCC* Bathurst-Bourke, 26 Oct. 1826, XXVIII, 277–78.
35. For further discussion of Xhosa raids and colonial commando reprisals, see Peires, *Phalo*, ch. VI, esp. pp. 80, 91–92.
36. A. Stockenstrom, *The Autobiography of Sir Andries Stockenstrom*, ed. C.W. Hutton (1887; repr. Cape Town, 1964), II, 349. For the origins of the Kat River settlement, see Stockenstrom-Bell, 22 Nov, 13 Dec. 1828 in Stockenstrom, *Autobiography*, I, 302; II, 350–51. These dispatches give the lie to Stockenstrom's later declaration that he only thought of settling Khoikhoi in the Ceded Territory *after* Maqoma had been expelled! Imperial Blue Book 538 of 1836, pp. 81–82. For the early history of the Kat River settlement, see also J.C. Visagie, 'Die Katriviernedersetting, 1829–1839,' (D.Litt. et Phil. Thesis; Unisa, 1978), ch. II and III.
37. CO 367, A. Stockenstrom-Government Secretary, 11 May 1829.
38. Deposition of Chief Botma, Imperial Blue Book 503 of 1837, p. 77.
39. Evidence of R. Aitchison, Imperial Blue Book 538 ot 1836, pp. 9–10.
40. Peires, *Phalo*, pp. 99–102; Donaldson, 'Council of Advice,' p. 313ff; S. Bannister, *Humane Policy* (1830; repr. London, 1968), pp. 114–29.

41. R. Bourke-Lord Bathurst, 30 June 1827, quoted in C.F.J. Muller, *Oorsprong*, p. 105.
42. S. Newton-King, 'The labour market of the Cape Colony, 1807–28,' *Economy and Society in Pre-Industrial South Africa*, ed. S. Marks and A. Atmore (London, 1980), p. 199; C.F.J. Muller, *Oorsprong*, ch. III; Bannister, *Humane Policy*, p. 101.
43. Peires, *Phalo*, pp. 86–89.
44. Evidence of W. Shaw, Imperial Blue Book 538 of 1836, pp. 56, 124–27.
45. J. Philip, *Researches in South Africa* (London, 1828), I, ix–x; D. Williams, 'The Missionaries on the Eastern Frontier of the Cape Colony, 1799–1853' (Ph.D. thesis, University of the Witwatersrand, 1959), pp. 238–45.
46. *Grahamstown Journal*, 11 May 1833; Peires, *Phalo*, pp. 101–03.
47. *Andrew Smith and Natal*, ed. P. Kirby (Cape Town, 1955), p. 68.
48. *Grahamstown Journal*, 24 July 1834.
49. Peires, *Phalo*, ch. V.
50. Williams, 'Missionaries,' ch. III.
51. Stockenström, *Autobiography*, I, 304; Cory Library, MS 14, 264, T. Philipps, 'Letters to my kinsfolk,' I–II, 114.
52. For a fuller account, see Peires, *Phalo*, pp. 108–15.
53. Cory Library, MS 2033, D'Urban Correspondence relating to Queen Adelaide Province, collected and edited by G.M. Theal; A. Harington, *Sir Harry Smith: Bungling Hero* (Cape Town, 1980), ch. IV.
54. For Glenelg's repudiation of D'Urban's measures, see also J.S. Galbraith, *Reluctant Empire* (Berkeley, 1963), ch. VII.
55. The secret was revealed to the British commander by Maria, a slave of one of the conspirators, John Truter, who was then Secretary to the Council of Policy. Truter, who later became Lord Charles Somerset's Chief Justice, got his revenge on Maria by obstructing British attempts to secure her freedom for no fewer than nine years. Lord Bathurst-C. Somerset, 9 Nov. 1814; *RCC*, J. Truter-Bathurst, 28 March 1815, X, 204, 282–87.
56. The description of the Cape's judicial system is based on *RCC*, Report of J.T. Bigge upon the Courts of Justice, 6 Sept. 1826, XXVIII, 1–111. The information on Truter's personal finances comes from *RCC*, XXVII, 334.
57. *RCC*, Report of the Commissioners of Inquiry to Lord Bathurst, 31 July 1826, XXVII, 177–94; *RCC*, Report . . . on the Finances, XXVII, 440; L.C. Duly, *British Land Policy at the Cape, 1795–1844* (Durham, N.C., 1968), p. 103.
58. *RCC*, Report . . . on the Finances, 6 Sept. 1826, XXVII, 438–40, 455–59; *RCC*, Report . . . upon the Administration of the Government, 6 Sept. 1826, XXVII, pp. 390–97.
59. *RCC*, R. Plaskett-W. Horton, 28 Sept. 1825, XXIII, 177. One prominent example of such a landdrost was J.G. Cuyler of Uitenhage. See *RCC*, Lord Bathurst-R. Bourke, 7 Aug. 1826 and Comm. of Inquiry-Bathurst, 6 Sept. 1826, XXVII, 241–42, 341.
60. *RCC*, Report upon the Administration, XXVII, 364–65.
61. *RCC*, Report . . . upon the Administration, XXVII, 342–97, esp. pp. 357–58; *RCC*, Report . . . upon the Finances, XXVII, 397–503, esp. pp. 406, 415–16, 428; Duly, *Land Policy*, ch. IV and V. The close relationship

between the leading families and the Cape administration has been noticed by Robert Ross in his important article, 'The Rise of the Cape Gentry,' *Journal of Southern African Studies*, IX (1983), p. 213. I am wary, however, about applying Ross's term 'gentry' (defined as 'relatively prosperous, market-orientated farm owner-operators') to the leading families of the eastern districts. And yet it seems to me that the leading families of the eastern districts were every bit as dominant in local administration as the 'gentry' of the southern and western Cape.

62. W. Macmillan, *The Cape Colour Question* (London, 1927), pp. 158–60; Newton-King, 'Labour market,' p. 182; *RCC*, Report of J.T. Bigge upon the Hottentot and Bushmen Population of the Cape of Good Hope [1830], XXXV, 314–325.

63. For a very detailed account of the currency question, M. Donaldson, 'Council of Advice', ch. IV and V, esp. p. 184.

64. *RCC*, R. Plaskett-W. Horton, 28 Sept. 1825, XXIII, 180; King, *Bourke*, p. 77.

65. *RCC*, Instructions to the Commissioners of Inquiry, 18 Jan. 1823, XV, 239; Donaldson, 'Council of Advice,' p. 267; King, *Bourke*, pp. 58–64.

66. King, *Bourke*, p. 87.

67. *RCC*, Report . . . upon the Administration, XXVII, 365–66, 375–76.

68. *Ibid.*, XXVIII, 17.

69. *Ibid.*, XXVIII, 1–111, esp. pp. 15–18.

70. *Ibid.*, XXVII, pp. 359–63, 396.

71. *Ibid.*, XXVII, pp. 377–90.

72. *Ibid.*, XXVII, pp. 345–47.

73. *RCC*, Report . . . upon the Finances, XXVII, 424; *RCC*, Report . . . upon the Courts of Justice, XXVIII, 13; *RCC*, Report upon a proposed Chartered South African Company, 30 Sept. 1825, XXIII, 196, 215; A Stockenstrom-R.Plaskett, 1 Dec. 1825, quoted in A. Du Toit and H. Giliomee, *Afrikaner Political Thought*, Vol I, 68 (Cape Town, 1983).

74. *RCC*, Report . . . upon the Courts of Justice, XXVIII, 36–38; Report 347–48.

75. *RCC*, Report . . . upon the Finances, XXVII, pp. 397–503, esp. pp. 407–09, 438, 444.

76. Donaldson, 'Council of Advice,' ch. VII.

77. Duly, *Land Policy*, ch. VII.

78. Stockenstrom, *Autobiography*, I, 391. See also Cory Library, MS 2033, J. Bell-B.D'Urban, 4 Dec. 1835.

79. Cory Library, MS 2033, P.L. Uys-B.D'Urban, 7 Aug. 1837.

80. The most significant exception to this generalisation is H. Giliomee, 'Processes in Development of the Southern African Frontier,' *The Frontier in History* (New Haven, 1981), ed. H. Lamar and L. Thompson, pp. 76–119. The standard work is now Muller's *Oorsprong van die Groot Trek*. The most recent work in English is still E.A. Walker's very dated *The Great Trek* (London, 1934). The best overview currently available is in Du Toit and Giliomee, *Afrikaner Political Thought*, vol I, ch. I.

81. 'Afer', [pseudonym], 'The Caffer Frontier,' *passim*. On Afrikaner reaction to the Somerset regime, see Cory, *Rise*, II, 245.

82. Quoted in Muller, *Oorsprong*, p. 206.

83. Too much emphasis has been placed on Theal's argument that 98 per cent of Voortrekkers came from districts containing only 16 per cent of the colony's slaves, quoted with approval by Muller, *Oorsprong*, p. 186. For the use of slaves by frontier farmers, see Newton-King, 'Labour Market', p.179. For a list of applicants for land in Somerset district, together with their holdings in slaves, see *RCC*, XXIII, 70–73.

84. Cory Library, MS 2033, J. Collett-B.D'Urban, 15 Dec. 1835.

85. Du Toit and Giliomee, *Afrikaner Political Thought*, I, 37.

86. Montgomery, *Reminiscences*, p. 103.

87. See Muller, *Oorsprong*, pp. 111–15. It should be noted, however, that many of the raids mentioned by Muller were due not to vagrancy or similar acts, but to the undeclared warfare which followed Maqoma's expulsion from the Kat River in 1829 or the annexation of Queen Adelaide Province in 1835. G.D.J. Duvenage, *Van die Tarka na die Transgariep*, pp. 79–82 falls into a similar trap. He does not seem to be aware that most of his evidence is drawn not from the Stockenström treaty period but from the D'Urban's Queen Adelaide Province which preceded it. His lengthy quotation from Field Commandant Van Wyk regarding the misbehaviour of the 'Mantatees' does not mention that Van Wyk was writing on behalf of a farmer charged with the murder of a 'Mantatee.'

88. A.J. Louw, quoted in Du Toit and Giliomee, *Afrikaner Political Thought*, p. 73. For illuminating discussions on the concept of vagrancy as applied to the Khoikhoi, see J.S. Marais, *The Cape Coloured People* (Longmans, 1939), pp. 125–26; N. Smit, quoted in Du Toit and Giliomee, *Afrikaner Political Thought*, pp. 123–24.

89. 'Herinneringe van J.H. Hatting, snr,' in G. Preller, *Voortrekkermense* (Cape Town, 1920–38), I, 114–15. For references to female and child labour during the Great Trek, Cory Library, MS 15,292, untitled MS by J. Ayliff [1851]; Montgomery, *Reminiscences*, p. 119.

90. *RCC*, Report . . . upon the Finances, XXVII, 404–06; Duly, *Land Policy*, chs. IV and V, esp. pp. 68, 77–78.

91. Land Board-J. Bell, quoted in Duly, *Land Policy*, p. 105.

92. Duly, *Land Policy*, ch. VI; Visagie, 'Katrivier', pp. 106–12.

93. Muller, *Oorsprong*, pp. 228–32; Stockenström, *Autobiography*, vol. I, ch. XVII.

94. Duly, *Land Policy*, ch. VI–VII.

95. Quoted by J.T. de Bruyn, 'The Great Trek' in *An Illustrated History of South Africa*, ed. T. Cameron and S.B. Spies (Johannesburg, 1986), p. 129.

96. Giliomee, 'Processes,' p. 97; Stockenström, *Autobiography*, I, 131.

97. P. Uys and C. Hattingh, quoted by Muller, *Oorsprong*, p. 184; Duvenage, *Tarka*, p. 23; C.F.J. Muller, *Leiers na die Noorde* (Cape Town, 1976), pp. 60–62. For the difficulties faced by the undercapitalised land applicant, see Visagie, 'Katrivier,' pp. 28–30.

98. Montgomery, *Reminiscences*, p. 121.

99. Duvenage, *Tarka*, ch. I; Muller, *Oorsprong*, pp. 177–78.

100. P. Swanepoel, quoted in Du Toit and Giliomee, *Afrikaner Political Thought*, p. 111; Duvenage, *Tarka*, pp. 34, 42, 68.

101. For other examples, see J.L.M. Franken, *Piet Retief se lewe in die kolonie* (Cape Town, 1949), pp. 268, 335; Montgomery, *Reminiscences*, p. 127.

102. J. Boshof, quoted in *Annals of Natal*, ed. J. Bird, (Repr. Cape Town, 1965), I, 506–07; Montgomery, *Reminiscences*, p. 126.
103. Muller, *Oorsprong*, pp. 186–87.
104. Muller, *Oorsprong*, pp. 246–48, 261, 273–75.
105. Franken, *Retief*, p. 328. The Retief-Stockenström correspondence is conveniently summarised in E. and J. Gledhill, *In the Steps of Piet Retief* (Cape Town, 1980), ch. XIII.
106. De Bruyn, 'Great Trek', p. 127; Muller, *Oorsprong*, p. 222.
107. Most of the information concerning Tregardt's early life is from Muller, *Oorsprong*, ch. IX.
108. For example, Muller, *Oorsprong*, p. 268.
109. Preller, *Voortrekkermense*, II, 5–6.
110. Deposition of Maqoma, 28 Apr. 1836 and Deposition of Tyali, 4 May 1836, in Imperial Blue Book 503 of 1837, pp. 232, 234; for the Afrikaner deputation to Hintsa, A.B. Armstrong-[no addressee], 21 Feb. 1835 in Imperial Blue Book 503 of 1837, pp. 216–17 and Hatting, 'Herinneringe,' p. 112.
111. For Mnyaluza's journey with Tregardt, Cory Library, MS 2033, H. Smith-B. D'Urban, 6 March 1836. For further references, see footnote 83 in Peires, *Phalo*, p. 238.
112. K. Tregardt, quoted in Muller, *Oorsprong*, p. 200; P. Retief, quoted in Du Toit and Giliomee, *Afrikaner Political Thought*, p. 112; A. Steenkamp in Bird, *Annals*, I, 459; E. Eybers, *Select Constitutional Documents* (London, 1918), p. 364.
113. J.S. Marais, *Maynier and the First Boer Republic* (Cape Town, 1944), p. 102; H.C.V. Leibbrandt, *The Rebellion of 1815* (Cape Town, 1902), pp. 278, 661, 745
114. M. Legassick, 'The Frontier Tradition in South African Historiography,' *Economy and Society*, ed. Marks and Atmore, esp. pp. 66–67. For Retief and Dingane, see Montgomery, *Reminiscences*, p. 118 and W. Wood, 'Statements respecting Dingaan,' in Bird, *Annals*, I, 380.
115. Quoted by R. Ross, *Adam Kok's Griquas* (Cambridge, 1976), p. 56.
116. I would like to express my admiration for the meticulous research of J.L.M. Franken.
117. E. and J. Gledhill, *Steps*, p. 96.
118. Franken, *Retief*, p. 71.
119. G. Wagenaar, 'Johannes Gysbertus van Reenen – Sy aandeel in die Kaapse Geskiedenis tot 1806' (M.A. thesis; University of Pretoria, 1976), pp. 43–57. This outstanding thesis deserves to be better known.
120. Franken, *Retief*, p. 80.
121. E. and J. Gledhill, *Steps*, p. 67; Franken, *Retief*, pp. 96, 115.
122. *RCC*, 'Reply to the Report of the Commissioners of Inquiry . . . by Mr Bishop Burnett,' XXIX, 85, 199. The important point here is that Retief tendered for the barracks contract at a price 'which would plunge an Englishman into ruin.' Burnett also claims that Retief paid 5,000 rixdollars for one of Somerset's private horses in order to secure the contract, and that he was the client and debtor of Robert Hart, the manager of the government farm at Somerset East. These allegations beg the question of why Retief fell out with Scott and Rivers, who were both Somerset men,

but they certainly fit in with the impression of Retief as an exponent of the 'old corruption' at the Cape.

123. Franken, *Retief*, pp. 159–217, esp. pp. 159, 172.
124. Franken, *Retief*, p. 186.

PART IV

An overview

The origins and entrenchment of European dominance at the Cape, 1652–c.1840[*]

Richard Elphick and Hermann Giliomee

A central concern of South African historiography is to understand how Europeans ('whites') gained control of society and created exclusivist institutions on which apartheid would be built in twentieth-century South Africa. This problem has concerned the authors of this book in their study of the pre-industrial Cape. In this final chapter we present views on this subject based on our own and others' research and on previous chapters in this book. This is not strictly speaking a conclusion: it presents our personal views, which differ at some points from those of other contributors.

Broadly speaking, there have been two influential schools of thought on the role of the pre-industrial Cape in creating European supremacy. The first view was propagated by the liberal historians of the 1920s and 1930s, beginning with W.M. Macmillan, who firmly planted the origins of the South African racial system in the Dutch period before 1795. Macmillan and his successors argued that Calvinism, isolation and frontier strife imprinted upon Europeans a strong sense of group identity, a consciousness of their destiny as a people, and a willingness to employ 'distinction of race and colour [as] devices for social and economic discrimination'. These liberals emphasized that racial dominance was born in South Africa, not imported, and that it was chiefly a product of frontier regions in the eighteenth century[1]. The

* This chapter incorporates some sections, substantially modified, of 'The Structure of European domination at the Cape, 1652-1820', which appeared in the first edition. Though the main thrust of our argument remains the same, we have reworked many aspects of it in light of recent research and have extended it to cover the period 1820-1840. We benefitted greatly from a discussion of this chapter at a workshop of the Yale-Wesleyan Southern African Research Program. We are especially grateful to Leonard Thompson and Leonard Guelke, the two respondents at the workshop, to John Edwin Mason, Jr. for sharing his unpublished research with us, and to Jeffrey Butler, Robert Harms, Jeanette Hopkins, and Ann Wightman, who provided us with detailed written critiques.

most influential exponent of this view was I.D. MacCrone, some of whose views are sympathetically assessed in this volume by Leonard Guelke (ch. 2).

In 1970 Martin Legassick, in reaction to the liberal school, rejected the 'frontier tradition', arguing that racism was not intensified on the frontier. His alternative view, subsequently taken up by a generation of revisionist historians, many of them Marxists, emphasized the role of post-1867 industrial capitalism and, by implication at least, deemphasized the formative influence of the pre-industrial period. Historians of this tradition, represented in this volume by Legassick (ch.8) and Freund (ch.7), tend to deny that a comprehensive racial order had formed in the earlier Dutch period.[2] Unlike the other liberals, who stressed the importance of racial identity in the social structure of the early Cape, these revisionists stress the importance of class.

A third, intermediate, position has recently been staked out by Van Arkel, Quispel and Ross. On the one hand, these authors agree with the liberals that the rigidity of the South African racial order originated in the pre-industrial period; on the other, they agree with the revisionists in placing emphasis neither on the frontier nor on the eighteenth century. For Van Arkel, Quispel and Ross the key impulse to European supremacy came from the Cape's integration into the world economy during the first half of the nineteenth century.[3]

Our own views bear some similarity to those of Van Arkel, Quispel and Ross, but unlike them we regard the racial order as largely in place by the end of the eighteenth century and we emphasize political intervention and other causes in addition to the world economy. On the race/class issue we argue that in the Cape society of 1840 race and class were both salient social groupings; in the all-important agricultural regions race and class reinforced each other at the top and bottom of society, with all landholders being European and almost all those other than Europeans being lowly paid unskilled labourers. We believe that scholars have asked the wrong question about the antecedents of this society, asking how it *emerged* in the course of South African history. We believe, rather, that it was *created* by legal fiat of the Dutch East India Company (VOC) in the first decade of colonization; the question is not how it emerged but how it survived two centuries of geographic expansion, economic development and demographic change.

Thus, in our view, the analysis should start neither with race nor class, but rather with the legal status groups that the VOC initially imposed on the Cape. From the beginning this legal status system fostered a social structure in which race and class were closely correlated. This social structure was constantly reinforced by patterns of recruitment to each legal status group and by economic and demographic forces to be discussed in this chapter. It remained fundamentally constant, though altered in detail, throughout the period 1652 to 1840. However, in the late eighteenth and early nineteenth century a series of crises began to challenge the long-established social order, and, to defend it, Europeans evolved an ideology of racism and indulged increasingly in racially discriminatory practices. In 1828 and 1838 the British government removed the legal scaffolding that had long upheld the old order; however, the old order remained largely intact, now sustained by extra-legal forces, especially the economy and Europeans' firmly held social ideology.

An implication of our view is that the original Cape racial order is one of the antecedents of the modern South African racial order. On this point we agree with the older liberals, without accepting, as MacCrone did, that the frontier influence was decisive. We take it for granted, as MacCrone apparently did not, that the old system was somewhat altered during the period of industrialization.

Throughout the period covered by this chapter colonial society was dominated by 'Europeans'†. They called themselves not only 'Europeans' but also 'colonists', 'inhabitants', 'Afrikaners', 'Christians', or 'whites.' They did not comprise an ethnic group as usually defined, for they spoke different languages (Dutch, German, French and later English, etc.), adhered to different religious traditions (Dutch Reformed and Lutheran, later Anglican, Methodist, etc.) and practised different cultures. Despite their diversity the Europeans remained distinct from other groups in the colony (slaves, free blacks, Khoisan, Bastaards, Prize Negroes and Xhosa).

We saw in chapter 4 (pp. 196–97) that there was a comparatively balanced sex ratio among the European population; thus only a small minority of Cape marriages was 'mixed'. Of a sample of 1,063 children

†We need a detailed study of this group's terms for itself. Our impression is that group identity rested on three characteristics: (1) common physical traits like 'white' skin, which made members of the group, in almost all cases, instantly recognisable; (2) common origin or ancestry in Europe (although Cape-born Europeans sometimes called themselves 'Afrikaners' to distinguish themselves from those born in Europe); (3) common European culture, of which Christianity formed the core. The term 'white', rarely used in the early decades of settlement, referred to physical type. The term 'colonist' denoted an origin overseas. So, too, did 'Christian', which affirmed not merely that one adhered to a particular creed and ritual, but also that one's origins were in Christendom (i.e., Europe or European civilization) and that one's culture derived from there. Baptized Khoisan and slaves, despite their religious profession, were not normally called Christians, except by the government. Unlike these terms, the word 'European' seems to have embraced all three criteria – appearance, origin and culture. Thus this is the term we shall generally use.

baptized in 1807 in the Reformed and Lutheran churches at the Cape, only about 5 per cent had a grandparent who was not European[4]. Moreover, children of extramarital mixing, though numerous, were not usually regarded as European. This high rate of endogamy confirms the impression we have gained from the documents that the European group was decidedly aware of its distinctive identity. It added to its members far more from further European immigration and from internal generation than from admitting outsiders through intermarriage. We call the European group a 'race' because membership in it was almost always determined by birth rather than by choice, because it embraced many European nationalities, and because physical appearance (which entailed more than skin colour) was an important badge of group membership.

Table 11.1 furnishes a rough breakdown of the colonial population between 1670 and 1840:[5] employees and slaves of the Company are omitted for the period before 1795.

Table 11.1   Population of the Cape Colony, 1670-1840

Year	European freeburghers	Burghers' slaves	Free Blacks	Khoikhoi and Bastaards
1670	125	52	13	not enumerated until 1798
1690	788	381	48	" "
1711	1,693	"	"	" "
1730	2,540	4,037	221	" "
1750	4,511	5,327	349	" "
1770	7,736	8,200	352	" "
1798	c20,000	25,754	c.1,700	" "
1820	42,975	31,779	1,932	25,975
1830	58,950	33,583	41,958	
1840	70,775	79,480*		

*This figure is for "Coloureds", a category including former slaves (emancipated in 1838), free blacks, Khoikhoi and Bastaards.

The European heritage and the social structure

Most Europeans who settled in South Africa in the seventeenth century were Dutch. The question has naturally been raised whether ideas or institutions imported from the Netherlands could have been decisive in the formation of South African society. Like all colonizing peoples of the period, the Dutch were convinced of the superiority of their culture and religion. Cultural chauvinism was an important component of racism; even before 1652 the Dutch had developed a strong aversion to Africans, attributing to them sexual licence, savagery, and a diabolical religion[6]. Some scholars of comparative race relations have concluded that racism was more intense in colonies of the Dutch and the English than in those of the French, Portuguese or Spanish.

They argue that the Dutch and English had moved beyond the spiritual unity of mediaeval Catholicism and the ordered hierarchy of feudalism, into the ferment of early capitalism, and hence that their populations had become more individualistic and more mobile, and their institutions more egalitarian and democratic. In this view Dutch and English society consisted not of a complex hierarchy of social ranks, but mainly of two classes: the respectable burghers who regarded themselves as industrious and the poor whom they despised.[7] In colonies, it is argued, this bifurcation was institutionalized into a rigid two-tiered society where Europeans dominated all others.

For the Cape Colony this analysis can be accepted only with modifications. Schutte points out (ch. 6, pp. 286–88) that the Netherlands itself was far from democratic. Moreover, the Cape *freeburghers* enjoyed none of the liberties or representative institutions found in some Anglo-American colonies of the time. But on the other hand, the Company was one of the most advanced commercial enterprises of the age, and as both Guelke and Schutte emphasize, (ch. 2, p. 67 and ch. 6, pp. 293–94) it offered opportunities for individual advancement that were rare in Europe. The democratic quality of the Netherlands is thus less important in analysing social stratification at the Cape than the commercial nature of the Cape government – its tendency to attract ambitious individualistic employees and colonists, more inclined perhaps than their Iberian counterparts to adopt the two-tier model of society.

Again, like other colonists, the Dutch arrived at the Cape with a 'somatic norm image' or a collectively held picture of ideal human appearance. In his investigation of New World societies, Harmannus Hoetink found that although certain persons of mixed ancestry were accepted as European by Spanish and Portuguese colonists, who were themselves swarthy and had a long history of mixing with the Moors in Europe, they were not accepted by the English and Dutch, who were among the whitest of Europeans[8]. According to Hoetink the Dutch in the New World stigmatized any person with the slightest trace of black ancestry and denied to mulattos any prospect of gradual progression towards the status of 'white'.[9]

Somatic preferences probably played some part in early Cape society. Sailors in Van Riebeeck's time called Khoisan 'black stinking dogs'[10]. In the eighteenth century colonists preferred blacks‡ over Khoisan as sexual partners and chose marriage partners roughly in this order of preference: Europeans, mixed-bloods, Asians, negro Africans and Khoisan (ch.4, pp. 197–99). It is hard to separate attitudes toward physical type from cultural prejudices: for example, the dress and skin-grease of Khoisan were powerful deterrents against miscegenation between European men and Khoisan women. Somatic preferences may also have influenced patterns of manumission, but here again cultural, and even more, economic considerations were also at work (ch. 4, pp. 204–14). Thus the Europeans' social evaluation of physical type had some influence on the social opportunities of other people in the colony, even in the seventeenth century, but the available evidence does not allow us to weigh this influence precisely.

Most historians have emphasized the role of religion, that is, Calvinism, more than the role of racism. Charles Boxer, a student of Dutch and Portuguese maritime empires, observed that the 'Portuguese, Spaniards, Dutch, English and French were nearly all convinced that a Christian European was *ipso facto* superior to members of any race . . . [This view] was inevitably strongest among Calvinists, who, consciously or subconsciously, were bound to believe that they were the Elect of the Lord and the salt of the earth.'[11] In her study of free blacks at the Cape, Sheila Patterson concluded that 'it would seem that primitive Calvinism, as modified by nearly two centuries of increasing isolation and dispersion, and the imported and increasingly ingrained habit of slave-owning, played a particularly important part in the ordering of attitudes and relationships . . . and in fostering the development of a bi-racial white/non-white society instead of the more flexible, pluralistic one imported from the Far East.'[12] Calvinism's role in structuring Cape society has been emphasized both by scholars who consider its impact harmful, and by whose who think it beneficial.[13]

There are serious problems with this argument. First, it is not yet clear

‡ By 'black' we mean persons of African, Madagascan or Asian origin; in practice most blacks were slaves or were wholly or partly descended from slaves. This was the usage in the Company period. Freed slaves were called 'free blacks' even if they were mulattos. Xhosa were seldom called 'blacks' until the late eighteenth century. The same was generally true of the Khoisan, despite the fact that their colour was often identified as black, as in the quotation just cited.

exactly how the Calvinist creed was more exclusivist than Roman Catholicism *vis-à-vis* people who were not European. Calvinist clergy at the Cape, like their Catholic counterparts in Latin America,[14] did not ban or discourage intermarriage, nor did they put less emphasis on the equality of all persons before God. Second, the adjectives 'primitive', 'fanatic', and 'fundamentalist', often attached to Calvinism at the Cape, have not been defined: the argument for Calvinist influence cannot be sustained until scholars abandon simplistic stereotypes and attempt a subtle analysis of Calvinist thought, both in Europe and at the Cape. Third, no one has yet shown what aspects of Calvinist doctrine permeated what regions and classes at the Cape, in what forms, and in what eras. It has not, in fact, been shown that Calvinism was influential at all in the era before the 1830s. One would naturally expect a high level of Calvinist influence in the pious seventeenth century, when most immigrants to the Cape were either Dutch or Huguenots fleeing France to preserve their religion. Yet in 1714 the well-travelled Rev. François Valentyn attended Holy Communion in Cape Town and reported:

> I found that the church members totalled 40 men and 48 women only, including those in the return-fleet, of whom there were a number, and it was entirely surprising that among those who approached the Table there was no Member of the Council of Policy [the ruling body], and apparently also none of them was a church member.
>
> Inland it may not be expected to be one-half so good.
>
> From this it can be seen, how little so many Preachers have gained in all these years by their toil among these [European] inhabitants, due in no wise to faltering of their zeal, but to the stupidity and insolence of the Burghers. I perceived also, that there are many Lutherans among the [Company] Servants.[15]

With the decline of religious commitment in eighteenth-century Europe, the increase of non-Dutch (hence largely non-Calvinist) immigration to the Cape, and the decrease in the ratio of clergy to laity, one would expect the influence of Calvinism to decline even further, at least until Evangelical influences arrived at the end of the century. The Cape, after all, was notoriously lacking in schools, churches and in vigorous intellectual life. Calvinist doctrine may have had some influence on social stratification in the early Cape, but the argument for such influence has yet to be made.

We are on surer ground when we look not at what Calvinism achieved, but at what it did not. Calvinism in general lacked missionary zeal, and before the 1790s the Cape clergy did not create a sizeable community of Christians other than Europeans. In contrast to the Catholic Church in Iberian America,[16] the Dutch Reformed Church at the Cape did not campaign on behalf of slaves for looser manumission regulations, milder treatment, or the right to marry. This inactivity was due in part to the church's organizational structure and to the context in which it operated. In Iberian colonies the clergy were guided and supported by the church in Europe, which was powerful enough to condemn the slave trade at an early stage and to dispatch religious orders, particularly the Jesuits, to the colonies to convert Indians. By contrast, the church at the Cape was decentralized. The *classis* (presbytery) of Amsterdam exercised only a nominal influence over it, and the Company would not allow the various congregations at the Cape to form their own classis.[17] Moreover, the Cape church was weak: contrary to Calvinist doctrine and practice in parts of Europe, it was dominated by the state. The Reformed clergy were employees of the VOC, which anticipated no profit in the evangelization of the Khoisan and had no intention of allowing its servants to challenge its regulations on manumission or to intercede on behalf of the slaves. In his study of the entire VOC empire, Charles Boxer found only one case of a church council attacking government policy, and that show of independence – in Batavia in 1653 – was quickly suppressed.[18]

It was the Company much more than the church that initially structured Cape society. It did so by creating distinctive legal status groups§ that remained in place until the 1820s and 1830s. The four main

§ Only one of the legal status groups – the slaves – corresponded roughly to a class, defined as a group with a common relationship to the means of production. The others – freeburghers, Company servants, Khoisan and, later, free blacks – were broad enough to encompass two or more fairly distinct classes.

We use the term *legal* status group to emphasize that the boundaries between groups were imposed more by law than by custom – a feature which somewhat distinguishes legal status groups from the 'orders' or 'estates' of early modern Europe. In any event the specific legal status groups at the Cape did not correspond closely to the various noble, clerical and bourgeois orders of contemporary Europe. Rather, they were products of the East India Company's conquests in Asia and at the Cape and of its decisions to create a freeburgher population and to acquire slaves. Perhaps the closest parallels are to be found in other pre-industrial colonies. For example, historians of the Spanish Empire in the Americas commonly refer to the transformation from a 'caste' society to a 'class' society during the seventeenth to the nineteenth centuries. 'Castes', on this definition, were bounded by legal restrictions and were largely, though not wholly, endogamous. Membership in a caste – with all its attendant privileges, disabilities and obligations – was inherited at birth, though one's caste status could sometimes be changed through legal procedures, as in the manumission of slaves. In these respects the Cape legal status group system approximates in general (though not in specifics) to the Spanish-American 'caste' system save that the status of Company servant was not inherited. See Kenneth Hughes' review of the first edition of this book in 1979 (*Social Dynamics*, V, 2 Dec. 1979), p. 44; and Raymond Mousnier, *Social Hierarchies, 1450 to the Present* (New York, 1973), pp. 23, 26, 67–89. We are grateful to Ann Wightman for information on the Latin American parallels: see her *Indigenous Migration and Social Change: The Forasteros of Cuzco, 1570– 1720* (Durham, N.C., forthcoming), ch. 3, 4.

groups, both in law and in practice, were Company servants (i.e., employees), freeburghers, slaves and 'Hottentots' (Khoisan)¶. The legal distinction between Company servants and freeburghers was familiar in Dutch-controlled Asia; it came into effect at the Cape when the first freeburghers were granted land in 1657 (ch. 6, pp. 298–303) and did not end until the demise of the VOC in 1795. The legal distinction between both free groups on the one hand, and slaves on the other, was also imported from the East (ch. 3, pp. 109–11), and endured until the ending of slavery in 1838. Finally, the distinction in law between all three groups in colonial society and the indigenous Khoisan outside it was at first simply a consequence of planting a colony overseas. But as the Khoisan were gradually incorporated into the Cape Colony their status changed from that of subjects of independent polities to subjects of the Company. The legal distinctions between Khoisan on the one hand and freeburghers, Company servants and slaves on the other gradually accumulated until the early nineteenth century when, as Susan Newton-King has noted, the term 'Hottentot' (which we translate as 'Khoisan') was more a legal category than an ethnic label.[19] By then Khoisan comprised a category of persons who held no land from the state, and were subject to various forms of labour coercion but were technically free. In the course of time a fifth category emerged, the free blacks, whose civil freedoms were slowly curtailed in the late eighteenth century, creating for them a status somewhat different from that of the freeburghers (pp. 544–45).

Colonial officials and colonial courts discriminated among the four status groups in many areas of daily life, such as domicile, right of marriage, right of movement, taxation, militia service, land ownership, and so on. In the official view one's legal status – more than one's race, religion, origin, culture or colour – determined one's opportunities for advancement: most important, before 1795 only Company servants, freeburghers and free blacks could hold land on secure tenure or gain political power in the official hierarchy of the colony.

It was of the highest importance for subsequent South African history that, in the seventeenth century, each of the legal status groups

¶ Khoisan is a portmanteau word devised by scholars to refer both to the pastoral Khoikhoi ('Hottentots') and the hunter-gatherer 'Bushmen' ('San'). As is explained in chapter 1 (pp. 4–7), there were many complex overlaps between these two groups both in reality and in Europeans' terminology. By the late eighteenth century people whom colonists and colonial law designated 'Hottentots' were largely of hunter-gatherer ancestry. Since the focus of this chapter is not on the indigenous people themselves but on their legal status in Cape society, we find it convenient to use 'Khoisan' throughout, except where the emphasis is clearly on the pastoral Khoikhoi alone.

corresponded almost exactly to a culturally and somatically distinct group. The Company servants and the freeburghers were almost all Europeans (though a few landowners were black and a very few Company servants had some Asian ancestry) and so from the beginning economic and political power was monopolized by Europeans. By contrast, no European was ever part of the slave force, which derived from Asia, Madagascar and distant parts of Africa. Slaves were readily distinguishable on sight from free Europeans and also from Khoisan; the slaves' cultures and languages were also different, underscoring the legal distinctions between them and the indigenous peoples. This initial correlation of race and legal status was constantly reinforced by the further incorporation of new individuals into Cape society. Slaves continued to be brought in from Asia, Madagascar and Africa until 1808, followed thereafter by Prize Negroes (ch. 3, p. 120), also distinct from whites in appearance and legal status; white Europeans continued to enter the freeburgher group throughout our period; Khoisan, and later Xhosa, were gradually incorporated into the labour force of the colony, also readily identifiable and with distinct legal status.

While immigration, importation and incorporation of new individuals did nothing to break down the correlation of race and legal status, other processes might well have done so. The three most important would have been racial mixture between members of different status groups, manumission of slaves, and economic advancement of members of lower status groups despite their legal disabilities. All three processes in fact occurred in Cape society, but our contention is that they undermined the original race-status overlap only marginally. Much of this chapter will be devoted to explaining why.

A society in formation, 1652- c.1720

Notwithstanding the racial assumptions embedded in the legal status system – such as the assumption that Asians and Africans, but never Europeans could be enslaved – the VOC had no intention of establishing a rigid European-dominated society at the Cape. Such societies were not common in Dutch-controlled Asia, where most Cape officials derived their understanding of what a colony should be. Moreover, although the legal status system was never in question, before c. 1720 there were many unresolved conflicts and ambiguities regarding the shape of future Cape society. The very economic basis of the colony was in dispute. At first the Company wished to create, not an expanding colony, but merely a refreshment station to victual passing ships with fruit and vegetables from its modest garden and with meat bartered from Khoisan. When it subsequently decided to entrust part of the settlement's food production to the freeburghers, it was not a foregone conclusion that all these burghers would be Europeans. Three of the most influential figures of the early colony – Van Riebeeck, Van Reede and Simon van der Stel – proposed that agricultural production be partly or even totally turned over to free blacks (ch. 4, p. 214). The Company also stumbled through various systems of landholding (ch. 2, pp. 69–78) and long refused to reconcile itself to new forms of extensive pastoralism developing on the colony's borders. Not until 1707 did it make the freeburghers the sole suppliers of food to Cape Town and the passing ships; in doing so it tightly circumscribed the opportunity of its own employees to become an entrepreneurial class competing with the freeburghers.

Even more vital was the indecision about the colony's labour force. As late as 1716 the Company was vacillating between two conflicting models of colonial development: assisted immigration of European artisans, agricultural labourers and farmers who would work their own lands, or the continued importation of slave labour. The future of at least the western part of the colony depended on the resolution of this issue. A decision in favour of European labour would make the western Cape a more self-sufficient European settlement with a large internal market. If the Company opted for slave labour, colonists would find it harder to obtain unskilled and some skilled jobs, leaving service occupations in Cape Town and farming in rural areas as their only opportunities.

Moreover, there were crucial ambiguities regarding the place of the Khoisan in the social structure of the seventeenth-century Cape. At first, individual clergy and officials held out the hope that Khoisan would adopt European culture and convert to Christianity; some tried to treat certain Khoisan (like Eva, see ch. 4, pp. 186–87) as members of elite European society. Although this policy of supervised assimilation failed, economic forces proved more efficacious: for most of this period the Khoisan were in transition from being regarded as members of independent polities to being a labouring class in the colony. The ambiguity of this transitional position was reinforced by the policies of the Company, which asserted that the Khoisan were a free and independent people but also, as early as 1672, established its authority to try them under Dutch law. By the turn of the century even relatively strong Khoisan rulers had been subordinated by the Company and were subject to interference in their daily lives.[20] The legal status of Khoisan continued to be distinct. They were no longer independent aliens; nor were they slaves who could be bought or sold; nor were they freeburghers who could hold land from the Company.

There were also uncertainties with respect to slaves. The conditions for freeing slaves were less clear than they would be after 1708 when government approval was required for each manumission. The official doctrine of the church was that baptized slaves were entitled to their freedom – as were slave children of European fathers, according to the influential commissioner H.A. van Reede in 1685. But most baptized slaves (including those with European fathers) were not in fact freed (ch. 4, pp. 189–90). There was a similar variance between the frequent regulations against miscegenation between Europeans and slaves, and the practice. Moreover, the future position of free blacks in Cape society was still uncertain; most were poor, but others appeared to be on the way to becoming successful agriculturalists, especially in Table Valley.[21] The shortage of European women enabled free black women to marry Europeans and thereby acquire wealth and status. However, the legal status of free blacks, unlike their social position, was quite clear: they were in law the equals of European burghers, and there is no evidence of official discrimination against them in the seventeenth century.[22]

Racial attitudes were not systematically expressed. Although Europeans frequently expressed disgust at the appearance of Khoisan and (less frequently) of slaves, these groups were not lumped together and castigated as different and inferior. Moreover, it was often changeable customs rather than biologically determined physical features which drew the Europeans' scorn. Most observers were horrified by the 'brutish' smell, apparel and customs of Khoisan but not by their brown colour.[23] There was no need for a systematic racial ideology to support the social order. Khoisan were 'heathen' and alien. Slaves were slaves. No further justification was needed to rule and exploit them. In short, the seventeenth-century Cape was unambiguously a European-dominated society, but also a society in formation. There were doubts about the future forms of European domination and – should the government opt for massive manumissions or importation of free blacks – even about European domination itself.

Cape society, c. 1720 – c. 1770: Economic and demographic forces

By about 1720 most of these major conflicts and contradictions had been resolved. It was clear that the economic base of the colony was to be farming. Intensive cultivation had been replaced by extensive arable and stock farming, almost all of which was in the hands of European burghers, especially in the newly occupied districts, where few free blacks settled and even fewer remained. In 1717 the government had decided that it would no longer assist the immigration of European families. The labour needs of the colony were to be met by the continued importation of slaves, and the government had tightened up manumission regulations so that few slaves were being freed. The smallpox epidemic of 1713 had completed the transformation of the sovereign Western Cape Khoisan into subordinated colonial 'Hottentots'.

In the eighteenth century certain forces, some of which had been incipient in the seventeenth century, became stronger and stabilized the European-dominated social structure. Particularly important were the economic forces. The productive capacity of the colony was greatly increased by the importation of slaves and by the steady growth of the European population (largely by internal generation). Before the 1770s the trekboers extended the land base of the colony more or less steadily. They encountered little resistance from the Khoikhoi (as opposed to the 'Bushmen'), whose pastoral economy limited the size of their population, inhibited the rise of effective military leadership and facilitated their absorption into the trekboers' labour force (ch. 1, p. 18–21). The economic base of indigenous society thus contributed substantially to the comparatively easy growth of the colony's land and labour base. This growth in turn resulted in a steady rise of agricultural production (ch. 5, pp. 248–53).

The relatively unhindered growth of the colony was one reason for the extreme simplicity of its economy. There was no internal stimulus for diversification in an economy which continued to expand without it. Also, the Company, guided by its mercantilist assumptions, did not encourage industry in the colony, and the crops planted at the Cape stimulated very little local processing such as, for example, created small industries in the sugar colonies of the Americas. The freeburghers in Cape Town engaged in commerce (including smuggling) and the provision of housing, entertainment and other services to visiting ships. But outside Cape Town there was little commerce, little building, no mining, and no professional military establishment. In the interior almost all freeburghers farmed, either as independent landholders, or as dependents or tenants of landholders (ch. 2, p. 91). There were few intermediate positions in the economy – work not suitable for either Europeans or slaves – apart from hauling or farm overseeing. The skilled trades – tasks which in other colonies were often performed by free people of colour – were performed by slaves at the Cape.

The nature of the economy largely determined the labour system. In Cape Town the economy was volatile. Demands for labour ebbed and flowed; slaves were speculative commodities; and manumissions were higher than in the rest of the colony. The agricultural regions, by contrast, required a stable labour supply and, particularly after the drastic decline of the Western Cape Khoikhoi, slaves were in demand. However, the small market, the system of partible inheritance (ch. 2, p. 81) and the shortage of imported capital all inhibited the rise of capitalist farming and the employment of large numbers of slaves on expanded plantations. While a small but wealthy 'gentry' did arise early in the eighteenth century, the productive forces of society continued to be widely distributed among whites. Fully 40 percent of all freeburgher households held land in 1731; and throughout the eighteenth century slightly more than a third of holders of arable farms possessed one to five adult male slaves, slightly less than a third had six to ten, and roughly a quarter had more than ten (ch. 2, p. 82 and ch. 3, p. 136). In the interior the rapid expansion from c. 1700 to c. 1770 of relatively few trekboers – an expansion which pushed the limits of European settlement 800 km eastward and 400 km northward – made it possible for European families to use land extensively, with unimproved pasture as the basic resource. The large extent of the farms, the low level of technology, and the Europeans' disdain for manual labour in the service of others, created the need for many shepherds and graziers. Here slaves were too expensive for most employers, and Khoisan were hired.

Thus the economy outside Cape Town was overwhelmingly agricultural, expanding, undiversified, and labour-intensive. Such economies have often appeared in colonial history. What distinguished the Cape economy was that it developed in the hinterland of a single port controlled by a giant mercantile concern with clear goals and tough methods. More interested in international commerce than in the interior of the Cape, the government intervened only when its narrowly defined interests were threatened. Yet it profoundly affected the stratification of Cape society in terms of its own priorities. For example, Cape Town's importance in the Company's global strategy made it the host for countless sailors and soldiers, who fathered many of the town's mixed-bloods. The Company also discouraged (or failed to encourage) the arrival of free blacks from the East, and thus helped create a society where the free population was predominantly European, unlike that in the Company's stronghold at Batavia. European immigration was largely the result of the Company's large employment roster, and its willingness to contract it periodically, causing a constant trickle of poor Europeans to enter the freeburgher population. Similarly, the Company's regular shipping made possible the arrival of European immigrants at the Cape, including significant numbers of women; but its lack of financial support for such immigration in the eighteenth century kept the European population fairly low and with an imbalance in favour of males.

Although the government did not consciously promote a European-dominated racial order, various of its economic policies facilitated just such an outcome. For example, by promulgating tough manumission regulations it undermined the official Reformed Church policy that slaves who were baptized should be freed. Similarly, while it upheld its traditional policy that Khoisan were free people who could not be enslaved, it did not defend their property or grant them land, thus conniving in their subordination to white landholders. It all but abandoned the interior to the colonists by turning over the vast areas – both Stellenbosch and Graaff-Reinet were larger than Portugal of today – to *landdrosts* who were assisted by only four or five mounted police, and thus it had to rely on burgher officers (*veldwachtmeesters*) to ensure compliance with Company laws. It was not that the government always favoured the colonists: Khoisan had access to the courts (ch. 1, p. 17), as did the slaves. Their evidence and complaints against their masters in court were sometimes upheld, since the VOC also wished to impose its authority on the burghers. Generally, however, the government sided with the owners in their efforts to control both the slaves and the Khoisan, and thus reinforced the tendencies, inherent in the hierarchy of legal status, to entrench Europeans at the top of society and Khoisan and slaves at the bottom.[23]

As an institutional force the state was much more important than the church, whose social role in the eighteenth century continued to be significant mainly in terms of what it did not accomplish. The church was not an avenue for blacks to reach positions of wealth or prestige; nor was it a countervailing force against the government or the slave-owners. As late as 1790 there were still fewer than ten Dutch Reformed ministers, all working for the Company, mainly among the colonists. Little mission work was undertaken by the Reformed Church before 1800. A visitor to Cape Town in the 1750s noted: 'The inhabitants have no care for the education of their slaves. No one ever speaks to them of religion, and those born in this country have no idea of it.'[25] Moreover, the church did not want missionary societies to perform the task it neglected, arguing that independent proselytisation would lead to religious schism. But even the overseas missionaries who led evangelization campaigns in the 1790s, apart from some 'radicals' like J.T. van der Kemp and James Read, had no intention of breaking down the racial order.[26] Their task was to save souls, thereby providing a spiritual haven in which slaves and Khoisan could escape from the hardships and humiliations of everyday life.[27] Thus neither missionaries nor official clergy overrode the impact on social structure of the simple, labour-intensive economy and the commercial concerns of the Cape government.

The stabilisation of European dominance

The forces we have described in the previous two sections affected the social structure in many interrelated ways. We will concentrate on three: (1) the continuing ability of Europeans to predominate over slaves and Khoisan, (2) the fact that the emerging free black and Bastaard groups did not rise high in colonial society, and (3) the fact that poor Europeans did not ally with free blacks and Bastaards against the ruling European classes.

Europeans were numerous enough throughout the eighteenth century to occupy all the key positions in the colony's political, economic and social structure. In the interior the veldwachtmeesters (later field-cornets), who represented the colonists as much as the government, settled the day-to-day disputes between colonists and their servants, and mobilized commandos. The business people, traders and slave-owners in Cape Town and the landholders and producers in the interior were, with the exception of some free black shopkeepers in Cape Town and the Bastaards on or beyond the colonial borders, almost all Europeans. The dominant position of Europeans confirmed and intensified feelings of European superiority. As the daughter of a European man and a Khoisan woman told a traveller in the 1780s: 'You know the profound contempt which the whites entertain for the blacks, and even for those of a mixed breed such as myself. To settle among them was to expose myself to daily disgrace and affronts.'[28]

It was of the utmost importance for later South African history that no group emerged in the eighteenth century outside the European group which could, like the free blacks in nineteenth-century Brazil, become numerous and powerful enough to break down the simple pattern of European dominance.[29] We shall consider three such groups: free blacks, i.e., black slaves who became free through manumission, chiefly in the southwestern Cape (ch. 4); colonial 'Hottentots', i.e., Khoisan who were subject to colonial laws (ch. 1); and baptized Bastaards, i.e., offspring of European fathers and Khoisan mothers who, mainly in trekboer regions, were members of the Christian church and enjoyed most of the privileges of Europeans (chs. 8 and 9).

As for the free blacks of Cape Town and the southwestern Cape, two features of their position suggest – at first glance – that Cape society was rather more like nineteenth-century Brazil, with its fluid racial pattern, than, say, the rigid caste system of the southern United States. These features were the rather high incidence of miscegenation in Cape Town, and the free blacks' considerable freedom from official discrimination before the mid-eighteenth century. In Brazil, however, a high rate of miscegenation was accompanied by a rate of manumission approximately six times greater than at the Cape (ch. 4, p. 206). As a result, the Brazilian free black population rapidly multiplied and the boundary between black and European ceased to correspond closely to the boundary between slave and free. In any event, the lines between races became blurred by the emergence of many intermediate shades, because interracial marriages were common, and many mixed-race children retained the social status of their white fathers. Thus, even though Europeans in Brazil were prejudiced against the colour and culture of blacks, it became possible for mulattos to rise in society and for criteria other than race (especially wealth) to determine status.

At the Cape, by contrast, the fairly high rates of miscegenation were coupled with rather low rates of manumission, with the result that the free blacks numbered only 8 percent of the free population in 1730 and only 4.4 per cent in 1770 (ch. 4, pp. 217–19). Hence interracial sex, quite common particularly in Cape Town, mostly involved European men and *slave* women. The mixed children of such unions inherited the status of their mothers and remained slaves. Furthermore, since at the Cape the fathers of these children were mainly passing sailors and soldiers or the poorest freeburghers, there was less likelihood of their being able to free these children after birth than was frequently the case in other parts of the world. Thus the main effect of miscegenation was the 'whitening' of the *slave* population. At the same time the free European community was also being 'darkened', but only very slightly. Because European males who did not find European wives were not allowed to marry slaves,[30] they had to choose from among the small free black population. And, as we saw in chapter 4 (pp. 197–99), such marriages, though legal, were fairly rare, apparently well below 5 per cent of all marriages: thus, for example, in 1731 only 2.3 per cent of all married European males had wives who were not pure Europeans.[31] Moreover, such marriages were disproportionately concentrated in one place, Cape Town.

Some historians have incorrectly concluded that mixed marriages were common at the Cape and have consequently overstated the 'openness' of early South African society.[32] The willingness of European men to have sexual relations outside their group was no sign of the fluidity of social boundaries. Only the willingness to allow the offspring of such unions to inherit one's name, fortune and community status would be signs of a breakdown of European group consciousness; all available evidence suggests that only the poorest European males and the most recent immigrants were willing to take such steps either by marrying those who were not European or by legitimating their mixed offspring. Thus as long as the majority of blacks were slaves, the legal boundaries of slavery allowed Europeans to propagate a mixed race within the slave population while keeping their own race relatively 'pure'. In effect, miscegenation was largely irrelevant to stratification in South African society.

Another seemingly flexible feature of Cape society – the colour-blind nature of laws affecting freeburghers – was also insufficient to make the free black community a major economic or political force at the Cape. This failure can be explained in four stages, of which stage two is the most important.

(1) Very few members of the free-black community were free when they came to the Cape. Though the Company often discussed importing free black labour, it never did so to any significant extent. The ready supply of Madagascan slaves made such an effort unnecessary, and in any case the Company may have feared creating a subversive population like the Chinese on Java. Hence it did not reproduce the social patterns of its Eastern capital at Batavia, where the many varieties of free persons of colour (many of whom were not ex-slaves), along with widespread miscegenation, gave rise to a spectrum of racial 'classes', in some respects like that of Brazil.

(2) Consequently almost all recruitment to the Cape free black population had to come from the limited ranks of the convicts and from the slave force. Yet comparatively few slaves were freed. The free black group was always small, and few freed slaves had prominent European fathers who could give them a good education or find them lucrative or prestigious positions.

(3) The birth rate among free blacks was much lower than among Europeans. Hence their numbers declined over the eighteenth century as a percentage of the total population.

(4) Free blacks briefly expanded into Stellenbosch in the period of early settlement. But by the early eighteenth century they were retreating to Cape Town and the Cape Peninsula,[33] separating themselves from the growing agricultural sector of South African society and sinking, in most cases, into poverty. As a result the small trickle of slaves into the free black community, and the full legal rights accorded them, did little to break down the pattern of European over black, and that only in Cape Town.

The most important of the foregoing points, the low rate of manumission, was due in part to the simple economy of the Cape, which, especially in rural areas, created few intermediate positions between landholders and unskilled labourers. Positions such as these, particularly in handicrafts, transportation and farm overseeing, were filled by free blacks elsewhere in the world. Furthermore, the Cape did not face such great dangers from other European powers that it needed to free slaves to augment its European militia. Nor was the slave population large enough in relation to Europeans, or sufficiently concentrated in any one place, to threaten a rising *en masse*: Europeans were not compelled, as in Brazil, to create a free black force to help them keep control.

The Company knew, then, that there were few positions for freed slaves and feared that easy manumission would lead to a large population of unemployed, destitute free blacks. This was the main reason why it progressively tightened manumission regulations for privately owned slaves, and one reason (along with its needs for labour) why it was reluctant to free its own. As for the freeburghers of the southwestern Cape, we have seen that they, too, needed large numbers of slaves (among whom mortality rates were high) and thus rarely freed them (ch. 4, p. 206). There were other economic disincentives to manumission. For example, the total absence of banks at the Cape until 1793 meant that Europeans sought other forms of investment, one of which was the slave force.

But the low manumission rates, like the low rate of mixed marriages, cannot be explained in economic or demographic terms alone. The values and attitudes of Cape society also played a role. For instance, the Cape church, unlike its Latin American counterpart, did not promote manumission by commending it to the laity as a noble act. Although there were some Cape colonists who wished to manumit their black mistresses and children,[34] few did so. This was perhaps because European women at the Cape, unlike their Brazilian counterparts,[35] enjoyed a strong social role and could evidently prevent their husbands from legitimizing the offspring of their extra-marital affairs. This was especially the case in the settled southwestern Cape, where the general prejudices against interracial sex (reflected even in official proclamations in the seventeenth century), combined with comparatively balanced sex ratios among Europeans, worked against the respectability of concubinage. The keepers of concubines tended to be either wealthy married men who, even if they wished, dared not free their mistresses and children, or poorer transitory Europeans who could not afford to do so. From the remarks of the traveller R. Percival, who visited the Cape at the end of the eighteenth century, one can deduce that many a poor European male would have manumitted and married a female slave but for the price of 800 to 1,000 rixdollars[36], equivalent to the cost of a farm in Graaff-Reinet.

We must now discuss a second group other than Europeans in the colony, that is, the Khoisan. After Khoisan had become subordinated to colonial rule they were no longer legal outsiders to the colony, but, as we noted, neither had they become freeburghers or slaves. Most crucially, they were excluded from the landholding system of the colony. Since they did not own the means of production, and since the government exercised little control in the trekboer regions, Khoisan were gradually reduced to a position not far removed from that of serfs. Various devices for keeping Khoisan on the farms were informally instituted long before their more formal counterparts (e.g., the pass system and indentureship) were entered into the law books (ch. 2, pp. 31–33 and ch. 9, pp. 448–50). Though Khoisan were not normally bought or sold like slaves, it was the direction of change that was crucial. Khoisan constantly moved downward in status toward the slaves, not upward toward the burghers. In racial terms the structure of trekboer society was thus roughly similar to that of the agrarian southwestern Cape: in both cases Europeans were free and most who were not European were totally or partially unfree.

In trekboer areas, especially in the northwestern Cape, there was considerable miscegenation. The so-called Bastaards, most of whom were children of European males and Khoisan females, and a few of whom were children of European males and slave females, were free. They tended to identify vigorously with Dutch culture and considered themselves superior to the Khoisan. Apparently those Bastaards who had been baptized in a Dutch Reformed (rather than a mission) church were regarded by the government, though perhaps not by many Europeans, as freeburghers. They had Dutch surnames, and sometimes appeared along with Europeans as taxpayers on the opgaaf rolls. A few held loan farms from the Company and some kept other Bastaards as tenants. Some moved into intermediate occupations in the economy, as supervisors on European farms or as wagon drivers.

On the Northern Frontier beyond the colony's boundaries, Bastaard families were able to establish a temporary hegemony by about 1800 (ch. 8, pp. 369–76). But within the colony itself, Bastaards, like the free blacks, did not break down the pattern of European domination over other groups. The reasons in each case were roughly the same. First, the Bastaards were too small a group, even in Graaff-Reinet. In 1798 there were only 136 baptized Bastaards on the Graaff-Reinet rolls compared to 4,262 Europeans, 8,947 Khoisan and 964 slaves. Although some Graaff-Reinet Bastaards owned considerable livestock, only a few held land. Second, the economy provided relatively few intermediate jobs for them to fill. And third, the degree of upward mobility offered by the 'open' frontier was soon lost as the frontier began to close in the 1790s: a shortage of land restricted opportunities for all groups, but chiefly for the Bastaards who found themselves squeezed out into new regions where the frontier was still open.

Thus the free blacks of the western Cape and the baptized Bastaards in trekboer regions found themselves ambiguously positioned between the Europeans in the top tier of society and the slaves and the Khoisan in the lowest tier. Both of these middle groups were small and localised, and their members, with few exceptions, poor; their social position tended to decline during the eighteenth century.

In all regions many Europeans were just as poor and powerless. In 1732 Governor de la Fontaine listed fifty-five 'poor, indigent, decrepit' European freeburghers as well as fifty-four free blacks in the Cape district (ch. 6, p. 300). In Cape Town European sailors, soldiers, artisans and labourers frequented the same lower-class taverns as free blacks and some slaves. In trekboer regions there was, in terms of landholding and wealth, little difference between the poor European knechts and ex-Company servants on the one hand, and the baptized Bastaards on the other. In certain periods the Company bracketed free blacks and European knechts on its rolls. Against this background we must discuss the third feature of the entrenchment of European domination; namely, that despite their similar legal and economic positions, poor Europeans, free blacks and Bastaards did not coalesce into a selfconscious class over against the European officials and landholders.

The effects of slavery penetrated far down the European social scale. Since slaves were well distributed among the colonists – by 1750 almost half the free male population had at least one slave (ch. 3, p. 135) – the status even of a European too poor to own a slave was bolstered by the demeaning features of others' servitude, such as a proclamation that 'no slave might jostle or otherwise behave in an ill-disposed way [qualyk te bejeegenen] towards a European even if he was of the meanest rank.'[38] In 1743 Baron Van Imhoff remarked:

> [Having] imported slaves every common or ordinary European becomes a gentleman and prefers to be served than to serve . . . The majority of the farmers in this colony are not farmers in the real sense of the word . . . and many of them consider it a shame to work with their own hands.

Furthermore, poor Europeans, free blacks and Bastaards competed for the same jobs, and in this competition the advantage of being European seems to have helped. In both psychological and material terms a racial order was beneficial to the poor Europeans.

Similarly, wealthier Europeans tended to identify more closely with poorer Europeans than with members of other groups. In choosing marriage partners and social equals they clearly preferred landless Europeans to Khoisan or ex-slaves. They made a similar decision in choosing tenant farmers, even though Khoisan would likely have been less rebellious than Europeans. Underpinning this trend were the racial attitudes of non-slaves in a slave society. Charles Boxer has observed in the context of Brazilian slavery: 'One race cannot systematically enslave members of another race for over three centuries without acquiring a conscious or unconscious feeling of racial superiority.'[40]

Many of the wealthy disapproved of miscegenation, and feared that persons of mixed race would pose a danger to them. In 1706 the leading farmers of Stellenbosch informed the Heren XVII that they feared the

> 'Kaffirs, Mulattoes, Mestiços, Castiços and all that black brood living among us, who have been bred from marriages and other forms of mingling with European and African Christians [i.e., colonists born in Europe and at the Cape]. To our amazement they have so grown in power, numbers and arrogance, and have been allowed to handle arms and participate with Christians in . . . military exercises, that they now tell us that they could and would trample on us . . . For there is no trusting the blood of Ham, especially as the black people are constantly being favoured and pushed forward.'[41]

Among 'respectable people' hostility was particularly intense against colonists who lived like, and with, Khoisan and Xhosa. In the 1780s some leading western Cape farmers referred to 'those who miscegenate with Hottentots and Kaffirs' and warned of 'a bastardization of morals' and the 'rise of a completely degenerate Nation which might become just as dangerous for the colony as the Bushmen-Hottentots are.'[42]

European solidarity and norms against miscegenation were reinforced in the eighteenth century by the substantial social and economic mobility available to poorer Europeans. Despite the dominance, in the western Cape, of a small urban elite of top government officials and merchants, and a rural gentry of large farmers who employed European foremen and owned many slaves, pastoralism nevertheless presented opportunities to ambitious young Europeans with little capital (ch. 2, pp. 86–87). The rapid expansion of the limits of the settlement from 1700 to 1770 brought into being a trekboer society which remained egalitarian as long as land was cheap and the market for produce limited. Only after the frontier had started to close late in the eighteenth century (ch. 9, p. 453) did considerable inequalities of wealth appear among trekboers. And even in circumstances in which every European male could not possibly have his own farm, the landless still seemed confident that they could acquire farms beyond the colonial borders and rise socially and economically. All this made for European solidarity and egalitarianism.** Despite some gradations of wealth and the intense status consciousness of top Company servants and some freeburghers near Cape Town (ch. 6, pp. 296–303), the opportunities created by Company land policy and the expanding frontier gradually produced an acceptance of the fundamental social equality of Europeans. Thus W.S. van Ryneveld, a high government official, remarked in 1805: 'Among the true [eigenlijke] inhabitants of this colony there is no real distinction of ranks among the white population.'[43] During the 1820s the traveller George Thompson observed that there was little or no gradation among the Europeans: 'Every man is a burgher by rank, and a farmer by occupation.'[44]

In short, then, the simplicity of the Cape economy, the absence of intermediate posts that could not be filled by Europeans, the rapid expansion of the colony until the 1770s, and the tradition of social mobility among settlers, combined to ensure that free blacks and Khoisan did not break through the disabilities first imposed on them by the hierarchy of legal status. These forces also prompted most Europeans of all ranks to retain closer ties with their fellow Europeans than with the other groups among whom they lived.

** The egalitarian, family-centered European society of the Cape has been explained by viewing the Cape colonists as a 'fragment' of the seventeenth-century Dutch bourgeoisie which had become immobilized because of its isolation from the European whole. See Louis Hartz, *The Founding of New Societies* (New York, 1964). This theory has been challenged by R. Cole Harris and Leonard Guelke, who have shown that colonial society both in New France and at the Cape, despite being very different fragments from different European heritages, remained unstratified and egalitarian as long as land was cheap and the market for produce poor. Only when the frontier 'closed' did society become diversified and did controls by the government and the wealthy become effective. See R. Cole Harris and Leonard Guelke, 'Land and society in early Canada and South Africa', *Journal of Historical Geography*, III (1977), pp. 135–53.

The colony in crisis, c. 1770 – c. 1814

The trends discussed so far operated over the long term. By the late eighteenth century race and class had overlapped for so long (in the sense that almost all landholders and officials were Europeans and almost all members of other racial groups were unfree or poor) that to many Europeans this social structure appeared to be natural or God-given. But between 1770 and c. 1814 this assumption was challenged by a crisis in the colony springing chiefly from accelerated economic development, from a blockage of frontier expansion and from a new shortage of both labour and land.

From the late 1770s the Cape economy gradually shed its fetters and became freer and more vigorous. Wars in North America and Europe brought ships and garrisons to the strategic outpost, stimulating investment and agricultural production. Wheat crops increased by more than 50 per cent between 1798 and 1820,[45] while wine production doubled between 1795 and 1804.[46] The British conquests of 1795 and 1806 incorporated the Cape into the British imperial system which, as Freund remarks, was much larger and more dynamic than that of the VOC. Exports rose from 180,000 rixdollars in 1807 to 1,320,000 rixdollars in 1815 (ch. 7, p. 329), while the Cape Town merchant and banking elite grew and prospered (ch. 5, pp. 261–63).

Farmers faced a shortage of slave labour. No slaves were imported between 1787 and 1795, and slaves entering the colony between 1795 and 1808 were bought mostly by Capetonians to be hired out as artisans. As a result of the dwindling supply, the price of slaves quadrupled between 1784 and 1804.[47] In 1808 the slave trade to the Cape was abolished by the British government, and owners increasingly feared for the security of their property. The restrictions on slave labour made landholders realize that Khoisan and Xhosa labour had to be harnessed more effectively.

In the interior, a crisis occurred not only in labour, but also in land. From 1700 to 1779 land resources in the colony had been virtually unlimited, but in about 1780 expansion was halted in the northeast by 'Bushman' hunters and in the southeast by Xhosa. For the next two decades no significant geographical expansion occurred, and by 1800 there was no suitable land for new farms within the limits of the colony.[48] Europeans sought out open spots between existing farms and pushed Khoisan and Bastaards out. Lichtenstein described this process during the first decade of the nineteenth century:

Many Hottentot families . . . had established themselves in the Lower Bokkeveld, when the increasing population of the colony occasioned new researches to be made after lands capable of cultivation, and the white children of the colonists did not hesitate to make use of the right of the strongest, and to drive their half yellow relations out of the places where they had fixed their abodes. These Bastaard Hottentots were then obliged to seek an asylum in more remote parts.[49]

By the end of the eighteenth century many Bastaards, Oorlams and Khoisan who had been forced off the land and compelled to work and fight for Europeans, trekked from Little Namaqualand to the Middle Orange (ch. 8, pp. 369–72). But some resisted. Trekboer expansion was stalled in the 1780s not only by 'Bushman' hunters and Xhosa, but also by persons fully or partially of Khoikhoi (pastoralist) descent who had formerly worked in the colony.

Khoisan labourers and slaves within the colony were also increasingly insubordinate. In the western part of the colony rumours circulated that the Khoisan were conspiring to murder all colonists. Bastaards of Khoisan-slave descent were in the vanguard of this resistance. As an official remarked: 'The true Hottentots are still governable whereas those who have interbred with slaves call the tune and pay no heed to any authority and even less to any kind of order.'[50]

As the century closed, the eastern part of the colony was also experiencing a crisis in master-servant relationships. Some Khoisan, finding themselves hemmed in between the Xhosa and the trekboers, tried to escape the constraints of colonial society. They found a leader in Klaas Stuurman, who sought to end their 'enslavement' in the massive rebellion of 1799–1803 on the Eastern Frontier (ch. 1, pp. 33–35). Trekboers further north in Sneeuwberg and Bruintjes Hoogte had to coax or cajole servants of other colonists to settle on their farms and protect their cattle against roving 'Bushmen' and Xhosa. In the southwestern Cape, where the ratio of male slaves to male freeburghers had risen sharply, slave-owners were sure that the slaves hated them and were preparing for an insurrection. With the institution of slavery under fire both in conservative Britain and on the revolutionary Continent, talk of emancipation inspired some slaves at the Cape to hold meetings 'to decide upon the fate of the free and independent burghers, when the happy days of their own emancipation should arrive.'[51] In 1808, after the abolition of the slave trade in the British Empire, the colony experienced its first serious slave revolt. It was led by the slave Louis van Mauritius, inspired by two Irish sailors and backed by some Khoisan (ch. 3, p. 161).[52]

After 1795 the British government, stronger than its VOC predecessor, added to the colonists' anxieties by asserting that the

Khoisan were a free people entitled to equal protection from the courts, if not full equality under the law. The 1790s also saw the arrival of the radical LMS missionaries J.T. van der Kemp and James Read, who insisted that 'the Hottentots should be perfectly free, upon an equal footing in every respect with Colonists, and by no sort of compulsion brought under a necessity to enter into their service.'[53]

These threats to the old Cape order and to the labour supply caused the elaboration and frequent expression of sentiments among Europeans, that slaves, free blacks, Khoisan and Xhosa were intrinsically inferior to the colonists. After returning from a visit to the interior in 1780, Governor van Plettenberg remarked that 'it would take more than human efforts to induce the colonists at large to accept Caffres as their fellow Christians, fellow men and brethren; the word heathen seems to be the device with which men in an unrestrained way like to give rein to their thirst for revenge and greed.'[54] Some twenty years later Governor Janssens observed on a visit to the frontier that the colonists called 'themselves men and Christians, and the Kaffirs and Hottentots heathens, and on the strength of this consider[ed] themselves entitled to anything.'[55] In the southwestern Cape one traveller encountered the opinion that the Khoisan 'in understanding and the powers of the mind . . . scarcely deserve to be ranked with human creatures; and are but little above the level of the brute creation.'[56] Another commented on the prevailing notion in Cape Town in 1805-06 that nature had drawn a fixed line between white and black and had destined the latter to be subservient for all time.[57]

Europeans reacted in a similar way when confronted with the government's policy of legal protection for the Khoisan. Landdrost Ludwig Alberti of Graaff-Reinet reported in 1803 that it was impossible to persuade the colonists that a judge should draw no distinction between them and Khoisan; in the colonists' view, 'a heathen was not actually human, although he could not be classified with the animals either.'[58] In 1797 the landdrost and heemraden of Stellenbosch objected when a Khoisan summoned his European employer before them. They doubted whether the Khoisan had the legal right to do so and pointed out that 'such practice would create the impression that a Hottentot was the equal of a burgher.'[59]

In this period the traditional hostility to miscegenation seemed more rampant and was more often extended to interracial marriages and to mixed offspring born from wedlock. Cape Town, it is true, remained more casual in its attitudes; but even here Lady Anne Barnard recorded that Cape Town Europeans snubbed Catherina van den Berg, the wife of an English officer, because her grandmother had been a slave.[60] In rural areas the prejudice was more severe. In the 1770s Anders Sparrman noted that 'a great many of the whites have so much pride, as to hinder, as far as lies in their power, the blacks or their offspring from mixing with their blood.'[61] In 1813 the missionary John Campbell encountered at the Orange River a European man who had fled the colony, ostracized for seeking to marry a black.[62] In 1809 an officer of the South African Missionary Society, concerned about the interracial marriages of Van der Kemp and other missionaries, commented that to take a 'black Hottentot is a great scandal among the people here and even the coloured people themselves.'[63]

Increasing tension between Europeans and persons of mixed blood was evident in disputes concerning the militia. In 1780 two burghers of Swellendam refused to let their sons do commando duty since they were considered 'Bastaards' and discriminated against while performing their military duties.[64] During a drill at Stellenbosch in 1788 some burghers refused to serve under their newly appointed corporal, Johannes Hartogh, because 'he was of a blackish colour and of heathen descent.'[65] In the previous year the so-called Free Corps had been formed in the Cape district as a separate unit for 'bastaards and mistiches' (i.e. mixed bloods) [66] The Free Corps ranked below the regular burgher companies, but above service in the fire brigade and in public works, which were compulsory for free blacks. By 1790 Jan Smook, the husband of a manumitted slave, was ordered by a militia officer to enroll his son in the Free Corps. He refused, claiming that his son did not belong to the category for whom the corps had been instituted. He was especially indignant because other young men with 'black blood' – Van Oudtshoorn, Oppel and Voges – were admitted to the (European) militia companies.[67]

There is also evidence of increasing discrimination in the church. As early as 1761 the Zwartland church had a separate section of the baptismal records for Bastaards and Khoisan; and after 1770 the Cape Town church records had a separate section for slaves. The evangelisation campaign of the 1790s, while actively supported by some colonists in the west, encountered stiff resistance from Europeans elsewhere, who feared that the mission stations would draw Khoisan from the farms and imbue the slaves with notions of equality and rebellion.[68] There was an uproar in Graaff-Reinet when Van der Kemp allowed Khoikhoi into the Reformed church. He noted that the Graaff-Reinet rebels complained that the 'government protected the Hottentots and the Caffres . . . [and] that they were instructed by us in reading, writing, and religion, and thereby put upon an equal footing with the Christians [that is, the Europeans].[69]

Finally, in this period colonial governments, both Dutch and British, introduced restrictions on the freedom of Khoisan and free blacks. Though the state continued to regard the Khoisan as free people who could not be enslaved, its chief concerns were to maintain order and encourage production. To attain these goals the government controlled the movements of Khoisan and forced them to work, thus combatting 'vagrancy' and theft. In 1787 it was decreed that vagrant Khoisan 'or bastards of these natives' in and about Cape Town be committed to the slave lodge and set to work for two months alongside slaves in government projects.[70] In the same period the government connived in the gradual decline of colonial Khoisan to a status approaching that of slaves. Through an informal extension of the indenture system (ch. 1, p. 32), Khoisan children were generally compelled until their twenty-fifth year to serve the master who had apprenticed them; this prompted Lady Anne Barnard to express the hope that the government would 'shorten the time of *slavery* to these oppressed creatures' [our emphasis].[71]

In 1797 and 1798 local authorities in Swellendam and Graaff-Reinet decided that Khoisan, like slaves, had to carry passes when travelling, so that burghers and officials could determine that they were not deserters.[72] The practice was confirmed by the colonial government in Caledon's Hottentot Proclamation of 1809. In 1811 W.J. Burchell remarked that 'every slave, or even Hottentot, who is found at a distance from home without a pasbrief, or passport signed by his master or some responsible person is liable to be taken into custody as a runaway or vagabond . . . It seems hardly fair to place a freeman, as the Hottentot is said to be, under the same restraint [as slaves].'[73] John Barrow commented that the Khoisan were not treated as favourably as the meanest of slaves.[74]

As for the free blacks, their first experience of legislative discrimination appears to have been in minor proclamations of 1765 and 1771 (ch. 4, p. 215). The documents of subsequent years yield evidence of more serious restrictions. In 1801 the government gave notice in Cape Town that, on account of recent robberies, the military guards and police officers 'have strict orders to apprehend and to commit to prison agreeable to the existing regulations of this colony *all slaves or people of colour* who shall be found in any of the streets after nine o'clock at night, without having lighted lanthorns' [our emphasis].[75] In 1816 Governor Lord Charles Somerset found it necessary to make the registration of slaves compulsory in order to prevent manumitted slaves, Prize Negroes and their offspring from 'merging into a state of slavery, or being confounded with the domestic or other slaves.'[76] The second clause of Ordinance 50, which in 1828 made Khoisan and free blacks equal with Europeans before the law, explained that by 'usage and custom of this Colony, Hottentots and other free persons of colour have been subjected to certain restraints as to their residence, mode of life, and employment, and to certain compulsory services to which others of His Majesty's subjects are not liable.'[77]

The prejudicial views and discriminatory acts which we have listed obviously reflect in part the material interests of landowners and government officials. However, these interests are expressed in racial terms, through a clear claim that whites *as whites* (not as free persons) were distinct from all other groups, upon whom disabilities of various sorts could legitimately be laid. The ideology of European supremacy that lay behind these opinions and regulations was not particularly coherent or systematically articulated. Slaves, free blacks, Khoisan and Bastaards were seldom lumped together and stereotyped as a uniform mass. Different stereotypes were held and different constraints were imposed, on the one hand on slaves amongst whom free blacks and Prize Negroes were sometimes included, and on the other hand on slaves amongst whom Bastaards and even Bantu-speakers were sometimes included. Whites also discriminated among different groups of slaves and ex-slaves, distinguishing for example between Madagascans, Mozambicans and Buginese. But occasionally, as in the pass system, all groups other than Europeans could be subjected to the same discriminatory treatment. It seems significant that in 1800 three opgaaf (tax enumeration) lists were compiled in Cape Town: one of Europeans who were permanent inhabitants, one of ex-Company servants, and one of 'those who belong to the Free Corps [for mixed-race people] as well as the free blacks, Bastaards and other Hottentots that live on their own and are not in the service of others'.[78] The scope of this third opgaaf list suggests that the catch-all category of 'non-European' was emerging in European thinking. However, it was not a uniform ideological casting of slaves, Khoisan, Bastaards etc. that made such a category possible, but a coherent assumption that *Europeans* were unique and special.

We think it appropriate to call this ideology of European supremacy 'racist'. This term draws attention to the fact that superior qualities and privileges were attributed not to a class (e.g. landowners) or to a legal status group (free persons), and not even to an ethnic group, since English and other European immigrants were easily assimilated to the privileges of the long-resident Dutch-speaking Europeans. Rather they were attributed to a 'race'. One must emphasize that many attributes mingled in the delineation of a race. Colour and appearance – the colour black was loosely applied to all who were not Europeans, even the Khoikhoi – were important badges of group membership. However, colour and other physical attributes were not at the core of the ideology of group identification; in fact revulsion against appearance may have been less common by 1800 than in the early days of the colony. Rather, by the beginning of the nineteenth century colour was increasingly linked with aspersions against the culture of slaves, free blacks and Khoisan, most frequently against their 'heathen' religion, 'wild' customs or alleged lack of humanity. Thus the Court of Justice, opposing the abolition of judicial torture of slaves, argued in 1796 that many of the slaves 'are descended from wild and rude nations, who hardly consider the privation of life as a punishment, unless accompanied by such cruel circumstances as [would] greatly aggravate their sufferings.'[79]

This last quotation displays another feature of the group stereotypes, namely aspersions against ancestry. In the evidence we have cited it is sometimes asserted that certain people deserved discriminatory treatment because their parents, grandparents, or more distant ancestors had been slaves, heathens, or Khoisan. We do not, however, agree with Van Arkel, Quispel and Ross that 'there is no indication of a taxonomy on the basis of race, but only of one derived from descent'.[80] To emphasize another person's ancestry is to emphasize the indelible, determined quality of his or her inferiority, which in the view of some scholars is an essential feature of racism.[81] At the Cape negative comments on appearance were mingled with pejorative comments on ancestry, as in the complaint against Johannes Hartogh, that 'he was of a blackish colour and of heathen descent' (p. 543). Appearance, culture, and ancestry were all components in the crude operative delineation of a race.

The ideology of European supremacy was widespread by the turn of the nineteenth century. However, there were distinct regional differences in how effectively it could be implemented. Cape Town continued to have a higher rate of miscegenation than the country districts, just as it had had throughout the VOC period. More crucially, the rate of mixed marriages continued to be much higher in Cape Town. The genealogical researcher J.A. Heese found that 15.9 per cent of marriages in the Cape Town Dutch Reformed church between 1800 and 1840 were mixed; by contrast in the same period in the rural areas of Tulbagh and Zwartland the percentages were, respectively, 3 per cent and 1.2 per cent.[82] The greater incidence of interracial marriage in Cape Town was both a cause and a reflection of comparative social fluidity. Passing for European on an individual basis was possible, and J.A. Vermaak, who had a grandparent who was not European, was prominent enough to be nominated by the Batavians to the *Raad der Gemeente* (the former Burgher Senate), though over the protests of some of his fellow burghers.[83] Freund has noted several other prominent Capetonians who had a black mother, and one businessman of Stellenbosch whose wife had been a slave.[84] In Cape Town Europeans and members of other groups sometimes lived in close proximity and slaves and Europeans attended the same schools. Samuel Hudson wrote: '. . . several persons in Cape Town of great wealth and respectability have been formerly slaves or descended from them. One generation does away the stain and though it may be remembered by some ill-natured persons they are generally received by the inhabitants according to their present situation in life'.[85]

There were other pockets of colonial life where the model of society envisaged in the ideology of European supremacy was not yet firmly established. That group which Guelke labels the eenlopendes (ch. 2, pp. 99–100) were poor Europeans, mostly in remote pastoral areas, who lived with Khoisan women and perhaps adopted some aspects of Khoisan culture. They were a threat both to their 'orthodox' neighbours, who maintained European endogamy, and to the authorities, who saw them as manifestations of the degeneracy of trekboer society. On the Northern Frontier (ch. 8, pp. 368–72) such Europeans lived interspersed with Khoisan, Bantu-speakers, Oorlams, and Bastaards. In this region, beyond the colonial boundaries, land was held both by Khoisan and Bastaards, sometimes with colonial approval.[86] Here 'orthodox' Europeans were able to establish their dominance only after an increase of European settlement during and after the Great Trek. On the Eastern Frontier, too, Bastaards held land and cattle. But here the orthodox Europeans were far more numerous and European endogamy became the norm far earlier. In 1798 only 5 or 6 per cent of burgher couples in Graaff-Reinet district were mixed (ch. 9, p. 455). By 1814 many Bastaards had sold their land in the eastern districts and had settled beyond the colonial boundary.

We must thus reject the view of I.D. MacCrone that conflict on the frontier was the cradle of the South African ideology of racial supremacy. The evidence we have cited of increasing racial prejudice and discrimination comes equally from the settled southwestern Cape and from the frontiers. Moreover, it is hard to see how the poorer, more sparsely inhabited areas could export their ideology to the more settled regions. In fact the frontier was an area where most Europeans tried to maintain social structures they had imported from the southwestern Cape. European supremacy was not a product of frontier violence. Instead it was the result of an agricultural system characterized by abundant land, scarce capital, and scarce labour. This economy developed within a political system that enabled Europeans to monopolize land and access to capital and that made it difficult to coerce whites to work as labourers. This social system was most firmly established in the arable regions of the southwestern Cape, and it was this region which developed the symbols of European identity and notions of superiority on which colonists relied when faced with the numerous new challenges of the period 1770-1814. Only in Cape Town, where the economic foundations were non-agricultural and where imported ideas could flourish, and in remote areas where Europeans, particularly European women, were still in short supply, was the dominant pattern of European white endogamy and European supremacy still subject to challenge.

The world market and a new legal order, c. 1814 – c. 1838

Central to the crisis that threatened the easy assumptions of European supremacy in the late eighteenth and early nineteenth centuries was the sudden check on the expansion of the colony and a consequent shortage both of land and labour. But two other facets of the crisis were economic growth through contacts with the world economy and a new willingness of governments, from the First British Occupation on, to intervene in matters of labour and frontier security. These new features, incipient before 1814, intensified greatly thereafter, as the Cape took its place permanently in the dynamic political and economic system of the British Empire. A crisis triggered by events within southern Africa was thus prolonged and brought to a climax by external forces.

As Robert Ross has shown (ch. 5, pp. 248–54), the Cape economy had grown gradually since 1652, but the rate of growth accelerated markedly in the early nineteenth century, especially in the production of wheat and wine. It also became more intimately interconnected with aspects of the world economy. Two consequences of this interconnection have attracted particular attention. Van Arkel, Quispel and Ross have noted the effects of British currency policy on Cape farmers and through them on relations between the races. The Cape rixdollar, a paper currency, suffered constant and drastic devaluation against the British pound sterling between 1792 and 1825. Cape farmers, they say, benefited far less from the rising revenue produced by exports to

European markets than they suffered from the rising cost of the goods they had to import and pay for in deflated rixdollars. Thus they were forced to increase production and curtail expenses in order just to maintain their level of profit. Since this currency crisis coincided with the closing of the slave trade, which took effect in 1808, the severely squeezed Cape farmers turned to Khoisan labour; unable to pay free market wages, they increasingly employed coercive measures. On the view of Van Arkel, Quispel and Ross, the firming up of the system of European supremacy was thus one effect of the Cape's incorporation into the world economy.[87]

Mary Rayner has also noted an effect of the world economy that, one could argue, intensified the crisis of the old order at the Cape during the 1810s and 1820s. From 1811 onward the British government encouraged wine exports by various measures, especially the institution of preferential access to British markets in 1813. The result was a boom in wine production, which by 1820-24 accounted for 72 per cent of the value of Cape exports. Because of the slow rate of growth of the slave population – a result of low birth rates among slave women and of the abolition of the slave trade – the brunt of the new expansion was borne by slaves, now driven harder than ever.[88] This could be regarded as another disruptive effect which exposure to the British imperial system had caused for Cape society.

However, one must not overstate the significance of the world economy for the social order at the Cape. The pressures delineated by Ross and Rayner were felt chiefly among the small minority of Cape farmers rich enough to provide for the world market, to import many goods and to afford large slave forces. The effects, positive or negative, of the world economy in the eastern districts were much less severe, at least until the 1840s when the export of Cape wool grew apace. Yet the repression of blacks and Khoisan, and the racist ideology that supported it, were equally present in the eastern and western districts.

Rather than external markets or economic forces it was political change within the colony which most severely intensified the crisis of the old order. Much of this change was a result of the Cape's new position in the British Empire, whose authorities had greater will and resources than the VOC to intervene in Cape society. Among the most important manifestations of this activism were the sweeping of the Xhosa out of the Zuurveld in 1811, which effectively 'closed' the Eastern Frontier; the intervention in Khoisan labour relations beginning with the Caledon Code of 1809 and culminating in Ordinance 50 of 1828; the abolition of slavery, beginning in 1834 and ending in 1838; the settlement of English immigrants in the eastern districts in 1820; and the restructuring of Cape governance in response to the Commission of Inquiry, appointed in 1822. All these actions had economic motivations to be sure, but they were also products of political pressures in South Africa, in Britain, and (in the case of slavery) in the West Indies. All, in one way or another, intensified the crisis of the old Cape order.

Governmental activism was in turn directed by new ideologies – liberalism, utilitarianism, and humanitarianism – which originated outside South Africa, and hence were experienced by the colonists as threatening and alien impositions. These ideologies overlapped in various ways so as to present a massive challenge to the assumptions and practices of the old Cape order. Liberalism provided the rising enthusiasm in Britain for freedom of labour, an important component in agitation for freeing the slaves and releasing the Khoisan from various forms of coercion. Utilitarianism provided some of the ideals behind the administrative revolution traced by Peires (ch. 10), such as an independent judiciary to guard against arbitrary and corrupt government and an honest and professional civil service to take away powers hitherto exercised by local farmers. It was the humanitarians, speaking through the missionaries, above all Dr. John Philip, who most clearly articulated the moral equality of all people, a principle which was enshrined in Ordinance 50 of 1828.

Central to the conflict between the old order and the brash new ideologies was the question of 'distinction of persons'. We have argued that Cape society was moulded since 1652 by the legal status distinctions between slaves, Khoisan, Company servants, and freeburghers and, after the mid-eighteenth century, free blacks. After 1795 the category of Company servant disappeared, but the other four remained, differentially affecting people's rights to land, to free movement, to marriage, to inheritance and to justice. We have noted that, abetted by demographic and economic forces, these distinctions shaped Cape society around a coalescence and mutual reinforcement of class and race (at the top and bottom of society, but not in the middle). The new British ideologies did not question most of the inequalities endemic in this situation. Rather they challenged statutory discrimination directed against groups on the basis of ascribed categories such as race or ancestry. More fundamentally they abhorred the legal status system which underpinned statutory discrimination and which defied the universalistic values of the Enlightenment and of radical evangelical Christianity. Very few of the reformers envisaged social, economic or political equality for blacks, Khoisan and Bastaards, but they did demand equal access to justice as well as laws which made no distinctions between persons. As Andries Stockenstrom, a colonist deeply influenced by the new values, put it in 1828: 'I . . . recommend the enactment of a law placing every free inhabitant in the colony on a level, in the eye of the law, as to the enjoyment of personal liberty and the security of his property.'[89] Advocates of this view tended to argue that blacks, Khoisan and Bastaards, though at present debased on the scale of civilization, could be raised through education and/or religion. Conservative colonists feared that this principle of *gelykstelling* or equalisation implied that people other than Europeans would become their social and political equals or that miscegenation would be forced upon the society – neither of which was envisaged by the reformers at all. Opponents of equalisation insisted that blacks and Khoisan were inherently wild, savage or lazy and that only by firmly subordinating them could one guarantee a peaceful society.[90]

While the old Cape order was threatened by new economic and ideological forces, it also faced increasing challenges from those who were not European. Khoisan and slaves were deeply inspired by the ideologies of free labour and equalization which reached them, often in fragmented or distorted form, from radical whites, from missionaries preaching the Gospel, from conversations they overheard among their masters and from newspapers they paid others to read to them. Various governmental proclamations ameliorating slavery and controlling labour conditions also served to advertise the new ideology, firing slaves and Khoisan with a sense, often exaggerated, of their rights under current law. Rayner has documented many cases of slaves taking their masters to court or demanding their freedom on the basis of legal arguments. Susan Newton-King has similarly suggested that much of the agitation against forced labour usually attributed by scholars to missionaries was actually undertaken by the Khoisan themselves.[91] The constant drumbeat of complaint and demand was a nuisance for individual masters; it was also a frightening sign that alien forces had allied with their labourers to challenge the masters' rights under the old order. During this period there was only one serious uprising among the labour force, in the Cold Bokkeveld in 1825. But it kept alive the memories of the far more serious Khoisan rising of 1799-1803 in the eastern Cape. As in 1808, so in 1825 some Khoisan joined the slaves in their rebellion.[92]

As the ameliorative legislation imposed on the Cape became tougher, colonists were faced with widespread desertion among their labourers and unwillingness to work. These phenomena, which Europeans typically called 'vagrancy', were of course a profound economic threat to those who relied on slave and coerced labour; but they were also a symbol of an old order in disintegration. 'Vagrancy' was a major issue after Ordinance 50 was proclaimed in 1828; as slavery was abolished in stages throughout the 1830s the anxieties of Europeans were increasingly deflected from the Khoisan to the slaves. Anti-vagrancy hysteria afflicted not only the country districts but also Cape Town, where it was closely linked to fear of crime. In Cape Town Europeans tended 'to regard all the poor as blacks and to attribute all criminal behaviour to them', even though as many as half of the convicted criminals in Cape Town were in fact European.[93]

Thus the 1820s and 1830s were a time of profound economic and social dislocation, as world markets, foreign ideologies and British imperial policy inflamed an already smouldering local conflict between master and servant. For many Europeans this was a period of anxiety, as the comfortable social order of their parents and grandparents was assailed by an alien government without and by resistance within. A society which, since its birth almost two centuries before, had known only growth within a constant pattern, now confronted the prospect of substantial change.

Yet the upshot of all this talk and tumult was meager. Leslie Duly, investigating the effects of Ordinance 50 during the 1830s, found that it lacked means of enforcement; the authorities were inaccessible to most Khoisan seeking redress. Duly also found that the Cape government did little to publicise the terms of the ordinance, even among its own departments; and that various justices of the Supreme Court showed little inclination to interpret the law on behalf of workers, or even to uphold the principle of equality before the law.[94] During the 1830s the British government, satisfied that it had resolved the 'Hottentot Question,' shifted its interest to the two-stage abolition of slavery. Thereafter its willingness to intervene at the Cape waned even further; by the early 1840s it was willing to ratify a Masters and Servants Ordinance (1841) which, though it was colour-blind and provided protection for labourers, imposed duties and penalties on servants which went far to allay the masters' alarm at abolition. Nonetheless, agitation for further regulation of labour continued throughout the 1840s. The British government waived much of its right to intervene when it granted Representative Government to the Cape in 1853. One of the first acts of the new legislature was a stiffer Masters and Servants Act (1856), which Rayner judges to have confirmed 'the habits of domination fostered under slavery' despite its nominally non-racial wording.[95]

With the proclamation of Ordinance 50 and the emancipation of the slaves, the legal mould which had first shaped Cape society fell away. What was revealed was a social structure which had hardened in the mould over the previous 180 years, a structure in which class and race coincided at the top and bottom of society. The judicial reform of the 1820s and 1830s failed to alter the social structure, in part because European settlers, galvanized by the struggles surrounding the reforms, were determined to shore up the system of labour repression. As Robert Ross has noted, the Masters and Servants Ordinance of 1841 was notable, not only for scotching any hopes of a truly free market in labour, but also for obliterating the distinctions that from the 1650s had made the Khoisan freer than the slaves.[96] Thus the ordinance further simplified Cape society and enhanced the polarization of Europeans versus all others.

In 1840 Cape Town continued to present a partial exception. Above all, its urban economy still allowed the emergence of skilled black workers and attracted white male immigrants who often married blacks and apparently suffered little discrimination for it. Nonetheless even in Cape Town there were no black or Khoisan professionals at the top of society (except clerks and Malay priests and teachers) and no European 'coolies' at the bottom. No blacks or Khoisan were bookkeepers or notaries, and none was employed in government departments. Black craftspeople were not numerous and were clustered in a few crafts where the cost of materials and equipment was relatively low. Members of the upper classes were almost all European, and they used a complex race and class terminology to describe the society below them. *The South African Commercial Advertiser*, for example, used such phrases as 'the poor or coloured population', 'the colored classes and poor generally' and 'the poorer classes, both black and white' – all of which indicate that it closely associated poverty with people of colour but still recognised that there were poor Europeans as well.[97] Many residential areas in the 1830s and 1840s seem to have been integrated, although the pattern was similar to what it had been in 1800 with the rich areas almost entirely European and the poorer areas mixed.[98] In their concern to uplift the poor, the elite of Cape Town founded schools in which Europeans and blacks studied together. And at least some segments of the elite looked benignly on the prospect of 'amalgamation' or integration; i.e., the union of 'all languages, colours, legal conditions, and religious creeds' in Cape society.[99]

Notwithstanding these sentiments, there was a lot of racial prejudice and racial discrimination in Cape Town. Differences in opportunity resulted from the fact that 'only whites (and possibly prize negroes) were indentured for crafts; for coloureds, apprenticeship meant indenture without the obligation to be taught a trade.'[100] A study of court sentences in the second half of 1844 showed that, while Europeans comprised 45 percent of those convicted in the police court, they received only 17 percent of corporal punishments. Moreover, black and European prisoners were separated in gaol.[101] For some years after 1829 slaves and free blacks were prohibited from attending the theatre for fear of bad behaviour.[102] Racist statements abound in the records, where blacks and Khoisan were associated with disorder and crime, and accused of 'relapsing into a state of savage barbarism'.[103] The police were suspicious of all black groups and feared collusion among them: a commission inquiring into the police reported that 'the connection between the Malays and Free Blacks professing the Mahommedan religion and the slaves, to whom also may now be added a large portion of Prize Negroes whose terms of apprenticeship have expired ... accounts for that marked distinction observed in the exposure of the houses and persons of these classes to entry and arrest, and the scrupulous protection of those of the Free Burghers.'[104] John Montagu, colonial secretary at the Cape from 1843 to 1852, summed up the situation by noting that 'colour had ceased to be the badge of civil disabilities and moral wrongs' but it 'still forms a bar to social intercourse and intimate relations far more formidable than any rising either from diversity of origin, language or religion.'[105]

A number of researchers have gained the impression that in Cape Town, too, polarisation on racial lines intensified in the 1830s and 1840s. J.A. Heese noted a decline in the rate of intermarriage in the period 1838–67,[106] a decline which would have affected chiefly Cape Town, since, as we have seen, the rate was already very low in other regions. Residential mixing also apparently declined between the 1830s and the 1870s. Moreover, Shirley Judges has argued that the tensions surrounding the gradual emancipation of slaves – resentments of slaves at the slow pace of reform and its implementation, resentments of owners at the loss of their property and the defiance of their former slaves – worsened Cape Town's social relations, which took an increasingly 'racial' form because free blacks and slaves increasingly coalesced. She goes on to assert that this polarisation was further intensified by the anti-vagrancy agitation among Europeans after 1834 and by the subsequent campaign for representative government.[107]

In short, Cape Town was not insulated from the rest of the colony; the racial prejudices and class conflicts of the agrarian areas were felt there too. But they were more attenuated because of the somewhat greater opportunities the town economy offered to blacks and because of the presence of a paternal elite with somewhat liberal notions. Even if the upheavals of the 1820s and 1830s intensified the tendency of Europeans to identify themselves by race and to stigmatize blacks, Cape Town society did not take for granted the identification of race and class that was characteristic of the countryside.

Conclusion

European supremacy in the colony was originally moulded by the VOC's system of legal status groups. Initially, both Company servants and freeburghers were almost all Christian and European; the members of the other two legal groups, the Khoisan and slaves, were not. Company servants and freeburghers were given preferential access both to land and to political office, and, as classes formed at the Cape, they coincided with race to a striking degree, particularly at the top and bottom of society.

Many developments might have broken down the correlation of class and race; among them, miscegenation, manumission, and the incorporation and acculturation of Khoisan and imported slaves. That they did so only to a limited degree was a function of many forces discussed in this chapter. Perhaps most important were (1) the economics of Cape agriculture, which, in the absence of sizable capital investment, had to rely on extensive use of land and semi-skilled labour); (2) the demographics of the European population, which was always small in relationship to the vast land it occupied and hence dependent on the labour of others, but large enough and with sufficient gender balance to maintain a high degree of endogamy and hence group identity; (3) the nature of Khoisan society – especially its pastoral economy – limited population growth, inhibited resistance to European expansion and fostered incorporation into white agricultural society; and (4) the economics of Cape slavery that made slaves available at comparatively cheap rates, not only to wealthy Europeans but to those of middling income as well, and hence broadened the number of Europeans with a stake in a racial order.

Thus there was no profound alteration of Cape society under the VOC. Despite widespread miscegenation – mostly outside wedlock – the Europeans maintained a clear group identity, admitting only a few black women to the group and regarding themselves as distinct even from those who, though not pure Europeans, were partially European in ancestry and Christian in religion. Throughout the eighteenth century Europeans held almost all the land and exercised all the power in the vast agricultural regions of the colony. Khoisan and slaves laboured in the service of others. True, in Cape Town a few free blacks, and, on the far northern frontiers, some Khoisan and Bastaards gained economic prominence. True too, there were class distinctions among whites – a wealthy gentry, many middling farmers, and substantial numbers of poor, landless, mostly unmarried men. But prosperous people other than Europeans were few and widely scattered, and their long-term impact on Cape social structure was slight; the poorer Europeans, though numerous, identified primarily with their wealthier fellow Europeans and made no significant alliances with poorer members of other groups. As the colony continued to expand with relative ease, the growing European population engrossed land, cattle, and indigenous labour. By 1770 there had been no effective challenge to the assumption that landholding was a prerogative of Europeans and that coerced labour was the natural lot of everyone else.

After 1770 these assumptions, nurtured in the easy expansion of the prior century, received several rude shocks. In the period from c. 1770 to c. 1815 these shocks were primarily local in origin. Most important were the checking of European advance first by the 'Bushmen', then by the Xhosa; the increasing militance of Khoisan labour; and the resultant shortage of both land and labour, especially on the Eastern Frontier but also throughout the colony. Even before 1815, but with increasing intensity thereafter, the local crises were complemented by an assault on the old Cape order by spokespeople for new liberal and humanitarian ideologies and by the British government, acting both for ideological and geopolitical reasons. In the course of these struggles the ideology of European identity and European supremacy hardened. New economic forces were also unleashed which in time might have shaken the old order. In the end, the structure of legal distinctions was removed from the colony, but the correlation of race and class – now entrenched in the economic life of the colony and safeguarded by a congealing ideology – remained firm.

In the mid-1830s emigrant Afrikaner farmers, the Voortrekkers, left the eastern regions of the Cape Colony to plant new societies in the interior of southern Africa. In large part they wished to restore the traditional social order of the Cape as they knew it – not only the labour repressive system but also the system of 'distinction of persons'. Their successful secession (acknowledged by the British government in 1852 and 1854) greatly expanded the area of extensive, low-capitalized agriculture, based on a large indigenous labour force. It also ensured the maintenance for several more generations of the European-dominated social order which had solidified at the Cape in the eighteenth century. Similarly but less dramatically, the Masters and Servants Ordinance in the Cape Colony (1841) and the granting of representative government to the colonists (1853) confirmed that British liberalism had not overturned major features of what we have called 'European domination'; this encompassed a conviction among whites, especially in agricultural regions, of their distinctiveness from the diverse peoples among whom they lived, their virtually exclusive access to power and wealth, and their expectation to be served by cheap labourers drawn from other groups. These convictions and social realities formed the fateful legacy of the pre-industrial Cape to the modern people of South Africa.

Chapter Eleven   Notes

1. See especially W.M. Macmillan, *The Cape Colour Question: A Historical Survey* (London, 1927), pp. 1-38; I.D. MacCrone, *Race Attitudes in South Africa: Historical, Experimental and Psychological Studies* (Johannesburg, 1937), pp. 1-136; C.W. de Kiewiet, *A History of South Africa, Social and Economic* (London, 1941), pp. 1–29. The quotation is from De Kiewiet, p. 22.
2. See especially a revision of Legassick's original 1970 paper: Martin Legassick, 'The frontier tradition in South African historiography', *Economy and society in pre-industrial South Africa*, ed. Shula Marks and Antony Atmore (London, 1980); W.M. Freund, 'Race in the social structure of South Africa, 1652–1836', *Race and Class*, XVIII (1976), pp. 53–67.
3. D. van Arkel, G.C. Quispel and R.J. Ross, *'De Wijngaard des Heeren?' Een onderzoek naar de wortels van 'die blanke baasskap' in Zuid-Afrika* (Leiden, 1983) pp. 17-72.
4. For approximately a further 5 per cent, one of the grandparents was of unknown (and possibly European) descent. The sample of 1,063 consisted of children whose descendants can be traced to the present and are now designated as white. In the baptismal records there are a total of 1,128 names of children with both parents' names recorded. These children, together with their parents, represented roughly 15 per cent of the 'Christian' population of 1807: G.F.C. de Bruyn, 'Die Samestelling van die Afrikaner', *Tydskrif vir Geesteswetenskappe*, XVI (1976), and personal communication on subsequent research; J.A. Heese, *Die Herkoms van die Afrikaner, 1652-1867* (Cape Town, 1971).
5. Figures for the Company period are based on the annual opgaafs. The number of free blacks has been subtracted from the total figures for freeburghers. On identifying free blacks, see chapter 4, pp. 217 and 238, n. 101. For 1798 the figure for the first column was calculated by subtracting

from Barrow's totals for 'free people of colour and servants'. The figure for the second column is only a rough indication: probably as much as half of the exact total of 1767 were European servants. Much more accurate census-taking in 1798 is mainly responsible for the sharp rise in totals since 1770. The heading of column one in the 1820 census reads only 'Christians' and probably includes all freemen other than free blacks, who are listed separately: See J. Barrow, *Travels in the Interior of South Africa* (London, 1806), I, 23, 67, 73, 82–83; *RCC*, XII, 354.

6. Ernst van den Boogaart, 'Colour Prejudice and the Yardstick of Civility: the Initial Dutch Confrontation with Black Africans, 1590-1635', *Racism and Colonialism: Essays on Ideology and Social Structure*, ed. R. Ross (The Hague, Boston and London, 1982), pp. 44-54.

7. Winthrop D. Jordan, *White Over Black: American Attitudes toward the Negro, 1550-1812* (Chapel Hill, 1968), pp. 40-43; George P. Rawick, *The American Slave: A Composite Autobiography* (Westport, 1972), I, 125-53. Eugene D. Genovese, *The World the Slaveholders Made* (New York, 1971), pp. 103-13; George M. Fredrickson, 'Toward a Social Interpretation of the Development of American Racism', *Key Issues in the Afro-American Experience*, ed. Nathan G. Huggins *et al.* (New York, 1971), I, 249-51.

8. H. Hoetink, *Caribbean Race Relations: A Study of Two Variants* (Oxford, 1967), and H. Hoetink, *Slavery and Race Relations in the Americas* (New York, 1973).

9. D.B. Davies, *The Problem of Slavery in Western Culture* (Ithaca, 1966), pp. 275-78.

10. Donald Moodie, *The Record* (Cape Town and Amsterdam, 1960), p. 250.

11. C.R. Boxer, *The Dutch Seaborne Empire* (London, 1965), p. 223.

12. Sheila Patterson, 'Some Speculations on the Status and Role of Free People of Colour in the Western Cape', *Studies in African Social Anthropology*, ed. M. Fortes and S. Patterson (London, 1975), p. 199. See also J.J. Loubser, 'Calvinism', *The Protestant Ethic and Modernisation*, ed. S.N. Eisenstadt (London, 1969), pp. 367-83.

13. F.A. van Jaarsveld, *From Van Riebeeck to Vorster, 1652-1974* (Johannesburg, 1975), pp. 37-38.

14. See for instance the comparative observations of Hoetink, *Caribbean Race Relations*, pp. 21, 49, 173-74.

15. François Valentyn, *Description of the Cape of Good Hope* . . . (Cape Town, 1973), II, 259.

16. Eugene D. Genovese, *Roll, Jordan, Roll: The World the Slaves Made* (London, 1975), p. 179; Frank Tannenbaum, *Slave and Citizen: The Negro in the Americas* (New York, 1946), pp. 62–65. For a brief summary of the debate on Tannenbaum's argument that the institutions of Latin America account for the differences between slavery in North and South America, see Carl N. Degler, *Neither Black nor White: Slavery and Race Relations in Brazil and the United States* (New York, 1971), pp. 19-21.

17. George McCall Theal, *History of South Africa under the Administration of the Dutch East India Company [1652-1795]* (London, 1897), I, 421.

18. Boxer, *Dutch Seaborne Empire*, pp. 137-38.

19. Susan Newton-King, 'The labour market of the Cape Colony, 1807-28', *Economy and society*, ed. Marks and Atmore, p. 201.

20. Richard Elphick, *Kraal and Castle: Khoikhoi and the Founding of White South Africa* (New Haven and London, 1977), pp. 188-92.
21. J.L. Hattingh, 'Grondbesit in die Tafelvallei. Deel I. Die Eksperiment. Grondbesit van Vryswartes', *Kronos*, X (1985), pp. 32-48.
22. For a fuller discussion, see A.J. Böeseken, 'Die Verhouding tussen Blank en Nie-Blank in Suid-Afrika aan die hand van die vroegste dokumente', *South African Historical Journal*, II (1970), pp. 3-18.
23. Elphick, *Kraal and Castle*, pp. 196-97.
24. Robert Ross, 'The Rule of Law at the Cape of Good Hope in the Eighteenth Century' (unpublished paper, 1977).
25. N.L. de la Caille, *Travels at the Cape, 1751-1753* (Cape Town, 1976), p. 35.
26. Some Khoisan, however, expected equalisation to result from conversion: a Khoisan was excluded from the congregation at Baviaanskloof because she boasted, while under the influence of liquor, that her baptism had made her an equal of the colonists. See Bernhard Krüger, *The Pear Tree Blossoms* (Genadendal, 1966), p. 59.
27. The Rev. M.C. Vos consoled himself with the thought that although the slaves were excluded from Communion, they would one day sit in the Kingdom of Heaven: M.C. Vos, *Merkwaardig Verhaal aangaande het Leven ende Lotgevallen van Michiel Christiaan Vos* (Cape Town, 1911), p. 138.
28. F. le Vaillant, *New Travels into the Interior Parts of Africa by way of the Cape of Good Hope in the Years 1783, 1784, and 1785* (London, 1976), II, 49-50.
29. In Brazil by 1800 the free coloured accounted for roughly a quarter to a third of the total 'coloured' population, by 1850 for a half, and by 1872 for three-quarters: Herbert S. Klein, 'Nineteenth Century Brazil', *Neither Slave Nor Free: The Freedman of African Descent in the Slave Societies of the New World*, ed. David W. Cohen and Jack P. Greene (Baltimore, 1972), pp. 312-16. Between 1798 and 1820 free blacks at the Cape accounted for little more than 5 per cent of the total free black and slave population. In the U.S.A. the free blacks numbered 11 per cent in 1860. See also Davies, *Problem of Slavery*, pp. 283-84.
30. Robert Ross, 'Sexuality and Slavery at the Cape in the Eighteenth Century', *Collected Seminar Papers on the Societies of Southern Africa* (Institute of Commonwealth Studies) VIII (1977), p. 22 and fn. 12.
31. Leonard Guelke, 'The Anatomy of a Colonial Settler Population: Cape Colony, 1657–1750', (unpublished paper), Table VI.
32. George Fredrickson, *White Supremacy: A Comparative Study in American and South African History* (New York and Oxford, 1981), ch. III, esp. pp. 108-24. For rebuttals of his view see Richard Elphick, 'A Comparative History of White Supremacy', *Journal of Interdisciplinary History*, XIII (1983), pp. 503-13; J.A. Heese, ' "Die Herkoms van die Afrikaner": 'n Nabetragting' *Familia*, XVII (1980), pp. 56–59; Hermann Giliomee, 'Eighteenth Century Cape Society: Culture, Race and Class,' *Social Dynamics*, IX (1983), pp. 18–29.
33. M. Cairns, 'Freeblack Landowners in the Southern Suburbs of the Cape Peninsula during the Eighteenth Century', *Kronos*, X (1985), pp. 23-31.
34. J. Hoge, 'Miscegenation in South Africa in the Seventeenth and Eighteenth Centuries', *New Light on Afrikaans and 'Malayo-Portuguese'*, ed. Marius F. Valkhoff (Louvain, 1972), pp. 99-118.

35. Degler, *Neither Black Nor White*, pp. 232-39.
36. R. Percival, *An Account of the Cape of Good Hope* (London, 1804), pp. 286–92.
37. O.F. Mentzel, *A Geographical and Topographical Description of the Cape of Good Hope* (Cape Town, 1925), II, 86.
38. *KP*, IV, Proclamation, 20 Aug. 1794, p. 249.
39. *The Reports of De Chavonnes and his Council, and of Van Imhoff on the Cape* (Cape Town, 1918), p. 137.
40. C.R. Boxer, *Race Relations in the Portuguese Colonial Empire* (Oxford, 1963), p. 56.
41. KA 4035, Adam Tas *et al.* – XVII, n.d., p. 1035v.
42. C 316, Memorial of J.M. Cruywagen and 14 other inhabitants – Governor and Council of Policy, 17 Feb. 1784.
43. W.S. van Ryneveld, 'Beschouwing over de veeteelt, landbouw, handel en finantie, van de kolonie de Kaap de Goede Hoop, in 1805', *Het Nederduitsch Zuid-Afrikaansch Tydschrift*, VIII (1831), p. 124.
44. George Thompson, *Travels and Adventures in Southern Africa* (London, 1827), p. 324. See also W. von Meyer, who stated that there were no other distinctions or ranks in Cape society but those indicated by the colour of the skin: *Reisen in Süd-Afrika während der Jahren 1840 und 1841* (Hamburg, 1843), p. 82.
45. D.J. van Zyl, 'Die Geskiedenis van Graanbou aan die Kaap, 1795-1826', *AYB* (1968), I, 178.
46. D.J. Van Zyl, *Kaapse Wyn en Brandewyn, 1795–1860* (Cape Town, 1975), p. 10.
47. Van Ryneveld, 'Schets', p. 196.
48. P.J. van der Merwe, *Trek* (Cape Town, 1945), p. 86.
49. H. Lichtenstein, *Travels in Southern Africa in the Years 1803, 1804, 1805 and 1806* (Cape Town, 1930), II, 303-04. For a succinct analysis of the processes by which the European ruling class established its dominance in South Africa over other groups, see Robert Ross, *Adam Kok's Griquas* (Cambridge, 1976), pp. 1-11, 134-38.
50. Hermann Giliomee, *Die Kaap tydens die Eerste Britse Bewind 1795-1803* (Cape Town, 1975), p. 21.
51. Barrow, *Travels*, II, 163.
52. Robert Ross, *Cape of Torments: Slavery and resistance in South Africa* (London, 1983), pp. 97–105.
53. *Transactions of the Missionary Society* (London, 1804), I, 494.
54. AR, Swellengrebel Archives, Van Plettenberg-Swellengrebel, 12 May 1770.
55. *Belangrijke Historische Dokumenten over Zuid-Afrika*, ed. George McCall Theal (Cape Town, 1911), III, 219.
56. Percival, *Account*, p. 92.
57. Cited by Michael Streak, *The Afrikaner as viewed by the English* (Cape Town, 1974), p. 20.
58. BR 68, Alberti-Janssens, 12 June 1805, pp. 280-81.
59. BO 50, Landdrost and Heemraden-Craig, 5 Feb. 1797, no. 33.
60. *The Letters of Lady Anne Barnard to Henry Dundas*, ed. A.M. Lewin Robinson (Cape Town, 1973), p. 174.

61. Anders Sparrman, *A Voyage to the Cape of Good Hope . . . from the Years 1772-1776* (Cape Town, 1975), I, 264.
62. Cited by Freund, 'Race in the Social Structure', p. 60.
63. LMS papers on South Africa, Box 4, Pacalt-Hardcastle, 18 Sept. 1809.
64. Moodie Afschriften: Extract Dagregister of Landdrost and Heemraden and Militia Officers, Swellendam, 16 June 1780.
65. MacCrone, *Race Attitudes*, p. 133.
66. *RCC*, I, 249.
67. Requesten or Memorials, 1787: Smook's petition, 19 Nov. 1792; C 93, Report of the Burgher Military Council; MacCrone, *Race Attitudes*, pp. 133-45.
68. In Roodezand the Rev. M.C. Vos was asked: why, if missionary work among slaves was necessary, did no minister advocate it before? The predecessors of Vos had not even instructed their own slaves in the Christian religion (Vos, *Merkwaardig Verhaal*, p. 119).
69. *Transactions*, I, 481-82.
70. *KP*, IV, 8-9.
71. *The Letters of Lady Anne Barnard*, p. 140.
72. Giliomee, *Eerste Britse Bewind*, p. 259.
73. W.J. Burchell, *Travels into the Interior of Southern Africa* (London, 1953), I, 29.
74. Barrow, *Travels*, I, 373.
75. *KP*, V, 255.
76. *RCC*, XI, 102.
77. G.W. Eybers, *Select Constitutional Documents Illustrating South African History* (London, 1918), p.26.
78. H.F. Heese, 'Die Inwoners van Kaapstad in 1800', *Kronos*, 7 (1983), p. 42.
79. *RCC*, I, Court of Justice – Craig, 14 Jan. 1796, p. 304.
80. Van Arkel, Quispel and Ross, '*Wijngaard des Heeren?*' p. 25.
81. John Rex, 'Racism and the Structure of Colonial Societies', *Racism and Colonialism*, ed. Ross, p. 199.
82. Heese, ''n Nabetragting', p. 57.
83. Giliomee, *Eerste Britse Bewind*, p. 22.
84. W.M. Freund, 'Race in the social structure', p. 59.
85. R. Shell, 'Introduction to S.E. Hudson's 'slaves',' *Kronos*, 9 (1984), p. 64. Spelling and capitalisation modernised in quotation.
86. Ch. 8, p. 373.
87. Van Arkel, Quispel and Ross, '*Wijngaard des Heeren?*', pp. 49-51.
88. Mary Isabel Rayner, 'Wine and Slaves: The Failure of an Export Economy and the Ending of Slavery in the Cape Colony, South Africa, 1806-1834' (Ph.D dissertation: Duke University, 1986), pp. 1-31, 66-72, 190ff.
89. André du Toit and Hermann Giliomee, *Afrikaner Political Thought: Analysis and Documents, Volume I, 1780–1850* (Berkeley, Los Angeles and London, 1983), p.105. Writing before the abolition of slavery, Stockenstrom qualifies the principle by advocating legal equality for all *free* persons. After abolition he demanded more forthrightly 'equal rights to all classes, without distinction' (p. 112).
90. *Ibid.*, pp. 86-88.

91. Rayner, 'Wine and Slaves,' pp. 152-89; Newton-King, 'Labour market', pp. 197-98.
92. Ross, *Cape of Torments*, pp. 112-13.
93. K.D. Elks, 'Crime, Community and Police in Cape Town, 1825-1850' (M.A. thesis: University of Cape Town, 1986), pp. 60-67, 80.
94. Leslie Clement Duly, 'A Revisit with the Cape's Hottentot Ordinance of 1828', *Studies in Economics and Economic History*, ed. Marcelle Kooy (Durham, N.C., 1972), pp. 34–56.
95. Rayner, 'Wine and Slaves', pp. 321-23; the quotation is on p.323.
96. Robert Ross, 'Pre-industrial and industrial racial stratification in South Africa', *Racism and Colonialism*, ed. Ross, pp. 85-86.
97. Shirley Judges, 'Poverty, living conditions and social relations – aspects of life in Cape Town in the 1830s' (M.A. thesis: University of Cape Town, 1977), pp. 7-9, 126.
98. Judges, 'Life in Cape Town', pp. 127-28; H.F. Heese, 'Inwoners van Kaapstad', pp. 45-46; E. Bradlow, 'Emancipation and Race Perceptions at the Cape', *South African Historical Journal*, XV (1983), p. 27.
99. Judges, 'Life in Cape Town', p.132.
100. Bradlow, 'Emancipation and Race Perceptions', p. 30.
101. Judges, 'Life in Cape Town', pp. 133-34; Bradlow 'Emancipation and Race Perceptions', p. 12.
102. Elks, 'Crime, Community and Police', pp. 65-66.
103. *Ibid.*, pp. 66-67.
104. Bradlow, 'Emancipation and Race Perceptions', p. 12.
105. *Ibid.*, p. 32.
106. Freund, 'Race in the social structure', p. 63.
107. Judges, 'Life in Cape Town', pp. 135-40, 144-47.

Glossary of foreign and technical terms

assegaai   spear used by Khoikhoi and Bantu-speakers

bandiet   'convict'; i.e., person convicted of a crime generally non-political, by the VOC in the East and sentenced to hard labour at the Cape

Bastaard   in the Cape district, a person born out of wedlock, in trekboer and frontier regions, a person of mixed Khoikhoi-European or, less frequently, slave-European descent; any person accepted as a member of a Bastaard community

bijwoner   tenant farmer

burgher   See *freeburgher*

burgerraad   Municipal Council of Cape Town comprised of *burgerraden*, some chosen by burghers and others appointed by government.

commando   a mounted fighting unit consisting at first of burghers and regular soldiers, but dominated by burghers by the late eighteenth century. Used to defend the colony and to attack indigenous people and seize their cattle

Corps Pandoeren   an auxillary corps established in 1781 in which Khoisan and 'Bastaards' were enrolled under white officers; later called the 'Cape Regiment'.

dagga   *Cannabis sativa*. Introduced from the East by the Portuguese; smoked as a drug.

drostdy   area of jurisdiction of a landdrost; also his official residence

droster   a slave, soldier or servant, who left service without permission; also indigent persons in general

eenlopendes   an officially unmarried white man, living on his own or with a woman who was not a European

fiscal   public prosecutor

freeburgher   (*vrijburger*); person not employed by the VOC and free to own or rent land, practice certain trades and hold office

heemraad   (pl. *heemraden*); member of the board of heemraden aiding the landdrost in the administration of a district

Heren XVII   'the Lords Seventeen'; the central board of directors of the VOC.

imam   Muslim religious leader

inboek	apprenticeship of a black youth as farm labourer until he or she reached a certain age; usually given no wages but food and clothes
kaffer	common name used both by government and colonists for a Bantu-speaking African, especially Xhosa
knecht	man usually white, employed by someone else, usually as overseer
kraal	a settlement, usually in circular form, of Khoikhoi huts; a livestock enclosure
landdrost	chief administrator and magistrate of a district
leningplaats	land given out by government for occupation subject to payment of rent
Mardijker	free black from VOC's Eastern territories
Mfecane	a series of wars leading to massive disruption and restructuring of African society in Natal and on the Highveld in the 1820s and 1830s
muid	dry measure roughly equivalent to one hectolitre
Oorlam	on the Northern Frontier, a person usually of Khoikhoi descent, previously in colonial service
opgaaf	enumeration of freeburghers, free blacks and their property for tax purposes
opstal	fixed improvements on a farm
ordonnantieruiter	a mounted police officer subject to the landdrost
pacht	trading rights in certain commodities; monopoly rented by VOC to *pachters* in return for *pachtgeld* (lit., 'monopoly money')
plakaat	proclamation with the force of law
platteland	countryside; during the seventeenth and eighteenth centuries effectively the entire interior of the colony beyond the limits of Cape Town
renosterbos	invasive shrub (*Elytropappus rhinocerotis*)
request	petition to the Council of policy for burgher rights, manumissions, monopoly rights, etc.
sekunde	second-in-command to the governor or commander; later lieutenant governor or deputy governor
sjambok	whip made of hide cut in strips
slachtersbrief	letter given by butchers or their servants in lieu of cash for cattle and sheep purchased in the interior. These letters had to be cashed in Cape Town
transport	deed of transfer
trekboer	semi-nomadic livestock farmer
veldschoenen	leather shoes; usually without heels
veldwachter	a police officer at the drostdy assisting the landdrost; later ordonnantieruiter

veldwachtmeester   freeburgher militia officer in rural areas; also responsible for some civil administrative duties in the division to which he was appointed

VOC   *(Verenigde Oost-Indische Compagnie)*; the Dutch East India Company

Bibliography

Only articles, books and theses referred to in this work are mentioned in this list. Archival sources are given in *Abbreviations* on p.xiii.

Books

Acocks, J.P.H.: *Veld Types of South Africa* (Pretoria, 1953)

Alberti, L.: *Account of the Tribal Life and Customs of the Xhosa in 1807* (Cape Town, 1968)

Anderson, H.J., ed.: *South Africa a Century Ago (1797–1801)* [Lady Anne Barnard] (Cape Town, n.d.)

Arbousset, T. and F. Daumas: *Narrative of an Exploratory Tour to the Northeast of the Colony of the Cape of Good Hope* (Cape Town, 1968)

Arkin, M.: *Storm in a Teacup: the Later Years of John Company at the Cape 1815–1836* (Cape Town 1973)

Arndt, E.H.D.: *Banking and Currency Development in South Africa* (Cape Town, 1928)

Atkinson, C.T., ed.: *The Maunscripts of Robert Graham, Esq., of Fintry* (London, 1942)

Bannister, S.: *Humane Policy, or Justice to the Aborigines of New Settlements . . .* (London, 1829, 1968)

Banton, M.: *Race Relations* (London, 1967)

[Barnard, Lady Anne]: *South Africa a Century Ago* (1797–1801), ed. H.J. Anderson (Cape Town, n.d.); *The Letters of Lady Anne Barnard to Henry Dundas*, ed. A.M. Lewin Robinson (Cape Town, 1973)

Barraclough, G.: *The Origins of Modern Germany*, 2nd edn. (Oxford, 1947)

Barrow, J.: *Voyage to Cochinchina* (London, 1806); *An Account of Travels into the Interior of Southern Africa Between the Years 1770 and 1779* (London, 1801; reprint New York, 1968); *An Account of Travels into the Interior of Southern Africa in the Years 1797 and 1798* (London, 1801; 1806)

Barth, Fredrik, ed.: *Ethnic Groups and Boundaries: The Social Organisation of Cultural Difference* (Boston, 1969)

Beinart, W., Peter Delius and S. Trapido, eds.: *Putting a Plough to the Ground: Accumulation and Dispossession in Rural South Africa, 1850–1930* (Johannesburg, 1986)

Bell, W. and W.F. Freeman, eds.: *Ethnicity and Nation Building* (Beverley Hills, 1974)

Beyers, C.: *Die Kaapse Patriotte Gedurende die Laaste Kwart van die Agtiende Eeu in die Voortlewing van hul Denkbeelde*, 2nd edn. (Pretoria, 1967)

Bird, J., ed.: *Annals of Natal* (reprint Cape Town, 1965)

[Bird, W.W.]: *State of the Cape in 1822 by a Civil Servant* (reprint Cape Town, 1966)

Blommaert, W.: *Die Joernaal van Dirk Gysbert van Reenen* (Cape Town, 1937)

Blussé, L. and F.S. Gaastra, eds.: *Companies and Trade, Essays on Overseas Trading Companies During the Ancien Régime* (Leiden, 1981)

Böeseken, A.J.: *Simon Van Der Stel en sy Kinders* (Cape Town, 1964); *Slaves and Free Blacks at the Cape, 1658–1700* (Cape Town, 1977); ed. *Suid-Afrikaanse Argiefstukke, Kaap: Resolusies van die Politieke Raad* (Cape Town, 1957; 1962); ed. *Suid-Afrikaanse Argiefstukke, Belangrike Kaapse Dokumente: Memoriën en Instructiën 1657–1699* (Cape Town, 1966

Bohannen, P. and F. Plogg, eds.: *Beyond the Frontier* (New York, 1967)

Bogaert, A.: *Historische Reizen door d'oostersche Deelen van Asia* . . .(Amsterdan, 1711)

Borcherds, P.B.: *An Autobiographical Memoir* (Cape Town, 1861)

Bosman, D.B.: *Briewe van Johanna Maria van Riebeeck en ander Riebeeckiana* (Amsterdam, 1952)

Bosman, D.B. and H.B. Thom, eds.: *Daghregister gehouden by den Oppercoopman Jan Antonisz van Riebeeck* (Cape Town, 1952; 1957)

Boserup, E.: *The Conditions of Agricultural Growth* (Chicago, 1965)

Botha, H.C.: *John Fairbairn in South Africa* (Cape Town, 1984)

Boucher, M.: *The Cape of Good Hope and Foreign Contacts 1735–1753* (Pretoria, 1985)

Boyce, W.B.: *Notes on South African Affairs* (Cape Town, 1971)

Boxer, C.R.: *The Dutch Seaborne Empire, 1600–1800* (New York, 1965); *Race Relations in the Portuguese Colonial Empire* (Oxford, 1963)

Bradlow, F. and M. Cairns: *The Early Cape Muslims* (Cape Town, 1978)

Bredekamp, H.C.: *Van Veeverskaffers tot Veewagters: 'n Historische Onderzoek na Betrekkinge Tussen die Khoikhoi en Europeëns aan die Kaap, 1662 – 1679* (Bellville, 1982)

Brink, A.: *Chain of Voices* (London, 1982)

Brugmans, I.T., ed.: *Welvaart en Historie* (The Hague, 1950)

Bruiijn, J.R. and Van Eyck van Heslinga, eds.: *Muiterij: Oproeren Bevechting op Schepen van de V.O.C.* (Haarlem, 1980)

Bryer, L. and K.S. Hunt: *The 1820 Settlers* (Cape Town, 1984)

Burchell, W.J.: *Travels in the Interior of Southern Africa* (London, 1822–1824)

Burrows, E.H.: *Overberg Outspan: A Chronicle of People and Places in the South Western Districts of the Cape* (Cape Town, 1952)

Cameron, T. and S.B. Spies: *An Illustrated History of South Africa* (Johannesburg, 1986)

Campbell, J.: *Travels in South Africa undertaken at the request of the London Missionary Society* (London, 1812); *Travels in South Africa . . . Second Journey* (London, 1822; reprint Cape Town, 1974)

Carstens, W.P.: *The Social Structure of a Cape Coloured Reserve* (Cape Town, 1966)

Cohen, D.W. and J. P. Greene: *Neither Slave Nor Free: The Freedman of African Descent in the Slave Societies of the New World* (Baltimore and London, 1972)

Colenbrander, H.T.: *De Afkomst der Boeren*, 2nd edn. (Cape Town, 1964)

Cory, G.: *The Rise of South Africa* (1910–1940) (reprint Cape Town, 1965)

Davies, D.B.: *The Problem of Slavery in Western Culture* (Ithaca, 1966); *The Problem of Slavery in the Age of Revolution, 1770–1823* (Ithaca, 1975)

Davies, D.B.: *Slavery and Human Progress*, part two (New York and Oxford, 1984)

Degler, C.N.: *Neither Black nor White: Slavery and Race Relations in Brazil and the United States* (New York, 1971)

Degrandpré, L.: *Voyage á la côte occidentale d'Afrique . . .* (Paris, 1801)

De Haan, F.: *Old Batavia: Gedenkboek*, 2 vols. (Jakarta, 1922)

De Heer, C.: *Bijdrage tot die Financiele Geschiedenis der Oost-Indische Compagnie* (The Hague, 1929)

De Jong, C.: *Reizen naar de Kaap de Goede Hoop, Ierland en Noorwegen in de jaren 1791 tot 1797* (Haarlem, 1802)

De Kiewiet, C.W.: *A History of South Africa, Social and Economic* (Oxford, 1942; 1946; 1957)

Dekker, R.: *Holland in Beroering. Oproeren in 17de en 18de Eeuw* (Baarn, 1982)

De Kock, V.: *Those in Bondage* (Cape Town, 1950; reprint 1963)

De Korte, J.P.: De Jaarlijkse Financiële Verantwoording in de Verenigde Oost-Indische Compagnie (Leiden, 1984)

De la Caille, A.N.L.: *Journal Historique du Voyage fait au Cap de Bonne–Espérance* (Paris, 1763); *Travels at the Cape, 1751–1753* (Cape Town and Rotterdam, 1976)

Delius, P.: *The Land Belongs to Us* (Johannesburg, 1983)

De Mist, J.A.: *The Memorandum of Commissary J.A. de Mist*, trans. K.M. Jeffreys (Cape Town, 1920)

De Villiers, C.C. and C. Pama: *Genealogies of Old South African Families* (Cape Town and Amsterdam, 1966)

De Vries, J.: *De Economische Achteruitgang der Republiek in de Achttiende Eeuw* (Leiden, 1968)

De Wet, G.C.: *Die Vryliede en Vryswartes in die Kaapse Nedersetting 1657–1707* (Cape Town, 1981)

Dictionary of South African Biography (Cape Town and Johannesburg, 1968; 1981)

Dominicus, F.C.: *Het ontslag van Wilhem Adriaen van der Stel* (Rotterdam, 1928)

Dreyer, A., ed.: *Boustowwe vir die Geskiedenis van die Nederduits–Gereformeerde Kerke in Suid-Afrika* (Cape Town, 1936)

Duly, L.C.: *British Land Policy at the Cape 1795–1844: A Study of Administrative Procedures in the Empire* (Durham, 1968)

Du Plessis, I.D.: *The Cape Malays: History, Religion, Traditions, Folk Tales, The Malay Quarter* (Cape Town, 1972)

Du Toit, A. and H. Giliomee, eds.: *Afrikaner Political Thought, Analysis and Documents, I: 1780–1850* (Cape Town, 1983)

Du Toit, P.S.: *Onderwys aan die Kaap onder die Bataafse Republiek 1803–1806* (Pretoria, 1944)

Duvenhage, G.D.J.: *Van die Tarka na die Transgariep*

Edwards, I.: *Towards Emancipation: A Study in South African Slavery* (Cardiff, 1942)

Ehret, C. and M. Posnansky, eds.: *The Archeological and Linguistic Reconstruction of African History* (Berkeley, Los Angeles and London, 1982)

Elias, J.E.: *Die Vroedschap van Amsterdam* (Amsterdam, 1923)

Elphick, R.: *Kraal and Castle: Khoikhoi and the Founding of White South Africa* (New Haven and London, 1977; new edn. Johannesburg, 1985)

Elphick, R. and H. Gilomee, eds.: *The Shaping of South African Society 1652 – 1820* (1st edn., Cape Town, 1979)

Engelbrecht, J.A.: *The Korana: An Account of their Customs and their History* (Cape Town, 1936)

Enloe, C.H.: *Police, Military and Ethnicity, Foundations of State Power* (New Brunswick, 1980)

Eybers, W.W., ed.: *Select Constitutional Documents Illustrating South African History* (London, 1918); *Bepalingen en Instructiën voor het Bestuur van de Buitendistricten van de Kaap de Goede Hoop* (Amsterdam, 1922)

Fairbairn, J.: *Five papers on the Slave Question* (Cape Town, 1831)

Filliot, J.M.: *La Traite des Esclaves ver les Mascareignes au XVIIIe siécle* (Paris, 1974)

Fischer, E.: Die Rehobother Bastards und das Bastardierungsproblem beim Menschen (Jena, 1913)

Foner, L. and E. Genovese: *Slavery in the New World: A Reader in Comparative History* (Englewood Cliffs, New Jersey, 1969)

Forbes, V.S.: *Pioneer Travellers in South Africa* (Cape Town and Amsterdam, 1965)

Forster, G.: *A Voyage Round the World . . . in His Brittannic Majesty's Sloop Resolution,* 3 vols. (London, 1977)

Fortes, M. and S. Patterson, eds.: *Studies in African Social Anthropology* (London, 1975)

Fouché, L.: *Dagboek van Adam Tas 1705–1706* (Cape Town, 1970); *Die Evolutie van die Trekboer* (Pretoria, 1909)

Frank, A.G.: *Capitalism and Underdevelopment in Latin America* (London, 1967)

Franken, J.L.M.: *Taalhistoriese Bydraes* (Amsterdam and Cape Town, 1953); *Piet Relief se lewe in die Kolonie* (Pretoria, 1949)

Freeman, J.J.: *A Tour in South Africa* (London, 1851)

Fredrickson, G., ed.: *White Supremacy. A Comparative Study in American and South African History* (New York and Oxford, 1981)

Gaastra, F.S.: *De Geschiedenis van de V.O.C.* Haarlem 1902; 1982)

Galbraith, J.S.: *Reluctant Empire* (Berkeley, 1963)

Gelman Taylor, J.: *The Social World of Batavia* (Madison, 1983)

Genovese, E.: *Roll, Jordan, Roll* (New York, 1974)

Geyer, A.L.: *Das wirtschaftliche System der Niederländisch Ostindischen Kompanie am Kap der Guten Hoffnung 1785–1795* (Munich and London, 1923)

Geyer, O.: *Die Ouhooggeregshofgebou; The History of the Old Supreme Court Building* (Cape Town, 1958)

Geyl, P.: *Revolutiedagen te Amsterdam, Aug.–Sept. 1748* (The Hague, 1936); ed.: *Pennestrijd over Staat en Historie* (Groningen, 1971)

Gie, S.F.N.: *Geskiedenis van Suid-Afrika of ons Verlede* (Stellenbosch, 1924)

Giliomee, H.: *Die Kaap tydens die Eerste Britse Bewind* (Cape Town and Pretoria, 1975)

Glaman, C.: *Dutch-Asiatic Trade, 1620–1740* (Copenhagen, 1958)

Glass, D.V. and D.E.C. Eversley: *Population in History: Essays in Historical Demography* (London, 1965)

Gledhill, E. and J.: *In the Steps of Piet Retief* (Cape Town, 1980)

Godëe Molsbergen, E.E.: *Reizen in Zuid-Afrika in de Hollandse Tijd,* 4 parts; *Linschotenvereniging* (The Hague, 1916; 1932)

Godlonton, R.: *Introductory Remarks to . . . the Irruption of the Kaffir Hordes* (1835; reprint Cape Town, 1965)

Golovnin, V.M.: *Detained in Simon's Bay* (Cape Town, 1964)

Grant, P.W.: *Considerations on the State of the Colonial Currency at the Cape of Good Hope* (Cape Town, 1825)

Greschat, H.J. and H. Jungraithmayr: *Wort und Religion: Kalima Na Dini* (Stuttgart, 1969)

Guelke, L.: *The Anatomy of a Colonial Settler Population: Cape Colony 1657–1750* (forthcoming)

Gutman, H.G.: *The black Family in Slavery and Freedom, 1750–1925* (New York, 1977)

Haafner, J.: *Lotgevallen en Vroegere Zeereizen van Jacob Haafner* (Amsterdam, 1820)

Hall, M. and Smith A.B., eds.: *Prehistoric Pastoralism in Southern Africa* (Goodwin Series 5, S.A. Archaeological Society, June 1986)

Hammond-Tooke, W.D., ed.: *The Bantu-speaking Peoples of Southern Africa* (London, 1974)

Hancock, W.K.: *Survey of Commonwealth Affairs* (London, 1940)

Harington, A.: *Sir Harry Smith: Bungling Hero* (Cape Town, 1980)

Harris, M.: *Patterns of Race in the Americas* (New York, 1974)   ·

Heese, H.F.: *Groep Sonder Grense* (Bellville, 1984)
Heese, J.A.: *Die Herkoms van die Afrikaner 1657–1867* (Cape Town, 1971); *Slagtersnek en sy Mense* (Cape Town, 1973)
Hobsbawm, E.J. and G. Rudé: *Captain and Swing* (1985)
Hoetink, H.: *Het Patroon van de Oude Curaçaose Samelewing* (Assen, 1958); *Carribbean Race Relations: A Study in Two Variants* (Oxford, 1967; New York, 1971); *Slavery and Race Relations in the Americas* (New York, 1973)
Hutton, C.W., ed.: *Autobiography of the Late Sir Andries Stockenstrom* (Cape Town, 1887, 1964)

Idenburgh, P.: *De Kaap de Goede Hoop Gedurende Laatste Jaren van het Nederlandsch Bewind* (Leiden, 1946)
Immelman, R.F.M.: *Men of Good Hope: The Romantic Story of the Cape Town Chamber of Commerce 1804–1954* (Cape Town, 1955)

Janowitz, M., ed.: *Civil-Military Relations, Regional Perspectives* (London, 1981)
Jeffreys, K.A., trans.: *The Memorandum of J.A. de Mist* (Cape Town, 1920); *Kaapse Argiefstukken, 1778–1783* (Cape Town, 1967); with S. D. Naudé, ed.: *Kaapse Argiefstukken: Kaapse Plakaatboek, 1652–1795* (Cape Town, 1944, 1949)
Jeffreys, M.K., ed.: *Kaapse Argiefstukken, 1783* (Cape Town, 1932)
Johnston, H.J.M.: *British Emigration Policy 1815–1830* (Oxford, 1972)
Jordan, W.D.: *White Over Black: American Attitudes Toward the Negro 1550–1812* (Chapel Hill, 1968)

Kennedy, R.F., ed.: *Journal of Residence in Africa, I, 1842–1853* [Thomas Baines] (Cape Town, 1961)
Khan, M.A.T.: *The Travels of Mirza Abu Taleb Khan in Asia, Africa and Europe in the years 1799, 1800, 1801, 1802 and 1803, written by himself in the Persian language and translated by Charles Stewart* (London, 1810)
King, H.: *Richard Bourke* (Melbourne, 1971)
Kirby, P., ed.: *Andrew Smith and Natal* (Cape Town, 1955)
Kolbe, P.: *Naaukeurige en Uitvoerige Beschrijving van de Kap de Goede Hoop* (Amsterdam, 1727)
Kotze, D.M., ed.: *Letters of the American Missionaries, 1835–1838* (Cape Town, 1950)
Kooy, M., ed.: *Studies in Economics and Economic History* (London, 1972)
Kruger, B.: *The Pear Tree Blossoms: A History of the Moravian Mission Stations in South Africa 1737–1869* (Genadendal, 1966)

Laidler, P.W.: *The Growth and Government of Cape Town* (Cape Town, 1939): *The African Court Calendar for 1814* (reprint Cape Town 1982)
Lamar, H. and L. Thompson, eds.: *The Frontier in History: North America and Southern Africa Compared* (New Haven and London, 1981)
Latrobe, C.I.: *Journal of a Visit to South Africa in 1815 and 1816 with some Account of the Missionary Settlements of the United Bretheren near the Cape of Good Hope* (New York, 1969)
Lattimore, O.: *Inner Asian Frontiers of China* (Clinton, 1940)
Le Cordeur, B.A.: *The Politics of Eastern Cape Separatism, 1820–1854* (Cape Town, 1981); with C. Saunders: *The Kitchingman Papers* (Johannesburg 1976)

Leeb, I.L.: *The Ideological Origins of the Batavian Revolution* (The Hague, 1973)

Leibbrandt, H.C.V.: *Précis of the Archives of the Cape of Good Hope: Letters and Documents Received 1649–1662* (Cape Town, 1896, 1899); ed.: *Précis of the Archives of the Cape of Good Hope, Letters Despatched 1652–1662* (Cape Town, 1900); *Précis of the Archives of the Cape of Good Hope, Journal 1662–1670* (28 Aug., 1670); *The Rebellion of 1815 generally known as Slachters Nek* (Cape Town, 1902); *De Rebellie van 1815 algemeen bekend als Slachtersnek* (Cape Town, 1903)

Lequin, F.: *Het personeel van de Verenigde Oost-Indische Compagnie in Azië in de Achttiende Eeuw, meer in het bijzonder in de vestiging Bengalen* (Leiden, 1982)

Le Roux, P.E.: *De Verdedigingstelsel aan die Kaap onder die Hollands-Oosindiese Kompanje 1652–1795* (n.p., 1925)

Le Vaillant, F.: *Voyage de Monsieur le Vaillant dans l'Interieur de l'Afrique* (Paris, 1790); *Travels into the Interior Parts of Africa by Way of the Cape of Good Hope in the Years 1780– 1785* (London, 1790); *New Travels into the Interior Parts of Africa by way of the Cape of Good Hope in the Years 1783, 1784 and 1785* (London, 1796)

Lichtenstein, H. [Martin Hinrich]: *Reisen in Südlichen-Afrika in den Jahren 1803, 1804, 1805 and 1806* (Berlin edition 1911, reprint Stuttgart 1967); *Travels in Southern Africa in the Years 1803, 1804, 1805 and 1806* (Cape Town, 1928, 1930)

Liesegang, G., H. Pasch and A. Jones, eds.: *Figuring African trade* (Cologne, 1985)

Lockyer, C.: *An Account of the Trade in India* (London, 1711); *Collectanea* (Cape Town, 1924)

MacCrone, I.D.: *Race Attitudes in South Africa: Historical, Experimental and Psychological Studies* (Johannesburg and Oxford, 1937)

Maclennan, B.: *A Proper Degree of Terror* (Johannesburg, 1985)

Macmillan, W.M.: *The Cape Colour Question* (Cape Town, 1969); *Bantu, Boer and Briton: The Making of the South African Native Policy* (London, 1923, 1963)

Mansvelt, W.M.F.: *Rechtsvorm en Geldelijk Beheer bij de Oost-Indische Compagnie* (Amsterdam, 1922)

Marais, J.S.: *Maynier and the First Boer Republic* (Cape Town, 1944, 1962); *The Cap Coloured People, 1652–1937* (London, 1939; Johannesburg, 1957, 1968)

Marks, S. and A. Atmore, eds.: *Economy and Society in pre-Industrial South Africa* (London, 1980)

Marx, G.T., ed.: *Racial Conflict* (Boston, 1971)

Maxwell, W.A. and R.T. McGeogh, eds.: *The Reminiscences of Thomas Stubbs* (Cape Town, 1978)

Mentzel, O.F.: *A Complete and Authentic Geographical and Topographical Description of the . . . Cape of Good Hope* (Cape Town, 1921, 1925, 1944); *Life at the Cape in the Mid-Eighteenth Century being the Biography of Rudolf Siegfried Alleman* (Cape Town, 1920)

Millar, A.: *Plantagenet in South Africa* (Cape Town, 1965)

Milo, T.H.: *De invloed van de Zeemacht op de geschiedenis der V.O.C.* (The Hague, 1946)

Moffat, R.: *Missionary labours and scenes in Southern Africa . . .* (London, 1842); *Apprenticeship at Kuruman: being the journals and letters of Robert and Mary Moffat, 1820 –1828*, ed.: J. Schapera (London, 1951)

Montgomery, J.: *The Reminiscences of John Montgomery*, ed. A. Gilfard (Cape Town, 1981)

Moodie, D. ed.: *The Record: or a series of official papers relative to the conditions and treatment of the native tribes of South Africa* (Cape Town, 1838, 1842; Amsterdam and Cape Town 1960, 1966)

Moore, B.: *Social Origins of Dictatorship and Democracy: Lord and Peasant in the Making of the Modern World* (Boston, 1966)

Moorees, A.: *Die Nederduitse Gereformeerde Kerk in Suid-Afrika, 1652–1873* (Cape Town, 1937)

Moritz, E., ed.: *Die Deutschen am Kap unter der Holländischen Herrschaft (1652–1806* (Weimar, 1938)

Mossop, E.E., ed.: *The Journals of Brink and Rhenius* (Cape Town, 1947); with A. W. van der Horst, ed.: *The Journal of Hendrik Jacob Wikar (1799) and the Journals of Jacobus Coetzé Jansz (1766) and Willem van Reenen (1791)* (Cape Town, 1935)

Muller, C.F.J.: *Johannes Frederik Kirsten oor die toestand van die Kaap-Kolonie in 1795* (Pretoria, 1966); *Leiers na die Noorde: Studies oor die Groot Trek* (Cape Town, 1976); ed.: *Vyfhonderd Jaar Suid-Afrikaanse Geskiedenis* (Pretoria and Cape Town, 1968)

Murray, A.H.: *The Political Philosophy of J.A. de Mist* (Cape Town, n.d.)

Namier, L.B.: *The Structure of Politics at the Accession of George III* (London, 1961)

Nash, M.D.: *Bailie's Party of 1820 Settlers* (Cape Town, 1982)

Neumark, S.D.: *Economic Influences on the South African Frontier, 1652–1836* (Stanford, 1957)

Newton-King, S. and W.C. Malherbe: *The Khoikhoi Rebellion in the Eastern Cape, 1799–1803* (Cape Town, 1984)

Nolthenius, R.J.P. Tutein: *Het Geslacht Nolthenius (Tutein Nolthenius)* (Haarlem, 1914)

Omer-Cooper, J.D.: *The Zulu Aftermath: a Nineteenth Century Revolution in Bantu Africa* (London, 1966)

Orpen, J.M.: *Reminiscences of Life in South Africa from 1846 to the Present Day* (London, 1908)

Pama, C.: *Geslagregisters van die ou Kaapse families* (Cape Town, 1966)

Palmer, R.R.: *The Age of Democratic Revolution* (Princeton, 1964)

Paravicini, W.B.E. di Capelli: *Reize in die Binnelanden van Zuid-Afrika* (Cape Town, 1965)

Paterson, W.: *A Narrative of Four Journeys into the Country of the Hottentots and Caffraria* (London, 1787, 1790)

Peires, J.B.: *The House of Phalo: A History of the Xhosa People in the Days of their Independence* (Johannesburg, 1981)

Percival, R.: *An Account of the Cape of Good Hope* (London, 1804)

Philip, J. *Researches in South Africa* (London, 1828)

Philip, P.: *British Residents at the Cape, 1795–1819* (Cape Town, 1981)

Porta, A.: *Johan en Gerrit Corver* (Assen, 1975)

Preller, G.: *Voortrekker Mense* (Cape Town, 1920, 1938)

Raven-Hart, R.: *Cape of Good Hope, 1652–1702: The First 50 Years of Dutch Settlement as seen by Callers*, 2 vols. (Cape Town, 1971)

Rawick, G.P.: *The American Slave: A Composite Autobiography* (Westport, 1972)

Reid, A., ed.: *Slavery, Bondage and Dependency in Southeast Asia* (St. Lucia, 1983)

Robinson, A.M. Lewin, ed.: *The Letters of Lady Anne Barnard to Henry Dundas* (Cape Town, 1973)

Roorda, D.J.: *Partij en Factie* (Gronigen, 1961)

Ross, A.: *John Philip, 1775–1851: Missions, Race and Politics in South Africa* (Aberdeen, 1986)

Ross, R.: *Adam Kok's Griquas: a Study in the Development of Stratification in South Africa* (London, 1976); *Cape of Torments: Slavery and Resistance in South Africa* (London, 1983)

Sales, J.: *Mission Stations and the Coloured Communities of the Eastern Cape, 1800–1852* (Cape Town, 1975)

Saunders, C. and R. Derricourt, eds.: *Beyond the Cape Frontier* (Cape Town, 1974)

Schapera, I., ed.: *The Khoisan Peoples of South Africa* (London, 1965); *Handbook of Tswana Law and Customs* (London, 1938); *Government and Politics in Tribal Societies* (London, 1956); ed.: *The Early Cape Hottentots* (Cape Town, 1933); *Apprenticeship at Kuruman: being the journals and letters of Robert and Mary Moffat 1820–1828* (London, 1951)

Scherzer, K.: *Narrative of the Circumnavigation of the Globe by the Austrian Frigate Novara in the Years 1857, 1858 and 1859*, 3 vols.: I (London, 1861)

Schollen, C.: *De Munten van de Nederlandse Gebiedsdeelen Overzee 1601–1948* (Amsterdam, 1951)

Scholtz, G.D.: *Die Ontwikkeling van die Politieke Denke van die Afrikaner* (Johannesburg, 1967)

Schrire, C., ed.: *Past and Present in Hunter-Gatherer Studies* (Orlando, 1984)

Schutte, G.J.: *De Nederlandse Patriotten en de Koloniën. Een Onderzoek naar hun Denkbeelden en Optreden, 1770–1800* (Groningen, 1974); ed.: *Briefwisseling van Hendrik Swellengrebel Jr. oor Kaapse sake 1778–1792* (Cape Town, 1982)

Shell, R.C.-H.: *De Meillon's People of Colour: Some Notes on their Dress and Occupations* (Johannesburg, 1978)

Shillington, K.: *The Colonisation of the Southern Tswana* (Johannesburg, 1985)

Shibutani, T.: *Improvised News: a Sociological Study of Rumor* (Indianapolis, 1966)

Smith, A.: *The Diary of Dr. Andrew Smith* (Cape Town, 1939)

Smith, J.M., ed.: *Seventeenth Century America* (Chapel Hill, 1959)

Soga, J.H.: *The South-Eastern Bantu* (Johannesburg, 1930)

Sparrman, Anders (André): *Voyage au Cap de Bonne-Espérance et autour du monde avec Capitaine Cook . . .* (Paris, 1787); *A Voyage to the Cape of Good Hope, 1772–1776*, 2nd edn. (London, 1785); *A Voyage to the Cape of Good Hope*, ed. V.S. Forbers (Cape Town, 1977); *A Voyage to the Cape of Good Hope towards the Antarctic polar circle; Round the world and to the country of the Hottentots and the Caffres from the year 1772– 1776* (Cape Town, 1975, 1977); *A Voyage to the Cape of Good Hope . . . chiefly into the country of the Hottentots and Caffres, from the year 1772 to 1776* (Dublin, 1775; Cape Town, 1975, 1977)

Spiers, E.M.: *The Army and Society 1815–1914* (London, 1980)

Spilhaus, M.W.: *South Africa in the Making 1652–1806* (Cape Town, 1966); *The First South Africans* (Cape Town and Johannesburg, n.d.)

Stavorinus, J.S.: *Voyages to the East Indies by the late John Splinter Stavorinus* (London, 1798); *Reize van Zeeland over de Kaap de Goede Hoop . . in de jaaren 1768 tot 1771 . . .* (Leiden, 1793); *Reize van Zeeland over de Kaap de Goede Hoop, . . . in de jaaren 1774 tot 1778 . .* (Leiden, 1798)

Steedman, A.: *Wanderings and Adventures in the Interior of Africa*, 2 vols. (London, 1835)

Steur, J.J.: *Herstel of Ondergang: De Voorstellen tot Redding van de V.O.C. 1740–1795* (Utrecht, 1984)

Stockenstrom, A.: *The Autobiography of the late Sir Andries Stockenstrom . . . (Cape Town, 1887)*, ed.: C.W. Hutton (Cape Town, 1964)

Stockenstrom, E.: *Vrystelling van die Slawe* (Stellenbosch, 1934)

Streak, M.: *The Afrikaner as viewed by the English* (Cape Town, 1974)

Tannenbaum, F.: *Slave and Citizen: The Negro in the Americas* (New York, 1947)

Taylor, J.G.: *The Social World of Batavian, European and Eurasian in Dutch Asia* (Madison, 1983)

Theal, G.M.: *Belangrijke Historische Dokeumenten over Zuid-Afrika* (Cape Town, 1896, 1911); *Basutoland Records* (Cape Town, 1883); *History of Africa South of the Zambesi from 1505–1795* (London, 1922); *History of South Africa before 1795* (London, 1927; Cape Town, 1964); *A History of South Africa under the Administration of the Dutch East India Company 1652–1795* (London, 1897); *A History of South Africa since 1706* (London, 1975)

Thom, H.B.: *Die Geskiedenis van die Skaapboerdery in Suid-Afrika* (Amsterdam, 1936); ed.: *Daghregister gehouden by den Oppercoopman Jan Anthonisz van Riebeeck* (Cape Town, 1952, 1957); ed.: *Journal of Jan van Riebeeck* (Cape Town, 1952, 1959)

Thompson, E.P.: *The Making of the English Working Class* (London, 1968)

Thompson, G.: *Travels and Adventures in Southern Africa* (London, 1827, Cape Town, 1967)

Thompson, L., ed.: *African Societies in Southern Africa* (London, 1969)

Thunberg, C.P.: *Voyages de C.P. Thunberg, au Japon, par le Cap de Bonne-Espérance* (Paris, 1796); *Travels in Europe, Africa, and Asia made between the years 1770 and 1779*, 3 parts (London, 1793, 1795)

Trotter, J.: *A Letter addressed to W. Robertson Esq. and the other members of a committee nominated on the part of the mercantile body of the Cape of Good Hope to draw up a report on the state of the commerce, finances and agriculture of that colony for the consideration of His Majesty's Commissioners of Enquiry* (Calcutta, 1825)

Turner, M.: *Slaves and Missionaries: The disintegration of Jamaican Slave Society 1787–1834* (Urbana, 1982)

Valentijn, F.: *Beschryvinge van de Kaap der Goede Hoope en de Zaaken Daartoe Behoorende* (Cape Town, 1971, 1973); *Description of the Cape of Good Hope with the matters concerning it* (Cape Town, 1971, 1973)

Valkhoff, M.F.: *Studies in Portugese and Creole, with Special Reference to South Africa* (Johannesburg, 1966); *New Light on Afrikaans and 'Malayo-Portuguese'* (Leuven, 1972)

Van Arkel, P., G.C. Quispel and R.J. Ross: *De Wijngaard des Heeren? Een onderzoek naar de wortels van 'die blanke baasskap' in Zuid-Afrika* (Leiden, 1983)

Van Dam, P.: *Beschrijvinge van de Oost-Indische Compagnie*, eds. F.W. Stapel and C.W. th. van Boetzelaer, 7 parts (The Hague, 1927; 1954)

Van Dantzig, A.: *Het Nederlandsch–Aandeel in de Slavenhandel* (Bossum, 1968)

Van der Bijl, M.: *Idee en interest. Voorgeschiedenis, verloop en achtergronden van de politieke twisten in Zeeland en vooral in Middelberg tussen 1702–1715* (Groningen, 1981)

Van der Chijs, J.A., ed.: *Nederlandsch-Indisch Plakaatboek 1602-1811* (The Hague, 1885, 1891; Batavia, 1893)

Van der Merwe, J.P.: *Die Kaap onder die Bataafse Republiek 1803–1806* (Amsterdam, 1926)

Van der Merwe, P.J.: *Die Noordwaartse Beweging van die Boere voor die Groot Trek 1770–1842* (The Hague, 1937); *Die Trekkoer in die Geskiedenis van die Kaapkolonie, 1657–1842* (Cape Town, 1938); *Die Kafferoorlog van 1793* (Cape Town, 1940); *Trek: Studies oor die Mobiliteit van die Pioniersbevolking aan die Kaap* (Cape Town, 1945)

Van Drillen, J.G.: *Van Rijkdom en Regenten: Handboek tot de Economische en Sociale Geschiedenis van Nederland Tijdens de Republiek* (The Hague, 1970)

Van Duin, P. and R. Ross: *The Economy of the Cape Colony in the Eighteenth Century*, Intercontinehtal No. VII (Leiden, 1987)

Van Jaarsveld, F.A.: *Van Van Riebeeck tot Verwoerd* (Johannesburg, 1971)
Van Leeuwen, S.: *Het Rooms–Hollands–Regt,* 10th edn. (The Hague, 1732)
Van Lier, R.A.J.: *Frontier Society: A Social Analysis of the History of Surinam* (The Hague, 1971)
Van Onselen, L.E.: *Cape Antique Furniture* (Cape Town, 1959)
Van Reenen, D.G.: *Die Joernaal van Dirk Gysbert van Reenen* (Cape Town, 1937)
Van Ryneveld, W.S.: *Aanmerkingen over die Verbetering van het Vee aan het Kaap de Goede Hoop, 1804* (Cape Town, 1942)
Van Warmelo, P.: *An Introduction to the Principles of Roman Law* (Cape Town, 1976)
Van Zurk, E.: *Codex Batavus* (Delft, 1711)
Van Zyl, D.J.: *Kaapse wyn en Brandewyn 1795–1860* (Cape Town, 1975)
Vedder, H.: *South West Africa in Early Times* (London, 1938)
Von Meyer, W.: *Reisen in Süd-Afrika während der Jahren 1840 und 1841* (Hamburg, 1843)
Vos, M.C.: *Merkwaardig Verhaal aangaande het Leven en de Lotgevallen van Michiel Christiaan Vos* (Cape Town, 1911)

Walker, E.A.: *A History of South Africa* (London, 1928); *The Great Trek* (London, 1960); *The Frontier Tradition in South Africa* (London, 1930); ed.: South Africa, vol. VII, *The Cambridge History of the British Empire,* 2nd imp. (Cambridge, 1963)
Wangemann, T.: *Geschichte der Berliner Mission Gesselschaft und ihrer Arbeiten in Süd-Afrika* (Berlin, 1872)
Ward, H.: *Five Years in Kaffirland, with sketches of the late War,* II (London, 1848)
Wertheim, H.A. and G. Weenink: *Democratische Bewegingen in Gelderland* (Amsterdam, 1973)
Wilberforce, B. and W.: *State of the Cape of Good Hope in 1822* (London, 1823)
Williams, J. B.: *British Commercial Policy and Trade Expansion, 1750–1850* (Oxford, 1972)
Wilson, G. and M.: *The Analysis of Social Change* (Manchester, 1945)
Wilson, M. and L. Thomson, eds.: *The Oxford History of South Africa* (Oxford, 1969, 1971)
Worden, N.A.: *Slavery in Dutch South Africa* (Cambridge, 1985)
Wright, W.: *Slavery at the Cape of Good Hope* (London, 1831)

Articles

Anon: 'The origin and incidence of miscegenation at the Cape during the Dutch East India Company's regime, 1652–1795', *Race Relations Journal,* XX (1953)
Aldridge, B.: 'Cape Malays in Action', *Quarterly Bulletin of the South African Library,* XXVII (1972)
Armstrong, J. C.: 'The Free Black Community at the Cape of Good Hope in the Seventeenth and Eighteenth Centuries (1973, unpublished paper); Madagascar and the slave trade in the Seventeenth Century' *Omaly sy Anio* nos. 17-20 (1983–1984); 'Malagasy slave names in the Seventeenth Century' *Omaly sy Anio* nos. 17-20 (1983–84)

Beck, R.: 'Edward Hanbury: Cape Town ship chandler and merchant, 1879–1925', *Quarterly Bulletin of the South African Library,* XXXIX (1984–1985)
Beeckman, capt. D.: 'A Voyage to Borneo in 1714', *Collectanea* (Cape Town, 1924)
Böeseken, A.J.: 'Die Nederlandse Kommissarisse en die 18e Eeuse samelewing aan die Kaap', *Archives Yearbook for South African History,* VII (1944); 'The meaning, origin and the use of the terms Khoikhoi, San and Khoisan', *Cabo* I, (1972, 1974) and II (1975); 'Die Verhouding Tussen Blank en Nie-Blank in Suid-Afrika aan die hand van die vroegste dokumente', *South African Historical Journal,* II (1970)

Boogman, J.C.: 'Die Hollandische Tradition in der Niederländischen Geschichte', *Westfälische Forschungen*, XV (1962)

Botha, C.G.: 'The Early Inferior Courts of Justice at the Cape', *South African Law Journal*, XXXVIII (1921)

Boucher, M.: 'The Cape and Foreign Shipping, 1714–1723', *South African Historical Journal*, 6 (Nov. 1974); 'The Voyage of a Cape Slaver in 1742', *Historia 24*, 1 (April 1979)

Bundy, C.: 'The Abolition of the Masters and Servants Act', *South African Labour Bulletin*, II (1975)

Bradlow, E.: 'Emancipation and Race Perceptions at the Cape', *South African Historical Journal*, XV (1983); 'The Khoi and the Proposed Vagrancy Legislation of 1834', *Quarterly Bulletin of the South African Library*, XXXIX (3), (Mar. 1985)

Bredenkamp, H. and S. Newton-King: 'Background to the Khoikhoi rebellion of 1799–1803', *Collected Seminar Papers of the Institute of Commonwealth Studies, London: The Societies of Southern Africa in the Nineteenth and Twentieth Centuries*, X (1981); 'The Subjugation of the Khoisan during the 17th and 18th Centuries', *Conference on Economic Development and Racial Domination, Bellville* I (1984)

Brownlee, J.: 'Account of the Amakosae or Southern Caffers', in G. Thompson: *Travels and Adventures in Southern Africa*, ed.: V. Forbes (1827; reprint Cape Town, 1967–1968)

Brugmans, I.J.: 'De Oost-Indische Compagnie en de Welvaart in de Republiek', *Welvaart en Historie*, ed. I. J. Brugmans (The Hague, 1950)

Cairns, M.: 'Freeblack Landowners in the Southern Suburbs of the Cape Peninsula during the Eighteenth Century, *Kronos*, X (1985)

Craton, M.: 'Slave culture, resistance and the achievement of emancipation in the British West Indies, 1783–1838', J. Walvin ed.: *Slavery and British Society 1776–1846* (London, 1982)

Davenport, T.R.H.: 'The Consolidation of a New Society: The Cape Colony, *The Oxford History of South Africa*, ed. M. Wilson and L. Thompson, 2 vols. (Oxford 1908, 1971)

De Bruyn, G.F.C.: 'Die Samestelling van die Afrikaner, *Tydskrif vir Geesteswetenskappe*, XVI (1976)

De Jong, C.: 'Walvisvangst bij de Kaap de Goede Hoop tijdens de Bataafse Republiek' *Historia*, XII (1967)

De Nettancourt, G.: 'Le Peuplement Néerlandais a l'Ile Maurice (1598–1710)' *Mouvements de Populations dans l'Océan Indien*, Actes du Quatrième Congres de l'Association Historique Internationale de l'Océan Indien et du Quatorzième Colloque de la Commission Internationale d'Histoire Maritime tenu á Saint-Dénis-de-la-Réunion du 4 au 9 Septembre 1972 (Paris, 1979)

Derricourt, R.: 'Settlement in the Transkei and Ciskei before Mfecane', *Beyond the Cape Frontier*, eds. C. Saunders and R. Derricourt (Cape Town, 1974)

Domar, E.D.: 'The Causes of Slavery or Serfdom: a Hypothesis', *The Journal of Economic History*, XXX (March 1970)

Duly, L.C.: 'A Revisit with the Cape's Hottentot Ordinance of 1828', *Studies in Economics and Economic History*, ed. M. Kooy (London, 1972, Durham, N.C., 1972)

Du Plessis, A.J.: 'Die Geskiedenis van die Graankultuur in Suid-Afrika, 1652-1752', *Annale van die Universiteit van Stellenbosch*, Series B1, II (Stellenbosch, 1933)

Ehret, C.: 'Patterns of Bantu and Central Sudanic Settlement in Central and Southern Africa', *Transafrican Journal of History*, III, 1973

Elkin, A.P.: 'Reaction and Interaction: A Food Gathering People and European Settlement in Australia', *Beyond the Frontier*, eds. P. Bohannen and F. Plogg (New York, 1967)

Elks, K.: 'Crime and Social in Cape Town, 1830–1850', unpublished paper, Fifth Workshop on the History of Cape Town (University of Cape Town, Dec., 1985)

Elphick, R.: 'Africans and the Christian Campaign in Southern Africa', H. Lamar and L. Thompson, eds.: *The Frontier in History; North America and Southern Africa Compared* (New Haven and London, 1981); A Comparative History of White Supremacy', *Journal of Interdisciplinary History,* XXII (1983)

Frederickson, G.M.: 'Toward a Social Interpretation of the Development of American Racism', *Key Issues in the Afro-American Experience,* eds. N.G. Huggins *et al.* (New York, 1971); 'The Uses of Antislavery', *The New York Review of Books,* 16 Oct. (1975, about D. B. Davis's *The Problem of Slavery in the Age of Revolution 1770–1823,* Ithaca, 1975)

Freund, W.M.: 'Race in the Social Structure of South Africa 1652–1836', *Race and Class,* XVII (1976); 'The Career of Johannes Theodorus van der Kemp and his role in the history of South Africa', *Tijdschrift voor Gescheidenis,* LXXXVI (1973); 'The Eastern Frontier of the Cape Colony during the Batavian Period 1803–1806', *Journal of African History,* XIII (1972)

Gaastra, F.S.: 'De V.O.C. in de Seventiende en Achttiende Eeu: de groei van een bedrijf; geld tegen goederen', *Bijdragen en Mededelingen betreffende de Geschiedenis der Nederlanden,* XCL (1975); 'The Shifting Balance of Trade of the Dutch East India Company', *Companies and Trade Essays on Overseas Trading during the Ancien Régime,* ed. L. Blussé and F. Gaastra (Leiden, 1981)

Genovese, E.: 'The treatment of slaves in different countries: Problems in the application of the comparative method', *Slavery in the New World: A Reader in Comparative History,* eds. L. Fouer and E. Genovese (Englewood Cliffs, New Jersey, 1969)

Geyl, P.: 'Democratische tendenties in 1672', *Pennestrijd over staat en historie,* ed. P. Geyl (Groningen, 1971)

Giliomee, H.: 'Democracy and the Frontier', *South African Historical Journal,* VI (1974); 'Die Administrasietydperk van Lord Caledon 1807–1811', *Argiefjaarboek van Suid-Afrikaanse Geskiedenis,* II (1966); 'Eighteenth Century Cape Society: Culture, Race and Class; *Social Dynamics* (1983); 'Processes in Development of the South African Frontier', *The Frontier in History* (New Haven, 1981) ed. H. Lamar and L. Thompson.

Guelke, L.: 'A Computer Approach to Mapping the Opgaaf: The Population of the Cape in 1731', *South African Journal of Photogrammetry, Remote Sensing and Cartography,* XIII (1983); 'The Anatomy of a Colonial Settler Population: Cape Colony, 1657–1750', unpublished paper, Table VI; 'The making of two Frontier Communities: Cape Colony in the Eighteenth Century', *Historical Reflections/Réflexions Historiques* XII (1985); with R.C.-H. Shell: 'An Early Colonial Landed Gentry: Land and Wealth in the Cape Colony (1652–1731)' *Journal of Historical Geography,* IX (1983)

Grandidier A., et al.: *Collection des ouvrages anciens concernant Madagascar,* VI (1913)

Greenstein, L. J.: 'Slave and Citizen: the South African Case', *Race,* XV (1970, 1971)

Haasbroek, D.J.P.: 'The Origin of Apartheid in South Africa', *Historia,* XV (1970, 1971)

Hajinal, J.: 'European marriage patterns in perspective', *Population in History: Essays in Historical Demography,* eds. D.V. Glass and D.E.C. Eversley (London, 1965)

Hammond-Tooke, W.D.: 'Segmentation and Fission in Cape Nguni Political Units', *Africa,* XXXV (1965)

Hancock, G.: 'Trek', *Economic History Review,* 2nd Series X (1958)

Harinck, G.: 'Interaction between Xhosa and Khoi: emphasis on the period 1620–1750', *African Societies in Southern Africa,* ed. L. Thompson (London, 1969)

Harlow, V.: 'The British Occupations in 1795–1806', *Cambridge History of the British Empire* (Cambridge, 1936)

Hattingh, J.L.: 'A.J. Böeseken se addendum van Kaapse slawe-verkooptransaksies foute en regstelling', *Kronos* IX (1984); 'Die Klagte oor Goewerneur W.A. van der Stel se slawebesit–'n beoordeling met behulp van kwantitiewe data, *Kronos,* VII (1983); 'Grondbesit in die Tafelvallei, Deel I. Die Experiment Grondbesit van Vryswartes', *Kronos* X (1985); 'n Ontleding van sekere aspekte van slawernij aan die Kaap in die sewentiende eeu', *Kronos* I (1979)

Heeres, J.E.: Artikel oor Kompanjie in Encyclopaedie van Nederlandsch-Indië (The Hague, 1917)

Heeringa, K.: 'De Nederlanders op Mauritius en Madagascar', *De Indische Gids* (1895)

Hesse, J.A.: ' "Die Herkoms van die Afrikaner": 'n Nabetragting', *Familia,* XVII, 1980

Hoetinck, H.: 'Surinam and Curaçao', *Neither Slave nor Free: The Freedman of African Descent in the Slave Societies of the New World,* eds. D.W. Cohen and J. P. Greene (Baltimore, 1972)

Hoge, J.H.: 'Martin Melck', *Tydschrift voor Wetenschap en Kuns,* XII (1934); 'Miscegenation in South Africa in the seventeenth and eighteenth centuries', *New Light on Afrikaans and 'Malayo-Portuguese',* ed. Marius F. Valkhoff (Louvain, 1972); 'Rassenmischung in Südafrika im 17. und 18. Jahrhundert', *Zeitschrift für Rassenkunde,* VIII (1938); 'Personalia of the Germans at the Cape, 1652–1804', *Archives Yearbook for South African History,* IX (1946)

Hulshof, A.: 'H.A. van Reede tot Drakenstein, Journaal van zijn verblijf aan de Kaap', *Bijdragen en mededelingen van het Historisch Genootschap te Utrecht* LXII (1941)

Kantor, B.: 'The Rixdollar and the Foreign Exchange', *South African Journal of Economics* XXXVIII (1970)

Katzen, M.F.: 'White Settlers and the Origin of a New Society', *The Oxford History of South Africa,* eds. W. Wilson and L. Thompson (Oxford, 1969)

Kirk, T.: 'Some Notes on the Financial State of the Eastern Cape, 1840–1850, and the Fate of the Kat River Settlement', *Collected Seminar Papers on the Societies of Southern Africa in the Nineteenth and Twentieth Centuries,* Institute of Commonwealth Studies (London, 1973)

Klein, H.S.: 'Nineteenth Century Brazil', *Neither Slave nor Free: The Freedman of African Descent in the Slave Societies of the New World,* ed. D.W. Cohen and J.P. Greene (Baltimore, 1972)

Kotalawele, D.A.: 'Agrarian Policies of the Dutch in South-West Ceylon, *A.A.G. Bijdragen,* XIV (1967)

Leibbrandt, H.C.V. and J.E. Heeres: 'Memoriën van den Gouverneur van de Graaf over de gebeurtenisse aan die Kaape de Goede Hoop in 1780–1806', *Bijdragen en Mededelingen van het Historisch Genootschap te Utrecht,* XV (1894)

Legassick, M.C.: 'The Frontier Tradition in South African Historiography', *Collected Seminar Papers on the Societies of Southern Africa,* II, Institute of Commonwealth Studies (London, 1970) and *Economy and Society in Pre-Industrial South Africa,* eds. S. Marks and A. Atmore (London, 1980); 'The Dynamics of Modernization in South Africa', *Journal of African History,* XIII, 1, 1972; *The Analysis of Racism in South Africa,* United Nations/African Institute for Economic Development and Planning, Dar-es-Salam (1975); 'Perspectives on African "Underdevelopment" ', *Journal of African History* XVII (1976); 'The Sotho-Tswana Peoples before 1800', *African Societies in Southern Africa,* ed.: L.M. Thompson (London, 1969)

Lewis, D.: 'Malay Arts and Crafts', *Handbook on Race Relations in South Africa,* ed. Ellen Hellmann (Cape Town, 1949)

Lopez, R.S.: 'The Origins of the Merino Sheep', *The Joseph Starr Memorial Volume* (New York, 1953)

Loubser, J.J.: 'Calvinism, Equality and Inclusion: The Case of Afrikaner Calvinism', The Protestant Ethnic and Modernisation, ed. S.N. Eisenstadt (London, 1969)

Lurie, N.O.: 'Indian Cultural Adjustments to European Civilisation', *Seventeenth Century America,* ed. J. M. Smith (Chapel Hill, 1959)

Lye, W.F.: 'The Difaqane: the Mfecane in the Southern Sotho Area 1822–1904', *Journal of African History,* VIII (1967)

Mabin, A.: 'The Rise and Decline of Port Elizabeth, 1850–1900', *International Journal of African Historical Studies,* XIX (1986)
MacCrone, I.D.: 'The Frontier Tradition and Race Attitudes in South Africa', *Race Relations Journal,* XXVII (1961)
Maingard, L.F.: 'Studies in Korana History, Customs and Language', *Bantu Studies,* VI (1932), 'The Lost Tribes of the Cape', *South African Journal of Science,* XXVII (1931)
Malherbe, V.C.: 'David Stuurman: "Last Chief of the Hottentots" ', *African Studies,* XXXIX (1980); 'Hermanus and His Sons: Khoi Bandits and Conspirators in the Post-rebellion Period 1803-1818', *African Studies,* XLI (1982)
Marks, S.: 'Khoisan Resistance to the Dutch in the Seventeenth and Eighteenth Centuries', *Journal of African History,* XIII (1972)
Mason, J.: 'Slaveholder resistance to the amelioration of slavery at the Cape' (unpublished paper, Western Cape: Roots and Realities Conference, University of Cape Town: July 1986); 'The amelioration of slavery and slaveholder resistance at the Cape', (unpublished paper, South African Research Seminar, Yale, revised edn., Feb. 1986)
Masson, F.: 'An account of three journeys from the Cape into the southern parts of Africa'. . . *Philosophical Transactions of the Royal Society,* LXVI (London, 1776)
Moerane, M.: 'Towards a Theory of Class Struggle in South Africa: Historical Perspectives', *Maji-Maji* (Dar-es-Salaam, 21 July, 1975)
Moller, H.: 'Sex Composition and Correlated Culture Patterns of Colonial America', *William and Mary Quarterley,* II (1945)

Newton-King, S.: 'Background to the Khoikhoi rebellion of 1799-1803', *Collected Seminar Papers of the Institute of Commonwealth Studies, London: The Societies of Southern Africa in the nineteenth and twentieth centuries,* X (1981); 'Commerce and Material Culture on the Eastern Cape Frontier, 1784-1812, (unpublished seminar paper, Institute of Commonwealth Studies, London, 1985, and presented to the History Workshop, University of Witwatersrand Feb. 1987); 'The labour market of the Cape Colony, 1807–1828', eds. S. Marks and A. Atmore, *Economy and Society in pre-Industrial South Africa* (London, 1980); 'Some thoughts about the Political Economy of Graaff-Reinet in the late Eighteenth Century', (unpublished paper 1984)

O'C Maggs, T.M.: 'Pastoral Settlements on the Riet River', *South African Archaeological Bulletin* (1971)

Palmier, L.H.: 'The Japanese Nobility Under the Dutch', *Comparative Studies in Society and History,* II (1959, 1960)
Parkington, J. and M. Hall, eds.: 'Papers in the Prehistory of the Western Cape, South Africa, *British Archaeological Reports,* series 332 (1987)
Patterson, S.: 'Some Speculations on the Status and Role of the Free People of Colour in the Western Cape', *Studies in African Social Anthropology,* eds. M. Fortes and S. Patterson (London, 1975)
Peires, J.B.: 'The Rise of the "Right-Hand House" in the history and historiography of the Xhosa', *History in Africa* (1975); 'Xhosa Expansion before 1800'; *Collected Seminar Papers on the Societies of Southern Africa,* Institute of Commonwealth Studies (London, 1976)
Penn, N.: 'Labour, Land and Livestock in the Western Cape during the Eighteenth Century: The Khoisan and the Colonists', (unpublished paper, Western Cape Roots and Realities Workshop, Centre for African Studies, University of Cape Town, 1986); 'The Frontier in the Western Cape, 1700–1740', (unpublished paper, Workshop on spatial Archaeology Research Unit, University of Cape Town, 1984)

Pheiffer, R.H.: 'Hernuwde aandag vir 'n Verloopte Fransman: Tekste in gebroke Nederlands van Estienne Barbier', *Tydskrif vir Geesteswetenskappe*, XV (1975)

Philip, P.: 'The Vicissitudes of the Early British Settlers at the Cape', *Quarterly Bulletin of the South African Library*, XL–XLI (1986)

Postma, J.: 'The Dutch Slave Trade, a quantitative assessment', *La Traite des noirs par l'Atlantique; nouvelles approches. The Atlantic slave trade; new approaches* (Paris, 1976)

Raum, O.F.: 'A Topological Analysis of Xhosa Society', *Wurt und Religion: Kalima Na Dini*, eds. H. J. Greschat and H. Jungraithmayer (Stuttgart, 1969)

Rayner, M.: '"Labourers in the Vineyard": work and resistance to servitude during the years of the wine-farming boom in the Cape Colony', (paper presented to third History Workshop, University of Witwatersrand 1984); 'Slave worker and free worker, an analysis of the content and significance of British anti-slavery ideology and legislation, 1816–1834', (unpublished paper); 'Slaves, slave owners and the British State: The Cape Colony, 1806–1834'; *The Societies of Southern Africa in the 19th and 20th Centuries*, University of Commonwealth Studies XII (1981)

Reyburn, H.A.: 'Studies in Cape Frontier History: Stockenstrom and Slagters Nek', *The Critic*, III (1935); 'Studies in Cape Frontier History: Land, Labour and the Law', *The Critic*, III (1934)

Rex, J.: 'Racism and the Structure of Colonial Societies', *Racism and Colonialism, Essays on ideology and social structure*, ed. R. Ross (Leiden, 1982)

Robertshaw, P.T.: 'The Origin of Pastoralism in the Cape', *South African Historical Journal*, X (1978)

Robertson, H.M.: 'The Economic Development of the Cape under Jan van Riebeeck', *South African Journal of Economics*, XIII (1945); '150 Years of Economic Contact between White and Black', *South African Journal of Economics*, II (1934) and III (1935)

Rochlin, S.A.: 'The first Mosque at the Cape', *South African Journal of Science*, XXXIII (1937)

Ross, R.: 'Assimilation and Collaboration: The Aspirations and Politics of the Griqua Captaincies of Mid-Nineteenth Century South Africa', (unpublished mimeo n.d.); 'Griqua Government', *African Studies* XXIII (1974); 'Griqua Power and Wealth: An Analysis of the Paradoxes of their Interrelationship; *Collected Seminar Papers on the Societies of Southern Africa*, Institute of Commonwealth Studies (London, 1974); 'Oppression, Sexuality and Slavery at the Cape of Good Hope'; *Historical Reflections/Reflexiones Historique*, VI (1979); 'Pre-industrial and industrial racial stratification in South Africa', *Racism and Colonialism: Essays on ideology and social structure* (Leiden, 1982); 'Smallpox at the Cape of Good Hope in the Eighteenth Century', C. Fyfe and D.M. McMasters, eds.: *African Historical Demography* (Centre of African Studies, University of Edinburgh, 1971); 'The Dutch on the Swahili Coast, 1776–1779: Two Slaving Journals'; *International Journal of African Historical Studies*, 19, 2 (1986) and 19, 3 (1986); 'The occupation of slaves in Eighteenth Century Cape Town', *Studies in the History of Cape Town* (Cape Town, 1988); 'The rise of the Cape Gentry', *Journal of Southern African Studies*, II (1983); 'The Rule of Law at the Cape in the Eighteenth Century', *Journal of Imperial and Commonwealth History* IX (1980); 'The "White" Population of the Cape Colony [South Africa] in the Eighteenth Century', *Population Studies* XXIX (1975)

Sansom, B.: 'Traditional Rulers and Realms'; 'Traditional Economic Systems', both in *The Bantu-speaking Peoples of Southern Africa*, ed. W.D. Hammond-Tooke (London, 1974)

Saunders, C.: 'Early Knowledge of the Sotho: Seventeenth and Eighteenth Century Accounts of the Tswana', *Quarterly Bulletin of the South African Library* (1966); 'Liberated Africans in the Cape Colony in the First Half of the Nineteenth Century', *International Journal of African Historical Studies*, 18 (1985)

Schapera, I.: 'A Short History of the Bangwaketse', *African Studies,* I (1942)

Schutte, G.J.: 'Johannes Henricus Redelinghuys: een Revolutionair Kapenaar', *South African Historical Journal,* III (1971)

Schwartz, S.B.: 'The manumission of slaves in colonial Brazil, 1684–1745', *Hispanic American Historical Review,* LIV (1974)

Shell, R.C.-H.: 'Auctions –their good and evil tendencies', *Quarterly Bulletin of the South African Library* XXIV–XL (1985); 'Rites and rebellion: Islamic conversion at the Cape, 1808–1915', *Studies in the History of Cape Town,* V (1984); 'The Impact of the Cape Slave Trade and its Abolition on the Demography, Regional Distribution and Ethnic Composition of the Cape Slave Population, 1652–1825', (unpublished seminar paper, Yale University 1979)

Slater, H.: 'Land, Labour and Capital in Natal', *Journal of African History* (1975)

'Slavernij': *Encylopaedie van Nederlandsch Indië* III, 621 (The Hague, Leiden, n.d.)

Smith, A.: 'Delagoa Bay and the Trade of South-Eastern Africa', *Pre-Colonial African Trade,* eds. R. Gray and D. Birmingham (London, 1970)

Somerville, W.: 'Cape of Good Hope', article in unknown encyclopaedia in c.a. 1803/1804, p.405 (South Africa Studies Library, University of Cape Town)

Stokes, R.G.: Afrikaner Calvinism and Economic Action: The Weberian Thesis in South Africa', *American Journal of Sociology* LXXXI (1981)

Sturgis, J.: 'Anglicisation at the Cape of Good Hope in the early Nineteenth Century', *Journal of Imperial and Commonwealth Studies* XI (1982)

Swellengrebel, H.: 'Joernaal van Swellengrebel', *Zuid-Afrika,* XI (1932)

Trapido, S.: 'The South African Republic: Class Formation and the State, 1850–1900', *Collected Seminar Papers on the Societies of Southern Africa in the Nineteenth and Twentieth Centuries,* Institute of Commonwealth Studies, (London, 1973); 'Aspects in the Transition from Slavery to Serfdom: The South African Republic', 1842–1902

Turner, L.C.F.: 'The Cape of Good Hope and the Anglo-French Conflict 1797–1806', *Historical Studies of Australia and New Zealand,* IX (1961)

Tylden, G.: 'The development of the Commando System in South Africa, 1715–1792', *Africana Notes and News,* XII (Dec. 1959); 'The Cape Coloured Regiments, 1793–1870', *Africana Notes and News,* VII, 2 (March, 1950)

Van den Boogaart, E.: 'Colour Prejudice and the Yardstick of Civility: the initial Dutch Confrontation with Black Africans, 1590–1635', *Racism and Colonialism: Essays on Ideology and Social Structure,* ed. R. Ross (The Hague, Boston and London, 1982)

Van der Merwe, P.J.: 'Van Verversingspos tot Landbou-Kolonie', *Geskiedenis van Suid-Afrika,* eds. A.J.H. Van der Walt, J.A. Wiid and A.L. Geyer (Cape Town, 1965)

Van Oordt, L.C.: 'Die Kaapse Taalargief: Een-en-Dertig Afrikaans–Hollandse briewe uit die jare 1712–1795, hoofsaaklik afkomstig van veldmagmeesters', *Tydskrif vir Wetenskap en kuns,* XVI (1956)

Van Reede, H.A.: '... Journaal van zijn verblijf aan de Kaap', ed. A. Hulshof, *Bijdragen en Mededelingen van het Historisch Genootschap te Utrecht,* LXIII (1941)

Van Rensburg, J.I.J.: 'Die Geskiedenis van die Wingerdkultuur in Suid-Afrika tydens die Eerste Eeu, 1652–1752', *Archives Yearbook for South African History,* II (1954)

Van Ryneveld, W.S.: 'Schets van den Staat der Kolonie in 1805', *Het Nederduitsch Zuid-Afrikaansche Tydschrift,* VII (1831)

Van Zyl, D.J.: 'Die Geskiedenis van Graanbou aan die Kaap, 1795–1826', *Archives Yearbook for South African History,* XXXI, 1 (1968)

Venter, P.J.: 'Die Inboekstelsel', Die Huisgenoot (1 June, 1934); 'Landdros en Heemrade', *Archives Yearbook for South African History,* III (1940)

Villiers, J.: 'Trade and Society in the Banda islands in the Sixteenth Century', *Modern Asian Studies,* XV (1981)

Visagie, J.C.: 'Die ontstaan van die Burgerraad', *Kleio:* Bulletin of the Department of History, University of South Africa, V (1973)

Wagner, R.: 'Coenraad de Buys in Transorangia', *Collected Seminar Papers on the Societies of Southern Africa in the Nineteenth and Twentieth Centuries,* IV, Institute of Commonwealth Studies (London, 1974)
Watermeyer, G.A.: 'The Rise and Early History of Graaff-Reinet', *The Graaff-Herald* (27 July, 1861)
Watson, R.L.: 'Religion and anti-slavery at the Cape of Good Hope', Discovering the African Past: Studies in honour of Daniel McCall (Boston, forthcoming); 'Slavery and ideology: the South African Case', *International Journal of African Historical Studies,* XX (1987)
Worden, N.A.: 'Adjusting to emancipation: freed slaves and farmers in the Western Cape', M. Simons and W.G. Janes, eds. *Essays in the social and economic history of the Western Cape* (Cape Town, 1989)

Theses

Appel, A.: 'Die Geskiedenis van houtvoorsiening aan die Kaap, 1652–1795' (M.A., University of Stellenbosch, 1966)
Beck, R.B.: 'The Legislation and development of trade on the Cape Frontier, 1817–1830' (Ph.D., University of Indiana, 1987)
Buirski, A.P.: 'The Barrys and the Overberg (M.A., University of Stellenbosch, 1952)
Coetzee, C.G.: 'Die Stryd om Delagoabaai en die Suidooskus, 1600–1800' (Ph.D., University of Stellenbosch, 1954)
Donaldson, M.: 'The Council of Advice at the Cape of Good Hope, 1825–1834' (Ph.D., Rhodes University, 1974)
Elks, K.D.: 'Crime, Community and Police in Cape Town, 1825–1850' (M.A., University of Cape Town, 1986)
Elphick, R.H.: 'The Cape Khoi and the First Phase of South African Race Relations' (Ph.D., Yale University, 1972)
Freund, W.M.: 'Society and Government in Dutch South Africa, The Cape and the Batavians, 1803–1806' (Ph.D., Yale University, 1972)
George, M.: 'John Bardwell Ebden; His business and political career at the Cape, 1806–1849' (M.A., University of Cape Town, 1980)
Grobler, J.C.H.: 'Die Arbeidsvraagstuk aan die Kaap, 1652–1662' (M.A., University of Stellenbosch, 1968)
Guelke, L.T.: 'The Early European Settlement of South Africa' (P.h.D., University of Toronto, 1974)
Heese, J.A.: 'Onderwys in Namakwaland: 1750–1940' (D.Ed., University of Stellenbosch, 1943)
Hengherr, E.: 'Emancipation and after: a study of Cape slavery and the issues arising from it, 1830–1843' (M.A., University of Cape Town, 1953)
Judges, S.: 'Poverty, living conditions and social relations–aspects of life in Cape Town in 1835' (M.A., University of Cape Town, 1977)
Jooste, G.J.: 'Die Geskiedenis van wynbou en wynhandel in die Kaap Kolonie, 1753–1795' (M.A., University of Stellenbosch, 1973)
Knaap, G.J.: 'Kruidnagelen en Christenen: De Verenigde Oos-Indische Compagnie en de bevolking van Ambon, 1656–1696' (Ph.D., Utrecht, 1985)
Legassick, M.: 'The Griqua, the Sotho Tswana and the Missionaries, 1780–1880: The Politics of a Frontier Zone' (Ph.D., University of California, Los Angeles, 1969)
Le Roux, H.J.: 'Die Toestand, Verspreiding en Verbrokkeling van die Hottentot-stamme in Suid-Afrika, 1653–1713' (M.A., University of Stellenbosch, 1945)

Malherbe, V.C.: 'Diversification and Mobility of Khoikhoi Labour in the Eastern Districts of the Cape Colony Prior to the Labour Law of 1 November, 1809' (M.A., University of Cape Town, 1978)

Marincowitz, J.: 'Rural production and labour in the Western Cape, 1838 — 1888, with special reference to the wheat growing districts (Ph.D., University of London, 1985)

Moorsom, R.: 'The Political Economy of Namibia until 1945' (M.A., Sussex University, 1973)

Oberholster, J.J.: 'Die Burger-Senaat 1795–1828' (M.A., University of Stellenbosch, 1936)

Postma, J.: 'The Dutch participation in the African slave trade: slaving on the Guinea Coast, 1695–1795' (Ph.D., Michigan State University, 1969–70)

Rayner, M.: 'Wine and Slaves: the failure of an export economy and the ending of slavery in the Cape Colony, South Africa 1806–1834' (Ph.D., Duke University, 1986)

Ross, R.J.: 'The Griquas of Philippolis and Kokstad, 1826–1879' (Ph.D., Cambridge University, 1974)

Schreuder, J.H.D.: 'Die geskiedenis van ons graanbou, 1752–1795' (M.A., University of Stellenbosch, 1948)

Selenes, R.W.: 'The Demography and Economics of Brazilian Slavery, 1850–1888' (Ph.D., Stanford University, 1975)

Shell, R.: 'Slavery at the Cape of Good Hope, 1680–1731' (Ph.D., Yale University, 1986); 'The Establishment and Spread of Islam at the Cape from the Beginning of Company Rule to 1838' (B.A. Hons., University of Cape Town, 1974)

Swart, H.L.G.: 'Developments in Currency and Banking at the Cape between 1782 and 1825, with an account of contemporary controversies' (Ph.D., University of Cape Town, 1953); 'Die ontwikkeling van handel aan die Kaap tussen die jare, 1795–1806' (M.A., University of Cape Town, 1949); 'Some Aspects of the History of the Cape Regiment 1806–1817' (B.A. Hons., University of Cape Town, Sept., 1978)

Visagie, J.C.: 'Die Katrivier nedersetting, 1829–1839' (D. Litt. et Phil., Unisa, 1978)

Wagenaar, G.: 'Johannes Gysbertus van Reenen: Sy aandeel in die Kaapse Geskiedenis tot 1806' (M.A., University of Pretoria, 1976)

Webb, A.C.M.: 'The Agricultural Development of the 1820 Settlement down to 1846' (M.A., Rhodes University, 1975)

Williams, D.: 'The Missionaries on the Eastern Frontier of the Cape Colony, 1799–1853' (Ph.D., University of the Witwatersrand, 1959)

Worden, N.A.: 'Rural slavery in the western districts of the Cape Colony during the nineteenth century' (Ph.D., Cambridge, 1982)

Index